Barrington
New Hampshire

Vital Records

Richard P. Roberts

HERITAGE BOOKS
2008

HERITAGE BOOKS
AN IMPRINT OF HERITAGE BOOKS, INC.

Books, CDs, and more—Worldwide

For our listing of thousands of titles see our website
at
www.HeritageBooks.com

Published 2008 by
HERITAGE BOOKS, INC.
Publishing Division
100 Railroad Ave. #104
Westminster, Maryland 21157

Copyright © 2000 Richard P. Roberts

All rights reserved. No part of this book may be reproduced or transmitted in any form or by any means, electronic or mechanical, including photocopying, recording or by any information storage and retrieval system without written permission from the author, except for the inclusion of brief quotations in a review.

International Standard Book Number: 978-0-7884-1552-4

CONTENTS

Introduction _____ 1

Births _____ 4

Marriages _____ 206

Deaths _____ 420

INTRODUCTION

Early vital records of many New Hampshire towns can be located either through the State's Vital Records Department or on microfilms made available through LDS Family History Centers. Some, however, have been lost or are inaccessible for various reasons. A valuable, but time-consuming, source of information for events occurring after 1886 is the vital statistics which are provided in a section of the Annual Town Reports of many New Hampshire towns. Many of these town reports have been collected at the New Hampshire State Library in Concord, as well as more local repositories.

The amount of information published in these Annual Town Reports varies tremendously over time. Early records are far more detailed and comprehensive. Recent records are rather cursory, but issues of confidentiality and sensitivity to the privacy of those residents still living offsets the lack of information of genealogical value.

While the information provided is often very helpful, one must remember that it is not fool-proof or universally accurate, nor is it the primary source or the actual vital record itself. The fact that much of the data is self-reported suggests that it is reliable. However, errors in transcription, spelling, and printing often are obvious. In addition, there may be, for example, two children listed as the third child of a particular couple, or the mother's maiden name, age or place of birth differs or is inconsistent from one entry to another. It is also important to note that a birth, marriage or death may have been reported in another town although the subject resided in Barrington, or the entry may not have been made in the first place.

Despite these shortcomings, the information contained in the Annual Town Reports can be a valuable tool for the genealogist. Marriage and death records from the late 1800's often identify parents who were married nearly a century before. In addition, due to the presence of numerous naval and military personnel during the period covered, many transient or temporary residents are covered by these records. Finally, those families that have remained in Barrington for several generations can be traced and connected to the present.

Births - To the extent the information is available, the entries in the list of births are given as follows: child's name; date of birth; place of birth (Barrington, unless otherwise indicated); the number of children in the family; father's name, place of birth, age and occupation; and the mother's maiden name, age and place of birth. The residence of the parents is sometimes given when it is shown as other than Barrington. As noted above, the amount of information in earlier records is substantially greater.

At times, the given names of many children are missing from the early reports. In this case, the sex of the child is given and they are listed chronologically at the beginning of the surname heading. On occasion, the child's name can be determined from marriage or death records, as well as secondary sources. These names are shown in brackets where available.

Marriages - To the extent the information is available, the entries in the list of marriages follow this format: groom's name; groom's residence; bride's name; brides residence; date of marriage; place of marriage (Barrington, unless otherwise indicated); H, signifying husband's information, and W, signifying wife's information, each in the following order - age, occupation, number of the marriage (if other than first), father's name, father's place of birth, father's occupation, mother's name, mother's place of birth, and mother's occupation. The name of the official conducting the marriage has been omitted but is generally provided in the original document. The records for several years do not provide the parents' surnames.

Deaths - To the extent available, the entries in the list of deaths contain the following information: name of decedent; place of death; date of death; age at death; cause of death; marital status; birthplace; father's name; father's place of birth; mother's name; and mother's place of birth. Later entries give the residence of the individual.

Most of the entries listing a cause of death are self-explanatory. In older entries, the phrase "senectus" is sometimes used and is essentially equivalent to "old age", and "phthisis" is similar to "consumption" and "tuberculosis". As one would expect, the death records often contain somber entries for young mothers and small children, as well as tragic instances of individuals passing before their time due to accidents or suicide.

There are additional resources which are certain to be useful in conjunction with the material contained in this book. The Strafford County Genealogical Society has recently concluded a transcription of many early vital and town records from the Barrington Town Clerk's Office. The time period covered by these records is the first half of the 19th Century. In addition, a fine book exists in several libraries which transcribes a large number of cemetery inscriptions. This volume may offer substantial information regarding family relationships and gaps can easily be filled by consulting this work. Finally, Morton Wiggin's History of Barrington, published in 1966, and Barrington, New Hampshire, 1722-1972, by Mary C. Emhardt and Louise F. Williams each provide a comprehensive history of the town as well as a good deal of documentary and genealogical information regarding the families who settled there and lived there.

ABBOTT,
Richard Thomas, b. 11/28/1947 in Exeter; second; George T. Abbott (buffer, Dover) and Ruth P. Ross (Lowell, MA)
Ruth-Ann Louise, b. 12/25/1946 in Exeter; first; George T. Abbott (in tannery, Dover) and Ruth P. Ross (Lowell, MA)

ACKERSON,
Adam David, b. 2/24/1977 in Rochester; Donna M. Ackerson

ADAMS,
Bryan George, b. 6/22/1970 in Dover; George K. Adams (MA) and Virginia E. Gibbs (MA)

AGNEW,
Elisha Paige, b. 6/10/1984 in Rochester; James D. Agnew, II and Jacqueline E. Powell
Kevin David P., b. 10/1/1987 in Hanover; James D. Agnew, II and Jacqueline E. Powell
Steven Alfred, b. 12/18/1985 in Rochester; James D. Agnew, II and Jacqueline E. Powell
Thomas Jay P., b. 10/1/1987 in Hanover; James D. Agnew, II and Jacqueline E. Powell

AIKEN,
Melissa Ann, b. 7/26/1985 in Rochester; Richard R. Aiken and Kathleen A. Tanguay

ALEX,
Theron Christopher, b. 6/22/1978 in Dover; William J. Alex and Debra G. Hillsgrove
William John, Jr., b. 8/5/1976 in Dover; William J. Alex and Debra G. Hillsgrove

ALLAIN,
Jennie Almira, b. 10/12/1983 in Dover; David J. Allain and Elizabeth G. Feuer
Peyton Hope, b. 7/20/1974 in Hanover; David Joseph Allain and Cecilia Moore

ALLAN,
Robert Douglas, b. 11/4/1953 in Dover; second; David N. Allan (soil conserv'ist, NH) and Natalie M. Chandler (NH)

ALLEN,
Donald Frank, b. 11/24/1937 in Rochester; second; Leighton O. Allen (farmer, Stockbridge, MA) and Muriel B. Shea (Wakefield, MA)
Rebecca Elizabeth, b. 10/31/1979 in Dover; Stephen L. Allen and Cheryl D. Bowles
Timothy Stephen, b. 3/17/1978 in Dover; Stephen L. Allen and Cheryl D. Bowles

ALONZI,
Derek Louis, b. 3/14/1986 in Dover; Brian L. Alonzi and Michelle M. Hopkins
Maegan Elizabeth, b. 12/26/1983 in Dover; Brian L. Alonzi and Michelle M. Hopkins

AMES,
Brook Leonard, b. 2/13/1981 in Exeter; David C. Ames and Diane J. Pratt

ANDERSEN,
Julie Marie, b. 9/10/1985 in Rochester; James W. Andersen and Cindy L. Dodge

ANDERSON,
James Walter, b. 5/8/1959 in Rochester; first; Albert J. Anderson (machinist, NY) and Betty A. Harding (NH)

Kenneth Paul, b. 3/8/1952 in Rochester; third; Carl V.
Anderson (self-employed, MA) and Louise M. Morin (MA)
Lucas Saul, b. 4/19/1977 in Dover; Bern E. Anderson and
Donna A. Cappiello

ANDRADE,
Matthew Johnson, b. 8/12/1959 in Rochester; second;
Joseph L. Andrade (engineer, MA) and Phyllis C.
Johnson (MA)

ANDREWS,
Myrtle L., b. 6/19/1918; third; Paul Y. Andrews (farmer,
Canterbury) and Sarah Mathews (Groton)

ARCHAMBAULT,
Brandon Joseph, b. 7/5/1979 in Exeter; Raymond F.
Archambault and Lynda L. St. Amour
Jamie Leigh, b. 9/1/1983 in Exeter; Walter J. Archambault
and Carol A. Frendh
Thais Rae, b. 5/13/1978 in Dover; Walter J. Archambault and
Debra L. Chase

ARLIN,
son, b. 1/12/1898; first; James C. Arlin (laborer, 22,
Barrington) and Neva Brown (25, Newmarket)
daughter, b. 6/1/1898; first; Berlie E. Arlin (shoe operative,
Barrington) and Addie Clarke (Boston, MA)
stillborn daughter, b. 1/9/1900; second; George A. Arlin
(farmer, 34, Barrington) and Julia F. Hart (24, Van
Buren, ME)
son, b. 10/25/1900; second; James C. Arlin (laborer, 25,
Barrington) and Neva J. Brown (28, Newmarket)
son, b. 1/21/1903; sixth; George Arlin (basket maker, 40,
Boston, MA) and Laura Freeman (38, Barrington)
son, b. 6/3/1903; third; James C. Arlin (laborer, 37,
Barrington) and Neva J. Brown (31, Newmarket)

daughter, b. 12/27/1904; fourth; Lorenzo D. Arlin (farmer, 49, Barrington) and Ida B. Whitehouse (28, Barrington)
Anna May, b. 8/2/1901; third; Lorenzo D. Arlin (laborer, 40, Barrington) and Ida Whitehouse (26, Barrington)
Dale Emily, b. 7/2/1946 in Rochester; second; Norman W. Arlin (mule fixer, Dover) and Dorothy H. Gibb (Atkinson)
Florence J., b. 1/16/1897; first; Lorenzo D. Arlin (farmer, 37, Barrington) and Ida B. Whitehouse (22, Barrington)
Florence May, b. 9/9/1896; first; George A. Arlin (laborer, 31, Barrington) and Julia E. Hart (21, Canada)
George McKinley, b. 3/1/1902; third; George Albert Arlin (Barrington) and Julia Hart (28, Van Buren, ME)
Leslie Charles, b. 6/20/1897; Eli A. Arlin (Barrington) and Ida B. Leighton (Strafford) (1946)
Mabel Gertrude, b. 3/5/1899; second; Lorenzo D. Arlin (laborer, 40, Barrington) and Ida Whitehouse (23, Barrington)
Niel Waldron, b. 8/27/1940 in Brentwood; first; Norman W. Arlin (Dover) and Dorothy H. Gibb (Atkinson)

ARMSTRONG,
Jacqueline Colette, b. 12/14/1982 in Portsmouth; Eugene C. Armstrong, Jr. and Jacqueline D. Mason

ARNOLD,
Allen A., b. 7/18/1969 in Rochester; Gerald R. Arnold (NH) and Lorraine G. Condon (NH)
David John, b. 3/31/1951 in Dover; sixth; Ralph W. Arnold (shoe cutter, MA) and Vira E. Neal (NH)
Edwin Samuel, b. 12/2/1948 in Dover; fourth; Ralph W. Arnold (shoe cutter, MA) and Vira Neal (NH)
Myra Sarah, b. 12/25/1949 in Dover; fifth; Ralph W. Arnold (shoe cutter, MA) and Vira Neal (NH)

ARSENAULT,
Sarah Johanna, b. 10/23/1986 in Concord; Steven N. Arsenault and Mari J. Samuels

ASHBURNER,
Aaron Steven, b. 1/17/1987 in Dover; Steven J. Ashburner and Tina M. Maskell

ATWOOD,
Brian Joseph, b. 4/3/1961 in Rochester; fifth; Robert H. Atwood (route salesman, MA) and Mary G. Pooler (MA)
Shine Walter, b. 8/4/1971 in Thailand; Milford W. Atwood (MA) and Pratoom Chandarussi (Thailand)
William Walter, b. 10/12/1959 in Rochester; fourth; Robert H. Atwood (milkman, MA) and Mary G. Pooler (MA)

AUBERT,
Aaron David, b. 11/27/1979 in Dover; David J. Aubert and Shelby J. Bragg

AUCELLA,
Jay Thomas, b. 6/13/1974 in Exeter; Paul Annis Aucella and Nancy Jewell Baker
Nathan Peter, b. 12/9/1981 in Exeter; Paul A. Aucella and Nancy J. Baker

AVERY,
Lloyd Allen, b. 6/16/1946 in Exeter; second; Elvin W. Avery (plumber, York Beach, ME) and Pauline Graham (Lynn, MA); residence - York Beach, ME

AYVAS,
Jody Lee, b. 11/6/1972 in Dover; Heinz K. Ayvas (Germany) and Marian T. Sunderland (NH)

AYVAZ,
Arthur John, b. 8/7/1984 in Dover; Arthur Ayvaz and Jane M. Glacken
Melissa Anne, b. 7/9/1981 in Dover; Arthur Ayvaz and Jane M. Glacken

BABB,
daughter, b. 10/4/1904; first; Frank H. Babb (farmer, 42, Barrington) and Esther J. Libbey (19, Dover)
daughter, b. 11/5/1908; third; Frank H. Babb (farmer, 46, Barrington) and Esther J. Libbey (23, Dover)
son [George], b. 11/14/1909; fourth; Frank H. Babb (farmer, 47, Barrington) and Esther Libbey (25, Dover)
son, b. 7/24/1913; fifth; Frank H. Babb (farmer, 50, Barrington) and Esther J. Libby (28, Dover)
daughter, b. 8/18/1914; seventh; Frank H. Babb (farmer, Barrington) and Esther Libby (Dover)
Frances Ella, b. 9/18/1906; second; Frank H. Babb (farmer, 44, Barrington) and Esther J. Libby (21, Dover)
Mary A., b. 2/17/1890; sixth; John O.F. Babb (farmer, Barrington) and Sarah A. Gray (Barrington)
Mary E., b. 8/10/1912; fifth; Frank H. Babb (farmer, 49, Barrington) and Esther J. Libby (27, Dover)

BABEL,
Brian James, b. 5/20/1974 in Dover; Donn Robert Babel and Anita Louise Dionne
Donn Robert, Jr., b. 1/13/1973 in Dover; Donn R. Babel, Sr. (NH) and Anita L. Dionne (NH)
Mark Alan, b. 9/4/1975 in Dover; Donn R. Babel, Sr. and Anita L. Dionne

BADEWICZ,
Matthew Benjamin, b. 12/10/1986 in Exeter; Benjamin F. Badewicz and Lorice A. Simmons

BAILEY,
daughter [Abbie], b. 12/21/1896; third; John W. Bailey (farmer, 31, Haverhill, MA) and Dora M. Warren (29, Chester)
Betty Christine, b. 12/17/1935; fourth; Raymond E. Bailey (farmer, Providence, RI) and Charlotte E. Goff (Andover, MA)
David Martin, b. 7/20/1954 in Rochester; first; Earl D. Bailey (printer, UNH, NH) and Martha Lee Faist (NH)
Earl Douglas, b. 4/20/1933; third; Raymond E. Bailey (farmer, Providence, RI) and Charlotte E. Goff (No. Andover, MA)
Effie Morse, b. 3/10/1895; second; John Bailey (farmer, 49, Haverhill, MA) and Dora Warren (28, Chester)
Irene Edith, b. 10/3/1942; fifth; Raymond E. Bailey (farmer, Providence, RI) and Charlotte E. Goff (No. Andover, MA)
Raymond E., b. 9/24/1931; second; Raymond Bailey (farmer, Providence, RI) and Charlotte Goff (No. Andover, MA)
Walter Douglas, b. 5/26/1960 in Rochester; third; Earl D. Bailey (IBM operator, NH) and Martha Lee Faist (NH)
Wanda Lynn, b. 10/21/1955 in Rochester; second; Earl D. Bailey (machine oper., NH) and Martha L. Faist (NH)

BAKER,
Carrie Nicole, b. 11/28/1976 in Exeter; Barry G. Baker and Sherri A. Rorer

BALBEN,
Philip Lawrence, b. 8/23/1981 in Dover; Lawrence D. Balben and Michele M. Scott

BARKER,
Barbara Anne, b. 8/4/1965 in Dover; fourth; Ralph Barker (stenciler, NC) and Elaine F. Sherry (NH)
Jessica Elaine, b. 2/15/1974 in Rochester; Ralph Barker and Elaine Frances Sherry

BARNARD,
child, b. 7/24/1892; fifth; Louis Barnard (laborer, 40, Canada) and Mary Bernier (30, Canada)
son, b. 3/11/1894; sixth; Louis Barnard (laborer, 41, Canada) and Mary Bernier (31, Canada)

BARRETT,
Katharine, b. 5/24/1973 in Exeter; Warren E. Barrett (NH) and Francesca LaGuardia (NH)

BARTELS,
Joan Merl, b. 10/4/1955 in Rochester; fifth; Wellington P. Bartels (service manager, MA) and Merl Seavey (NH)
Richard Ernest, b. 7/26/1948 in Concord; third; Wellington P. Bartels, Jr. (mechanic, Boston, MA) and Merl L. Seavey (Northwood)
Thomas Donald, b. 4/7/1953 in Concord; fourth; Wellington P. Bartels (mechanic, MA) and Merl L. Seavey (NH)

BARTOSIEWICZ,
Elizabeth Ann, b. 9/29/1982 in Dover; Robert L. Bartosiewicz and Constance M. Larock
Jeffrey Aaron, b. 10/6/1981 in Dover; Robert L. Bartosiewicz and Constance M. Larock
Ryan Michael, b. 10/19/1979 in Dover; Robert L. Bartosiewicz and Constance M. Larock

BARTOSZAK,
Francis John, b. 10/29/1984 in Rochester; John F. Bartoszak and Lisa A. Gagnon

BASSETT,
Justin Sherburne, b. 11/10/1987 in Dover; Russell E. Bassett and Ann M. Zerbinopoulos

BASTON,
Nellie E., b. 1/22/1900; first; Stephen A. Baston, Jr. (painter, 28, So. Berwick, ME) and Alvina Marston (20, No. Hampton)

BATEMAN,
Jason Foss, b. 9/16/1980 in Concord; John F. Bateman and Gail E. Emerson
Sarah Jean, b. 7/22/1978 in Dover; Charles R. Bateman and Gloria J. Craig

BAXTER,
Brenda Lee, b. 5/24/1952 in Rochester; third; Alden E. Baxter (poultry inspector, NH) and Geraldine E. Swain (NH)
Carolyn Lou, b. 7/22/1950 in Rochester; third; Sherman L. Baxter (truck driver, NH) and Luverne C. Swain (NH)
Jean Esther, b. 11/19/1945 in Rochester; first; Alden E. Baxter (US Army, Madbury) and Geraldine E. Swain (Dover)
John Allen, b. 12/14/1956 in Rochester; fifth; Sherman L. Baxter (grain store, NH) and Luverne C. Swain (NH)
Linda May, b. 12/13/1947 in Rochester; second; Alden E. Baxter (poultry tester, Madbury) and Geraldine E. Swain (Dover)
Lori Susan, b. 4/30/1954 in Rochester; stillborn; fourth; Sherman L. Baxter (store mgr., NH) and Luverne C. Swain (NH)
Melvin Sherman, b. 5/17/1949 in Exeter; second; Sherman L. Baxter (truck driver, NH) and Luverne C. Swain (NH)
Sharon Ann, b. 4/13/1947 in Exeter; first; Sherman L. Baxter (truck driver, Madbury) and Luverne C. Swain (Barrington)
Tara Anne, b. 10/20/1981 in Dover; John A. Baxter and Lori J. Gray

Troy David, b. 9/13/1979 in Dover; John A. Baxter and Lori J. Gray

Velma Evelyn, b. 2/28/1941 in Exeter; second; Alfred W. Baxter (poultryman, Madbury) and Leota L. Davis (Barrington)

BEAL,

Elizabeth Jean, b. 5/18/1949 in Dover; third; Edward R. Beal (shipfitter, MA) and Margaret G. Thomas (CT)

Ellen Louise, b. 8/23/1947 in Newburyport, MA; Edward R. Beal (student, Newburyport, MA) and Margaret G. Thomas (Hartford, CT)

Joel Christopher, b. 6/5/1951 in Dover; fourth; Edward R. Beal (shipfitter, MA) and Margaret G. Thomas (CT)

Margaret Maud, b. 6/16/1953 in Dover; fifth; Edward R. Beal (shipfitter, MA) and Margaret G. Thomas (CT)

Stacy Lee, b. 9/6/1984 in Exeter; Harold L. Beal and Bonnie M. Chase

Stephen Daniel, b. 1/25/1982 in Dover; Harold L. Beal and Bonnie M. Chase

BEAN,

son, b. 10/3/1890; Edward Bean (brickmaker, Canada) and Ellen Renney (Canada)

BEARDSLEY,

son, b. 2/15/1958 in Rochester; second; Warren H. Beardsley (Air Force, OH) and Rhea E. Smith (GA)

BEAULIEU,

Brian, b. 6/28/1979 in Dover; Denis A. Beaulieu and Marilyn B. Hatch

BEERS,

Shane Boudreau, b. 11/23/1974 in Exeter; Alan George Beers and Patricia Ellen Mann

BELANGER,
Heather Leigh, b. 8/11/1986 in Exeter; Richard R. Belanger and Martha E. Klopp

BELIVEAU,
John Albert, b. 9/19/1964 in Rochester; second; Richard R. Beliveau (store manager, CT) and Lucille L. Bellemore (NH)

BELL,
Byron George, b. 11/16/1966 in Portsmouth; first; Norman B. Bell (welder, Rochester) and Madeline E. Wells (Rochester)
Cathy Sue, b. 2/13/1968 in Rochester; Norman B. Bell (NH) and Madeline E. Wells (NH)

BELLIVEAU,
Jennifer Marie, b. 10/22/1975 in Portsmouth; Paul A. Belliveau and Joanne Evans
Paul Allaine, Jr., b. 10/22/1975 in Portsmouth; Paul A. Belliveau and Joanne Evans

BENGTSON,
Rebecca May, b. 7/7/1966 in Exeter; third; Richard C. Bengtson (tool & die maker, Manchester, CT) and Marion L. Bryson (Exeter)

BENNETT,
Andrew Lawrence, b. 11/16/1963 in Rochester; first; Joseph A. Bennett (dairyman, WV) and Sally C. Pelletier (IL)
Catalee Catherine, b. 6/16/1965 in Rochester; second; Joseph A. Bennett (carpenter, WV) and Sally C. Pelletier (IL)
Christine Jessie, b. 2/13/1963 in Rochester; fourth; Philip Bennett (dairy farmer, WV) and Jacqueline F. Marble (NH)

John Gabriel, b. 4/29/1962 in Kittery, ME; third; William A.
Bennett (USAF, CA) and Angelina Corradin (Italy)
John Lawrence, b. 8/31/1979 in Dover; John F. Bennett, Jr.
and Arlinda Van Liere
Joseph Aaron, b. 5/22/1969 in Rochester; Joseph A. Bennett
(WV) and Sally C. Pelletier (IL)
Philip Harold, b. 4/21/1965 in Rochester; fifth; Philip Bennett
(dairyman, WV) and Jacqueline F. Marble (NH)

BENNINGTON,
Jeffrey Michael, b. 8/26/1982 in Rochester; Brian R.
Bennington and Laurie J. Willett
Joshua Andrew, b. 9/22/1980 in Rochester; Brian R.
Bennington and Laurie J. Willett

BENSON,
Brad Michael, b. 5/20/1987 in Dover; Cecil A. Benson and
Rebecca A. Houle

BERGERON,
Samuel Lawrence, b. 3/23/1987 in Dover; Gerard L.
Bergeron and Dawn S. Seaver

BERNIER,
son [Fred J.], b. 8/31/1893; first; Theodore Berniel (sic)
(laborer, Canada) and M. E. Pumbank (Canada)
stillborn son, b. 8/3/1898; third; Theodore Bernier (railroad
man, 30, Canada) and Delvena Pomolo (26, Canada)
Arthur, b. 12/25/1899; fourth; Theodore Bernier (section
hand, 33, Canada) and Delvine Pomarlo (28, Canada)
Stephanie Michelle, b. 11/1/1980 in Dover; Gary W. Bernier
and Gabriella Boldi

BERRY,
daughter, b. 8/13/1893; first; Elmer Berry (farmer, Strafford)
and Laura Corson (Barrington)

son, b. 4/19/1895; first; Alvin F. Berry (farmer, 19, Barrington) and Mary Hughes (21, Boston, MA)

son, b. 8/27/1895; third; Charles Berry (farmer, 37, Barrington) and Emma Morrison (34, Barrington)

son, b. 1/8/1896; second; Albert C. Berry (laborer, 22, Strafford) and Nellie C. Weeden (23, Somersworth)

son [Clifton B.], b. 5/31/1896; second; Alvin T. Berry (laborer, 21, Barrington) and Mary A. Hughes (22, Boston, MA)

daughter, b. 9/21/1896; first; Lewis C. Berry (laborer, 27, Barrington) and Sadie J. Perkins (18, Barrington)

son, b. 7/1/1897; third; Alvin T. Berry (farmer, 22, Barrington) and Mary A. Hughes (23, Boston, MA)

son [William], b. 3/15/1898; third; Albert C. Berry (farmer, 24, Strafford) and Nellie A. Weeden (26, Strafford)

daughter, b. 4/1/1901; second; Elmer Berry (farmer, 37, Strafford) and Lura D. Carson (26, Barrington)

son, b. 11/23/1903; fifth; Alvin T. Berry (farmer, 29, Barrington) and Mary A. Hughes (30, Boston, MA)

son, b. 11/4/1904; eighth; Alvin T. Berry (farmer, 29, Barrington) and Mary Hughes (31, East Boston, MA)

son [Clarence L.], b. 2/25/1905; second; Lewis Berry (laborer, 35, Farmington) and Sadie Perkins (26, Barrington)

daughter, b. 1/24/1909; first; Warren W. Berry (farmer, 21, Barrington) and Eva Mattox (21, Lee)

son, b. 4/12/1909; seventh; Alvin T. Berry (farmer, 33, Barrington) and Mary A. Hughes (36, Boston, MA)

daughter, b. 5/6/1910; second; Warren W. Berry (farmer, 23, Barrington) and Eva Mattox (24, Lee)

daughter, b. 9/17/1914; third; Warren W. Berry (farmer, Barrington) and Eva Mattox (Lee)

Arline E., b. 5/20/1922; third; Franklin L. Berry (farmer, Weymouth, MA) and Anna E. Rawson (Paris, ME)

Christine F., b. 7/4/1921; fourth; Warren Berry (farmer, Barrington) and Eva M. Mattox (Lee)

Clarence Lewis, Jr., b. 3/20/1934; third; Clarence L. Berry (laborer, Barrington) and Estelle Mary Pay (Wolfeboro)
Daniel Edwards, b. 10/29/1987 in Dover; Jonathan D. Berry and Diane E. Edwards
Doris May, b. 4/25/1937; eighth; Clarence Berry (farmer, Barrington) and Edith M. King (Wolfeboro)
Elizabeth, b. 12/23/1900; first; Flavius J. Berry (farmer, 41, Barrington) and Nellie N. Glidden (29, Lee)
Harold Linwood, b. 10/4/1898; fourth; Alvin Berry (farmer, Barrington) and Anna M. Hughes (Boston, MA)
Janice Janet, b. 7/19/1935; seventh; Clarence L. Berry (farmer, Barrington) and Edith M. King (Wolfeboro Falls)
Jill Kelli, b. 4/2/1982 in Portsmouth; Stephen M. Berry and Verna M. Jennings
Kenneth Bruce, b. 10/11/1941 in Brentwood; third; Willis Berry (garage wkr.) and Vira E. Neal (Barrington)
Lucille A., b. 4/24/1912; second; Irving B. Berry (farmer, 44, Strafford) and Delia Foss (32, Strafford)
Mary Margery, b. 8/17/1909; third; Flavius J. Berry (farmer, 51, Barrington) and Nellie E. Glidden (38, Lee)
Norman J., b. 5/31/1903; second; Flavius J. Berry (lumber, farmer, 45, Barrington) and Nellie Glidden (32, Lee)
Norman J., b. 6/22/1929 in Rochester; first; N. J. Berry (farmer, Barrington) and Dorothy Burpee (Exeter)
Percy N., Jr., b. 4/3/1930 in Rochester; third; Percy N. Berry (farmer, Barrington) and Stella Hall (Dover)
Percy Nelson, b. 9/13/1908; third; Lewis C. Berry (laborer, 38, Farmington) and Sarah J. Perkins (31, Barrington)
William Edward, b. 4/22/1940; ninth; Clarence L. Berry (farmer, Barrington) and Edith M. King (Wolfeboro)

BERTHIAUME,
Stephanie Lara, b. 4/4/1986 in Dover; Robert P. Berthiaume and Myra K. Wagener

BERUBE,
Bradford Michael, b. 4/11/1973 in Kittery, ME; Michael R. Berube (NH) and Theresa A. Garneau (NH)

BICKERSTAFFE,
Daniel David, b. 1/5/1976 in Dover; Daniel W. Bickerstaffe and Mary E. O'Brien

BICKFORD,
son [John Hart], b. 2/22/1902; first; Herbert Bickford (chopper, 30, Farmington) and Lizzie H. Perkins (26, Barrington); residence - Northwood
Duane David, b. 12/8/1970 in Rochester; David L. Bickford (ME) and Julia S. Hilton (ME)
Kevin Thomas, b. 12/28/1970 in Rochester; Wesley B. Bickford (NH) and Sally Bowyer (NH)
Penny Lynn, b. 10/12/1968 in Rochester; Wesley B. Bickford (NH) and Sally Bowyer (NH)
Wendy Jo, b. 3/6/1967 in Rochester; second; Wesley B. Bickford (research chem., Rochester) and Sally Bowyer (Derry)
Wesley Bruce, Jr., b. 7/1/1965 in Rochester; first; Wesley B. Bickford (research chem., NH) and Sally Bowyer (NH)

BILODEAU,
Robert Allen, b. 11/4/1979 in Dover; Ronald L. Bilodeau and Diane L. Gray

BIRKEMOSE,
Kevin Wayne, b. 4/12/1956 in Rochester; second; Robert J. Birkemose (ROTC office, MA) and Joan B. Hooper (ME)

BISBING,
Phaedra Michelle, b. 2/5/1977 in Portsmouth; William F. Bisbing and Pamela Allen

BISHOP,
Cheryl Ruth, b. 10/26/1981 in Dover; Roger C. Bishop and Virginia N. Ramsdell

BISSELL,
Amanda Dianna, b. 4/8/1979 in Dover; Gary A. Bissell and Martha K. Phinney
Andrew Gibson, b. 6/3/1983 in Dover; Gary A. Bissell and Martha K. Phinney
Raymond Edwin, b. 10/18/1949 in Dover; sixth; William O. Bissell (truck driver, MA) and Ethel M. Marshall (NH)

BISSON,
Randy Lee, b. 6/1/1982 in Rochester; Terry A. Bisson and LuAnn M. Forbes
Shane Paul, Jr., b. 10/6/1979 in Rochester; Shane P. Bisson and Mable R. Elliott

BLAIR,
Lynda Lee, b. 10/30/1962 in Dover; first; Thomas F. Blair (shipper, ME) and Mary E. Hichens (NH)

BLAISDELL,
Mabel Mary Elizabeth, b. 6/16/1881; Arthur T. Blaisdell (Deerfield) and Mary Blaisdell (Barrington) (1947)
Matie A., b. 3/21/1892; first; Oliver Blaisdell (farmer, 23, Barrington) and Rosina Grey (24, Greenland)

BLANCHETTE,
Craig Charles, b. 6/1/1960 in Portsmouth; second; Ronald C. Blanchette (guidance councelor, NH) and Patricia E. Bailey (NH)

BLISS,
Elijah Grahame, b. 4/9/1976 in Exeter; Michael G. Bliss and Ann C. Greenberg

Samantha Matin, b. 3/23/1972 in Dover; Michael G. Bliss (OH) and Ann C. Greenberg (NY)

BLODGETT,
Melissa Anne, b. 4/19/1982 in Dover; Daniel R. Blodgett and Nikki Tatakes

BLOSSOM,
Rebecca Lynn, b. 2/10/1985 in Concord; Wilbur A. Blossom and Phyllis L. Brown

BLOUNT,
Ralph Woods, b. 11/13/1985 in Dover; Joseph P. Blount and Mary A. Records

BODGE,
daughter [Ethel M.], b. 3/30/1890; fourth; Charles F. Bodge (farmer, Barrington) and Mary F. Curley (Brighton, MA)
daughter [Mary Ruth], b. 5/20/1893; C. F. Bodge (farmer, Barrington) and Mary F. Curley (Brighton, MA)
daughter [Gertrude G.], b. 3/6/1895; sixth; Charles F. Bodge (farmer, 38, Barrington) and Mary Carley (32, Brighton, MA)
son [James], b. 3/7/1898; seventh; Charles Bodge (farmer, 41, Barrington) and Mary Carley (33, Brighton, MA)
son, b. 5/31/1910; first; John Bodge (farmer, 24, Barrington) and E. Josephine Daly (25, Brighton, MA)
Carl Andrew, b. 12/12/1961 in Rochester; second; Carl J. Bodge (maint. man, NH) and Eunice B. Wilkins (NH)
Charles A., b. 4/1/1914; second; John W. Bodge (farmer, Barrington) and Winfied J. Daley (Brighton, MA)
Connie Sue, b. 5/31/1956 in Rochester; first; John L. Bodge (farm work, NH) and Gloria A. Bennett (WV)
Dexter Philip, b. 8/23/1961 in Rochester; second; John L. Bodge (laborer, NH) and Gloria A. Bennett (WV)

James Michael, b. 12/29/1945 in Dover; first; James C.
Bodge (mechanic, Barrington) and Doris A. Fogarty
(Dover)
John Lawrence, Jr., b. 1/11/1948 in Rochester; second; John
L. Bodge (const. co., Dover) and Mary E. Ward
(Pembroke, ME)
Linda Marie, b. 3/20/1967 in Rochester; fifth; Carl J. Bodge
(maintenance man, Manchester) and Eunice B. Wilkins
(Farmington)
Mary Elizabeth, b. 12/18/1946 in Rochester; first; John L.
Bodge (woodsman, Dover) and Mary E. Ward
(Pembroke, ME)
Nancy Jean, b. 8/1/1950 in Rochester; third; John L. Bodge
(unemployed, NH) and Mary E. Ward (ME)
Terrilynn Marie, b. 7/14/1985 in Dover; Michael G. Bodge
and Kimberly L. Geer

BODUCH,
Anastasia Elizabeth, b. 10/15/1973 in Dover; Thaddeus R.
Boduch (MA) and Janet Collins (NH)
Samuel Thaddeus, b. 1/8/1984 in Dover; Thaddeus S.
Boduch and Janet Collins
Stanley Joseph, II, b. 1/22/1977 in Dover; Thaddeus S.
Boduch and Janet Collins
Stephanie Joan, b. 2/9/1975 in Dover; Thaddeus S. Boduch
and Janet B. Collins
Stephen James, b. 6/13/1979 in Dover; Thaddeus S. Boduch
and Janet Collins

BOGGS,
Brandon Dean, b. 6/4/1983 in Dover; Dean F. Boggs and
Jean E. Van Nest
Daniel George Edwin, b. 2/13/1985 in Dover; Dean F. Boggs
and Jean E. Van Nest

BOISVERT,
Fara Dianne, b. 3/24/1972 in Dover; Alan R. Boisvert (NH) and Carolyn F. Knights (NH)
Kregg Alan, b. 2/14/1971 in Dover; Alan R. Boisvert (NH) and Carolyn F. Knights (NH)

BOLDUC,
Benjamen William, b. 11/8/1979 in Dover; Edward D. Bolduc and Donna L. Hayes
Tonya Darcell, b. 2/21/1977 in Dover; Edward D. Bolduc and Donna L. Hayes

BOOD[E]Y,
son, b. 8/31/1907; fifth; John Y. Boody (farmer, 38, Strafford) and Alice I. Arlin (26, Strafford)
son [Ralph J.], b. 7/11/1923; sixth; John W. Boody (farmer, Barrington) and Alice Arlin (Strafford)
Alice Lucille, b. 12/5/1920; fifth; John U. Boody (farmer, Barrington) and Alice I. Arlin (Strafford)
Julia Eileen, b. 7/13/1948 in Rochester; second; Ralph J. Boodey (farmer, Barrington) and Pauline Beauchain (E. Wallingford, VT)
Michael Hester, b. 9/23/1976 in Rochester; Philip J. Boodey and Karen M. Shorry
Philip John, b. 3/23/1945 in Rochester; first; Ralph J. Boodey (farmer, Barrington) and Pauline E. Beauchain (E. Wallingford, VT)
Susan May, b. 12/10/1950 in Rochester; third; Ralph J. Boodey (farmer, NH) and Pauline E. Beauchain (VT)
Timothy Main, b. 9/23/1976 in Rochester; Philip J. Boodey and Karen M. Shorry

BOOTH,
Bonnie Lou, b. 4/6/1949 in Rochester; second; George W. Booth, Jr. (salesman, NH) and Elizabeth M. Francis (NH)

BORRAZAS,
Andrea Marie, b. 12/22/1984 in Concord; Lawrence H. Borrazas and Holly A. Howard
Meghan, b. 5/22/1986 in Concord; Lawrence H. Borrazas and Holly A. Howard

BOSTON,
Bertha May, b. 10/29/1896; first; Charles Boston (laborer, 30, Barrington) and Laura Smith (29, Deerfield)
Flossie, b. 6/14/1890; twelfth; Stephen A. Boston (farmer, So. Berwick, ME) and Hannah Giles (Nottingham)

BOSTROM,
Susan, b. 4/20/1965 in Rochester; second; David A. Bostrom (lineman, MA) and Gladys A. Campbell (ME)

BOUCHARD,
Joy Jessica, b. 10/7/1968 in Rochester; George I. Bouchard (NH) and Jacqueline A. Turner (NH)

BOUCHER,
Brian Normand, b. 1/31/1981 in Rochester; Normand H. Boucher and Marianne S. Cromwell
Christopher Michael, b. 8/28/1983 in Portsmouth; Raymond L. Boucher and Vickie M. Caskie
Thomas Anthony, b. 9/22/1985 in Dover; Raymond L. Boucher and Vicki M. Caskie

BOUDREAU,
Kelly Marie, b. 9/22/1977 in Rochester; Joseph V. Boudreau and Grace O. Poliquin

BOURGEOIS,
Jeremy Ryan, b. 12/19/1986 in Rochester; James R. Bourgeois and Deborah S. Smith

BOWER,
Martha Huntley, b. 2/14/1952 in Exeter; second; Warren C. Bower (UNH, NY) and Mary E. Swain (NH)
Warren Cornell, Jr., b. 1/16/1951 in Exeter; first; Warren C. Bower (psychologist, NH) and Mary E. Swain (NH)

BOWICK,
Blake Richard, b. 8/11/1987 in Exeter; Walter K. Bowick, Jr. and Marilyn J. Qua

BOWLEN,
Amy Elizabeth, b. 10/4/1972 in Portsmouth; Kenneth C. Bowlen (MA) and Priscilla A. Brown (NH)

BOYCE,
Jarrod Thomas, b. 5/11/1982 in Rochester; Thomas E. Boyce and Victoria S. Latella

BOYLE,
Ivan Patrick, b. 2/24/1972 in Rochester; Sean M. Boyle (NH) and Susan J. Doran (MA)
Michael Barney, b. 8/25/1978 in Rochester; Sean M. Boyle and Susan J. Doran
Nancy Arline, b. 8/24/1936 in Dover; second; Warren A. Boyle (farmer, Charlestown, MA) and Mildred French (Dover)
Shawna Colleen, b. 9/18/1975 in Rochester; Sean M. Boyle and Susan J. Doran

BRADIE,
Michael Robert, b. 8/20/1975 in Dover; Ross L. Bradie and Karen A. Pereiva

BRAMAN,
Jonathan David, b. 2/27/1979 in Rochester; Grenville J.F. Braman and Suzanne M. Doughlin

BRANT,
Margaret Baldwin, b. 6/30/1951 in Rochester; third; John M. Brant (lawyer, NY) and Constance Cronin (MA)

BRENNON,
son, b. 8/4/1895; second; Comfort Brennon (26, England)

BRETON,
Cynthia Merle, b. 5/18/1959 in Rochester; second; John T. Breton (insurance agent, MA) and Marilyn M. Bodge (NH)

BREUNIG,
Bethany Lynn, b. 6/14/1978 in Rochester; David D. Breunig and Linda J. Hodge

BREWSTER,
Steven Darrell, b. 5/29/1965 in Dover; fourth; Ronald W. Brewster (electronics, NH) and Ida Marlene Hale (NH)
Tricia Ann, b. 8/9/1985 in Rochester; Steve D. Brewster and Stacey D. Goff

BRISSON,
Todd Michael, b. 9/19/1976 in Exeter; Claude A. Brisson and Susan A. Rickards

BROADBENT,
Melissa Sue, b. 2/21/1978 in Dover; Gary R. Broadbent and Linda J. Normand
Troy Mathew, b. 1/31/1979 in Dover; Gary R. Broadbent and Linda J. Normand

BROCK,
daughter, b. 9/21/1890; first; Charles E. Brock (laborer) and Abbie L. Avery (Strafford)

John Richard, b. 6/1/1983 in Dover; John P. Brock and Margaret A. Tobin

BROOKS,
Daniel Christopher, b. 7/10/1984 in Exeter; Gary A. Brooks and Holly A. Howard
Kathi Jane, b. 7/24/1961 in Rochester; fourth; Richard S. Brooks (electrician, MA) and Ann K. Johnson (VT)
Keith Paige, b. 5/14/1959 in Rochester; third; Richard S. Brooks (electrician, MA) and Ann K. Johnson (VT)
Kim Kra-Veiling, b. 5/3/1956 in Rochester; second; Richard S. Brooks (electrician, MA) and Ann K. Johnson (VT)
Lorrine A., b. 6/27/1932; third; Ernest Brooks (box maker, Rockland, MA) and Mildred B. Jollymore (Cambridge, MA); residence - East Rochester
Whitney Renee, b. 2/3/1986 in Portsmouth; Vernon W. Brooks and Denise M. Leon

BROWN,
son, b. 9/27/1890; third; Thomas F. Brown (farmer, Newburyport, MA) and Ann Mary Brown (Barrington)
son, b. 5/7/1892; fifth; Joseph Brown (laborer, 31, Canada) and Rose Rauleau (31, Canada)
son [George T.], b. 5/14/1892; fourth; Frank Brown (laborer, 23, Barrington) and Annie Arlin (22, Barrington)
son [Chester], b. 4/11/1899; first; John Brown (laborer, 22, Barrington) and Iza May Harvell (20, Barrington)
child, b. 4/12/1899; eighth; Frank Brown (laborer, 30, Barrington) and Eliza A. Allen (27, Barrington)
son [Harold], b. 4/23/1901; second; John Brown (laborer, 24, Barrington) and Iza Harnell (22, Barrington)
daughter, b. 8/17/1901; ninth; Frank R. Brown (laborer, 32, Cambridgeport, MA) and Eliza A. Brown (32, Barrington)
son [Everette], b. 3/16/1903; third; John Brown (laborer, 26, Barrington) and Iza Harwell (24, Barrington)

daughter, b. 3/27/1903; tenth; Frank Brown (laborer, 34, Barrington) and Eliza A. Allen (34, Barrington)
son, b. 5/27/1907; first; Orison J. Brown (shoemaker, 48, Barrington) and Bertha Rand (26, Rochester)
daughter, b. 6/27/1910; sixth; John A. Brown (laborer, 33, Haverhill, MA) and Iza M. Harvell (28, Barrington)
daughter, b. 7/17/1910; third; Henry E. Brown (farmer, 40, Strafford) and Grace B. Corson (33, Barrington); residence - Strafford
son [Orrin], b. 12/21/1910; first; Edgar F. Brown (teamster, 25, Barrington) and Edna Buzzell (16, Barrington)
daughter, b. 8/23/1912; second; Edgar F. Brown (farmer, 24, Barrington) and Edna Buzzell (18, Barrington)
daughter, b. 3/27/1913; seventh; John A. Braum (sic) (millman, 36, Haverhill, MA) and Iza M. Harvell (34, Barrington)
son, b. 12/25/1915; eighth; John A. Brown (mill operator, Haverhill, MA) and Iza M. Harvell (Barrington)
son [Thomas], b. 4/14/1920; first; Chester Brown (lumberman, Barrington) and Iva S. McKay (Barrington)
Aaron Alden, b. 7/16/1979 in Hanover; Lewis P. Brown, Jr. and Brenda L. Baxter
Alberta S., b. 8/26/1926; seventh; Edward Brown (laborer, 32, Lee) and Margaret McDonald (Barrington)
Alice May, b. 2/6/1890; Frank Brown (Haverhill, MA) and Eliza Ann Allen (Barrington) (1943)
Ashley Krista, b. 11/15/1985 in Dover; Lewis P. Brown and Brenda L. Baxter
Barbara J., b. 8/24/1931; ninth; Edward E. Brown (laborer, Lee) and Margaret McDonald (Barrington)
Benjamin Augustus, b. 9/11/1895; Frank Brown (MA) and Eliza A. Allen (NH) (1957)
David Forrest, b. 4/26/1947 in Rochester; second; Earl H. Brown (farmer, Barrington) and Shirley M. Pearson (Lawrence, MA)

Dora, b. 3/27/1905; eleventh; Frank Brown (laborer, 37, Barrington) and Eliza A. Allen (37, Barrington)

Doris Irene, b. 10/16/1932 in Dover; third; Harold G. Brown (truck driver, Barrington) and Irene A. Stimpson (Weathersfield, VT)

Earl H., b. 1/9/1922; tenth; John A. Brown (lumber op., Haverhill, MA) and Iza M. Harwell (Barrington)

Esther Nellie, b. 1/22/1894; Frank Brown (MA) and Eliza A. Allen (NH) (1955)

Ethel Lucy, b. 3/27/1891; Frank Brown (MA) and Eliza A. Allen (NH) (1955)

Flora Bell, b. 10/29/1901; William H. Brown (farmer, Barrington) and Sarah P. Reed (Barrington)

Florence J., b. 12/4/1923; fifth; Edward Brown (woodchopper, Lee) and Margaret McDonald (Barrington)

Georgianna L., b. 9/11/1919; fifth; Edgar F. Brown (farmer, Barrington) and Edna L. Buzzell (Barrington)

Gordon W., b. 7/2/1937; fifth; Harold G. Brown (laborer, Barrington) and Irene A. Stimpson (Weathersfield, VT)

Guy Nelson, b. 11/8/1910; William H. Brown (farmer, Barrington) and Sarah P. Reed (Barrington)

Ina Elizabeth, b. 8/31/1928; first; Warren Brown (Barrington) and Evelyn Buzzell (Barrington)

James Clifford, b. 11/4/1969 in Dover; Robert A. Brown (OH) and Arline M. Lirette (NH)

James Elwood, b. 2/10/1959 in Concord; third; Earl A. Brown (truck driver, NH) and Mary E. Bateman (NH)

Jeffrey William, b. 11/4/1969 in Dover; Robert A. Brown (OH) and Arline M. Lirette (NH)

Jill Marie, b. 1/26/1975 in Rochester; Charles L. Brown, Jr. and Sarah Bronson

Kady Jeanne, b. 12/5/1984 in Portsmourh; Kirk D. Brown and Carol J. Wentworth

Laforest W., b. 3/18/1915; third; Edgar Fox Brown (farmer, Barrington) and Edna Buzzell (Barrington)

Lawrence Kingman, III, b. 4/11/1969 in Rochester; Lawrence K. Brown II (NH) and Linnie A. Sanborn (NH)

Linda Alice, b. 4/28/1949 in Rochester; first; Robert F. Brown (carpenter, NH) and Irene A. Meattey (NH)

Lloyd Harold, b. 10/27/1958 in Rochester; seventh; Lawrence K. Brown (foreman, MA) and Barbara F. Wakefield (MA)

Martha Louise, b. 8/22/1945 in Rochester; first; Earl H. Brown (mover, Barrington) and Shirley M. Pearson (Lawrence, MA)

Melvin Henry, b. 3/11/1920; third; Edward E. Brown (lumberman, Lee) and Margaret McDonald (Lee)

Nancy Ellen, b. 3/7/1943 in Rochester; third; Richard E. Brown (boxmaker, Barrington) and Florence E. Wells (Northwood)

Oscar, b. 8/5/1921; fifth; Edward E. Brown (laborer, Lee) and Margaret McDonald (Barrington)

Patricia Mary, b. 3/26/1928; eighth; Edward Brown (laborer, Barrington) and Margaret McDonald (Barrington)

R[aymond]. C., b. 6/26/1917; fourth; Edgar Fox Brown (millhand, Barrington) and Edna Buzzell (Barrington)

R. Edward, b. 2/20/1915; first; Edward E. Brown (laborer, Lee) and Margaret McDonald (Barrington)

Randall Denis, b. 11/2/1956 in Rochester; fourth; Robert F. Brown (truck driver, NH) and Irene A. Meattey (NH)

Robert, b. 3/20/1917; second; Edward E. Brown (laborer, Lee) and Margaret McDonald (Barrington)

Robert Francis, Jr., b. 12/6/1951 in Rochester; second; Robert F. Brown (truck driver, NH) and Irene A. Meattey (NH)

Rodney Alan, b. 6/24/1953 in Rochester; third; Robert F. Brown (truck driver, NH) and Irene A. Meattey (NH)

Roland Everett, b. 11/28/1941 in Rochester; second; Richard E. Brown (laborer, Barrington) and Florence E. Wells (Northwood)

Stephen Donald, b. 12/7/1969 in Dover; Kenneth W. Brown (MA) and Alice N. LePelley (MN)

Tamara Leigh, b. 7/7/1966 in Rochester; second; Charles L. Brown, Jr. (substitute clerk, Bellefontaine, OH) and Sarah Bronson (Rochester)

Valarie Ann, b. 7/19/1938; fourth; Lester A. Brown (laborer, Rome, ME) and Winona E. Sterling (Saco, ME) (1942)

Waldron Augustus, b. 11/16/1918; ninth; John A. Brown (lumberman, Haverhill, MA) and Iza M. Harvell (Barrington)

Warren R., b. 4/17/1908; William H. Brown (farmer, Barrington) and Sarah P. Reed (Barrington)

Warren Raymond, b. 7/23/1940 in Rochester; first; Warren R. Brown (saw mill prop., Barrington) and Fannie L. Brown (Barrington)

Weston Frank, b. 6/9/1898; Frank Brown (Haverhill, MA) and Eliza Ann Allen (Barrington)

William Alfred, III, b. 9/9/1972 in Rochester; William A. Brown, Jr. (NH) and Janet M. Potter (ME)

BRUCE,

Carol Ann, b. 12/2/1967 in Concord; second; Allan D. Bruce (student, Winchester, MA) and Diane S. Twombly (Nottingham)

BRYSON,

Charles Frazer, b. 3/25/1932 in Dover; second; Melvin Frazer Bryson (laborer, Dover) and Evelyn M. Green (Barrington); residence - S. Barrington

Marion, b. 5/19/1941 in Exeter; fourth; Melvin F. Bryson (laborer) and Evelyn M. Green

Ruth Evelyn, b. 12/29/1938 in Exeter; third; Melvin Frazer Bryson (laborer, Dover) and Evelyn May Green (Barrington)

William Frazer, b. 7/22/1969 in Dover; Charles F. Bryson (NH) and Jane E. Tufts (RI)

BUCZEK,
Aaron Michael, b. 4/28/1985 in Portsmouth; Todd M. Buczek and Leah L. Gifford
Barry Kenneth, b. 4/12/1972 in Dover; Theodore J. Buczek (NH) and Linda L. Warnecke (NH)
Donald Joseph, b. 9/26/1967 in Rochester; second; Theodore J. Buczek (trouble shooter, Dover) and Linda L. Warnecke (Rochester)

BULLIS,
Jared Adam, b. 8/13/1987 in Dover; Roger D. Bullis and Traci L. Steele
Lindsay Marie, b. 11/1/1985 in Dover; Roger D. Bullis and Traci L. Steele

BUMFORD,
son [Grover C.], b. 1/4/1893; C. W. Bumford (farmer, Barrington) and Helen M. Hodgdon (Greenland)
Paul Woodrow, b. 4/5/1926; first; Roland W. Bumford (farmer, 39, Barrington) and Stella Lorange (St. Hyacinth, Canada)
Stacy Lynn, b. 9/7/1978 in Dover; William R. Bumford and Cheryl A. Morrow

BUNDZA,
David Michael, b. 8/4/1985 in Keene; Robert M. Bundza and Anne M. Donahe
John Leo, b. 1/18/1957 in Rochester; third; Joseph T. Bundza (dispatcher, MA) and Claire M. Noble (MA)
Robert Michael, b. 7/8/1958 in Rochester; fourth; Joseph T. Bundza (machinist, MA) and Claire M. Noble (MA)

BURGIO,
Matthew Evan, b. 1/20/1978 in Dover; Ralph E. Burgio and Catherine J. Paulgaard

BURKE,
son, b. 1/11/1948; seventeenth; Everett H.W. Burke (mechanic, Milton) and Ora B. Chase (Skowhegan, ME)
Aaron David, b. 6/1/1984 in Portsmouth; David G. Burke and Janice M. Murray
Joseph Jewell, b. 1/11/1948; sixteenth; Everett H.W. Burke (mechanic, Milton) and Ora B. Chase (Skowhegan, ME)

BURLEIGH,
Naomi Nichole, b. 9/22/1987 in Dover; Jeffrey W. Burleigh, Sr. and Bonnie M. Raymond

BURROWS,
Cynthia Jean, b. 2/22/1964 in Rochester; fourth; Edgar E. Burrows (laborer, NH) and Miriam A. Huse (NH)
Julia Ann, b. 3/13/1973 in Dover; William R. Burrows, Sr. (NY) and Julia M. Lowe (NY)
William Richard, b. 8/30/1971 in Portsmouth; William R. Burrows (NY) and Julia M. Lowe (NY)

BUSH,
Sarah Marie, b. 4/4/1987 in Dover; Douglas H. Bush and Valerie E. Jock
Wesley Alvie, b. 6/22/1897; Joseph Bush and Ella F. Rowe (Barrington) (1942)

BUTLER,
Annette May, b. 1/23/1951 in Rochester; third; Roy W. Butler, Jr. (minister, MA) and Harriet C. Bruce (MA)

BUZZELL,
daughter, b. 4/14/1894; second; Orrin P. Buzzell (farmer, 34, Barrington) and Jennie E. Trask (27, Berwick, ME)
son [Clarence T.], b. 12/13/1900; first; Levi H. Buzzell (blacksmith, 23, Barrington) and Bessie Arlin (21, Strafford)

daughter, b. 4/17/1901; second; Charles E. Buzzell (farmer, 35, Barrington) and Adeline Curris (29, Boston, MA)
son, b. 5/1/1905; third; Levi Buzzell (farmer, 29, Barrington) and Bessie Arlin (26, Strafford)
son, b. 4/19/1907; fourth; Levi Buzzell (farmer, 31, Barrington) and Bessie Arlin (28, Strafford)
daughter, b. 6/11/1909; fifth; Levi H. Buzzell (farmer, 32, Barrington) and Bessie Arlin (30, Strafford)
daughter [Eleanor L.], b. 2/3/1912; sixth; Levi H. Buzzell (farmer, 35, Barrington) and Bessie M. Arlin (33, Strafford)
daughter [Eloise J.], b. 10/1/1913; seventh; Levi Buzzell (farmer, 36, Barrington) and Bessie M. Arlin (34, Strafford)
Arthur Lewis, b. 6/20/1955 in Rochester; second; Arthur J. Buzzell (laborer, NH) and Annie A. Dodge (NH)
Edith Genrose, b. 3/27/1942 in Brentwood; sixth; Harold B. Buzzell (laborer, Barrington) and Serena W. Ball (NS)
George Malcolm, b. 4/14/1959 in Rochester; fifth; Arthur J. Buzzell (laborer-constr., NH) and Annie A. Dodge (NH)
Harold Burton, b. 7/6/1934; second; Harold B. Buzzell (truck driver, Barrington) and Lerena Ball (Yarmouth, NS)
Helen Hope, b. 3/21/1925; Maurice T. Buzzell (farmer, 45, Lee) and Laura Edney (33, Colorado Springs, CO)
James, b. 10/31/1916; first; Maurice T. Buzzell (farmer, Lee) and Laura C. Edney (CO)
Karen Dale, b. 7/14/1957 in Rochester; fourth; Arthur J. Buzzell (self-employed, NH) and Annie A. Dodge (NH)
Levi Stanley, b. 9/28/1937; third; Harold B. Buzzell (mechanic, Barrington) and Serena Ball (NS)
Marian C., b. 6/19/1897; first; Charles E. Buzzell (farmer and carpenter, 31, Barrington) and Adeline Curris (26, Boston, MA)
Mary E., b. 10/8/1890; first; Orin P. Buzzell (farmer, Barrington) and Jennie E. Trask (Berwick, ME)

Mildred Ann, b. 5/9/1954 in Rochester; first; Arthur J. Buzzell (laborer, NH) and Annie A. Dodge (NH)
Rebecca Hope, b. 5/6/1956 in Rochester; third; Arthur J. Buzzell (laborer, NH) and Annie A. Dodge (NH)
Sarah Elizabeth, b. 9/8/1920; third; Maurice T. Buzzell (farmer, Lee) and Laura C. Edney (Colorado Springs, CO)

CABRAL,
James Joseph, b. 12/18/1980 in Dover; Joseph E. Cabral and Deborah A. Reynolds

CAFASSO,
Scott Michael, b. 8/9/1982 in Dover; John J. Cafasso and Cynthia A. Soule

CAIN,
Jonathan Roland, b. 8/8/1980 in Dover; Kenneth C. Cain, Sr. and Carline J. Naglie

CALDWELL,
son [Dexter H.], b. 3/17/1911; first; Harold D. Caldwell (farmer, 19, Barrington) and Mabel F. Kenniston (18, Lee)
Mabell Gertrude, b. 5/15/1899; third; Edwin Caldwell (farmer, 30, Barrington) and Clara Biederman (34, Saxony, Germany)
William D., b. 9/6/1891; second; Edwin D. Caldwell (farmer, Barrington) and Clara A. Beederman (Lawrence, MA)

CALEF,
son, b. 3/30/1901; fifth; Austin L. Calef (merchant, 30, Barrington) and Clellie M. Chesley (28, Barrington)
son [A. Harlan], b. 6/27/1910; sixth; Austin L. Calef (merchant, 39, Barrington) and Cellie M. Chesley (37, Barrington)

Andrea Elizabeth, b. 9/16/1949 in Rochester; first; Roger L. Calef (clerk, NH) and Alberta M. Whitham (NH)

Bradley John, b. 10/25/1966 in Dover; third; John M. Calef (poultryman, Dover) and Shirley A. McKenna (Rochester)

Diane Jean, b. 5/6/1959 in Rochester; second; John M. Calef (poultryman, NH) and Shirley A. McKenna (NH)

Dorothy, b. 3/7/1899; fourth; Austin L. Calef (merchant, 28, Barrington) and Clellie M. Chesley (25, Barrington)

George Austin, b. 9/16/1939 in Dover; first; A. Harlin Calef (salesman, East Barrington) and Irene M. Holmes (Everett, MA); residence - East Barrington

James Austin, b. 5/1/1962 in Rochester; first; George A. Calef (meat cutter, NH) and Arvilla M. twombly (NH)

Jere Clarence, b. 7/24/1958 in Rochester; third; Roger L. Calef (clerk, NH) and Alberta M. Witham (NH)

John Morrell, b. 6/24/1935 in Dover; second; Leon C. Calef (chicken dlr., NH) and Ruth Morrell (NH) (1962)

Karen Lynne, b. 5/14/1965 in Rochester; second; George A. Calef (meat cutter, NH) and Arvilla M. Twombly (NH)

Leon Chesley, b. 9/24/1897; Austin L.F. Calef (NH) and Clellie M. Calef (NH) (1963)

Linda Leigh, b. 9/7/1948 in Rochester; first; Leon C. Calef (poul. dealer, Barrington) and Arlene E. Rowe (Madbury)

Patricia Lee, b. 7/18/1930 in Dover; first; Leon Calef (merchant, NH) and Ruth Morrell (NH) (1962)

Paul Holmes, b. 4/4/1943 in Rochester; second; Austin Harlan Calef (clerk, Barrington) and Irene May Holmes (Everett, MA)

Ruth, b. 3/21/1895; second; Austin Calef (merchant, 24, Barrington) and Clellie Chesley (21, Barrington)

William Roger, b. 3/19/1953 in Rochester; second; Roger L. Calef (clerk, NH) and Alberta M. Witham (NH)

CALETTE,
son, b. 10/6/1891; second; David Calette (laborer, St. Charles, NB) and Require Gray (St. Charles, NB)

CALL,
Erica Jean, b. 10/23/1970 in Concord; Winfield S. Call (ME) and Ruth M. Grover (ME)

CAMIRE,
Erica Patricia Ann, b. 1/3/1975 in Lawrence, MA; William P. Camire, Jr. and Deborah M. Chute

CAMPBELL,
Richard Calvin, b. 10/8/1971 in Rochester; Richard D. Campbell (NH) and Cheryl L. Wentworth (NH)

CAMPOS,
Stephanie Jeanne, b. 1/19/1977 in Dover; Calixtro V. Campos and Pamela J. Clay

CANNEY,
son [Clifford], b. 4/24/1908; first; Norman Canney (blacksmith, 21, Barrington) and Minnie Waterhouse (21, Barrington)
Alfred Benjamin, Jr., b. 10/28/1971 in Rochester; Alfred B. Canney (NH) and Patricia A. Tebbetts (NH)
Deborah Marilyn, b. 4/15/1959 in Rochester; first; Jerome E. Canney, Jr. (truck driver, NH) and Marilyn M. Corbett (NH)
Jerome Edcil, III, b. 12/5/1961 in Rochester; third; Jerome E. Canney, Jr. (truck driver, NH) and Marilyn M. Corbett (NH)
Theryl May, b. 5/14/1960 in Rochester; second; Jerome Edcil Canney, Jr. (truck driver, NH) and Marilyn M. Corbett (NH)

CAPEN,
son [Everett], b. 10/17/1899; second; Levi Capen (laborer, 33, Somerville, MA) and Laura Freeman (23, Barrington)

CAPPIELLO,
Benjamin Dolphin, b. 5/9/1986 in Concord; Daniel M. Cappiello and Joyce A. Dolphin
Lena, b. 9/28/1981 in Concord; Daniel M. Cappiello and Joyce A. Dolphin

CARDIN,
Jonathan Edward, b. 9/28/1976 in Exeter; Roger E. Cardin, Jr. and Deanna O. Tremblay

CAREY,
Shawn Ryan, b. 9/5/1982 in Portsmouth; Scott A. Carey and Rosemary J. Crocker

CARLL,
George Harold, b. 8/25/1913; first; Irving R. Carll (stable keeper, 29, Springvale, ME) and Harriet M. Marston (22, Strafford); residence - Rochester
Lawrence, b. 5/29/1917; second; Irvin R. Carll (garage worker, So. Waterboro, ME) and Harriet Marrison (Barrington); residence - Rochester

CARLSON,
Adam Erik, b. 11/6/1982 in Portsmouth; John E. Carlson and Laurette A. Loveall
Esther Rose A., b. 4/4/1927; sixth; Carl R. Carlson (farmer, Sweden) and Gerlie Walgoest (Sweden)
Hilary Joy, b. 3/12/1986 in Dover; John W. Carlson and Barbara E. Hicks
Richard V., b. 6/6/1924; fifth; Carl R. Carlson (farmer, Sweden) and Gurlie Walquist (Sweden)

CARNEY,
Maura Cathleen, b. 6/13/1974 in Exeter; John Joseph Carney and Heather Campbell
Patrick Conor, b. 12/5/1978 in Exeter; John J. Carney and Heather Campbell
Sean Campbell, b. 5/28/1976 in Exeter; John J. Carney and Heather Campbell

CARON,
Linda, stillborn, b. 4/25/1956 in Dover; third; Lucien Caron (shoe worker, ME) and Lillian Michaud (ME)

CARR,
Eliza Jane, b. 8/13/1896; first; Curtis G. Carr (sawyer, 26, Manchester) and Carrie B. Boston (19, Barrington)

CARROLL,
Andrew David, b. 2/17/1985 in Dover; David J. Carroll and Mary J. Shea
Jennifer Elizabeth, b. 111/19/1986 in Dover; David J. Carroll and Mary J. Shea

CARTER,
son, b. 8/25/1901; tenth; Louis Carter (laborer, 30, Boston, MA) and Minnie Contutier (30, Canada)

CASE,
Chad Vernon, b. 1/28/1980 in Dover; Paul F. Case and Frances J. Bogan
Mackenzie Louis, b. 7/15/1983 in Dover; Reginald L. Case and Michael A. Bauman

CASEY,
daughter, b. 2/9/1897; third; Patrick Casey (railroad man, 33, Ireland) and Mary Morehead (28, Ireland)

Bridget Terese, b. 11/25/1893; first; Patrick Casey (section hand, Ireland) and Mary Morehead (Ireland)
Patrick F., b. 10/21/1894; second; Patrick Casey (section boss, 28, Ireland) and Mary Moreland (26, Ireland)

CASSELL,
Patrick M., b. 11/4/1970 in Exeter; Michael A. Cassell (NH) and Yvonne M. Lebeau (NH)

CASWELL,
daughter [Helen E.], b. 8/20/1909; first; Frank A. Caswell (laborer, 22, Dover) and Mary E. Buzzell (18, Barrington)
son, b. 7/16/1911; second; Frank Caswell (teamster, 25, Goffstown) and Mary Buzzell (20, Barrington)
Kirsten Marie, b. 5/22/1967 in Portsmouth; third; Dana F. Caswell (foreman, Portsmouth) and Beverly A. Swain (Exeter)
Paul David, b. 5/3/1965 in Portsmouth; second; Dana F. Caswell (technician, NH) and Beverly A. Swain (NH)
Shawn Justin, b. 10/13/1979 in Rochester; Ray A. Caswell, Jr. and Dianne K. Fryer

CATE,
son [Herman], b. 7/15/1899; second; Clarence E. Cate (shoemaker, 33, Strafford) and Mattie E. Wood (23, Barrington)
son [Herbert C.], b. 7/15/1899; third; Clarence E. Cate (shoemaker, 33, Strafford) and Mattie E. Wood (23, Barrington)

CATER,
daughter, b. 9/8/1903; first; Harry B. Cater (farmer, 23, Barrington) and May Belle Jordan (23, Biddeford, ME)
daughter, b. 7/29/1907; second; Harry B. Cater (farmer, 25, Barrington) and May Belle Jordan (26)

Perley, b. 4/27/1897; seventh; Albert H. Cater (farmer, 43, Barrington) and Cathie McDonald (40, Fredericton, NB)

CAVERLY,
Arthur Lendall, b. 8/19/1983 in Dover; Lendall R. Caverly, Jr. and Karen D. Buzzell
Robert Alan, b. 11/18/1984 in Dover; Lendall Caverly, Jr. and Karen D. Buzzell

CAVERNO,
Monique Marie, b. 11/4/1979 in Portsmouth; Thomas Caverno and Lyn M. Chantre
Pike, b. 4/9/1900; second; John L. Caverno (laborer, 27, Barrington) and Mabel Harvey (26, Nottingham)

CEPKAUSKAS,
Matthew Michael, Jr., b. 2/21/1972 in Dover; Matthew M. Cepkauskas (PA) and Cinda J. LaFleur (CT)

CHADWICK,
Elicia Marie, b. 4/1/1987 in Rochester; Norman L. Chadwick and Kimberly A. Couture

CHALBER,
Burton D., b. 10/9/1914 in Dover; first; Burton R. Chalber (box maker, Madison, CT) and Hazel Hull (Guilford, CT); residence - Madison, CT

CHAMBERLAND,
Joseph Anthony, b. 7/26/1980 in Exeter; Donald G. Chamberland and Joann Joyce
Justin Thomas, b. 2/17/1978 in Exeter; Donald G. Chamberland and Joann Joyce

CHAMPEON,
Corinne Anne, b. 9/1/1943 in Rochester; first; Thayne E. Champeon (elec. mach., Dexter, ME) and Dorothy F. McKenney (Lawrence, MA)

CHANTRE,
Nicklaus Steven, b. 6/17/1987 in Portsmouth; Steven N. Chantre and Julianne Morin

CHAPLIN,
Sharon Ann, b. 4/15/1956 in Rochester; second; Harold N. Chaplin (box maker, VT) and Julia M. Stiles (NH)

CHAPMAN,
Alice Elizabeth, b. 2/17/1935 in Rochester; fourth; Harris Chapman (farmer, Canada) and Dorothy Roberts (England)
Lori Jill, b. 8/29/1960 in Rochester; fifth; Paul R. Chapman (shoe cutter, NH) and Florence J. Dyment (OH)
Sally Jean, b. 8/23/1958 in Rochester; fourth; Paul R. Chapman (shoe cutter, NH) and Florence J. Dyment (OH)

CHAREST,
Angela Monique, b. 4/15/1968 in Exeter; Peter I. Charest (NH) and Christine Mills (NH)

CHASE,
Amanda Lynn, b. 12/15/1986 in Dover; James P. Chase and Dale E. Wells
Sandra Ann, b. 1/5/1959 in Dover; third; Gilbert L. Chase (dry cleaner, NH) and Helen L. Stewart (ME)

CHATMAN,
Chesley F., b. 10/1/1915; third; Joseph C. Chatman (farmer, Newfoundland) and Carrie E. Preston (Manchester, MA)

CHELLIS,
David Paul, b. 6/30/1944 in Concord; first; Virginia Cora Chellis (Grafton)

CHICOINE,
Danielle Renee, b. 10/23/1983 in Portsmouth; Walter Chicoine, Jr. and Julie A. Judd

CHIPMAN,
Miles Nathaniel, b. 5/17/1981 in Dover; Eric J. Chipman and Joan E. Gustin

CHRETIEN,
Amanda Leigh, b. 2/1/1974 in Dover; Leroy Gerard Chretien and Bonnie Faye Berry
Marissa Beth, b. 6/10/1977 in Dover; Leroy G. Chretien and Bonnie F. Berry

CINFO,
Anthony R.K., b. 6/7/1977 in Dover; Leo P. Cinfo and Patricia Clee

CIOFFI,
Robert Louis, b. 10/1/1982 in Manchester; Grant L. Cioffi and Ann M. Whitehall

CLARK,
daughter [Evelyn Esther], b. 3/16/1904; third; Arthur M. Clark (farmer, 30, Barrington) and Emma C. Kendall (25, St. Johns, NB)
son [Melvin], b. 5/2/1909; fifth; Arthur M. Clark (farmer, 35, Barrington) and Emma Kendall (30, St. Johns, NB)
stillborn daughter, b. 7/29/1913; seventh; Marshall Clark (farmer, Barrington) and Ada Freeman (39, Barrington)
child, b. 10/8/1916; third; Frank Clark (farmer, Canin) and Agnes Baxter (Scotland)

Agnes B., b. 12/14/1914; second; Frank F. Clark (farmer, Burlingham, MA) and Agnes Baxter (Scotland)

Brenden Tyler, b. 1/12/1981 in Portsmouth; Gordon C. Clark and Carol L. Simpson

Carol Delia, b. 1/23/1943 in Wolfeboro; fourth; Melvin Arthur Clark (farmer, Barrington) and Olive M. Cleveland (Boscawen)

Crystal Rose, b. 2/3/1980 in Exeter; Gary M. Clark and Jolene C. Peterson

Gregg Patrick, b. 6/21/1974 in Dover; Ernest William Clark, Jr. and Susan Rita Hatch

John Edward, b. 8/13/1951 in Exeter; third; Ernest W. Clark (lumber jack, NH) and Viola G. Elliott (NH)

John William, b. 5/3/1899; Marshall R. Clark (NH) and Ada Freeman (NH) (1949)

Murial Mildred, b. 11/29/1906; fourth; Arthur M. Clark (farmer, 34, Barrington) and Emma S. Kendell (St. Johns, NB)

Myrtie Ada, b. 10/28/1910; Marshall R. Clark (Barrington) and Ada Freeman (Barrington)

CLARKE,

Beulah Bernice, b. 10/14/1898; second; Arthur M. Clarke (farmer, Barrington) and Emma C. Kendall (St. John, NS)

CLAUSS,

son, b. 2/21/1979 in Dover; Allan B. Clauss and Laura J. Miller

daughter, b. 2/21/1979 in Dover; Allan B. Clauss and Laura J. Miller

Christopher Allan, b. 2/26/1974 in Dover; Allan Barry Clauss and Laura Jean Miller

CLAY,

Willis Herbert, b. 4/5/1890; Harry P. Clay (farmer, Lee) and Nellie Hanscom (Barrington) (1942)

CLEMENT,
stillborn son, b. 12/12/1955 in Dover; third; George E.
  Clement (US Army, NH) and Kathleen Cates (ME);
  residence - Dover
Robert Allan, b. 10/30/1970 in Dover; Raymond W. Clement
  (NH) and Janice L. Irons (MA)

CLOUTIER,
Mackenzie Morgan, b. 4/6/1983 in Exeter; Christopher A.
  Cloutier and Deborah Lucas

COLCORD,
Kelsey Marisa, b. 9/28/1987 in Exeter; John T. Colcord and
  Mary M. Day

COLE,
Louis Gardiner, b. 8/22/1981 in Dover; Michael L. Cole and
  Theresa M. Ottati
Stephen Thomas, b. 3/15/1971 in Dover; Forrest G. Cole
  (NH) and Jean L. Patch (NH)

COLETY,
Matthew William, b. 9/26/1984 in Dover; Marc S. Colety and
  Alice Hodgins
Rebecca, b. 11/14/1982 in Dover; Marc S. Colety and Alice
  Hodgins

COLLINS,
Caitlin Ann, b. 2/16/1983 in Rochester; Jacky R. Collins and
  Cathi V. O'Neill

COLWELL,
Derek John, b. 4/20/1985 in Dover; Robert P. Colwell and
  Darlene G. Towle
Douglas Milton, b. 2/6/1983 in Dover; Robert P. Colwell and
  Darlene G. Towle

COMSTOCK,
Wesley Scott, b. 5/22/1957 in Manchester; second; Richard D. Comstock (manager, NH) and Florence A. Jolin (NH)

COMTOIS,
Alan Benjamin, b. 12/31/1976 in Exeter; Paul O. Comtois and Dianne J. Roy

CONANT,
Breton Mansfield, b. 12/11/1934; fourth; Paul A. Conant (laborer, Wells, ME) and Edith E. Brown (Farmington)
Dwayne Albertus, b. 4/30/1932; second; Atlee P. Conant (laborer, Wells, ME) and Edith E. Brown (Farmington)

CONLEY,
Arianne Calef, b. 7/15/1976 in Dover; Martin W. Conley and Andrea E. Calef

CONRAD,
Corinne Loudon, b. 8/22/1982 in Exeter; Richard H. Conrad and MaryJo London

CONROY,
Brian Robert, b. 7/20/1986 in Dover; Edward A. Conroy and Karin J. McLeod
Ryan Edward, b. 10/5/1985 in Portsmouth; Terrence E. Conroy and Lauren E. Gallant
Tyler Eugene, b. 4/27/1983 in Portsmouth; Terrance E. Conroy and Lauren E. Gallant

COOK,
Arlene Beverly, b. 8/3/1953 in Rochester; tenth; John W. Cook (foundry, NH) and Louise Dionizio (MA)
Corey Ames, b. 8/14/1977 in Rochester; Howard L. Cook and Emma J. Hartford

David Ronald, b. 8/8/1945 in Rochester; seventh; John W. Cook (sawmill work, South Lee) and Louise Dionizio (East Boston, MA)

Ernest Everett, b. 1/26/1949 in Rochester; ninth; John W. Cook (molder, NH) and Louise Dionizia (MA)

George Peter, b. 5/25/1943 in Rochester; sixth; John William Cook (saw mill, South Lee) and Louise Dionizio (East Boston, MA)

Helen Roberta, b. 8/4/1946 in Rochester; seventh; John W. Cook (foundry, Lee) and Louise Dionizio (East Boston, MA)

Robert Daniel, b. 10/18/1941 in Brentwood; fourth; John W. Cook (navy yard, South Lee) and Louise Dionejo (East Boston, MA)

Tammy Rose, b. 7/31/1965 in Rochester; third; George P. Cook (poultryman, NH) and Ramona R. Wentworth (NH)

Vanessa Kelli, b. 1/2/1973 in Rochester; John W. Cook (MA) and Alice L. Thomas (NH)

Vaughn Kelley, b. 5/29/1966 in Rochester; second; John W. Cook, Jr. (oiler, Boston, MA) and Alice L. Thomas (Gonic)

CORBETT,

Marilyn May, b. 5/22/1943 in Concord; second; Hollie Burt Corbett (farmer, Colebrook) and Doris May Drake (Campton)

CORBIN,

Craig Robert, b. 8/8/1984 in Dover; Albert L. Corbin and Diane J. Larochelle

Randy Leo, b. 8/8/1984 in Dover; Albert L. Corbin and Diane J. Larochelle

CORMIER,

Danielle Nicole, b. 3/13/1983 in Dover; Denis G. Cormier and Lisa M. Kaler

CORRIGAN,
David Matthew, b. 3/15/1977 in Portsmouth; Robert L. Corrigan and Susanne Irish

CORSON,
son, b. 10/5/1894; fourth; Henry Corson (laborer, 41, Barrington) and Cora Cater (38, Barrington)
Nathan Lewis, b. 1/30/1984 in Dover; Galen L. Corson and Bette E. McClain

COSTA,
Amy Lee, b. 1/25/1982 in Exeter; Robert J. Costa and Robin H. Smith

COSTLOW,
Heather Marie, b. 11/16/1982 in Portsmouth; William J. Costlow and Diana M. Deangelo

COTIC,
Jon Marc, b. 6/27/1959 in Dover; first; William L. Cotic (student, MA) and Jacklyn Laser (CT)

COTTON,
Kathleen Elizabeth, b. 2/13/1970 in Rochester; Chester A. Cotton (NH) and Florence L. LeClair (NH)

COUGHLIN,
Catherine Anne, b. 10/11/1970 in Rochester; Arthur C. Coughlin (MA) and Donna J. Begin (NH)
Frederick Daniel, b. 5/25/1950 in Rochester; fifth; David F. Coughlin (electric plater, MA) and Florence E. Bell (MA)
Lisa-Marie, b. 2/18/1976 in Rochester; David F. Coughlin, III and Heidi L. Cutter
Rae-Anne Carol, b. 11/30/1976 in Dover; David F. Coughlin, Jr. and Anita S. Bourque

Rebecca Lyn, b. 12/2/1973 in Dover; David F. Coughlin, Jr. (MA) and Anita S. Bourque (NH)

COUTURE,
Amy Beth, b. 8/14/1976 in Portsmouth; James J. Couture and Diane L. Fernald

Elizabeth Grace, b. 8/15/1945; second; Armand L. Couture (disch. marine, Berlin) and Evelyn G. Elliott (Worcester, MA); residence - Revere, MA

Matthew James, b. 11/19/1980 in Portsmouth; James J. Couture and Diane L. Fernald

COYNE,
Sarah Helen, b. 11/11/1980 in Dover; John W. Coyne, III and Jaimie S. Wolf

CREMER,
Kirsten Alexis, b. 9/14/1983 in Exeter; Vivian G.N. Cremer and Margie A. Shaw

CREPEAU,
Danielle Heath, b. 6/6/1987 in Rochester; Gary R. Crepeau and Sheila A. Heath

Lauren Elizabeth, b. 4/14/1986 in Rochester; Gary R. Crepeau and Sheila A. Heath

CRITCHETT,
son [Frank], b. 3/11/1893; second; J. L. Critchett (farmer, Barrington) and Emma F. Sewall (Barrington)

son [Dwight], b. 11/11/1905; fourth; John L. Critchett (farmer, 51, Barrington) and Emma F. Sewall (38, Barrington)

Blanche, b. 4/28/1897; third; John L. Critchett (farmer and miller, 41, Barrington) and Emma F. Sewall (30, Newmarket)

CROSBY,
daughter, b. 4/18/1893; first; J. F. Crosby (minister, Naponsett, IL) and Eva E. Hale (Barrington)
Crystal Lee, b. 5/12/1985 in Portsmouth; Carl W. Crosby, Jr. and Lori A. Dowd

CROSS,
Brittney Meredith, b. 6/2/1985 in Manchester; David M.J. Cross and Robin G. Olmsted

CROTHERS,
Amanda Joy, b. 11/24/1979 in Rochester; David L. Crothers and Carol M. McCarthy
Michelle Lindsay, b. 12/3/1987 in Dover; Jeffrey J. Crothers and Patricia C. Creighton

CROUCH,
Carroll George, b. 3/26/1953 in Dover; second; Floyd K. Crouch (truck driver, NH) and Lorraine M. Turcotte (NH)

CUEVAS,
Jose Luis, II, b. 7/8/1984 in Portsmouth; Jose L. Cuevas and Krystina J. Krysiak

CUI,
Jeremy Kyle, b. 1/6/1987 in Portsmouth; Dan C. Cui and Debra M. Pratt

CUNNINGHAM,
Matthew Shane, b. 10/16/1979 in Rochester; Wilfred M. Cunningham and Marsha G. Hodge

CURRAN,
Colleen Elizabeth, b. 4/19/1976 in Portsmouth; George S. Curran and Norma M. Smith

CUTLER,
Cassandra Christina, b. 9/26/1985 in Exeter; Richard P. Cutler and Barbara A. Theriault
Eileen Timm, b. 2/18/1969 in Rochester; Alan S. Cutler (NH) and Patricia A. Timm (NY)
Richard William, b. 9/29/1983 in Exeter; Richard P. Cutler and Barbara A. Theriault

CUTTER,
Timothy Stephen, b. 12/25/1984 in Rochester; Timothy S. Cutter and Tammy J. Gardner

CYR,
Emily Rose, b. 7/3/1981; Edward N. Cyr, III and Robyn M. Payne
Jada Rae, b. 9/24/1977; Edward N. Cyr, III and Robyn M. Payne

DAHOWSKI,
Laura Beth, b. 4/28/1979 in Dover; John H. Dahowski and Dolores J. Chmielewski

DAIGLE,
Richard Philip, b. 3/9/1965 in Portsmouth; first; Richard R. Daigle (plumber, NH) and Gail C. Rousseau (ME)
Susan Lynn, b. 1/14/1970 in Portsmouth; Richard R. Daigle (NH) and Gail C. Rousseau (ME)

DAISEY,
Joshua Chase, b. 5/14/1979 in Dover; Richard E. Daisey and Donna J. Tirrell

DAME,
Beverly Ruth, b. 7/4/1971 in Dover; Robert W. Dame (NH) and Eva M. Blais (NH)

Robert Daniel, b. 5/22/1974 in Dover; Robert Warren Dame and Eva Marie Flint

Sherri Lynn, b. 10/17/1968 in Kittery, ME; Forrest F. Dame (NH) and Beverly L. Wells (NH)

DARLING,
Brian, b. 2/24/1958 in Dover; fifth; David A. Darling (poultry raiser, MA) and Arlene C. Patrone (MA)

Diane, b. 9/24/1956 in Dover; fourth; David A. Darling (poultry raising, MA) and Arlene A. Patrone (MA)

Jeff, b. 6/10/1959 in Dover; seventh; David A. Darling (truck driver, MA) and Arlene C. Patrone (MA)

Keith, b. 2/27/1953 in Dover; second; David A. Darling (chicken farmer, MA) and Arlene C. Patrone (MA)

Korey Ryan, b. 7/3/1983 in Portsmouth; Brian Darling and Theresa M. Lalancette

Nancy, b. 8/3/1954 in Dover; third; David A. Darling (poultry breeder, MA) and Arlene C. Patrone (MA)

Susan, b. 6/10/1959 in Dover; sixth; David A. Darling (truck driver, MA) and Arlene C. Patrone (MA)

DAVIS,
son [Archie], b. 5/26/1905; third; Frank E. Davis (farmer, 45, Dover) and Lizzie E.M. Chesley (35, Barrington)

son, b. 6/9/1906; third; Gerald B. Davis (clerk, 33, Bethel, ME) and Vinnie M. Smallcon (32, Barrington); residence - Portsmouth

daughter, b. 1/17/1908; fourth; Frank Davis (farmer, 48, Dover) and Lizzie E.W. Chesley (37, Barrington)

son, b. 11/7/1910; fifth; Frank E. Davis (farmer, 50, Dover) and Lizzie Chesley (40, Barrington)

Alyson Beth, b. 1/1/1982 in Dover; Irving R. Davis and Susan A. Nichols

Marlo Roscoe, b. 2/11/1904; second; Frank E. Davis (farmer, 44, Dover) and Lizzie E.M. Chesley (33, Barrington)

Norman Howe, b. 8/6/1910; fifth; Gerald B. Davis (clerk, 37, Bethel, ME) and V. May Smallcon (36, Barrington); residence - Portsmouth

Sadie Belle, b. 4/20/1891; first; Samuel F. Davis (weaver, Craftsbury, VT) and Olive E. Woodward (NH)

Vinnie Geraldine, b. 5/13/1909; fourth; Gerald B. Davis (clerk, 35, Bethel, ME) and V. May Smallcon (35, Barrington); residence - Portsmouth

DAY,
Dianne Lynn, b. 5/12/1960 in Dover; first; Everett H. Day, Jr. (milk route, MA) and Ruthann G. Welch (NH)

DEAN,
Michael David, b. 8/12/1955 in Kittery, ME; first; Donald F. Dean (USN, NJ) and Patricia J. Weeden (NH)

William Geary, b. 8/22/1986 in Dover; William L. Dean and Patricia A. Geary

DEBUTTS,
Carol Ann, b. 9/1/1952 in Rochester; first; John M. DeButts (laborer, MA) and Margaret Smith (NH)

John Mitchell, Jr., b. 3/4/1958 in Rochester; second; John M. DeButts (machinist, MA) and Margaret Smith (NH)

Kayla Marie, b. 3/8/1987 in Rochester; Daniel J. DeButts and Pammy J. Hemeon

DECKER,
Mark Timothy, b. 4/26/1982 in Rochester; Bruce M. Decker and Holly J. Hatch

DEELY,
Abigail Mae, b. 5/6/1982; Joseph J. Deely, Jr. and Bonnylou Anderson

DELONG,
Jeremy Thomas, b. 4/1/1985 in Dover; Thomas H. Delong and Kathleen R. Mynahan
Kellie Mynahan, b. 10/2/1980 in Dover; Thomas H. Delong and Kathleen R. Mynahan

DELUDE,
Jamie Anne, b. 10/5/1976 in Rochester; Joseph F. Delude, Jr. and Lorraine A. Peare

DEMARIS,
Anthony Michael, b. 4/16/1979 in Dover; Alfred G. Demaris, Jr. and Sue A. Bernabo
Jennifer Leigh, b. 9/3/1976 in Dover; Alfred G. Demaris, Jr. and Sue Ann M. Barnabo

DEMER[R]ITT,
daughter [Mabel], b. 6/27/1894; fifth; S. P. Demeritt (farmer, 38, Barrington) and Lizzie S. Locke (29, Dover)
son [Maurice], b. 5/6/1908; eighth; Samuel P. Demeritt (farmer, 52, Barrington) and Lizzie S. Locke (43, Dover)
son [Philip O.], b. 3/29/1910; first; John W. Demeritt (laborer, 27, Barrington) and Alice M. Whitehouse (20, Barrington)
son, b. 3/29/1916; fourth; John W. Demeritt (farmer, Barrington) and Alice M. Whitehouse (Barrington)
Dorothy, b. 10/27/1918; fifth; John Demeritte (wood cutter, Barrington) and Alice M. Whitehouse (Barrington)
Earl Isaac, b. 4/30/1936 in Malden, MA; first; Earl DeMeritt (farmer, Barrington) and Jennie Bell (Malden, MA)
Florence, b. 3/3/1898; sixth; S. P. Demeritt (farmer, 42, Barrington) and Lizzie S. Locke (33, Dover)
Gerald Edward, b. 3/25/1954 in Rochester; eighth; Earl I. DeMeritt (uncmployed, NH) and Jennie M. Bell (MA)
Helen, b. 10/2/1913; third; John W. Demeritt (laborer, 31, Barrington) and Alice Whitehouse (24, Barrington)

May Belle, b. 5/2/1900; Plummer Demeritt (NH) and Ethel
　　May Hall (NH) (1957)
Nelson Locke, b. 4/3/1904; seventh; Samuel Demerritt
　　(farmer, 48, Barrington) and Frances Locke (39, Dover)
Pitman, b. 5/5/1910; ninth; Samuel Demeritt (farmer, 54,
　　Barrington) and Lizzie D. Locke (45, Dover) (see below)
Robert George, b. 4/1/1948 in Rochester; sixth; Earl I.
　　Demeritt (auto mechanic, Strafford) and Jennie M. Bell
　　(Malden, MA)
Roscoe Pitman, b. 5/6/1910; Samuel Demeritt and Lizzie
　　Locke (1980 - see above)
Ruth, b. 11/29/1911; second; John W. DeMeritt (lumberman,
　　28, Barrington) and Alice M. Whitehouse (21, Barrington)

DENICOURT,
Dustin Andrew, b. 8/13/1986 in Dover; Gary F. Denicourt and
　　Patricia M. Noble

DESHARNAIS,
Casey Morgan, b. 1/18/1979 in Dover; Robert H. Desharnais
　　and Lynn J. Morrill
Erin Morrill, b. 9/17/1981 in Dover; Robert H. Desharnais and
　　Lynn J. Morrill

DESHONG,
Kelsey Hayes, b. 1/2/1987 in Rochester; George A. Deshong
　　and Lisa G. Ainsworth
Troy Lee, b. 6/17/1962 in Rochester; third; George H.
　　Deshong (machine oper., PA) and Germaine R. Gardner
　　(ME)
Wendy Joy, b. 9/4/1965 in Rochester; fourth; George H.
　　Deshong (laborer, PA) and Germaine R. Gardner (ME)

DEVER,
Stacey, b. 7/13/1979 in Rochester; Michael J. Dever and
　　Diane M. DeLuca

DEWILDT,
Keri Ann, b. 8/29/1987 in Dover; John D. deWildt and
  Kathleen M. Fogarty

DEWITT,
Julie Ann, b. 8/15/1970 in Portsmouth; Henry F. DeWitt (NH)
  and Susan M. Laney (NH)
Kerry Lynn, b. 12/1/1975 in Dover; Henry F. DeWitt and
  Susan M. Laney
Wendy Elaine, b. 12/10/1973 in Dover; Henry Francis DeWitt
  and Susan Martha Lamay

DEXTER,
son, b. 2/17/1890; second; Foster Dexter (teamster, NS) and
  Jane Crowell (NS)

DIAMENT,
Allison Sarah, b. 12/11/1979 in Dover; Joseph Diament and
    Pattie S. Streiff
Julia Deborah, b. 12/28/1982 in Dover; Joseph Diament and
    Patti S. Strieff

DIBERTO,
Natalie Marie, b. 6/21/1984 in Dover; Robert L. DiBerto and
    Gail S. Perrault

DIETEL,
Catherine Marie, b. 1/21/1973 in Rochester; James M. Dietel
  (MA) and Paulette E. Rehkugler (PA)

DIETTERLE,
Hans Kurtis, b. 10/23/1980 in Dover; Paul H. Dietterle, Jr.
  and Laura L. Oakes

DIGREGORIO,
Danielle Marie, b. 9/17/1980 in Dover; Joseph S. DiGregorio and Madeleine A. Seeber

DILLON,
Kevin Charles, b. 6/26/1987 in Dover; James P. Dillon and Melinda G. Grant
Samuel James, b. 1/8/1985 in Dover; James P. Dillon and Melinda J. Grant

DINING,
Tamara Kelly, b. 12/6/1971 in Portsmouth; Paul H. Dining (NH) and Kathleen L. McAdams (NH)

DINWOODIE,
Donald Arthur, Jr., b. 7/12/1957 in Dover; fifth; Donald A. Dinwoodie (painter, RI) and Barbara L. Lucas (NH)

DIONNE,
Raymond Joseph, Jr., b. 6/10/1979 in Dover; Raymond J. Dionne, Sr. and Ellen J. Russell

DIVIRGILIO,
Alan David, b. 8/12/1963 in Rochester; fourth; Nicholas DiVirgilio (pipe fitter, MA) and Barbara A. Milne (MA)
Caitlin Ann, b. 2/25/1987 in Dover; Alan D. DiVirgilio and Tina M. Labrie

DODGE,
son, b. 10/26/1891; thirteenth; Frank S. Dodge (farmer, New Durham) and Rusella Pearl (Rochester)
son [Harry], b. 1/28/1904; fifth; Herbert Dodge (chopper, 21, Rochester) and Alice Garland (28, Farmington)
Amy Katherine, b. 1/11/1979 in Dover; George E. Dodge and Nancy A. O'Connell

Bernice Priscilla, b. 11/20/1908; third; Herman Dodge (farmer, 25, Barrington) and Louise G. Babb (20, Barrington)

Charles F., b. 1/18/1916; sixth; Herman Dodge (farmer, Rochester) and Louise G. Babb (Barrington)

Dorothy, b. 8/3/1910; fourth; Herman A. Dodge (farmer, 27, Barrington) and Louise G. Babb (22, Barrington)

Elaine Jean, b. 7/18/1975 in Dover; Philip C. Dodge and Elona J. Estes

Ernest, b. 12/17/1894; first; Edwin S. Dodge (laborer, 21, New Durham) and Mary Lingard (18, Barrington)

Frederick Herman, b. 10/9/1940 in Dover; first; Robert A. Dodge (farmer, Barrington) and Mary E. Conway (Lawrence, MA)

Idella Blanche, b. 9/27/1907; second; Herman A. Dodge (farmer, 24, Rochester) and Louise G. Babb (19, Barrington)

Kenneth Kingsley, b. 11/2/1980 in Dover; Clinton P. Dodge and Sandra L. Spinney

Philip Charles, b. 11/29/1945 in Exeter; fourth; Robert A. Dodge (laborer, Barrington) and Mary E. Conway (Lawrence, MA)

Robert A., b. 9/10/1911; fifth; Herman A. Dodge (farmer, 28, Rochester) and Louise G. Babb (23, Barrington)

Robert Lewis, b. 4/26/1938 in Exeter; first; Robert Alvin Dodge (farmer, Barrington) and Mary Elizabeth Conway (Lawrence, MA)

DOLAN,
Matthew James, b. 12/8/1983 in Exeter; Timothy B. Dolan and Suzanne Vorrilas

DONAHUE,
Sean Patrick, b. 5/9/1977 in Concord; David B. Donahue and Cathy L. Perkins

DOODA,
Darien Marie, b. 6/14/1978 in Portsmouth; James Dooda and
   Roxanne M. Cummings
Matthew James, b. 5/27/1980 in Portsmouth; James Dooda
   and Roxanne M. Cummings

DORE,
Evelyn Gladys, b. 3/11/1899; first; Elmer H. Dore (farmer, 23,
   Barnstead) and Florence Blackmer (17, Rochester)

DOUCET,
Edward Christopher, b. 6/19/1983 in Manchester; Wayne F.
   Doucet and Pamela J. Nicoll

DOUCETTE,
Dwayne Arthur, b. 4/7/1977 in Exeter; Richard A. Doucette
   and Barbara M. Jennison

DOW,
Nichole Amanda, b. 5/19/1986 in Dover; Ronald A. Dow and
   Dawn M. Gallagher

DOWNAR,
James Bradley, III, b. 9/5/1973 in Dover; James B. Downar,
   Jr. (MA) and Susan A. Kingsbury (NH)
Lynda Susan, b. 10/13/1971 in Dover; James B. Downar, Jr.
   (MA) and Susan A. Kingsbury (NH)

DOWNIE,
Dorothy Anne, b. 7/25/1936 in Dover; second; Ralph Downie
   (oper. fill sta., Lynn, MA) and Alice Culleton (Canada)

DOWNING,
son, b. 7/10/1904; first; Arthur T. Downing (physician, 27,
   Hanover) and Mabel Moore (24, Plymouth, VT)

Alexander Corwin, b. 6/10/1981 in Exeter; Vincent B. Downing and Donna L. Johnson
Alexander Jenness, b. 11/4/1976 in Exeter; Vincent B. Downing and Donna L. Johnson
Donna Lee, b. 12/1/1977 in Exeter; Vincent B. Downing and Donna L. Johnson
Evelyn May, b. 2/12/1972 in Exeter; Vincent B. Downing (NH) and Donna L. Johnson (NH)
Justin Miles, b. 11/3/1981 in Rochester; Robert F. Downing and Marilyn G. Litchfield
Katie Briana, b. 10/6/1977 in Portsmouth; Robert F. Downing and Marilyn G. Litchfield
Sarah Beverly, b. 10/21/1984 in Exeter; Vincent B. Downing and Donna L. Johnson
Vincent Bryant, Jr., b. 9/27/1974 in Exeter; Vincent Bryant Downing and Donna Lee Johnson

DOWNS,
Courtnee Colleen, b. 9/27/1982 in Concord; Joseph Downs and Shirley L. Fife
Daniel Joseph Roscoe, b. 1/29/1986 in Exeter; Joseph Downs and Shirley M.S. Fife
Kelly Rae, b. 4/17/1985 in Dover; William E. Downs, Jr. and Karen L. Hanson
Robert Willis, b. 11/30/1956 in Rochester; sixth; Bernard W. Downs (laborer, NH) and Marion L. Foster (NH)

DOYLE,
Laird Raymond, b. 1/9/1976 in Dover; Lawrence R. Doyle and Jackie A. Snow

DRAPEAU,
Roxanne Sharon, b. 4/8/1971 in Dover; Kenneth R. Drapeau (NH) and Raylene E. Quinn (NH)

DREW,
child [Joseph], b. 8/9/1897; sixth; Greenlief S. Drew (farmer, 30, Barrington) and Noma S. Miles (35, Perryville, MO)
Christine A., b. 11/4/1930 in Dover; third; Fred Drew (merchant, MO) and Lydia Anderson (MA)
Christopher Steven, b. 4/22/1978 in Portsmouth; Steven A. Drew and Carol A. Labbe
Cory Michael, b. 9/29/1980 in Portsmouth; Steven A. Drew and Carol A. Labbe
Eric Harold, b. 7/18/1955 in Rochester; second; Robert V. Drew (GE Co., MA) and Esther J. Flower (MA)
Frederick Elmer, 3d, b. 8/11/1954 in Rochester; third; Frederick E. Drew, Jr. (civil engineer, NH) and Mary C. Hough (MA)
Gladys Evans, b. 5/27/1905; third; Ellen Drew (34, Chichester)
Jonathan Woodbury, b. 11/13/1952 in Rochester; second; Frederick E. Drew, Jr. (civil engineer, NH) and Mary C. Hough (MA)
Theresa E., b. 4/14/1966 in Rochester; eighth; Donald M. Drew (utility man, Hyde Park, NY) and Florence M. McIntosh (New York, NY)

DRISCOLL,
Samantha Kristin, b. 9/28/1981 in Dover; Edmond W. Driscoll and Deborah E. Harris

DROWN,
Richard Earl, b. 9/15/1956 in Concord; second; Earl A. Drown (truck driver, NH) and Mary E. Bateman (NH)

DRUMMOND,
Michael Feitelson, b. 3/4/1987 in Dover; Edward H. Drummond and Amy S. Feitelson

DUBE,
Peter Raymond, b. 1/31/1952 in Rochester; second; Raymond E. Dube (shoeworker, NH) and Ethrilla A. Eveleth (MA)

DUBOIS,
Andrea Robin, b. 9/15/1976 in Dover; Robert A. DuBois and Brenda M. Beaulieu

DUBUCLET,
Adam Charles, b. 2/8/1971 in Dover; Michael A. Dubuclet (CA) and Patricia J. Velasco (MI)
Allanna Teresa, b. 7/8/1975 in Dover; Michael A. DuBlucet and Patricia J. Velasco
Vance P., b. 5/10/1973 in Dover; Michael A. DuBlucet (CA) and Patricia J. Velasco (MI)

DUCHARME,
James George, b. 7/17/1969 in Dover; Bruce W. Ducharme (ME) and Mary F. Riordan (NH)

DUCKWORTH,
Jennifer Marie, b. 3/28/1984 in Rochester; Joseph B. Duckworth and Jasmine M. Miller

DUDLEY,
son, b. 10/21/1935 in Rochester; second; Randolph Dudley (mill worker, Deerfield) and Helen Caverly (Strafford)
Guy H., b. 5/20/1906; first; Charles C. Dudley (sawyer, 35, Danbury) and Maud A. Davis (26, Deerfield)
Robert Oliver, Jr., b. 7/18/1986 in Exeter; Robert O. Dudley and Angela L. Desjardins

DUFRESNE,
Sylvia Ellen, b. 3/1/1950 in Rochester; first; Chandler A. Dufresne (shipping clerk, NH) and Shirley E. Robie (NH)

William Allan, b. 9/28/1951 in Rochester; second; Chandler A. Dufresne (pipe fitter, NH) and Shirley E. Robie (NH)

DUGAL,
Erik Thomas, b. 5/31/1982 in Dover; Jay T. Dugal and Donna E. Caswell

DULUDE,
Mary J., b. 8/11/1911; second; Philip A. Dulude (tel. operator, 27, Canada) and Eugenie Beliveau (22, Canada)

DUPONT,
Christopher Jon, b. 1/6/1987 in Dover; David P. Dupont and Carolyn J. Watkins

DUREAU,
daughter, b. 5/24/1979 in Dover; Paul G. Dureau and Julie A. Clay

DURGIN,
son, b. 1/22/1898; first; Albert S. Durgin (clerk, 21, Greenland) and Mabell Blaisdell (16, Barrington)

DUTILE,
Joshua Paul, b. 10/6/1977 in Dover; Paul D. Dutile and Kim C. Hanefeld

DYER,
son [Joseph], b. 8/2/1901; fifth; Joseph N. Dyer (laborer, 36, Chesterville, ME) and Mary Billington (33, Weld, ME)
Sonja Jean, b. 5/25/1971 in Rochester; Ronald S. Dyer (ME) and Patricia L. Moulton (ME)

EATON,
Francis Forrest, b. 1/21/1944 in Dover; first; Robert Wilson Eaton (US Army, Hartford, CT) and Eloise J. Buzzell (Barrington)
Richard Thomas, b. 4/15/1983 in Concord; Robert A. Eaton and Leslie A. Head

EDDINGTON,
Joshua John, b. 12/12/1986 in Dover; John A. Eddington, Jr. and Kimberley A. Pevear

EDDY,
Kasey Lynn, b. 5/20/1981 in Dover; Cyril W. Eddy and Susan T. Ellis

EDGECOMB,
Christopher Charles, b. 1/5/1984 in Dover; Terrance C. Edgecomb and Virginia E. Roya

EDMUNDS,
Garth Chester, II, b. 8/24/1979 in Dover; Garth C. Edmunds, I and Michelle C. Cyr

EICKLER,
Anna Eva, stillborn, b. 4/23/1915; second; Herbert W. Eickler (laborer, Plantsville, CT) and Jennifer A. Wheeler (Orange, MA)

ELDREDGE,
Kurt Randall, b. 1/9/1972 in Dover; Glen E. Eldredge (NH) and Ellen A. Stackpole (NH)
William Lester, III, b. 4/11/1953 in Dover; second; William L. Eldredge, Jr. (truck driver, ME) and Florence E. DeMeritt (NH)

ELLIOTT,
son, b. 8/4/1892; first; G. S. Elliott (laborer, 40, Concord) and Ida Nealy (20, Lowell, MA)
Alice Maude, b. 10/14/1944; fourth; Franklin Earl Elliott (lumberman, Raymond) and Georgia Eva Davis (Lee)
Angela Marie, b. 11/20/1975 in Rochester; Arthur J. Elliott and Lorraine M. Brown
Arthur James, b. 1/8/1941; tenth; Kelly E. Elliott (saw mill wkr., Canaan) and Susan N. Sargent (Danville)
Betty Ann, b. 10/2/1955 in Dover; first; Clarence G. Elliott (lumberjack, NH) and Beatrice H. Cofferen (ME)
Cathrine I., b. 10/19/1933; seventh; Kelley Elliott (laborer, Orange) and Susie Sargent (Kingston)
Charles Henry, Jr., b. 2/22/1949 in Exeter; second; Charles H. Elliott (lumberman, NH) and Ruth E. Forrest (ME)
Clayton Roy, b. 4/8/1943; eleventh; Kelly Edward Elliott (wood chopper, Canaan) and Susan Norris Sargent (Danville)
Doris Evelyn, b. 2/16/1951 in Exeter; third; Charles H. Elliott (millworker) and Ruth E. Forrest (ME)
Edgar Eugene, b. 10/16/1943 in Exeter; third; Earl Franklin Elliott (lumberman, Raymond) and Georgia Eva Davis (Lee Hill)
Edward John, b. 7/12/1976 in Exeter; John A. Elliott, Jr. and Jane Fenderson
Everett Ashley, b. 3/25/1954 in Exeter; fourth; Charles H. Elliott (laborer, NH) and Ruth E. Forrest (ME)
Gerald George, b. 9/3/1936; seventh; Herbert W. Elliott (carpenter, Canaan) and Lora M. Hartford (Deerfield)
Ginger Lee, b. 5/26/1970 in Exeter; Augustus Elliott (NH) and Corliss A. Currier (NH)
Helen Jennie, b. 6/1/1936; eighth; Kelly E. Elliott (farmer, Canaan) and Susan Sargent (Danville)
Jeannine Lauranne, b. 7/29/1961 in Rochester; third; Robert E. Elliott (laborer, NH) and Carolyn J. Bellen (NH)
John David, b. 8/14/1985 in Dover; Lisa P. Elliott

Jonathan Andrew, b. 11/20/1971 in Exeter; Charles H. Elliott (NH) and Mary J. Eaton (NH)

Katherine Louise, b. 11/9/1947 in Exeter; first; Charles H. Elliott (lumberman, Hampstead) and Ruth E. Forest (Stowe, ME)

Keith Michael, b. 1/2/1979 in Portsmouth; Michael A. Elliott and Diane L. Davis

Kelly Ellsworth, b. 9/7/1962 in Rochester; second; Clayton R. Elliott (lumberman, NH) and Priscilla P. Libby (ME)

Laurie Anne, b. 1/16/1973 in Dover; Charles H. Elliott (NH) and Mary J. Eaton (NH)

Louise Eva, b. 2/10/1920; Earl Franklin Elliott (wood chopper, Raymond) and Georgia Eva Elliott (Newfields)

Raymond Arthur, b. 7/18/1956 in Exeter; fifth; Charles H. Elliott (laborer, NH) and Ruth E. Forrest (ME)

Robert Eugene, b. 11/6/1938; eighth; Kelly Edward Elliott (wood chopper, Canaan) and Susie Norris Sargent (Danville)

Shane Robert, b. 7/8/1977 in Portsmouth; Michael A. Elliott and Diana L. Davis

Tara Ann, b. 5/4/1983 in Concord; Eric T. Elliott and Annette M. Masten

ELLIS,
Amy Marie, b. 11/5/1977 in Exeter; Raymond B. Ellis and Linda S. Freeman

Scott Richard, b. 6/12/1967 in Rochester; first; Richard F. Ellis (draftsman, Berlin) and Norma L. Jenness (Dover)

Terry Charles, b. 7/26/1967 in Dover; third; Warren F. Ellis (commercial mgr., Providence, RI) and Jane J. Clark (Norwalk, CT)

ELLISON,
son [William F.], b. 9/17/1899; fifth; Willie Ellison (lumberman, 35, Nottingham) and Etta M. Drew (32, Dover)

daughter, b. 1/12/1904; first; Ernest Ellison (farmer, 18, Barrington) and Maude Morrison (19, Nottingham)

son, b. 12/3/1905; third; Ernest Ellison (lumberman, 19, Barrington) and Maude Morrison (21, Nottingham)

daughter, b. 5/30/1908; first; Walter Ellison (fireman, 38, Nottingham) and Alta Glover (20, Nottingham)

son, b. 8/31/1909; fourth; Ernest Ellison (fireman, 23, Barrington) and Maude Morrison (24, Nottingham)

daughter, b. 5/28/1911; fifth; Ernest Ellison (fireman, 25, Barrington) and Maude Marrison (26, Nottingham)

son [Charles], b. 1/17/1912; second; Walter S. Ellison (fireman, 42, Nottingham) and Alta Glover (24, Nottingham)

son, b. 9/3/1914; third; Walter Ellison (fireman, Nottingham) and Alta Glover (Nottingham)

son [Edgar E.], b. 1/19/1915; seventh; Ernest Ellison (sawyer, Barrington) and Maud M. Morrison (Nottingham)

son [George W.], b. 7/3/1915; fourth; Walter Ellison (lumberman, Nottingham) and Alta Glover (Nottingham)

Beverly Jean, b. 2/7/1946 in Exeter; fifth; George W. Ellison (laborer, Barrington) and Evelyn E. Elliott (Kensington)

Chester, b. 7/12/1917; fifth; Walter A. Ellison (lumberman, Nottingham) and Alta Glover (Nottingham)

Doris Rita, b. 8/3/1908; fourth; Ernest Ellison (fireman, 22, Barrington) and Maud N. Morrison (24, Nottingham)

Elizabeth M., b. 12/5/1920; sixth; Walter A. Ellison (lumberman, Barrington) and Alta M. Glover (Nottingham)

George Wood, b. 6/20/1935; second; George W. Ellison (wood chopper, Barrington) and Evelyn Elliott (Kingston)

Georgia Anna, b. 6/15/1896; fourth; Willie A. Ellison (sawyer, 31, Nottingham) and Etta M. Drew (29, Dover)

Gordon Kelley, b. 4/22/1950 in Exeter; sixth; George W. Ellison (truck driver, NH) and Evelyn E. Elliott (NH)

Linda Lee, b. 8/8/1952 in Exeter; eighth; George W. Ellison (woodsman, NH) and Evelyn E. Elliott (NH)

Pearl E., b. 4/11/1928; second; William F. Ellison (trucking, Barrington) and Margaret Campbell (Dover)
Rosemary, b. 8/3/1948 in Exeter; sixth; George W. Ellison (mill worker, Barrington) and Evelyn E. Elliott (Kensington)
Ruth Evelyn, b. 3/4/1934; first; George W. Ellison (laborer, Barrington) and Evelyn E. Elliott (Kensington)
Sarah Josephine, b. 2/4/1921; eighth; Ernest Ellison (lumberman, Barrington) and Maude Morrison (Nottingham)
Shirley Anne, b. 12/19/1937; third; George W. Ellison (laborer, Barrington) and Evelyn Elliott (Kensington)
Stella, b. 6/23/1902; sixth; William Ellison (mill owner, 37, Nottingham) and Etta May Drew (35, Dover)
Thelma A., b. 10/6/1925; eighth; Walter A. Ellison (laborer, 54, Nottingham) and Alta M. Glover (38, Nottingham)
William Scott, b. 9/24/1943 in Exeter; fourth; George Walter Ellison (saw mill, Barrington) and Evelyn Eloise Elliott (Kensington)

ELWELL,
Daniel Lawrence, b. 7/16/1979 in Dover; Lawrence M. Elwell and Hope L. Rousseau
Nicholas Glenn, b. 2/6/1986 in Rochester; Anthony G. Elwell and Mary E. Bernier

EMERSON,
son [Bert W.], b. 4/24/1890; fifth; John Emerson (laborer, Lee) and Elmira Arlin (Nottingham)
George Wentworth, Jr., b. 8/18/1987 in Dover; George W. Emerson, Jr. and Kathleen A. Stevens

EMERY,
son [Harry E.], b. 2/16/1899; first; Fred E. Emery (laborer, 23, Manchester) and Sadie Lingard (17, Barrington)

EMMETT,
Ashley Brooks, b. 10/26/1972 in Exeter; Jay A. Emmett (ME) and Ruth D. Sickel (NJ)

EMMONS,
Jessica Marie, b. 9/19/1985 in Dover; Edwin R. Emmons and Robin L. Kimball

ERICKSON,
Joanne Elizabeth, b. 7/24/1961 in Rochester; fourth; Earl R. Erickson (self-employed, MA) and Elizabeth S. Folsom (LA)

ESTES,
Christopher Paul, b. 8/25/1985 in Dover; Wayne M. Estes and Dierdre C. Seaver

Craig Wayne, b. 5/20/1983 in Dover; Wayne M. Estes and Dierdre C. Seaver

Eleona Jean, b. 10/21/1935; second; Elmer H. Estes (shoeworker, Epping, ME) and Hilda Kahps (Roxbury, MA)

Meaghan Elizabeth, b. 12/5/1986 in Exeter; Philip D. Estes and Katherine B. O'Connell

EVANS,
son, b. 3/23/1890; second; Frank S. Evans (farmer, Barrington) and Rebecca Ludd (Epping)

FAIST,
James David, b. 12/10/1957 in Rochester; first; David O. Faist (student, NH) and Beverly L. Clough (NH)

Jeffrey Herbert, b. 9/18/1964 in Rochester; second; Walter H. Faist (pipefitter, NH) and Madelynn M. Nason (NH)

Martha Lee, b. 8/8/1935 in Pittsfield; second; Walter H. Faist (laborer, Dorchester, MA) and Frances L. Ball (Yarmouth, NS)

Robert Lee, b. 11/7/1961 in Rochester; first; Walter H. Faist (plumber's hlpr., NH) and Madelynn M. Nason (NH)
Walter Herbert, b. 11/11/1939 in Dover; third; Walter H. Faist (dyer, Boston, MA) and Frances L. Ball (Canada)

FALL,
Timothy Edward, b. 7/18/1968 in Rochester; Kenneth C. Fall (ME) and Marian A. Bronson (NH)

FANNING,
Mary, b. 12/17/1916; fourth; John A. Fanning (shoemaker, NS) and Mary J. Metcalf (England)

FARMER,
Shirley June, b. 6/3/1934 in Rochester; first; Henry Farmer (farmer, East Providence, RI) and Blanch Moreau (Pontiac, RI)

FARRELL,
Alison, b. 8/17/1979 in Dover; Michael E. Farrell and Nancy A. Brown

FARRIS,
Kenneth Eugene, b. 9/12/1957 in Rochester; first; Eugene Farris (Air Force, KY) and Mary T. Eldridge (MA)

FARROW,
Katherine Leigh, b. 9/22/1951 in Dover; first; George T. Farrow (laborer, VT) and Lugina C. Gutowski (MA)
Thomas George, b. 12/30/1952 in Dover; second; George T. Farrow (Navy Yard, VT) and Lugina C. Gutowski (MA)

FAULKINGHAM,
Ashley Beth, b. 9/30/1984 in Exeter; Jeffrey A. Faulkingham and Jean R. Dore

FAWNING,
Francis Marie, b. 4/12/1913; first; Manson H. Fawning (farmer, 39, NS) and Jennie E. Day (20, Cambridge, MA)

FEE,
Rebecca Charlotte, b. 5/26/1942 in Exeter; first; Thomas H. Fee (Lynn, MA) and Helen H. Buzzell (Barrington); residence - Lynn, MA

FEELEY,
Edward Michael, b. 9/7/1977 in Portsmouth; Edward W. Feeley and Margie E. Durden
Jennifer Lee, b. 8/10/1980 in Dover; Robert J. Feeley and Nancy E. Grinshaw
Jill Marie, b. 7/9/1983 in Dover; Robert J. Feeley and Nancy E. Grimshaw

FELKER,
Elizabeth Anne, b. 7/3/1976 in Dover; Elliott H. Felker and Shirley A. Gaffney
Mary Susan, b. 4/14/1964 in Dover; second; Martin J. Felker (gov't worker, NH) and Jean E. Blankenship (NH)

FENERTY,
Jeffrey Scott, b. 10/17/1963 in Exeter; first; Ronald L. Fenerty (teacher, NH) and Linda C. MacDonald (ME)

FERNALD,
Gary Paul, b. 10/14/1952 in Dover; second; Paul F. Fernald (General Electric, NH) and Ada M. Neal (NH)
Harold Lewis, b. 5/25/1960 in Dover; third; Paul F. Fernald (paint sprayer, NH) and Ada M. Neal (NH)
Larry Frederick, b. 12/3/1949 in Dover; first; Paul F. Fernald (general helper, NH) and Ada M. Neal (NH)

FERRARINI,
Elizabeth Marie, b. 3/23/1981 in Dover; Joseph A. Ferrarini, Jr. and Mary E. Spencer

FERRY,
Eugene A., b. 3/27/1923; second; Eugene Ferry (laborer, Hillsboro) and Leona Strachan (Barrington)
Forrest Edward, b. 8/15/1920; first; Eugene F. Ferry (laborer, Hillsboro) and Leona W. Strachn (Barrington)

FIELD,
son, b. 9/9/1979 in Concord; Jonathan R. Field and Carol G. Korenstein

FILIAULT,
Rose M. Delina, b. 6/29/1882; Alexander Filiault (woodsman, Canada) and Lucy Houle (Canada) (1942)

FILIEO,
Sherri Marie, b. 2/4/1972 in Dover; Bernard R. Filieo (ME) and MaryRose J. Colello (ME)

FILLMORE,
Becky Lynn, b. 10/4/1977 in Dover; David L. Fillmore and Monica L. Vose

FINCHUM,
Amanda Rachel, b. 3/14/1985 in Dover; Gary L. Finchum and Constance J. Myers
David Benjamin, b. 3/14/1985 in Dover; Gary L. Finchum and Constance J. Myers

FISTER,
Bernice Addie, b. 11/30/1932 in Rochester; first; Frank G. Fister (laborer, Leominster, MA) and Bernice Howard (Strafford)

FLETCHER,
Jemila Maryam, b. 12/12/1973 in Exeter; William Charles
Fletcher and NancyAnne DeFelice

FLOOD,
James Francis, b. 4/29/1980 in Rochester; Lawrence C.
Flood and Priscilla J. Millette

FLORENCE,
Candace Jean, b. 11/30/1986 in Dover; William B. Florence
and Cassie J. Edwards
Matthew Roger, b. 1/19/1978 in Exeter; Roger H. Florence
and Mary K. Long

FOGARTY,
Diane Lynne, b. 12/27/1964 in Dover; third; David M. Fogarty
(insurance man, MA) and Loretta D. DiCicco (NH)
Eva Theresa, b. 4/8/1948 in Rochester; first; Leonard C.
Fogarty (lumber foreman, Barrington) and Theresa M.
Hill (Manchester)
Guy Cecil, b. 7/5/1949 in Rochester; second; Leonard C.
Fogarty (foreman, NH) and Marie T. Hill (NH)
Ivan Paul, b. 12/7/1957 in Dover; second; Ivan T. Fogarty
(lineman, NH) and Gail P. Rogers (NH)
Lauretta E., b. 6/5/1930; fifth; Leonard L. Fogarty (farmer,
PEI) and Laura Ploude (Gonic)
Leonard C., b. 7/11/1928; fourth; Leonard Fogarty (farmer,
PEI) and Laura Plonde (Gonic)
Lydia Mackay, b. 3/23/1982 in Rochester; F. Urban Fogarty
and Judy M. Musler
Patrick Michael, b. 10/6/1980 in Rochester; Michael W.
Fogarty and Cindy J. Willett
Justin Urban, b. 1/9/1980 in Rochester; Frederick U. Fogarty
and Judy M. Musler (1983)

FOGG,
Connie May, b. 4/22/1959 in Dover; third; Donald W. Fogg (draftsman, NH) and Barbara J. Thompson (OH)
Kelly Samuel, b. 12/25/1962 in Dover; eighth; Russell L. Fogg (machinist, NH) and Rose L. Ellis (NH)
Sara Elizabeth, b. 9/1/1986 in Dover; James L. Fogg and Karen S. Johnson

FOLEY,
Kerrie Ann, b. 9/27/1978 in Exeter; Donald P. Foley and JoAnn L. Miesowicz
Peter Michael, b. 12/31/1981 in Exeter; Donald P. Foley and JoAnn L. Miesowicz

FOLSOM,
Stephany Jane, b. 1/9/1978 in Exeter; Stephen D. Folsom and Colleen F. Olcott

FONTAINE,
Jon Stephen, b. 5/29/1974 in Rochester; Russell John Fontaine, Jr. and Mary Ada York

FOOTE,
Nichole Holly, b. 6/16/1984 in Manchester; Joel L. Foote and Allyson C. Wells

FORCIER,
Leigh Anne, b. 6/13/1974 in Haverhill, MA; Edward C. Forcier and Faye A. Brooks

FORTIER,
Benjamin Joseph, b. 10/24/1981 in Dover; Louis W. Fortier, Jr. and Deborah J. Libby
Sarah Elizabeth, b. 12/4/1983 in Nashua; John B. Fortier and Brenda K. Stark

Shanda Ann, b. 3/4/1984 in Dover; Thomas W. Fortier and Corina J. Lavertue

FOSS,
daughter, b. 4/28/1894; second; Fred Foss (farmer, 25, Strafford) and Esther Hayes (18, Dover)
Shirley Ann, b. 12/30/1941; Albert G. Foss (laborer, Strafford Ridge) and Grace M. Bond (Haverhill, MA)
Sylvia May, b. 6/7/1893; first; Fred R. Foss (farmer, Strafford) and Esther J. Hayes (Strafford)

FOURNIER,
Jared Dennis, b. 11/3/1977 in Exeter; Dennis A. Fournier and Anna R. Polychronis

FOWLER,
Donald Edward, b. 2/12/1981 in Portsmouth; Donald E. Fowler, II and Brenda K. Palmer

FRANCESCHINI,
Scott Gregory, b. 9/6/1984 in Portsmouth; Paul G. Franceschini and Julie L. Oliver

FRANZEN,
William Frederick, b. 10/2/1932; second; William Everett Franzen (boat captain, Providence, RI) and Viola G. Gahan (Divide, CO)

FRASE,
Kristen Rana, b. 2/13/1970 in Rochester; James R. Frase (PA) and Sabra A. Gelatt (NY)
Michael Ross, b. 6/18/1987 in Dover; Stephen F. Frase and Judith A. Ross

FREDETTE,
Joseph Leland, b. 9/20/1980 in Dover; Vincent L. Fredette
and Marilyn G. Turcotte
Leonie M., b. 5/30/1905; second; Joseph Fredette (farmer,
31, Canada) and Elmire Bernier (29, Canada)
Vincent Leon, b. 5/9/1978 in Exeter; Vincent L. Fredette and
Marilyn G. Turcotte

FREEMAN,
son, b. 2/7/1897; first; Walter Freeman (laborer, 25,
Barrington) and Eva Hanscomb (18, Barrington)
daughter [Josephine], b. 4/14/1901; first; Walter Freeman
(laborer, 22, Barrington) and Effie Tyler (20, Barrington)
son [Harry], b. 7/8/1901; first; Willie H.C. Freeman (laborer,
28) and Julia Capen (29)
son, b. 3/4/1902; fifth; John Freeman (laborer, 40,
Barrington) and Mary E. Richardson (23, Somerville, MA)
son [Gussie], b. 3/17/1902; third; Arthur Freeman (laborer,
24, Barrington) and Vina Stanley (20, Barrington)
daughter [Josephine], b. 9/20/1902; second; Walter Freeman
(laborer, 23, Barrington) and Effie Tyler (20, Barrington)
daughter, b. 4/14/1904; third; Walter Freeman (laborer, 23,
Barrington) and Effie Tyler (20, Barrington)
daughter, b. 1/7/1905; fourth; Arthur Freeman (laborer, 26,
Barrington) and ----- Stanley (24, Cambridge, MA)
daughter, b. 5/6/1912; seventh; Walter Freeman (laborer, 34,
Barrington) and Effie Tyler (30, Barrington)
daughter, b. 7/20/1912; second; Augustus Freeman (laborer,
30, Barrington) and Gladys Twombly (19, Nottingham)
Amie Estelle, b. 2/12/1969 in Dover; Arthur W. Freeman (NH)
and Jacqueline D. Goulet (NH)
Beatrice, b. 12/14/1907; first; Ellen L. Freeman (19,
Somerville, MA)
Charles David, b. 4/9/1916; eighth; Walter Freeman (laborer,
Barrington) and Effie E. Grey (Barrington) (1942 and
1978)

Chester Arthur, b. 8/16/1899; first; Arthur Freeman (farmer) and Lavina Freeman (1942)

Clarence, b. 2/12/1912; Arthur Freeman (laborer, 26, Barrington) and Eva Hanscam (25, Barrington)

Elaine Leah, b. 4/8/1940 in Rochester; first; Herbert W. Freeman (laborer, Rochester) and Roxanna O. Lemere (Sanford, ME)

Flora F., b. 6/4/1903; third; Arthur Freeman (farmer, Boston, MA) and Lavina Freeman (Boston, MA) (1918)

Kelly Ann, b. 8/2/1965 in Kittery, ME: second; Dennis H. Freeman (US Navy, NH) and Patricia L. Maxwell (NY)

Lillian R., b. 11/19/1920; first; Albert Freeman (laborer, Barrington) and Lottie R. Emerson (Barrington)

Lori Ann, b. 3/30/1970 in Dover; Wesley J. Freeman, Jr. (NH) and Ruth M. Bridges (ME)

Morton, b. 7/23/1922; second; Albert Freeman (laborer, Barrington) and Lottie Emerson (Barrington)

Nicholas Ronald, b. 2/2/1986 in Dover; Tony D. Freeman and Pamela D. Dube

FRIEL,
Jennifer Eileen, b. 8/5/1974 in Portsmouth; Gerard James Friel and Joan Esther Robie

FRIELINGSDORF,
Alexander Michael, b. 5/5/1977 in Portsmouth; Michael T. Frielingsdorf and Joanne L. Sage

FROST,
Jennifer Lynn, b. 11/6/1973 in Dover; Ernest L. Frost (NH) and Patricia A. Tarmey (NH)

FROTTON,
John Matthew, b. 8/10/1987 in Exeter; Michael J. Frotton and Jill M. Eckhardt

GAETJENS,
John Brett B., b. 8/9/1984 in Exeter; Robert E. Gaetjens and Noreen T. Brophy
Patrick Robert Brophy, b. 7/21/1982 in Exeter; Robert E. Gaetjens and Noreen T. Brophy

GAGNE,
Corie Elizabeth, b. 5/1/1987 in Dover; Steven A. Gagne and Donna V. Nadeau

GAGNON,
Nicole Marie, b. 5/4/1985 in Dover; Donald C. Gagnon and Linda M. Stanley

GALE,
stillborn daughter, b. 3/12/1944 in Brentwood; seventh; Frank Gale (laborer, Amesbury, MA) and Sarah Green (Rochester)
Annett Marie, b. 4/6/1955 in Rochester; fifth; Warren E. Gale (machinist, NH) and Frances L. Wallingford (ME)
Clarice Maxine, b. 2/16/1962 in Dover; fifth; Warren E. Gale (contractor, NH) and Frances L. Wallingford (ME)
Edward Martin, b. 7/23/1957 in Rochester; fourth; Warren E. Gale (machinist, NH) and Frances L. Wallingford (ME)
Marc Anthony, b. 3/2/1965 in Dover; sixth; Warren E. Gale (machinist, NH) and Frances L. Wallingford (ME)
Warren E., b. 5/30/1930; third; Franklin C. Gale (laborer, Amesbury, MA) and Sarah M. Green (Rochester)
Warren Edward, Jr., b. 10/12/1953 in Rochester; second; Warren E. Gale (Kidder Press, NH) and Frances L. Wallingford (ME)

GALVIN,
Amanda Marie, b. 11/10/1985 in Portsmouth; Sean A. Galvin and Fawn E. Norton

Sarah Ann, b. 11/10/1985 in Portsmouth; Sean A. Galvin and Fawn E. Norton

GAMPBELL,
Ryan Curtis, b. 1/8/1984 in Dover; Wayne C. Gampbell and Karen A. Radtke

GARBOSKI,
Bethany Elka, b. 2/25/1985 in Rochester; Stephen E. Garboski and Eunice R. Brown

GARDNER,
Tammy Jean, b. 7/28/1966 in Rochester; fourth; Gerard M. Gardner (sole layer, Richmond, ME) and Virginia E. Caswell (Dover)

GARLAND,
Herbert A., stillborn, b. 7/14/1897; second; James N. Garland (farmer, 23, Farmington) and Nellie M. Henderson (17, Farmington)
Robert Verne, b. 11/12/1970 in Dover; Robert E. Garland (NH) and Jacqueline R. Kelley (NH)

GARNETT,
Alyssa Dawn, b. 1/3/1984 in Dover; James E. Garnett and Heidi D. Purington
John Joseph, b. 8/20/1965 in Dover; third; Clarence J. Garnett (electronics, NH) and Alice M. O'Neill (NH)

GARRITY,
Tina Michelle, b. 6/12/1987 in Dover; James A. Garrity and Carol A. Boroom

GASOWSKI,
Carl Walter, b. 1/31/1982 in Dover; Paul L. Gasowski and Annamarie Magdik

Jeremy Milan, b. 4/1/1979 in Dover; Paul L. Gasowski and Annamarie Magdik

GAUDETTE,
Christopher, b. 9/17/1979; Edward A. Gaudette and Linda A. Joyce

GAUNYA,
Crystal Marie, b. 6/12/1982 in Dover; James T. Gaunya and Lenor F. Lago
Janet Elaine, b. 8/30/1942 in Dover; fifth; Roswell G. Gaunya (carpenter, Rutland, VT) and Lillian A. Bonneau (Dover)
Nancy Barbara, b. 11/8/1936; second; Roswell A. Gaunya (carpenter, Salisbury, VT) and Lillian A. Bonneau (Dover)
Shirley Madeline, b. 6/20/1935; second; Roswell A. Gaunya (carpenter, Salisbury, VT) and Lillian A. Bonneau (Dover)

GAY,
Alvina Florence, b. 8/22/1884; Frank Gay (Canada) and Octave Cote (Canada) (1943)

GELDART,
Danielle Marie, b. 8/24/1981 in Portsmouth; Val A. Geldart and Denise N. Bilodeau

GEOFFRION,
Samantha Jean, b. 8/13/1987 in Exeter; Gary M. Geoffrion and Michele R. Bonenfant

GEORGE,
Andrew Edgerton, b. 11/7/1986 in Dover; Douglas E. George and Mary C. Edgerton
Robert James, b. 9/15/1987 in Dover; Robert P. George and Cassandra L. Shanklin

GIALOUSIS,
Sara, b. 5/25/1981 in Exeter; Paul G. Gialousis and Ellen Fowler

GIBB,
Donald Glenn, b. 3/2/1951 in Rochester; first; Glenn C. Gibb (plumber, NH) and Ethelyn Emerson (NH)
Joanne Gloria, b. 8/26/1955 in Rochester; fourth; Neil H. Gibb (garage owner, NH) and Shirley G. Witham (NH)
Jonathan Neil, b. 9/12/1957 in Rochester; fifth; Neil H. Gibb (garage owner, NH) and Shirley Witham (NH)
Kenneth Edward, b. 3/18/1941 in Brentwood; second; Roger W. Gibb (spinner, Manchester) and Priscilla A. Hayes (Madbury)
Laurin Ann, b. 6/7/1975 in Rochester; Jonathan N. Gibb and Debra J. Sanborn
Linda Dallas, b. 5/1/1951 in Rochester; second; Neil H. Gibb (garage owner, NH) and Shirley G. Witham (NH)
Michael Allen, b. 11/27/1967 in Dover; first; Richard A. Gibb (electrician hlpr., Rochester) and Laurette R. Caron (Dover)
Neil Joseph, b. 12/12/1970 in Rochester; Richard A. Gibb (NH) and Laurette R. Caron (NH)
Pamela Jane, b. 10/16/1952 in Rochester; second; Glenn C. Gibb (plumber, NH) and Ethelyn Emerson (NH)
Ruth Evelyn, b. 4/10/1937 in Rochester; first; Roger W. Gibb (woolen mill, Manchester) and Priscilla Hayes (Nashua)
Susan Dorothy, b. 9/20/1954 in Rochester; third; Neil H. Gibb (garage owner, NH) and Shirley G. Witham (NH)
Timothy Jonathan, b. 6/29/1972 in Rochester; Richard A. Gibb (NH) and Laurette R. Caron (NH)

GIBNEY,
Alyssa Marie, b. 4/14/1974 in Dover; Patrick Gibney and Diane Marie Hamel

GILE,
June L., b. 6/1/1925; fourth; Leroy S. Gile (chauffeur, 32, Rochester) and Ella Goutier (32, Hampton Falls)

GILLEN,
Jessica Lynn, b. 1/4/1974 in Exeter; Michael John Gillen and Victoria Charlene Porter

GILLILAND,
Jaime Lyn, b. 12/3/1976 in Exeter; Robert J. Gilliland and Brenda G. Schilling

GILPATRICK,
daughter, b. 4/17/1892; third; George Gilpatrick (laborer, 29, Nottingham) and Ida Boston (27, Barrington)

GIRARD,
Stephen Patrick, b. 9/22/1983 in Rochester; Patrick H. Girard and Mary-Jayne Duyon

GLENISTER,
Erik Westman, b. 11/15/1982 in Portsmouth; Thomas E. Glenister and Birgit M. Westman

GLIDDEN,
Chris Edward, b. 9/29/1968 in Rochester; Reynard F. Glidden (NH) and Sandra J. Pratt (NH)
Donna May, b. 3/28/1972 in Rochester; Roger F. Glidden (NH) and Marlene E. Fortier (ME)
Electa Bell, b. 9/23/1896; second; William H. Glidden (laborer, 27, Farmington) and Ella L. Otis (24, Gonic)
Jane Leslie, b. 4/25/1962 in Dover; seventh; Robert L. Glidden, Jr. (yard switcher, NH) and Ruth E. Stadlg (NH)

GLODE,
Barbara Mary, b. 3/27/1973 in Concord; Charles J. Glode, Jr. (CT) and Laurie G. Knouse (CT)
Charles Andrew, b. 8/9/1974 in Dover; Charles Joseph Glode, Jr. and Laurie Gertrude Knouse
Matthew Peter, b. 9/2/1982 in Dover; Charles J. Glode, Jr. and Laurie G. Knouse

GODDARD,
Kali Elizabeth, b. 6/1/1983 in Dover; Timothy A. Goddard and Susan P. Locke

GOOCH,
Emily Rose, b. 6/13/1987 in Dover; Theodore A. Gooch and Sharon C. Wise
Holly Lorna, b. 7/6/1984 in Dover; Theodore A. Gooch and Sharon C. Wise

GOODE,
Suzanne Ellen, b. 11/12/1977 in Exeter; Malcolm E. Goode and Jane S. Mori

GOODELL,
Brett Steven, b. 5/26/1981 in Portsmouth; Steven B. Goodell and Jacquelyn M. Grimbilas
Matthew Ryan, b. 3/11/1979 in Dover; Michael S. Goodell and Dawn E. Hooker

GOODMAN,
Donna Lee, b. 11/2/1948 in Rochester; first; Albert M. Goodman (US Navy, Roxbury, MA) and Doris L. Meattey (Fitzwilliam)
Steven Michael, b. 7/11/1950 in Rochester; second; Albert M. Goodman (US Navy, MA) and Doris L. Meattey (NH)
Susan Elaine, b. 6/3/1954 in Kittery, ME; fourth; Albert M. Goodman (MA) and Doris L. Meattey (NH)

GOODWIN,
Karli Nicole, b. 6/19/1985 in Exeter; Michael E. Goodwin and
   Karen N. Roberts

GORHAM,
Christopher Michael, b. 1/28/1983 in Rochester; Dennis R.
   Gorham and Nancy L. Chasse

GOSCINSKI,
Louis James, Jr., b. 3/4/1987 in Dover; Louis J. Goscinski,
   Sr. and Donna H. Henkel

GOSSELIN,
stillborn son, b. 11/12/1904; first; Edla Gosselin (16,
   Barrington)
Kendra Rondra, b. 7/29/1980 in Dover; Kenneth R. Gosselin
   and Deborah M. Canney
Madeline M., b. 9/18/1899; fifth; Ella F. Gosselin (36,
   Strafford)

GOUDREAU,
Sarah Elizabeth, b. 5/18/1984 in Dover; Robert G. Goudreau
   and Candice M. Colburn

GOULD,
Adam Charles, b. 12/29/1980 in Dover; David S. Gould and
   Cynthia J. Sullivan
Amanda Jean, b. 6/24/1976 in Dover; Adrian R. Gould and
   Carolyn L. Baxter

GOULET,
Kori Dotson, b. 11/5/1981 in Dover; Ronald M. Goulet and
   Bonnie J. Dotson
Toby Dotson, b. 5/8/1980 in Dover; Ronald M. Goulet and
   Bonnie J. Dotson

GRANT,
Christopher Edward, b. 2/20/1984 in Rochester; Kenneth E. Grant and Linda A. Wagner
Daren Robert, b. 8/16/1983 in Portsmouth; Charles C. Grant and Diana R. Beaucage
Keri Beth, b. 2/12/1980 in Dover; Kenneth E. Grant and Linda A. Wagner
Robert Douglas, b. 11/16/1981 in Rochester; Douglas J. Grant and Susan E. Magowan
Ryann Natalie, b. 12/28/1984 in Concord; Douglas J. Grant and Susan E. Magoun

GRAY,
child, b. 10/28/1899; first; Frank H. Gray (painter, 39, Barrington) and Sophronia Cilley (40, Barnstead)
Lauren Elsworth, b. 4/6/1913; third; Frank L. Gray (farmer, 56, Barrington) and Susie Cady (25, Providence, RI)
Thomas Arthur, b. 11/22/1945; John F. Gray (engineer, Northwood) and Ruth T. Bell (Malden, MA) (1947)
William Frederick, b. 3/29/1981 in Exeter; William E. Gray and Cassie L. Delsoldato

GRECO,
Adam Richard, b. 2/15/1980 in Dover; Thomas J. Greco and Kathleen A. O'Brien
Thomas William, b. 5/13/1978 in Rochester; Thomas J. Greco and Kathleen A. O'Brien

GREEN,
stillborn daughter, b. 1/15/1916; fourth; George Green (theatre operator, Haverhill, MA) and Lillie Waterhouse (Barrington)
Evelyn M., b. 8/6/1911; third; George A. Green (stage manager, 30, Haverhill, MA) and Lilla Waterhouse (30, Barrington)

Sharon Elaine, b. 9/23/1947 in Rochester; first; Michael D. Green (chef, Presque Isle, ME) and Elaine A. Turner (Dover)

Thomas George, b. 7/30/1935; third; Harold C. Green (farmer) and Margaret Ellison (Barrington)

GREENE,
son [Charles J.], b. 5/11/1908; second; George A. Greene (farmer, 27, Haverhill, MA) and Lilla Waterhouse (27, Barrington)

GREENWOOD,
Kaitlyn Abby, b. 8/9/1985 in Exeter; Mark E. Greenwood and Janet A. Asamus

GRENIER,
Tricia Leigh, b. 9/20/1985 in Rochester; Roland R. Grenier, Jr. and Robbin J. Richards

GRIFFIN,
son, b. 8/13/1891; second; Herbert E. Griffin (farmer, Strafford) and Mamie Hanson (Strafford)
son [Clarence], b. 6/4/1894; third; Herbert Griffin (shoemaker, 33, Strafford) and Mary E. Hanson (23, Strafford)
son [Robert C.], b. 10/31/1899; fifth; Herbert E. Griffin (farmer, 39, Strafford) and Mary E. Hanson (29, Strafford)
daughter, b. 1/22/1905; sixth; Herbert Griffin (farmer, 44, Strafford) and Mamie Hanson (34, Strafford)
son [Norman E.], b. 5/26/1907; seventh; Herbert E. Griffin (farmer, 46, Barrington) and Mamie E. Hanson (36, Strafford)
John Joseph, b. 8/17/1893; fourth; Martin Griffin (laborer on RR, Ireland) and Delia Ferry (Ireland)

Katherine, b. 7/1/1895; fourth; Martin Griffin (RR station boss, 34, Ireland) and Delia Forey (33, Ireland)

Lillian B., b. 3/17/1897; fourth; Herbert E. Griffin (farmer, 36, Barrington) and Mary E. Hanson (26, Strafford)

Roger Caverly, b. 3/19/1933 in Rochester; second; Norman C. Griffin (box shop, Barrington) and Katherine V. Hussey (Rochester)

GROEN,

Joseph Mark, b. 9/17/1981; Fenton L. Groen and Shirley K. Van Otterloo

Martha, b. 2/12/1986 in Rochester; Fenton L. Groen and Shirley K. Van Otterloo

Phoebe Kaye, b. 2/21/1979 in Rochester; Fenton L. Groen and Shirley K. Van Otterloo

Susanna Alice, b. 12/22/1983 in Rochester; Fenton L. Groen and Shirley K. Van Otterloo

GRONDIN,

Nathan Andre, b. 8/22/1982 in Dover; Louis O. Grondin and Carol A. Doering

Nicholas Alexander, b. 8/22/1982 in Dover; Louis O. Grondin and Carol A. Doering

GROSSMAN,

Joseph Winston, b. 8/13/1983 in Concord; Kenneth W. Grossman and Holly M. Nichols

Sadie Blanca, b. 2/22/1982 in Dover; Kenneth W. Grossman and Holly M.A. Nichols

GROTH,

Nathan John, b. 8/24/1975 in Dover; Herman J. Groth and Jeanne E. Croteau

GROULX,
Patrick Michael, b. 6/15/1982 in Rochester; Michael A. Groulx and Dorothy J. Girard

GRUPE,
Heather Rose, b. 10/2/1986 in Dover; Karl A. Grupe and Deborah A. Taranowski

GUBELLINI,
John Michael, Jr., b. 5/30/1981 in Dover; John M. Gubellini, Sr. and Linda S. Fischer

GUIMOND,
Chadd, b. 8/19/1987 in Portsmouth; Maurice N. Guimond and Betsy L. Hippensteel

GUPTILL,
Melanie Myrtle, b. 12/4/1963 in Rochester; second; Philip J. Guptill (excavating, NH) and Audrey L. Clark (NH)

GUSTAFSON,
Contessina Leigh, b. 3/6/1965 in Rochester; third; Gerald D. Gustafson (printer, MA) and Sylvia A. Sim (NH)

GUYER,
Darin Marc, b. 4/25/1969 in Dover; Michael S. Guyer (VT) and Carolyn A. Brown (NH)
Dawyne Mathew, b. 8/6/1973 in Rochester; Michael S. Guyer (NH) and Delphine M. Guillemette (NH)

HAGAR,
Jill Samantha, b. 7/16/1979 in Dover; William S. Hagar and Jeninne L. Miner

HALE,
Matthew Steven, b. 10/2/1977 in Dover; Mitchell E. Hale and Carol A. Connelly

HALEY,
Alan Dodge, b. 5/2/1955 in Rochester; third; Waldron B. Haley (dentist, NH) and Grace M. McDaniel (NH)

Donetta Jean, b. 9/3/1952 in Rochester; second; Waldron B. Haley (dentist, NH) and Grace M. McDaniel (NH)

Dwight H., b. 10/8/1922; second; William A. Haley (mechanic, Boston, MA) and Gertrude Hayes (Barrington)

Garth Eric, b. 9/18/1972 in Exeter; Gregory A. Haley (ME) and Lee A. Pleadwell (RI)

James Waldron, b. 10/1/1958 in Rochester; fourth; Waldron B. Haley (dentist, NH) and Grace M. McDaniel (NH)

Lawrence George, b. 8/5/1948 in Rochester; first; Waldron B. Haley (student, Dover) and Grace M. McDaniel (Barrington)

Melinda Leah, b. 12/3/1973 in Exeter; Gregory A. Haley (ME) and Lee A. Pleadwell (RI)

Vanessa Jane, b. 10/30/1960 in Rochester; fifth; Waldron B. Haley (dentist, NH) and Grace M. McDaniel (NH)

HALL,
daughter, b. 4/2/1892; third; G. A. Hall (farmer, 48, Barrington) and Carrie E. Richardson (32, Northwood)

son [Linza O.], b. 1/1/1893; third; Charles T. Hall (farmer, Barrington) and Christina Gray (Barrington)

son [Kenneth A.], b. 8/26/1896; third; Charles S. Hall (farmer, 35, Strafford) and Emma F. Caverly (37, Strafford)

daughter, b. 9/21/1897; second; Minnie L. Hall (23, Barrington)

daughter, b. 12/29/1897; first; Alice E. Hall (20, Barrington)

son [Fred], b. 6/14/1903; first; Walter F. Hall (farmer, 29, Barrington) and Mertie E. Young (19, Barrington)

son [Fred], b. 4/12/1905; second; Walter F. Hall (laborer, 30, Barrington) and Mertie Young (21, Barrington)
son [Clifton], b. 11/25/1906; first; Warren Hall (farmer, 28, Barrington) and Inez Chesley (21, Barrington)
son [Chester], b. 3/24/1909; first; Anderson Hall (farmer, 28, Barrington) and Agnes Stevens (30, France)
stillborn daughter, b. 7/8/1918; Herbert Hall (express driver, Haverhill, MA) and Eunice Ross (Barrington); residence - Portsmouth
son, b. 7/5/1921; second; John C. Hall (laborer, Rochester) and Jenefer R. Wheeler (Orange, MA)
stillborn son, b. 11/19/1931; second; Kenneth Hall (shoe cutter, Barrington) and Ruth Hall (Dover)
Charles M., b. 3/9/1908; second; Warren C. Hall (farmer, 31, Barrington) and Inez Chesley (24, Barrington)
Clifton Everett, b. 2/13/1942; Kenneth A. Hall (NH) and Ruth E. Hall (NH) (1957)
Edna Dora, b. 4/1/1894; seventh; Charles F. Hall (NH) and Christiana V. Gray (NH) (1959)
Eleanor M., b. 2/10/1930; first; Kenneth H. Hall (farmer, Barrington) and Ruth Ellen Hall (Dover)
Florence Almira, b. 6/9/1910; second; Anderson Hall (photographer, 30, Strafford) and Florence A. Stevens (32, France)
Henry E., b. 2/16/1895; second; Henry Hall (laborer, 24, Barrington) and Emma Rust (31, Barrington)
Kenneth Alonzo, b. 12/7/1943; Kenneth A. Hall (NH) and Ruth E. Hall (NH) (1957)
Madeline, b. 7/2/1934; third; Kenneth Hall (shoe maker, Barrington) and Ruth Hall (Dover)

HAM,
son, b. 6/14/1897; second; Foster Ham (farmer, 50, No. Billerica, MA) and Gertie B. Howard (17, Barrington); residence - No. Billerica, MA

daughter, b. 12/29/1899; second; George S. Ham (farmer, 23, Barrington) and Lillian E. Jukes (21, Andover, England)
son, b. 7/26/1902; third; George S. Ham (farmer, 25, Barrington) and Lillian Jukes (23, Andover, England)
son [Roger], b. 11/19/1904; third; George S. Ham (farmer, 27, Barrington) and Lillian Jukes (26, Andover, England)
daughter [Christabel], b. 5/23/1911; fifth; George S. Ham (farmer, 34, Barrington) and Lillian Jukes (32, England)
Frances, b. 1/2/1916; eighth; George S. Ham (farmer, Barrington) and Lillian Jukes (Andover, England)
Harold Rudman, b. 1/2/1899; first; George S. Ham (farmer, 22, Barrington) and Lillian E. Jukes (20, Andover, England)

HAMEL,
Adam Wilfrid, b. 12/7/1985 in Exeter; Michael L. Hamel and Pamela J. Lang
Erica Rose, b. 9/24/1985 in Exeter; Paul J. Hamel and Deborah A. Laroche
Kendra Nicole, b. 2/2/1986 in Rochester; Allen A. Hamel and Cynthia A. Wenzl

HANSCOM[B],
son, b. 1/12/1896; tenth; Leander Hanscomb (laborer, 43, Barrington) and Nellie Story (40, Boscawen)
daughter, b. 9/10/1898; first; Marinda Hanscomb (Barrington)
daughter, b. 6/15/1903; first; Henry Hanscam (sic) (laborer, 23, Barrington) and Lillian E. Stanley (17, Catskill, NY)
son, b. 10/18/1904; second; Henry Hanscom (laborer, 24, Barrington) and Ella Stanley (18, Catskill, NY)
Arthur, b. 10/18/1875; Alvie Hanscom (Barrington) and Prudy Allen (Lowell, MA) (1942)
Bertha Lillian, b. 4/23/1891; Leander Hanscom (Barrington) and Lucy Storey (Concord) (1942)

Edith Mazie, b. 6/15/1899; Leander Hanscom (Barrington) and Nellie Storey (Concord) (1943)
Kristin Ann, b. 9/29/1979 in Portsmouth; Gregory F. Hanscom and Kim A. Wooley

HANSON,
stillborn son, b. 4/29/1916; second; Clarence F. Hanson (farmer-teamster, Strafford) and Dora E. Philbrick (Epsom); residence - Strafford
Olive F., b. 4/8/1916; second; Lewis Hanson (farmer, Strafford) and Beatrice Hall (Lynn, MA)

HARDING,
Betty Ann, b. 5/9/1934 in Rochester; second; Walter Harding (electrician, Newton, MA) and Cora Tibbetts (Barrington)
David Wayne, b. 12/16/1974 in Rochester; Arthur F. Harding and Eleanor L. Blaisdell
Laura Lee, b. 5/1/1971 in Rochester; Arthur F. Harding (MA) and Eleanor L. Blaisdell (NH)
Richard Walter, b. 11/10/1932 in Rochester; first; Walter M. Harding (electrician, Newton, MA) and Cora Tebbets (Barrington)

HARDY,
Dawn Elizabeth, b. 1/5/1970 in Dover; Craig C. Hardy (DC) and Doris A. Benson (NY)
Joy Christine, b. 11/25/1976 in Dover; Craig C. Hardy and Doria A. Benson
Laura Austin, b. 8/24/1985 in Dover; Roy E. Hardy and Marie McKone
Todd Gilman, b. 10/8/1975 in Rochester; Joseph W. Hardy and Gemma J. Gilman
Warren Benson, b. 6/17/1974 in Dover; Craig Castle Hardy and Doris Anne Benson

HARMANSKY,
Drew Anne, b. 7/14/1985 in Dover; George N. Harmansky and Karen A. McManus

HARMON,
Sean Wilder, b. 12/3/1969 in Rochester; Wayne M. Harmon (NH) and Patricia A. Davis (NH)

HARRIMAN,
Earl, b. 7/30/1922; second; Earl H. Harriman (box maker, Lisbon) and Eleanor J. Gay (Cambridge, MA)

HARRIS,
Allan Raymond, b. 1/15/1947 in Rochester; first; Raymond T. Harris (filling sta., Mexico, ME) and Stella Berry (New Durham)
David Andrew, b. 8/17/1983 in Rochester; Michael S. Harris and Andrea M. Miller
Tony Raymond, b. 5/1/1973 in Rochester; Wayne G. Harris (NH) and Carolyn M. Mailhot (NH)
Wayne Guy, b. 1/10/1949 in Rochester; second; Raymond F. Harris (woodsman, ME) and Stella Berry (NH)

HART,
Benjamin Louis Wolak, b. 4/25/1986 in Concord; John L. Hart and Janis Wolak

HARTFORD,
son [Grover], b. 2/24/1893; third; Clement Hartford (farmer, Hiram, ME) and Mamie Jewell (Sebago, ME)
son [Norman], b. 5/30/1896; third; Samuel B. Hartford (farmer, 42, Hiram, ME) and Evelyn Pearson (32, Rawdon, NC)
daughter, b. 2/23/1908; fourth; Wilbur S. Hartford (teamster, 30, Barrington) and Marie Pearson (29, NS)

Frances C., b. 6/18/1934; fourth; Gordon Hartford (store mgr., Rochester) and Lillian Griffin (Barrington); residence - Exeter

Greta H., b. 9/7/1903; second; Wilbur Hartford (teamster, Barrington) and Marie Pearson (NS) (1918)

Herbert C., b. 5/3/1919; second; Gordon B. Hartford (teamster, Rochester) and Lillian Griffin (Barrington); residence - Rochester

Irene, b. 10/15/1901; first; Wilbur Hartford (teamster, 25, Barrington) and Maria Pearson (23, NS)

Kelly Robin, b. 2/25/1971 in Rochester; Albion R. Hartford (NH) and Dorothy P. Dufault (ME)

Samuel, b. 4/12/1892; third; Samuel Hartford (farmer, 39, Hiram, ME) and Jennie A. Seavey (38, Dover)

Samuel A., b. 2/21/1900; fourth; Samuel B. Hartford (farmer, 46, Hiram, ME) and Evelyn Pearson (36, NS)

Stanley, b. 12/3/1916; first; Gordon B. Hartford (expressman, Rochester) and Lillian B. Griffin (Barrington); residence - Rochester

Wilbur S., b. 6/4/1876; Samuel Hartford (farmer, Barrington) and Jennie Seavey (Barrington)

HARTY,
Thomas Jerry, b. 5/29/1970 in Rochester; Martin C. Harty (MA) and Arlene F. Joyal (VT)

HASHEM,
Talitha Nina, b. 1/14/1982 in Dover; Michael A. Hashem and Charlotte A. Andruskiewicz

HATCH,
Bennett Douglas, b. 12/9/1982 in Dover; Douglas N. Hatch, Jr. and Natalie E. Larson

Daphne Foster, b. 8/18/1961 in Rochester; second; Douglas N. Hatch (truck driver, ME) and Dawn Foster (NH)

Darin Frank Matthew, b. 5/18/1967 in Rochester; third; Douglas N. Hatch (heavy equip. op., So. Berwick, ME) and Dawn Foster (Rochester)

Douglas Neal, Jr., b. 4/22/1958 in Exeter; first; Douglas N. Hatch (truck driver, ME) and Dawn Foster (NH)

Justin Neal, b. 4/12/1981 in Dover; Douglas N. Hatch, Jr. and Natalie E. Larson

HAYES,

daughter [Marion B.], b. 9/4/1890; third; Ivory Hayes (farmer, Newington) and Martha Daniels (Nottingham)

daughter, b. 9/25/1897; first; Charles H. Hayes (farmer, 25, Barrington) and Judith J. Bennett (25, Dover)

Dulcie, b. 7/16/1899; second; Charles H. Hayes (belt maker, 27, Barrington) and Judith J. Bennett (27, Dover); residence - Dover

Gerald Garland, b. 7/27/1908; first; Arthur D. Hayes (farmer, 25, Barrington) and Helen V. Garland (20, Strafford)

Hamilton Lee, b. 2/1/1942 in Rochester; second; Jack G. Hayes (student, Barrington) and Betty E. Gentry (Sapulpa, OK)

Rodney Garland, b. 6/10/1943 in Dover; second; Sumner Arthur Hayes (joiner, Somerville, MA) and Pauline M. Wiggin (Barrington)

Russell Dudley, b. 6/21/1938 in Dover; first; Sumner A. Hayes (carpenter, Somerville, MA) and Pauline M. Wiggin (Barrington)

Travis Converse, b. 1/24/1972 in Dover; Haven H. Hayes (NH) and Barbara Rising (NH)

HEMEON,

Jeffrey Paul, b. 8/30/1984 in Wolfeboro; Stephen D. Hemeon and Therese A. Meattey

HENDERSON,
Coleen Elaine, b. 5/25/1964 in Dover; fifth; Joseph R. Henderson (water dept. emp., NH) and Martha E. Segee (NH)
Helen Marcia, b. 1/13/1940 in Dover; third; Harold W. Henderson (grocer, Spofford) and Katherine H. Wiggin (East Barrington); residence - East Barrington
Janet Amelia, b. 7/23/1934 in Dover; second; Harold Henderson (postmaster, Spofford) and Katherine Wiggin (Barrington)
Kristin Gale, b. 3/21/1979 in Dover; Dana G. Henderson and Roberta A. Marchiony
Nicholas Steven, b. 2/28/1986 in Dover; Steven R. Henderson and Diane L. Lennon

HENLEY,
Elizabeth Ann, b. 12/4/1961 in Manchester; first; Zenas R. Henley (minister, NH) and Louise M. Scott (ME)
Scott Ray, b. 3/19/1963 in Manchester; second; Zenas R. Henley (teacher, NH) and Louise M. Scott (ME)

HESELTON,
Jesse James, b. 3/16/1981 in Rochester; Dana J. Heselton and Marlene E. Miller

HEWITT,
Megan Jesse, b. 11/1/1986 in Exeter; Mark A. Hewitt and Mae B. Kater

HEY,
Jesse William, III, b. 7/2/1976 in Dover; Jesse W. Hey, Jr. and Jean E. VanNest

HIBBARD,
Patti Ruth, b. 12/15/1985 in Exeter; Andrew S. Hibbard and Deborah R. McKnight

HILDRETH,
Tasha Ann, b. 8/20/1986 in Rochester; Daniel S. Hildreth and Sue A. Yoder

HILL,
Helen Marion, b. 1/20/1889; Charles J. Hill (Barrington) and Addie J. Evans (Madbury) (1945)

HILLSGROVE,
Crystal Lee, b. 5/21/1980 in Portsmouth; Darryl W. Hillsgrove and Karen L. Holland
Kelly Marie, b. 5/17/1983 in Dover; David R. Hillsgrove and Dorene D. LaPete
Kristy Lynn, b. 7/3/1980 in Dover; David R. Hillsgrove and Dorene D. LaPete

HINCH,
Tiffany Mae, b. 1/8/1974 in Rochester; Jonathan Bennett Hinch and Debra Ann Watson

HODGDON,
Amanda Lyn, b. 3/2/1985 in Dover; Gary A. Hodgdon and Teryl M. Canney
Sara May, b. 12/19/1980 in Dover; Gary A. Hodgdon and Teryl M. Canney

HOEY,
Leah Victoria, b. 7/24/1961 in Rochester; fourth; Donald J. Hoey (supervisor, NH) and Edith V. Crosby (MA)

HOITT,
A. Michelle Lee, b. 3/31/1973 in Dover; Walter B. Hoitt (NH) and Donna L. Roberts (NH)
Rebecca Marie, b. 3/31/1973 in Dover; Walter B. Hoitt (NH) and Donna L. Roberts (NH)

HOLLAND,
Rodney Arnold, b. 2/11/1967 in Rochester; second; Arnold R. Holland (machinist, Sanford, ME) and Elaine M. Pelletier (Rochester)

HOLLIS,
Amanda Lillian, b. 2/10/1980 in Dover; Robert C. Hollis, III and Deborah L. Bemis

HOLMES,
Pearl Elwood, b. 3/30/1894; second; Fred E. Holmes (engineer, 36, Portsmouth) and Jennie Hilton (35, No. Berwick, ME); residence - Portsmouth

HOLT,
Bradley Sean, b. 8/8/1981 in Exeter; Bradley G. Holt and Mary J. Shea
Brian Sean, b. 6/14/1983 in Exeter; Bradley G. Holt and Mary J. Shea

HOOKER,
Charles Alexander, b. 10/4/1959 in Kittery, ME; fourth; Duane A. Hooker (USAF, PA) and Elizabeth J. Parshall (NY)

HORGEN,
Jon David, b. 1/28/1974 in Dover; John Melvin Horgen and Diane Jean Jongeward
Ruth Elizabeth, b. 8/22/1975 in Dover; John M. Horgen and Diana J. Jongewaard
Stephen Paul, b. 9/10/1979 in Dover; John M. Horgen and Diana J. Jongewaard

HOTCHKISS,
Kathleen Grace, b. 9/21/1978; Michael L. Hotchkiss and Margaret Rohan

HOUK,
Karl Nathan, b. 4/14/1980; Donald R. Houk and Katherine A. Winter
Simon Willoughby, b. 12/15/1982; Donald R. Houk and Katherine A. Winter

HOULE,
Melinda Marie, b. 12/20/1985 in Dover; Scott R. Houle and Sandra L. Stone

HOWARD,
son [Llewellyn], b. 8/11/1893; sixth; E. Howard (laborer, Barrington) and Emma Kenney (Madbury)
son, b. 1/27/1897; twelfth; Emery Howard (laborer, 46, Barrington) and Emma Kennedy (45, Madbury)
son [Earl L.], b. 7/18/1898; second; Ernest Howard (laborer, 24, Dover) and Lilla M. Reed (17, Barrington)
daughter [Mary G.], b. 9/16/1900; second; Levi Howard (laborer, 35, Rochester) and Clara B. Foss (27, Barrington)
daughter, b. 5/19/1901; third; Ernest Howard (laborer, 27, Dover) and Lilla M. Reed (19, Barrington)
daughter [Celia], b. 4/21/1903; third; Ernest Howard (chopper, 29, Barrington) and Lillian Reed (21, Barrington)
stillborn daughter, b. 3/12/1905; third; John Howard (laborer, 50, Barrington) and Annie Calan (43, Boston, MA)
son, b. 8/1/1912; second; Fred W. Howard (laborer, 44, Farmington) and Elizabeth Howard (39, Barrington)
Arthur Waite, b. 10/23/1880; William Howard (Rochester) and Elizabeth A. Parshley (Strafford) (1946)
Charlie Edmond, b. 7/11/1898; second; Charles Howard (laborer, 27, Dover) and Genese Hart (31, Van Buren, ME)

George N., b. 12/15/1901; fourth; Charles F. Howard (laborer, 30, Barrington) and Denise Hart (36, Van Buren, ME)

Lisa Beth, b. 7/21/1983 in Exeter; Kevin Howard and Judy A. Heath

Mabel, b. 3/17/1901; second; William I. Howard (laborer, 30) and Bertha S. Goodwin (20, Barrington)

Mabel C., stillborn, b. 1/7/1897; first; Ernest Howard (laborer, 22, Dover) and Lilla M. Reed (16, Barrington)

Nellie, b. 4/20/1903; second; Levi Howard (farmer, 38, Rochester) and Cora B. Foss (29, Barrington)

William S., b. 9/19/1900; first; Harry W. Howard (farmer, 22, Barrington) and Sadie G. Eaton (19, Strafford)

HOWE,
Andrew Bradford, b. 9/5/1986 in Exeter; Roger B. Howe, II and Lynne B. Painting

HOWES,
Courtney Elizabeth, b. 6/15/1985 in Dover; Robert A. Howes and Elaine E. Beal

Rachel Mariana, b. 4/6/1987 in Dover; Robert A. Howes and Elaine E. Beal

HOYT,
Raymond Joseph, b. 9/6/1983 in Exeter; Joseph W. Hoyt, Jr. and Brenda J. Pasch

Rebekka Ann, b. 12/30/1980 in Dover; Benjamin W. Hoyt and Petra I. Posner

Stephanie Christine, b. 5/30/1983 in Dover; Benjamin W. Hoyt and Petra I. Posner

HUDSON,
Kathryn Anastatia, b. 8/29/1984 in Dover; William R. Hudson and Deborah M. Anglia

Todd Jeffrey, b. 7/29/1982 in Dover; William R. Hudson and Deborah M. Anglia

HUGHES,
Eva B., b. 4/7/1916; second; Henry Hughes (section hand, Dover) and Gertrude Ross (Barrington)
Frances, b. 9/13/1917; third; Henry Hughes (laborer, Dover) and Gertrude E. Ross (Barrington)

HULME,
Richmond Fisk, b. 11/7/1951 in Rochester; fourth; Russell C. Hulme (electrician, MA) and Alice E. Butterfield (MA)

HUNT,
Kenneth Paul, b. 8/2/1914; fourth; John P. Hunt (laborer, Greenville, NH) and Blanche T. Mayberry (Mechanics Falls, ME)
Phyllis E., b. 4/28/1912; second; John P. Hunt (farmer, 34, Abbott, ME) and Blanche T. Maberry (23, Mechanics Falls, ME)

HUNTER,
Stephen Earle, Jr., b. 2/15/1981 in Dover; Stephen E. Hunter, Sr. and Kim M. Early

HURLBURT,
Vicki Lynn, b. 3/15/1974 in Dover; Richard Paul Hurlburt and Robin Elaine Wood

HUSSEY,
Esther, b. 4/18/1916; second; Charles W. Hussey (painter, Cambridge, MA) and Mildred Smith (Hingham, MA)

HUTCHINSON,
Dean Douglas, b. 6/26/1971 in Dover; Douglas H. Hutchinson (VT) and Cynthia D. Derby (VT)

HYRE,
Christopher Lloyd, b. 2/3/1987 in Portsmouth; Daniel L. Hyre and Barbara J. Hodgens

IBER,
Ashlee Morgan, b. 3/10/1985 in Dover; Jonathan O. Iber and Carol A. Jones

INGHAM,
Kimberly Anne, b. 7/19/1984 in Dover; William E. Ingham and Margaret A. Cole

INGRAM,
John Stephen, b. 6/5/1986 in Rochester; John S. Ingram and Wendy J. Prine

INHOFF,
Marika Connine, b. 10/9/1987 in Dover; Albrecht W. Inhoff and Cynthia M. Connine

IOTT,
Andrew Peter, b. 2/20/1974 in Exeter; David Michael Iott and Nancy Caroline Wise

IRONS,
Asa McQueeney, b. 7/24/1981 in Exeter; Henry M. Irons and Mary D. McQueeney
Kelley MacAllister, b. 7/22/1977 in Rochester; Anthony E. Irons and Janet L. Douglas
Lydia Rhea, b. 10/1/1986 in Dover; Henry M. Irons and Mary D. McQueeney
Moses Ewing, b. 5/29/1973; Anthony E. Irons (WA) and Janet L. Douglas (NH)

IRVINE,
Thomas Craige, Jr., b. 5/13/1984 in Rochester; Thomas C. Irvine and Barbara J. Nasuti

JACKSON,
Amory Leigh, b. 11/11/1973 in Exeter; William S. Jackson (RI) and Ethel M. Hutchinson (MA)
Brian Dennis, b. 12/24/1985 in Portsmouth; David A. Jackson and Susan L. Clement
Brian Scott, b. 10/31/1950 in Rochester; second; Frederick L. Jackson (lineman, FL) and Ina E. Brown (NH)
Craig Martin, b. 6/28/1954 in Rochester; third; Frederick L. Jackson (line foreman, FL) and Ina E. Brown (NH)
Curtis George, b. 5/21/1959 in Rochester; fifth; Frederick L. Jackson (line foreman, FL) and Ina E. Brown (NH)
Danielle Leann, b. 5/16/1986 in Rochester; Curtis G. Jackson and Robin M. Pelletier
Frederick Lensworth, Jr., b. 11/19/1956 in Rochester; fourth; Frederick L. Jackson (line foreman, FL) and Ina E. Brown (NH)
Jamie Lee, b. 5/9/1981 in Dover; Frederick L. Jackson, Jr. and Julie E. Fitzgerald
Kari Ann, b. 12/23/1977 in Dover; Craig M. Jackson and Kim E. Knight
Keith Frederick, b. 9/4/1947 in Rochester; first; Frederick L. Jackson (foreman, FL) and Ina E. Brown (Barrington)
Lisa Evelyn, b. 7/29/1961 in Rochester; sixth; Frederick L. Jackson (line foreman, FL) and Ina E. Brown (NH)
Melissa Anne, b. 5/25/1984 in Portsmouth; David A. Jackson and Susan L. Clement
Mindy Lee, b. 7/9/1979 in Dover; Craig M. Jackson and Kim E. Knight
Nichole Marie, b. 1/1/1970 in Rochester; Brian S. Jackson (NH) and Deborah E. Weeks (NH)
Seth Stanworth, b. 4/12/1969 in Dover; William S. Jackson (RI) and Ethel M. Hutchinson (MA)

JACQUES,
David McKenzie, b. 4/26/1940 in Exeter; third; Theodore J. Jacques (laborer, Manchester) and Muriel T. Robbin (Danvers, MA)
Kevin Roger, b. 10/20/1973 in Dover; Paul B. Jacques (NH) and Judy A. LaPanne (NH)
Timothy Tyler, b. 8/30/1964 in Rochester; third; David M. Jacques (cashier, NH) and Patricia R. Carpenter (ME)

JAMES,
Rebecca Ann, b. 2/18/1981 in Rochester; Kevin G. James and Kathleen L. Miller

JANELLE,
Charles Jonathan, b. 9/7/1977 in Dover; Charles P.F. Janelle and Nilda R. Taylor

JEFFERY,
Gwendolyn Leigh, b. 3/6/1986; Stephen P. Jeffery and Katherine L. Smith
Kirsten Merinda, b. 7/5/1984; Stephen P. Jeffery and Katherine L. Smith

JENNESS,
daughter, b. 7/22/1893; first; Louis Jenness (music teacher, Nottingham) and Lula Rowe (Barnstead)

JENNINGS,
Melinda Anne, b. 11/15/1977 in Portsmouth; William D. Jennings and Susan M. Matson

JENNISON,
Adam Winthrop, b. 11/20/1978 in Rochester; Martin P. Jennison and Karen L. Deane
Christie Ann, b. 1/22/1977 in Rochester; Bruce R. Jennison and Janice A. Jewell

Diane Elizabeth, b. 12/21/1975 in Exeter; Dan A. Jennison and Pamela A. Sumner
Kimberly Marion, b. 5/10/1977 in Exeter; Dan A. Jennison and Pamela A. Sumner
Steven Arthur, b. 12/27/1975 in Dover; Steven A. Jennison and Linda J. Abbott
Victoria Faith, b. 5/19/1974 in Exeter; Dan Arthur Jennison and Pamela Ann Sumner

JERABEK,
Bryan William, b. 9/6/1978 in Portsmouth; William L. Jerabek and Dolores M. Levesque
Sarah Dale, b. 6/24/1980 in Portsmouth; William L. Jerabek and Dolores M. Levesque

JOHN,
Philip Ray, b. 1/25/1985 in Dover; Richard E. John and Betsy E. Bormann
Timothy Jacob, b. 1/25/1985 in Dover; Richard E. John and Betsy E. Bormann

JOHNSEN,
Karli Dawn, b. 1/17/1983 in Rochester; Gregory T. Johnsen and Dorothy E. Bogoslawski
Kristian Gregory, b. 1/22/1985 in Rochester; Gregory T. Johnsen and Dorothy E. Bogoslawski

JOHNSON,
stillborn son, b. 9/17/1913; first; Charles E. Johnson (barber, 24, Greece) and Laurel Burleigh (17, Dover)
son, b. 11/10/1914; second; Ernest Johnson (salesman, Old Town, ME) and Winnie F. Welman (Winthrop, ME); residence - Hartland, NH
Donna Lee, b. 2/25/1952 in Exeter; fifth; Alexander J. Johnson (fireman, MA) and Evelyn M. Green (NH)

Janice Louise, b. 7/26/1939 in Exeter; ninth; Alexander J.
    Johnson (chemical plant, Melrose, MA) and Marion E.
    Ineson (Weare)
Richard Arthur, b. 6/10/1938 in Exeter; eighth; Alexander J.
    Johnson (chemical plant, Melrose, MA) and Marion E.
    Inman (East Weare)
Seth Samuel, b. 8/24/1982 in Rochester; Samuel O. Johnson
    and Mary M. Kathios

JOHNSTONE,
Bobbie-Jo Marie, b. 8/28/1977 in Lawrence, MA; Robert J.
    Johnstone and Sharon L. Fortier

JONCAS,
Kate Elizabeth, b. 5/8/1977 in Dover; Mark S. Joncas and
    Trudy G. Goodwin
Troy Stephen, b. 7/26/1975 in Dover; Mark S. Joncas and
    Trudy G. Goodwin

JONES,
Daniel Douglas, b. 1/23/1977 in Exeter; Gregory M. Jones
    and Patricia D. Dunham
Jennifer Kristen, b. 3/27/1981 in Dover; Robert E. Jones, Jr.
    and Gloria A. Scarborough
Kelly Elizabeth, b. 8/1/1977 in Exeter; John K.M. Jones and
    Karen L. Callahan
Kimberly Alyson, b. 5/11/1983 in Dover; Robert E. Jones and
    Gloria A. Scarborough
Mark Woodrow, b. 3/1/1965 in Kittery, ME; second; Elwood
    C. Jones (USAF, PA) and Megumi Fukui (Japan)

JOSELIN,
Edla Esther, b. 8/12/1915; second; Joseph R. Joselin
    (laborer, Barrington) and Nellie M. Brown (Madbury)

JOUBERT,
Ted William, b. 6/20/1987 in Portsmouth; Scott C. Joubert and Anne R. Guerette

JOY,
Jennifer Mimi, b. 9/25/1975 in Dover; Alan D. Joy and Nancy C. Bondelevitch

JOYAL,
Renee Lynne, b. 2/21/1986 in Dover; Robert J. Joyal, Jr. and Flora N. LaPierre
Ryan James, b. 2/21/1986 in Dover; Robert J. Joyal, Jr. and Flora N. LaPierre

JUNKINS,
son, b. 6/3/1895; third; Frank Junkins (41, No. Berwick, ME) and Addie Jano (20, Wolfeboro)

JUSTICE,
Lisa Kathleen, b. 7/12/1972 in Dover; Russell E. Justice (NH) and Kathleen F. Paul (NH)

KAPSIMALIS,
Corey William, b. 3/10/1987 in Portsmouth; William P. Kapsimalis, Jr. and Helene F. Moore
Shane Peter, b. 3/10/1987 in Portsmouth; William P. Kapsimalis, Jr. and Helene F. Moore

KARAVICH,
Peter William, Jr., b. 2/9/1967 in Rochester; first; Peter W. Karavich (welder, Queen City, NY) and Patricia A. Proctor (Dover)

KARMERIS,
Tyson Gregory Parks, b. 6/3/1981 in Dover; Theodore J. Karmeris and Susan J. Parks (see below)

Tyson Gregory Parks, b. 7/30/1981 in Dover; Theodore J. Karmeris and Susan J. Parks (see above)

KAUFHOLD,
Benjamin Thomas, b. 6/12/1985 in Dover; Thomas J. Kaufhold and Mary P. Tebo

KAY,
Darcy Ryan, b. 8/28/1983 in Dover; David D. Kay and Donna L. Newsky
Dustin Dean, b. 4/2/1982 in Dover; David D. Kay and Donna L. Newsky

KEEFE,
Peter Thomas, b. 12/4/1957 in Dover; first; Thomas P. Keefe (with gas co., ME) and Anita M. Martel (NH)

KEESEE,
Linda Michelle, b. 8/2/1975 in Rochester; Thomas G. Keesee and Linda R. Nettleton

KELLEY,
Ashlie Anne, b. 10/1/1985 in Rochester; John L. Kelley, III and LouAnne M. Wilbur
Heather Lee, b. 3/28/1975 in Dover; Alan A. Kelley and Elinor M. Palmer
Kristen Lara, b. 12/4/1978 in Dover; Alan A. Kelley and Elinor M. Palmer
Marnie Elinor, b. 9/22/1976 in Dover; Alan A. Kelley and Elinor M. Palmer
Patricia Vina, b. 8/14/1964 in Concord; second; Verne C. Kelley (US Army, NH) and Anita Rost (Germany)
Sean Richard, b. 12/3/1981 in Dover; Alan A. Kelley and Elinor M. Palmer

KENNEY,
Nancy Ann, b. 7/29/1972 in Dover; William M. Kenney (MA) and Barbara A. Wallingford (NH)

KESSLER,
Andrew Eric, b. 10/2/1986 in Dover; Harry E. Kessler and Jacqueline E. Neal
Donald Edwin, b. 2/6/1980 in Dover; Harry E. Kessler and Jacqueline E. Neal

KIERSTEAD,
Alex David, b. 9/4/1986 in Exeter; David W. Kierstead, Jr. and Elizabeth P. Pretty

KIMBALL,
Brett Allan, b. 3/9/1980 in Rochester; Robert E. Kimball and Mona L. Houde

KITTREDGE,
Jessica Marie, b. 2/18/1987 in Rochester; Van R. Kittredge and Lynn M. Hatch
Tabor James, b. 12/6/1987 in Dover; James K. Kittredge and Cynthia L. Cummings

KLUESENER,
daughter, b. 2/7/1979 in Dover; David R. Kluesener and Sherri A. Hull
Joshua, b. 9/12/1977 in Dover; David R. Kluesener and Sherri A. Hull

KNOX,
Evelyn M., b. 2/20/1912; first; Harley Knox (lumberman, 22, Epping) and Lois Ellison (18, Nottingham)

KOST,
daughter, b. 8/21/1982 in Dover; Dennis D. Kost and Ann L. Warren
Amanda Jean, b. 1/1/1984 in Dover; Dennis D. Kost and Ann L. Warren

KOSTIEW,
Katherine Elizabeth, b. 1/5/1986 in Concord; Michael S. Kostiew and Judith L. Cirella
Kristal Marie, b. 1/8/1982 in Concord; Michael S. Kostiew and Judith L. Cirella
Matthew Joseph, b. 2/5/1984 in Concord; Michael S. Kostiew and Judith L. Cirella
Michael Angelo, b. 1/25/1978 in Dover; Michael S. Kostiew and Judith L. Cirella

KOUFOS,
Christine Ruth, b. 5/13/1964 in Kittery, ME; eighth; Theodore Koufos (USAF, MA) and Gisele A. Henke (Germany)
Doreen Giselle, b. 1/30/1963 in Kittery, ME; seventh; Theodore Koufos (USAF, MA) and Gisela I.A. Henke (Germany)
Michael Ted, b. 4/15/1960 in Kittery, ME; sixth; Theodore Koufos (USAF, MA) and Gisela I.A. Henke (Germany)

LABRECQUE,
Lorie Ann, b. 12/12/1972 in Rochester; Donald R. Labrecque (CA) and Shirley A. Grenier (NH)

LADUCI,
Mary R., b. 5/24/1892; first; Louis Laduci (laborer, 24, Canada) and Lora Decatur (20, Canada)

LAFERTE,
Janet Susan, b. 9/29/1972 in Rochester; Robert H. Laferte (NH) and Susan P. Clements (NH)

LAFRANCE,
Mary Margaret, b. 5/26/1955 in Dover; fifth; Joseph G. LaFrance (electronic tech., Canada) and Elyse A. Hamilton (IA)
Robert Gerard, b. 12/29/1948; fourth; Joseph G. LaFrance (electrician, Canada) and Elsie Hamilton (IA)

LAGASSE,
Stephen Charles, b. 3/24/1959 in Dover; first; Raymond A. Lagasse (student, DC) and Marie A. Doherty (NH)

LAKEMAN,
Stephanie Helen, b. 5/4/1983 in Dover; Frederick W. Lakeman and Donna M. Smith

LALANCETTE,
Kari Dawn, b. 10/7/1986 in Portsmouth; Roland P. Lalancette and Stephanie S. Caldwell

LANCIANO,
Alisha Marie, b. 3/29/1986 in Dover; Francis B.M. Lanciano and Ronna M. McBride

LANDRY,
Cynthia Joyce, b. 6/29/1939; third; James W. Landry (shoe wkr., Landaff) and Barbara N. Walker (Pike)
Dana Allen, b. 6/14/1964 in Rochester; second; James W. Landry (salvage yard, NH) and Joan M. Loring (MA)
Darcy Ann, b. 6/8/1962 in Rochester; first; James W. Landry (garage mech., NH) and Joan M. Loring (MA)
Daryl Aaron, b. 9/21/1965 in Rochester; third; James W. Landry, Jr. (self employed, NH) and Jean M. Loring (MA)
Eugene Richard, b. 12/30/1935 in Rochester; first; James W. Landry (shoeworker, Landaff) and Barbara Walker (Pike)

Eugene Richard, Jr., b. 12/10/1960 in Rochester; third; Eugene R. Landry (mechanic, NH) and Doris E. Alty (MA)
Kasey Leigh, b. 8/7/1968 in Dover; Eugene R. Landry (NH) and Doris E. Alty (MA)
Korey Lugene, b. 11/14/1962 in Rochester; fourth; Eugene R. Landry (mechanic, NH) and Doris E. Alty (MA)
Kristina Loren, b. 6/29/1965 in Rochester; fifth; Eugene R. Landry (self employed, NH) and Doris E. Alty (MA)
Ronald David, b. 10/1/1942; fifth; James W. Landry (shoe worker, Landaff) and Barbara N. Walker (Pike)

LANGELIER,
Alicia Marie, b. 11/27/1985 in Rochester; Laurice A. Langelier and Carol J. Colby
Jeffrey Laurice, b. 3/22/1981 in Dover; Laurice A. Langelier and Carol J. Colby

LANGEVIN,
Bree Anne, b. 11/22/1981 in Dover; Jeffrey D. Langevin and Kimberly J. Tuttle

LANGLEY,
daughter, b. 9/9/1902; first; Percy Langley (farmer, 24, Barrington) and Josephine Brown (19, Northwood)

LANGLOIS,
Robert Michael, b. 11/8/1985 in Dover; Michael R. Langlois and Karen M. Waida

LAPANNE,
Donald Robert, b. 3/22/1960 in Dover; sixth; Simon E. LaPanne (machinist, CT) and Alice J. Grenier (NH)
Heidi Marie, b. 2/4/1986 in Dover; Marc A. LaPanne and Donna M. Breton

Julie Anne, b. 5/22/1956; third; Nelson H. LaPanne
(carpenter, CT) and Lorraine M. Joyal (NH)
Paul Anthony, b. 12/11/1957 in Dover; fourth; Nelson H.
LaPanne (shoe worker, CT) and Lorraine M. Joyal (NH)
Richard Raymond, b. 3/23/1961 in Dover; seventh; Simon E.
LaPanne (machine oper., CT) and Alice J. Grenier (NH)
Ryan Luke, b. 5/21/1985 in Rochester; Luke J. LaPanne and
Penelope A. Thurston
Tara-Lee Ann, b. 3/17/1984 in Rochester; Luke J. LaPanne
and Penelope A. Thurston

LAPHAM,
Erin Leigh, b. 6/19/1984 in Concord; Warren E. Lapham and
Cheryl L. McKerley

LAPIERRE,
Gina Marie, b. 4/15/1976 in Rochester; Paul M. Lapierre and
Rosanne M. Trudel
Joshua Vaughn, b. 10/31/1985 in Dover; Jeffrey D. LaPierre
and Kimberly D. Poulin

LAPLANTE,
Elana Estelle, b. 7/23/1983 in Dover; Roy A. LaPlante and
Danielle L. McMurchy

LAPRADE,
Todd Patrick, b. 1/31/1980 in Dover; Roland P. Laprade and
Rachel A. Primeau

LAROCHE,
Amanda Leigh, b. 8/11/1978 in Dover; Thomas A. Laroche
and Cheryl R. Newhall
Melissa Lynn, b. 11/4/1983 in Dover; Thomas A. Laroche
and Cheryl R. Newhall
Thomas Alan, Jr., b. 9/12/1981 in Dover; Thomas A.
Laroche, Sr. and Cheryl R. Newhall

LAROCHELLE,
Erik James, b. 10/1/1977 in Dover; James E. LaRochelle and Kathleen G. King

LAVIGNE,
Matthew Joseph, b. 2/10/1986 in Rochester; Joseph L. Lavigne and Martha K. Wentworth

LAVOIE,
Erica Lynn, b. 11/27/1976 in Dover; Patrick P. Lavoie and Gail I. Saunders
Patrick Paul, Jr., b. 3/17/1978 in Dover; Patrick P. Lavoie, Sr. and Gail I. Saunders

LAW,
George William, b. 2/18/1915; second; Reginald S. Law (laborer, Boston, MA) and Frances Twombly (Nottingham)

LAWRENCE,
Timothy Adams, b. 10/31/1976 in Exeter; James E. Lawrence and Linda S. Roberson
Tonia Marie, b. 8/28/1981 in Dover; Donald C. Lawrence and Lois E. Brown

LAWRY,
Stephanie Anne Eliza, b. 7/26/1973 in Portsmouth; Donald E. Lawry (NH) and Marie T. Fox (ME)

LEAHY,
Jarrett Ernest, b. 2/21/1983 in Exeter; Timothy F. Leahy and Karen A. Scafidi
Regina Marie, b. 10/29/1972 in Rochester; Tommi J. Leahy (NH) and Marie T. Watts (PA)
Sandra Mary, b. 10/27/1953 in Rochester; third; John J. Leahy (auto supply, NH) and Gloria A. Witham (NH)

Tommie John, II, b. 11/13/1980 in Dover; Tommie J. Leahy, Sr. and Debra A. Guppy

LEAK,
Christopher William, b. 12/15/1965 in Rochester; second; William B. Leak (research lab chief, Mahwah, NJ) and Shirley A. Garland (Rochester)
Timothy Irving, b. 7/26/1975 in Rochester; William B. Leak and Shirley A. Garland

LECLAIR,
son [Allison], b. 1/21/1923; fifth; Frank LeClair (farmer, Canada) and Bessie Whalen (NS)
Corrine Christina, b. 7/11/1982 in Dover; John A. LeClair, Jr. and Maureen E. Joyce
William, b. 5/19/1924; sixth; Frank LeClair (farmer, Canada) and Bessie Whalen (Canada)

LEDUC,
William Vincent, III, b. 1/16/1984 in Rochester; William V. Leduc and Susan T. Carroll

LEE,
Christopher George, b. 7/12/1972 in Portsmouth; George F. Lee (MA) and Joyce A. McKenna (ME)
Eric Wayne, b. 5/31/1967 in Dover; second; Denneth W. Lee (foreman, Rochester) and Judith M. West (York, ME)
Jason Clarendon, b. 2/11/1972 in Dover; Denneth W. Lee (NH) and Judith M. West (NH)
Linda Ann, b. 1/21/1966 in Kittery, ME; first; Kenneth W. Lee (landscape foreman, NH) and Judith M. West (York, ME)
Robert Edward, III, b. 6/18/1986 in Rochester; Robert E. Lee, Jr. and Brenda L. Reed
Tabitha Ann, b. 7/22/1985 in Rochester; Robert E. Lee, Jr. and Brenda L. Reed

Wendy Sue, b. 4/21/1979 in Dover; Denneth W. Lee and
  Judith M. West
William Joseph, b. 1/14/1983 in Dover; Denneth W. Lee and
  Judith M. West

LEEMAN,
Aaron J., b. 5/27/1975 in Dover; Dennis A. Leeman and
  Linda A. Tetreault

LEFAVE,
John Michael, b. 5/17/1984 in Rochester; Robert A. Lefave
  and Lee A. Howland

LEFEBRVRE,
Richard Daniel, b. 7/10/1960 in Rochester; first; Albert R.J.
  Lefebvre (carpenter, NH) and Carol F. Hogan (NH)

LEIGHTON,
son [Albert J.], b. 6/13/1890; third; J. Herbert Leighton
  (farmer, Strafford) and Mary E. Holmes (Barrington)
Kara Shea, b. 1/7/1985 in Rochester; Thomas C. Leighton
  and Darlene L. Toof
Lucas Frazer, b. 2/22/1971 in Rochester; Warren C. Leighton
  (NH) and Ruth E. Bryson (NH)

LEMAY,
Jean Francis, b. 7/24/1972 in Rochester; Jean M. Lemay
  (NH) and Dorothy F. Duvall (NY)

LEMELIN,
daughter, b. 11/23/1987 in Dover; Roger D. Lemelin and
  Sally A. Fitz
Christopher David, b. 4/16/1982 in Dover; Roger D. Lemelin
  and Sally A. Fitz
Elaine Marie, b. 2/18/1981 in Dover; Raymond A. Lemelin
  and Carol L. Poplett

LENSI[E],
Frank Gordon, b. 12/6/1913; first; George Lensi (farmer, 22, Boston, MA) and Ruth Bodge (20, Barrington)
George Robert, b. 4/5/1915; second; George F. Lensie (farmer, Boston, MA) and Ruth Bodge (Barrington)

LENZI,
Andrea Ruth, b. 8/23/1975 in Dover; Steven F. Lenzi and Pamela M. Caron
Brian Douglas, b. 5/23/1948 in Rochester; second; George R. Lenzi (laborer, Barrington) and Evaline E. Baker (Yonkers, NY)
Jessica Ann, b. 10/13/1973 in Dover; Steven F. Lenzi (NH) and Pamela M. Caron (NH)
Mark Douglas, b. 7/12/1974 in Dover; Brian Douglas Lenzi and Rebecca Mae Walker
Patrice Agnes, b. 3/15/1951 in Rochester; fourth; George R. Lenzi (ass't patrolman, NH) and Evaline E. Baker (NY)
Robert George, b. 7/16/1946 in Rochester; first; George R. Lenzi (resort, Barrington) and Evaline E. Baker (Yonkers, NY)
Steven Francis, b. 7/2/1949 in Rochester; third; George R. Lenzi (laborer, NH) and Evaline E. Baker (NY)

LEOCHA,
Alice Muriel, b. 8/30/1946 in Rochester; first; Mitchell J. Leocha (US Army, Claremont) and Muriel L. Turner (Madbury)
Diane Valerie, b. 8/7/1955 in Rochester; second; Mitchell J. Leocha (machinist, NH) and Muriel L. Turner (NH)
Leona Denise, b. 1/5/1957 in Rochester; third; Mitchell J. Leocha (machinist, NH) and Muriel L. Turner (NH)
Mitchell John, II, b. 10/18/1960 in Rochester; fourth; Mitchell J. Leocha (qtrmn. machinist, NH) and Muriel L. Turner (NH)

LEONARD,
son, b. 3/10/1970 in Dover; Richard D. Leonard, Jr. (NH) and Kathleen A. Murphy (NH)

LEROY,
Katy Lynn, b. 6/25/1987 in Haverhill, MA; James H. LeRoy and Tammy A. MacLeen
Stephanie Marie, b. 8/26/1985 in Haverhill, MA; James H. LeRoy and Tammy A. MacLean

LESLIE,
Andrea Kate, b. 1/25/1986 in Portsmouth; James B. Leslie and Susan F. Clock

LESSARD,
Drina Lee, b. 8/14/1968 in Rochester; Paul E. Lessard (NH) and Joan E. Vass (NH)
Nicole Dee, b. 12/9/1970 in Rochester; Paul E. Lessard (NH) and Joan E. Vass (NH)
Peter Jay, b. 7/28/1969 in Rochester; Paul E. Lessard (NH) and Joan E. Vass (NH)

LEVASSEUR,
Sonya Jean, b. 1/19/1987 in Dover; Leo H. Levasseur and Natasha A. Itchkavich

LEVENDAHL,
Chivon Janie, b. 5/2/1983 in Manchester; David R. Levendahl and Shari L. Knoth
Ryan Robert, b. 12/5/1984 in Manchester; David R. Levendahl and Shari L. Knoth

LEVESQUE,
Peter Michael, b. 8/1/1981 in Dover; Michael J. Levesque and Sara L. Watson

LEWIS,
Ashley Nicole, b. 10/19/1986 in Exeter; Jeffrey B. Lewis and Victoria L. Chase
Paula Ann, b. 1/3/1966 in Dover; first; Paul H. Lewis (auto machinist, Dover) and Sylvia A. Soames (Dover)

LEY,
Christine Chantal, b. 1/29/1981 in Dover; David A. Ley and Colleen A. Windorf

LIBBY,
Leo Richard, Jr., b. 10/9/1981 in Portsmouth; Leo R. Libby, Sr. and Lisa E. Jackson

LIMANNI,
Angela Marie, b. 1/8/1983 in Rochester; Charles M. Limanni and Lynda K. Chase
Nicholas Charles, b. 9/7/1981 in Portsmouth; Charles M. Limanni and Lynda K. Chase

LINCOLN,
Betty Sue, b. 11/28/1947 in Rochester; twelfth; Robert A. Lincoln (truck driver, Red Beach, ME) and Helena M. Durgin (Chelsea, MA)
Carol Theresa, b. 12/2/1946 in Rochester; eleventh; Robert A. Lincoln (truck driver, Red Beach, ME) and Helena M. Durgin (Chelsea, MA)
Cora May, b. 11/22/1890; first; Levi T. Lincoln (farmer, Lowell, MA) and Susie B. Lincoln (Germany)

LINGARD,
Kendra Jennie, b. 5/1/1979 in Rochester; Kenneth R. Lingard and Cynthia J. Wheeler

LINZI,
child, b. 6/21/1916; third; George Linzi (farmer, Boston, MA) and Ruth Bodge (Barrington)

LITTLEFIELD,
Robin Hunter, b. 9/8/1984 in Concord; Frederick H. Littlefield and Virginia L. Sleamaker
Robin Sue, b. 8/26/1967 in Dover; second; Raymond S. Littlefield (designer, Bridgton, ME) and Bonita L. Eastman (No. Conway)

LITZENBERGER,
Scott Edward, b. 3/1/1980 in Rochester; Edward L. Litzenberger and Donna E. Lund

LLOYD,
Shaina Faye, b. 11/6/1987 in Dover; Jacob S. Lloyd and Sandra L. Routhier

LOCKE,
daughter [Gertrude], b. 3/24/1893; third; A. B. Locke (farmer, Barrington) and Mary A. Waterhouse (Barrington)
stillborn daughter, b. 8/30/1902; first; Stanley A. Locke (farmer, 32, Barrington) and Isabel Thompson (32, Lee)
Clarence Bryan, b. 3/10/1898; first; Irving M. Locke (lumber dealer, 34, Barrington) and Linna M. Buzzell (20, Barrington)
Eva May, b. 6/9/1901; second; Irving M. Locke (farmer, 37, Barrington) and Linna M. Buzzell (23, Barrington)
Everett I., b. 10/2/1930 in Rochester; first; Clarence B. Locke (farmer and lum., Barrington) and Lillian F. Morrison (East Boston, MA)
James Samuel, b. 2/11/1945 in Rochester; third; Clarence B. Locke (fireman, Barrington) and Eva M. Clow (Claremont)

Mary Linna, b. 2/16/1942 in Rochester; third; Clarence B. Locke (lumberman, Barrington) and Eva M. Clow (Claremont)

Mildred, b. 11/11/1895; fourth; A. B. Locke (butter maker, 46, Barrington) and Mary Waterhouse (44, Barrington)

Stanley Ellsworth, b. 6/3/1906; first; Stanley Locke (farmer, 35, Barrington) and Isabelle Chesley (29, Boston, MA)

LOISELLE,
Nicholas James, b. 12/7/1981 in Dover; Peter A. Loiselle and Diane L. Huston

LOMBARDO,
Nicholas Michael, b. 8/31/1985 in Rochester; Steven E. Lombardo and Ann M. Pike

LORANGER,
Elizabeth Anne, b. 8/27/1980 in Exeter; Roger R. Loranger and Jennifer O. Redding

Jessica Susan, b. 11/22/1981 in Exeter; Roger R. Loranger and Jennifer O. Redding

LORING,
Anda Lucia, b. 7/22/1976 in Exeter; Justin C. Loring and Janice A. Crossley

Burlen Clay, b. 7/19/1975 in Dover; Justin C. Loring and Janice A. Crossley

Kirt Lydell, b. 4/12/1978 in Dover; Justin C. Loring and Janice A. Crossley

Meredith, b. 7/16/1979 in Dover; Justin C. Loring and Janice A. Crossley

Prentice Chandler, b. 12/9/1973 in Rochester; Justin Charles Loring and Janice Anne Crossley

LOWRY,
Andrea Kay, b. 7/18/1966 in Kittery, ME; fifth; Ellis C. Lowry (USAF, MA) and Beverly A. McGregor (NH)
Austin, b. 8/21/1983 in Portsmouth; Mark K. Lowry and Anita M. Geldart
Ilene Edith, b. 7/12/1959 in Kittery, ME; third; Ellis C. Lowry (USAF, MA) and Beverly A. McGregor (NH)
James Michael, b. 1/14/1986 in Rochester; Scott C. Lowry and Carol L. Brown
Marion Frances, b. 7/8/1946 in Rochester; second; Leo K. Lowry (farmer, Revere, MA) and Marion V. Benson (Whitman, MA)
Mark Kenneth, b. 7/18/1962 in Kittery, ME; third; Ellis C. Lowry (USAF, MA) and Beverly A. McGregor (NH)
Scott Curtis, b. 1/20/1964 in Rochester; fourth; Ellis C. Lowry (USAF, MA) and Beverly A. McGregor (NH)

LOWY,
Pamela Ann, b. 7/25/1973 in Dover; John J. Lowy (NY) and Margaret E. Wilson (England)

LUOMA,
Janna Marie, b. 2/12/1987 in Dover; William A. Luoma and Kelly M. Girard

LYNCH,
Dylan Thomas, b. 10/9/1985 in Rochester; Mark W. Lynch and Joanne B. Baldwin

LYONS,
Donald Richard, Jr., b. 8/9/1959 in Rochester; second; Donald R. Lyons (carpenter, NH) and Gail J. Small (NH)

MACDONALD,
Peter Martin, b. 3/26/1970 in Rochester; Charles J. Macdonald, II (MA) and Jean L. Babson (NH)

MACEACHERN,
Amanda Suzanne, b. 9/11/1980 in Portsmouth; Donald L. MacEachern and Michele J. Lambert

MACKENZIE,
Kyle Steven, b. 8/13/1986 in Rochester; Steven G. MacKenzie and Candace E. DeVries
Ryan George, b. 6/8/1984 in Rochester; Steven G. MacKenzie and Candace E. deVries

MACLEAN,
Carly Elizabeth, b. 6/26/1984 in Rochester; David A. MacLean and Jane E. Rowell
Jeffrey John, b. 6/11/1979 in Dover; Brian L. MacLean and Nancy E. Simpson
Tammy Elizabeth, b. 1/13/1978 in Dover; Brian L. MacLean and Nancy E. Simpson

MACPHERSON,
Casey Lee, b. 3/13/1982 in North Conway; Scott P. MacPherson and Tracey A. Benson
Joshua Parker, b. 7/15/1983 in Exeter; Scott P. MacPherson and Tracey A. Benson

MACRAE,
Alice Mae, b. 2/7/1886; Thomas E. MacRae (Cape Breton, NS) and Clarinda Richardson (Woburn, MA) (1943)
Hilda A., b. 10/8/1918; first; Kenneth MacRae (farmer, Barrington) and Ethel L. Brown (Barrington)
Josephine Elizabeth, b. 6/7/1888; Thomas E. MacRae (Cape Breton, NS) and Clarinda Richardson (Woburn, MA) (1943)
Kenneth, b. 4/8/1890; Thomas E. MacRae (Cape Breton, NS) and Clarinda Richardson (Woburn, MA) (1943)

MADARIAGA,
Megan Grace, b. 6/11/1985 in Dover; Jorge E. Madariaga and Diane M. Valinski

MAGNUSON,
Conan Ernest, b. 5/2/1982 in Rochester; Gary W. Magnuson and Jennifer A. Coyne

MAGUIRE,
Linda Ellen, b. 4/30/1963 in Dover; second; Joseph F. Maguire (carpenter, PA) and Pamela J. Hughey (MA)

MAHONEY,
Brett James, b. 8/11/1981 in Exeter; James J. Mahoney and Cheryl L. Follansbee
Matthew Follansbee, b. 11/6/1978 in Exeter; James J. Mahoney and Cheryl L. Follansbee

MALIK,
Matthew Robert, b. 8/12/1987 in Exeter; Perry R. Malik and Joan M. Green

MALONE,
Adam Christopher, b. 3/29/1980 in Rochester; Gary R. Malone and Jacqueline G. Grant
Christina Eva, b. 3/14/1976 in Rochester; Wayne E. Malone and Carmen I. Mueller
Jared Christopher, b. 9/1/1976 in Rochester; Gary R. Malone and Jacqueline G. Grant
Lindsay Rachel, b. 8/18/1981 in Rochester; Gary R. Malone and Jacuqeline G. Grant

MALONEY,
Cara Ann, b. 12/14/1978 in Dover; John E. Maloney and Barbara A. Hoey

MANSFIELD,
Albert Hussey, b. 1/31/1953 in Dover; fourth; Benjamin W. Mansfield, Jr. (pressman, NH) and Barbara L. Lucas (NH)
Jacqueline Susan, stillborn, b. 5/2/1956 in Dover; fifth; Benjamin W. Mansfield, Jr. (printer, NH) and Barbara L. Lucas (NH)
Judith Ann, b. 12/29/1948 in Dover; first; Benjamin W. Mansfield, Jr. (truck driver, NH) and Barbara Lucas (NH)
Lois Arlene, b. 8/23/1951 in Dover; third; Benjamin W. Mansfield, Jr. (circulation mgr., NH) and Barbara L. Lucas (NH)
Nancy Jean, b. 1/27/1950 in Dover; second; Benjamin W. Mansfield, Jr. (electrician, NH) and Barbara L. Lucas (NH)

MARCOTTE,
John Joseph, b. 12/17/1982 in Rochester; Dennis J. Marcotte and Connie S. Bodge
Sarah Ann, b. 3/3/1979 in Rochester; Dennis J. Marcotte and Connie S. Bodge

MARCOUX,
Paula Lynn, b. 12/3/1968 in Dover; Richard A. Marcoux (ME) and Pauline L. Couture (NH)

MARINO,
Ricardo Charles, b. 4/10/1976 in Dover; Anthony F. Marino and Anna J. Bergeron
Tino Anthony, b. 8/1/1978 in Exeter; Anthony F. Marino and Anna J. Bergeron

MARIOTTI,
Daniel Charles, b. 8/18/1975 in Rochester; Judson E. Mariotti and Linda A. Brown

Edward Charles, b. 12/25/1939 in Exeter; first; Darius C.
Mariotti (farmer, Newmarket) and Fern York (Elmwood,
WI); residence - East Barrington

Jason Edward, b. 3/26/1971 in Rochester; Judson E. Mariotti
(NH) and Linda A. Brown (NH)

Judson Edward, b. 11/24/1943 in Exeter; second; Darius C.
Mariotti (farmer, Newmarket) and Fern Mary York
(Elmwood, WI)

MAR[R]ISON,
Bernard Louis, b. 1/29/1920; second; Lindley J. Marison
(farmer, Strafford) and Mary C. Louis (Nottingham)

Helen, b. 11/15/1917; first; Lindley Marrison (farmer,
Strafford) and Mary C. Lewis (Northwood)

MARKEY,
Zachary Nicholas, b. 2/3/1987 in Dover; Thomas G. Markey
and Debra A. Frey

MARKHAM,
Tyler Benjamin, b. 5/6/1984 in Exeter; Arthur C. Markham
and Sharon L. Butler

MARQUETTE,
Daniel Edward, b. 11/9/1977 in Exeter; Joseph A. Marquette,
Jr. and Sheila M.L. Mainville

Elizabeth Christina, b. 7/9/1979 in Rochester; Joseph A.
Marquette, Jr. and Sheila M.L. Mainville

Tobias Andrew, b. 11/29/1980 in Rochester; Joseph A.
Marquette, Jr. and Sheila M. Mainville

MARSH,
Michael David, b. 9/2/1965 in Rochester; first; Earl L. Marsh,
Jr. (shoe worker, NH) and Jean F. Hall (NH)

Shawn Earl-Edward, b. 1/13/1967 in Rochester; second; Earl L. Marsh, Jr. (shoe worker, Farmington) and Jean F. Hall (Dover)

MARSHALL,
son, b. 8/21/1894; fifth; Thomas Marshall (farmer, 38, Digby, NS) and Ina J. Fullmore (30, Five Island, NS)
son [Benjamin], b. 7/28/1902; first; Frank Marshall (teamster, 30, NS) and Cora Willey (25, Barrington); residence - Dover

MARSOLAIS,
Nathan Daniel, b. 11/1/1987 in Exeter; Timothy W. Marsolais and Cheryl A. Davis

MARTEL,
Anthony James, b. 12/25/1981 in Dover; Dana P. Martel and Celeste M. Mone
Jamie Lynn, b. 6/15/1980 in Dover; Dana P. Martel and Celeste M. Mone

MARTIN,
Benjamin H., b. 4/19/1931; first; Harry B. Martin (laborer, Hudson, MA) and Loretta Sardiff (Burlington, VT)
Julie Margaret, b. 6/2/1981 in Portsmouth; William T. Martin and Gail F. Trowell

MASKELL,
Regina Lucy, b. 9/9/1959 in Rochester; third; Albert A. Maskell (art. well driller, MA) and Doreen Lord (ME)

MASON,
Tammy Marie, b. 2/3/1967in Rochester; fourth; Thomas E. Mason (salesman, Portsmouth) and Madelyn E. Webber (Pittsfield, MA)

Timothy Edwin, b. 1/9/1966 in Rochester; third; Thomas E. Mason (carpenter, Portsmouth) and Madelyn E. Webber (Pittsfield, MA)

MATTOX,
son [Leroy], b. 6/21/1904; first; William Mattox (shop hand, 23, Brentwood) and Lottie Hall (30, Charlestown, MA)
Alfred Atwood, b. 9/14/1899; tenth; William Mattox (section hand, 42, Lynn, MA) and Sarah Jane Davis (42, Raymond)
Helen Augusta, b. 9/2/1896; ninth; William Mattox (railroad, 40, West Lynn, MA) and Sarah J. Davis (40, Raymond)

MAURAIS,
Jared Robert Ross, b. 7/16/1983 in Rochester; Marc-Andre G. Maurais and Margaret I. Ross

MAWSON,
Thomas Arthur, b. 4/7/1987 in Exeter; Michael J. Mawson and Julia M. Steed

McARDLE,
son [Clyde], b. 10/8/1908; first; Clyde McArdle (salesman, 19, Lowell, MA) and Dora Ragg (18, Lowell, MA); residence - Lowell, MA

McCART[H]Y,
Carol Marie, b. 2/24/1947 in Rochester; third; Gilbert L. McCarthy (mill worker, Nottingham) and Muriel L. Lowry (Revere, MA)
David Bruce, b. 3/13/1943 in Rochester; third; Joseph J. McCarthy (truck driver, Epping) and Anna Marie Delenco (Salisbury, MA)
Donald Jeffrey, b. 6/20/1944 in Rochester; fourth; Joseph J. McCarthy (truck driver, Epping) and Anna Marie Delenco (Salisbury, MA)

Florance Clara, b. 5/16/1926; fifth; William B. McCarty (farmer, 46, Dunlyn, Scotland) and Dora M. Cheltry (Brandon, VT)

Franklin R., b. 2/10/1923; fourth; William E. McCarthy (lumberman, Scotland) and Dora Chiltuf (Brandon, VT)

Frederick Albert, b. 10/24/1932; eighth; William E. McCarthy (laborer, Dunlyn, Scotland) and Dora M. Cheltry (Brandon, VT)

James Henry, b. 7/31/1939 in Rochester; second; Joseph J. McCarthy (finisher, Epping) and Anna M. Delenco (Salisbury, MA); residence - East Barrington

John Harry, b. 7/28/1936; tenth; William E. McCarthy (laborer, Barrington) and Dora M. Cheltry (Brandon, VT)

Leo Edward, b. 2/26/1935; ninth; William E. McCarthy (laborer, Scotland) and Dora M. Chiltry (Brandon, VT)

Michael William, b. 1/30/1951 in Rochester; sixth; Gilbert L. McCarthy (millworker, NH) and Muriel L. Lowry (MA)

Olive K., b. 3/16/1928; sixth; William E.E. McCarty (laborer, Dunlys, Scotland) and Dora Cheltry (Brandon, VT)

Raymond Napoleon, b. 2/3/1938 in Rochester; eleventh; William Ernest McCarthy (laborer, Syracuse, NY) and Dora Marion Cheltry (Brandon, VT)

Sandra Elaine, b. 6/21/1943 in Rochester; first; Gilbert L. McCarthy (army, Nottingham) and Muriel Lois Lowry (Revere, MA); residence - Gonic

Wayne Gilbert, b. 10/27/1945 in Rochester; second; Gilbert L. McCarthy (US Army, Barrington) and Murial L. Lowry (Revere, MA)

William E., b. 11/20/1930; seventh; William E. McCarthy (laborer, Scotland) and Dora M. Chiltry (Brandon, VT)

William Joseph, b. 4/25/1937; first; Joseph J. McCarthy (laborer, Epping) and Anna M. Delenco (Salisbury, MA)

McCOY,
Joshua Alexander, b. 5/29/1980 in Rochester; Richard T. McCoy and Denise M. Guay

McDANIEL,
son, b. 3/29/1899; seventh; Frank McDaniel (farmer, 44, Barrington) and Ruth A. Small (38, Epping)
daughter, b. 7/3/1901; eighth; Frank McDaniel (farmer, 47, Barrington) and Ruth A. Small (40, Epping)
Grace M., b. 5/20/1921; second; George T. McDaniel (farmer, Nottingham) and Grace E. Dodge (Somerville, MA)
Mildred E., b. 1/1/1919; first; George McDaniel (farmer, Nottingham) and Grace Dodge (Somerville, MA)

McDONALD,
daughter [Margaret E.], b. 10/6/1893; first; C. McDonald (farmer, Barrington) and Nellie Whitehouse (Barrington)

McFARLAND,
Devin Michael, b. 6/17/1983; John McFarland and Maybeth Anderson

McGEE,
Kevin David, b. 1/23/1986 in Portsmouth; Kevin E. McGee and Linda A. Pottle

McGLONE,
Daniel Hubert, b. 6/20/1956 in Exeter; fourth; Hubert J. McGlone (machinist, NH) and Barbara E. Chase (MA)
David Paul, b. 4/22/1958 in Exeter; fifth; Hubert J. McGlone (machinist, NH) and Barbara E. Chase (NH)
Debra Marie, b. 12/16/1965 in Dover; seventh; Hubert J. McGlone (machinist, NH) and Barbara E. Chase (NH)
Phyllis R., b. 9/5/1926; first; Arthur G. McGlone (laborer, 20, Dover) and Doris Ellison (Barrington)

McGOWEN,
Jennifer Lynn, b. 11/19/1973 in Portsmouth; William J. McGowen (NH) and Julie A. Allard (NH)

McKAY,
Cheryl Ann, b. 11/8/1967 in Dover; fourth; Robert E. McKay (inspector, Dover) and Marilyn I. Sawyer (Dover)
Douglass Eugene, b. 6/29/1898; second; William McKay (farmer, 45, NS) and Martha Dexter (25, NS)
Ina Lucretia, b. 2/20/1902; third; William McKay (lumberman, 53, NS) and Martha Dexter (27, NS)
Robert Wayne, b. 9/17/1964 in Dover; third; Robert E. McKay (inspector, NH) and Marilyn I. Sawyer (NH)
William H., b. 3/29/1895; first; William H. McKay (laborer, 21, Shelburne, NS) and Martha Dexter (40, Shelburne, NS)

McKENNA,
Blanche Marie, b. 5/13/1946; eighth; John J. McKenna (truck driver, Dover) and Blanche Perron (Lowell, MA)
Kelly Rose, b. 1/16/1961 in Rochester; first; Raymond F. McKenna (truck driver, NH) and Carolyn A. Gosselin (NH)
Kerrie Melissa, b. 8/17/1984 in Dover; Joseph J. McKenna and Kristen M. Swanson
Lisa Lee, b. 5/17/1962 in Rochester; second; Raymond F. McKenna (truck driver, NH) and Carolyn A. Gosselin (NH)
Mary Margaret, b. 10/22/1949; tenth; John J. McKenna (truck driver, NH) and Blanche Perron (MA)
Theresa Louise, b. 2/10/1945; seventh; John J. McKenna (truck driver, Dover) and Blanche Perron (Lowell, MA)
Thomas Henry, b. 7/2/1948; ninth; John J. McKenna (truck driver, Dover) and Blanche Perron (Lowell, MA)

McKETON,
Kara Leigh, b. 4/29/1986 in Dover; Donald McKeton and Nancy A. Pustis
Lindsay Anne, b. 8/9/1983 in Dover; Donald McKeton and Nancy A. Pustis

McLAREN,
Jason Robert, b. 1/17/1982 in Rochester; Donald J. McLaren and Stephanie A. Morris

McLEAN,
Ernest Paul, b. 10/2/1948 in Exeter; first; Donald T. McLean (US Army, Johnston, RI) and Fay E. Johnson (Hopkinton)

McLELLAN,
Jared Eben, b. 1/22/1987 in Rochester; Robert M. McLellan and Susan A. McLaughlin
Nathan Robert, b. 2/8/1985 in Rochester; Robert M. McLellan and Susan A. McLaughlin

McMANUS,
Kate Cynthia, b. 3/2/1979 in Hanover; Henry E. McManus and Diane I. Wiggin

McMULLEN,
Scott Thomas, b. 6/13/1972 in Rochester; Patrick A. McMullen (NY) and Judith A. Hayes (NH)
Stephen Patrick, b. 11/27/1966 in Rochester; second; Patrick A. McMullen (serviceman, Ticonderoga, NY) and Judith A. Hayes (Rochester)

McNEIL,
Matthew Paul, b. 4/22/1982 in Exeter; Paul J. McNeil and Suzanne Wyer
Peter David, b. 5/28/1984 in Exeter; Paul J. McNeil and Suzanne Wyer

McSHANE,
Neil James, b. 7/9/1986 in Dover; Kevin P. McShane and Anne M. Guazzo

MEATTEY,

Bonnie Lou, b. 2/24/1958 in Rochester; fourth; Herbert E. Meattey, Jr. (welder, NH) and Lillian E. Moody (NH)

Debra Lynne, b. 3/9/1960 in Dover; first; Richard R. Meattey (truck driver, NH) and Jacqueline A. Stacy (NH)

Donald Edmond, b. 12/11/1970 in Rochester; Russell L. Meattey (NH) and Mary A. Morrow (NH)

Mark Lyndon, b. 3/9/1964 in Dover; third; Richard R. Meattey (maint. man, NH) and Jacquelyn A. Stacy (NH)

Matthew John, b. 5/6/1969 in Dover; Richard R. Meattey (NH) and Jacquelyn A. Stacy (NH)

Michael Christopher, b. 1/30/1962 in Dover; second; Richard R. Meattey (maint. man, NH) and Jacqueline A. Stacy (NH)

Mildred Alice, b. 7/23/1960 in Rochester; sixth; Herbert E. Meattey, Jr. (machinist, NH) and Lillian E. Moody (NH)

Rebecca Lynne, b. 12/3/1970 in Dover; Richard R. Meattey (NH) and Jacquelyn A. Stacy (NH)

Reginald Allen, b. 5/25/1951 in Rochester; eighth; Herbert E. Meattey (sawyer, NH) and Mildred A. Deshan (NH)

Russell Louis, b. 11/14/1945 in Rochester; seventh; Herbert E. Meattey (mill sawyer, Fitzwilliam) and Mildred A. Deshan (Washington)

Suzanne Marie, b. 1/10/1966 in Dover; fourth; Richard R. Meattey (maintenance man, Fitzwilliam) and Jacqueline A. Stacy (Barrington)

Therese Anne, b. 5/27/1959 in Rochester; fifth; Herbert E. Meattey (machine shop, NH) and Lillian E. Moody (NH)

MEDINA,

Nelson Anthony, b. 12/2/1986 in Portsmouth; Nelson A. Medina and Miriam Romain

MELANSON,

Alicia Lynn, b. 2/25/1986 in Dover; Jeffrey P. Melanson and Elizabeth A. Chubbuck

MENTER,
Florence Helen, b. 2/24/1955 in Rochester; third; Everett P. Menter (mechanic, NH) and Rita T. Lessard (NH)

MERCER,
Donald Edward, b. 7/16/1935; Elijah Mercer (carpenter, Newfoundland) and Nellie May (Newfoundland)
Norman, b. 7/16/1935; sixth; Elijah Mercer (carpenter, Newfoundland) and Nellie M. May (Newfoundland)

MERRILL,
John Thomas, b. 6/16/1986 in Rochester; John A. Merrill and Roseann P. Murphy
Karen Marie, b. 2/21/1967 in Rochester; fourth; Brenton L. Merrill (wire & cable, Lebanon, ME) and Roxanna M. Brazeau (Rochester)

MERTON,
Gabriel Richard, b. 5/23/1979 in Concord; Andrew H. Merton and Gail J. Kelley
Rachel Felice Kelley, b. 8/21/1982 in Concord; Andrew H. Merton and Gail J. Kelley

METCALF,
Susan Louise, b. 4/7/1966 in Dover; first; Bertram H. Metcalf (shoe worker, Perry, ME) and Gail I. Freeman (Rochester)

MEYER,
Billie Jo, b. 2/10/1973 in Portsmouth; Herbert W. Meyer (ME) and Barbara A. Sawyer (NH)

MICHAUD,
Joshua Ronald, b. 11/3/1987 in Dover; Ronald P. Michaud and Sharon R. Grenier

MICHENER,
Kirsten Laurel, b. 11/25/1987 in Dover; R. Dean Michener and Nancy M. McLaughlin

MIEKLE,
Marjorie May, b. 5/15/1959 in Kittery, ME; first; Robert Miekle (USAF, MI) and Marjorie M. Timm (NY)

MILBURY,
Shawna Anissa, b. 10/11/1971 in Dover; Everett L. Milbury (ME) and Geraldine C. Stewart (NH)

MILLER,
Benjamin Edward, b. 3/21/1986 in Concord; David F. Miller and Barbara Courtney
Dawn Andrea, b. 11/15/1974 in Dover; Mitchel Charles Miller and Susan Fern Hoffman
Hugh Ronald, Jr., b. 7/3/1960 in Rochester; first; Hugh R. Miller (truck driver, NH) and Elaine E. McKenna (NH)
Kimberly Ann, b. 7/14/1972 in Dover; Wayne C. Miller (NH) and Carol J. Veno (NH)
Linda Marie, b. 1/16/1949 in Rochester; second; Malcolm W. Miller (Spalding Fibre Co., NH) and Mary Y. Labrie (NH)
Marlene Elizabeth, b. 11/9/1955 in Rochester; third; Malcolm W. Miller (poultry business, NH) and Mary Y. Labrie (MA)
Megan Rose, b. 10/15/1984 in Dover; Bruce E. Miller and Pamela R. Nye
Nancy Jane, b. 6/12/1957 in Rochester; fourth; Malcolm W. Miller (poultry raiser, NH) and Mary Y. Labrie (NH)
Sean Douglas, b. 7/24/1980 in Exeter; George D. Miller and Doreen T. Loranger

MILNE,
Aaron Anton, b. 4/27/1982 in Rochester; Jonathan Milne and Cynthia F. Palumbo

Tamara Miller, b. 1/26/1980 in Rochester; Jonathan Milne and Cynthia F. Palumbo

MINOR,
Scott Carl, b. 9/20/1975 in Exeter; Larry R. Minor and Patricia A. Coolbaugh

MITCHEL,
Allen Irving, b. 3/14/1909; first; Harry I. Mitchel (farmer, 21, Boston, MA) and Bertha Button (23, Westford, VT)

MOFFETT,
John Lee, b. 11/4/1966 in Rochester; third; Joseph H.F. Moffett (carpenter, Gonic) and Madalene L. Rouleau (Wolfeboro)
Kathleen Mary, b. 2/9/1964 in Dover; fourth; Nelson J. Moffett (machinist, NH) and Karen M. Weeden (NH)
Kelly Anne, b. 6/27/1969 in Rochester; Joseph H.F. Moffett (NH) and Madelene L. Rouleau (NH)
Melissa Mae, b. 2/22/1971 in Rochester; Joseph H. Moffett (NH) and Madelene L. Rouleau (NH)
Wendy Susan, b. 12/11/1/967 in Rochester; fourth; Joseph H. Moffett (NH) and Madelene L. Rouleau (NH)

MONAGHAN,
Christopher Ryan, b. 1/30/1974 in Exeter; Frank Wayne Monaghan and Edith Yvonne Euson

MOODY,
Katie Lynn, b. 7/11/1986 in Dover; Paul D. Moody and Madalyn M. Frost

MOORE,
Catherine Mary, b. 11/22/1986 in Dover; Timothy D. Moore and Mary C. Lemay

Rebecca Ann, b. 9/14/1981 in Dover; Timothy D. Moore and Mary C. Lemay

MOORS,
Alison Lynn, b. 1/19/1971 in Dover; Kent F. Moors (MA) and Claudette J. Simard (ME)

MOREAU,
Jacob Daniel, b. 6/5/1979 in Rochester; Daniel L. Moreau and Deborah A. George

MOREL,
John Davis, b. 3/14/1986 in Dover; David B. Morel and Nancy J. Calhoun

MORGANELLI,
Anthony Nicholas, b. 9/5/1987 in Rochester; Nicholas A. Morganelli and Sharon A. Proulx

MORGRIDGE,
Julie Ann, b. 10/3/1981 in Dover; William H. Morgridge and Debra A. Van Geyte
Roy Leonard, b. 1/26/1980 in Dover; William H. Morgridge and Debra A. Van Geyte

MORIARTY,
Kenneth Warren, b. 4/2/1965 in Dover; second; David N. Moriarty (laborer, NH) and Karen G. Quintal (NH)
Tammy Lee, b. 7/9/1966 in Dover; third; David N. Moriarty (construction worker, Dover) and Karen G. Quintal (Exeter)

MORIN,
Cody Adams, b. 9/11/1983 in Rochester; Raymond A. Morin and Cathy D. Hutchins

MORRISON,
son, b. 7/23/1890; second; George W. Morrison (farmer, Shapleigh, ME) and Viola Willey (Barrington)
child, b. 10/26/1891; third; George W. Morrison (laborer, Nottingham) and Viola Willey (Barrington)
Michael Ross, b. 8/2/1986 in Dover; James R. Morrison and Valerie A. Parker

MORRISSEY,
Kaylin Dawn, b. 6/9/1983 in Dover; Michael S. Morrissey and Kathleen A. Morrison

MORSE,
Lisa Jean, b. 3/19/1986 in Hanover; Russell W. Morse and Jean A. Huppe

MOSLEY,
Samantha Kyong, b. 11/10/1986 in Portsmouth; Scott A. Mosley and Kyong S. Pae

MOTT,
Heather Elizabeth, b. 7/24/1986 in Dover; David G. Mott, V and Bonnie S. Schaffer

MOUNTAIN,
David John, b. 9/13/1967 in Portsmouth; fourth; Joseph F. Mountain (truck driver, Whitefield) and Catherine M. McGee (Twin Mountain)
Mathew Thomas, b. 1/17/1985 in Dover; Fulton T. Mountain and Lisa M. Garren

MUDGETT,
Elizabeth Ann, b. 4/23/1985 in Dover; Peter K. Mudgett and Lisa C. Canfield
Peter Kenton, Jr., b. 9/24/1987 in Dover; Peter K. Mudgett, Sr. and Lisa C. Canfield

MULCAHY,
William Shawn, b. 7/7/1971 in Dover; John J. Mulcahy (MA) and Deanna M. Manson (ME)

MUMFREY,
Gerardino Paul, Jr., b. 11/9/1981 in Portsmouth; Gerardino P. Mumfrey and Mildred A. Meattey
Stacia Nicole, b. 12/21/1980 in Rochester; Gerardino P. Mumfrey and Mildred A. Meattey

MUMME,
Ryan Douglas, b. 9/16/1971 in Dover; Christian F. Mumme (NY) and Gail Regione (NH)

MUNOZ,
John Michael, Jr., b. 7/19/1987 in Portsmouth; John M. Munoz, Sr. and Karen L. Dillingham

MUNROE,
Brandon Douglas, b. 6/30/1985 in Dover; Steven D. Munroe and Sandra M. Gregoire
Brian Frederic, b. 4/8/1962 in Rochester; second; James A. Munroe (truck driver, NH) and Joanne E. Cookson (NH)
David Leslie, b. 3/5/1964 in Exeter; third; James A. Munroe (truck driver, NH) and Joanne E. Cookson (NH)
Russell James, b. 6/8/1960 in Rochester; first; James A. Munroe (student, NH) and Joanne E. Cookson (NH)

MURDO,
Dana Scott, b. 11/4/1966 in Rochester; second; Albert T. Murdo (supervisor, So. Berwick, ME) and Rebecca K. Hartford (Rochester)
Dean Shane, b. 2/28/1964 in Rochester; first; Albert T. Murdo (supervisor, ME) and Rebecca K. Hartford (NH)

MURPHY,
Christopher Ryan, b. 4/2/1984 in Rochester; Leon E. Murphy and Crystal L. Senter
Sarah Mary St. John, b. 5/14/1985 in Rochester; William S. Murphy and Adele C. Davis

MURRAY,
Joseph William, Jr., b. 10/4/1984 in Portsmouth; Joseph W. Murray and Susan M. Donovan
Melissa Sue, b. 3/28/1980 in Portsmouth; Joseph W. Murray and Susan M. Donovan

MUSLER,
Deidre Darcel, b. 12/5/1986 in Rochester; Gary T. Musler and Cindy L. Greenwood
Gary Thomas, b. 1/22/1962 in Rochester; third; George T. Musler (engineer, MA) and Helen I. Mackay (MA)

NASON,
son, b. 2/24/1893; fifth; W. H. S. Nason (farmer, Barrington) and E. F. Gray (Barrington)
daughter, b. 12/16/1896; seventh; William H. S. Nason (farmer, 38, Rochester) and Ellen F. Gray (32, Farmington)
son [James W.], b. 5/13/1900; ninth; W. H. S. Nason (farmer, 42, Rochester) and Ellen F. Gray (36, Farmington)
Amanda Lee, b. 10/17/1987 in Rochester; Ricky D. Nason and Jo-Ellen Eliopoulos
Bernard Foss, b. 1/25/1926; third; Charles E. Nason (mechanic, 33, Barrington) and Minnie Foss (Strafford)
Kenneth Ernest, b. 11/19/1964 in Rochester; third; Raymond C. Nason (operations mgr., NH) and Lillian A. Wilds (NY)
Maria, b. 9/12/1898; eighth; W. H. S. Nason (farmer, 40, Rochester) and Ellen F. Gray (Farmington)
Michael Bruce, b. 12/1/1963 in Rochester; second; Raymond C. Nason (oper. mgr., NH) and Lillian A. Wilds (NY)

Raymond Oscar, b. 11/7/1960 in Rochester; first; Raymond C. Nason (truck driver, NH) and Lillian A. Wilds (NY)

NASUTI,
Jessica Lynn, b. 10/23/1980 in Dover; Anthony J. Nasuti, Jr. and Michele B. Lacroix

NEAL,
daughter, b. 1/11/1930; first; Vira Neal (Barrington)
son (Baby Neal) [Richard], b. 2/23/1933; first; Willis Berry and Viva E. Neal (Barrington)
Alden Arthur, b. 1/7/1943 in Franklin; second; Arthur Glidden Neal (teamster, Concord) and Effie Agnes Cooper (Boston, MA)
Audry Myrtle, b. 1/9/1944 in Wolfeboro; third; Arthur Glidden Neal (teamster, Concord) and Ettie Agnes Cooper (Boston, MA)
Carl Albert, b. 10/1/1952 in Dover; third; Roger E. Neal (weaver, NH) and Laura C. Wheeler (NH)
Catherine Elizabeth, b. 8/1/1938 in Rochester; seventh; Natt Jacob Neal (truck driver, Barrington) and Carrie L. Twombly (Northwood)
Daniel Roger, b. 5/10/1951 in Dover; second; Roger E. Neal (washer, NH) and Laura C. Wheeler (NH)
Frank Langley, b. 3/19/1908; third; Edwin C. Neal (farmer, 29, Voluntown, CT) and Myra Hanson (21, Strafford)
Howard Knight, b. 2/24/1907; second; Edwin C. Neal (farmer, 28, Voluntown, CT) and Myra Hanson (20, Strafford)
Jacob Louis, b. 2/17/1955 in Rochester; fifth; Roger E. Neal (weaver, NH) and Laura C. Wheeler (NH)
Jacqueline Ellen, b. 7/11/1959 in Dover; seventh; Roger E. Neal (shipper, shoe, NH) and Laura C. Wheeler (NH)
Jeffery Michael, b. 8/15/1975 in Dover; Daniel R. Neal and Debra J. Neal
Jeremy Daniel, b. 8/15/1975 in Dover; Daniel R. Neal and Debra J. Neal

Melissa Alice, b. 5/22/1969 in Exeter; Alden A. Neal (NH) and Constance A. Holmes (NH)
Melissa Debra, b. 9/3/1973 in Dover; Daniel R. Neal (NH) and Debra J. Neal (CA)
Michael, b. 2/5/1954 in Rochester; fourth; Roger E. Neal (weaver, NH) and Laura C. Wheeler (NH)
Muriel Elizabeth, b. 4/23/1937; seventh; Nathaniel J. Neal (truckman, Barrington) and Carrie L. Twombly (Northwood)
Natt T., b. 8/20/1904; first; Edwin C. Neal (farmer, 25, Voluntown, CT) and Myra Hanson (17, Strafford)
Patricia Laura, b. 8/28/1949 in Dover; first; Roger E. Neal (NH) and Laura C. Wheeler (NH)
Paul Jacob, b. 5/25/1934; Natt J. Neal and Carrie Twombly (1983)
Pauline Hope, b. 11/30/1956 in Rochester; sixth; Roger E. Neal (shipping, NH) and Laura C. Wheeler (NH)
Pauline Louise, b. 3/12/1936; sixth; Nathaniel J. Neal (truck driver, Barrington) and Carrie L. Neal (Barrington)
Robert Elwood, b. 3/23/1933; fourth; Wat. J. Neal (laborer, Barrington) and Carrie L. Twombly (Northwood)
Thomasine Jeanne, b. 9/23/1962 in Exeter; second; Thomas J. Neal (deceased, IN) and Marion L. Bryson (NH)
Vira Elizabeth, b. 7/23/1909; fourth; Edwin C. Neal (farmer, 30, Voluntown, CT) and Myra Hanson (22, Strafford)

NEWELL,
Gerald Harvey, b. 1/25/1920; second; Arlin Newell (farmer, Canada) and Emeroy F. Brock (Canada)
Lynn Francis, b. 5/23/1951 in Rochester; second; Donald F. Newell (clerk, ME) and Beverly L. Anderson (NH)
Rowena, b. 11/19/1917; first; Arlin M. Newell (farmer, Providence, Quebec) and Emeroy Brock (Providence, Quebec)

NEWMAN,
Earl Raymond, IV, b. 2/12/1987 in Exeter; Earl R. Newman, III and Elizabeth J. Oliver
Kyra Lynne, b. 4/7/1986 in Exeter; David A. Newman and Margaret M. McDonald

NEWSKY,
Joseph Thomas, b. 6/16/1959 in Dover; second; Michael L. Newsky (machinist, NH) and Barbara E. Neal (NH)
Kristin Elise, b. 9/25/1987 in Dover; Michael Newsky and Susan V. Labrie
Linda Jean, b. 6/26/1964 in Dover; fifth; Michael L. Newsky (machinist, NH) and Barbara E. Neal (NH)

NEWTON,
Justin Thomas, b. 5/4/1983 in Dover; Mark T. Newton and Nancy L. Frizzell
Tyler Jameson, b. 4/7/1985 in Dover; Mark T. Newton and Nancy L. Frizzell

NICHOLS,
Zachary David, b. 8/8/1986 in Dover; David P. Nichols and Deborah K. Densmore

NIENHOUSE,
Andrea Ann, b. 5/3/1976 in Dover; Ralph Nienhouse, Jr. and Linda M. Baxter

NOBLE,
Jessica Ann, b. 6/15/1974 in Rochester; William James Noble and Diane Jean Long

NORMAN,
Harvey Edward, b. 11/8/1934; fourth; John Norman (carpenter, Madbury) and Clara A. Varney (Barrington)

NORMAND,
Erika Lynn, b. 8/11/1978 in Dover; Robert W. Normand and
　　Carmel J. Benson

NOYES,
daughter, b. 4/29/1892; sixth; John M. Noyes (laborer, 40,
　　Nottingham) and Annie Stevens (30, Raymond)

NYE,
Barry Evan, b. 8/12/1981 in Dover; George E. Nye and
　　Sharon E. Inniss
Shane Michael, b. 9/2/1980 in Dover; Philip R. Nye and
　　Diane L. Albert

O'BRIEN,
Brandon Conor, b. 9/22/1978 in Exeter; John F. O'Brien and
　　Carla C. Brasseur
Eric Thomas, b. 2/11/1978 in Dover; Thomas F. O'Brien and
　　Carol D. Brown
Kayla Marie, b. 4/1/1983 in Dover; Thomas F. O'Brien and
　　Carol D. Brown

O'CONNOR,
Crystal Lea, b. 12/23/1983 in Dover; John L. O'Connor and
　　Brenda L. Hardy
Michael Albert, b. 3/11/1977 in Rochester; John T. O'Connor
　　and Irene M. Sasseville

O'DONNELL,
daughter, b. 3/10/1895; first; John O'Donnell (laborer, 18)
　　and Minnie L. Hall (21, Barrington)

O'FLAHERTY,
Gillian Elizabeth, b. 6/26/1983 in Manchester; Thomas E.
　　O'Flaherty and Virginia E. Boyd

Thomas Emmett, III, b. 10/15/1986 in Exeter; Thomas E.
O'Flaherty, Jr. and Virginia E. Boyd

O'MALLEY,
Jennifer Maureen, b. 9/8/1979 in Hanover; Desmond F.
O'Malley and Kathryn L. Farrow
Marianne Meghan, b. 2/17/1982 in Dover; Desmond F.
O'Malley and Kathryn L. Farrow
Patrick Desmond, b. 11/10/1983 in Dover; Desmond F.
O'Malley and Kathryn L. Farrow

O'NEILL,
Christina Marie, b. 2/21/1981 in Exeter; Stephen J. O'Neill
and Mary D. Francis

O'REAR,
Jon Robert, b. 7/28/1984 in Portsmouth; Robert A. O'Rear
and Monika Lohrmann

OAKLEY,
James Allen, b. 2/25/1983 in Exeter; Richard B. Oakley and
Carol A. Holroyd

OATES,
Lance Michael, b. 11/29/1976 in Dover; Walter T. Oates and
Diane M. Mantos

OLIVER,
Adam, b. 1/6/1987 in Dover; Stanley H. Oliver and Claire E.
DeFeo

OLIVIER,
Anique Julienne, b. 6/1/1980 in Dover; Julien L. Olivier and
Jane E. Duddy
Danielle Jane, b. 6/6/1978 in Dover; Julien L. Olivier and
Jane E. Duddy

Jennifer Kathleen, b. 10/24/1973 in Dover; Julien L. Olivier (NH) and Jane E. Duddy (ME)
Nicole Marie, b. 4/28/1975 in Dover; Julien L.A. Olivier and Jane E. Duddy

OLSEN,
Elizabeth A., b. 9/13/1924; second; Elmer F. Olsen (shoe operative, Norway) and Ella F. Howard (Rochester)
Eric Dahlberg, b. 7/10/1968 in Dover; Bjorn D. Olsen (Norway) and Margaret L. Heanssler (ME)
Jennifer Jill, b. 10/1/1977 in Dover; Bjorn D. Olsen and Margaret L. Heanssier
Oscar W., b. 6/5/1922; first; Elwin F. Olsen (shoemaker, Norway) and Ella F. Howard (Rochester); residence - Rochester
Robin Timothy, b. 3/16/1974 in Dover; Bjorn Dehlberg Olsen and Margaret Lillian Heanssler

ORKIN,
Jessica Bounds, b. 7/23/1975 in Dover; Eric B. Orkin and Linda A. Bounds
Joshua Bounds, b. 6/25/1977 in Exeter; Eric B. Orkin and Linda A. Bounds

ORMES,
Leighton, b. 12/9/1934 in Rochester; first; Leighton O. Ormes (farmer, Stockbridge, MA) and Muriel Shea (Wakefield, MA)

OSBORNE,
Jessica Marie, b. 1/19/1977 in Rochester; Mary E. Osborne
Shane Thomas, b. 6/22/1980 in Exeter; Michael C. Osborne, Sr. and Cynthia A. McMahon

OSGOOD,
Christopher Paul, b. 10/23/1974 in Exeter; Richard Paul
   Osgood and Barbara Louise Hill

OTT,
Wendy Ann, b. 7/9/1979 in Rochester; Wayne R. Ott and
   Susan A. Hamel

OUELLETTE,
Mary Arline, b. 11/26/1948 in Rochester; second; Eugene J.
   Ouellette (log trucker, Berwick, ME) and Lena M. Plourde
   (Auburn, ME)

OWENS,
Joshua Robert, b. 3/21/1983 in Rochester; Kenneth P.
   Owens and Marcia I. Johnson

OXNER,
Jesse Caleb Evan, b. 9/17/1985 in Salem, MA; Ralph W.
   Oxner and Patricia A. Linacre

PAITON,
Andrew Barrington, b. 6/1/1984 in Dover; Peter S. Paiton and
   Barbara A. Bristol

PALMER,
daughter, b. 3/24/1896; second; Burton R. Palmer
   (brakeman, 26, Dover) and Bertha S. Folsom (31,
   Ossipee)
son [Raynor], b. 5/1/1914; second; William Palmer
   (lumberman, Dover) and Addie Canney (Dover)
Eloise, b. 8/20/1910; first; William Palmer (blacksmith, 33,
   Dover) and Addie M. Canney (23, Dover)
John R., b. 4/7/1916; third; William Palmer (blacksmith,
   Dover) and Addie Canney (Dover)

PARENTEAU,
Dennis Raymond, Jr., b. 6/8/1984 in Dover; Dennis R. Parenteau, Sr. and Kathy J. Fowler
Shirley Debra, b. 10/6/1983 in Dover; Patrick M. Parenteau and Debra A. Letourneau

PARKER,
Carol Jean, b. 12/25/1938; first; Stanley Harvey Parker (wool spinner, Charlestown, MA) and Rose Alma St. John (Suncook)
Nancy Ellen, b. 3/27/1958 in Rochester; fourth; Norman E. Parker (lining cutter, NH) and Alice J. Hilliard (NH)

PARSHLEY,
son [Joseph F.], b. 7/17/1904; eleventh; Charles E. Parshley (shoemaker, 45, Strafford) and Mary E. Jewell (41, Strafford)
son, b. 9/1/1920; first; Robert Parshley (farmer, Strafford) and Mary G. Howard (Barrington)

PARSONS,
Amanda May, b. 2/3/1986 in Dover; Mason H. Parsons and Laura S. Akeley
Kelley Marie, b. 10/15/1982 in Dover; Mason H. Parsons and Laura S. Akeley
Kevin Ian, b. 5/10/1984 in Exeter; John W. Parsons and Jean M. Monteverde

PATCH,
Carol Ann, b. 7/23/1951 in Rochester; fourth; Raymond L. Patch (laborer, ME) and Edith M. Appleby (MA)
David Raymond, b. 7/3/1946 in Rochester; first; Raymond L. Patch (carpenter, Sanford, ME) and Edith M. Appleby (Needham, MA)
Jean Elizabeth, b. 1/9/1949 in Rochester; third; Raymond L. Patch (carpenter, ME) and Edith M. Appleby (MA)

PATERSON,
Caleb John, b. 1/29/1986 in Portsmouth; Derrick J. Paterson and Sherryl T. Maddock

PATRICK,
Kyle Daniel, b. 1/18/1986 in Dover; Daniel J. Patrick and Sharon M. Middaugh

PATTERSON,
Jill Suzanne, b. 7/31/1981 in Dover; Robert W. Patterson and Barbara S. Nichols

PEABODY,
Rebecca Pearl, b. 5/21/1986 in Dover; Bradley S. Peabody and Cydney E. Klipp

PEARSON,
Adam Benjamin, b. 10/15/1979 in Dover; Steven P. Pearson and Jo A. Laansma
Adam Charles, b. 2/24/1970 in Concord; Michael E. Pearson (ME) and Evelynn M. Nolin (NH)
Joseph Zachary, b. 6/1/1984 in Dover; Steven P. Pearson and Jo A. L. Laansma
Margaret Anne, b. 6/7/1987 in Dover; Steven P. Pearson and Jo A. Laansma

PEASE,
Penny Ann, b. 1/25/1965 in Dover; third; Dennis S. Pease, Sr. (truck driver, ME) and Margueritte E. Lemire (ME)

PECK,
David Taylor, b. 9/5/1984 in Exeter; Stephen M. Peck and Nancy M. Orzechowski

PELLETIER,
Lawrence Paul, b. 2/21/1949 in Rochester; second; Lawrence P. Pelletier (teamster, NY) and Catherine Mariotti (NH)

PERKINS,
Rebecca Holly, b. 12/22/1978 in Rochester; Ralph H. Perkins and Barbara L. Johnson
Rebecca Lynn, b. 3/15/1977 in Rochester; Donald A. Perkins and Doreen Lord

PERRON,
Gregory Ryan, b. 10/14/1984 in Dover; Kevin R. Perron and Kathy A. Gauvin

PERRY,
Andrea Lynn, b. 4/8/1985 in Dover; Stephen M. Perry and Kathleen A. Webber
Dorothy M., b. 4/5/1912; first; Harry H. Perry (farmer, 30, Lynn, MA) and Ethel A. Morrison (20, Dover)

PETERS,
Dennis Lawerance, Jr., b. 1/12/1980 in Dover; Dennis L. Peters, Sr. and Lynn A. Gregoire

PHILBRICK,
Sherri Lynn, b. 1/13/1969 in Dover; Wesley A. Philbrick (NH) and Georgia D. Perkins (NH)

PIERCE,
Alfred L.A., b. 5/21/1868; Curtis H. Pierce (Barrington) and Charlotte L. Hill (Barrington) (1945)
Mary Jane, b. 6/23/1883; Curtis H. Pierce (Barrington) and Izora Zetta Prescott (Appleton, ME) (1943)

PIKE,
Mary Ann, b. 3/18/1956 in Rochester; third; Alvah B. Pike (carpenter, ME) and Mary L. Dunlap (ME)
Nancy Susan, b. 1/24/1957 in Rochester; fourth; Alvah B. Pike (shoe worker, ME) and Mary L. Dunlap (ME)
Peter, b. 10/24/1953 in Rochester; seventh; Arthur E. Pike (auto salesman, NY) and Barbara Morris (Washington, DC)

PILGRIM,
Donna Lee, b. 6/3/1963 in Dover; second; Peter Q. Pilgrim (mech. engineer, NH) and Patsy L. Ramsay (NH)

PILLER,
Sheri Lynne, b. 12/31/1976 in Dover; Scott G. Piller and Beth M. Fitch

PILOTTE,
Amanda Joy, b. 6/1/1980 in Dover; Lemuel F. Pilotte and Betty J. Dufour

PINKHAM,
John Arthur, b. 7/16/1940 in Dover; first; John H. Pinkham (counter mkr., Haverhill, MA) and Ethel L. McAllister (Pittsfield, ME)

PINZARI,
Jack Mathew, b. 8/6/1969 in Rochester; Gerald J. Pinzari (MA) and Priscilla J. Osgood (MA)

PLANTE,
Alyssa Marie, b. 3/16/1981 in Dover; Rene P. Plante and Carleen J. Fogarty
Julia Renee, b. 8/16/1982 in Dover; Rene P. Plante and Carleen J. Fogarty

PLIMPTON,
Nathan Henry, b. 6/19/1987 in Dover; Brian H. Plimpton and
 Nancy E. Talbot

PLOU[R]DE,
Cecile Yvonne, b. 12/11/1936; seventh; Alfred Ploude
 (farmer, Gonic) and Olivine Dalpe (Canada)
Frederick, b. 8/7/1940; eighth; Alfred Plourde (farmer, Gonic)
 and Olivine Dalpe (St. John, Canada)
Jeannette R.A., b. 10/1/1932; fifth; Alfred Plourde (farmer,
 Gonic) and Olivine Dalpe (Canada)
Paul Luger, b. 9/1/1937; sixth; Rose Plourde (Gonic)
Shelli Marie, b. 7/10/1983 in Rochester; David E. Plourde
 and Debra A. McKay
Theresa Irene, b. 3/6/1929; Alfred J. Plourde (Rochester)
 and Olivine M. Dalpee (Canada) (1945)

PLUMER,
Christopher Otis, b. 7/4/1981 in Exeter; Craig O. Plumer and
 Susan M. Garrison

PLUMMER,
Amie Arvilla, b. 11/12/1987 in Rochester; Richard L.
 Plummer and Karen L. Calef

POIRE,
Brian Gene, b. 12/17/1976 in Rochester; Gene R. Poire and
 Ann E. Ouimette

POIRIER,
Seth Terry, b. 2/9/1982 in Dover; Terry R. Poirier and Janice
 E. Westgate

PORTER,
Christopher Alan, b. 11/12/1976 in Dover; Ronald A. Porter
 and Sharon A. Baxter

POTTER,
Adam Patrick, b. 5/13/1968 in Portsmouth; Alfred R. Potter (MA) and Judith A. Hall (NH)
Jessica Angela, b. 6/2/1970 in Portsmouth; Alfred R. Potter (MA) and Judith A. Hall (NJ)

POTVIN,
Andrew Wayne, b. 12/14/1984 in Dover; Wayne R. Potvin and Carol A. Spear

POULIN,
Marie Olivine, b. 5/13/1890; Jacob Poulin (Canada) and Agnes Pallardy (Canada) (1946)

POULIOT,
Gavin William, b. 8/30/1982 in Dover; Mike W. Pouliot and Deborah A. Perusse
Shelby Lynn, b. 7/10/1985 in Dover; Mike W. Pouliot and Deborah A. Perusse

POULTON,
Gregory Scott, b. 1/30/1987 in Exeter; Jeffrey J. Poulton and Maribeth L. Coughlin

POWER,
Ryan Drew, b. 12/4/1973 in Dover; Edwin R. Power (NH) and Alex A. Flarford (NH)

PRAKOP,
Ashleigh Anne, b. 9/27/1984 in Exeter; Michael J. Prakop and Dorothy E. Nixon

PRATT,
Curtis James, b. 12/19/1983 in Rochester; Leonard D. Pratt and Jeanette L. Sullivan

Paul Everett, b. 9/30/1967 in Dover; first; Harvey W. Pratt (laborer, Dover) and Sandra L. Smith (Rochester)

PREBLE,
Michael David, b. 5/12/1978 in Exeter; Ivon S. Preble, Jr. and Linda D. Marston

PRESTAGE,
Jennifer Leigh, b. 7/28/1979 in Dover; Jonathan P. Prestage and Kathleen A. Bourbeau

PRESTON,
Carrie Belle, b. 2/18/1889; Alberton D. Preston (NH) and Fannie Perkins (NH) (1954)
David Lund, b. 9/30/1935; first; John Preston (farmer, Barrington) and Vida Lund (Newport)
Loren John, b. 11/21/1936; second; John D. Preston (farmer, Barrington) and Vida C. Lund (Newport)
Vivian May, b. 2/24/1908; first; Herbert M. Preston (farmer, 21, Rochester) and Gertrude Jacobs (18, Rochester)
Walter Jewell, b. 1/7/1906; fifth; Alburton D. Preston (farmer, 44, Barrington) and Fannie Perkins (43, Strafford)

PRIDHAM,
Lora Lee, b. 7/1/1971; Lawrence M. Pridham (ME) and Frances L. Dubois (NH)

PUNSKY,
Elizabeth Waldron, b. 9/29/1986 in Rochester; Howard T. Punsky and Lynne A. Waldron

PURDY,
Frank S., b. 8/22/1914; third; Roger B. Purdy (farmer, Boston, MA) and Louise G. Corr (St. Johns, NB)
Robert D., b. 10/25/1920; first; Robert P. Purdy (laborer, Lowell, MA) and Ruth S. Berry (Rochester)

PURVIS,
Charles David, b. 2/28/1953 in Rochester; fourth; Carlyle S. Purvis (Kidder Press, NH) and Dorothy A. Littlefield (NH)
Ruth May, b. 7/28/1956 in Rochester; fifth; Carlyle S. Purvis (assembler, NH) and Dorothy A. Littlefield (NH)

RADLOFF,
Jamie John, b. 2/10/1972 in Rochester; James E. Radloff (OH) and Gaye P. Bronson (NH)
Michelle Marie, b. 4/2/1968 in Rochester; James E. Radloff (OH) and Gaye P. Bronson (NH)

RAICHE,
Raymond Joseph, b. 8/16/1982 in Portsmouth; Raymond A. Raiche and Tanya S. McClure

RAINVILLE,
Michelle Elaine, b. 5/16/1969 in Dover; Raymond E. Rainville (NH) and Barbara A. Mudarri (MA)

RAMBOLT,
Katherine Nolan, b. 10/11/1966 in Exeter; second; Wynn M. Rambolt (teacher, Flushing, NY) and Eleanor Hunt (New York, NY)

RAMSDELL,
Brandie Lynn, b. 7/27/1977 in Rochester; Gary E. Ramsdell and Faith J. Littlefield
Dana William, b. 10/14/1950 in Rochester; third; William C. Ramsdell (painter, MA) and Muriel Buck (MA)
Gary Earle, b. 12/13/1945 in Exeter; second; William C. Ramsdell (farmer, Pt. Independence, MA) and Muriel Buck (Norton, MA)
George William, b. 6/26/1970 in Dover; John B. Ramsdell (NH) and Janet M. Rollins (MA)

James Brooks, b. 7/27/1967 in Dover; first; John B. Ramsdell (draftsman, Dover) and Janet M. Rollins (Somerville, MA)
John Brooks, b. 6/26/1943 in Dover; first; William C. Ramsdell (farmer, Pt. Indep., MA) and Murial Buck (Norton, MA)
Marcia Jane, b. 12/24/1943 in Exeter; first; Frederick Ramsdell (US Army, Wareham, MA) and Annie Naomi Taylor (Chelsea, MA)
Sandra Mae, b. 7/20/1946 in Exeter; second; Frederick M. Ramsdell (electrician, Wareham, MA) and Annie N. Taylor (Chelsea, MA)
Virginia Norma, b. 2/21/1948 in Exeter; third; Frederick M. Ramsdell (electrician, Wareham, MA) and Annie N. Taylor (Chelsea, MA)

RAND,
Clyde Leroy, III, b. 10/11/1981 in Dover; Clyde L. Rand, Jr. and Deborah L. Crawford

RAYMOND,
Brandon Thomas, b. 10/7/1985 in Exeter; Calvin L. Raymond, Jr. and Marie L. McCabe

REARDON,
Ryan Turner, b. 6/30/1977 in Dover; Charles R. Reardon and Michelle M. Turner

RECKARD,
Mark David, b. 6/18/1986 in Portsmouth; Richard D. Reckard and Lynn A. Pepe

REDHOUSE,
Rebecca Olive, b. 4/14/1985 in Exeter; Daniel J. Redhouse, Jr. and Margaret O. Woodward
Sarah Irene, b. 1/4/1983 in Exeter; Daniel J. Redhouse, Jr. and Margaret O. Woodward

REED,
stillborn son, b. 5/16/1914; Dexter C. Reed (teamster, Cambridge, MA) and Alice May Morley (Charlestown, MA)
Addie, b. 9/1/1877; Charles Reed (shoemaker, Barrington) and Annie B. Seavey (1941)
Ian Augustus, b. 11/20/1983 in Exeter; Royal F. Reed and Donna M. Frye
Lilla M., b. 12/23/1882; Charles Reed (shoemaker, Barrington) and Annie B. Seavey (1941)
Sarah P.H., b. 6/17/1885; Charles Reed (shoemaker, Barrington) and Annie B. Seavey (1941)

REGOULINSKY,
Wendy Ann, b. 11/6/1986 in Exeter; Mark W. Regoulinsky and Anita B. McNally

REID,
Jodie Lynn, b. 8/6/1968 in Dover; Douglas S. Reid (RI) and Lois K. Armstrong (RI)
Stefanie Jo, b. 6/17/1967 in Dover; third; Douglas S. Reid (union laborer, Warwick, RI) and Lois K. Armstrong (Providence, RI)
Stuart William, b. 5/13/1965 in Dover; second; Douglas S. Reid (union laborer, RI) and Lois K. Armstrong (RI)

REIMERS,
Nicholas Raymond, b. 10/16/1987 in Rochester; Richard R. Reimers and Barbara J. Littlefield

REINHARDT,
Jamie Aaron, b. 3/6/1974 in Dover; Werner Andrew Reinhardt and Barbara Louise Sanborn
Robin Louise, b. 12/3/1975 in Dover; Werner A. Reinhardt and Barbara L. Sanborn

Werner Andrew, Jr., b. 4/25/1972 in Dover; Werner A. Reinhardt, Sr. (NY) and Barbara L. Sanborn (NH)

RENAUD,
Benjamin Michael, b. 7/5/1983 in Dover; Dale P. Renaud and Holly M. Fenn
Kelly Jane, b. 7/5/1983 in Dover; Dale P. Renaud and Holly M. Fenn
Stuart Copeland, b. 3/18/1985 in Dover; Dale P. Renaud and Holly M. Fenn

RHINES,
Sarah Nichole, b. 7/15/1985 in Concord; Peter C. Rhines and Judith A. Lust

RICARD,
Dominique Louise, b. 1/8/1983 in Dover; Roderick R. Ricard, III and Tracy L. White

RICHARD,
Alaina Carole, b. 4/18/1987 in Portsmouth; Wayne A. Richard and Christina E. Lopez
Jillian Christine, b. 9/16/1983 in Exeter; Wayne A. Richard and Christina E. Lopez
Maxine Rita, b. 10/17/1932; second; Emile J. Richard (laborer, Rochester) and Violet J. Wiggin (Barrington)

RICHARDSON,
David Arthur, b. 5/23/1973 in Rochester; James P. Richardson (VT) and Thomasine Fisher (NH)
Jeffrey Gunnar, b. 6/13/1955 in Rochester; second; Harry Richardsen (sic) (minister, NY) and Ingrid Aasby (NY)
Ruth Ingrid, b. 10/24/1956 in Rochester; third; Harry Richardson (minister, NY) and Ingrid Aasby (NY)
Wesley Craig, b. 10/18/1958 in Rochester; fourth; Harry Richardson (minister, NY) and Ingrid Aasby (NY)

RICHER,
Brian Daniel, b. 6/18/1968 in Dover; Donat D. Richer (ME) and Vera H. Clark (MA)
Jennifer Ann, b. 3/3/1973 in Rochester; Donat D. Richer (ME) and Vera H. Clark (MA)

RICKER,
Cortney Beth, b. 5/25/1980 in Dover; Bruce R. Ricker and Kay E. Turcotte
Jessica Lee, b. 1/16/1978 in Dover; Bruce R. Ricker and Kay E. Turcotte

RILEY,
Charles W., b. 9/21/1908; first; Charles Riley (wood chopper, 32, OH) and Nellie Bartlett (20, OH)

RIVET,
Michael James, b. 4/17/1977 in Dover; James A. Rivet and Elizabeth A. McLearney

ROBERTS,
Matthew John, b. 9/21/1984 in Rochester; John Roberts and Cheryl A. McKay

ROBICHEAU,
Dianna Marie, b. 6/28/1986 in Portsmouth; Richard J. Robicheau and Marie B. Moroney

ROBIDOUX,
Lee Patrick, b. 3/28/1985 in Rochester; Douglas E. Robidoux and Sandra M. Law
Stacia Anne, b. 3/15/1982 in Dover; Robert V. Robidoux and Julia E. Maderos

ROBIE,
Catherine Elizabeth, b. 3/1/1968 in Dover; Lawrence C.
   Robie (NH) and Roberta H. Bassett (NH)
Cheryl Diane, b. 7/8/1953 in Newport, RI; first; Wayne A.
   Robie (USN, NH) and Phyllis A. Seavey (NJ)
Karen Roberta, b. 8/9/1962 in Dover; first; Lawrence C.
   Robie (laborer, NH) and Roberta H. Bassett (NH)
Laurie Christine, b. 6/8/1964 in Dover; second; Lawrence C.
   Robie (tannery emp., NH) and Roberta H. Bassett (NH)

ROBINSON,
Erika Jill, b. 2/12/1980 in Dover; William S. Robinson and
   Maureen A. Nichols
James Herbert, b. 4/30/1952 in Rochester; second; Herbert
   L. Robinson (student, MA) and Audrey S. Winlock (MA)
Matthew Bruce, b. 1/9/1987 in Portsmouth; Bruce G.
   Robinson and Kathleen M. Meehan
Sherman Lunt, b. 5/11/1950 in Rochester; first; Herbert L.
   Robinson (student, MA) and Audrey S. Winlock (MA)

ROCK,
Christopher William, b. 12/9/1983 in Portsmouth; Stanley W.
   Rock and Charlotte A. Doran

ROLLINS,
Beverly Joyce, b. 3/1/1946 in Rochester; fourth; Herbert L.
   Rollins (US Army, Nottingham) and Dorothy L. Jenness
   (Gonic)
Lewis Wilbur, b. 4/16/1902; third; Walter Rollins (laborer, 30,
   Nottingham) and Marinda Hanscom (27, Barrington)

ROLLISON,
Virginia Mae, b. 12/13/1986 in Dover; Paul S. Rollison and
   Marcia R. Kisner

ROSS,
son [Charles E.], b. 5/26/1892; fifth; Amasa Ross (laborer, 49, Topsfield, ME) and Abbie Brown (39, Barrington)
daughter, b. 4/23/1895; sixth; Amasa Ross (farmer, 51, Shapleigh, ME) and Abbie Brown (42, Barrington)
Doris M., b. 6/26/1916; first; Charles E. Ross (farmer, Barrington) and Florence Arlin (Barrington)
Freddie, b. 1/4/1890; fourth; Amasa L. Ross (laborer, Topsfield, ME) and Abbie M. Brown (Barrington)
George E., b. 2/3/1918; second; Charles E. Ross (farmer, Barrington) and Florence J. Arlin (Barrington)
Karen Lee, b. 6/26/1963 in Exeter; fourth; Shepley L. Ross (assoc. prof., ME) and Virginia Rivinius (MA)

ROULEAU,
James Stephen, b. 8/10/1980 in Dover; Paul D. Rouleau and Barbara D. Hill
Jeffrey Nelson, b. 12/7/1976 in Rochester; David E. Rouleau and Pamela S. Mattes
Megan Dawn, b. 1/22/1985 in Dover; Paul D. Rouleau and Barbara D. Hill
Stanley Harold, b. 6/13/1974 in Dover; David Ernest Rouleau and Pamela Sue Mattes

ROUNDY,
Stephani Jane, b. 4/1/1985 in Dover; Edward K. Roundy, Jr. and Vicki A. Stueve

ROUX,
Arthur, b. 11/1/1930; second; Mary M. Roux (Kingsfield, ME); residence - Kingsfield, ME

ROWE,
son [Alton], b. 12/26/1890; fifth; John F. Rowe (laborer, Barrington) and Mary A. Arlin (Barrington)

daughter, b. 3/28/1893; sixth; J. F. Rowe (farmer, Barrington) and Mary A. Arlin (Barrington)

daughter, b. 5/25/1904; fourth; John Rowe (mill hand, 46, Barrington) and Julia Hart (29, Van Buren, ME)

son, b. 9/14/1905; second; John F. Rowe (sawyer, 46, Barrington) and Julia E. Hart (30, Van Buren, ME)

Ralph Raymond, b. 12/18/1913; third; Walter Henry Rowe (farmer, 28, Barrington) and Myrtle M. Downs (25, So. Lebanon, ME)

Vesta A., b. 1/8/1876; George F. Rowe (farmer, Holderness) and Elizabeth Brown (Salem, MA) (1941)

Walter Henry, b. 9/23/1885; Henry E. Rowe (Barrington) and Emma J. Kingman (Barrington) (1942)

ROWELL,
Jane Elizabeth, b. 1/7/1957 in Rochester; sixth; Edward R. Rowell (truck driver, MA) and Ruth E. Taylor (MA)

Julie Ann, b. 4/3/1961 in Rochester; seventh; Edward R. Rowell (laborer, MA) and Ruth E. Taylor (MA)

Patricia Jean, b. 3/22/1950 in Rochester; second; Edward R. Rowell (sales clerk, MA) and Ruth E. Taylor (MA)

Peter Edward, b. 3/17/1949 in Rochester; first; Edward R. Rowell (garage man, MA) and Ruth E. Taylor (MA)

Peter Fielding, b. 5/10/1980 in Exeter; Peter E. Rowell and Lauren C. Chase

Scott Richard, b. 6/27/1983 in Dover; Stephen T. Rowell and Pamela J. Small

Seth Edward, b. 9/1/1983 in Concord; Peter E. Rowell and Lauren C. Chase

Stephen Taylor, b. 7/23/1951 in Rochester; third; Edward R. Rowell (truck driver, MA) and Ruth E. Taylor (MA)

Stephen Taylor, Jr., b. 8/21/1981 in Dover; Stephen T. Rowell, Sr. and Pamela J. Small

Thomas Richard, b. 4/12/1955 in Rochester; fifth; Edward R. Rowell (truck driver, MA) and Ruth E. Taylor (MA)

Timothy Earle, b. 12/18/1952 in Rochester; fourth; Edward R. Rowell (truck driver, MA) and Ruth E. Taylor (MA)

ROWH,
Adam Michael, b. 7/18/1985 in Manchester; Michael E. Rowh and Katherine A. DiMaria
Johnathon Arnett, b. 9/10/1983 in Manchester; Michael E. Rowh and Katherine A. Dimaria

ROY,
David Leon, b. 1/10/1949; eighth; Clarence E. Roy (lumber laborer, NH) and Hazel E. Farrington (ME)

ROYCE,
Brian Jeffrey, b. 6/12/1980 in Dover; Peter W. Royce and Nona A. Bean
Jonathan Tyler, b. 7/4/1976 in Dover; Peter W. Royce and Nona E. Bean

RUEL,
Christopher Gareth, b. 10/8/1982 in Dover; David P. Ruel and Lisa A. Addison
Deborah Ruth, b. 4/28/1982 in Dover; Robert A. Ruel and Lisa B. Stimpson
Meredith Lynn, b. 7/24/1987 in Dover; Robert A. Ruel and Lisa B. Stimpson
Rachel Ann, b. 9/26/1983 in Dover; Robert A. Ruel and Lisa B. Stimpson

RUSSELL,
Arlene, b. 9/1/1952 in Rochester; first; Eldridge E. Russell (farmer, MA) and Edith Doremus (MA)
Dorothy Althea, b. 12/2/1914; Simon O. Russell (ME) and Alice I. Houghton (MA) (1956)
Jamie Scott, b. 12/15/1981 in Dover; Bruce Russell and Cynthia L. Kelly

Mikell Bruce, b. 5/2/1980 in Dover; Bruce A. Russell and
Cynthia L. Kelly

RYEA,
son, b. 6/9/1980 in Dover; Allen M. Ryea and Vicky S.
Estabrook
Jennifer Louise, b. 9/29/1981 in Dover; Allan M. Ryea and
Vicky S. Estabrook

ST. JEAN,
Aaron Daniel, b. 6/28/1979 in Rochester; Ronald A. St. Jean
and Diane M. Sawicki
Andrew Todd, b. 3/7/1984 in Rochester; Ronald A. St. Jean
and Diane M. Sawicki

ST. ONGE,
Katie Lyn, b. 1/17/1985 in Dover; Steven W. St. Onge and
Patricia A. Morin
Kristen Marie, b. 1/30/1983 in Dover; Steven W. St. Onge
and Patricia A. Morin

ST. PIERRE,
Suzette Nicole, b. 8/5/1984 in Exeter; Gary M. St. Pierre and
Jean Ann Rotonda

SABIN,
Jennifer Ann, b. 11/30/1986 in Dover; Robert C. Sabin and
Donna L. Bonneau

SALIGA,
Leah Anne, b. 6/22/1982 in Dover; Daniel R. Saliga and
Maryann Robert

SALTMARSH,
David John, b. 3/13/1964 in Kittery, ME; first; Stephen J.
Saltmarsh (USAF, NH) and Mary Burgin (England)

SAMARAS,
Albert, b. 6/14/1969 in Dover; Andrew Samaras (MA) and Carol L. Benger (CT)

SANBORN,
Bertha, b. 3/6/1930 in Rochester; second; Guy Sanborn (farmer, Boston, MA) and Mabel Morrill (Rochester)

SANDERS,
David Charles, b. 5/3/1962 in Rochester; second; John H. Sanders (plumber, NH) and Lynda L. Gagne (NH)
David Peter, b. 7/3/1979 in Dover; Donald P. Sanders and Helen C. Raff
Erik Scott, b. 9/24/1977 in Exeter; Dan H. Sanders and Ruthellen Higgins
Heather Ann, b. 2/17/1977 in Dover; Donald P. Sanders and Helen C. Raff
Jared Benjamin, b. 3/21/1981 in Dover; Albert N. Sanders and Ellen Beam
John Hayes, III, b. 3/21/1961 in Rochester; first; John H. Sanders, Jr. (plumber, NH) and Lynda L. Gagne (NH)
Katherine Joanna, b. 3/23/1979 in Exeter; Dan H. Sanders and Ruthellen Higgins
Liza Ann, b. 7/14/1964 in Rochester; fourth; John H. Sanders, Jr. (plumber, NH) and Lynda L. Gagne (NH)
Pamela Jean, b. 6/13/1963 in Rochester; third; John H. Sanders, Jr. (plumber, NH) and Lynda L. Gagne (NH)
Paul Edward, b. 7/17/1970 in Rochester; John H. Sanders, III (NH) and Lynda L. Gagne (NH)
Sarah Rebecca, b. 10/9/1984 in Dover; Albert N. Sanders and Ellen Beam

SANTANA,
Angelina Marie, b. 1/22/1981 in Portsmouth; Raul F. Santana and Rebecca L. Mynatt

SATTERFIELD,
Kevin Dana Alexandrov, b. 11/6/1981 in Dover; John Satterfield and Madelyn E.L. Pirupshvarre

SAUCIER,
Randy Joseph, b. 12/16/1972 in Dover; Roger J. Saucier (NH) and LuAnn Bromfield (NH)

SAVAGE,
Anna Evangeline, b. 7/4/1982; John F. Savage and Patricia E. DeGruttula
Jonathan Andrew, b. 7/24/1976 in Exeter; James W. Savage and Lois E. Lind

SAVAGEAU,
Michael Joseph, b. 5/10/1987 in Portsmouth; Richard D. Savageau and Kelly A. Damato

SAWYER,
Chad Henry, b. 7/7/1976 in Dover; Eugene F. Sawyer and Priscilla S. Pattee
Tyler Ryan, b. 5/16/1987 in Portsmouth; Bradley W. Sawyer and Michelle L. Knapp

SCARKS,
Stefan Joseph, b. 5/2/1984 in Dover; Karol M. Scarks and Julianne Crockett

SCHEN,
Carol Lesly, b. 2/17/1942; fourth; Arnold L. Schen (meat cutter, Chelsea, MA) and Louise F. Letteney (Malden, MA)

SCHEU,
Ronald Edward, b. 4/16/1953 in Rochester; fifth; Arnold L. Scheu (construc. co., MA) and Louise F. Letteney (MA)

SCHNOOR,
Bryan James, b. 7/29/1986 in Rochester; William K. Schnoor, Sr. and Bettiejo M. Souza

SCHOLL,
Serena Jean, b. 10/29/1976 in Portsmouth; Carl E. Scholl and Mary J. Hutchinson

SCHONTAG,
Nathan Robert, b. 10/27/1976 in Dover; John H. Schontag and Patricia A. Elliott

SCHRIER,
Adam Michael, b. 8/20/1984 in Dover; David A. Schrier and Coleen E. McKay
David Alan, II, b. 11/28/1980 in Dover; David A. Schrier, Sr. and Coleen E. McKay
Kimberly Ann, b. 1/8/1986 in Dover; David A. Schrier and Coleen E. McKay
Peter Lee, Jr., b. 9/4/1985 in Exeter; Peter L. Schrier and Carol L. Nicholas
Rebecca Lynn, b. 7/24/1983 in Exeter; Peter L. Schrier and Carol L. Nicholas

SCHULTE,
Frederick William, b. 10/25/1971 in Exeter; Alfred W. Schulte (MA) and Nancy Adikson (FL)

SCHULTZ,
Karla Marie, b. 12/27/1986 in Portsmouth; Brian K. Schultz and Virginia C. Merry
Renate Christine, b. 1/24/1984 in Portsmouth; Brian K. Schultz and Virginia C. Merry

SCIABARRASI,
Marisa Lynne, b. 6/26/1985 in Portsmouth; Michael R.
   Sciabarrasi and Gail A. Touchette
Miranda Leigh, b. 6/1/1987 in Portsmouth; Michael R.
   Sciarabarrasi and Gail A. Touchette

SCLINERR,
stillborn daughter, b. 9/28/1915; fifth; Joseph J. Sclinerr
   (laborer, Shrewsbury, PA) and Louisa M. Hutchinson
   (Bethel, ME)

SCOTT,
June Lee, b. 6/15/1971 in Dover; David R. Scott (NH) and
   Margaret E. Martineau (NH)

SEARLES,
Jason Eric, b. 1/16/1980 in Dover; Ronald L. Searles and
   Bonnie E. Bryar

SEAVER,
David Colby, b. 2/17/1964 in Rochester; third; Ronald P.
   Seaver (trucker, NH) and Elizabeth A. Witham (NH)
Jennifer Marguerite, b. 4/10/1967 in Rochester; fourth;
   Ronald P. Seaver (mail carrier, Dover) and Elizabeth A.
   Witham (Portsmouth)
Tracy Jean, b. 4/18/1962 in Rochester; second; Ronald P.
   Seaver (asst. manager, NH) and Elizabeth A. Witham
   (NH)

SEAVEY,
John Stark, b. 12/4/1893; first; S. C. Seavey (farmer,
   Barrington) and Mignonette Moore (Mattapoisett, MA)

SEFOROVITCH,
Antonio V.S., b. 6/15/1914; first; Antonio Seforovitch (army officer, Montenegro) and Bertha G. Hayes (Philadelphia, PA)

SEVERENCE,
Herbert Elwin, b. 7/23/1937; Leroy A. Severence (laborer, Whitman, MA) and Harriet J. Wiggins (Holbrook, MA) (1944)

SEWARD,
John E., b. 4/3/1935 in Pittsfield; first; John E. Seward (laborer, Barrington) and Velna Clark (Pittsfield)

SHANNON,
Denise Lee, b. 7/29/1968 in Rochester; Daniel C. Shannon (NH) and Sharon L. Millette (NH)

SHARMAN,
Dwight Bradley, b. 9/28/1977 in Dover; Bradley D. Sharman and Dorothy D. Salmon
Nathaniel Dean, b. 12/31/1974 in Dover; Bradley D. Sharman and Dorothy D. Salmon

SHARON,
Michael Allen, b. 8/2/1968 in Dover; Edward M. Sharon (CT) and Jane E. Allen (MA)

SHAW,
Amy Elizabeth, b. 11/10/1974 in Dover; Richard Alan Shaw and Sara Jane Strachan
Vanessa Joy, b. 6/19/1961 in Rochester; first; Loren T. Shaw (laborer, NH) and Susan J. Leffel (NJ)

SHEEHAN,
Jennifer Lynn, b. 10/12/1979 in Portsmouth; James M. Sheehan and Mary E. Pease
Tadd Jason, b. 12/5/1977 in Rochester; Mark R. Sheehan and Sabrina M. Cray

SHELLY,
Julie Ann, b. 2/27/1984 in Exeter; Jerry L. Shelly and Eileen M. Vaughan

SHEPARD,
Eric William, b. 12/30/1981 in Rochester; Robert W. Shepard and Sandra L. Hooper
Judith, b. 7/24/1978; Scott H. Shepard and Jane Whitfield

SHERBURNE,
Joel William, b. 11/21/1940 in Rochester; first; J. Ralph Sherburne (carpenter, Barrington) and Flora B. Brown (Barrington)

SHERER,
Jeremiah Kriner, b. 3/10/1979 in Dover; John T. Sherer and Deanna M. Trefry

SHERRILL,
Corey Richard, b. 4/15/1981 in Exeter; Richard E. Sherrill and Jeanine T. Endres

SHERWOOD,
Michael John, b. 2/14/1975 in Rochester; Bradbury E. Sherwood and Beverly I. Robinson

SHEVENELL,
Jessie Lynn, b. 9/18/1984 in Rochester; Guy P. Shevenell and Deborah A. Sexton

Krista Lee, b. 1/20/1984 in Dover; Brian K. Shevenell and
    Kelly L. Landry
Travis Keith, b. 3/8/1980 in Dover; Brian K. Shevenell and
    Kelly L. Landry

SHONK,
Dana Emmett, b. 10/12/1970 in Exeter; Bronson Shonk (VA)
    and Mary H. Robinson (NH)

SHORTLE,
Abigail Grace, b. 9/9/1977 in Dover; Walter C. Shortle and
    Elizabeth Stickney
Emily Rebekah, b. 1/5/1979 in Rochester; Walter C. Shortle
    and Elizabeth Stickney

SIMMONS,
Dana Charles, b. 2/1/1978 in Dover; Gary P. Simmons and
    Peggy A. Nealand
Peter George, b. 6/6/1971 in Dover; Gary P. Simmons (NH)
    and Peggy A. Nealand (NH)

SIMON,
Yves Phillippe Francois, b. 1/27/1983 in Dover; Francois Y.
    Simon and Karen I. Perschy

SINK,
Juliet Anja, b. 11/27/1973 in Rochester; Theodore W. Sink
    (NY) and Karen J. Eldridge (NY)

SIROIS,
Adam Blain, b. 12/24/1983 in Dover; Richard L. Sirois and
    Paulette G. Blais
Richard Louis, b. 8/30/1986 in Dover; Richard L. Sirois and
    Paulette G. Blais

SIRRELL,
Curt Francis, b. 11/18/1943 in Rochester; first; Curt Francis Sirrell (lumberman, Southbridge, MA) and Goldie Mary Emmons (Tilton)
Francis Curt, b. 11/18/1943 in Rochester; second; Curt Francis Sirrell (lumberman, Southbridge, MA) and Goldie Mary Emmons (Tilton)

SKOOLICAS,
Christina Laura, b. 2/4/1986 in Dover; George C. Skoolicas and Linda K. Mortensen

SLOPER,
son [Myron J.], b. 5/15/1898; first; Joshua Sloper (laborer, 36, Strafford) and Ada Willey (29, Barrington)

SMALL,
Blanche, b. 1/1/1905; first; Frank Small (laborer, 27, Barnstead) and Nellie F. Howard (15, Dover)

SMALLCON,
Alta Esmeralda, b. 1/8/1890; George A. Smallcon (NH) and Esmeralda J. Howe (NH) (1958)

SMITH,
daughter, b. 7/31/1895; fourth; Frank Smith (carpenter, 27, Barrington) and Alice Philbrick (29, Campton)
son, b. 7/16/1904; first; Lewis L. Smith (farmer, 23, Barrington) and Stella Drysdale (25, East Boston, MA)
daughter, b. 4/27/1910; third; Fred B. Smith (laborer, 31, Newmarket) and Jessie M. Libby (25, Somersworth); residence - Lee
son, b. 3/8/1913; fourth; Fred D. Smith (laborer, 34, Newmarket) and Jessie May Libby (28, Berwick, ME)
Allen Todd, b. 2/1/1972 in Dover; Stephen W. Smith (NH) and Diane I. Turcotte (NH)

Beatrice, b. 5/29/1916; sixth; Fred Smith (woodchopper, Newmarket) and Jennie Libby (Berwick, ME)

Betty Ann, b. 4/6/1961 in Rochester; first; Adriel C. Smith (mechanic, NH) and Mary L. Locke (NH)

Cheryl Diane, b. 7/15/1952 in Exeter; third; Leroy F. Smith (General Electric, NH) and Therese L. Hamel (NH)

David James, b. 1/29/1979 in Rochester; David W. Smith and Susan J. Post

Dorothy Anne, b. 7/25/1936 in Dover; second; Leo Francis B. Smith (rest. manager, Revere, MA) and Alice L. Culliton (York Co., NB)

Erin Elizabeth, b. 5/4/1982 in Dover; Richard W. Smith and Penny E. Preve

Everett Donald, b. 10/8/1940 in Exeter; first; Donald H. Smith (woolen mill, Holderness) and Elizabeth McRae (Lee)

Jacob Tyler, b. 12/24/1985 in Dover; Randall C. Smith and Debbie L. Hendrickx

James Ivory, b. 1/11/1919; eighth; Fred D. Smith (farmer, Newmarket) and Jessie M. Smith (Brunswick, ME)

Johana Marcia, b. 7/29/1945 in Rochester; fourth; John M. Smith (machinist, Chelsea, MA) and Barbara Morris (Washington, DC)

John Dana, b. 2/5/1910; John Dana Smith (Haverhill, MA) and Bessie Hanscom (Somerville, MA) (1942)

John Mark, III, b. 3/11/1948 in Rochester; fifth; John M. Smith, Jr. (post engineer, Chelsea, MA) and Barbara Morris (Washington, DC)

Kris Allen, b. 12/10/1960 in Dover; first; Stephen W. Smith (laborer, NH) and Carol L. Ryan (MA)

LeRoy Frank, b. 8/30/1939 in Dover; third; LeRoy F. Smith (truck driver, Epping) and Mary C. Thomas (Rollinsford); residence - East Barrington

Lewis, b. 7/24/1917; seventh; Fred D. Smith (laborer, Newmarket) and Jessie M. Libbey (Berwick, ME)

Mark Alan, b. 10/12/1979 in Dover; David A. Smith and Kathleen G. Greene

Mary Louise, stillborn, b. 6/22/1944 in Exeter; fifth; Leroy Frank Smith (electrician, Epping) and Mary Claire Smith (Rollinsford)
Matthew David, b. 8/4/1978 in Dover; David A. Smith and Kathleen G. Greene
Richard Lee, b. 1/17/1964 in Rochester; first; Leroy F. Smith (supervisor, NH) and Donna M. Garland (NH)
Roxanne Muriel, b. 3/4/1965 in Rochester; second; Leroy F. Smith, Jr. (supervisor, NH) and Donna M. Garland (NH)
Ruth, b. 12/16/1917; first; Lloyd B. Smith (mail carrier, Barrington) and Edna B. Chapman (Coaticook, PQ)
Sandra Robin, b. 2/19/1976 in Dover; Charles H. Smith and Linda J. Miller
Shawn Richard, b. 7/2/1979 in Dover; Richard W. Smith and Penny E. Preve
Stefanie Lyn, b. 3/11/1984 in Dover; Steven E. Smith and Marguerite A. O'Sullivan
Stella Emelia, b. 9/2/1906; first; Frank P. Smith (29, Barrington) and Jennie E. Mattox (21, Lee)
Sydney Dodd, b. 11/24/1950 in Rochester; sixth; John M. Smith, Jr. (machinist, MA) and Barbara Morris (Washington, DC)
Wendy Anne, b. 11/19/1964 in Rochester; fourth; Leroy F. Smith, Sr. (production dept., NH) and Therese L. Hamel (NH)

SOLOMON,
Ruth Ella, b. 11/13/1947 in Rochester; first; James M. Solomon (bus driver, Cincinnati, OH) and Ella C. Lenzi (Suncook)

SOUDER,
Morning-Glory Akhola, b. 8/18/1974; Stephen Paul Souder and Laura Wyatt

SOULE,
Emily, b. 5/8/1894; first; Hallarn Soule (laborer, 30, Auburn) and Delia Hart (26, Auburn)

SOUTHARD,
Robert, b. 3/13/1944; Edward Southard (salesman, NY) and Gertrude Wagner (NY)

SPAULDING,
Roberta Mae, b. 1/12/1951 in Exeter; first; Richard M. Spaulding (US Air Force, ME) and Doris I. Brown (NH)

SPELLMAN,
Adam Richard, b. 10/23/1979 in Rochester; Richard L. Spellman and Jean E. Van Nest

SPENCER,
son, b. 7/1/1907; first; Harry Spencer (teamster, 29, Berwick, ME) and Bessie Chesley (26, Barrington)

SPINALE,
Charles Eric, b. 10/1/1982 in Rochester; Charles E. Spinale and Betty L. Moronie
Erin, b. 1/17/1980 in Rochester; Charles E. Spinale and Betty L. Moronie

SPROWL,
Jennifer Lynn, b. 3/22/1983 in Rochester; Timothy A. Sprowl and Pamela J. Hasty
Katherine Ann, b. 1/25/1985 in Rochester; Timothy A. Sprowl and Pamela J. Hasty

STACY,
Jacqueline Alice, b. 4/7/1940; fourth; Earl C. Stacy (laborer, Newfields) and Ruth Theresa Bell (Barrington)

Thomas Arthur, b. 11/22/1945; fifth; Earl C. Stacy (clerk, Newmarket) and Ruth T. Bell (Malden, MA); residence - Milford

STAFFORD,
Katelyn Elizabeth, b. 1/21/1987 in Dover; Scott R. Stafford and Carrie L. Stockwell

STANLEY,
daughter, b. 6/2/1904; twelfth; Jack Stanley (basket maker, 55, NS) and Mary Capen (40, Charlestown, MA)
Everett Anthony, b. 1/13/1951 in Rochester; seventh; Herbert A. Stanley (teamster, VT) and Anna M. Drysdale (MA)

STAPLEY,
Mark George, b. 12/30/1983 in Exeter; Douglas R. Stapley and Lois V. Hodgdon

STEEL,
Katherine Lynn, b. 10/19/1965 in Saco, ME; third; David C. Steel (laborer, ME) and Janice K. Morse (NH)

STEERE,
Kristen Ann, b. 6/25/1975 in Portsmouth; Clark D. Steere and Mary Ann E. Giran

STEINHART,
Sharna Lee, b. 4/7/1985 in Dover; Stephen L. Steinhart and Rosanne L. Berube

STEVENSON,
Carolyn, b. 4/6/1930; first; Douglas M. Stevenson (teacher, Concord) and Eva M. Locke (Barrington)

STEWART,
Jessica Anne, b. 11/13/1980 in Portsmouth; John R. Stewart and Darlene A. Russo

STILES,
Lillian Bessie, b. 1/5/1913; first; Walter T. Stiles (farmer, 47, Lunenburg, MA) and Flora Ella Cater (22, Barrington)

STIMPSON,
Cora Evelyne, b. 1/31/1925; seventh; Urbana Stimpson (farmer, 37, Charlestown) and Maude A. Bellows (36, Weathersfield, VT)

STONE,
daughter [Emma], b. 4/29/1892; first; Fred Stone (laborer, 20, Manchester) and Lillie Bernier (21, Canada)
daughter, b. 9/28/1894; second; Fred Stone (laborer, 22, Manchester) and Lillie Bernier (23, Canada)
son [Harry], b. 7/2/1900; third; Fred Stone (miller, 28, Manchester) and Leo Bernier (27, Canada)
daughter, b. 5/23/1914; fifth; Fred Stone (farmer, Manchester) and Leo Burnier (Canada)
Eric Richard, b. 10/3/1977 in Rochester; Richard H. Stone and Myra S. Arnold
Jared Douglas, b. 9/14/1972 in Exeter; Lewis A. Stone (ME) and Anita C. Ferland (NH)
Trevor Sheldon, b. 1/6/1982 in Hanover; Albert E. Stone and Elizabeth A. Atwood

STRACH[A]N,
daughter, b. 8/18/1900; fourth; Charles E. Strachn (farmer, 36, Strafford) and Addie M. Arlin (26, Barrington)
son [George C.], b. 12/23/1904; sixth; Charles E. Strachn (farmer, 40, Strafford) and Addie M. Arlin (30, Barrington)

son, b. 7/29/1907; seventh; Charles E. Strachn (farmer, 42, Strafford) and Addie M. Arlin (33, Barrington)
daughter, b. 6/23/1911; eighth; Charles E. Strachan (carpenter, 46, Strafford) and Mary Addie Arlin (36, Barrington)
Charles W., b. 6/17/1892; first; Charles Strachan (laborer, 27, Strafford) and Addie Arlin (18, Barrington)
Florence May, b. 1/20/1895; second; Charles Strachn (laborer, 30, Barrington) and Addie Arlin (21, Barrington)
Lottie Hazel, b. 11/12/1897; third; Charles E. Strachn (farmer, 32, Strafford) and Addie E. Arlin (24, Barrington)
Ray, b. 11/24/1902; fifth; Charles E. Strachn (farmer, 37, Strafford) and Addie M. Arlin (27, Barrington)

STRONG,
Alberta Ruth, b. 11/10/1959 in Rochester; third; Leonard Strong (tile mechanic, NH) and Ruth A. Erickson (MA)
Marlene Anne, b. 4/10/1963 in Dover; second; Leonard Strong (tile mechanic, NH) and Ruth Alberta Erickson (MA)

STULTZ,
Patricia Kay, b. 11/21/1966 in Rochester; second; Peter E. Stultz, Sr. (USN, Yarmouth, ME) and Cheryl L. Wentworth (Rochester)

STURMER,
Joshua David, b. 12/29/1981 in Rochester; John R. Sturmer and Jamie L. Boudreau

STYLES,
Julia Maude, b. 3/21/1923; second; Walter F. Styles (farmer, Lunenburg, MA) and Flora E. Cater (Barrington)

SVENSON,
Garth William, b. 4/7/1975 in Dover; John P. Svenson and
 Linda L. Calef
Mark Chesley, b. 8/31/1976 in Exeter; John P. Svenson and
 Linda L. Calef

SWAIN,
son, b. 1/22/1891; fourth; L. F. Swain (farmer, Barrington)
 and Carrie I. Hoitt (Bangor, ME)
daughter, b. 1/20/1896; fifth; Llewellyn Swain (farmer, 38,
 Barrington) and Carrie Hoitt (32, Barrington)
son, b. 12/31/1897; sixth; Llewellyn F. Swain (farmer, 40,
 Barrington) and Carrie Hoyt (34, Barrington)
son, b. 7/31/1934; seventh; William S. Swain (farmer,
 Barrington) and Mary Sanders (Madbury)
stillborn daughter, b. 5/19/1936; eighth; William Sherburne
 Swain (farmer, Barrington) and Mary E. Sanderson
 (Madbury)
son, b. 3/20/1939; first; Dorothy E. Swain (Barrington)
Beverly Ann, b. 8/7/1941 in Exeter; second; Ralph W. Swan
 (sic) (laborer, Barrington) and Pauline A. Swenson
 (Everett, MA)
Calvin S., b. 12/3/1927; sixth; N. Sherburn Swain (farmer,
 Barrington) and Mary E. Saunders (Madbury)
Dorothy E., b. 12/23/1921; fourth; W. Sherburne Swain
 (farmer, Barrington) and Mary E. Sanders (Madbury)
Geraldine, b. 11/20/1917 in Dover; W. Sherbourne Swain
 (NH) and Mary Sanders (NH) (1970)
Luverne C., b. 11/6/1920; third; Sherburne Swain (farmer,
 Barrington) and Mary Saunders (Madbury)
Mauriah Lee, b. 5/30/1971 in Dover; Ralph M. Swain (NH)
 and Katherine M. Redden (NH)
Nancy Elizabeth, b. 6/8/1950 in Exeter; fourth; Ralph W.
 Swain (mechanic, NH) and Pauline A. Swenson (MA)

Ralph Malcolm, b. 9/24/1944 in Exeter; third; Ralph William Swain (elec. welder, Barrington) and Pauline A. Swenson (Everett, MA)

Ralph William, b. 3/11/1919; second; Sherburne Swain (farmer, Barrington) and Mary E. Sanders (Madbury)

Richard Bennett, b. 12/14/1936 in Exeter; first; Ralph W. Swain (laborer, Barrington) and Pauline Sevenson (Everett, MA)

William Sherburn, b. 2/26/1896; first; William B. Swain (farmer, 34, Barrington) and Effie A. Locke (34, Barrington)

SWENSON,

Andrea Lynn, b. 12/2/1968 in Dover; Harold W. Swenson (NH) and Dale E. Arlin (NH)

Harold Walter, b. 12/23/1944; first; Harold M. Swenson (US Navy, Haverhill, MA) and Madelyn L. Hopey (Madbury)

Joseph Edward, b. 1/12/1986 in Dover; Joseph T. Swenson and Kim A. Kusnierz

Joseph Thomas, b. 12/18/1956 in Exeter; first; Joseph J. Swenson (janitor, NH) and Marion T. McEachern (MA)

TAATJES,

Cheryl Lynn, b. 2/10/1960 in Rochester; second; Robert D. Taatjes (elec. engineer, NH) and Norma F. Simes (NH)

TABOR,

Jennifer Louise, b. 7/3/1980 in Rochester; Ernest E. Tabor, Jr. and Janice L. Grochmal

TAPPIN,

Jesse Stephen, b. 9/28/1980 in Dover; Stephen S. Tappin and Ruth M. Rogers

TARBELL,
Cynthia Susan, b. 11/20/1965 in Dover; first; Terry C. Tarbell (univ. student, OK) and Susan A. Horner (NH)

TARMEY,
Meghan Jade, b. 1/8/1985 in Dover; John A. Tarmey and Dawn B. Tilton

TASKER,
Doreen Susan, b. 8/24/1960 in Concord; second; Cecil W. Tasker (tree surgeon, NH) and Barbara J. Corbett (NH)
Michael Walter, b. 3/12/1959 in Concord; first; Cecil W. Tasker (truck driver, NH) and Barbara J. Corbett (NH)

TAYLOR,
Brian John, b. 11/27/1979 in Rochester; William H. Taylor and Martha L. Skelton
Colby Joseph, b. 11/12/1985 in Dover; Kevin M. Taylor and Robin R. Mattingly
Daniel David, b. 6/21/1984 in Exeter; Lee C. Taylor and Barbara J. Bagnell
Donald George, b. 12/12/1960 in Dover; sixth; Harold R. Taylor (poultry serv. man, MA) and Mildred E. McDaniel (NH)
Joyce May, b. 1/28/1942 in Dover; first; Harold R. Taylor (salesman, Chelsea, MA) and Mildred E. McDaniel (Barrington)
Judith Anne, b. 11/1/1947 in Dover; second; Harold R. Taylor (asst. mgr., Chelsea, MA) and Mildred E. McDaniel (Barrington)
Katherine Amy, b. 1/9/1981 in Exeter; Lee C. Taylor and Barbara J. Bagnell
Keith Allen, b. 8/5/1984 in Rochester; Terry A. Taylor and Christine Vanscoder
Marilyn Anne, b. 9/23/1958 in Dover; fifth; Harold R. Taylor (farmers exch., MA) and Mildred E. McDaniel (NH)

Rebecca Lou, b. 12/11/1978 in Dover; Frederick H. Taylor, Jr. and Cindy L. Voye

Robert Rowe, b. 11/4/1953 in Dover; third; Harold R. Taylor (poultryman, MA) and Mildred E. McDaniel (NH)

William Harold, b. 9/25/1956 in Dover; fourth; Harold R. Taylor (poultryman, MA) and Mildred E. McDaniel (NH)

TEBBETS,
daughter, b. 10/26/1898; first; Frank E. Tebbets (farmer, Madbury) and Annabel McRae (Barrington); residence - Madbury

TEBBETTS,
daughter, b. 3/31/1890; first; Charles A. Tebbetts (farmer, Barrington) and Etta J. Ham (Rochester)

son, b. 4/29/1892; first; John Tebbetts (farmer, 23, Barrington) and Fanny Laine (20, Lee)

son [Harold], b. 10/14/1899; second; Frank E. Tebbetts (farmer, 33, Madbury) and Anna B. McRea (23, Barrington); residence - Madbury

TEMPLAR,
son, b. 6/5/1903; first; Fred Templar (teamster, 32, Boston, MA) and Bertha M. Stiles (21, Lunenburg, MA)

THEBEAULT,
Helen Marie, b. 5/20/1932; first; Henry A. Thebeault (glove maker, Brooklyn, NY) and Rowea Laforme (Lowell, MA)

THEODORE,
Timothy Stephen, b. 12/8/1983 in Dover; Stephen F. Theodore and Sharon L. Marmen

THERIAULT,
Diana Sue, b. 11/30/1982 in Dover; Maurice H. Theriault and Jane A. Mooney

THIBEAULT,
Bruce Joseph, b. 11/7/1973 in MA; Bruce W. Thibeault (NH) and Barbara A. Goyette (MA)

THIBODEAU,
Nichole Suzanne, b. 9/4/1976 in Rochester; Paul L. Thibodeau and Marie E. Bedard

THOMAS,
Adam James, b. 1/19/1984 in Rochester; James L. Thomas and Suzanna C. Hamilton
Alex William, b. 10/15/1985 in Rochester; James L. Thomas and Suzanne C. Hamilton

THOMPSON,
son [Lester], b. 1/3/1891; second; H. T. Thompson (farmer, Barrington) and L. V. Raynes (Bangor, ME)
daughter, b. 8/1/1894; second; W. I. N. Thompson (farmer, 33, Barrington) and Ida Payme (33, Bangor, ME)
daughter, b. 8/19/1896; fourth; H. T'lm'n Thompson (fax, 31, Barrington) and Lanzara Raynes (37, Bangor, ME)
daughter, b. 6/28/1906; fourth; Roscoe P. Thompson (farmer, 28, Barrington) and Fannie Freeman (25, Barrington)
daughter, b. 9/23/1907; second; Roscoe Thompson (workman, 30, Barrington) and Fannie Freeman (26, Barrington)
Brian Herbert, b. 7/26/1958 in Dover; second; Herbert A. Thompson (cable splicer, ME) and Joan H. Smith (NH)
Susan Marie, b. 2/3/1961 in Dover; third; Herbert A. Thompson (maint. man, ME) and Joan H. Smith (NH)
Vera A., b. 1/9/1901; fourth; H. T. Thompson (farmer, 35, Barrington) and Lausarah Raynes (41, Bangor, ME)

THORN,
James Adam, b. 2/1/1985 in Dover; James E. Thorn, Jr. and Darlene M. Gordon

THORNE,
Jeffrey Robert, b. 4/10/1954 in Rochester; second; George W. Thorne (carpenter, NH) and Olive H. Shiere (MA)

THURSTON,
Dennis Freeman, b. 3/4/1952 in Wolfeboro; second; Walter S. Thurston (electrician, NH) and Rachael F. Roberts (NH)
Rebecca Lynn, b. 6/2/1972 in Rochester; Dennis F. Thurston (NH) and Monda O. Grondin (ME)
Steven Warren, b. 3/2/1959 in Rochester; second; Calvin W. Thurston (machine operator, NH) and Grace S. Roberts (NH)

TIBBETS,
son, b. 5/17/1898; first; John Tibbets (farmer, 29, Barrington) and Fanny M. Lane (25, Lee Hill)

TIBBETTS,
daughter, b. 9/28/1893; first; Era L. Tibbetts (shoemaker, Barrington) and Gertrude Dixon (Barrington)
daughter [Cora E.], b. 5/11/1895; third; Charles Tibbetts (farmer, 33, Barrington) and Etta Ham (33, Rochester)
Christina Lynn, b. 5/22/1978 in Rochester; Gary L. Tibbetts and Linda D. Woolson

TIBBITTS,
daughter, b. 11/3/1894; second; John Tibbitts (farmer, 25, Barrington) and Fannie Lane (21, Lee)

TILTON,
Joshua Christian, b. 12/9/1985 in Dover; Jeffrey P. Tilton and Kathryn M. Eder

TIMM,
Kathryn Irene, b. 2/4/1947 in Rochester; fifth; Frederick N. Timm (investigator, Brooklyn, NY) and Marjorie M. Boyce (Brooklyn, NY)

TINKER,
Peter John, b. 11/1/1967 in Dover; first; Arthur R. Tinker (machinist, Dover) and Vicki M. Emerson (Concord)

TOCZKO,
Eric Andrew, b. 4/25/1986 in Rochester; Gary M. Toczko and Pamela A. Penas
Holly Ellen, b. 12/10/1984 in Rochester; Gary M. Toczko and Pamela A. Penas

TOOCH,
Dylan Eli, b. 2/21/1986 in Dover; David E. Tooch and Rochelle L. Gagnon
Nathan Edward, b. 11/26/1983 in Dover; David E. Tooch and Rochelle L. Gagnon

TOWLE,
Bryan Lindsay, b. 1/18/1983 in Dover; Dennis L. Towle and Deborah L. Taylor
James Daniel, II, b. 3/2/1986 in Dover; James D. Towle, Sr. and Darlene M. Brown
Jessica Ann, b. 3/2/1986 in Dover; James D. Towle, Sr. and Darlene M. Brown

TOWNSEND,
Timothy Scott, b. 12/7/1980 in Rochester; Scott T. Townsend and Celia M. Baker

TREADWELL,
Dwight Howard, b. 12/2/1973 in Rochester; Gordon B. Treadwell (NH) and Cynthia L. Brown (CT)
Keith Brian, b. 3/16/1976 in Dover; Gordon B. Treadwell and Cynthia L. Brown

TREBLE,
Rita Joan, b. 9/8/1943 in Rochester; third; Kenneth Brian Treble (asst. mgr., Lisbon Falls, ME) and Geraldine B. Stone (Barrington)
Vickie Jean, b. 8/14/1957 in Rochester; second; Kenneth B. Treble, Jr. (inspector, ME) and Jeanne M. Gaulin (NH)

TREFETHEN,
Valerie Jeanne, b. 5/16/1987 in Rochester; Bruce Trefethen and Pamela J. Bowley

TRIPP,
Rose Judy, b. 1/5/1978 in Rochester; Henry A. Tripp and Yvonne E. Forrest

TRUEWORTHY,
daughter, b. 10/4/1903; fourth; William L. Trueworthy (shoemaker, 40, Washington, DC) and Ada M. Howard (26, Barrington)
Eva May, b. 1/9/1899; second; William L. Trueworthy (shoemaker, 33, Waldboro, ME) and Ada M. Howard (23, Barrington)

TRUFANT,
Jocelyn Leigh, b. 9/26/1979 in Dover; Peter W. Trufant and Laurel A. Warren

TSAKIRIS,
Jeremy George, b. 8/17/1977 in Rochester; Dennis J. Tsakiris and Christina M. Chick

TUCK,
stillborn son, b. 6/3/1908; first; Percey H. Tuck (RR fireman, 21, Mapleton, ME) and Florence E. Griffin (19, Barrington)
Betty Anne, b. 4/4/1947; fourth; Gordon Tuck (Navy Yard, Ware, MA) and Beatrice Beriault (Canada); residence - Strafford
Cecelia Florence, b. 3/5/1951 in Rochester; seventh; Gordon C. Tuck (machinist, MA) and Beatrice Beriault (Canada)
Helen Marie, b. 3/15/1952 in Rochester; eighth; Gordon C. Tuck (machinist, MA) and Beatrice Beriault (Canada)
Joseph, b. 11/22/1948 in Rochester; fifth; Gordon C. Tuck (machinist, Ware, MA) and Beatrice Beriault (Canada)
Margery Anne, b. 2/18/1950 in Rochester; sixth; Gordon C. Tuck (machinist, MA) and Rose Beriault (Canada)

TUCKER,
daughter, b. 5/15/1899; sixth; Charles H. Tucker (minister, 35, Thornton) and Angie E. Clay (34, West Concord)
daughter, b. 7/23/1900; eighth; Charles H. Tucker (clergyman, 36, Thornton) and Angie E. Clay (34, West Concord)
Carrie Ellen, b. 12/4/1971 in Dover; Freeman J. Tucker, Jr. (MA) and Ruth M. Burgess (Canada)

TURNER,
Bruce Wellington, b. 6/15/1938 in Dover; second; Arthur James Turner (electrician, Staten Island, NY) and Virginia F. Ramsdell (Wareham, MA)
Florence E., b. 5/24/1924; third; Arthur W. Turner (mechanic, Staten Island, NY) and Alice V. Hopey (Canada)
Jacqueline Ann, b. 4/12/1945 in Rochester; third; Arthur J. Turner (electrician, Staten Island, NY) and Virginia F. Ramsdell (Wareham, MA)

Roberta Ramsdell, b. 7/21/1936 in Exeter; first; Arthur J. Turner (truck driver, Staten Island, NY) and Virginia Ramsdell (Wareham, MA)

TUTTLE,
daughter [Gladys May], b. 2/16/1896; second; Joseph H. Tuttle (merchant, 25, Dover) and Caroline Arlin (22, Barrington)
daughter, b. 4/15/1897; second; Fred F. Tuttle (shoemaker, 31, Nottingham) and Maud E. Chesley (22, Barrington)
son [Merlon], b. 7/2/1898; second; Owen S. Tuttle (farmer, 34, Barnstead) and Nettie F. Foss (36, Strafford)
daughter, b. 6/5/1900; third; Owen H. Tuttle (farmer, 25, Barnstead) and Nettie Foss (37, Strafford)
stillborn daughter, b. 12/17/1901; third; Joseph H. Tuttle (postmaster, 31, Dover) and Carrie E. Arlin (28, Barrington)
Adam Roy, b. 8/24/1979 in Concord; Glen R. Tuttle and Dawn Z. Pero
Audrey Lee, b. 2/4/1942 in Pittsfield; third; Chester R. Tuttle (tractor driver, Barrington) and Alice M. Clark (Pittsfield); residence - North. Ridge
C[hester]. R., b. 8/17/1911; second; Alpha O. Tuttle (farmer, 33, Strafford) and Eva May Hall (26, Strafford)
Ellen Rosila, b. 4/26/1909; first; Alpha D. Tuttle (farmer, 30, Strafford) and Eva M. Hall (23, Strafford)
John Michael, b. 3/10/1975 in Concord; Glen R. Tuttle and Dawn Z. Pero
John Wilder, b. 5/25/1972 in Rochester; John W. Tuttle (ME) and Claire J. Johnston (NY)
Ralph Nelson, b. 8/16/1938; first; Ellen Rosila Tuttle (Barrington)
Wendell Thomas b. 3/1/1906; fourth; Joseph H. Tuttle (clerk, postmaster, 36, Dover) and Carrie E. Arlin (33, Barrington)

TWOMBLEY,
daughter, b. 11/11/1896; first; Albert H. Twombley (farmer, 39, Madbury) and Lizzie O. Caswell (16, Barrington)

TWOMBLY,
son, b. 7/27/1897; first; William Twombly (stone cutter, 32, Washington) and Aela Howard (22, Barrington); residence - Somersworth

son, b. 11/12/1900; fifth; Charles Twombly (teamster, Madbury) and Alice Caswell (Northwood)

daughter, b. 12/17/1902; seventh; Charles E. Twombly (teamster, 36, Madbury) and Mary A. Twombly (24, Northwood)

son, b. 9/21/1906; fourth; Albert H. Twombly (laborer, 49, Madbury) and Lizzie O. Caswell (26, Barrington)

son [Harold Ford], b. 7/9/1908; fifth; Albert H. Twombly (laborer, 51, Madbury) and Lizzie O. Caswell (28, Barrington)

daughter, b. 5/4/1911; thirteenth; Charles E. Twombly (teamster, 45, Madbury) and Mary A. Caswell (33, Northwood)

Annie E., b. 1/25/1912; fourth; Albert D. Twombly (laborer, 23, Fremont) and Nellie L. Freeman (24, Somerville, MA)

Arvilla May, b. 1/30/1942 in Dover; Merton D. Twombly (truck driver, Barrington) and Villa M. Johnson (Wakefield)

Charles Franklin, b. 7/26/1944 in Dover; second; Merton D. Twombly (buffer, Barrington) and Villa Mae Johnson (Wakefield)

Charles Irving, b. 3/7/1905; ninth; C. E. Twombly (farmer, 39, Madbury) and Mary A. Caswell (27, Northwood)

Chelsie Elice, b. 5/6/1987 in Dover; Stephen L. Twombly and Laurie C. Robie

Clarence Eugene, b. 6/10/1913; fourteenth; Charles Edgar Twombly (teamster, 47, Madbury) and Mary Alice Caswell (35, Northwood)

Clayton Bennett, b. 10/26/1914; second; Frank O. Twombly
(laborer, Nottingham) and Georgianna Ellison
(Barrington)

Dudley, b. 4/23/1912; first; Frank O. Twombly (laborer, 18, Nottingham) and Georgianna Ellison (16, Barrington)

Edgar Caswell, b. 3/28/1907; tenth; Charles E. Twombly (laborer, 41, Barrington) and Mary A. Caswell (29, Northwood)

George W.A., b. 1/1/1910; first; Albert Twombly, Jr. (laborer, 21, Fremont) and Ellen L. Freeman (22, Somerville, MA)

Hermon C., b. 6/21/1918; fifth; David O. Twombly (farmer, Strafford) and Bernice M. Brown (Northwood)

Ida A., b. 9/29/1918; seventeenth; Charles E. Twombly (teamster, Madbury) and Mary A. Caswell (Northwood)

Joel, b. 12/6/1903; eighth; Charles S. Twombly (farmer, 37, Madbury) and Alice Caswell (25, Northwood)

Lucille Estelle, b. 1/24/1947 in Dover; third; Merton Twombly (scanister, Barrington) and Villa Johnson (Whitefield)

Merton Daniel, b. 11/29/1908; eleventh; Charles E. Twombly (laborer, 42, Madbury) and Mary A. Caswell (30, Northwood)

Shawn Allen, b. 2/2/1971 in Dover; Frederick P. Twombly (NH) and Naomi Martin (MA)

Stephen Lawrence Clarkson, b. 3/6/1986 in Hanover; Stephen L. Twombly and Laurie C. Robie

Waldo H. Fernald, b. 12/23/1909; twelfth; Charles E. Twombly (teamster, 42, Madbury) and Mary Alice Caswell (31, Northwood)

TYLER,
daughter, b. 5/10/1904; second; Lizzie Tyler (30)
daughter, b. 5/22/1906; first; John Tyler (laborer, 21) and ----- (18)

TYRE,
Erica Danielle, b. 8/31/1979 in Dover; Patrick A. Tyre and Carolyn I. Flinn

UDALL,
Timothy Cushing, b. 8/3/1950 in Rochester; first; John L. Udall, Jr. (clergyman, MA) and Marjorie L. Cushing (NH)

URQUHART,
James Henry, IV, b. 4/30/1982 in Exeter; James H. Urquhart, III and Kimberly A. Jordan

VALLEY,
Annie, b. 8/4/1873; Michael Valley (Canada) and Emma Grenier (Canada) (1944)

VAN ENGEN,
Heidi Jo, b. 7/3/1975 in Portsmouth; Jered H. Van Engen and Marcia L. Koele
Melanie Lynn, b. 4/21/1974 in Dover; Jerod Henry Van Engen and Marcia Lynn Koele

VAN HORN,
son, b. 4/12/1930; seventh; Walter Van Horn (lumberman, Portland, MI) and Annie Smith (Deerfield)

VANCE,
Joshua, b. 12/1/1985 in Dover; William B. Vance and Carol L. Briggs

VARNEY,
Clara Augusta, b. 8/15/1937; second; Nolan Varney (farmer, Farmington) and Lucy M. Hall (Barrington)
George Edward, b. 3/4/1908; first; George E. Varney (lumberman, 42, Madison) and Emma F. Demeritt (18, Lebanon, ME)

Jill Margaret, b. 9/21/1978 in Dover; Timothy W. Varney and Sally J. Watson
Sarah Jeanne, b. 11/10/1976 in Dover; Timothy W. Varney and Sally J. Watson

VELEZ,
Anita Luisa, b. 1/4/1980 in Dover; Lishenel Velez and Lyndie L. Brooke

VESTAL,
Sherry Lee, b. 12/17/1976 in Exeter; David L. Vestal and Kathleen A. Cheever

VIGUE,
Andrew Larry, b. 2/5/1987 in Exeter; Larry A. Vigue and Diane M. Beauchesne

VIOLETTE,
Tina Marie, b. 5/22/1968 in Dover; Anthony G. Violette (ME) and Janice K. Lewis (NH)

VOROSMARTY,
Daniel Robert, b. 10/30/1982 in Concord; Charles J. Vorosmarty and Lorraine M. Eckland

WAITE,
Erika Lee, b. 4/11/1978 in Concord; Terry A. Waite and Louise A. Planchet

WAKEFIELD,
Howard Leroy, III, b. 4/6/1958 in Dover; third; Howard L. Wakefield, Jr. (machinist, MA) and Lorna L. Boucher (NH)

WAKEMAN,
Bethany Rose, b. 5/11/1987 in Hanover; Kenneth J. Wakeman and Patricia L. Djerf

WALKER,
Cory Patrick, b. 3/9/1985 in Dover; Robert C. Walker and Janet L. Comtois
Richard Arthur, Jr., b. 9/19/1959 in Rochester; first; Richard A. Walker (shoe worker, NH) and Irene H. Beaulieu (NH)
Seth Robert, b. 10/4/1981 in Dover; Robert C. Walker and Janet L. Comtois
William Henry, Jr., b. 4/5/1951 in Dover; first; William H. Walker (fireman, NH) and Jeannine R. Laurent (France)

WALLACE,
Kelly Ann, b. 10/19/1976 in Portsmouth; Terrance N. Wallace and Sylvia A. Ingerson

WALLINGFORD,
Barbara Ann, b. 7/18/1954 in Exeter; first; Richard E. Wallingford (woodsman, ME) and Helen J. Elliott (NH)
Bonnie Lou, b. 5/29/1961 in Exeter; fourth; Richard E. Wallingford (lumber pit man, ME) and Helen J. Elliott (NH)
Richard Everett, Jr., b. 11/29/1956 in Exeter; third; Richard E. Wallingford (woodsman, ME) and Helen J. Elliott (NH)
Russell James, b. 9/19/1959 in Exeter; fourth; Richard E. Wallingford (lumberjack, ME) and Helen J. Elliott (NH)
Susan Emily, b. 6/30/1955 in Exeter; second; Richard E. Wallingford (saw mill worker, ME) and Helen J. Elliott (NH)
Tammy Rose, b. 8/8/1968 in Dover; Richard E. Wallingford (ME) and Helen J. Elliott (NH)
Tina Marie, b. 1/13/1966 in Dover; fifth; Clifford E. Wallingford (tanner, Lebanon, ME) and Sandra L. Clark (Dover)

WALTER,
Laura Ann, b. 5/28/1960 in Rochester; second; Richard A. Walter, Sr. (shoe worker, NH) and Irene H. Beaulieu (NH)

WALTON,
Christopher Brian, b. 12/2/1957 in Dover; first; Alfred C. Walton (student, UNH, MA) and Vilma E. Grube (NH)

WARD,
stillborn daughter, b. 10/24/1955 in Dover; first; William R. Ward (poultryman, ME) and Marjorie Lirette (NH)
Aaron David, b. 6/27/1971 in Rochester; William R. Ward (ME) and Marjorie M. Lirette (NH)
Chester W., b. 6/4/1903; first; Roy J. Ward (physician, 27, Johnson, VT) and Mary Downing (29, Hanover)
Cindy Lee, b. 1/28/1971 in Rochester; Stephen R. Ward (ME) and Lorraine E. Wilson (NY)
Donald Alan, b. 3/11/1971 in Kittery, ME; John A. Ward (ME) and Payso Montong (Thailand)
Glenn Peter, b. 12/20/1958 in Dover; second; William R. Ward (truck driver, ME) and Marjorie M. Lirette (NH)
Jason Michael, b. 10/31/1977 in Dover; Stephen L. Ward and Deborah L. Georgantis
Jennifer Lynn, b. 9/26/1978 in Dover; Stephen L. Ward and Deborah L. Georgantis
Pauline Ann, b. 6/4/1951 in Rochester; third; Rogers A. Ward (gas cutter, ME) and Pauline R. Collins (ME)
Shirley Jean, b. 8/28/1952 in Rochester; fourth; Rogers A. Ward (gas burner, ME) and Pauline R. Collins (ME)
Stacy Marline, b. 12/2/1968 in Rochester; William R. Ward (ME) and Marjorie M. Lirette (NH)
Telisha Marie, b. 3/8/1978 in Dover; William H. Ward and Vicki J. Small
Vickie Ann, b. 4/5/1953 in Rochester; second; Stephen R. Ward (truck driver, ME) and Dorothy A. Norman (NH)

Wendy, b. 12/27/1954 in Rochester; third; Steven R. Ward (carpenter, ME) and Dorothy A. Norman (NH)

WARREN,
son [George], b. 11/10/1896; first; Frank E. Warren (laborer, 30, So. Berwick, ME) and Belle Austin (23, Hudson)
Ann Lee, b. 6/26/1948 in Exeter; fourth; Richard Warren (poultry spec., Ithaca, NY) and Dorothy E. Brown (Winchendon, MA)
Derrick Matthew, b. 8/10/1982 in Portsmouth; Richard V. Warren, Jr. and Lori L. Dixon
Richard Randall, b. 3/5/1951 in Exeter; fourth; Richard Warren (NH Exten. Ser., NY) and Dorothy E. Brown (MA)

WATERHOUSE,
daughter, b. 6/3/1891; fourth; Charles F. Waterhouse (farmer, Barrington) and Laura J. Hill (Strafford)
stillborn son, b. 11/11/1895; fifth; C. F. Waterhouse (farmer, 36, Barrington) and Laura Hill (44, Strafford)
daughter, b. 3/5/1901; second; Arthur C. Waterhouse (farmer, 28, Barrington) and Mattie G. Young (23, Boston, MA)
daughter, b. 8/14/1904; first; J. H. Waterhouse (farmer, 29, Barrington) and Myra N. Gage (28, Hopkinton)
son [Maurice], b. 11/10/1906; third; Arthur C. Waterhouse (farmer, 33, Barrington) and Mattie E. Young (28, Boston, MA)
son [Merton A.], b. 10/10/1910; fourth; Arthur Waterhouse (farmer, 37, Barrington) and Mattie Young (32, Boston, MA)
Ann Leslie, b. 4/17/1955 in Exeter; fourth; Lester A. Waterhouse (truck driver, NH) and Barbara A. Brown (NH)

Carl Albert, b. 10/10/1946 in Exeter; second; Lester A.
Waterhouse (truck driver, Rochester) and Barbara A.
Brown (Dover)
Daniel Lester, b. 10/23/1970 in Rochester; Lester A.
Waterhouse (NH) and Barbara A. Brown (NH)
Eileen Mae, b. 1/22/1945; first; Lester A. Waterhouse (US
Army, Rochester) and Barbara A. Brown (Dover)
Gail Lynn, b. 2/3/1957 in Exeter; fifth; Lester A. Waterhouse
(truck driver, NH) and Barbara A. Brown (NH)
Lester D., b. 3/13/1900; first; Arthur C. Waterhouse
(blacksmith, 26, Barrington) and Mattie E. Young (22,
Boston, MA)
Stuart J., b. 11/14/1947 in Exeter; third; Lester A.
Waterhouse (truck driver, Rochester) and Barbara A.
Brown (Dover)

WATTERS,
John Michael, b. 6/26/1970 in Dover; Raymond J. Watters
(NH) and Linda L. Jenness (NH)

WEEDEN,
Brandie Lynn, b. 6/22/1984 in Dover; Albert S. Weeden and
Deborah L. Anderson
Lucas Steven, b. 3/14/1987 in Hanover; Albert S. Weeden
and Deborah L. Anderson

WEEKS,
daughter, b. 11/7/1891; first; Charles A. Weeks (grocer,
Dover) and Aline E. Hull (Unadilla, NY); residence -
Dover
Albion Locke, b. 11/10/1921; second; Albion G. Weeks
(farmer, Barrington) and Gertrude Locke (Barrington)
Brian Robert, Jr., b. 4/4/1973 in Rochester; Brian R. Weeks
(MA) and Elizabeth I. McCarthy (NY)
Dorothy, b. 10/25/1918; first; Albion G. Weeks (farmer,
Barrington) and Gertrude Locke (Barrington)

Lindsey Jane, b. 7/2/1987 in Dover; Brian J. Weeks and Janet L. Hill

Robert, b. 2/18/1927; third; Albion Weeks (farmer, Barrington) and Gertrude Locke (Barrington)

Stacey Ellen, b. 8/5/1981 in Rochester; Steven M. Weeks and Silvia R. Figueredo

Tia Renae, b. 3/24/1980 in Dover; Brian J. Weeks and Janet L. Hill

WEESNER,
Steven Conrad, b. 3/7/1967 in Dover; third; Theodore W. Weesner (writer-teacher, Flint, MI) and Sharon L. Long (Omaha, NE)

WEINER,
Bertha C., b. 3/1/1902; fifth; Thomas Weiner (carpenter, 38, Halifax, NS) and Maggie Beaton (31, Cape Breton, NS)

WEISS,
Sarah Catherine, b. 11/26/1984 in Portsmouth; David A. Weiss and Mary A. Vogel

WELCH,
Mason Michael, b. 4/13/1987 in Exeter; George M. Welch and Bethann Markiewicz

WELLS,
Anne, b. 1/25/1978 in Dover; Donald D. Wells and Mary K. Pattie

Donald Earl, b. 8/3/1938; first; Chester Earl Wells (truck driver, Northwood) and Elizabeth E. Brown (Barrington)

Joyce Ann, b. 12/13/1939; second; Chester E. Wells (truck driver, Northwood) and Betty E. Brown (Barrington)

Madeline Edla, b. 9/16/1938 in Rochester; first; George Edelbert Wells (shoe worker, Concord) and Lillian Bessie Stiles (Barrington)

WENTWORTH,
son, b. 7/16/1906; third; Charles A. Wentworth (farmer, butcher, 26, Dover) and Alice M. Sargent (25, Sanford, ME)
Norman Frederick, b. 5/10/1903; second; Charles A. Wentworth (farmer, 23, Dover) and Alice M. Sargent (22, Sanford, ME)
Ryan Keith, b. 4/6/1970 in Dover; Roy E. Wentworth (MA) and Janice M. Tarbox (MA)

WESCOTT,
daughter, b. 7/23/1921; third; Fred H. Wescott (laborer, Berwick, ME) and Bessie H. Smith (Nottingham)

WEST,
Amy Melissa, b. 2/24/1978 in Portsmouth; David F. West and Anne Carmichael
Eliot Warren, b. 2/10/1985 in Dover; Richard W. West and Joyce A. Mailhot
Jason Alan, b. 6/11/1981 in Portsmourh; David F. West and Anne Carmichael
Madison Troy, b. 6/19/1983 in Dover; Richard W. West and Joyce A. Mailhot

WHEELER,
Adam Daniel, b. 11/15/1983 in Rochester; Alan J. Wheeler and Karen S. Tarlton
Alan John, b. 2/28/1956 in Dover; second; Arthur J. Wheeler (truck driver, NH) and Adeline J. Norman (NH)
Angela Jean, b. 5/14/1979 in Rochester; Arthur J. Wheeler and Frances Ferraro
Bradley Allan, b. 1/22/1959 in Rochester; third; Maurice J. Wheeler (laborer, NH) and Barbara A. Levasseur (MA)
Brenda Ann, b. 1/28/1970 in Rochester; Maurice J. Wheeler (NH) and Barbara A. Levasseur (NH)

Cynthia Jean, b. 8/31/1954 in Rochester; first; Maurice J. Wheeler (roller, saw mill, NH) and Barbara A. Levasseur (MA)
Daniel John, b. 11/15/1980 in Dover; Alan J. Wheeler and Karen S. Tarlton
Jessica Lynn, b. 5/17/1982 in Dover; Alan J. Wheeler and Karen S. Tarlton
Kevin Scott, b. 8/2/1971 in Dover; Chester H. Wheeler, Jr. (NH) and Karen L. Morrill (ME)
Paula Marie, b. 11/17/1961 in Rochester; fourth; Maurice J. Wheeler (foreman, NH) and Barbara Ann Levasseur (MA)
Richard Maurice, b. 7/10/1956 in Rochester; second; Maurice J. Wheeler (lineman, NH) and Barbara A. Levasseur (MA)

WHITE,
Lisa Elizabeth, b. 5/10/1967 in Dover; third; Melvin C. White (food serv. dept., Greenfield) and Shirley E. Twombly (Berlin)
Michael Francis, b. 7/9/1985 in Rochester; Michael M. White and Janis D. Hubert

WHITEHOUSE,
daughter [Alice M.], b. 3/28/1890; second; John T. Whitehouse (laborer, Barrington) and Ida Brown (Barrington)
son [Andrew J.], b. 11/28/1891; third; John T. Whitehouse (laborer, Barrington) and Ida Brown (Barrington)
son [Herbert G.], b. 9/26/1893; fourth; J. Whitehouse (farmer, Barrington) and Ida Brown (Barrington)
daughter [Lottie B.], b. 4/11/1895; fifth; John Whitehouse (laborer, 30, Barrington) and Ida Brown (25, Barrington)
son [Clarence D.], b. 11/16/1898; seventh; John Whitehouse (laborer, Barrington) and Ida M. Brown (Barrington)

son [Merle], b. 8/14/1900; eighth; John Whitehouse (laborer, 37, Barrington) and Ida Brown (31, Barrington)
son [Jasper], b. 2/21/1904; ninth; John Whitehouse (laborer, 39, Barrington) and Ida Brown (34, Barrington)
stillborn daughter, b. 6/20/1911; tenth; John Whitehouse (farmer, 45, Barrington) and Ida M. Brown (42, Barrington)
Clyde Richard, b. 4/10/1954 in Exeter; fifth; Merle Whitehouse (farmer, NH) and Mary G. Groundry (MA)
Edna F., b. 12/13/1896; sixth; John Whitehouse (laborer, 32, Barrington) and Ida Brown (27, Barrington)
Robert Thomas, b. 12/14/1966 in Rochester; first; Robert E. Whitehouse (truck driver, Salem, MA) and Sharon L. Vittum (Rochester)
Russell Milton, b. 11/26/1955 in Rochester; sixth; Merle Whitehouse (junk dealer, NH) and Mary G. Goundry (NH)

WHITNEY,
Christine Michel, b. 7/25/1952 in Laconia; fifth; Howard A. Whitney (electrician, NH) and Irene Beard (MA)

WICKERS,
Rachel Lynn, b. 11/11/1987 in Dover; George E. Wickers and Cheryl A. Schneider

WICKLOW,
Cormac McKinley, b. 6/18/1985; Barry J. Wicklow and Patricia A. Snow

WIDHOLM,
Julie Taylor, b. 5/1/1983 in Exeter; Mark R. Widholm and Jill C. Taylor

WIGGIN,
son [Otto S.], b. 3/19/1899; fourth; George W. Wiggin (farmer, 47, Barrington) and Marcilla Verne (26, Salem, MA)
daughter, b. 5/2/1905; eighth; George Wiggin (farmer, 48, Barrington) and Marcella Verne (32, Salem, MA)
Edward Norman, b. 6/20/1936; second; Jasper R. Wiggin (painter, Barrington) and Frances M. Downing (Barrington)
Jasper R., b. 6/29/1900; fifth; George W. Wiggin (farmer, 49, Barrington) and Marcille Verne (27, Salem, MA)
Katherine, b. 12/8/1900; third; Elmer E. Wiggin (station agent, 39, Barrington) and Bertha M. Reynolds (29, Milton)
Leo Carlton, b. 8/31/1897; third; George Wiggin (farmer, 45, Barrington) and Marcelle Vern (25, Beverly, MA)
Morton Hayes, b. 11/6/1894; first; E. E. Wiggin (station agent, 33, Barrington) and Bertha M. Reynolds (23, Dover)
Myra Reynolds, stillborn, b. 6/15/1896; second; Elmer E. Wiggin (station agent, 34, Barrington) and Bertha M. Reynolds (24, Milton)
Pauline, b. 8/30/1909; third; Elmer E. Wiggin (station agent, 48, Barrington) and Bertha M. Reynolds (38, Milton)
Robert Lawrence, b. 5/26/1934 in Rochester; first; Jasper Wiggin (mill worker, Barrington) and Frances Fanning (Barrington)
Ruby May, b. 5/5/1902; sixth; George Wiggin (farmer, 51, Barrington) and Marcella Verne (30, Beverly, MA)
Ruth F., b. 2/10/1912; third; William E. Wiggin (laborer, 25, Lee) and Elizabeth McIntire (25, Lebanon, ME)
Viola Auleta, b. 3/20/1896; second; George W. Wiggin (farmer, 44, Barrington) and Marcelia Vorn (24, Barrington)

WILCOX,
Lisa Jean, b. 8/5/1976 in Portsmouth; James A. Wilcox and Lynne M. Surprenant

WILKINS,
Dennis Frank, b. 5/11/1964 in Rochester; third; Robert R. Wilkins (shoe worker, NH) and Patricia B. Walker (NH)

WILLEY,
son, b. 1/31/1904; first; George H. Willey (engineer, 23, Biddeford, ME) and Jennie Q. Ham (19, Salem, MA)

WILLIAMSON,
Christian Wade, b. 12/16/1967 in Exeter; second; Murray R. Williamson (MA) and Gail E. Haley (ME)

WILSON,
Amy Elizabeth, b. 1/18/1985 in Dover; Scott D. Wilson and Janet E. Owens
Emery Russ, b. 4/9/1974 in Dover; Warren James Wilson and Jennifer Ellen Russ
Mark Samuel, b. 7/14/1967 in Dover; first; Howard T. Wilson (assembly worker, Dade City, FL) and Karen E. Pigeon (Dover)
Wesley James, b. 11/19/1971 in Dover; Warren J. Wilson (NY) and Jennifer E. Russ (NY)

WINKLEY,
son [Ernest], b. 4/21/1896; second; Leroy A. Winkley (laborer, 27, Strafford) and Jennie H. Gray (20, Barrington)
Willard C., b. 6/1/1885; John L. Winkley (Barrington) and Sarah Ellen Young or Ellen S. Young (Barrington) (1944)

WITT,
Michelle Lee, b. 8/18/1977 in Portsmouth; Richard T. Witt and Bonnie L. Hall

WOJTYSIAK,
Anthony William, Jr., b. 4/7/1984 in Rochester; Anthony W. Wojtysiak and Lisa J. Lesperance

WOLF,
Brian Edward, b. 5/31/1977 in Rochester; Richard L. Wolf and Cheryl M. Smith
Heather Marie, b. 2/4/1975 in Rochester; Richard L. Wolf and Cheryl M. Smith
Richard Leo, Jr., b. 11/25/1971 in Rochester; Richard L. Wolf (IL) and Cheryl M. Smith (NH)

WOOD,
Kelly Marie, b. 8/8/1979 in Dover; Peter S. Wood, Sr. and Diane L. Purington
Maud Emily, b. 4/5/1877; third; Hiram H. Wood (farmer, Boston, MA) and Lydia S. Ham (Dover) (1942)

WOODMAN,
son [Lawrence], b. 6/2/1890; second; George E. Woodman (farmer, Strafford) and Clista Chesley (Barrington)

WOODS,
stillborn son, b. 9/27/1922; fifth; Jacob Woods (carpenter, Canada) and Mary Bishop (Canada)
son, b. 10/13/1937 in Rochester; William J. Woods (farmer, Glasgow, Scotland) and Edith M. Adair
Eunice Arline, b. 4/13/1913; first; Joseph D. Woods (laborer, 20, Somersworth) and Florence M. White (19, Barrington)

George Henry, b. 5/16/1921; sixth; Charles Wood (sic) (woodchopper, So. Berwick, ME) and Lucy Hall (Rochester)

Lawrence J., b. 8/2/1914; second; Joseph D. Woods (shoemaker, Somersworth) and Florence M. White (Barrington)

Leo, b. 7/22/1917; second; Wilfred L. Woods (laborer, Rochester) and Viola A. Wiggin (Barrington)

Margaret E., b. 12/17/1918; fifth; Charles J. Woods (laborer, So. Berwick, ME) and Lucy Hall (Rochester)

Virginia May, b. 5/21/1915; first; Wilfred L. Woods (laborer, Rochester) and Viola A. Wiggin (Barrington)

William, b. 6/24/1917; fourth; Charles James Woods (laborer, So. Berwick, ME) and Lucy M. Hall (Rochester)

WOODWORTH,
Sandra Jean, b. 4/28/1977 in Rochester; Daryl T. Woodworth and Gail P. Bowman

WORMELL,
Stephen Brian, b. 4/28/1955 in Dover; fourth; John P. Wormell (TV service, NH) and Ruth E. Tinker (NH)

WORMHOOD,
Nancy Irene, b. 8/21/1945 in Rochester; first; Leman Wormhood, Jr. (laborer, Rochester) and Norah G. Chapman (Dover)

WROBEL,
Timothy Charles, b. 3/15/1964 in Rochester; second; Anthony W. Wrobel (computer eng., CT) and Evelyn M. Greene (GA)

WRONSKI,
Samuel Loudon, b. 9/5/1980 in Exeter; Jeffrey R. Wronski and Vida Loudon

WYATT,
Barbara T., b. 4/3/1918; first; Ralph E. Wyatt (farmer, Farmington) and Ellen E. Thompson (Barrington); residence - Farmington
Clarence T., b. 1/21/1921; third; Ralph F. Wyatt (farmer, Farmington) and Ellen E. Thompson (Barrington); residence - Farmington

YEATON,
Robert Laurent, b. 12/19/1983 in Rochester; Michael J. Yeaton and Lise-Marie C. Descoteaux

YORK,
Amy M., b. 6/28/1983 in Rochester; George K. York and Sally L. Musler
Cora Bell, b. 2/26/1905; first; William York (laborer, 38, Pittsfield) and Mary York (28, Canada)
James Arthur, b. 4/23/1980 in Rochester; George K. York and Sally L. Musler

YOUNG,
son, b. 4/14/1903; first; Lendel A. Young (teamster, 23, Scituate, MA) and Ella Drew (15, Boston, MA)
Anthony Nelson, b. 11/11/1984 in Dover; Ralph N. Young, Jr. and Michele L. Garland
Ethel, b. 9/18/1890; first; David Young (blacksmith, Barrington) and Mary Calligan (No. Hanover, MA)
Fred L., b. 5/15/1892; Jeremiah K. Young (Barrington) and Fannie Locke (Dover) (1942)
George Everett, b. 10/15/1932; fourth; Ivory Young (truck driver, Barrington) and Nancy Brock (Pittsfield)
Mertie Ethel, b. 2/28/1884; Jeremiah K. Young (Barrington) and Fannie A. Locke (Dover) (1942)
Roberta Elaine, b. 5/25/1949 in Dover; fourth; Kenneth F. Young (cross dopher, ME) and Elizabeth O'Neil (NH)

Scott Michael, b. 10/3/1985 in Manchester; Scott L. Young and Grace K. Porter

ZAMPA,
Anthony William, b. 2/15/1962 in Rochester; third; Gino P. Zampa (mechanic, NY) and Claire J. Johnston (NY)

ZANES,
Daniel Edgerly, b. 11/8/1961 in Exeter; first; John P. Zanes (student, NH) and Elizabeth H. Nichols (MA)

ZELIE,
Mary Helen, b. 10/19/1985 in Rochester; David A. Zelie and Susan Brand

ZIELFELDER,
Kelsey Margaret, b. 5/7/1987 in Dover; Ross M. Zielfelder and Sharon L. Evans
Ronald James, Jr., b. 1/3/1971 in Dover; Ronald J. Zielfelder, Sr. (MA) and Suzanne M. Comtois (NH)
Timothy Ross, b. 7/26/1976 in Portsmouth; Ross M. Zielfelder and Dianne M. Fogg
Toby Philip, b. 6/11/1974 in Dover; Ronald James Zielfelder and Suzanne Marie Comtois
Tonia Charlene, b. 3/30/1971 in Rochester; Robert C. Zielfelder (MA) and Wava M. Braman (WA)

FATHER'S NAME OMITTED,
child, b. 12/10/1966; father (foreman rubber ind., Lansing, MI) and Charlynn M. Constantine (Milford, CT)
child, b. 3/4/1981, "Not published per request of parents"

ACETO,
Charles J. of Barrington m. Lynne D. **Danforth** of Barrington 2/16/1985

ADAMS,
John J. of MA m. Christine A. **Hanley** of MA 9/19/1984

AGNEW,
James D., II of TX m. Jacqueline E. **Powell** of Barrington 2/1/1984

AIKEN,
Richard R. of Rochester m. Kathleen A. **Tanguay** of Barrington 12/19/1981

ALCOTT,
James R. of Barrington m. Darlene L. **Nolf** of Barrington 1/30/1981

ALDRICH,
James S. of Dover m. Helen E. **Smith** of Barrington 9/15/1956 in Dover; H - 32, journalist, b. NH, s/o A. J. Aldrich (VT) and Jessie Welsh (NH); W - 20, waitress, b. Panama Canal Zone, d/o Thomas D. Flynn and Barbara Morris (WA)
Paul R. of Eliot, ME m. Jean K. **Downs** of Barrington 6/21/1986 in Northwood

ALLAIN,
David J. of Barrington m. Elizabeth G. **Feuer** of Barrington 6/26/1982

ALLARD,
John M. of Barrington m. Marlene R. **MacGown** of Barrington 10/13/1979 in Amesbury, MA

William Jeffrey of Durham m. Elizabeth Mary **Baird** of Barrington 5/24/1975 in Littleton

ALLEN,
James W., Jr. of RI m. Sylvia M. **Evans** of Barrington 4/26/1984 in Middleton
Michael E. of Barrington m. Helen M. **Delude** of Barrington 12/26/1981 in East Rochester

ALLERSON,
Walter S. of Barrington m. Altie E. **Glover** of Barrington 10/30/1907; H - 37, fireman, b. Barrington, s/o Frank Allerson (Barrington, teamster) and Georgianna Emerson (Madbury); W - 20, at home, b. Barrington, d/o Woodbury Glover (Nottingham, teamster) and Ida Leathers (Nottingham)

ALTMAN,
Jack E. of Barrington m. Cathie V. **Cook** of Barrington 10/11/1986

AMBROSE,
Frank E. of Barrington m. Lillian S. **Schuman** of Barrington 4/4/1957; H - 60, farmer, 2d, b. MA, s/o Albion N. Ambrose (NH) and Susie F. Coburn (MA); W - 70, at home, 3rd, b. NH, d/o Joseph F. Lingard (NH) and Sarah A. Hall (NH)

AMERO,
John V. of Rochester m. Madlyn P. **Ross** of Barrington 6/26/1982

AMES,
David C. of Barrington m. Diane J. **Pratt** of Barrington 10/6/1979 in Durham

ANDERSEN,
James W. of Barrington m. Cindy L. **Dodge** of Barrington 7/2/1983 in Strafford

ANDERSON,
Albert J. of Manchester, CT m. Betty A. **Harding** of Barrington 6/21/1958; H - 28, lathe oper., b. NY, s/o Alf G. Anderson (Norway) and Johanna Swenson (NY); W - 24, mica worker, b. NH, d/o Walter M. Harding (MA) and Cora E. Tebbets (NH)
Dana H. of Barrington m. Vickie L. **Clark** of Gretna, LA 12/29/1979
Kenneth P. of Barrington m. Ann A. **Cheverie** of Kittery, ME 9/27/1986 in Wolfeboro
Thomas F. of Barrington m. Sally J. **Perez** of Barrington 7/9/1986

ANDRADE,
Mark G. of Barrington m. Heather C. **Lewis** of Belmont 8/22/1987 in Nashua

ANDRUSKIEWICZ,
Joseph M. of Barrington m. Marjorie E. **Wharmby** of Lee 6/12/1976 in Durham

ANGEVIN,
Richard E. of Concord m. Miriam I. **Buzzell** of Barrington 7/1/1943; H - 24, Coast Guard, b. Concord, s/o William J. Angevin (Concord) and Marjorie Douglas (Bethlehem, VT); W - 24, armature opr., b. Dover, d/o Maurice T. Buzzell (Lee) and Laura C. Edney (Colorado Springs, CO)

ANGUS,
Henry H. of Boston, MA m. Eva Mae **Egell** of Boston, MA 6/29/1946; H - 59, carpenter, b. Norfolk, MA, s/o James

H. Angus (NS) and Annie S. MacDonald (PEI); W - 58, waitress, 2d, b. Revere, MA, d/o Gideon C. Porter (NS) and Charlotte Sylvester (Revere, MA)

ARKERSON,
Gary L. of Barrington m. Judith E. **Lee** of Barrington 9/1/1978

ARKWELL,
Gary H. of Barrington m. Donna L. **Lyons** of Rochester 7/4/1981 in Rochester

ARLIN,
Austin H. of Barrington m. Nellie **Holbrook** of Barrington 4/8/1895; H - 27, laborer, b. Barrington, s/o Daniel (Barrington, laborer) and Laura (Barrington); W - 31, housemaid, b. Galveston, TX, d/o William Hughes and Mary

Frank H. of Barrington m. Emma **Stone** of Barrington 7/18/1925 in Gonic; H - 43, farmer, b. Barrington, s/o Daniel W. Arlin (Barrington, farmer) and Larosa Esters (Barrington, housewife); W - 33, store clerk, b. Barrington, d/o Fred L. Stone (Manchester, farmer) and Lou Bernier (Canada, housewife)

George A. of Barrington m. Delia **Hart** of Barrington 5/4/1895; H - 28, laborer, b. Barrington, s/o William and Jane; W - 20, housemaid, b. Van Buren, ME, d/o Frank and Annie

James C. of Barrington m. Neva J. **Brown** of Barrington 3/23/1897 in Strafford; H - 21, farmer, b. Barrington, s/o Daniel (Barrington, farmer) and Laura (Rochester, housewife); W - 24, domestic, b. Barrington, d/o Jared (Strafford, farmer) and Sarah (housewife)

John W. of Barrington m. Melissa J. **Evans** of Barrington 12/25/1899; H - 44, laborer, 2d, b. Barrington, s/o John (deceased) and Hannah; W - 42, domestic, 2d, b. Strafford

Leslie C. of Barrington m. Amy R. **Brown** of Barrington 7/14/1923; H - 26, farmer, b. Barrington, s/o Eli Arlin (Barrington, farmer) and Ida Leighton (Strafford, housewife); W - 19, at home, b. Barrington, d/o William Brown (Barrington, farmer) and Sarah Reed (Barrington, housewife)

Lorenzo D. of Barrington m. Ida **Whitehouse** of Barrington 5/16/1896; H - 37, farmer, b. Barrington, s/o William and Jane; W - 21, housewife, b. Barrington, d/o Lenod and Eliza (Strafford)

Neil W. of Barrington m. Ardys J. **Jacobs** of Rochester 9/22/1962; H - 22, US Army, b. NH, s/o Norman W. Arlin (NH) and Dorothy H. Gibb (NH); W - 20, student, b. NH, d/o John A. Jacobs (NH) and Lucille Cater (NH)

Norman W. of Rochester m. Dorothy H. **Gibb** of Barrington 11/4/1935 in Rochester; H - 22, mechanic, b. Dover, s/o Norman W. Arlin (Steep Falls, ME) and Jessie F. Sanborn (Somersworth); W - 22, teacher, b. Atkinson, d/o Oscar E. Gibb (Orleans, VT) and Nellie M. Jones (Lyndonville, VT)

ARLING,
John of Hampstead m. Faithe Sharon **Hallows** of Barrington 7/18/1976 in Hampstead

ARNOLD,
Ralph W. of Dover m. Vira E. **Neal** of Barrington 3/22/1947 in Rochester; H - 41, shoe cutter, 2d, b. So. Brunswick, ME, s/o S. V. Arnold (NS) and Sharron Godfrey (NS); W - 37, shoe shop, b. Barrington, d/o Edwin C. Neal (Voluntown, CT) and Myra Hanson (Strafford)

ARSENAULT,
George of Rochester m. Cecelia F. **Tuck** of Barrington 10/4/1969 in Dover; H - b. 6/1/1945 in Canada, s/o George Arsenault, Sr. (Canada) and Cherubine Dedam

(Canada); W - b. 3/5/1951 in NH, d/o Gordon C. Tuck
(MA) and Rose M.B. Beriault (Canada)

ASHBURNER,
Steven J. of Barrington m. Tina M. **Colbath** of Barrington 3/27/1986

ATWOOD,
Brian J. of Barrington m. Terri L. **Ford** of Rochester 12/12/1981 in Rochester
Richard S. of Plymouth m. Edith V. **Hoey** of Barrington 3/18/1973 in Plymouth; H - 2d, b. 4/15/1914 in MA, s/o Carl W. Atwood (MA) and Marianne Stearns (MA); W - 2d, b. 4/19/1929 in MA, s/o Albert N. Crosby (MA) and Edith M. MacArthur (MA)
William of Barrington m. Florence **Talbott** of Boston, MA 11/25/1925; H - 62, farmer, 3rd, b. Middleton, MA, s/o Morrison Atwood (Thornton, wheelwright) and Mary Fairfield (Salem, MA, housewife); W - 65, at home, 2d, b. Shuyler Falls, NY, d/o William Otis (Shuyler Falls, farmer) and Lovina Garlick (Shuyler Falls, housewife)
William W. of Barrington m. Pamela A. **Moody** of Rochester 11/11/1983 in Rochester

AUCELLA,
Paul A. of Barrington m. Mary A. **Leighton** of Barrington 9/19/1987 in Strafford

AUSTIN,
Burton J. of Barrington m. Lula V. **Welch** of Exeter 9/8/1946 in Strafford; H - 23, truck driver, b. Bristol, s/o George Austin (Dover) and Amy Caldon (Plymouth); W - 20, at home, b. Exeter, d/o Worth D. Welch (O'Brien, FL) and Wilhelmina Brienn (Exeter)
Donald B. of Barrington m. Patricia A. **Schnelle** of Exeter 10/18/1958 in Exeter; H - 23, retreader, b. NH, s/o

Ugene Austin (NH) and Ida R. Charest (NH); W - 18, clerk, b. VA, d/o Earl Schnelle (VA) and Edna Gamble (VA)

AVERY,
Alan R. of Barrington m. Kimberly A. **Hinkefente** of Barrington 11/29/1985

AYERS,
John F. of Barrington m. Mary L. **Tibbetts** of Dover 6/30/1903 in Madbury; H - 47, farmer, b. Barrington, s/o Joseph Ayers (Barrington, farmer) and Mary Henderson (Barrington); W - 40, dressmaker, b. Dover, d/o Fred B. Tibbetts (Dover) and Caroline Lafevor (Dover)

AYVAZ,
Steven L. of Barrington m. Tammy H. **Hartford** of Barrington 6/2/1984 in Dover

BABB,
Frank H. of Barrington m. Esther J. **Libbey** of Barrington 12/24/1903; H - 41, farmer, b. Barrington, s/o Joseph T. Babb (Barrington, farmer) and Abigail Kimball (Strafford); W - 19, at home, b. Dover, d/o Reuben A. Libbey (Wolfeboro, farmer) and Ella Davis (England)

BAER,
Brian D. of Raymond m. Michelle A. **Willett** of Barrington 4/24/1982

BAILEY,
Earl D. of Barrington m. Martha L. **Faist** of Barrington 8/1/1953; H - 20, farm worker, b. NH, s/o Raymond E. Bailey (MA) and Charlotte E. Goff (MA); W - 17, secretary, b. NH, d/o Walter H. Faist (MA) and Frances L. Ball (Canada)

John W. of Barrington m. Martha W. **Moulton** of Newmarket 3/10/1897 in Newmarket; H - farmer; W - domestic

John W., Jr. of Barrington m. Dora **Warren** of Barrington 12/28/1892; H - 42, shoemaker, b. Haverhill, s/o John W. and Susan; W - 26, housekeeper, b. Chester, d/o George W. and Sarah

Raymond E., Jr. of Barrington m. Edith T. **Norris** of Portsmouth 2/26/1955 in Portsmouth; H - 23, truck driver, b. NH, s/o Raymond E. Bailey (MA) and Charlotte E. Goff (MA); W - 19, hairdresser, b. NH, d/o Freeman E. Norris (NH) and Edith B. Taylor (NH)

BAKER,
Alan L. of Barrington m. Ailsa G. **Bernell** of Barrington 12/15/1983

BALDWIN,
Melvin K. of Barrington m. Barbara A. **Kwok** of Barrington 1/1/1979

BALFANY,
Gregory J. of Barrington m. Martha **Blood** of Portsmouth 12/16/1978 in Durham

BALL,
Leon J. of Bellows Falls, VT m. Ethel Maude **Decatur** of Barrington 6/16/1904; H - 28, clerk, b. Athens, VT, s/o Joseph R. Ball (Athens, VT, manufacturer) and Augusta S. Bowles (Bethlehem); W - 25, stenographer, b. Rochester, d/o Frank I. Decatur (Barrington, merchant) and Nellie S. Hall (Barrington)

BARBIN,
Daniel J. of Barrington m. Jean L. **Cadorette** of Barrington 10/24/1987 in Rochester

BARCHAND,
Clifton W. of Malden, MA m. Teri A. **Smith** of Malden, MA 7/25/1987

BARDEN,
Brian M. of Keene m. Jean E. **Baxter** of Barrington 6/29/1968; H - b. 10/26/1941 in NH, s/o Charles D. Barden (NH) and Lois P. Mitchell (NH); W - b. 11/19/1945 in NH, d/o Alden E. Baxter (NH) and Geraldine E. Swain (NH)

BARISH,
Abraham of Portsmouth m. Marion A. **Flynn** of Barrington 4/25/1937; H - 52, salesman, b. Russia, s/o Joseph Barish (Russia) and Sarah Levine (Russia); W - 38, at home, 2d, b. Boston, MA, d/o Patrick Flynn (Ireland) and Mary Dunn (Ireland)

BARKER,
Fred R. of Johnston, RI m. Eleanor M. **Ford** of Middleboro, MA 9/28/1957; H - 23, surveyor, b. ME, s/o Fred R. Barker (ME) and Marda I. Lougee (ME); W - 18, at home, b. MA, d/o Arthur L.D. Ford (NH) and Jean P. Corey (MA)

BARNABY,
Roland T. of Hampton m. Ina H. **Taylor** of Barrington 5/11/1940; H - 27, mason, b. Greenland, s/o Lewis A. Barnaby (deceased) and Charlotte Thompson (England); W - 20, waitress, b. Revere, MA, d/o H. Fielding Taylor (Newfoundland) and Emily Rowe (deceased)

BARNES,
Robert O. of Barrington m. Denise M. **Bessette** of Barrington 8/17/1985 in Dover

Ronald E. of Rochester m. Mary L. **Cook** of Barrington 12/17/1958 in Gonic; H - 24, shoe worker, b. NH, s/o Robert E. Barnes (NH) and Jeanne I. Drouin (ME); W - 18, waitress, b. NH, d/o John W. Cook (NH) and Louise Duesine (MA)

BARRETT,
Raymond L. of Barrington m. Mary E. **McEvoy** of Nashua 2/1/1969 in Nashua; H - b. 11/20/1943 in NH, s/o Leslie Barrett (ME) and Florence Chadwick (ME); W - b. 4/18/1947 in NH, d/o Weston McEvoy (NH) and Edith Holt (NH)

BARRY,
Donald Wayne of Barrington m. Kathleen Elizabeth **Klucik** of Portsmouth 7/22/1976 in Newington

BARTELS,
Wellington P., Jr. of Barrington m. Merl L. **Seavey** of Northwood 10/7/1942 in Center Strafford; H - 18, truck driver, b. Boston, MA, s/o Wellington P. Bartels (Boston, MA) and Idlene M. Streeter (Boston, MA); W - 18, housemaid, b. Northwood, d/o Ralph C. Seavey (Northwood) and Grace M. Atkins (Northwood)
Wellington P., III of Barrington m. Gloria A. **Witham** of East Rochester 6/11/1962; H - 38, US Army, 2d, b. MA, s/o Wellington P. Bartels, Sr. (MA) and Ideline M. Streeter (TN); W - 30, assembly wkr., 2d, b. NH, d/o Albert M. Witham (NH) and Marguerite A. Ball (Canada)
Wellington P., III of Barrington m. Sally L. **Avery** of Pittsfield 7/10/1964; H - 21, lab. tech., b. NH, s/o Wellington P. Bartels, Jr. (MA) and Merl L. Seavey (NH); W - 18, clerk-typist, b. NH, d/o Nolan Avery (NH) and Naomi R. Mitchell (NH)

BARTLETT,
Gary F. of Dover m. Marie M. **Gitschier** of Barrington 1/22/1983 in Dover
George A., Jr. of Northwood m. Joyce **Bigelow** of Barrington 12/24/1954; H - 25, auditor, b. ME, s/o George A. Bartlett (NH) and Nellie C. Mason (NH); W - 18, student, b. MA, d/o Victor L. Bigelow (MA) and Bernice E. Ramsdell (ME)
Steven A. of Kingston m. Vicki-Lynn **Brewer** of Barrington 7/26/1986 in Kingston

BASCOM,
Kevin T. of Nottingham m. Diana J. **Glidden** of Barrington 6/11/1977 in Dover

BASSETT,
Russell E. of Barrington m. Ann M. **Zerbinopoulos** of Barrington 5/17/1986 in Dover

BATCHELDER,
Bradford P., Jr. of Nottingham m. Betty C. **Bailey** of Barrington 6/9/1956; H - 27, engineer, b. NH, s/o Bradford P. Batchelder (NH) and Liza Berg (Sweden); W - 20, hair dresser, b. NH, d/o Raymond E. Bailey (MA) and Charlotte E. Goff (MA)

BAUD,
Richard Paul of Farmington m. Debra Lee **Zampa** of Barrington 2/2/1974

BAXTER,
Alden E. of Barrington m. Geraldine E. **Swain** of Dover 9/4/1937; H - 22, farmer, b. Madbury, s/o Nahum Baxter (Wolfeboro) and Alta Mattox (Lee); W - 19, at home, b. Barrington, d/o William Swain (Barrington) and Mary Sanders (Madbury)

Alfred W. of Barrington m. Evelyn M. **Kitchens** of Newington 11/22/1952 in Dover; H - 42, truck driver, 2d, b. NH, s/o Nahum W. Baxter (NH) and Alta M. Mattox (NH); W - 44, cook, 3rd, b. ME, d/o Ransom Nason (ME) and Luella Cameron (ME)

John Allen of Barrington m. Lori Jeanne **Gray** of Barrington 9/19/1975 in Rochester

Sherman L. of Barrington m. Luverne C. **Swain** of Barrington 10/6/1945; H - 26, veteran, b. Barrington, s/o Nahum W. Baxter (Wolfeboro) and Alta M. Mattox (Lee); W - 24, at home, b. Barrington, d/o William S. Swain (Barrington) and Mary E. Sanders (Madbury)

BEACH,
Kenneth of Barrington m. Martha **Whitney** of Rochester 10/8/1928 in Dover; H - 22, mechanic, b. Rochester, s/o Frank E. Beach (carpenter) and Daisey D. Heeney (domestic); W - 26, nurse, b. Wilton, d/o James E. Whitney (farmer) and Mary Purcell (domestic)

BEARD,
John W. of Little Rock, AR m. Gloria J. **Bonser** of Barrington 7/24/1964; H - 20, member US Navy, b. AR, s/o Carl W. Beard (AR) and Lula Woodall (AR); W - 18, rubber industry worker, b. NH, d/o Elmer D. Bonser (NH) and Jeannette A. Maxfield (NH)

BEAUDONA,
Raymond A., Jr. of Rochester m. Grace L. **Johnson** of Barrington 7/27/1950 in No. Berwick, ME; H - 24, b. NH; W - 18, b. NH

BEAUREGARD,
William E. of Manchester m. Jennie **Mitchell** of Manchester 10/1/1930; H - 45, chauffeur, b. Canada, s/o Charles Beauregard (carpenter) and Jennie L. Burke

(housewife); W - 41, housekeeper, b. Andover, d/o George E. Mitchell (caretaker) and Emma Rowe (housewife)

BEDARD,
Maurice J. of Rochester m. Gladys M. **Smith** of Barrington 9/18/1982 in Rochester

BEDFORD,
Thomas A. of Barrington m. Carolyn B. **Dehls** of Bridgewater 8/25/1973 in Concord; H - b. 7/21/1952 in VT, s/o Clay P. Bedford (NY) and Carolyn Stevenson (NH); W - b. 12/16/1953 in NH, d/o Alan W. Dehls (NJ) and Virginia Ely (NJ)

BELANGER,
Ronald A. of West Lebanon, ME m. Margaret L. **Heath** of Barrington 7/28/1979 in Farmington

BELL,
Norman B. of Dover m. Madeline E. **Wells** of Barrington 6/4/1966; H - 19, repairman, b. Rochester, s/o Byron F. Bell (NH) and Ethel L. Nason (ME); W - 27, instructor, b. Rochester, d/o George A. Wells (NH) and Lillian B. Stiles (NH)

BELLEVILLE,
Ernest L. of Rochester m. Nancy A. **Mazur** of Barrington 8/28/1965; H - 19, shoe worker, b. NH, s/o Ernest L. Belleville (NH) and Juliette Letourneau (NH); W - 19, secretary, b. NH, d/o Adam Mazur (NY) and Clara E. Hull (ME)

BELLUCCI,
Stephen M. of Dover m. JoAnne J. **Gero** of Barrington 8/1/1981

BELVILLE,
Walter H. of Barrington m. Estelle V. **Grenier** of East Rochester 11/11/1937 in East Rochester; H - 26, mch. operator, 2d, b. Pittsfield, s/o Fred H. Belville (Rumney) and Flora Hannah (Laconia); W - 28, shoe worker, b. East Rochester, d/o Wilfred Grenier (Canada) and Bertha McCrilles (East Rochester)

BENGSTON,
Richard C. of Northwood m. Marian L. **Neal** of Barrington 10/2/1965; H - 30, tool & die maker, b. CT, s/o Carl R. Bengston (CT) and Helen M. Spencer (CT); W - 24, housewife, 2d, b. NH, d/o Melvin F. Bryson (NH) and Evelyn M. Green (NH)

BENNETT,
Joseph A. of Barrington m. Sally C. **Pelletier** of Barrington 8/4/1962; H - 23, dairyman, b. WV, s/o Calvin Bennett (WV) and Roxie R. Sheaves (WV); W - 16, student, b. IL, d/o Lawrence V. Pelletier (NY) and Catherine Mariotti (NH)

BENSON,
Fred W. of Malden, MA m. Mary K. **Fletcher** of No. Weymouth, MA 12/30/1950; H - 20, Marine, b. MA, s/o Joseph W. Benson (MA) and Rozilla Cushing (MA); W - 23, waitress, 2d, b. MN, d/o Chauncey Brockway (MN) and Katherine Merkl (MN)

BERG,
Hakon H. of Barrington m. Diane E. **Dean** of Barrington 9/24/1982

BERGERON,
Gerard L. of Rochester m. Dawn M. **Seaver** of Barrington 11/10/1985 in Durham

BERKY,
   Timothy J. of Barrington m. Diane B. **Apt** of Portsmouth 4/20/1985 in Portsmouth

BERNIER,
   Alfred of Barrington m. Amelia **Clements** of Clinton 7/23/1900; H - 24, laborer, b. Montreal, s/o Joseph (Canada, farmer) and Filiman; W - 21, mill hand, b. Clinton, d/o John (Canada, carpenter) and Mary
   Earle W. of Rochester m. Charlene M. **Atkinson** of Rochester 6/21/1980

BERRY,
   Alvin T. of Barrington m. Mary A. **Hughes** of Strafford 9/16/1894; H - 19, farmer, b. Barrington, s/o D. R. (Barrington, farmer) and Elizabeth (Barrington); W - 22, housekeeper, b. Barrington
   Clarence L. of Barrington m. Edith M. **Twombly** of Barrington 6/17/1933 in Strafford Corners; H - 28, farmer, b. Barrington, s/o Lewis C. Berry (Barrington) and Sara Perkins (Barrington); W - 29, housewife, 3rd, b. Wolfeboro, d/o Fred King (Canada) and Emma Paugutt (Salmon Falls)
   David A. of Barrington m. Sylvia Ann **Lyons** of Manchester 4/16/1955 in Manchester; H - 23, US Army, b. NH, s/o Norman J. Berry (NH) and Dorothy F. Burpee (NH); W - 20, nurse, b. NH, d/o Clarence H. Lyons (NH) and Angie L. Watts (NH)
   Elmer of Barrington m. Laura **Corson** of Barrington 5/2/1892; H - 28, farmer, b. Strafford, s/o James and Louise; W - 19, housemaid, b. Barrington, d/o Oscar and Ann
   Flavius J. of Barrington m. Nellie E. N. **Glidden** of Barrington 12/25/1899; H - 40, lumberman, b. Barrington, s/o Jonathan (Barrington, lumberman) and Mary (Barrington); W - 28, teacher, b. Lee, d/o James (Durham, deceased) and Elizabeth (Lee)

Lewis C. of Barrington m. Sadie J. **Perkins** of Barrington 10/14/1895; H - 26, laborer, b. Barrington, s/o Daniel (Barrington, farmer) and Elizabeth; W - 17, at home, b. Barrington, d/o Charles (Barrington, laborer) and Ersilla

Louis C. of Barrington m. Mary A. **Hanscom** of Barrington 11/11/1891; H - 22, b. Barrington, s/o Daniel R. and Elizabeth; W - 16, b. Barrington, d/o Nathan and Eliza

Norman J. of Barrington m. Dorothy **Burpee** of Exeter 6/22/1928; H - 25, farmer, b. Barrington, s/o Flavius J. Berry (farmer) and Nellie Glidden (domestic); W - 22, teacher, b. Exeter, d/o Leroy B. Burpee (postal clerk) and Belle Tuck (domestic)

Norman J., Jr. of Barrington m. Patricia M. **Cortez** of Durham 3/28/1953 in Durham; H - 23, US Army, b. NH, s/o Norman J. Berry (NH) and Dorothy Burpee (NH); W - 21, student, b. NH, d/o Edmund A. Cortez (PA) and Evelyn E. Willis (ME)

BICKFORD,

Andrew of Dover m. Lizzie **Perkins** of Barrington 7/11/1896; H - 21, mechanic, b. Fryeburg, ME, s/o Henry (Dover, mechanic) and Ida (Ossipee); W - 21, domestic, b. Barrington, d/o Charles (Barrington, laborer) and Ersilla (Barrington)

Carl Albert of Dover m. Lois Elaine **Brown** of Barrington 6/15/1974

BICKNELL,

Lee R. of Durham m. Sarah A. **Poirier** of Barrington 5/5/1984 in Rye

BIGONIA,

Allan R. of Barrington m. Susan B. **Reuell** of Lee 3/24/1973 in Lee; H - b. 9/30/1948 in WI, s/o John F. Bigonia (WI) and Darlene Eichorn (WI); W - b. 4/23/1945 in MA, d/o William L. Reuell (MA) and Helen Warren (MA)

BILLS,
William C. of Barrington m. Lizzie A. **Canney** of Barrington 11/4/1890; H - 40, b. NY; W - 24, b. Barrington

BILODEAU,
Arthur A. of Rochester m. Barbara A. **Felong** of Barrington 7/2/1983 in Dover

BIOTEAU,
Francois Gilbert of Barrington m. Cynthia Ann **Brown** of Exeter 6/29/1974 in Exeter

BIRT,
James M. of Portsmouth m. Rebecca H. **Buzzell** of Barrington 9/29/1984

BISCHOFF,
James A. of Barrington m. Laurette P. **Gagnon** of Barrington 5/4/1985

BISHOP,
Daniel M. of Seattle, WA m. Mary E. **Menten** of Barrington 7/6/1957 in Dover; H - 27, forester, b. WA, s/o Ned Bishop (MO) and Hilder Swanson (WA); W - 26, home ec., b. IL, d/o Thomas H. Menten (MO) and Gladys E. Keller (IL)
Roger C. of Mountain View, WY m. Virginia N. **Ramsdell** of Barrington 10/18/1969; H - b. 10/23/1945 in WY, s/o Cecil L. Bishop (WY) and Mabel R. Spracklen (WY); W - b. 2/21/1948 in NH, d/o Frederick M. Ramsdell (MA) and Annie N. Taylor (MA)

BISSON,
Sylvain J. of Rochester m. Kim L. **Landry** of Barrington 10/25/1980

BLAIR,
Theodore W., Jr. of Rochester m. Judith A. **Mansfield** of Barrington 6/29/1968 in Rochester; H - b. 7/30/1946 in RI, s/o Theodore W. Blair, Sr. (NE) and Helen Lathrop (RI); W - b. 12/29/1948 in NH, d/o Benjamin W. Mansfield, Jr. (NH) and Barbara L. Lucas (NH)
Thomas F. of Barrington m. Mary E. **Hichens** of Eliot, ME 6/9/1962; H - 18, shipper, b. ME, s/o Theodore W. Blair (NE) and Helen L. Lathrop (MA); W - 18, at home, b. NH, d/o Walter W. Hichens (MA) and Elmira Ballard (ME)

BLAISDELL,
Willis m. Hannah **Jacobs** 11/1/1929; H - 38, farmer, 2d, b. Belfast, Ireland, s/o William Blaisdell (Somersworth) and Jennie Hoyt (Rochester); W - 36, school teacher, b. Rochester, d/o Moses Jacobs (Shapleigh, ME) and Mary Clark (No. Lebanon, ME)

BLAKE,
Lewis A. of Barrington m. Alice A. N. **Haseltine** of Barrington 6/10/1939; H - 46, salesman, 2d, b. Newburyport, MA, s/o George B. Blake (Hampton) and Mary E. Lamprey (Hampton); W - 39, hairdresser, 2d, b. Anson, ME, d/o William H. Nicholson (Rutland, VT) and Lura C. Hutchins (Kingfield, ME)

BLANCHETTE,
Arthur L. of Dover m. Drina M. **Perkins** of Barrington 3/15/1947 in Milton; H - 27, laborer, b. Plymouth, s/o Arthur J. Blanchette (Salmon Falls) and Ruth E. Morse (Fitchburg, MA); W - 22, teacher, b. Auburn, ME, d/o Earl L. Perkins (Auburn, ME) and Blanche Y. Croteau (Auburn, ME)

BLINN,
Edward J., Jr. of Barrington m. Barbara A. **Larock** of Barrington 10/31/1981

BLOUNT,
Joseph P. of MN m. Mary A. **Records** of Barrington 6/9/1984 in Durham

BOCHER,
Frederick, Jr. of Exeter m. Arlene M. **Flower** of Barrington 7/24/1942 in Durham; H - 20, Marine, b. Cambridge, MA, s/o Frederick Bocher (Cambridge, MA) and Dorothy Bruce (York, ME); W - 20, switchbd. opr., b. Lynn, MA, d/o Harold E. Flower (Bethel, VT) and Addie M. Carter (Strafford)

BODGE,
Carl J. of Barrington m. Eunice J. **Wilkins** of Somersworth 8/5/1961; H - 27, maint. worker, b. NH, s/o James C. Bodge (NH) and Marie Warren (NH); W - 21, rubber worker, b. NH, d/o Richard Wilkins (NH) and Irma Place (NH)

Charles A. of Barrington m. Mildred E. **Emerson** of Rochester 2/7/1942 in Rochester; H - 27, machinist, b. Barrington, s/o John W. Bodge (Barrington) and Winifred J. Daley (Brighton, MA); W - 29, shoe worker, b. Nashua, d/o George Y. Emerson (Stoughton, MA) and Sarah F. Corbett (Stoughton, MA)

James C. of Barrington m. Doris A. **Fogarty** of Dover 12/27/1943 in Dover; H - 43, mechanic, b. Barrington, s/o Charles Bodge (Barrington) and Mary Carley (Brighton, MA); W - 20, shoe worker, b. Dover, d/o Leonard L. Fogarty (PEI) and Laura Plourde (Gonic)

John L. of Barrington m. Mary E. **Ward** of Barrington 1/26/1946 in Rochester; H - 21, farmer, b. Dover, s/o John W. Bodge (Barrington) and Winifred J. Daly

(Brighton, MA); W - 18, at home, b. Pembroke, ME, d/o John Ward (Eastport, ME) and Dorothy Rogers (St. Paul, MN)

John L. of Barrington m. Gloria A. **Bennett** of Rochester 9/17/1955 in Gonic; H - 31, farmer, 2d, b. NH, s/o John W. Bodge (NH) and Winifred J. Daly (MA); W - 20, b. WV, d/o Calvin Bennett (WV) and Roxie Sheaves (WV)

John W. of Barrington m. Winifred J. **Daley** of Barrington 6/23/1909 in Rochester; H - 23, farmer, b. Barrington, s/o Charles F. Bodge (Barrington, farmer) and Mary Carley (Barrington, housewife); W - 24, boxmaker, b. Brighton, ME, d/o Thomas F. Daley and Winifred E. Gaffey (Brighton, MA, housewife)

BODINE,
John J. of CT m. Wilhelmina T. **Bijlefeld** of CT 9/15/1984

BOGGS,
Dean F. of Barrington m. Jean E. **Spellman** of Barrington 11/27/1982

BONAMO,
Robert F. of Barrington m. Ethrilla A. **Eveleth** of Barrington 6/22/1935 in Rochester; H - 21, shipper, b. Roxbury, MA, s/o Samuel Bonamo (Italy) and Anna Bowen (Roxbury, MA); W - 18, unemployed, b. Malden, MA, d/o Frank E. Eveleth (Lynn, MA) and Ida A. Crowell (Barrington, NS)

BOOD[E]Y,
C. W. of Barrington m. Sadie **Cunliffe** of Barrington 8/11/1894; H - 17, farmer, b. Barrington, s/o D. W. (Barrington, farmer) and Ann (Barrington, housewife); W - 21, at home, b. England, d/o James (England) and Lucy (England)

John U. of Barrington m. Alice I. **Arlin** of Barrington 5/1/1899; H - 30, teamster, b. Barrington, s/o Daniel (Barrington,

farmer) and Marilla (Durham); W - 18, domestic, b.
Strafford, d/o Eli (Barrington, farmer) and Ida (Strafford)
Ralph J. of Barrington m. Pauline E. **Beauchain** of Strafford
5/1/1944 in Rochester; H - 20, farmer, b. Barrington, s/o
John V. Boodey (Barrington) and Alice I. Arlin (Strafford);
W - 22, hairdresser, b. E. Wallingford, VT, d/o Philip H.
Beauchain (Providence, RI) and Marguerite C. Bulley (E.
Wallingford, VT)

BOOTH,
Douglas B. of Fargo, ND m. Laura J. **Tubbs** of Federal Way,
WA 9/4/1983

BOSCH,
Joseph L. of North Hampton m. Jeanne M. **Meuse** of
Barrington 5/8/1982 in Nashua

BOSTON,
Charles H. of Barrington m. Laura M. **Smith** of Dover
4/29/1890 in Dover; H - 23, b. Barrington, s/o S. A. and
Hannah Boston; W - 20, b. Dover, d/o Elizabeth Smith
Kenneth Lee, Sr. of Berwick, ME m. Olive Marie **Belanger** of
Barrington 7/3/1976
Stephen A. of Barrington m. Mamie F. **Richardson** of
Northwood 1/1/1895 in Northwood; H - 23, painter, b.
Barrington, s/o S. A. (So. Berwick, ME, farmer) and
Hannah; W - 19, s. teacher, b. Northwood, d/o Oliver
(Northwood, shoemaker) and Abbie (Northwood)

BOUCHARD,
George I. of East Rochester m. Jacqueline A. **Turner** of
Barrington 9/10/1966; H - 23, machine oper., b.
Rochester, s/o Robert E. Bouchard (ME) and Eleanore
M. Nickerson (ME); W - 21, payroll clerk, b. Rochester,
d/o Arthur J. Turner (NY) and Virginia F. Ramsdell (MA)

BOUCHER,
Edward C. of Cranston, RI m. Holly **Wallace** of Barrington 5/30/1981 in Durham
Norman Ernest of Barrington m. Marlene Jane **Townsend** of Barrington 11/13/1976 in Madbury

BOUDREAU,
Francis J., III of Barrington m. Carol A. **Moreau** of Rochester 4/6/1985 in Rochester
William J. of Rochester m. Lillian M. **Brooks** of Barrington 4/22/1955 in Rochester; H - 26, shoe work, 2d, b. NH, s/o Joseph A. Boudreau (NH) and Patricia L. Lonegren (NY); W - 25, shoe work, b. NH, d/o George H. Brooks (Canada) and Isabelle Fanning (NH)

BOURKE,
Nicholas R. of Montague, MA m. Marlene E. **Zakon** of Montague, MA 8/7/1977

BOUTHOT,
Leopold J. of Barrington m. Debra J. **Barker** of Rochester 10/19/1985 in Rochester

BOYLE,
Paul E. of Boston, MA m. Rosalie D. **Hicker** of Saugus, MA 11/11/1937; H - 37, dentist, 2d, b. Somerville, MA, s/o John A. Boyle (IA) and Olive M. Berry (Milton, MA); W - 34, at home, 2d, b. MI, d/o Frederick Dunlap (Chicago, IL) and Eleanor Baldwin (MA)
Sean M. of Dover m. Susan J. **Doran** of Barrington 8/6/1971; H - b. 4/20/1952 in NH, s/o John B. Boyle (NH) and Loretta E. Fogarty (NH); W - b. 5/1/1952 in MA, d/o Louis N. Doran (MA) and Marjorie A. Hurd (MA)
Terry J. of Barrington m. Patricia A. **Ash** of Barrington 9/16/1978

BRADBURY,
Mark H. of Berwick, ME m. Sandra A. **Witmer** of Barrington 8/21/1965; H - 26, college student, b. ME, s/o Frank R. Bradbury (ME) and Gertrude E. Tripp (NH); W - 20, store clerk, b. NH, d/o Carl T. Witmer (IN) and Leah M. Clark (NH)

BRADLEY,
Robert A., Jr. of ME m. Theresa J. **Lambert** of Barrington 9/1/1984

BREWSTER,
Steve D. of Barrington m. Stacey D. **Goff** of Rochester 6/29/1985

BROOKS,
Richard S. of Barrington m. Ann K. V. **Johnson** of Boston, MA 4/5/1952 in Dover; H - 25, electrician, b. MA, s/o Ernest P. Brooks (MA) and Mildred B. Jollymore (MA); W - 19, student nurse, b. VT, d/o Chester F. Johnson (ME) and Dorothy D. Morris (ME)

BROWN,
Arthur H. of Barrington m. Lizzie I. **Willey** of Barrington 1/1/1890 in Rochester; H - 23, b. Barrington, s/o James E. and Clara Brown; W - 17, b. Barrington, d/o George W. and Olive Willey

Charles of Barrington m. Florence **Dustin** of Manchester 10/19/1895; H - 21, farmer, b. Barrington, s/o Isaac (Barrington, farmer) and Sarah; W - 24, at home, b. Manchester, d/o Peter and Mary

Chester G. of Barrington m. Gladys M. **Cates** of Strafford 11/24/1935; H - 36, stm. engineer, 2d, b. Barrington, s/o John A. Brown (Haverhill, MA) and Iza Harvell (Strafford); W - 30, housework, 2d, b. Barrington, d/o

Millard Thompson (Strafford) and Ellen Drew (Chichester)

Earl H. of Barrington m. Shirley M. **Pearson** of Barrington 9/6/1944; H - 22, mover, b. Barrington, s/o John A. Brown (Haverhill, MA) and Iza M. Harvell (Barrington); W - 18, inspector, b. Lawrence, MA, d/o Carl W. Pearson, Sr. (No. Andover, MA) and Martha M. Taplin (Lawrence, MA)

Edgar F. of Barrington m. Edna **Buzzell** of Barrington 12/18/1909 in Dover; H - 23, farmer, b. Barrington, s/o George F. Brown and Julia Waterhouse (housekeeper); W - 18, at home, b. Barrington, d/o Orrin P. Buzzell and Jennie Trask (Dover, housekeeper)

Edward Everett of Barrington m. Margaret E. **McDonald** of Barrington 2/18/1915; H - 20, laborer, b. Lee, s/o Henry M. Brown (Barrington, laborer) and Evilla Morrison (Epping, housekeeper); W - 21, at home, b. Barrington, d/o Cornelius McDonald (Portland, ME, laborer) and Nellie Whitehouse (Barrington, deceased)

Everette of Barrington m. Doris T. **Rudd** of Somerville, MA 6/28/1928 in Somerville, MA; H - 25, engineer, b. Barrington, s/o John A. Brown (steam mill owner) and Iza Harvell (domestic); W - 26, teacher, b. Somerville, MA, d/o James J. Rudd and Geor'am B. Hayes

Guy of Barrington m. Kathryn **Lenfest** of Gonic 3/26/1932 in Dover; H - 21, truck driver, b. Barrington, s/o William Brown (Barrington) and Sarah Reed (Barrington); W - 24, bookkeeper, b. Wakefield, MA, d/o Harry Lenfest (Rockland, ME) and Theresa McDermot (Ireland)

Henry M. of Barrington m. Ervilla **Morrison** of Barrington 9/14/1893; H - 44, farmer, s/o Dennis (Barrington, farmer) and Mehitable (Strafford); W - 17, at home, d/o G. W. (Nottingham, farmer) and Emma (Nottingham)

James D. of Barrington m. Denise I. **Barbin** of Barrington 5/6/1984 in Lebanon

John A. of Barrington m. Iza May **Harvell** of Strafford 3/6/1898 in Northwood; H - 21, fireman, b. Haverhill, MA, s/o George T. (Barrington, deceased) and Julia (housewife); W - 19, at home, b. Barrington, d/o Ghersom (Strafford, farmer) and Elizabeth (housewife)

Lawrence K. of Dover m. Barbara K. **Wakefield** of Barrington 8/16/1947; H - 27, laborer, b. Haverhill, MA, s/o George A. Brown and Dorothy Mooney; W - 17, at home, b. Haverhill, MA, d/o Edgar Wakefield and Serena Ball (Canada)

Lawrence K., II of Barrington m. Linnie A. **Sanborn** of Dover 1/3/1969; H - b. 12/25/1948 in NH, s/o Lawrence K. Brown, Sr. (MA) and Barbara F. Buzzell (MA); W - b. 10/5/1948 in ME, d/o Richard Sanborn (NH) and Gertrude E. Baron (NH)

Lawrence K., Jr. of Barrington m. Diane G. **Ward** of Rochester 2/10/1979 in Rochester

Leonard C. of Barrington m. Debra A. **Reynolds** of East Rochester 7/26/1971; H - b. 1/16/1952 in NH, s/o Lawrence K. Brown, Sr. (MA) and Barbara F. Buzzell (MA); W - b. 9/14/1954 in MA, d/o Burton K. Reynolds (MA) and Theresa L. Mahair (MA)

Lester J. of Barrington m. Elsie **Stimpson** of Barrington 6/1/1927; H - 22, lumberman, b. Barrington, s/o John Brown (lumberman) and Iza M. Harvel (deceased); W - 18, at home, b. Wethersfield, VT, d/o Urban Stimpson (farmer) and Maude Bellows (domestic)

Lewis Plummer, Jr. of Dover m. Brenda Lee **Baxter** of Barrington 6/26/1976

Orison J. of Barrington m. Bertha **Rand** of Rochester 11/25/1903 in Rochester; H - 42, shoemaker, 2d, b. Barrington, s/o James E. Brown (Barrington) and Clara A. Hall (Barrington); W - 22, school teacher, b. Rochester, d/o Bickford Rand (farmer) and Mary A. Berry (Strafford)

Richard E. of Barrington m. Elinor F. **Wells** of Barrington 11/19/1939 in Gonic; H - 24, truck driver, b. Barrington, s/o Edward E. Brown (Lee) and Margaret E. McDonald (Barrington); W - 19, at home, b. Northwood, d/o William Wells (Oxford, CT) and Nancy E. Wallace (Northwood)

Rob T. of Greenhurst, NY m. Ruth T. **Purvis** of Barrington 8/4/1979

Robert F. of Dover m. Irene A. **Meattey** of Barrington 12/4/1948 in Rochester; H - 21, carpenter, b. Dover, s/o George A. Brown and Dorothy Mooney; W - 16, at home, b. Fitzwilliam, d/o Herbert Meattey (Fitzwilliam) and Mildred DeShan (Washington)

Robert Francis, Jr. of Rochester m. Joanne Marie **Schanda** of Barrington 2/22/1975

Roscoe of Strafford m. Lena F. **Waterhouse** of Barrington 12/25/1916; H - 21, farmer, b. Strafford, s/o Henry E. Brown (Strafford, farmer) and Grace D. Corson (Barrington, housewife); W - 16, at home, b. Barrington, d/o Arthur C. Waterhouse (Barrington, farmer) and Mattie E. Young (Boston, MA, housewife)

Willie H. of Barrington m. Sarah P. H. **Reed** of Barrington 11/16/1900; H - 34, laborer, b. Barrington, s/o George (Barrington, deceased) and Julia; W - 15, housework, b. Barrington, d/o Charles (Barrington, shoemaker) and Annie

BRUCE,

Edward A. of Rochester m. Mildred E. **Berry** of Barrington 11/1/1947; H - 31, laborer, b. Saranac. NY, s/o Harry L. Bruce (Saranac, NY) and Emma McClain (Belknap); W - 18, at home, b. Rochester, d/o Percy N. Berry (Barrington) and Stella M. Hall (Dover)

BRYANT,

Douglas Frederick of Barrington m. Janice Scully **Realey** of Exeter 5/3/1975 in Exeter

BRYSON,
Edward J. of Newton, MA m. Florence E. **Gentile** of W. Newton, MA 4/20/1954; H - 23, laborer, b. MA, s/o William J. Bryson (MA) and Margaret Durno (Scotland); W - 18, student, b. MA, d/o Napoleon P. Gentile (Italy) and Santa Guzzi (MA)

Melvin of Barrington m. Evelyn **Green** of Barrington 10/27/1927; H - 36, farmer, b. Dover, s/o Frazer Bryson (farmer) and Etta Norton (domestic); W - 16, at home, b. Barrington, d/o George Green (stage electrician) and Lilla Waterhouse (domestic)

BUCHANAN,
George D. of Barrington m. Loretta G. **Poole** of Barrington 6/8/1985 in Durham

BUCHANON,
Warren C. of Alton m. Edwina **Gilman** of Alton 4/3/1937 in Rochester; H - 27, mechanic, 2d, b. Sussex, NB, s/o Herbert Buchanon (Sussex, NB) and Elmira Buchanon (Mapleton, ME); W - 18, at home, b. Alton, d/o Fred Gilman and Etta Gilman (Alton)

BUCK,
Richard L. of Greenville Jct., ME m. Rebecca E. **Hixon** of Greenville Jct., ME 10/1/1983

BUCZEK,
Todd M. of Barrington m. Leah L. **Gifford** of Barrington 10/1/1983 in Dover

BULLIS,
Roger D. of Barrington m. Traci L. **Steele** of Barrington 6/1/1985

BUMFORD,
Brian P. of Barrington m. Brenda B. **Grass** of Somersworth 9/25/1982 in Dover

Roger C. of Barrington m. Lorraine B. **Bennett** of Dover 2/4/1956 in Dover; H - 25, meat cutter, b. NH, s/o Roland W. Bumford (NH) and Stella G. Lorange (Canada); W - 19, waitress, b. NH, d/o John J. Bennett (NH) and Mary Gauvin (ME)

Roger C. of Barrington m. Alma E. **Demyanovich** of Raymond 8/15/1959; H - 28, truck driver, 3rd, b. NH, s/o Roland W. Bumford (NH) and Stella G. Lorange (Quebec); W - 28, shoe worker, 3rd, b. NH, d/o Clifford M. Hendrick (RI) and Iola D. Rowe (NH)

Roger C. of Barrington m. Lorraine B. **Gravel** of Rochester 7/1/1961; H - 30, truck driver, 4th, b. NH, s/o Roland W. Bumford (NH) and Stella G. Lorange (Canada); W - 25, secretary, 2d, b. NH, d/o Homer L. Parker (NH) and Jeannette V. Marcotte (NH)

Roger C. of Barrington m. Pauline M. **LaRochelle** of Rochester 10/19/1964; H - 33, truck driver, 5th, b. NH, s/o Roland W. Bumford (NH) and Stella G. Lorange (Canada); W - 34, at home, 2d, b. NH, d/o Joseph E. LaRochelle (NH) and Eva M. Rand (NH)

Roland of Barrington m. Sarah J. **Townsend** of Barrington 11/10/1908; H - 22, farmer, b. Barrington, s/o Charles W. Bumford (Barrington, farmer) and Ellen M. Hodgdon; W - 21, domestic, b. Boston, MA, d/o James Townsend and Ella F. Robinson

William R. of Barrington m. Cheryl A. **Morrow** of Barrington 7/16/1977

BUNDZA,
Joseph T. of Barrington m. Sylvia J. **Attanasio** of Barrington 5/4/1984 in Rochester

Thomas J. of Barrington m. Juanita M. **Lord** of Dover 7/21/1973 in Dover; H - b. 7/9/1951 in MA, s/o Joseph

Bundza (MA) and Claire Noble (MA); W - b. 8/31/1951 in NH, d/o Armand Lord (NH) and Cecelia Moreau (NH)

BUNTEN,
Dennis H. of East Meadow, Long Island, NY m. Marcia J. **Ramsdell** of Barrington 8/5/1967; H - 22, teacher, b. Jamaica, NY, s/o Howard E. Bunten (NY) and Alice M. Oppenheim (NY); W - 23, teacher, b. Exeter, d/o Frederick Ramsdell (MA) and Annie N. Taylor (MA)

BURBANK,
William G. of Durham m. Carol A. **Middaugh** of Barrington 2/28/1962; H - 19, member USN, b. NH, s/o Clair G. Burbank (Canada) and Dorothy M. Anderson (NH); W - 16, at home, b. ME, d/o Raymond E. Middaugh (ME) and Theresa Pasquill (MA)

BURGESS,
Tab M. of Somersworth m. Cathy A. **Fitzgerald** of Barrington 8/30/1981

BURLEIGH,
Jeffrey W. of Barrington m. Bonnie M. **Raymond** of Barrington 2/14/1987 in Barnstead

BURNS,
George H. of Barrington m. Yvette M. **Goulet** of Barrington 3/5/1977 in Dover

Patrick of Rochester m. Gina M. **Freeman** of Barrington 8/20/1983

Raymond J. of Barrington m. Alice B. **Howard** of Strafford 3/11/1935 in Rochester; H - 21, mechanic, b. Swanton, VT, s/o Edward Burns (Rutland, VT) and Alice Burns (Taffield, CT); W - 20, housekeeper, b. Strafford, d/o Harry Howard (Strafford) and Sadie E. Howard (Barrington)

BUTCHER,
Robert Arthur of Barrington m. Tevis **Kraft** of Barrington 10/12/1974 in Wakefield

BUTLER,
Clifford S. of Barrington m. Lula B. **Wakefield** of Lyman, ME 11/24/1965; H - 66, ret. laborer, 3rd, b. NH, s/o Hosiah Butler (NH) and Maria Debelle (NH); W - 70, ret. mach. oper., 4th, b. ME, d/o Byron Taylor (ME) and Jennie F. Stoddard (ME)
John T., Jr. of Barrington m. Tabatha E. **Thyng** of Barrington 4/25/1987

BUZZELL,
Arthur J. of Barrington m. Marian M. **Dudley** of Barrington 12/15/1944 in Gonic; H - 27, US Army, b. Suncook, s/o Clarence Buzzell (Epping) and Grace Bodge (Barrington); W - 30, clerk, b. Lee, d/o Darius C. Mariotti (Italy) and Edna C. Proctor (Durham)
C. E. of Barrington m. Adeline **Kurris** 6/23/1894; H - 28, grain dealer, b. Barrington, s/o William H. (Barrington, wheelwright) and Ellen (Amherst, at home); W - 23, at home, b. Boston, MA, d/o David (Boston, MA) and Annie (NY)
Levi H. of Barrington m. Bessie M. **Arlin** of Barrington 10/4/1899 in Strafford; H - 22, blacksmith, b. Barrington, s/o John (Barrington, farmer) and Annie (Madbury); W - 20, at home, b. Strafford, d/o Eli (Barrington, farmer) and Ida (Strafford)
Maurice T. of Barrington m. Laura C. **Edney** of Rochester 2/6/1916 in Rochester; H - 36, farmer, b. Lee, s/o James Buzzell (Lee, blacksmith) and Martha E. Tuttle (Barrington, housewife); W - 24, teacher, b. Colorado Springs, CO, d/o James M. Edney (Rochester, decorator) and Clara Coen (Des Moines, IA, housewife)

Walter E. of Barrington m. Nellie M. **Gibb** of Barrington 11/26/1936 in Rochester; H - 46, farmer, 2d, b. Wilton, s/o Arthur E. Buzzell and Ellen M. Buzzell (Greenfield); W - 50, tel. operator, 2d, b. Lyndonville, VT, d/o Willard H. Jones (Wilder, VT) and Emily E. Simpson (Sheffield, VT)

CABLE,
George B., Jr. of NY m. Olevia J. **Haley** of New York, NY 8/8/1953; H - 45, credit man, b. WV, s/o George B. Cable (WV) and Nancy L. Ryan (MO); W - 30, credit woman, b. NH, d/o Lawrence D. Haley (NH) and Cassie M. Hall (NH)

CAFASSO,
John J. of Rochester m. Cynthia A. **Soule** of Barrington 10/20/1979 in Rochester

CALDWELL,
Harold of Barrington m. Nellie **Curtis** of Barrington 8/20/1922 in Dover; H - 30, farmer, 2d, b. Barrington, s/o Edwin D. Caldwell (Barrington, farmer) and Clara Beiderman (Germany, housewife); W - 32, housewife, 2d, b. Somerville, MA, d/o George L. McIver (Scotland, carpenter) and Mary S. Bremner (Scotland, housewife)

CALEF,
A. Harlan of Barrington m. Irene M. **Holmes** of Everett, MA 10/13/1937 in Everett, MA; H - 27, clerk, b. Barrington, s/o Austin Calef (Barrington) and Clellie Chesley (Barrington); W - 29, bookkeeper, b. Everett, MA, d/o Joseph Holmes (Boston, MA) and Paul Zwicker (NS)
Alan D. of Barrington m. Donna **Young** of Somersworth 11/5/1977
Austin L. of Barrington m. Clellie **Chesley** of Barrington 2/14/1893 in Dover; H - 22, merchant, s/o J. R. Calef

(Barrington, merchant) and M. E.; W - 20, at home, d/o George O. A. (Barrington, farmer) and Sarah

Clarence L. F. of Barrington m. Mildred **Locke** of Barrington 10/2/1920; H - 26, clerk, b. Barrington, s/o Austin Calef (Barrington, merchant) and Clellie Chesley (Barrington, housewife); W - 24, at home, b. Barrington, d/o Alphonso Locke (Barrington, farmer) and Mary Waterhouse (Barrington, housewife)

George A. of Barrington m. Arvilla M. **Twombly** of Dover 5/6/1961; H - 21, meat cutter, b. NH, s/o A. Harlan Calef (NH) and Irene M. Holmes (MA); W - 19, rubber worker, b. NH, d/o Merton D. Twombly (NH) and Villa M. Johnson (NH)

Jere C. of Barrington m. Jane M. **Jacques** of Gonic 10/4/1986 in Strafford

John M. of Barrington m. Shirley A. **McKenna** of Barrington 9/5/1955 in Dover; H - 20, poultry work, b. NH, s/o Leon C. Calef (NH) and Ruth Morrell (NH); W - 19, b. NH, d/o John J. McKenna (NH) and Blanche Perron (NH)

Leon C. m. Ruth **Morrell** 10/5/1929 in Rochester; H - 31, poultry dealer, b. Barrington, s/o Austin L. Calef (Barrington) and Clellie M. Chesley (Barrington); W - 18, at home, b. Rochester, d/o Charles Morrell (ME) and Fannie Jenkins (Plymouth, MA)

Roger L. of Barrington m. Alberta M. **Witham** of Barrington 6/4/1948; H - 23, store clerk, b. Rochester, s/o Clarence L. Calef (Barrington) and Mildred Locke (Barrington); W - 19, receptionist, b. Exeter, d/o Albert M. Witham (Northwood) and Marguerite Ball (NS)

CALLAN,

David W. of Stoneham, MA m. Ione F. **Crowell** of Stoneham, MA 7/4/1964; H - 22, elec. eng., b. MA, s/o Samuel Callan (Ireland) and Eliza J. Smyth (Ireland); W - 23, teacher, b. MA, d/o Everett W. Crowell (MA) and Thelma I. Maxfield (MA)

CALLANAN,
Walter L. of Barrington m. Ruth H. **Callanan** of Barrington 6/25/1943 in Rochester; H - 42, machinist, 2d, b. Salem, MA, s/o Lafayette T. Callanan (Salem, MA) and Annie L. Fall (Salmon Falls); W - 35, nurse, 2d, b. Auburn, ME, d/o Albert W. Ham (Lewiston, ME) and Edith A. Walsh (Newton, MA)

CAMILIE,
Charles of Barrington m. Florence Emily **Day** of Barrington 5/5/1915; H - 36, laborer, b. Italy, s/o Rock Camilie (Italy, farmer) and Bllina ----- (Italy, housewife); W - 25, housekeeper, b. St. John's, NB, d/o William Day (St. Johns, NB, blacksmith) and Margaret Cooper (St. Johns, NB, housewife)

CANNEY,
Alfred B. of Barrington m. Patricia A. **Howard** of Rochester 8/22/1970 in Rochester; H - 2d, b. 10/20/1942 in NH, s/o Jerome E. Canney (NH) and Elizabeth A. Hayes (NH); W - 2d, b. 7/12/1942 in NH, d/o Parker N. Tebbetts (ME) and Martha L. Smith (NH)

Charles A. of Barrington m. Adah Swain **Jones** of Dover 4/23/1905 in Dover; H - 52, farmer, 2d, b. Strafford, s/o Alvah V. Canney (Strafford, farmer) and Sophronia E. Hill (Strafford); W - 44, housewife, 2d, b. Barrington, d/o John Q.A. Swain (Barrington, farmer) and Sarah Jane Swain (Barrington)

Jerome E., Jr. of Lee m. Marilyn M. **Corbett** of Barrington 1/17/1959; H - 20, highway dept., 2d, b. NH, s/o Jerome E. Canney, Sr. and Elizabeth Hayes; W - 15, housewife, b. NH, d/o Hollie Corbett (NH) and Doris Drake (NH)

Norman A. of Barrington m. Minnie M. **Waterhouse** of Barrington 10/20/1907; H - 21, farmer, b. Barrington, s/o Charles A. Canney (Strafford, blacksmith) and Victoria

Chesley; W - 21, at home, b. Barrington, d/o Benjamin A. Waterhouse (Barrington, farmer) and Mary Downing

CANTIN,
Real Richard of Barrington m. Avis Jean **Young** of Barrington 7/6/1975 in Farmington

CANTWELL,
Edward D. of East Orange, NJ m. Cynthia J. **Landry** of Barrington 7/6/1957 in Rochester; H - 21, USAF, b. NJ, s/o Edward G. Cantwell (NJ) and Muriel E. Startup (NJ); W - 18, at home, b. NH, d/o James W. Landry (NH) and Barbara N. Walker (NH)

CAPEN,
Arthur of Barrington m. Alice **Miller** of Boston, MA 6/21/1911; H - 21, farmer, b. Barrington, s/o Levi Capen (farmer) and Clara Freeman (housewife); W - 17, housework, b. Worcester, MA, d/o Wilbur Miller (painter) and ----- Miller (housewife)

CAPON,
Dana K. of Barrington m. Julia A. **Jeffrey** of Barrington 9/20/1987 in Madbury

CAPPIELLO,
Daniel Mauro of Barrington m. Joyce Ann **Dolphin** of Barrington 8/9/1975

CARL,
Christopher M. of Ocean Springs, MS m. Tammy L. **George** of Barrington 11/23/1985 in Somersworth

CARMODY,
Patrick J. of Barrington m. Harriet M. **Carmody** of Barrington 2/18/1978 in Rochester

CARON,
Leo J. of Barrington m. Elaine Y. **Badger** of E. Lebanon, ME 12/3/1966; H - 19, machine oper., b. Dover, s/o Lucien J. Caron (ME) and Lillian R. Michaud (ME); W - 17, shoe worker, b. Dover, d/o Arthur I. Badger (NH) and Jeannette M. Dionne (NH)
Leo Joseph of Barrington m. Nancy A. **McAvoy** of Lawrence, MA 5/3/1970 in Salem; H - 2d, b. 6/11/1947 in MA, s/o Lucien J. Caron (ME) and Lillian R. Michaud (ME); W - b. 7/27/1950 in MA, d/o Edward L. McAvoy (MA) and Helen F. Lane (NH)

CARPER,
Harry Lee of Barrington m. Peggy Lee **McKeown** of Barrington 5/17/1975 in Center Strafford

CARRACINO,
Robert G. of No. Reading, MA m. Pamela E. **Eschman** of No. Reading, MA 7/20/1985

CARRIER,
Harold E. of Dover m. Eleanor M. **Rivers** of Barrington 8/13/1949 in Dover; H - 22, carp. helper, b. ME, s/o Wilfred Carrier (Canada) and Nora Thibeault (MA); W - 18, at home, b. NH, d/o Lewis E. Rivers (NH) and Marion E. Hope (MA)

CARSON,
Christopher L. of Barrington m. Elizabeth **Marancik** of Barrington 1/24/1981 in Rye

CASE,
Versel Thomas of Lansing, MI m. Irene **Whitten** of Barrington 8/1/1976

CASWELL,
Dana F. of Barrington m. Beverly A. **Swain** of Barrington 7/8/1961; H - 24, member USCG, b. NH, s/o Earle W. Caswell (ME) and Effie Archibald (NH); W - 19, dental asst., b. NH, d/o Ralph W. Swain (NH) and Pauline A. Swenson (MA)

Dana Fenton of Barrington m. Denise Anne Marie **Routhier** of Barrington 9/21/1974

Joseph A. of Barrington m. Marion L. **Palmer** of Deerfield 5/25/1973 in Deerfield; H - b. 12/21/1947 in ME, s/o Kenneth A. Caswell (NH) and Theresa M. Kelley; W - b. 2/14/1955 in NH, d/o Frederick M. Palmer (NH) and Lilla M. Heath (VT)

CATER,
Harry B. of Barrington m. May Belle **Jordan** of Rochester 6/11/1902; H - 21, farmer, b. Barrington, s/o Henry F. Cater (Barrington, farmer) and Augusta F. Rollins; W - 22, at home, b. Biddeford, ME, d/o James Jordan and Isabelle Jordan

CATTANERO,
Enrico of Epping m. Elizabeth **Tyler** of Barrington 12/27/1895; H - 24, laborer, b. Italy, s/o Rachele (Italy) and Rachole; W - 22, domestic, b. Barrington, d/o Hiram (Barrington, laborer) and Liza

CAVERLY,
Lendall R., Jr. of Exeter m. Ellen L. **Beal** of Newburyport, MA 9/29/1966 in Brentwood; H - 22, member USN, b. Exeter, s/o Lendall R. Caverly (NH) and Cecelia Niemi (NH); W - 19, student, b. Newburyport, MA, d/o Edward R. Beal (MA) and Margaret Thomas (CT)

Lendall R., Jr. of Barrington m. Karen D. **Buzzell** of Barrington 6/20/1981 in Dover

Leslie D. of Strafford m. Irene E. **Bailey** of Barrington 6/25/1960; H - 22, truck driver, b. NH, s/o Leslie J. Caverly (MA) and Lorraine Allen (MA); W - 17, secretary, b. NH, d/o Raymond E. Bailey (RI) and Charlotte E. Goff (MA)

CERNEY,
Myron of San Francisco, CA m. Mary L. **Emhardt** of San Francisco, CA 9/5/1969; H - b. 8/10/1930 in Czechoslovakia, s/o John Cernslovsky (Ukraine) and Karla Reichrich (Czechoslovakia); W - b. 8/27/1943 in NH, d/o William H. Emhardt (DE) and Mary C. Hough (MA)

CHALTAS,
John G. of Barrington m. Joy P. **Savage** of Barrington 5/1/1983 in Rye

CHAPMAN,
Harris W. of Barrington m. Dorothy M. **Roberts** of Wilmington, MA 7/12/1920; H - 30, farmer, b. Barnston, PQ, s/o Jonathan Chapman (Barnston, PQ, farmer) and Ella J. Snow (Compton, PQ, housewife); W - 22, nurse, b. Wales

Harris W. of Barrington m. Beulah K. **Strong** 12/12/1947 in Rochester; H - 58, mechanic, 2d, b. Canada, s/o Jonathan Chapman (Canada) and Ella J. Snow (Canada); W - 42, teacher, 3rd, b. Portland, ME, d/o John F. Kennedy (Portland, ME) and Alice M. Libby (Buxton, ME)

Paul R. of Barrington m. Olga P. **Osepchook** of Madbury 1/29/1944 in Madbury; H - 19, soldier, b. Rochester, s/o Harris W. Chapman (Coaticook, PQ) and Dorothy M. Roberts (Bristol, England); W - 19, weaver, b. Newfields, d/o William J. Osepchook (Romania) and Catherine W. Fresno (Austria)

CHARETTE,
Charles E. of Barrington m. Sandra J. **MacIver** of Barrington 9/16/1977

CHASE,
Arthur M. of Barrington m. Mary L. **Charles** of Rochester 4/21/1950 in Dover; H - 20, US Navy, b. NH, s/o Arthur M. Chase (NH) and Mabel Demeritt (NH); W - 19, at home, b. NH, d/o Russell D. Charles (NH) and Florence M. Demers (MA)

Clayton Edward of Foxborough, MA m. Helen Elizabeth **Moltedo** of Foxborough, MA 1/17/1976

Fred of Barrington m. Mary Ann **Langley** of Nottingham 11/2/1924 in Newmarket; H - 53, farmer, 2d, b. Parsonsfield, ME, s/o James P. Chase (Parsonsfield, ME, farmer) and Henrietta Sanborn (Parsonsfield, ME, housewife); W - 46, housekeeper, b. Nottingham, d/o David Langley (Nottingham, farmer) and Martha Welch (Nottingham, housewife)

Kendall of Epping m. Gail **Peabody** of Barrington 3/2/1969; H - 2d, b. 12/9/1913 in MA, s/o Frank R. Chase (NH) and Winnifred B. Kendall (MA); W - b. 5/8/1932 in MA, d/o Myron F. Peabody (MA) and Olive P. Hunter (Canada)

CHESLEY,
Daniel S. of Barrington m. Gertrude S. **Drew** of Madbury 3/24/1908; H - 57, farmer, 2d, b. Barrington, s/o Joseph W. Chesley (Barrington, farmer) and Margaret A. Swain; W - 21, housekeeper, b. Cape Girardeau, MO, d/o Greenlief S. Drew (Barrington, farmer) and Neoma Miles (Perry Mills, MO, housewife)

CHICK,
Michael E., Jr. of Rochester m. Diane L. **Doucette** of Barrington 6/27/1987

CHICOINE,
Anthony F. of Barrington m. Francesca **Barrett** of Barrington 12/15/1984 in Wolfeboro

CHITTICK,
Claude Samuel of Barrington m. Patricia May **Chamberlain** 12/30/1976

CHURCH,
John E. of Barrington m. Martha S. **Hayes** of Barrington 1/4/1900 in Boston, MA; H - 45, farmer, b. Barrington, s/o John (Barrington, farmer) and Nancy; W - 48, at home, 2d, b. Barrington, d/o Joseph (deceased) and Eliza

CINFO,
Norman P. of Barrington m. Cecelia M. **Duffy** of Barrington 7/4/1987 in Lee

CLAFLIN,
Frederick E., Jr. of Southboro, MA m. Bernadine J. **Lindquist** of Southboro, MA 1/28/1957; H - 35, salesman, 2d, b. MA, s/o Frederick E. Claflin (MA) and Dorothy B. Dempsey (IL); W - 32, housewife, 2d, b. MA, d/o Edward M. Cross (MA) and Lauretta Renaud (MA)

CLARK,
Ernest W., Jr. of Barrington m. Susan R. **Hatch** of Newmarket 5/22/1965; H - 21, member US Army, b. NH, s/o Ernest W. Clark, Sr. (NH) and Viola G. Elliott (NH); W - 19, student, b. ME, d/o William F. Hatch (NH) and Lillian E. Pettingill (NH)

Everett E. of Barrington m. Mary I. **Daniels** of Barrington 6/17/1931 in Rochester; H - 43, farmer, b. Barrington, s/o Frank Clark (Dover) and Lizzie Swain (Barrington); W

- 47, at home, b. Barrington, d/o John C. Daniels (Strafford) and Cora Arlin (Barrington)

Garrick D. of Barrington m. Luanne K. **Loranger** of Barrington 5/17/1986 in Newmarket

Herbert of Barrington m. Gladys May **Tuttle** of Barrington 4/29/1915; H - 20, shoemaker, b. Barrington, s/o Marshall R. Clark (Barrington, farmer) and Ada Freeman (Barrington, deceased); W - 19, at home, b. Barrington, d/o Joseph H. Tuttle (Dover, farmer) and Carrie E. Arlin (Barrington, domestic)

John E. of Barrington m. Sharon A. **Lance** of Rochester 6/18/1983

John W. of Barrington m. Mary A. **Hargraves** of Nottingham 6/18/1919; H - 20, teamster, b. Barrington, s/o Marshall Clark (Barrington, farmer); W - 23, shoe factory, 2d, b. Taftsville, CT, d/o Arthur Hargraves (England, farmer)

Marshall K. of Barrington m. Ada **Freeman** of Barrington 7/4/1891 in Northwood; H - 29, b. Barrington, s/o Dennis; W - 19, b. Barrington, d/o Wilbur

Steven A. of Somersworth m. Nadine **Stickles** of Somersworth 5/16/1987

CLARKE,

Daniel of Barrington m. Nancy **Richardson** of Barrington 6/24/1895; H - 77, laborer, b. Barrington, s/o John and Betsy; W - 74, housemaid

John C. of Center Strafford m. Susan **Asquith** of Barrington 8/19/1972 in Exeter; H - b. 8/19/1948 in NH, s/o John L. Clarke (MA) and Mildred E. Buker (CT); W - b. 11/24/1944 in MA, d/o John F. Asquith (MA) and Charlotte E. Swett (MA)

CLAY,

Harry P. of Barrington m. Jennie **Leslie** of Lee 9/1/1905; H - 34, teamster, 2d, b. Lee, s/o Job Clay (Barrington, farmer) and Alta Glover; W - 29, housework, 2d, b. Holyoke, MA, d/o Frank Riley and Margaret Smith

Robert S. of Barrington m. Katherine E. **Mitchell** of Barrington 5/2/1981 in Durham

CLEMENT,

Paul W. of Dover m. Anna M. **Hopey** of Barrington 4/7/1942 in Ossipee; H - 23, soldier, b. Quechee, VT, s/o Frank Clement (VT) and Mary Parker (VT); W - 21, bookkeeper, b. Madbury, d/o Walter C. Hopey (NY) and Bessie Bradeen (Dover)

Raymond S. of Barrington m. Cheryl A. **Morrow** of Barrington 8/15/1981

CLOUGH,

Barry Lenwood of Farmington m. Jenneke Margery **Finlay** of Barrington 6/21/1975

Jay Scott of Londonderry m. Paulette Ruth **Tucker** of Barrington 5/17/1975 in Dover

CLOUTHIER,

Christopher A. of Barrington m. Deborah **Lucas** of Barrington 2/14/1981 in Dover

COBBAN,

James S. of Barrington m. Emily J. **Ramsey** of Goffstown 4/21/1956 in Goffstown; H - 22, USAF, b. ME, s/o Douglas Cobban (MA) and Isabel Seagers (Canada); W - 21, medical sec., b. MA, d/o Fred E. Ramsey (MA) and Lena E. Maxwell (NH)

COLDWELL,

James of TN m. Eunice **Durrell** of Barrington 5/25/1915 in Portsmouth; H - 80, merchant, 3rd, b. TN, s/o William Coldwell (TN, farmer) and Rhoda Wildman (TN, housewife); W - 60, at home, 2d, b. Biddeford, ME, d/o

Daniel Durell (Kennebunk, ME, carpenter) and Sarah Downing (Alewive, ME, housewife)

COLE,

James A. of Barrington m. Mary E. **Haskell** of Barrington 8/11/1901; H - 70, farmer, 2d, b. Wells, ME, s/o Samuel Cole (Wells, ME, farmer) and Eleanor Cole; W - 68, housekeeper, 3rd, d/o Ephraim Haskell (Barrington, farmer) and Mary Haskell

Jimmy D. of Barrington m. Mary J. **Fortier** of Dover 5/7/1977 in Dover

Scott D. of Barrington m. Marguerite L. **Blanchette** of Dover 9/7/1985 in Dover

William D. of Barrington m. Sandra J. **Rollins** of Nottingham 10/7/1978 in Lee

COLLINS,

Daniel J. of Wells, ME m. Kim M. **Elliott** of Wells, ME 6/14/1986

James F. of Wolfeboro m. Blanche C. **Critchett** of Barrington 12/13/1915 in Dover; H - 24, lineman, b. Somersworth, s/o Stephen Collins (Berwick, ME, moulder) and Annie Simpson (Somersworth, housewife); W - 18, teacher, b. Barrington, d/o Loring Critchett (Barrington, farmer) and Emma Sewell (Newmarket, housewife)

COLPRIT,

James D. of Madbury m. Carol L. **McKenna** of Barrington 11/28/1959; H - 17, student, b. NH, s/o James H. Colprit (NH) and Emily Bickford (NH); W - 16, rose packer, b. NH, d/o John J. McKenna (NH) and Blanche M. Perron (NH)

COMLEY,

Martin W. of Durham m. Andrea E. **Calef** of Barrington 7/25/1970; H - b. 2/7/1950 in NY, s/o Francis W. Comley

(ME) and Phyllis L. Graham (MA); W - b. 9/16/1949 in
NH, d/o Roger L. Calef (NH) and Alberta M. Witham
(NH)

CONRAD,
Richard H. of Barrington m. Mary-Jo **Standifer** of Barrington
7/10/1982 in Nottingham

CONSTANTINE,
Parker A. of Rochester m. Lorraine **Stevenson** of Barrington
9/3/1949 in Rochester; H - 24, bookkeeper, b. NH, s/o
Melvin L. Constantine (NH) and Madge McFee (NS); W -
19, clerical work, b. NH, d/o Alexander Stevenson (MA)
and Vera A. Thompson (NH)

COOK,
Albert J. of Barrington m. Lena A. **Pomerleau** of Gonic
9/10/1960; H - 21, utility man, b. NH, s/o John W. Cook
(NH) and Louise B. Dionizio (MA); W - 17, at home, b.
MA, d/o Joseph N. Pomerleau (Canada) and Elsie
Tremblay (MA)
Dwayne E. of Barrington m. Jody L. **Harmon** of Rochester
11/7/1986
Ernest E. of Barrington m. Florence I. **Gagnon** of Gonic
9/12/1970 in Wolfeboro; H - b. 1/26/1949 in NH, s/o
John W. Cook, Sr. (NH) and Louise Dionizio (MA); W - b.
7/30/1951 in NH, d/o Pierre B. Gagnon (ME) and Lucille
E. Nadeau (NH)
George P. of Gonic m. Ramona R. **Wentworth** of Barrington
2/24/1961; H - 17, wool dyer, b. NH, s/o John W. Cook
(NH) and Louise B. Dionizio (MA); W - 17, at home, b.
NH, d/o George Wentworth (NH) and Katherine C. Blais
(NH)
John W., Jr. of Barrington m. Alice L. **Thomas** of Gonic
10/14/1961; H - 24, wool dyer, b. MA, s/o John W. Cook,
Sr. (NH) and Louise Dionizio (MA); W - 18, shoe worker,

b. NH, d/o William L. Thomas (MA) and Eleanor B. Terrill (NH)

Peter C. of Barrington m. Victoria L. **Hamilton** of Rochester 2/26/1982 in Rochester

Robert W. of Barrington m. Margaret A. **Slaney** of Barrington 9/5/1987

Roderick W. of Amesbury, MA m. Nancy L. **Millette** of Amesbury, MA 11/26/1983

Roy H. of Barrington m. Carol E. **Heyl** of Barrington 12/24/1983

COOPER,
Matthew O. of Durham m. Carmen M. **Vanca** of Barrington 3/9/1971 in Durham; H - b. 6/4/1943 in NY, s/o Robert I. Cooper (NY) and Hannah Miller (NY); W - b. 11/27/1949 in Brazil, d/o Stanley Vanca (Czechoslovakia) and Beate Mrazek (Czechoslovakia)

CORBIN,
Albert L. of Barrington m. Diane J. **Larochelle** of Barrington 4/27/1984

CORMIER,
Joseph O. of Barrington m. Louise M. **Bishop** of Barrington 11/28/1972 in Durham - H - 4th, b. 8/21/1920 in ME, s/o Wilfred J. Cormier (Canada) and Marion Lagasse (Canada); W - 3rd, b. 4/22/1921 in NH, d/o Wilfred J. Paquette (NH) and Lena Labranche (NH)

CORSON,
James W. of Barrington m. Emma M. **Rust** of Barrington 3/31/1890 in Rochester; H - 30, b. Barrington, s/o D. and Malinda Corson; W - 26, b. Dover, d/o Charles H. and Mary Rust

Meldean R. of Lynn, MA m. Eleanor R. **Bailey** of Barrington 2/5/1950; H - 23, apprentice, b. NH, s/o Edward R.

Corson (NH) and Grace M. Randall (NH); W - 21, nurse, b. CT, d/o Raymond E. Bailey (RI) and Charlotte E. Goff (MA)

Oliver P. of Barrington m. Elizabeth A. **Howard** of Barrington 7/26/1904 in Rochester; H - 46, farmer, 2d, b. Exeter, s/o Lorenzo D. Corson and Melinda Arlin (Barrington); W - 50, housewife, 2d, b. Strafford, d/o Stephen Howard and Mary J. Parshley (Center Harbor)

Richard J. of Dover m. Elaine A. **Whittier** of Barrington 4/16/1966; H - 34, elec. technician, 3rd, div., b. Dover, s/o Frank H. Corson (NH) and Georgianna Souza (MA); W - 33, at home, 2d, div., b. ME, d/o B. Burgess (ME) and Lillian G. Ames (ME)

COUGHLIN,

David F., Jr. of Barrington m. Jacqueline M. **Moreau** of Dover 3/11/1955 in Rochester; H - 18, student, b. MA, s/o David F. Coughlin (MA) and Florence E. Bell (MA); W - 15, student, b. NH, d/o William Moreau (VT) and Frances L. Ellis (NH)

David F., Jr. of Barrington m. Anita S. **Clark** of Somersworth 7/4/1972; H - 2d, b. 7/4/1936 in MA, s/o David Coughlin (MA) and Florence Bell (MA); W - 2d, b. 3/29/1948 in NH, d/o John Bourque (NH) and Anita LaRoche (NH)

David F., III of Barrington m. Heidi L. **Cutter** of Barrington 9/29/1973 in Dover; H - b. 9/6/1955 in NH, s/o David F. Coughlin, Sr. (MA) and Jacqueline Ellis (NH); W - b. 5/26/1955 in NH, d/o Jackson G. Cutter (NH) and Sharon L. Crosby (NH)

COWLING,

Mark D. of OH m. Corbett **Gordon** of OH 12/24/1980

COX,

Larry G. of Barrington m. Linda L. **Weiss** of Greenland 3/2/1979 in Portsmouth

COYNE,
James M. of So. Lebanon, ME m. Debra L. **Fabian** of So. Lebanon, ME 11/9/1985
John W., III of Barrington m. Jaimie S. **Wolf** of Barrington 12/11/1979 in Portsmouth

CROCKETT,
George W. of Barrington m. Janet E. **Wichmann** of Somersworth 1/11/1986 in Portsmouth

CROSBY,
John F. of Barrington m. Eva E. **Hale** of Barrington 6/22/1892; H - 30, clergyman, b. Neponset, IL, s/o Thomas and Eliza; W - 22, lady, b. Barrington, d/o Thomas and Eliza

CROWERS,
Alexander W. of Barrington m. Lurleane **Harden** of Barrington 10/10/1987

CROWLEY,
Roland V. of Barrington m. Sara B. **Gallant** of Barrington 10/20/1984 in Harrisville

CUEVAS,
Jose L. of Barrington m. Krystyna J. **Krysiak** of Barrington 6/5/1982

CULBERT,
Frank J., Jr. of Barrington m. Gloria **DiFazio** of Barrington 5/15/1971; H - 3rd, b. 11/25/1916 in MA, s/o Frank J. Culbert (MA) and Sarah Nolan (MA); W - b. 6/1/1932 in MA, d/o Louis DiFazio (Italy) and Susan ----- (Italy)

CUMMINGS,

George N. of Barrington m. Ella H. **Partlow** of Portland, ME 5/29/1900; H - 30, farmer, 2d, b. Milton Mills, s/o Lewis (Canada, laborer); W - 20, housework, b. Portland, ME, d/o Justice (NY, machinist) and Emma

Harry W. of Dover m. Sadie E. **Morley** of Barrington 7/21/1921 in Milton; H - 37, postal clerk, b. Dover, s/o Frank Cummings (Dover, belt maker) and Carrie Nourse (Fox Lake, WI, housewife); W - 22, at home, b. Charlestown, MA, d/o Joseph Morley (Halifax, NS, retired) and Mary Fanning (Halifax, NS, housewife)

CUNNINGHAM,

Wilfred M. of Barrington m. Marsha G. **Hodge** of Rochester 9/11/1971 in Milton; H - b. 4/2/1947 in NH, s/o Wilfred M. Cunningham (NH) and Gladys F. Marden (NH); W - b. 3/23/1947 in MA, d/o Stuart I. Hodge (VT) and Marion L. Hockaday (MA)

CURTIS,

Arthur B. of Abington, MA m. Ruth **Bateman** of Abington, MA 10/12/1935 in Northwood; H - 46, salesman, 2d, b. Elmwood, MA, s/o Lucius J. Curtis (Elmwood, MA) and Rosetta Baker (Hyannis, MA); W - 45, buyer, b. Lynn, MA, d/o James F. Bateman (Dover) and Ella Teeling (Houlton, ME)

CUSICK,

Leslie W. of Taunton, MA m. Catherine E. **McClellan** of Taunton, MA 5/13/1937; H - 25, bartender, b. Taunton, MA, s/o Eugene Cusick (Taunton, MA) and Maud Alexander (Taunton, MA); W - 20, at home, b. Norton, MA, d/o William McClellan (Taunton, MA) and Katherine Driscoll (Taunton, MA)

CUTLER,
Alan S. m. Patricia A. **Timm** of Barrington 8/19/1961; H - 23, teacher, b. NH, s/o Frank R. Cutler (MA) and Alma Smith (NH); W - 19, payroll clerk, b. NY, d/o Frederick M. Timm (NY) and Marjorie M. Boyce (NY)

CUTTER,
Edward H. of Rochester m. Audrey M. **Neal** of Barrington 3/16/1963; H - 17, pulp cutter, b. NH, s/o George H. Cutter (NH) and Helen B. Barber (NH); W - 19, waitress, b. NH, d/o Arthur G. Neal (NH) and Ettie A. Cooper (NH)
Timothy S. of Barrington m. Tammy J. **Gardner** of Nottingham 11/12/1982
Timothy S. of Barrington m. Michalene J. **Leba** of Dover 11/14/1987 in Rochester

DAIGNEAU,
Mark of Barrington m. Tina M. **Bruce** of Barrington 7/11/1987 in Dover

DALZELL,
Hugh M. of Southboro, MA m. Donna N. **Whitehead** of Southboro, MA 8/14/1986

DAME,
Forrest F. of Rochester m. Beverly L. **Wells** of Barrington 12/30/1967 in Rochester; H - 19, b. NH, s/o Forrest P. Dame (NH) and Hazel E. Fritz (MA); W - 18, b. NH, d/o Chester E. Wells (NH) and Elizabeth E. Brown (NH)

DANFORTH,
Francis J. of Barrington m. Jennie **Hayes** of Barrington 7/30/1891 in Rochester; H - 33, b. Barrington, s/o Betsey; W - 39, 2d, b. NY

DANIELS,

Arthur C., Jr. of Barrington m. Jeanne F. **McKowen** of North Hampton 5/8/1977 in Gonic

Frank A. of Barrington m. Martha E. **Swasy** of Barrington 10/12/1898; H - 21, miller, b. Barrington, s/o John C. (miller) and Cora A. (Barrington, housewife); W - 21, domestic, b. Scarboro, ME, d/o Allen (Ossipee, farmer) and Martha

DARLING,

Brian of Dover m. Ann Leslie **Waterhouse** of Barrington 9/11/1976

Charles Barry of Center Sandwich m. Linda Louise **Farr** of Barrington 10/3/1976 in Moultonboro

DAUDELIN,

Ricky P. of Barrington m. Mary E. **Sartain** of England 1/16/1982

DAVIS,

Charles W. of Barrington m. Phebe A. **Dodge** of Lebanon, ME 10/10/1904; H - 58, farmer, 3rd, b. Barrington, s/o Daniel Davis and Mary A. Corson; W - 63, housework, 2d, b. Acton, ME, d/o Simon Brackett and Sarah Brackett

Dennis J. of Dover m. Pamela A. **Shute** of Barrington 6/25/1983

Kenneth Eugene of Barrington m. Rita Virginia **Eaton** of North Conway 8/21/1976

Russell A., Jr. of Lakeport m. Jeanette E. **Stevenson** of Barrington 6/20/1959; H - 21, civil eng., b. NH, s/o Russell A. Davis (NH) and Violetta P. Rogers (NH); W - 21, teacher, b. NH, d/o Marshall M. Stevenson (MA) and Freda E. Billeter (FL)

DAY,
Troy S. of Portsmouth m. Diane M. **Beauchemin** of Barrington 4/20/1984 in Portsmouth

DEAN,
Carl B. of Dover m. Winifred E. **Leffel** of Barrington 4/15/1967; H - 53, mach. oper., 3rd, widower, b. Peterborough, s/o Truman F. Dean (NH) and Harriette M. Cilley (MA); W - 51, assembler, 2d, widow, b. Hackensack, NJ, d/o Willard K. Conrad (SD) and Grace M. Soley (NJ)

Donald F. of Belvidere, NJ m. Patricia J. **Weeden** of Barrington 9/26/1954; H - 20, US Navy, b. NJ, s/o Donald L. Dean (NJ) and Gladys P. Linnaberry (NJ); W - 19, US Navy, b. NH, d/o Albert E. Weeden (NH) and Thelma Richards (ME)

Kevin A. of Barrington m. Susan D. **Creighton** of Dover 4/7/1984 in Dover

DEARBORN,
Simeon D. of Barrington m. Hattie M. **Clark** of Barrington 2/16/1891; H - 32, 2d, b. Cornish, ME, s/o Isaac and Eliza; W - 57, b. Strafford, d/o John and Polly

DEBUTTS,
Daniel J. of Strafford m. Pammy J. **Hemeon** of Barrington 9/1/1986

DECATUR,
Roland W. of Barrington m. Beulah H. **Winsor** of Duxbury, MA 10/16/1907; H - 25, engineer, b. Barrington, s/o Frank I. Decatur (Barrington, merchant) and Nellie S. Hall (Barrington); W - 22, bookkeeper, b. Duxbury, MA, d/o Fred R. Winsor (Duxbury, MA, driver) and Caroline M. Glass (Duxbury, MA)

DECESARE,
William Anthony of Fresno, CA m. Carol Lynn **Porter** of Barrington 12/27/1976 in Durham

DECHEN,
Martial of Barrington m. Blanche **Davis** of Barrington 4/23/1905 in Lee; H - 27, laborer, b. Canada, s/o Martial Dechen (Canada, farmer) and Clarise Fournier (Canada); W - 16, at home, b. Dover, d/o Frank Davis (Dover, farmer) and Emma Willey (Barrington)

DEELY,
Joseph J., Jr. of Barrington m. Bonnylou **Roberts** of Barrington 6/28/1980

DEHARO,
Jean P. of Dover m. Lois A. **Mansfield** of Barrington 5/28/1970 in Dover; H - b. 3/20/1948 in MA, s/o Manuel Deharo (Algeria) and Rita Jacques (MA); W - b. 8/23/1951 in NH, d/o Benjamin Mansfield (NH) and Barbara Lucas (NH)

DELTWAS,
Julius A. of Lawrence, MA m. Diane P. **Bennett** of Lawrence, MA 8/3/1985

DELUCA,
Richard J. of Barrington m. Andrea M. **Bergin** of Barrington 2/15/1980

DEMASKY,
Wayne N. of Barrington m. Sherry A. **Dion** of Barrington 12/29/1984 in Newmarket

DEMER[R]ITT,
John W. of Barrington m. Alice M. **Whitehouse** of Barrington 5/12/1909 in Strafford; H - 26, farmer, b. Barrington, s/o Samuel P. Demeritt (Barrington, farmer) and Sarah E. Locke (Dover, housewife); W - 19, domestic, b. Barrington, d/o John T. Whitehouse (Barrington, laborer) and Ida Brown (Barrington, housewife)

Maurice of Barrington m. Ada T. **Fuller** of Cochituate, MA 4/2/1927 in Dover; H - 19, farmer, b. Barrington, s/o Samuel P. Demeritt (farmer) and Sarah E. Locke (domestic); W - 19, domestic, b. Dorchester, MA, d/o Timothy Fuller (lecturer) and Evelyn Costigan (deceased)

Philip O. of Rochester m. Beatrice **MacMullen** of Dover 9/1/1934 in Rochester; H - 24, lumberman, b. Barrington, s/o John W. DeMerritt (Barrington) and Alice Whitehouse (Barrington); W - 18, at home, b. Dover, d/o Samuel MacMullen (VT) and Charlotte Caldwell (St. Johns, Newfoundland)

Plummer of Nottingham m. Ethel M. **Hall** of Barrington 4/19/1899 in Northwood; H - 39, farmer, b. Nottingham, s/o Jacob (Nottingham) and Olive (Epping); W - 27, domestic, b. Barrington, d/o George (Barrington, farmer) and Chloe (Strafford)

Roscoe P. of Barrington m. Edna E. **Soule** of Dover 11/5/1937 in Dover; H - 27, lumberman, b. Barrington, s/o Samuel Demeritt (Barrington) and Sarah Locke (Dover); W - 21, at home, b. Brockton, MA, d/o Alton L. Soule (Boston, MA) and Katherine Donahee (Brockton, MA)

Walter C. of Barrington m. Margaret A. **Gulant** of Jackson 5/18/1906 in Strafford; H - 21, farming, b. Barrington, s/o Samuel P. DeMeritt (Barrington, farming) and Lizzie S. DeMeritt (Dover); W - 20, housework, b. Jackson, d/o Gilman Gulant (Jackson, hotel keeper) and Mary Gulant (Jackson)

DENHARD,
Bruce D. of Barrington m. Karen E. **Collins** of Barrington 5/2/1981

DENYOU,
John M., Jr. of Barrington m. Donna M. **Elliott** of Nottingham 3/19/1983

DESHONG,
George A. of Barrington m. Lisa G. **Ainsworth** of Barrington 12/7/1985

DESJARDINS,
Dennis H. of Dover m. Jean **Finlay** of Barrington 7/8/1983 in Dover

DESMARAIS,
Paul A. of Barrington m. Susan E. **Drew** of Barrington 6/6/1981

DEVER,
Michael J. of Barrington m. Diane M. **DeLuca** of Medford, MA 8/19/1973 in Plaistow; H - 2d, b. 12/10/1945 in MA, s/o Lawrence Dever (MA) and Gladys A. DeMaso (MA); W - b. 11/14/1953 in MA, d/o Thomas J. DeLuca (MA) and Gladys A. Knight (MA)

DEXTER,
John W. of Barrington m. Margaret E. **McDonald** of Barrington 9/30/1907 in Gonic; H - 44, farmer, b. Shelburne, NS, s/o James Dexter (Shelburne, NS) and Sarah A. Davis (Shelburne, NS); W - 44, domestic, b. Fredericton, NB, d/o Cornelius McDonald (Ireland) and Nora McDonald (Ireland)

DIBERTO,
Robert L. of Barrington m. Gail S. **Delisle** of Barrington 12/3/1983

DIMAMBRO,
Donald V. of Barrington m. Marcia D. **Moore** of Barrington 10/8/1983

DINGLE,
Stephen L. of Colchester, VT m. Cuc K. **Huynh** of Colchester, VT 6/5/1982

DINWOODIE,
Donald A. of Ashway, RI m. Barbara L. **Mansfield** of Barrington 10/19/1956 in So. Berwick, ME; H - 27, painter, 2d, b. RI, s/o Theodore Dinwoodie (CT) and Hannah White (CT); W - 28, housewife, 2d, b. NH, d/o Irving F. Lucas (NH) and Rachel J. Clark (Ireland)

DIONNE,
Raymond J. of Barrington m. Terry J. **Gaetz** of Barrington 7/10/1985 in Milton

DIVIRGILIO,
Alan D. of Barrington m. Tina M. **Labrie** of Barrington 6/29/1985 in Rochester
Mark Nicholas of Barrington m. Corinne **Drapeau** of Rochester 10/2/1976 in Rochester

DOBSON,
Mark P. of Barrington m. Cheryl M. **Mielke** of Barrington 4/9/1983

DODGE,
Charles F. of Barrington m. Dorothy E. **Hunter** of Dover 9/16/1938 in Dover; H - 22, chauffeur, b. Barrington, s/o

Herman E. Dodge and Louise G. Babb (Barrington); W - 20, mill worker, b. Dover, d/o Thomas Hunter (Belfast, Ireland) and Florence Greenway (Dover)

Edwin S. of Barrington m. Mary A. **Lingard** of Barrington 12/31/1893; H - 20, laborer, s/o Frank (New Durham, farmer) and Rosalia (Barrington); W - 17, at home, d/o Joseph (Barrington, farmer) and Sarah (Barrington)

Ernest m. Pauline W. **Card** 10/29/1929 in Rochester; H - 36, farmer, 3rd, b. Barrington, s/o Edwin Dodge (Rochester) and Mary Lingard (Barrington); W - 32, housework, 2d, b. Berwick, ME, d/o Archie Williams (Ossipee) and Caro Robinson

Forest M. m. Mertie F. **Jackson** 1/3/1903

Frederick H. of Barrington m. Stella L. **McGuinness** of Gonic 3/3/1962; H - 21, maint. wkr., b. NH, s/o Robert A. Dodge (NH) and Mary E. Conway (MA); W - 20, shoeworker, b. NH, d/o James F. McGuinness (MA) and Florida Payeur (ME)

Herman of Rochester m. Lillian E. **Rowe** of Barrington 12/22/1900; H - 17, shoemaker, b. Rochester, s/o Frank (New Durahm, farmer) and Rose; W - 14, housework, b. Barrington, d/o Henry (Barrington, farmer) and Emma

John R. of Barrington m. Louise M. **St. Cyr** of Dover 8/31/1963; H - 20, hosp. worker, b. NH, s/o Robert A. Dodge (NH) and Mary Conway (NH); W - 19, hair dresser, b. NH, d/o Henry J. St. Cyr (NH)

Robert A. of Barrington m. Mary E. **Conway** of Dover 7/10/1937 in Dover: h - 25, farmer, b. Barrington, s/o Herman Dodge (Gonic) and Louise Babb (Barrington); W - 18, at home, b. Lawrence, MA, d/o Frederick Conway (Ogdensburg, NY) and Grace Pierce (Andover, MA)

Robert L. of Barrington m. Elona J. **Estes** of Barrington 6/18/1960; H - 22, poultryman, b. NH, s/o Robert A. Dodge (NH) and Mary E. Conway (MA); W - 24, nurse, b. NH, d/o Elmer H. Estes (ME) and Hilda E. Kahps (MA)

DODSON,
Charles M. of Barrington m. Joan H. **Ascheim** of Barrington 6/22/1985 in Durham

DOHERTY,
Dale M. of East Rochester m. Virginia A. **Bodge** of Barrington 4/5/1986 in Rochester

DOLAN,
Albert of Billerica, MA m. Jane Alta **Brisbane** of Billerica, MA 4/8/1976

DONADIO,
Francis M. of Barrington m. Laurette R. **Gibb** of Barrington 7/2/1977

DORE,
Elmer H. of Barrington m. Florence **Blackmer** of Madbury 4/18/1898 in Rochester; H - 22, farmer, b. Pittsfield, s/o Herbert (Alton, farmer) and Susie (housewife); W - 16, at home, b. Gonic, d/o Charles (Madbury, farmer) and Anna (housewife)

DOTSON,
Edward J., II of Barrington m. Beverly A. **Landers** of Rochester 10/27/1973 in Rochester; H - b. 2/24/1948 in NY, s/o Edward Dotson (NJ) and Jean Chadbourne (NH); W - b. 5/19/1955 in ME, d/o John Landers and Helen Simmons (ME)

DOUCETTE,
Richard A. of Lee m. Barbara M. **Jennison** of Barrington 7/26/1969; H - b. 2/7/1947 in NH, s/o Gerard Doucette (NH) and Barbara Bennett (NH); W - b. 5/15/1950 in NH, d/o Roger D. Jennison (NH) and Beatrice Dennett (NH)

DOUGHTY,
Charles T. of Nottingham m. Barbara L. **Litchfield** of Barrington 7/2/1987

DOUGLAS,
Howard William of New Milford, CT m. Barbara Preston **Joy** of Barrington 6/27/1936; H - 27, school teacher, b. Barre, VT, s/o Walter C. Douglas and Elizabeth Douglas (Edinboro, Scotland); W - 27, librarian, b. Warner, d/o Clarence L. Joy and Lena Joy

William H. of Strafford m. Edith E. **Miller** of Barrington 2/4/1961; H - 20, heel factory, b. NH, s/o Charles F. Douglas (NH) and Alice E. King (MA); W - 18, shoe factory, b. NH, d/o Douglas F. Miller, Jr. (NH) and Barbara M. Young (ME)

DOW,
Ronald A. of Barrington m. Dawn M. **Gallagher** of Barrington 1/25/1986

DOWLING,
John J., Jr. of Somersworth m. Laura A. **Parsons** of Barrington 11/22/1986 in Somersworth

DOWNING,
Robert F. of Barrington m. Marilyn G. **Litchfield** of Barrington 6/4/1971 in Dover; H - b. 10/26/1949 in NH, s/o Wesley A. Downing (NH) and Beverly C. Whitcher (NH); W - b. 5/23/1952 in ME, d/o Robert G. Litchfield (ME) and Rebecca M. Reeve (ME)

Vincent B. of Barrington m. Donna L. **Johnson** of Barrington 7/16/1970; H - b. 12/12/1951 in NH, s/o Wesley A. Bryant (NH) and Beverly C. Whitcher (NH); W - b. 2/25/1952 in NH, d/o Alexander J. Johnson (MA) and Evelyn M. Green (NH)

DOWNS,
Chester K. of Milton m. Hannah M. **Boyce** of Barrington 7/9/1970 in Milton; H - 3rd, b. 10/26/1892 in NH, s/o Frank L. Downs (NH) and Augusta Kimball (NH); W - 2d, b. 6/28/1880 in CT, d/o Frank Smith (MA) and Hannah Reiter (NY)
Joseph of Barrington m. Shirley **Fife** of Pittsfield 9/5/1981
Michael J. of Barrington m. Suzanne E. **Cooper** of Rochester 6/4/1977 in Dover
Peter J. of Barrington m. Maureen A. **Neal** of Concord 8/10/1985

DREW,
Albert A. of Barrington m. Velma M. **Ruff** of S. Berwick, ME 1/20/1956 in So. Berwick, ME; H - 27, laborer, b. NH, s/o Freeman Drew (NH) and Doris R. Pray (NH); W - 20, clerk, b. NY, d/o George H. Ruff (NY) and Hazel Skinner (NY)
Albert A. of Barrington m. Lois A. **Goss** of Dover 3/9/1968 in Dover; H - 2d, b. 11/19/1928 in NH, s/o Freeman Drew (NH) and Doris R. Pray (NH); W - 2d, b. 2/19/1942 in NH, d/o E. Stanley Merrill (NH) and Alice E. Amazeen (NH)
Frederick E. of Barrington m. Lydia C. **Anderson** of Everett, MA 6/29/1920 in Everett, MA; H - 31, farmer, b. Cape Girardeau, MO, s/o Greenleaf Drew (Barrington, farmer) and Neoma Miles (Mobile, AL, housewife); W - 33, teacher, b. Everett, MA, d/o Gustaf Anderson (Engelholm, Sweden, painter) and Selma England (Gottenburg, Sweden, housewife)
Frederick E. of Barrington m. Mary H. **Emhardt** of Barrington 2/27/1950 in New Haven, CT; H - 27, civil engineer, b. NH, s/o Frederick Drew and Lydia Anderson; W - 30, at home, 2d, b. MA, d/o Woodbury Hough and Lucia Cartland

George of Barrington m. Lucy **Clay** of Barrington 6/6/1893; H - 30, laborer, s/o William (Barrington, farmer); W - 22, at home, 2d, d/o Horace (laborer) and Cynthia

DROUN,
Hollis A. of Lyman, ME m. Mary Cecelia **Condon** of Saco, ME 1/10/1942; H - 21, appren. mach., b. Lyman, ME, s/o Lawrence W. Droun (Lyman, ME) and Edna M. Stevens (Kennebunk, ME); W - 19, clerk, b. Saco, ME, d/o Francis M. Condon (Canada) and Helen Murphy (Lawrence, MA)

DROWN,
Richard Earl of Barrington m. Robin Leigh **Burklund** of Northwood 10/9/1976 in Northwood

Thomas M. of Barrington m. Mary S. **Baker** of Deerfield 2/21/1977 in Deerfield

DUBE,
Peter R. of Rochester m. Susan **Bostrom** of Barrington 7/19/1986 in Rochester

DUBOIS,
Albert L. of Rochester m. Pauline H. **Neal** of Barrington 6/10/1972 in Rochester; H - b. 2/14/1948 in NH, s/o Eugene Dubois (NH) and Bertha Masse (NH); W - b. 11/30/1956 in NH, d/o Roger Neal (NH) and Laura Wheeler (NH)

Girard W. of Lexington, MA m. Murielle R. **Boucher** of Barrington 8/23/1985

DUFFY,
Daniel T. of Barrington m. Cynthia L. **Watson** of Somersworth 7/25/1982 in Rochester

James M. of Barrington m. Viola A. **Trenholm** of Newmarket 6/23/1984

DUFRESNE,
Chandler of Farmington m. Shirley E. **Robie** of Barrington 9/11/1949; H - 24, carpenter, b. NH, s/o Henry D. Dufresne (VT) and Silver Caswell (NH); W - 19, student, b. NH, d/o Lloyd A. Robie (NH) and Bernice Clarkson (NH)

DUGAL,
Jay T. of Barrington m. Donna E. **Caswell** of Barrington 7/19/1980 in Newmarket

DUNTON,
Kenneth I., Jr. of Barrington m. Coreen J. **Goodrow** of Rochester 8/30/1985 in Rochester
Kenneth I., Jr. of Barrington m. Kathryn M. **Trott** of Dover 8/8/1987 in Dover

DUPLAICE,
William of Kennebunk, ME m. Delia **Languirand** of Kennebunk, ME 8/17/1902; H - 28, teamster, 2d, b. Canada, s/o Alick Duplaice (Canada, laborer) and Lena Duplaice (Canada); W - 24, at home, b. Worcester, MA, d/o John Languirand and Phebe Lord

DUREAU,
Paul G. of Barrington m. Julie A. **Clay** of Barrington 4/14/1979 in Dover

DUROCHER,
David R. of Barrington m. Deborah A. **Hadfield** of Dover 2/27/1983 in Dover

DUSTIN,
Charles P. of Barrington m. Grace **Trafton** of Dover 1/4/1892 in Dover; H - 34, farmer, b. Barrington, s/o Mary B. Dustin; W - 32, dressmaker, 2d, b. Dover

EASON,
Robert E. of Farmington m. Dorothy E. **Griffin** of Barrington 8/12/1966 in Milton; H - 34, electronic tech., 3rd, div., b. Portland, ME, s/o Walter R. Eason and Mary A. Shapleigh (ME); W - 22, shoe worker, b. Rochester, d/o Elmer G. Griffin (ME) and Nellie C. Belleville (NH)

EATON,
John P. of Barrington m. Beth K. **Davis** of Barrington 11/12/1977 in East Rochester
Robert W. of Strafford m. Eloise J. **Buzzell** of Barrington 11/10/1942 in Dover; H - 25, US Army, b. Hartford, CT, s/o Charles L. Yeaton (Nashua) and Dorothy Caverly (London, England); W - 29, at home, b. Barrington, d/o Levi H. Buzzell (Barrington) and Bessie M. Arlin (Barrington)

EDDY,
Mathew H. of Barrington m. Susan F. **Kingsland** of Barrington 7/8/1983

EDGECOMB,
Lewis O. of Barrington m. Alfrida E. **Smith** of Barrington 11/8/1924; H - 32, farm helper, b. Sanford, ME, s/o Eben Edgecomb (Lovell, ME, retired) and Georgiana Worthern (Cambridge, MA); W - 16, housework, b. Lee, d/o Fred D. Smith (Barrington, woodchopper) and Jessie M. Libby (Berwick, ME, housewife)

EDMUNDS,
Garth C. of Barrington m. Michelle C. **Cyr** of Barrington 10/29/1977

ELLIOTT,
Charles H. of Barrington m. Ruth E. **Forest** of Barrington 8/19/1947 in Eliot, ME; H - 22, lumbering, b. Hampstead,

s/o Kelley E. Elliott (Canada) and Susie N. Sargent (Danville); W - 19, housework, b. Stowe, ME, d/o Charles E. Forest (Tamworth) and Rose E. Wiggins (Stowe, ME)

Clarence G. of Barrington m. Beatrice H. **Cofferen** of Barrington 1/1/1955 in Raymond; H - 25, woodsman, b. NH, s/o Kelley E. Elliott (NH) and Susan Norris (NH); W - 18, shoeworker, b. ME, d/o Maurice F. Cofferen (ME) and Alnora Damien (ME)

Earl F. of Barrington m. Georgia E. **Davis** of Nottingham 8/21/1939 in Eliot, ME; H - 18, cutting lum., b. Raymond, s/o Kelly E. Elliott (Orange) and Susie N. Sargent (Danville); W - 18, at home, b. Newfields, d/o Charles Davis and Mabel Clark

Gregory P. of Barrington m. Cynthia J. **Allis** of Barrington 5/26/1984 in Dover

Robert E. of Barrington m. Carolyn J. **Bellen** of Lebanon, ME 3/3/1956 in Berwick, ME; H - 17, woodsman, b. NH, s/o Kelly Elliott (NH) and Susan N. Sargent (NH); W - 16, at home, b. NH, d/o Harry E. Bellen (NH) and Martha J. Smith (NH)

Robert E. of Barrington m. Jeannine E. **Cross** of Durham 5/7/1966 in Durham; H - 27, orchard worker, 2d, div., b. Barrington, s/o Kelley E. Elliott (NH) and Susie N. Sargent (NH); W - 26, LPN, b. Exeter, d/o Clayton R. Cross (NH) and Eleanor B. Ellison (NH)

Robert N. of Barrington m. Juanita M. **Ricker** of Barrington 7/22/1978 in Raymond

ELLIS,
Steven H. of Barrington m. Kathy-Rae **Barnes** of Nottingham 6/3/1977 in Rochester

ELLISON,
Chester J. of Barrington m. Virginia B. **Tuttle** of Eliot, ME 6/4/1966 in Portsmouth; H - 48, inspector, 2d, widower,

b. Barrington, s/o Walter S. Ellison (NH) and Alta M. Glover (NH); W - 46, at home, 2d, widow, b. Jefferson, d/o Frank Kenison (NH) and Alice M. Blair (VT)

Ernest of Barrington m. Maude **Morrison** of Nottingham 12/19/1903; H - 18, fireman, b. Barrington, s/o William A. Ellison (Nottingham, lumberman) and Etta Drew (Dover); W - 19, at home, b. Nottingham, d/o John Morrison (carpenter) and Sarah Ellison (Barrington)

George E. of Barrington m. Mary Jane **Heath** of Northwood 4/15/1955 in No. Berwick, ME; H - 21, truck driver, b. NH, s/o George W. Ellison (NH) and Evelyn Elliott (NH); W - 18, at home, b. NH, d/o Robinson Heath (NH) and Elsie C. Mudgett (NH)

George W. of Barrington m. Evelyn E. **Elliott** of Barrington 12/18/1933 in Kingston; H - 18, laborer, b. Barrington, s/o Walter E. Ellison (Nottingham) and Alla Glover (Nottingham); W - 17, housework, b. Kingston, d/o Kelley Elliott (Kingston) and Susie Sargent (Danville)

Gordon K. of Barrington m. Minnie E. **Bryant** of Raymond 10/5/1968 in Raymond; H - b. 4/22/1950 in NH, s/o George W. Ellison (NH) and Evelyn L. Elliott (NH); W - 2d, b. 1/19/1946 in NH, d/o George A. Eaton (NH) and Lauretta E. Jones (NH)

Lewis H. of Barrington m. Sadie B. **Fogg** of Durham 3/7/1903 in Lee; H - 25, sawyer, b. Barrington, s/o Frank B. Ellison (Lee, teamster) and Georgianna Emerson (Lee); W - 28, dressmaker, b. Durham, d/o H. Freeman Fogg (Lowell, MA, farmer) and Abbie Bennett (Northwood)

William F. of Barrington m. Margaret E. **Campbell** of Dover 9/12/1925 in Dover; H - 25, gen. trucking, b. Barrington, s/o William A. Ellison (Nottingham, farmer) and Etta M. Drew (Dover, housewife); W - 24, clerk, b. Dover, d/o Walter C. Campbell (Poland, ME, supt. water works) and Viola C. Marshall (Digby, NS, housewife)

EMERSON,

Albert D. of Madbury m. Bertha L. **Berry** of Barrington 9/26/1898 in Dover; H - 25, farmer, b. Madbury, s/o Laban (Madbury, farmer) and Electa (Lee, housewife); W - 19, housekeeper, b. Barrington, d/o Alonzo (Strafford, farmer) and Olive (deceased)

Morris E. of Barrington m. Annie E. **Parshley** of Barrington 5/26/1932 in Rochester; H - 22, farmer, b. Manchester, s/o Edward S. Emerson (Rochester) and Etta M. Bickford (Rochester); W - 20, at home, b. Strafford, d/o Alvin C. Parshley (Strafford) and Elizabeth Gibson (Strafford)

Robert Scott of Northwood m. Joan Marjorie **Carr** of Barrington 2/28/1974 in Nottingham

ENDERSON,

George A. of Barrington m. Norma J. **Frost** of Rochester 6/26/1982

ENTWISTLE,

John L. of Saugus, MA m. Jean Y. **Johnston** of Saugus, MA 6/13/1957; H - 36, machinist, 2d, b. MA, s/o John Entwistle (England) and Alice Woodard (MA); W - 31, typist, 2d, b. MA, d/o Walter Y. Smith (MA) and Estelle Gray (MA)

ERICKSON,

Earl R. of Barrington m. Beatrice M. **Tirrell** of Saugus, MA 8/2/1942 in Gonic; H - 20, mill worker, b. Malden, MA, s/o Emrick E. Erickson (Lynn, MA) and Ida A. Eveleth (Chelsea, MA); W - 21, candy wrapper, b. Saugus, MA, d/o James T. Tirrell (Boston, MA) and Beatrice Bragg (St. Johns, Newfoundland)

Emrick E. of Barrington m. Hilda E. **Estes** of Barrington 4/24/1958 in Rochester; H - 58, carpenter, 2d, b. MA, s/o Emil Erickson (Sweden) and Hannah O. Glantz

(Sweden); W - 45, supervisor, 2d, b. MA, s/o Christopher Kahps (Latvia) and Emma Damburg (Latvia)

ESTES,
Alfred of Barrington m. Barbara J. **Sullivan** of Somersworth 10/4/1958 in Rochester; H - 24, air force, b. NH, s/o Elmer E. Estes (NH) and Hilda E. Kahps (MA); W - 25, IBM, b. NH, d/o John L. Sullivan (NH) and Hazel Thompson (NH)

Daniel J. of Dover m. Julie A. **Brown** of Barrington 5/25/1985

Robert I. of Barrington m. Cheryl C. **Gordon** of Rochester 6/21/1985

EVANS,
George E. of Barrington m. Mabel L. **Stilson** of Epping 1/1/1959; H - 56, mechanic, 2d, b. PA, s/o George Evans (Czechoslovakia) and Mary Breha (Czechoslovakia); W - 54, housewife, 2d, b. NH, d/o Justin G. Morrison (NH) and Maude I. Glover (NH)

FAIST,
David O. of Barrington m. Beverly L. **Clough** of Rochester 1/15/1955 in Rochester; H - 20, US Army, b. NH, s/o Walter H. Faist (MA) and Frances L. Ball (NS); W - 18, at home, b. NH, d/o Gilbert C. Clough (MA) and Hazel M. Holland (NH)

Robert L. of Barrington m. Jodie A. **Ward** of Milton 7/25/1981 in Milton

Walter H. of Barrington m. Madelynn M. **Nason** of Barrington 5/27/1961; H - 21, plumber, b. NH, s/o Walter H. Faist (MA) and Frances L. Ball (Canada); W - 19, at home, b. NH, d/o Ernest E. Nason (NH) and Dorothy O. Thyng (NH)

FANNING,
Monson H. of Barrington m. Jennie E. **Day** of Cambridge, MA 6/19/1912 in Rochester; H - 38, farmer, b. NS, s/o James Fanning (steam engineer) and Mary Swihamer; W - 19, housekeeper, b. Cambridge, MA, d/o Will Day (watchman) and Margaret Crawford

FARINA,
James Salvatore of Barrington m. Janet Irene **Foster** of Rochester 11/29/1976 in Rochester
Joseph Robert of Barrington m. Rose Marie **Letendre** of Rochester 6/29/1976 in Rochester

FARRIS,
Eugene of Leitchfield, KY m. Mary T. **Eldridge** of Barrington 3/2/1957 in Dover; H - 21, USAF, b. KY, s/o Ezra Farris (KY) and Martha Arsborn (KY); W - 17, student, b. MA, d/o Daniel F. Eldridge (MA) and Celia Dionizio (MA)

FARROW,
Thomas G. of Barrington m. Lydia A. **Cook** of Barrington 8/7/1982

FAVASSA,
Salvatore C. of Gloucester, MA m. Mary L. **Brigham** of Salem, MA 9/24/1960; H - 21, truck driver, b. MA, s/o Michael A. Favassa (Italy) and Nina R. Orlando (MA); W - 18, medical secr., b. MA, d/o Elliott W. Brigham (MA) and Marjorie E. Webber (MA)

FECTEAU,
Bruce D. of Barrington m. Linda A. **Pease** of Newmarket 10/2/1971 in Newmarket; H - b. 6/4/1952 in NH, s/o Leon Fecteau (NH) and Florence Laliberty (NH); W - b. 9/27/1952 in NH, d/o Arthur Pease (NH) and Grace Wojnar (NH)

Stephen N. of Rochester m. Marlene E. **Miller** of Barrington 9/1/1973 in Rochester; H - b. 12/19/1954 in NH, s/o Norman Fecteau (NH) and Marion Dehart (NH); W - b. 11/9/1955 in NH, d/o Malcolm W. Miller (NH) and Mary Y. Labrie (NH)

FEELEY,
Edward William, Jr. of Barrington m. Margie Ethelene **Honeycutt** of Barrington 11/1/1975 in Newington

FELKER,
Andrew L. of Barrington m. Eva J. **Perkins** of Meredith 12/4/1894 in Meredith; H - 25, bookkeeper, b. Barrington, s/o A. J. (Barrington, farmer) and Lydia (Barrington, at home); W - 23, school teacher, b. Meredith, d/o Benjamin (Meredith, farmer) and Eva T. (Meredith, at home)
Lafayette of Barrington m. Ida May **Varney** of Barrington 11/26/1894; H - 23, mechanic, b. Barrington, s/o A. J. (Barrington, farmer) and Lydia (Barrington, at home); W - 23, at home, b. Barrington, d/o Charles (Barrington, electrician) and Mary (Haverhill, MA)
William H. of Barrington m. Annie L. **Brown** of Strafford 8/13/1905 in Strafford; H - 31, farmer, b. Barrington, s/o Andrew J. Felker (Barrington, farmer) and Lydia A. Seavey (Dover); W - 24, sch. teacher, b. Strafford, d/o Levi W. Brown (Strafford, farmer) and Lydia A. Smith (Barrington)

FENERTY,
Stanley W. of Barrington m. Irene A. **Brown** of Barrington 2/15/1968 in Madbury; H - b. 12/28/1926 in ME, s/o Frank Fenerty (MA) and Ruby L. Tetley (ME); W - 2d, b. 4/14/1932 in NH, d/o Herbert E. Meattey (NH) and Mildred A. Deshan (NH)

FERNALD,
Gary P. of Barrington m. Virginia L. **Boyle** of Plymouth 6/30/1973; H - b. 10/14/1952 in NH, s/o Paul F. Fernald (NH) and Ada M. Neal (NH); W - b. 10/15/1952 in NH, d/o Francis L. Boyle (NH) and Thelma M. York (NH)
Herbert Albert of Barrington m. Lucille Norma **Fernald** of Barrington 10/16/1974 in Newmarket

FERRIS,
William L. of Rochester m. Helen M. **Tuck** of Barrington 3/12/1971 in Rochester; H - b. 4/7/1951 in MA, s/o Francis Ferris (MA) and Elsie Madirous (MA); W - b. 3/15/1952 in NH, d/o Gordon Tuck (MA) and Beatrice Beriault (Canada)

FERRY,
Guy M. of Barrington m. Lillian **Asel** of Barrington 2/19/1921; H - 22, construction worker, b. Hillsboro, s/o Albert C. Ferry (VT, trapper) and Eva Scribner (Chester, housewife); W - 21, waitress, 2d, b. Nashua, d/o Napoleon Dumas (ND, foundry) and Pamela Galipeau (Montreal, bookkeeper)

FIELD,
Jonathan R. of Barrington m. Carol G. **Weeks** of Barrington 9/7/1979 in Portsmouth
Jonathan R. of Barrington m. Pamela G. **Ward** of Barrington 8/16/1986 in Madison

FIFE,
Minot R. of Pembroke m. Katherine **Gallivan** of East Barrington 10/7/1930 in Dover; H - 65, farmer, b. Pembroke, s/o Ruben S. Fife (farmer) and Kate A.E. Worth (deceased); W - 56, housekeeper, b. Boston, MA, d/o Thomas Gallivan (deceased) and Julia M. Murphy (deceased)

FILLEY,
Ralph C. of Barrington m. Elaine K. **Emerson** of Northwood 7/4/1980 in Northwood

FITTS,
Michael K. of Nottingham m. Trudy A. **Desaulnier** of Barrington 9/24/1977

FITZGERALD,
William A. of Barrington m. Susan M. **Harlow** of Barrington 12/1/1979

FLAHERTY,
Wallase J. of Barrington m. Laurette R. **Donadio** of Barrington 12/19/1981

FLINT,
Daniel, Jr. of Dover m. Corinne A. **Edin** of Barrington 11/3/1945; H - 24, millhand, b. Boscawen, s/o Daniel Flint (Boscawen) and Hazel Hill (Henniker); W - 18, clerk, b. Malden, MA, d/o Reuben Edin (Newport, RI) and Martha Johnson (Sweden)

FLOOD,
Lawrence Charles of Barrington m. Priscilla Joan **Millette** of Barrington 10/4/1976
Martin James, Jr. of Barrington m. Sharon Elizabeth **Stuver** of Barrington 6/25/1976

FLORES,
James S. of Ft. Edward, NY m. Kathy L. **Woodard** of Ft. Edward, NY 6/4/1977

FOGARTY,
Frederick U. of Barrington m. Judy M. **Musler** of Barrington 4/30/1977

Leonard C. of Barrington m. Theresa M. **Hill** of Somersworth 1/17/1948 in Somersworth; H - 19, lumbering, b. Barrington, s/o Leonard L. Fogarty (PEI) and Laura M. Plourde (Rochester); W - 17, at home, b. Manchester, d/o Ernest E. Hill (Manchester) and Eva Metivier (Ossipee)

Michael W. of Barrington m. Cindy J. **Willett** of Lee 4/18/1980

FOGMAN,
Jeffrey R. of Barrington m. Jeannie M. **Fine** of Barrington 10/14/1977

FOLSOM,
Waynard Winston of Barrington m. Joyce Marie **Janelle** of Barrington 1/27/1975

FORBES,
Douglas L. of Barrington m. Pamela J. **Campos** of Barrington 3/30/1985

FORD,
Arthur L. D. of Taunton, MA m. Jean P. **Corey** of Taunton, MA 1/26/1952; H - 43, inspector, 2d, b. NH, s/o Rupert H. Ford (NH) and Daisy E. Camp (CA); W - 20, student, b. MA, d/o Carl W. Corey (NH) and Lilly L. Almquist (NY)

FORNWALT,
Thomas S. R. of Barrington m. Janet D. **Johnson** of Durham 7/4/1982 in Durham

FORTESCUE,
Henry M. of Barrington m. Marianne **Bucklin** of Barrington 10/16/1981 in Alexandria

FORTIER,
Thomas W. of Barrington m. Corina J. **Dunton** of Barrington 1/9/1984

FOSS,
Edwin S. of Barrington m. Mabel **Hodgdon** of Barrington 5/19/1892 in Strafford; H - 28, farmer, b. Barrington, s/o James S. and Martha J.; W - 22, teacher, b. Barrington, d/o Darius

Irvin C. of Sabattus, ME m. Annie E. **Felker** of Barrington 12/23/1901 in Pailland, ME; H - 25, teacher, b. Strafford, s/o Mark Foss (Strafford, farmer) and Lavinia Foss (Durham); W - 24, at home, b. Barrington, d/o Andrew Felker (Barrington, farmer) and Lydia Felker (Dover)

Oliver M. of Barrington m. Abbie L. **Avery** of Barrington 11/18/1893; H - 28, farmer, 2d, s/o W. H. (Lee, carpenter) and Fannie D. (So. Berwick, ME); W - 26, housemaid, d/o S. D. (Barnstead, farmer) and M. E.

William S. of Barrington m. Emma F. **Brown** of Barrington 11/20/1909; H - 83, farmer, 2d, b. Barrington, s/o Samuel H. Foss and Charlotte Nute; W - 55, domestic, b. Barrington, d/o Hezekiah Brown and Augusta E. Sylvester

FOWLER,
Aaron L. of Newmarket m. Tammy A. **Robidoux** of Barrington 2/12/1982

Clarence D. of Farmington m. Marion M. **Parsley** of Barrington 12/25/1914 in Strafford; H - 25, steamfitter, 2d, b. Strafford, s/o Arthur Fowler (Barrington, sawyer); W - 17, at home, b. Strafford, d/o Charles E. Parsley (Barrington, laborer) and Mary E. Jewell (Barrington, housewife)

William H. of New Durham m. Bertha G. **Shackford** of East Wakefield 1/3/1897; H - 26, lumber man, b. Rockland, ME, s/o Leroy (Waldoboro, ME, farmer) and Ellen (Ft.

Fairfield, ME, housewife); W - 16, housekeeper, b. Freedom, d/o Stephen (Eaton, farmer) and Ada (Waterboro, ME, housewife)

FOX,
Ronald G. of Bedford m. Sandra M. **Ramsdell** of Barrington 6/22/1968; H - b. 4/14/1944 in NH, s/o George A. Fox (PA) and Christina S. Clark (NH); W - b. 7/20/1946 in MA, d/o Frederick M. Ramsdell (MA) and Annie N. Taylor (MA)

FRANCIS,
Clayton J. of Barrington m. Sharon L. **Clough** of Barrington 4/7/1969 in Lee; H - 2d, b. 10/25/1923 in VT, s/o Solomon Francis (VT) and Mary Hoos (VT); W - 2d, b. 12/22/1940 in CA, d/o Maurice D. Meader (NH) and Loraine Brock (NH)

FRASE,
Stephen F. of Barrington m. Judith A. **Ross** of Barrington 6/30/1984

FRASER,
Thomas A. of Barrington m. Constance J. **Nadeau** of Nashua 7/16/1983 in Nashua

FREED,
Jeffrey L. of Barrington m. Kelly-Sue **Skimin** of Barrington 5/16/1987 in Durham

FREEMAN,
Albert of Barrington m. Lottie R. **Emerson** of Barrington 2/26/1919; H - 21, farmer, b. Barrington, s/o Charles Freeman (Barrington, laborer); W - 18, shop girl, b. Barrington, d/o George Emerson (Lowell, MA, laborer)

Arthur of Barrington m. Vinia **Freeman** of Barrington 10/30/1898 in Strafford B.L.; H - 22, laborer, b. Boston, MA, s/o Wilbur (Barrington, laborer) and Melissa; W - 18, domestic, b. Barrington, d/o John (Barrington, laborer) and Mary (housewife)

Arthur of Barrington m. Eva **Hanscom** of Barrington 5/29/1909 in Strafford; H - 23, farmer, 2d, b. Boston, MA, s/o Wilbur Freeman (Barrington, laborer) and Melissa Waterhouse; W - 23, domestic, b. Barrington, d/o Samuel Hanscom and Bridget Mahoney

Arthur W. of Barrington m. Jacqueline D. **Goulet** of Somersworth 11/9/1963; H - 20, member US Navy, b. NH, s/o Herbert Freeman (NH) and Rose Lemire (ME); W - 20, secretary, b. NH, d/o Roger B. Goulet (NH) and Gennita Letendre (NH)

Arthur W. of Barrington m. Maureen B. **Stabile** of Barrington 8/2/1986 in Portsmouth

George S. of Barrington m. Gertrude **Hanscom** of Barrington 10/12/1902; H - 24, laborer, b. Barrington, s/o Stephen Freeman (Barrington, laborer) and Fanny Chamberlain; W - 16, at home, b. Hartford, CT, d/o Leander Hanscom (Barrington, laborer) and Nellie Story

Herbert W. of Barrington m. Roseanna **Lemire** of Sanford, ME 7/1/1939 in Sanford, ME; H - 21, laborer, b. Rochester, s/o Arthur Freeman (Barrington) and Eva Hanscom (Barrington); W - 18, housework, b. Sanford, ME, d/o Ovila Lemire (Canada) and Lea Lavoie (New Durham)

Herbert W. of Barrington m. Barbara L. **Plante** of Alton Bay 10/3/1985 in Alton

Paul J. of Rochester m. Cathy L. **Wilkins** of Barrington 7/13/1985 in Dover

Perley of East Barrington m. Emma M. **Tuttle** of Epping 4/30/1922; H - 30, jobber, b. E. Barrington, s/o Charles Freeman (E. Barrington, jobber) and Mary Capen (Lynn, MA, housewife); W - 20, shoemaker, 3rd, b. Epping, d/o

Horace Davis (Raymond, laborer) and Mary E. Currier (Strafford, housewife)

Perley m. Mabel **Clark** 5/11/1929 in Dover; H - 36, lumberman, 2d, b. Barrington, s/o Charles Freeman (Barrington) and Mary Capen (Barrington); W - 29, housekeeper, 2d, b. Newmarket, d/o John Clark (Suncook) and Anna Stimpson (Stratham)

W. H. of Barrington m. Julia A. **Capur** of Barrington 9/3/1894; H - 21, farmer, b. Methuen, MA, s/o S. R. (Barrington, farmer) and Fannie (Barrington, at home); W - 22, at home, b. Somerville, MA, d/o Eben (Barrington, farmer) and Rhoda (Barrington, at home)

Walter of Barrington m. Effie E. **Tyler** of Barrington 12/27/1900 in Northwood; H - 22, laborer, b. Barrington, s/o Charles (Barrington, laborer) and Mary; W - 19, at home, b. Barrington, d/o George (Barrington) and Abbie

FRIEL,

Gerard J. of Barrington m. Joan E. **Robie** of Durham 5/29/1971 in Durham; H - b. 7/8/1943 in NY, s/o James P. Friel (MA) and Edna M. McFadden (MA); W - b. 9/23/1948 in NH, d/o Frank D. Robie (NH) and Joan Couture (ME)

FRIEND,

Alan R. of Rochester m. Julie A. N. **Bergeron** of Barrington 9/13/1986 in Rochester

FROST,

Ernest L. of Rochester m. Patricia A. **Tarmey** of Barrington 4/27/1973; H - b. 2/28/1952 in NH, s/o Lyle Frost (NH) and Dorothy Coffin (ME); W - b. 3/5/1954 in NH, d/o John Tarmey (NH) and Carol Brassaw (NH)

Fred R. of Barrington m. Esther J. **Hayes** of Barrington 1/6/1892; H - 23, farmer, b. Strafford, s/o William and

Fannie; W - 17, housemaid, b. Dover, d/o Enoch and Elizabeth

FRY,
Mark W. of Quincy, MA m. Virginia D. **LaCombe** of Barrington 5/19/1979

FULLINWIDER,
John Alexander of San Diego, CA m. Sylvia Ann **Fletcher** 3/27/1975 in Rochester

GAGNE,
Henri L. of Dover m. Theresa L. **Plourde** of Barrington 8/7/1948 in Gonic; H - 24, coal dealer, b. Dover, s/o John H. Gagne (Canada) and Elsa Cyr (Canada); W - 19, Gen. Elec., b. Barrington, d/o Alfred J. Plourde (Gonic) and Olivine M. Dalpie (Canada)

GAGNON,
Michael H. of Barrington m. Andrea T. **Provencher** of Rochester 8/27/1983 in Rochester

GAHAN,
Scott W. of Madbury m. Marjorie E. **Morgan** of Barrington 8/17/1985 in Durham

GARBOSKI,
Stephen E. of Barrington m. Eunice R. **Horton** of Barrington 7/11/1981 in Jackson

GARDNER,
Gary E. of Barrington m. Pamela G. **Randall** of Barrington 3/22/1987
Gerard M. of Barrington m. Mary L. **Gorman** of Rochester 12/10/1960; H - 24, heel turner, b. ME, s/o Armand W. Gardner (ME) and Ruth Lloyd (ME); W - 20, heel sander,

b. MA, d/o Philip F. Gorman (CT) and Evelyn Gilbert (NH)

GARLAND,
Alan G. of Madbury m. Cheryl D. **Smith** of Barrington 1/31/1970; H - b. 10/27/1948 in NH, s/o Frank E. Garland (NH) and Muriel Clark (NH); W - b. 7/15/1952 in NH, d/o Leroy F. Smith, Sr. (NH) and Therese L. Hamel (NH)
Alan G. of Barrington m. Jean **Gonzales** of Dover 9/2/1983
Robert E. of Madbury m. Jacqueline R. **Kelley** of Barrington 1/21/1962; H - 19, auto mechanic, b. NH, s/o Frank E. Garland (NH) and Muriel B. Clark (NH); W - 16, at home, b. NH, d/o Reginald E. Kelley (MA) and Vina L. Caverly (NH)

GARNETT,
James E. of Barrington m. Heidi D. **Purington** of Barrington 3/19/1983 in Weare
John J. of Barrington m. Christine M. **Bertrand** of Barrington 7/19/1986

GARVEY,
William F., Jr. of Barrington m. Rita M. **Hodges** of Dover 5/30/1951 in Dover; H - 21, USMC, b. NY, s/o William F. Garvey (NH) and Florence E. DeMeritt (NH); W - 18, student, b. NH, d/o George W. Hodges (Canada) and Elsie Wallace (NH)

GASKIN,
Robert W. of Coalinga, CA m. Deborah L. **Huntley** of Richmond, VA 5/30/1981

GAUNYA,
Alfred R. of Barrington m. Leona E. **Watts** of So. Berwick, ME 5/26/1951 in So. Berwick, ME; H - 18, clerk, b. NH,

s/o Roswell Gaunya (CT) and Lillian Bonneau (NH); W - 19, yarn inspector, b. NH, d/o Archie H. Watts (ME) and Lena Belliveau (ME)

GAUTHIER,
George Elmer of Barrington m. Nancy Louise **Plante** of Barrington 6/7/1975

GENDRON,
Paul E. of Sanford, ME m. Evangeline **Desroche** of Barrington 11/28/1927 in Gonic; H - 20, carpenter, b. Sanford, ME, s/o N. J. Gendron (lumberman) and Suzanne Langlois (domestic); W - 19, clerk, b. Barrington, d/o Fred Desroche (farmer) and Lea Bernier (domestic)

Roland N., Jr. of Barrington m. Paulette L. **Chase** of Barrington 3/10/1970; H - b. 12/29/1949 in MA, s/o Roland N. Gendron, Sr. (MA) and Lillian L. Rines (MA); W - b. 11/7/1951 in NH, d/o George L. Chase (MA) and Elfride M. Niedergesass (Austria)

Thomas of Barrington m. Irene M. **York** of Barrington 3/27/1948 in Berwick, ME; H - 59, moulder, 4th, b. Millbury, MA, s/o Joseph Gendron (Canada) and Melvina Devol (Newfoundland); W - 36, shoe worker, 2d, b. Rochester, d/o Hormidas Plourde (Canada) and Desauge Rioux (Canada)

GEOFFRION,
Allen F. of Barrington m. Donna L. **Wells** of Lee 5/20/1978 in Newmarket

Gary M. of Barrington m. Michele R. **Bonenfant** of Epping 6/7/1980 in Durham

GEORGE,
Robert P. of Barrington m. Cassandra L. **Shanklin** of Newmarket 6/30/1978

GERVAIS,
Donald G. of Barrington m. Claire L. **Willey** of Barrington 8/4/1984 in Madbury
Gerald R. of Barrington m. Diane L. **Gray** of Barrington 5/10/1986

GIBB,
Neil H. of Barrington m. Shirley G. **Witham** of Barrington 8/25/1945; H - 21, US Army, b. Enfield, s/o Oscar E. Gibb (Orleans, VT) and Nellie M. Jones (Lyndon, VT); W - 18, tel. oper., b. Northwood, d/o Albert M. Witham (Claremont) and Marguerite A. Ball (Canada)
Richard A. of Barrington m. Laurette R. **Caron** of Barrington 4/22/1967 in Dover; H - 19, master maker, b. Rochester, s/o Neil H. Gibb (NH) and Shirley G. Witham (NH); W - 18, at home, b. Dover, d/o Lucien J. Caron (ME) and Lillian R. Michaud (ME)
Roger W. of Lee m. Mary G. **Whitehouse** of Barrington 11/18/1967 in Lee; H - 51, transportation, 2d, widower, b. Manchester, s/o Oscar E. Gibb (VT) and Nellie M. Jones (VT); W - 47, at home, 4th, widow, b. Lawrence, MA, d/o James I. Goundrey (NY) and Ethel M. Russell (ME)
Roger Wendall of Barrington m. Priscilla Alma **Hayes** of Madbury 9/7/1936 in Dover; H - 20, spinner, b. Manchester, s/o Oscar E. Gibb and Nellie M. Gibb (Lyndonville, VT); W - 18, at home, b. Nashua, d/o Arthur Hayes (Madbury) and Irene Hayes (Quebec)

GILBRIDE,
Robert P. of Ogunquit, ME m. Barbara A. **Felong** of Barrington 10/26/1985 in Dover

GILMORE,
Richard E. of Rochester m. Shirley L. **Landry** of Barrington 11/27/1958 in Rochester; H - 23, shoe worker, b. NH, s/o

William L. Gilmore (Scotland) and Mary F. Witham (NH); W - 20, office work, b. NH, d/o James W. Landry (NH) and Barbara N. Walker (NH)

GILPATRICK,
Fred R. of Barrington m. Mildred M. **Howard** of Northwood 8/21/1919 in Northwood; H - 29, shoemaker, b. Barrington, s/o George Gilpatrick (Strafford, farmer); W - 18, shoe operator, b. Barrington, d/o Ernest Howard (Dover, surveyor)

GINGRAS,
Mark S. of Barrington m. Jennifer L. **Simpson** of Barrington 4/5/1986 in Exeter

GIROUARD,
Claude Yves of Nashua m. Jeannette Marie **Phillips** of Barrington 2/15/1975 in Rochester

GITSCHIER,
Stephen P. of Dover m. Deborah H. **Tucker** of Barrington 6/10/1978 in Dover

GLADHILL,
Charles W., Jr. of Portsmouth m. Carol L. **Anderson** of Barrington 12/26/1961; H - 25, univ. student, b. NH, s/o Charles W. Gladhill, Sr. (IA) and Ethel M. Palmer (England); W - 19, univ. student, b. MA, d/o Carl V. Anderson (MA) and Louise M. Morin (MA)

GLIDDEN,
Arthur F. of Rochester m. Gloria J. **Waterhouse** of Barrington 9/26/1964; H - 20, oven operator, b. NH, s/o Clarence A. Glidden (NH) and Mary A. Webber (NH); W - 18, rubber industry worker, b. NH, d/o Lester D. Waterhouse (NH) and Ethel C. Pike (NH)

Arthur Francis of Barrington m. Marcia Elizabeth **Wojtysiak** of Dover 7/20/1974

Danny K. of Barrington m. Jean M. **Stanley** of Rochester 7/3/1982 in Rochester

GLINES,
Roy of Barrington m. Dora **Clark** of Northwood 9/11/1926 in Northwood; H - 34, laborer, 2d, b. Springfield, MA, s/o Edward Glines (laborer) and Mary Kidder (at home); W - 18, at home, b. Deerfield, d/o George H. Clark (farmer) and Mary Young (at home)

GOLDEN,
Anthony W. of Portsmouth m. Toni-Jo **Nasuti** of Barrington 9/26/1987 in Portsmouth

GOLLEDGE,
Gary A. of Farmington m. Carol D. **Clark** of Barrington 9/5/1964; H - 22, welder, b. ME, s/o Charles Golledge (MA) and Ida Wellman (VT); W - 21, secretary, b. NH, d/o Melvin A. Clark (NH) and Olive M. Cleveland (NH)

GOODELL,
Michael Stephen of Dover m. Nola Jeanne Marie **DiVirgilio** of Barrington 9/6/1975

GOODFIELD,
Clarence of S. Lebanon, ME m. June B. **French** of E. Lebanon, ME 1/17/1949; H - 20, veteran, b. MA, s/o Nelson P. Goodfield (MA) and Florence Ballou (MA); W - 18, at home, b. NH, d/o Ernest H. French (ME) and Mildred G. Nowhall (ME)

GOODMAN,
Albert M. of Everett, MA m. Doris L. **Meattey** of Barrington 8/5/1948 in Rochester; H - 25, Navy, b. Roxbury, MA, s/o

Nathan Goodman (Roxbury, MA) and Anna Glazer (Russia); W - 17, at home, b. Fitzwilliam, d/o Herbert Meattey (Fitzwilliam) and Mildred DeShan (Washington)

GOODWILL,
Lloyd T. of Barrington m. Carolyn L. **Wynott** of Rye 7/13/1963; H - 41, electrician, b. MA, s/o Thomas M. Goodwill (Canada) and Edna Wynot (Canada); W - 40, teacher, b. NH, d/o Garland F. Wynott (Canada) and Ester L. Baker (NH)

GOODWIN,
Derald H. of Rochester m. Madeline **Hall** of Barrington 4/17/1953 in Rochester; H - 18, woodsman, b. NH, s/o John F. Goodwin (NH) and Odabelle M. Willey (NH); W - 18, shoeworker, b. NH, d/o Kenneth A. Hall (NH) and Ruth E. Hall (NH)

GOOSSENS,
Timothy W. of Dover m. Wendy A. **Smith** of Barrington 10/27/1984 in Dover

GORDON,
Neal H. m. Marie L. **Michaud** 5/19/1929 in Dover; H - 35, farmer, 2d, b. St. L. Co., NY, s/o W. J. Gordon (Felchville, VT) and Nattie Dean (NY); W - 25, at home, b. Quebec, d/o Joseph Michaud (Canada) and Anna Bossy (Canada)

Neil H. of Barrington m. Grace E. **Shepherd** of Portsmouth 6/26/1960; H - 66, ret. carpenter, 3rd, b. NY, s/o William J. Gordon (NY) and Nettie Dean (NY); W - 69, housewife, 4th, b. MA, d/o Albert H. Healey (NH) and Hattie Ladd (NH)

Richard P. of Somersworth m. Esther E. **Neal** of Barrington 8/31/1951; H - 28, butler, b. NH, s/o George Gordon

(NH) and Maxine S. York (NH); W - 20, dipper, b. NH, d/o Vira E. Neal (NH)

GORRILL,
Harry J. of Plymouth, MA m. Elaine A. **Turner** of Barrington 10/13/1956; H - 41, employer, 2d, b. Canada, s/o Roy H. Gorrill (Canada) and Sylvia Williams (Canada); W - 29, at home, 2d, b. NH, d/o Arthur W. Turner (NY) and Alice V. Hopey (Canada)

GOSS,
Vinal S. of Lee m. Madeline R. **Dubey** of Barrington 8/21/1970 in Farmington; H - 2d, b. 8/28/1938 in ME, s/o Charles S. Goss (ME) and Madeline M. Page (ME); W - 3rd, b. 10/13/1941 in NH, d/o Chester E. Wells (NH) and Elizabeth E. Brown (NH)

GOSSELIN,
Carlton R., Jr. of Gonic m. Marilyn M. **Canney** of Barrington 9/3/1966 in Gonic; H - 25, laborer, 2d, div., b. Rochester, s/o Carlton R. Gosselin (NH) and Viola V. Chase (NH); W - 23, at home, 2d, div., b. Concord, d/o Hollie Corbett (NH) and Doris Drake (NH)

GOULD,
Adrian R. of Keene m. Carolyn L. **Baxter** of Barrington 6/20/1970; H - b. 4/1/1947 in NH, s/o Adrian N. Gould (NH) and Barbara P. Donovan (NH); W - b. 7/22/1950 in NH, d/o Sherman L. Baxter (NH) and Luverne C. Swain (NH)

GOULET,
Ronald M. of Barrington m. Bonnie J. **Topliffe** of Barrington 11/11/1978

GOWIN,
David E. of Barrington m. Linda J. **Thurber** of Northwood 7/9/1983 in Northwood

GRACE,
William P. of Barrington m. Virginia A. **Maguire** of Barrington 7/9/1983 in Durham

GRAMMAS,
George A. of Gloucester, MA m. Trudi F. **Grier** of Gloucester, MA 4/7/1979

GRANT,
David R. of Northwood m. Irene E. **Caverly** of Barrington 7/6/1962; H - 28, plumber, 2d, b. MA, s/o Russell B. Grant (MA) and Dorothy F. Kelley (NH); W - 19, secretary, 2d, b. NH, d/o Raymond E. Bailey (RI) and Charlotte E. Goff (MA)

Roger Elton of York Harbor, ME m. Mildred P. **Clark** of Sanford, ME 12/6/1941; H - 26, contractor, b. Kennebunk, ME, s/o Harold H. Grant (Kennebunk, ME) and Ina E. Wakefield (Sanford, ME); W - 21, student, b. Sanford, ME, d/o George O. Clark (Sanford, ME) and Mildred Shaw (Sanford, ME)

GRAY,
Frank N. of Barrington m. Jean C. **Chretien** of Rochester 10/29/1955 in Rochester; H - 21, truck driver, b. NH, s/o John F. Gray (NH) and Edythe Langmaid (MA); W - 17, shoe worker, b. NH, d/o Eugene V. Chretien (Canada) and Madeline R. Hall (NH)

John F. of Barrington m. Ruth T. **Stacy** of Barrington 4/23/1946; H - 40, engineer, 2d, b. Northwood, s/o Fred L. Gray (Strafford) and Anna Clough (Rochester); W - 37, housewife, 2d, b. Malden, MA, d/o Clarence F. Bell

(Pleasant Valley, NY) and Mary Colclough (Patterson, NJ)

John W. of Barrington m. Ella G. **Spofford** of Barrington 1/14/1909; H - 52, farmer, 2d, b. Dover; W - 51, housekeeper, 2d, b. St. Johns, NB

Paul S. of Barrington m. Frances E. **Wroblewski** of Greenland 6/9/1979 in Greenland

Robert L. of East Rochester m. Marilyn E. **Stacy** of Barrington 6/30/1951; H - 20, weaver, b. NH, s/o John F. Gray (NH) and Edythe M. Langmaid (MA); W - 18, at home, b. MA, d/o Earle C. Stacy (NH) and Ruth T. Ball (MA)

GREELEY,

Robert M. of Rochester m. Barbara M. **Parker** of Barrington 8/27/1946 in Plaistow; H - 21, bus driver, b. Brockton, MA, s/o Arthur M. Greeley (Chester, VT) and Clara L. Williams (Brockton, MA); W - 22, at home, b. Littleton, d/o Albert E. Parker (Canada) and Ada M. Hopkins (Lowell, MA)

GREEN,

George A. of Haverhill, MA m. Lilla **Waterhouse** of Barrington 8/19/1903; H - 22, stage carp., b. Haverhill, MA, s/o Joseph Green and Adeline King; W - 22, at home, b. Barrington, d/o Benjamin Waterhouse (Boston, MA, farmer) and Loveling Downing

James B. of Dover m. Gladys F. **Cunningham** of Barrington 6/24/1967; H - 43, night watchman, 2d, div., b. Jacksonville, FL, s/o Walter D. Green (FL) and Mamie C. Weeks (FL); W - 42, at home, 2d, widow, b. Dover, d/o Harold C. Marden (NH) and Fannie B. Walch (NH)

Michael D. of Rochester m. Elaine A. **Turner** of Barrington 3/23/1947; H - 27, restaurateur, 2d, b. Merrill, ME, s/o Angus F. Green (Perth, Canada) and Louise M. York (Ashland, ME); W - 20, stenographer, b. Dover, d/o

Arthur W. Turner (Staten Island, NY) and Alice V. Hopey (Canada)

GREENE,
Frank E. of Moultonboro m. Edith L. **Smith** of Barrington 6/24/1978 in Exeter

GREENWOOD,
Charles E. of Bristol m. Elizabeth Jane **Albert** of Barrington 6/15/1957; H - 24, teacher, b. NH, s/o Joseph L. Greenwood (NH) and Estelle Robert (NH); W - 21, student, b. MA, d/o Russell A. Albert (MA) and Elizabeth J. Stewart (MA)

GRIESEMER,
Manfred R. of Barrington m. Charlene J. **Libby** of Barrington 4/6/1986

GRIFFIN,
Clarence W. of Barrington m. Mabelle B. **Jackson** of Rochester 9/13/1925 in Portsmouth; H - 30, farmer, b. Barrington, s/o Herbert E. Griffin (Strafford, farmer) and Mary E. Hanson (Strafford, housewife); W - 19, nurse, b. Dover, d/o Leslie E. Jackson (Madison, mechanic) and Annie Taylor (England, housekeeper)
Elmer G. of Springvale, ME m. Nellie C. **Belville** of Barrington 11/27/1936; H - 29, shoe maker, 2d, b. No. Berwick, ME, s/o Harry L. Griffin (So. Berwick, ME) and Annie Canney (No. Berwick, ME); W - 29, shoe shop, d/o Fred H. Belville (Keene) and Flora Hanna (Laconia)
Norman E. of Barrington m. Katherine **Hussey** of Rochester 4/6/1927 in Rochester; H - 20, farmer, b. Barrington, s/o Herbert E. Griffin (farmer) and Mary Hanson (domestic); W - 19, domestic, b. Rochester, d/o John W. Hussey (mason) and Sarah E. Garland (domestic)

GRISWOLD,
Ronald A. of Newmarket m. Madlyn P. **Walker** of Barrington 5/4/1963; H - 20, member US Army, b. CT, s/o George E. Griswold (NH) and Jennie J. Polyott (CT); W - 20, mica worker, b. NH, d/o Frank E. Walker (NH) and Blanche R. Brogan (NH)

GROETZ,
John D. of Exeter m. Mary A. **Drew** of Barrington 10/16/1954; H - 23, NHANG, b. NH, s/o Harry T. Grotz (OH) and Jennie A. Daughenbaugh (MN); W - 19, clerk, b. NH, d/o Freeman Drew (NH) and Doris R. Pray (NH)

GRONDIN,
Louis of Barrington m. Carol A. **Doering** of Barrington 7/12/1981 in Durham

GROSSMAN,
Kenneth W. of Barrington m. Arlys J. **Manning** of Barrington 8/21/1973 in Rochester; H - 2d, b. 3/8/1943 in NY, s/o Barney Grossman (NY) and Mollie Schuster (NY); W - 3d, b. 3/27/1935 in NE, d/o Malcolm D. Biery (IA) and Florence M. Kangan (NE)

GUBELLINI,
John M. of Barrington m. Linda F. **Wright** of Gulfport, FL 8/22/1978 in Portsmouth

GUIMOND,
Maurice N. of Barrington m. Betsy L. **Hippensteel** of Barrington 9/1/1984 in Durham

GUPTILL,
Paul J. of Barrington m. Marsha L. **Kiehl** of Gonic 12/1/1979 in Conway

Philip J. of Northwood m. Audrey L. **Clark** of Barrington 12/16/1955; H - 21, truck driver, b. NH, s/o Clyde T. Guptill (ME) and Helen O. Gerrish (NH); W - 19, secretary, b. NH, d/o Melvin A. Clark (NH) and Myrle O. Cleveland (NH)

GURNEY,
Glenn A. of Barrington m. Cynthia R. **Hildreth** of Rochester 10/5/1985 in New Durham

GUSTAFSON,
Carl Bertel of Barrington m. Meta Helene **Sexton** of Barrington 8/10/1974 in Strafford

GUYER,
Michael S. of Barrington m. Delphine **Evans** of Rochester 4/17/1971 in Durham; H - 2d, b. 7/16/1945 in VT, s/o Simeon J. Guyer (NH) and Mildred I. Bixby (ME); W - 2d, b. 2/5/1945 in NH, d/o George E. Guillmette (MA) and Delphine Mauzerolle (Canada)

HAECK,
Mark H. of Barrington m. Debra L. **Lafrance** of Bradford, MA 3/14/1981 in Dover

HAGERMAN,
Ronald E. of Kezar Falls, ME m. Marjorie L. **Wyant** of Barrington 6/11/1983 in Durham

HALE,
Samuel of Bar Mills, ME m. Lucia C. **Hough** of Barrington 7/9/1952 in Lee; H - 68, insurance salesman, 2d, b. NH, s/o Samuel Hale (NH) and Eva Cressey (NH); W - 61, housewife, 2d, b. NH, d/o Charles S. Cartland (NH) and Julia H. Wallingford (NH)

Thomas J. of Dover m. Marsha L. **Clay** of Barrington 5/10/1986 in Dover

HALEY,

Dwight H. of Barrington m. Shirley G. **Gibb** of Barrington 7/2/1977

Gregory A. of Barrington m. Lee A. **Pleadwell** of Fremont 10/16/1971 in Exeter; H - b. 6/1/1947 in ME, s/o Hubert C. Haley (ME) and Louise E. Nile (ME); W - b. 8/25/1952 in RI, d/o George E. Pleadwell (MA) and Mariana A. Possante (MA)

Leo M. of Rochester m. Florence E. **Turner** of Barrington 8/31/1942 in Berwick, ME; H - 21, fitter, b. Rochester, s/o Joseph L. Haley (Winchester, MA) and Ella Boudrane (Winchester, MA); W - 18, unemployed, b. Barrington, d/o Arthur W. Turner (Staten Island, NY) and Alice V. Hopey (NS)

Philip of Barrington m. Mary Jane **Howard** of Barrington 1/30/1902; H - 34, laborer, b. Haverhill, MA, s/o John Haley (Ireland, shoemaker) and Julia Canners (Ireland); W - 48, housework, 2d, b. Rochester, d/o Ira T. Howard (farmer) and Sarah Leathers

Sumner Abbott of East Barrington m. Rena Henderson **Wiley** of St. George, ME 8/26/1913 in Wiley's Corner, ME; H - 29, clerk, B&M, b. East Barrington, s/o George Benton Haley (grain dealer) and Mary Josephine Ham (Housewife); W - 27, teacher, b. St. George, ME, d/o John Fairfield Wiley (retired) and Mary G. Watts (deceased)

Waldron B. of Barrington m. Grace M. **McDaniel** of Barrington 3/17/1943; H - 23, US Army, b. Dover, s/o Lawrence D. Haley (Barrington) and Cassie Hall (Nottingham), W - 21, calculator, b. Barrington, d/o George T. McDaniel (Nottingham) and Grace E. Dodge (Somerville, MA)

William A. of Lowell, MA m. Gertrude V. **Hayes** of Barrington 7/31/1918 in Lowell, MA; H - 26, fireman, b. Boston, MA, s/o G. B. Haley (Lee, merchant) and Josephine Ham (Rochester, housekeeper); W - 26, housekeeper, b. Barrington, d/o Ivory Hayes (farmer) and Martha Daniels (housekeeper)

HALL,

Anderson C. of Barrington m. Agnes C. **Stevens** of Worcester, MA 6/13/1908; H - 28, engineer, b. Barrington, s/o George A. Hall (Barrington, farmer) and Elmira Berry; W - 30, artist, b. France, d/o Walter Stevens and Anne Pritchard

Fred C. of Barrington m. Ida E. **Smith** of Northwood 6/17/1916 in Northwood; H - 27, shoemaker, b. Northwood, s/o Charles S. Hall (Strafford, farmer) and Emma F. Caverly (Strafford, housewife); W - 23, housekeeper, b. Lowell, MA, d/o Samuel Smith (Lowell, MA) and Emma L. Price (Gilmanton, housekeeper)

Fred G. of Rollinsford m. Ruth E. **Wheeler** of Barrington 9/10/1960; H - 55, mechanic, 2d, b. NH, s/o Walter F. Hall (NH) and Mertie E. Young (NH); W - 48, elec. worker, 2d, b. NH, d/o John W. Demeritt (NH) and Alice M. Whitehouse (NH)

Harry of Barrington m. Aldona B. **Florence** of Deerfield 6/26/1954 in Rochester; H - 17, poultryman, b. NH, s/o Kenneth A. Hall (NH) and Ruth E. Hall (ME); W - 18, at home, b. NH, d/o Wilfred H. Florence (NH) and Marjorie N. Stevens (NH)

John E. of Barrington m. Mary A. **Dodge** of Barrington 9/22/1921; H - 71, farmer, b. Barrington, s/o George W. Hall (Barrington, farmer) and Lucinda Hall (Barrington, at home); W - 45, at home, 2d, b. Barrington, d/o Joseph Lingard (Switzerland, farmer) and Sarah Hall (Barrington, at home)

Kenneth of Barrington m. Ruth E. **Hall** of Barrington 9/3/1927
in Northwood; H - 31, truckman, b. Barrington, s/o
Charles Hall (real estate) and Emma Caverly (domestic);
W - 21, housekeeper, b. Dover, d/o Herbert Hall
(teamster) and Eunice Ross (deceased)
Robert L. of Barrington m. Joanne F. **Berry** of Dover
8/30/1973 in Dover; H - 2d, b. 1/6/1946 in CA, s/o
George Hall (NE) and Josephine Gales (ND); W - b.
4/20/1952 in NH, d/o John Berry (NH) and Pat Muciollo
(MA)
Walter F. of Barrington m. Mertie E. **Young** of Barrington
8/28/1901 in Rochester; H - 27, laborer, b. Barrington,
s/o David Hall (Barrington, shoemaker) and Mary E. Hall
(Strafford); W - 18, at home, b. Barrington, d/o Kingman
Young (Barrington, farmer) and Fannie Young
Warren C. of Barrington m. Inez C. **Chesley** of Barrington
10/4/1905 in Rochester; H - 28, farmer, b. Barrington,
s/o James C. Hall (Barrington, farmer) and Nancy J.
Chesley; W - 21, at home, b. Barrington, d/o Daniel S.
Chesley (Barrington, farmer) and Clara J. Hall

HAMBLETON,
James Thomas of Barrington m. Mary Ann **Morelle** of Lyme
8/25/1974

HAMILTON,
Charles E. of Cambridge, MA m. Addie M. **Dearborn** of
Barrington 8/10/1909 in W. Barrington; H -31, truckman,
2d, b. Limington, ME, s/o Solomon Hamilton and
Alsereta Sawyer; W - 24, domestic, b. Bridgton, ME, d/o
Simeon Dearborn (Barrington, farmer) and Lizzie M.
Brown

HAMMOND,
Howard F. of Dover m. Nancy J. **Mansfield** of Barrington
10/18/1969 in Dover; H - b. 9/16/1946 in NH, s/o Howard

E. Hammond (NH) and Leone Clifford (NH); W - b. 1/27/1950 in NH, d/o Benjamin W. Mansfield (NH) and Barbara Lucas (NH)

HANSCOM[B],
Charles of Barrington m. Julia **Capen** of Barrington 6/11/1911; H - 37, farmer, b. Somerville, MA, s/o Alva Hanscomb (Barrington, farmer) and Prudence Arlin (Barrington, housewife); W - 22, housework, b. Barrington, d/o Levi Capen (farmer) and Clara Freeman (housewife)

Henry of Barrington m. Lillian **Stanley** of Barrington 6/29/1902 in Rochester; H - 22, laborer, b. Barrington, s/o Leander Hanscom (Barrington, laborer) and Lucy Story (Barrington); W - 16, at home, b. Hudson, NY, d/o John Stanley (Boston, MA, farmer) and Ella Stanley (Barrington)

Irving of Barrington m. Nellie **Brown** of Madbury 3/17/1910; H - 31, farmer, b. Barrington, s/o Samuel Hanscom; W - 16, at home, b. Madbury, d/o Thomas Brown (Newburyport, MA, farmer) and Mary Brown (Barrington, housewife)

John H. of Barrington m. Lucy Mabel **Caswell** of Madbury 9/1/1906 in Exeter; H - 34, farmer, b. Somerville, MA, s/o Samuel Hanscomb (Barrington, farmer) and Bridget Mahoney (Lawrence, MA); W - 34, housekeeper, 2d, b. Dover, d/o Luther Brackett (Acton, ME, mechanic) and Emily J. Goodwin (So. Berwick, ME)

HANSON,
Edwin of Barrington m. Hattie **Carter** of Barrington 11/14/1899 in Rochester; H - 45, farmer, b. Barrington, s/o Moses (deceased) and Eliza; W - 35, domestic, b. Newton, d/o Moses (deceased) and Eliza

HARDENBROOK,
Bruce N. of Dover m. Janet M. **Hubbard** of Barrington 6/8/1974 in Dover

HARDING,
Edwin K., III of Barrington m. Sheila M. **Devine** of Hampton 8/22/1987 in Durham
Richard W. of Barrington m. Evelyn A. **Towle** of Concord 7/31/1963; H - 30, electrician, b. NH, s/o Walter M. Harding (MA) and Cora E. Tebbetts (NH); W - 40, secretary, 2d, b. MA, d/o Edward D. McGown (MA) and Pauline C. Rost (CT)
Richard W. of Barrington m. Ruth M. **Ruel** of Barrington 11/18/1978
Walter M. of Rochester m. Cora E. **Tebbetts** of Barrington 9/17/1931 in Dover; H - 36, electrician, b. Newton, MA, s/o Stewart Harding (Canada) and Margaret Peacock (Canada); W - 36, at home, b. Barrington, d/o Charles A. Tebbetts (Barrington) and Etta J. Ham (Rochester)

HARMON,
Arthur E. of Barrington m. Reta M. **Stevens** of Rochester 6/15/1947 in Rochester; H - 48, box maker, 2d, b. Springvale, ME, s/o Levi Harmon and Corris C. Cate (Plattsburgh, NY); W - 35, shoe worker, 2d, b. Center Ossipee, d/o Everett S. Eldridge (Ossipee) and Nettie Pike (Center Ossipee)

HARRIS,
Bradley S. of Barrington m. Darlene M. **McCann** of Barrington 9/1/1984
Delbert W. of Barrington m. Lillian E. **Martin** of Rochester 10/11/1947 in Rochester; H - 20, laborer, b. Mexico, ME, s/o John A. Harris (Camelton, NB) and Pearl Endmen (PEI); W - 18, at home, b. Tewksbury, MA, d/o Edgar Beaulieu (Rochester) and Cecile Martin (Lowell, MA)

Delbert W. of Barrington m. Lillian E. **Meattey** of Barrington 12/23/1977 in Lee

Wayne G. of Barrington m. Carolyn M. **Mailhot** of Rochester 4/11/1969 in Farmington; H - b. 1/10/1949 in NH, s/o Raymond F. Harris (ME) and Stella Berry (NH); W - b. 9/27/1951 in NH, d/o Leo P. Mailhot (NH) and Madeline M. Novinsky (NJ)

HART,

Stephen J. of Portsmouth m. Susan **Newsky** of Barrington 9/24/1983 in Dover

HARTFORD,

Albion R., Jr. of Barrington m. Kathleen A. **Rickrode** of Barrington 7/15/1972 in Rochester; H - b. 2/17/1952 in NH, s/o Albion R. Hartford, Sr. (NH) and Dorothy P. Dufault (ME); W - b. 3/18/1953 in CA, d/o James Rickrode (PA) and Joanna Rodgers (CA)

HARTON,

Thomas W. of Barrington m. Karen L. **Ross** of Barrington 11/30/1985

HARTRICH,

Jerald Jean of Andover, MA m. Shirley Ann **Cowgill** of Barrington 4/5/1975

HARTY,

Neil T. of Barrington m. Laura L. **Beeman** of Barrington 6/2/1973; H - b. 9/1/1954 in MA, s/o Martin C. Harty (MA) and Arlene F. Joyal (VT); W - b. 2/2/1956 in MI, d/o Darwin D. Beeman (MI) and Esther R. Kurkjian (MA)

HARVEY,

Benjamin F. of Barrington m. Valerie J. **Kubik** of Barrington 5/24/1980

Daniel S. of Barrington m. Theresa R. **Lemieux** of Barrington 12/17/1977 in Newmarket

HARWAY,
Oscar of Barrington m. Edith M. **Reed** of Madbury 3/29/1945 in Dover; H - 59, US Navy, ret., 2d, b. Jersey City, NJ, s/o Charles Harway (New York, NY) and Caroline (Jersey City, NJ); W - 44, teacher, 2d, b. Lee, d/o Loren Fernald (Nottingham) and Cylena DeMerritt (Lee)

HASKINS,
Robert H. of Barrington m. Pauline E. **Labrecque** of Barrington 1/2/1982

HASTINGS,
Neal H. of Strafford m. Madeline R. **Wells** of Barrington 7/9/1960; H - 23, baker, b. CT, s/o Henry L. Hastings (Canada) and Vivian G. Hopps (Canada); W - 18, office worker, b. NH, d/o Chester E. Wells (NH) and Elizabeth E. Brown (NH)

HATCH,
Douglas N. of Rochester m. Dawn **Foster** of Barrington 10/10/1954 in Berwick, ME; H - 21, woodsman, b. ME, s/o Ellis R. Hatch (ME) and Anna I. Neal (ME); W - 18, student, b. NH, d/o G. Frank Foster, Jr. (MA) and Bernice E. Howard (NH)
Douglas N. Jr. of Barrington m. Natalie E. **Larson** of Barrington 3/21/1980
Jeffrey E. of Barrington m. Teresa L. **McKay** of Rochester 4/27/1985 in Rochester

HAUGHEY,
John J. of Dover m. Denise H. **Kapsimalis** of Barrington 1/2/1982 in Portsmouth

HAWKINS,
Frankie David of Athens, GA m. Lorraine Victoria **Binette** of Barrington 8/23/1974 in Gonic

HAY,
George E. of Barrington m. Janet M. **Overlock** of Barrington 9/17/1983 in Hampton

HAYES,
Arthur D. of Barrington m. Helen V. **Garland** of Strafford 10/30/1907 in Strafford; H - 24, farmer, b. Barrington, s/o Ivory Hayes and Martha Daniels; W - 19, at home, b. Strafford, d/o Charles Garland (Strafford, farmer) and Ada Thompson (Northwood)
Brian R. of Rochester m. Korey L. **Landry** of Barrington 7/20/1985 in Dover
Charles H. of Barrington m. Judith J. **Bennett** of Dover 2/18/1897 in Dover; H - 24, farmer, b. Barrington, s/o Aleazor (Barrington, farmer) and Elizabeth (housewife); W - 25, b. Dover, d/o Andrew (Dover, shoemaker) and Jennie
Elihu W. of Rochester m. Ella F. **Howard** of Barrington 4/27/1904; H - 22, farmer, b. Rochester, s/o Benjamin F. Hayes (Rochester, farmer) and Clara L. Watson (Rochester); W - 21, housework, b. Rochester, d/o William H. Howard (Rochester, farmer) and Lizzie A. Parshey (Strafford)
Rodney G. of Barrington m. Patricia C. **Jones** of Madbury 4/3/1965; H - 21, electrician, b. NH, s/o Sumner A. Hayes (MA) and Pauline M. Wiggin (NH); W - 18, at home, b. NH, d/o Harold S. Jones (NH) and Lola A. Elkins (NH)
Stephen R. of Barrington m. Carolyn A. **Hershey** of Mt. Carmel, IL 3/1/1986
Sumner B. of Center Strafford m. Ada E. **Dean** of Center Strafford 5/18/1935 in Northwood; H - 21, farmer, b.

Center Strafford, s/o Berton Hayes (Center Strafford) and Blanche J. Hall (Bow Lake); W - 29, teacher, b. Dublin, d/o Freeman Dean (Francestown) and Harriett Cilley (Lowell, MA)

HAYNES,
George H. of Epsom m. Margaret D. **Waterhouse** of Barrington 8/19/1903; H - 25, farmer, b. Epsom, s/o Henry D. Haynes (Epsom, farmer) and Eliza A. Atwood (Alexandria); W - 26, school teacher, b. Boston, MA, d/o Thomas F. Dowd (Boston, MA, letter carrier) and Catherine Guilfoyle (England)

HAYWARD,
Guy D. of Barrington m. Phyllis E. **Dudley** of Dover 7/10/1981

HEALEY,
Randy L. of Barrington m. Cathleen M. **Ranagan** of Rochester 9/22/1984 in Rochester

HEATH,
Dana K. of Barrington m. Catherine F. **Ward** of Atkinson 7/21/1984 in Plaistow
Fred E. of Dover m. Lizzie E. **Tibbetts** of Barrington 8/5/1893; H - 60, shoe cutter, s/o Charles (Belmont, farmer) and Ellen (Exeter); W - 58, house maid, d/o Hiram (Barnstead, farmer) and Jennie (Barrington)
Joseph P. of Barrington m. Mary A. **Hayes** of Barrington 12/30/1983

HEATHFIELD,
Robert W. of Barrington m. Nancy M. **Nutter** of Barrington 12/19/1982

HEBERT,

Dennis W. of Rochester m. Pamela D. **Walker** of Barrington 10/3/1964; H - 20, barber, b. NH, s/o Wilfred J. Hebert (Canada) and Emily M. Lizotte (Canada); W - 20, rubber industry worker, b. NH, d/o Frank E. Walker (NH) and Blanche R. Brogan (NH)

HEDLEY,

Byron L. of Barrington m. Sheila A. **Shaw** of Barrington 10/20/1984

HELFGOTT,

Paul C. of Oakland, CA m. Patricia A. **Engel** of Mamaroneck, NY 9/27/1970; H - b. 3/6/1946 in DE, s/o Meyer Helfgott (Poland) and Gertrude D. Rotfuss (NY); W - b. 5/17/1948 in NY, d/o Morton H. Engel (NY) and Barbara A. Rossman (NY)

HEMEON,

David A. of Barrington m. Sabrina D. **Taylor** of Barrington 12/1/1973; H - b. 11/26/1954 in NH, s/o Howard J. Hemeon, Jr. (NH) and Ida A. Phelps (MA); W - b. 7/23/1956 in IL, d/o Charles R. Taylor (OK) and Macel E. Gamble (NE)

David Alan of Barrington m. Deborah Lee **Eschmann** of Barrington 7/5/1975

Howard J., III of Barrington m. Theresa M. **Wheeler** of Rochester 2/13/1972 in Rochester; H - b. 3/18/1950 in NH, s/o Howard J. Hemeon, Jr. (NH) and Ida A. Phelps (NH); W - b. 3/9/1954 in NH, d/o Charles W. Wheeler (NH) and Mildred Sullivan (MA)

Steven D. of Barrington m. Therese A. **Meattey** of Barrington 7/8/1978 in Durham

HENDERSON,
Dana D. of Barrington m. Roberta A. **Lemke** of Barrington 10/13/1978 in Durham
Harold of Keene m. Katherine H. **Wiggin** of Barrington 6/29/1923; H - 26, shoe finisher, b. Spofford, s/o William Henderson (England, woodworker) and Amelia Traynor (England); W - 22, teacher, b. Barrington, d/o Elmer E. Wiggin (Barrington, sta. agent) and Bertha Reynolds (Milton, housewife)
James A., Jr. of Miami, FL m. Marcia E. **Dustan** of Barrington 9/10/1960; H - 22, law student, b. FL, s/o James A. Henderson (GA) and Ruth Taylor (WI); W - 23, chartist, b. NH, d/o George R. Dustan (NH) and Elizabeth M. Knowlton (VT)
Samuel L. of Barrington m. Jennie **White** of Barrington 8/11/1903 in Dover; H - 29, shoemaker, b. Barrington, s/o Samuel Henderson (Eaton, farmer) and Sarah Locke (Barrington); W - 23, at home, b. Boston, MA
Steve R. of Barrington m. Diane L. **Lennon** of Dover 8/17/1985 in Dover

HENDRICKSON,
Edward P. of Barrington m. Linda C. **Hendrickson** of Dover 9/1/1979 in Dover
Wesley L. of Barrington m. Joan F. **Walters** of Rochester 5/14/1977 in Milton

HERTEL,
Van E. of Barrington m. Constance R. **Anderson** of Tilton 1/24/1984 in Tilton

HESELTON,
Dana J. of Rochester m. Marlene E. **Miller** of Barrington 1/26/1980

HILL,
Daniel C. of Winchester m. Lucille A. **Boodey** of Barrington 6/26/1948 in Richmond; H - 30, farmer, b. Winchester, s/o Cecil D. Hill (Winchester) and Jennie L. Thompson (Winchester); W - 27, teacher, b. Barrington, d/o John U. Boodey (Barrington) and Alice I. Arlin (Strafford)

George C. of Rochester m. Joan B. **Morrow** of Barrington 5/10/1979

J. W. of Barrington m. Cynthia **Winkley** of Strafford 7/27/1896 in Strafford; H - 63, farmer, 5th, b. Strafford, s/o Stephen and Mahala; W - 74, domestic, 5th

James R. of Nottingham m. Dorothy B. **Adams** of Barrington 4/9/1973; H - 4th, b. 4/3/1926 in ME, s/o Charles B. Hill (IL) and Bessie James (IL); W - 2d, b. 12/29/1930 in NH, d/o Charles Stilson (NH) and Mabel L. Morrison (NH)

HILLS,
Reid Anthony of Barrington m. ----- (name illegible) 12/27/1976 in Somersworth

HILLSGROVE,
Darryl W. of Somersworth m. Karen L. **Holland** of Barrington 5/26/1979

HINTON,
Dennis G. of Barrington m. Linda K. **Weeden** of Barrington 4/25/1987

HOBART,
Kenneth Clinton of Barrington m. Cecelia Margaret **Keefe** of Barrington 2/16/1975 in Durham

HOBBS,
Richard Alvin of Barrington m. Estelle Emerence **St. Laurent** of Hartford, CT 6/14/1975

HODGDON,
Gary A. of Strafford m. Teryl M. **Canney** of Barrington 7/28/1979 in Northwood

HOLMES,
Charles H. of Barrington m. Lillian **Hogan** of Dover 11/12/1905; H - 24, laborer, b. Crosby, VT, s/o Albert W. Holmes (Strafford, laborer) and Mary McDonald (Portland, ME); W - 19, at home, b. Dover, d/o Patrick Hogan (weaver) and Joanna Hogan

Fred W. of Barrington m. Minnie M. **Davis** of Barrington 5/27/1935 in Dover; H - 63, laborer, 4th, b. Nottingham, s/o Charles P. Holmes (Randolph) and Arvilla L. Foss (Strafford); W - 50, housekeeper, b. Pittsfield, d/o Horace Davis (Barnstead) and Martha J. Bridges (Levant, ME)

HOLT,
Bradley G. of Barrington m. Mary J. **Shea** of Wakefield 8/6/1978 in Durham

HORNE,
Philip D. of Sandown m. Gayle S. **Blidberg** of Barrington 10/5/1985

HOSIER,
Carl D. of Barrington m. Justine D. **DiFruscio** of Lawrence, MA 2/6/1960; H - 22, member Army, b. OK, s/o Robert D. Hosier (CA) and Alice Babar (VA); W - 25, shoe worker, b. MA, d/o Frank DiFruscio (Italy) and Josephine Fuschi (Italy)

HOUDE,
Andrew R. of Dover m. Kathy J. **LaBelle** of Barrington 12/12/1970 in Dover; H - b. 7/22/1947 in NH, s/o Alfred H. Houde (NH) and Louise Gagnon (NH); W - b.

8/4/1951 in IL, d/o Boyd H. LaBelle (IL) and Wilma Truman (WI)

HOUK,
Donald R. of Barrington m. Katherine A. **Winter** of Barrington 10/4/1979

HOULE,
Richard H. of Barrington m. Elizabeth A. **Staryk** of Barrington 1/4/1980
Scott R. of Barrington m. Sandra L. **Stone** of Barrington 6/15/1985 in Somersworth

HOUSTON,
Darrell S. of Barrington m. Rhonda L. **Cilley** of Barrington 9/29/1984 in Penacook

HOWARD,
Arthur W. of Barrington m. Laura L. **Wingate** of Barrington 11/25/1904; H - 24, farmer, b. Barrington, s/o William H. Howard and Elizabeth A. Parshley; W - 45, housewife, 2d, b. Strafford, d/o Asa Jewell and Marion Thompson
Arthur W. of Barrington m. Abbie E. **Willand** of Rochester 9/9/1933 in Dover; H - 52, farmer, 2d, b. Rochester, s/o William Howard (Barrington) and Elisabeth Parshley (Strafford); W - 51, shoe operator, 2d, b. Rochester, d/o Augustus E. Horne (Wolfeboro) and Nellie Johnson (Brookfield)
Charles of Barrington m. Genese **Harte** of Barrington 4/18/1898; H - 27, farmer, b. Dover, s/o Emery (Barrington, farmer) and Emma H. (housewife); W - 32, domestic, b. Van Buren, ME, d/o Frank (farmer) and Annie (deceased)
D. M. of Barrington m. Isadore **Malonzo** of Barrington 11/9/1893; H - 48, harness maker, 3rd, s/o Joel (Rochester, farmer) and Harriet (Barrington); W - 43, at

home, 2d, d/o Israel (River Lew, farmer) and Angie (Canada)

Ernest of Barrington m. Lilla **Reed** of Barrington 11/25/1895; H - 22, laborer, b. Dover, s/o Emery (Barrington, laborer) and Emma; W - 17, at home, b. Barrington, d/o Charles (Barrington, laborer) and Anna

Fred W. I. M. of Barrington m. Bertha S. **Goodwin** of Barrington 10/11/1896 in Strafford; H - 25, laborer, b. Farmington, s/o Edwin and Mary (Rochester, housewife); W - 16, domestic, b. Strafford, d/o George and Christaing (Barrington, housewife)

Harry W. of Barrington m. Sadie **Eaton** of Strafford 4/26/1899 in Rochester; H - 20, farmer, b. Barrington, s/o William and Elizabeth; W - 18, domestic, b. Strafford, d/o Samuel and Evelyn

John W. of Barrington m. Anna **Farrel** of Boston, MA 5/20/1890; H - 33, b. Barrington, s/o Emery Howard; W - 26, b. Boston, MA, d/o Michael and Mary Farrel

Levi of Barrington m. Cora B. **Howard** of Barrington 2/4/1892 in Strafford; H - 21, farmer, b. Rochester, s/o A. B. Howard and Nancy; W - 18, lady, b. Barrington, d/o Joel N. and Jane L.

Michael C. of Barrington m. Melissa F. **Jayes** of Barrington 2/15/1986

Ray F. m. Ruth C. **Falk** 7/14/1949; H - 45, phys. therapist, 3rd, b. ME, s/o Joseph J. Howard (ME) and Ada Cooper (ME); W - 50, none, 2d, b. NY, d/o Austin Hopey (Canada) and Margaret Arseneau (Canada)

Stephen of Barrington m. Lola Ethel **Pike** of Rochester 11/5/1905; H - 26, laborer, b. Dover, s/o Emery Howard (Barrington, laborer) and Emma Canney (Dover); W - 18, domestic, b. Farmington, d/o George H. Pike (Middleton, teamster) and Cynthia A. Pike (Wells, ME)

William I. of Barrington m. Lydia F. **Clough** of Alton 7/3/1906 in Strafford; H - 36, laborer, 2d, b. Farmington, s/o Mary I. Howard (Rochester); W - 48, domestic, 2d, b. Alton, d/o Charles E. Young (Alton, farmer) and Mary E. Jones (Alton)

HOWCROFT,
Michael A. of Barrington m. Sharon E. **Jackson** of Barrington 7/5/1985 in Farmington

HOWE,
Elmer C. of Waltham, MA m. Annie J. **Adams** of Waltham, MA 9/22/1890; H - 29, b. Barrington, s/o Daniel and Sarah Howe; W - 25, b. Waltham, MA, d/o Mary Adams
Frank R. of Barrington m. Ethel L. **Boyle** of Boston, MA 8/4/1899; H - 17, farmer, b. Farmington, s/o Frank (Barrington, furniture) and Ida (Sanford, ME); W - 16, domestic, b. Lynn, MA, d/o Daniel (Halifax, NS, engineer) and Charlotte

HOYT,
Benjamin W., Jr. of Barrington m. Petra I. **Posner** of Barrington 2/3/1979
Charles L. of Barrington m. Mary **Chamberlain** of Weston, MA 9/23/1913 in Gonic; H - 64, farmer, 2d, b. Rochester, s/o Rufus Hoyt (farmer) and Lovey Tebbetts (deceased); W - 63, housework, 2d, b. Cambridge, MA, d/o Luther Townsend (deceased) and Mary Nichols (deceased)
Frank D. of Barrington m. Adeline **Green** of Haverhill, MA 8/6/1901; H - 43, farmer, 2d, b. Barrington, s/o Charles Hoyt (Barrington, farmer) and Rosetta Hoyt (Loudon); W - 44, housekeeper, 2d

HUBBARD,
Daniel H. of Barrington m. Pamela J. **Johnson** of Coral Gables, FL 8/21/1971; H - b. 12/4/1944 in CT, s/o Harry B. Hubbard (CT) and Jessie A. MacFarlane (Canada); W - b. 4/23/1946 in VT, d/o Ovid Armis Johnson (MN) and Amy Gladys Osgood (VT)

HUBERT,
Steven M. of Rochester m. Patricia M. **White** of Barrington 4/16/1985

HUCKINS,
Thomas E. of Barrington m. Sandra L. **Smith** of Barrington 2/23/1980 in Rochester

HUDSON,
Roderick W. of Barrington m. Barbara E. **Costa** of Barrington 8/4/1985 in Dover

HUGGARD,
Daniel Clayton of Rochester m. Susan Dale **Purvis** of Barrington 8/17/1974

HUGHES,
Daniel P. of Dover m. Cynthia L. **Eschmann** of Barrington 2/27/1965; H - 21, Gen. Elec. emp., b. NH, s/o John J. Hughes (NH) and Evelyn Lamie (NH); W - 20, secretary, b. ME, d/o Leon J. Eschmann (NH) and Louise Elliott (NH)

HUGHEY,
Lewis R. of Barrington m. Frances C. **Arsenault** of Freeport, ME 4/14/1965; H - 50, contractor, 3rd, b. ME, s/o Henry J. Hughey (Canada) and Berniece Orr (Canada); W - 41, secretary, b. ME, d/o Joseph D. Arsenault (Canada) and Sarah J. LeClair (Canada)

HUNTOON,
Roger J., Jr. of Barrington m. Lisa A. **Brown** of Strafford 3/28/1987

HUPPE,
Paul R. of Berwick, ME m. Janice R. **Patry** of Berwick, ME 6/6/1987

HUSSEY,
Charles William of Cambridge, MA m. Mildred May **Smith** of Barrington 6/4/193 in Rochester; H - 26, painter, b. Cambridge, MA, s/o Ruel W. Hussey (painter) and Ella F. Pierce (housewife); W - 17, no occ., b. Hingham, MA

HUTCHINS,
Charles H. of So. Berwick, ME m. Elaine L. **Freeman** of Barrington 6/22/1957; H - 21, painter, b. ME, s/o Charles H. Hutchins (ME) and Gertrude Adams (ME); W - 17, at home, b. NH, d/o Herbert W. Freeman (NH) and Roseanna Lemire (ME)

HUTCHINSON,
Perne of Berlin m. Ruth **Calef** of Barrington 2/27/1918; H - 22, forester, b. Berlin, s/o Louis A. Hutchinson (Milan, banker) and Clarice Mitchell (Dummer, housewife); W - 22, at home, b. Barrington, d/o Austin Calef (Barrington, merchant) and Clillie Chesley (Barrington, housewife)

IBER,
Jonathan O. of Barrington m. Carol A. **Jones** of Barrington 6/25/1983

IKEWOOD,
Dean J. of Barrington m. Susan M. **Lipsey** of Barrington 8/16/1985

INSALACCA,
Guy of Gonic m. Thesa **Mana** of Gonic 8/14/1936; H - 19, truck driver, b. Gonic, s/o Joseph Insalacca (Gonic) and

Josephine Insalacca (Gonic); W - 23, at home, b. Dover, d/o John Mana (Gonic) and Marion Mana (Gonic)

IOCONO,
Gino A. of Barrington m. Bethany D. **Reed** of Barrington 9/29/1984 in Dover

IRONS,
Anthony E. of Barrington m. Janet L. **Navin** of Barrington 12/30/1972 in Newfields; H - b. 8/13/1948 in WA, s/o Davison E. Irons (PA) and Alda G. Hanlon (MA); W - 3d, b. 1/20/1940 in NH, d/o Kenneth F. Douglas (MA) and Doris Coe (MA)
Davison R. of Durham m. Carolina **Bodner** of Barrington 9/5/1971; H - b. 10/21/1941 in MA, s/o Davison E. Irons (PA) and Alda G. Hanlon (MA); W - b. 7/29/1946 in NH, d/o Walter F. Bodner (NJ) and Adela W. Sienko (NH)

IRVIN,
Roger M. of Dover m. Susan J. **Digman** of Barrington 12/20/1968 in Durham; H - b. 9/11/1948 in MN, s/o Willis Irvin (AR) and Mary Barrett (MN); W - b. 1/16/1946 in ME, d/o Ralph Digman (WI) and Patricia McNally (ME)

IRVINE,
Thomas C. of Barrington m. Barbara J. **Nasuti** of Barrington 8/16/1980 in Dover

ISEMAN,
Donald L. of Freeport, PA m. Susan E. **Phillips** of Barrington 11/9/1968; H - b. 12/6/1944 in PA, s/o Clifford Iseman (PA) and Verna R. Van Dyke (PA); W - b. 1/31/1946 in MA, d/o Harry Phillips, Jr. (NH) and Elizabeth M. King (MA)

JABLONSKI,
Robert J. of Barrington m. Julia E. **Robidoux** of Barrington 7/31/1982

JACKSON,
Brian S. of Barrington m. Deborah E. **Weeks** of Barrington 8/2/1969; H - b. 10/31/1950 in NH, s/o Frederick L. Jackson (FL) and Ina E. Brown (NH); W - b. 11/9/1951 in NH, d/o Robert E. Weeks (NH) and Betty M. Scott (MA)
Craig Martin of Barrington m. Kim Elaine **Knight** of Barrington 8/7/1976
Curtis G. of Barrington m. Robin M. **Pelletier** of Dover 6/12/1981 in Dover
Frederick L. of Barrington m. Ina E. **Brown** of Barrington 9/22/1946 in Dover; H - 20, mechanic, b. Melbourne, FL, s/o Everett C. Jackson (Dover) and Ella Lear (Dover); W - 18, at home, b. Barrington, d/o Warren Brown (Barrington) and Evelyn Buzzell (Barrington)
Frederick L. Jr. of Barrington m. Julie E. **Fitzgerald** of Barrington 6/28/1980 in Rochester
Frederick Lensworth, Jr. of Barrington m. Marlene Elisa **Harty** of Barrington 10/16/1976
Keith F. of Barrington m. Audrey M. **Perry** of Milton 7/15/1967 in Milton; H - 19, mechanic, b. Rochester, s/o Frederick Jackson (FL) and Ina E. Brown (NH); W - 17, student, b. Rochester, d/o Charles E. Perry, Jr. (NH) and Eva M. Pearson (NH)

JACQUES,
Philip R. of Dover m. Sherry A. **Osborne** of Barrington 4/25/1979
Theodule J. of Barrington m. Muriel T. **Robbins** of Barrington 4/23/1937 in Nottingham; H - 32, laborer, 2d, b. Manchester, s/o Theodule Jacques (St. Sov'r'n, PQ) and Delia Grenier (St. Sov'r'n, PQ); W - 18, at home, b.

Danvers, MA, d/o Charles Robbins (Moncton, NB) and Mildred Mackenzie (Danvers, MA)

JAMES,
Mark D. of Barrington m. Linda A. **Fowler** of Exeter 4/8/1978 in Exeter

JEFFERS,
Robert M., Jr. of Barrington m. Joyce W. **Pelletier** of Barrington 2/14/1985 in Portsmouth

JEFFERY,
Stephen P. of Barrington m. Katherine L. **Smith** of Barrington 6/25/1983 in Durham

JENNESS,
John of Barrington m. Emily S. **Hurd** of Rochester 9/21/1892 in Pittsfield; H - 28, laborer, b. Rochester, s/o Paul L. and Susan; W - 22, housemaid, b. Rochester, d/o John W. and Ann

Lewis B. of Barrington m. Lula M. **Rowe** of Barrington 9/20/1892 in Dover; H - 23, music teacher, b. Nottingham, s/o George W. and Mary C.; W - 16, music teacher, b. Barnstead, d/o Charles C. and Mary L.

JENNISON,
Dan A. of Barrington m. Pamela A. **Sumner** of Durham 1/13/1973 in Durham; H - b. 9/18/1952 in NH, s/o Roger Jennison (NH) and Bertrice Dennett (NH); W - b. 10/14/1950 in NH, d/o Donald M. Sumner (NH) and Margaret Strong (NH)

Douglas R. of Barrington m. Merry F. **Graves** of Northwood 1/6/1968 in Northwood, H - 19, b. NH, s/o Roger D. Jennison (NH) and Beatrice M. Dennett (NH); W - 18, b. NH, d/o Robert W. Graves (MA) and Dorothy M. McKay (MA)

Robert E. of Madbury m. Louise M. **Meattey** of Barrington 4/3/1953 in Dover; H - 19, mechanic, b. NH, s/o Harold F. Jennison (MA) and Sarah E. Gilmore (MA); W - 17, at home, b. NH, d/o Herbert E. Meattey (NH) and Mildred A. Deshane (NH)

JESSEMAN,
Melton A. of Bristol, CT m. Shirley R. **Roberts** of Barrington 6/14/1986 in Rochester

JESSING,
David W. of Barrington m. Candace G. **Hurst** of Barrington 5/17/1987

JOHNS,
Joel E. of Marlboro, MA m. Nancy M. **Hodsdon** of Barrington 7/14/1979

JOHNSON,
Alexander J. of Barrington m. Evelyn M. **Bryson** of Barrington 5/4/1951 in Dover; H - 45, fireman, 2d, b. MA, s/o Ernest F. Johnson (MA) and Lulu P. Hogle (Canada); W - 39, factory worker, 2d, b. NH, d/o George A. Green (MA) and Lilla Waterhouse (NH)
David F. of Jacksonville, FL m. Laurie M. **Nasuti** of Barrington 12/30/1983
Ernest B. of Barrington m. Vera Helen **Locke** of Barrington 7/28/1920 in Rochester; H - 42, farmer, 2d, b. Fryeburg, ME, s/o Isachar Johnson (Jackson, farmer) and Jennie Ross (Lebanon, ME, housewife); W - 43, housekeeper, 2d, b. Milton, d/o Ephraim Ellis (Milton, farmer) and Hannah Jones (Milton, housewife)
Ovid A. of Rochester m. Shirley E. **Rowell** of Barrington 11/22/1983 in Rochester
Ralph Wallace of Lynn, MA m. Harriette Mae **Norton** of Lynn, MA 9/15/1915; H - 29, telephone, b. Almena, KS, s/o

Frederick C. Johnson (Lowell, MA) and Lydia B. Johnson (Somersworth, housewife); W - 35, housewife, 2d, b. Exeter, d/o Philip H. Curley (VT) and Helen May Curley (England, housewife)

Rodney A. of Barrington m. Nancy A. **Keen** of Barrington 5/10/1986

Thomas F. of Dover m. Carol L. **Scheu** of Barrington 6/22/1963; H - 21, shoe worker, b. NH, s/o John J. Johnson (NH) and Lucia E. Wiggin (NH); W - 21, secretary, b. NH, d/o Arnold L. Scheu (MA) and Louise F. Lettrey (MA)

JONES,

Kenneth A. of Barrington m. Bonnie L. **Eldredge** of Dover 10/23/1982 in Dover

Moulton R. of Barrington m. Dorothy M. **Brooks** of Barrington 10/11/1967; H - 44, carpenter, 2d, div., b. E. Lebanon, ME, s/o Moulton R. Jones, Sr. (ME) and Erma M. Hemingway (ME); W - 51, waitress, b. Dover, d/o Irving E. Brooks (ME) and Pearl H. Gordon (ME)

JOY,

Ephraim of Barrington m. Olive A. **Fling** of Barrington 4/25/1896 in So. Berwick, ME; H - 56, farmer, 2d, b. So. Berwick, ME, s/o Asa and Dorcas; W - 59, housekeeper, d/o Sewall and Joan

Ephraim of Barrington m. Maria **Allard** of Berwick, ME 4/15/1902 in Berwick, ME; H - 64, farmer, 3rd, b. Berwick, ME, s/o Asa Joy (York Co., ME, farmer) and Dorcas Joy (York Co., ME); W - 65, housewife, 3rd, b. NS, d/o William Buckman (NS, farmer)

JULIN,

Ben L. of Barrington m. Sandra R. **Pease** of Barrington 8/27/1983

JUNKINS,
Guy D., Jr. of Somersworth m. Paula **Johnson** of Barrington 6/29/1985 in Dover

KANE,
Paul Daniel of Portsmouth m. Laurie Margaret **Johnson** of Barrington 9/6/1975

KAY,
David D. of Dover m. Donna L. **Newsky** of Barrington 8/26/1978 in Dover

KEAYS,
William E. of Dover m. Bette M. **Clayton** of Barrington 10/27/1950 in Dover; H - 22, mason, b. NH, s/o Walter Keays (NH) and Annie Ferns (NH); W - 18, student, b. MA, d/o Max Clayton (NY) and Norma Perry (ME)

KEESEE,
Thomas G. of Chilhowie, VA m. Linda R. **Nettleton** of Barrington 9/9/1972 in Portsmouth; H - b. 7/23/1949 in VA, s/o Luther E. Keesee (VA) and Lula Sessor (VA); W - b. 2/7/1953 in PA, d/o John T. Nettleton (CT) and Elaine G. Shannon (PA)

KELLER,
Stephen E. of Rochester m. Susan D. **Gibb** of Barrington 9/22/1972; H - b. 12/8/1954 in PA, s/o ----- Keller and Doris F. Fallon (PA); W - b. 9/20/1954 in NH, d/o Neil H. Gibb (NH) and Shirley G. Witham (NH)

KELLEY,
Dennis W. of Farmington m. Joanne G. **Gibb** of Barrington 2/5/1977

George W. of Barrington m. Joanne T. **Bourque** of Dover 8/24/1963; H - 19, member US Army, b. NH, s/o

Reginald Kelley (MA) and V. L. Caverly (NH); W - 18, tel. operator, b. OH, d/o Raymond Bourque (NH) and Gertrude T. Laughlan (NH)

KELLY,
Robert F. of Northwood m. Addie Lora **Smith** of Concord 10/9/1937 in Gonic; H - 21, iron moulder, b. Northwood, s/o Bert O. Kelly (Strafford) and Mary McLaughlin (Brookline, MA); W - 18, at home, b. Groton, d/o Lewis Smith (Orange) and Bernice Hill (Grafton)

KENDALL,
Raymond R. of Brockton, MA m. Gladys E. **Nute** of Brockton, MA 8/14/1943 in Rochester; H - 41, weaver, b. Boston, MA, s/o George F. Kendall (Boston, MA) and Helen McBride (NH); W - 36, tel. operator, b. W. Bridgewater, MA, d/o Clarence J. Nute (E. Bridgewater, MA) and Ethel G. Babcock (NS)

KENISTON,
Robert L., Jr. of Dover m. Mary E. **Clancy** of Barrington 12/29/1972; H - 2d, b. 12/22/1932 in NH, s/o Robert Keniston (NH) and Euna Wilkie (NH); W - b. 6/27/1942 in NH, d/o Thomas Clancy (NH) and Helen Hughes (NH)

KENNEY,
William M. of York, ME m. Barbara A. **Wallingford** of Barrington 4/8/1972; H - b. 7/26/1948 in NH, s/o John F. Kenney (MA) and Norma Rice (MA); W - b. 7/18/1954 in NH, d/o Richard E. Wallingford (ME) and Helen J. Elliott (NH)

KERN,
John J., Jr. of Barrington m. Teresa A. **King** of Exeter 4/6/1985 in Portsmouth

KERR,
Daniel E. of Berwick, ME m. Lucy P. **Gordon** of Barrington 10/11/1909; H - 54, mill operator, 2d, b. Boston, MA, s/o Daniel Kerr and Catherine Lambert; W - 57, domestic, 2d, b. Barrington, d/o Hezekiah Brown and Augusta B. Parson

KESSLER,
Harry E. of Barrington m. Jacqueline E. **Neal** of Barrington 8/11/1979

KETCHEN,
Richard L. of Carlisle, MA m. Anne E. **Dearstyne** of Danvers, MA 8/20/1983

KIMBALL,
Paul A. of Wolfeboro m. Patricia A. **Waterhouse** of Barrington 7/22/1961; H - 20, carpenter, b. NH, s/o John P. Kimball (NH) and Mary E. LeVangie (MA); W - 18, at home, b. NH, d/o George L. Waterhouse (NH) and Elsie F. Whitaker (NH)

KINCAID,
Clifford G. of Dover m. Gladys **Crawbuck** of Barrington 6/6/1980 in Dover

KINERSON,
Russell S., Jr. of Barrington m. Michelle **Zenon** of Barrington 9/15/1979 in Durham

KING,
Stephen C. of Somersworth m. Donna L. **Moore** of Barrington 6/3/1978

KINNEY,
Andrew C. of Barrington m. Cheryl A. **Twomey** of Barrington 8/2/1987 in Dover

KISOR,
William M. of Barrington m. Karen L. **McElmurry** of Barrington 10/29/1987

KITTREDGE,
Scott G. of Barrington m. Janet L. **Merrill** of Barrington 8/19/1983 in Strafford
Van R. of Barrington m. Lynn M. **Hatch** of Barrington 7/23/1983

KNIGHT,
David T. of Barrington m. Gail **Sirviris** of Somersworth 8/19/1978 in Somersworth
David T. of Barrington m. Joy C. **Page** of Somersworth 2/28/1986 in Madbury
Fred W. of Durham m. Roberta R. **Turner** of Barrington 6/2/1956; H - 23, mechanic, b. NH, s/o John B. Knight (NH) and Florence Crouch (NH); W - 19, hair dresser, b. NH, d/o Arthur J. Turner (NY) and Virginia F. Ramsdell (MA)
Harold R. of Durham m. Florence E. **Haley** of Barrington 9/14/1947 in Center Sandwich; H - 35, machinist, 2d, b. Newmarket, s/o Fred W. Knight (Newmarket) and Evelyn E. Bentley (NS); W - 23, sales agt., 2d, b. Barrington, d/o Arthur W. Turner (Staten Island, NY) and Alice V. Hopey (Ontario)
John A. of Wakefield m. Sandra L. **Evenson** of Barrington 6/9/1985 in Strafford

KNOOP,
William E. of Durham m. Elaine M. **Gardner** of Barrington 12/4/1973 in Durham; H - 2d, b. 4/24/1936 in OH, s/o

Russell H. Knoop (MO) and Laura Morrow (OH); W - 2d, b. 3/20/1947 in MA, d/o Alexander Cooper (Newfoundland) and Frances Warner (MA)

KNOX,
Harley of Miami, FL m. Lois **Kimball** of Barrington 4/12/1945 in Dover; H - 55, farmer, 3rd, b. Epping, s/o Fred P. Knox (Epsom) and Carey Chamberlain (Oakland, CA); W - 51, housewife, 3rd, b. Nottingham, d/o William Ellison (Lee) and Etta Drew (Dover)

KOH,
Chang H. of Barrington m. Mi K. **Kim** of Barrington 11/1/1982

KUDER,
Gregory T. of Barrington m. Brenda L. **Maurice** of Farmington 10/29/1982 in Milton

KUNZ,
Frederick W., Jr. of Barrington m. Ginelle L. **Emerson** of Barrington 8/16/1986 in Alton

KYLE,
Paul Edward of W. Nottingham m. Mariann **Downs** of Barrington 5/29/1976

LABONTE,
Richard B. of Dover m. B. Ellen **Clouthier** of Barrington 1/26/1980

LABRECQUE,
Alfred of Barrington m. Shirley F. **Dougherty** of New Brunswick, Canada 5/27/1972 in Dover; H - 2d, b. 2/7/1922 in MA, s/o Honore Labrecque (Canada) and Angelina Robitaille (Canada); W - b. 12/2/1934 in

Canada, d/o Hazen L. Dougherty (Canada) and Jessie K. Fisher (Canada) Donald R. of Rochester m. Angela M. **Mountain** of Barrington 7/16/1983 in Rochester

LACOMBE,
James of Barrington m. Catherine Jane **McCusker** of Claremont 1/25/1975 in Durham

LAFLAMME,
Wayne L. of Barrington m. Linda M. **Thibeault** of Barrington 9/13/1985

LAFLEUR,
Donald E. of Barrington m. Valerie A. **Kenney** of Rochester 4/21/1979 in Rochester

LAFOND,
Gerard L. of Barrington m. Wanda M. **Maynard** of Manchester 3/8/1984 in Manchester

LAFRAMBOISE,
Frederick B. of Newmarket m. Helen H. **Fee** of Barrington 9/2/1953 in Rochester; H - 36, manager, 2d, b. NH, s/o Benjamin F. LaFramboise (Canada) and Lena M. Duguay (NH); W - 28, receptionist, 2d, b. NH, d/o Maurice T. Buzzell (NH) and Laura C. Edney (CO)

LALOS,
Thomas K., Jr. of Barrington m. Elaine A. **Hyde** of Hanover 5/5/1967 in Durham; H - 21, power linesman, b. Manchester, s/o Thomas K. Lalos (MA) and Vasilku Georgu (NH); W - 21, univ. student, b. Taunton, MA, d/o Ralph E. Hyde (MA) and Edith L. Bennett (MA)

LAMBERT,

Donald R. of Rochester m. Donnine **Schofield** of Barrington 8/26/1966 in Farmington; H - 26, board scaler, 2d, div., b. Rochester, s/o Albert G. Lambert (NH) and Phyllis Shorey (NH); W - 19, IBM student, b. Rochester, d/o Donald E. Schofield (VT) and Nadine B. Currier (NH)

LANDERS,

Steven William of Barrington m. Donna Lynn **Craig** of Rochester 7/10/1976

LANDRY,

Eugene R. of Barrington m. Doris E. **Alty** of Dover 3/17/1956 in Dover; H - 20, USAF, b. NH, s/o James Landry (NH) and Barbara Walker (NH); W - 20, at home, b. MA, d/o Joseph Alty (MA) and Beatrice Paul (MA)

Francis A. of Barrington m. Elizabeth J. **Albert** of Barrington 4/23/1946; H - 35, fireman, 2d, b. Bethlehem, s/o Joseph V. Landry (Canada) and Mary Bodrew (Canada); W - 40, housewife, 2d, b. Boston, MA, d/o Elias B. Stewart (Canada) and Lena D. Allen (Helena, NY)

James W., Jr. of Barrington m. Joan Marie **Loring** of Gonic 2/10/1962; H - 21, gas sta. attnd., b. NH, s/o James Wilfred Landry, Sr. (NH) and Barbara N. Walker (NH); W - 18, at home, b. MA, d/o Norman A. Loring (MA) and Sylvia B. Orpik (MA)

LANG,

George F., III of Barrington m. Joanne **Piper** of Barrington 5/16/1987

LANGELIER,

Laurice A. of Barrington m. Carol J. **Colby** of Barrington 11/18/1978 in Greenland

Michael J. of Rochester m. Lisa M. **Hill** of Barrington 8/28/1982 in Rochester

LANGLEY,
Percy of Barrington m. Josephine **Brown** of Northwood 7/10/1902; H - 24, farmer, b. Barrington, s/o Gilbert Langley (Nottingham, farmer) and Charlotte Langmaid (Lee); W - 19, at home, b. Northwood, d/o Samuel Brown (Barrington) and Sophia Canney

LANGMAID,
Charles A. of Lee m. Louise C. **Dodge** of Barrington 6/30/1925; H - 42, laborer, 2d, b. Lee, s/o Alonzo Langmaid (Lee, farmer) and Legetta Wiggin (Lee, housewife); W - 37, at home, 2d, b. Barrington, d/o John C. Bodge (Barrington, farmer) and Sarah I. Gray (Strafford, housewife)

LAPANNE,
Luke J. of Strafford m. Penelope A. **Thurston** of Barrington 5/14/1983 in Rochester

LAPIERRE,
Kevin H. of Barrington m. Doreen M. **Cary** of Barrington 8/25/1979 in Lee

LAROCHE,
Robert J. of Durham m. Linda D. **Gibb** of Barrington 8/6/1971 in Durham; H - b. 2/3/1950 in NH, s/o Roger LaRoche (Canada) and Laura Cote (NH); W - b. 5/1/1951 in NH, d/o Neil Gibb (NH) and Shirley Witham (NH)

LAROCHELLE,
Armand J., Jr. of Rochester m. Joyce A. **Wells** of Barrington 6/27/1959; H - 21, shoe worker, b. NH, s/o Armand J. Larochelle (NH) and Agnes E. Pike (NH); W - 19, shoe worker, b. NH, d/o Chester E. Wells (NH) and Elizabeth E. Brown (NH)

LATHROP,
Herbert N. of Barrington m. Diana **Warburton** of Barrington 1/14/1983

LAURION,
Henry of Gonic m. Rosamond C. **Champagne** of Barrington 7/4/1959; H - 26, barber, b. NH, s/o Adelard Laurion (NH) and Eva Berthiaume (Canada); W - 20, office worker, b. NH, d/o Damus W. Champagne (NH) and Ruth Osgood (NH)

Victor V. of Rochester m. Mary A. **Roulx** of Barrington 10/30/1937 in Gonic; H - 24, spinner, b. Gonic, s/o Israel Laurion (Canada) and Emma Landry (Canada); W - 19, housemaid, b. Barrington, d/o Ferdinand Roulx (Canada) and Mary Bishop (Canada)

LAVALLIERE,
Frank D. of Barrington m. Diane F. **MacEachern** of Barrington 12/11/1987

LAVOIE,
Dennis J. of Barrington m. Dorothy G. **McGuirk** of Barrington 6/11/1977 in Nottingham

LAWRENCE,
Michael P. of Manchester m. Penny D. **Zsigray** of Barrington 6/7/1986 in Dover

LAWSON,
Fred W. of Manchester m. Helen E. **Vallee** of Barrington 7/5/1947 in Manchester; H - 48, fruit buyer, 3rd, b. Calais, ME, s/o Christopher Lawson (St. Johns, NB) and Bessie Johnson (Perry, ME); W - 34, at home, 2d, b. Northwood, d/o Frank N. Pender (Northwood) and Mabel Bryant (Northwood)

LAYNE,
Benton E. of Lee m. Mabel L. **Wheeler** of Barrington 12/20/1899 in Dover; H - 31, farmer, 2d, b. Lee, s/o Samuel (Lee, farmer) and Susan (Nottingham); W - 25, teacher, b. Lowell, MA, d/o Jessie (deceased) and Laura

LAZARO,
Barry C., Sr. of Barrington m. Karen E. **Stender** of Somersworth 5/25/1979 in Rochester

LEAHY,
Daniel J. of Barrington m. Ruby C. **Redden** of Dover 7/15/1982 in Lee

John G. of Manchester m. Debra **Low** of Barrington 6/22/1957; H - 25, claim adj., b. MA, s/o John L. Leahy (MA) and Dorice Tozier (MA); W - 22, student, b. MA, d/o Frederick B. Low and Irene Beard (MA)

John J. of Madbury m. Gloria A. **Witham** of Barrington 12/31/1949 in Dover; H - 22, student, b. NH, s/o John W. Leahy (NH) and Marie A. Ouellette (NH); W - 18, tester, b. NH, d/o Albert M. Witham (NH) and Marguerite A. Ball (Canada)

John J. of Barrington m. Grace M. **Wynn** of Dover 8/24/1963; H - 35, auto worker, 2d, b. NH, s/o John W. Leahy (NH) and Marie A. Ouelette (NH); W - 30, rubber ind., 2d, b. NH, d/o Edward Stillwagon (PA) and Mildred Brennan (NH)

Tommie J. of Barrington m. Debra A. **Guppy** of Barrington 8/5/1978 in Dover

LEBLANC,
Robert G. of Lee m. Andrea R. **Youngren** of Barrington 2/24/1973; H - 2d, b. 10/28/1930 in NH, s/o John S. LeBlanc (Canada) and Lea Plouff (NH); W - 2d, b. 4/23/1944 in IL, d/o Ralph A. Nelson (IL) and Eleanore Braun (IL)

LECLAIR,
John A., Jr. of Barrington m. Maureen E. **Joyce** of Weymouth, MA 6/30/1979

LEDINGTON,
Gary W. of Newport, MI m. Deborah L. **Laroy** of Monroe, MI 10/19/1985

LEE,
James E. of Barrington m. Beverly J. **Braley** of Barrington 4/25/1981
Robert E. of Lee m. Brenda L. **Reed** of Barrington 9/29/1984 in Hanover

LEEPER,
Verne P. of Barrington m. Dorothy M. **Codyer** of Dover 12/5/1969 in Dover; H - 3rd, b. 10/4/1931 in SC, s/o Durwood Leeper (CT) and Mary Spise (CT); W - 3rd, b. 5/1/1928 in MA, d/o John Chiasson (Canada) and Edith Lambert (ME)

LEFEBVRE,
Timothy T. of Rochester m. Carolyn M. **Hooper** of Barrington 8/16/1986 in Rochester

LEFFEL,
Alfred W., Jr. of Barrington m. Patricia R. **Aikin** of Northwood 3/21/1964; H - 25, truck driver, b. NJ, s/o Alfred W. Leffel (NJ) and Winifred W. Conrad (NJ); W - 22, nurse, 2d, b. NV, d/o Ray J. Flynn (OR) and Georgalee A. Crider (MO)
Barry L. of Barrington m. Joan D. **Pease** of Northwood 3/14/1959; H - 18, US Navy, b. NJ, s/o Alfred W. Leffel (NJ) and Winifred C. Conrad (NJ); W - 19, at home, b. NH, d/o George Pease (NH) and Dorothy M. Corliss (NH)

LEIGHTON,
Warren C. of Dover m. Ruth E. **Bryson** of Barrington 10/8/1960; H - 22, shovel oper., b. NH, s/o Warren A. Leighton (NH) and Florence O. Chandler (NH); W - 21, stenographer, b. NH, d/o Melvin F. Bryson (NH) and Evelyn M. Green (NH)

LENZI,
Brian D. of Barrington m. Rebecca M. **Walker** of Newmarket 8/18/1973 in Newmarket; H - b. 5/23/1948 in NH, s/o George R. Lenzi (NH) and Evaline B. Baker (NY); W - b. 9/14/1948 in NH, d/o Richman G. Walker (NH) and Theresa A. Bourgoin (NH)
George Francis of Boston, MA m. Mary Ruth **Bodge** of Barrington 2/5/1913; H - 21, clerk, b. Boston, MA, s/o Frank Lenzi (meat cutter) and Mary Sullivan (housekeeper); W - 19, milliner, b. Barrington, d/o Charles F. Bodge (farmer) and Mary C. Carly (housekeeper)
Steve F. of Barrington m. Pamela M. **Caron** of Dover 6/16/1973 in Dover; H - b. 7/2/1949 in NH, s/o George Lenzi (NH) and Evanor Baker (NJ); W - b. 10/15/1950 in NH, d/o William Caron (MA) and Barbara Saisen (MA)

LEOCHA,
Mitchell J. of Portsmouth m. Muriel L. **Turner** of Barrington 5/5/1945 in Rochester; H - 26, machinist, b. Claremont, s/o Zenon Leocha (Warsaw, Poland) and Saturninga Jasinski (Warsaw, Poland); W - 26, clerk-typist, 2d, b. Madbury, d/o Arthur W. Turner (Staten Island, NY) and Alice V. Hopey (St. Johns, Canada)
Mitchell J., II of Barrington m. Julie A. **Parker** of Gonic 5/27/1984 in Rochester

LESLIE,
James B. of Barrington m. Susan F. **Clock** of Hampton
9/24/1983 in Exeter

LEVASSEUR,
Leo H. of Barrington m. Natasha A. **Itchkawich** of Barrington
8/25/1985 in New Durham

LEVENDAHL,
David R. of Barrington m. Kathleen M. **Deely** of Rochester
10/14/1987 in Newington

LEVESQUE,
Louis A., Sr. of Salem m. Starr R. **Kelley** of Barrington
9/29/1979 in Northwood

LEWIS,
Paul Herbert of Barrington m. Sandra Arlene **Selig** of Dover
12/29/1973
Wayne E. of Kaiserslauten, West Germany m. Yvonne M.
Larocca of Barrington 6/27/1987 in Hampton Falls

LIBBY,
Leo R. of Rochester m. Lisa E. **Jackson** of Barrington
8/4/1979

LIGHT,
Donald W., Jr. of Cambridge, MA m. Nancy L. **Knott** of
Stanford, CA 1/4/1964; H - 21, research asst., b. MA, s/o
Donald W. Light, Sr. (KS) and Helen Downs (NJ); W -
24, college student, b. WA, d/o Harold R. Knott (WA)
and Agnes G. Smick (WA)

LINGARD,
Ralph E. of Barrington m. June T. **Lund** of Rochester
12/10/1966 in Manchester; H - 51, carpenter, 3rd, div., b.

Strafford, s/o Grover C. Lingard (NH) and Josie M. Bushway (NH); W - 31, shoe worker, 2d, div., b. Rochester, d/o James H. Willard (MA) and Cancia A. Thivierge (NH)

LINSCOTT,
Fred E. of Barrington m. Grace G. **Hanson** of Strafford 1/1/1906 in Strafford; H - 24, farmer, b. Northwood, s/o Albert Linscott (Rochester, farmer) and Josephine Linscott; W - 24, at home, b. Strafford, d/o Charles Hanson (Strafford, machinist) and Vina Tebbetts (Barrington)

LIPE,
Bradley A. of Barrington m. Linda A. **Tamulonis** of Barrington 10/20/1979

LITTLEFIELD,
Frederick E., Jr. of Barrington m. Virginia L. **Smith** of Barrington 3/18/1983

LOCHREN,
Lawrence D. of Barrington m. Carol L. **Gowin** of Barrington 2/14/1985 in Dover

LOCKE,
Clarence B. of Barrington m. Eva May **Forsaith** of Barrington 12/16/1939 in Dover; H - 41, farmer, 2d, b. Barrington, s/o Irving M. Locke (Barrington) and Linna Buzzell (Barrington); W - 34, housewife, 2d, b. Claremont, d/o Samuel Clow (PEI) and Mary Duffany (Northfield, VT)
Eben S. of Barrington m. Marguerite **Hanna** of Barrington 4/20/1905; H - 40, farmer, b. Barrington, s/o Samuel A. Locke (Barrington, farmer) and Sophronia A. Sherburne (Barrington); W - 40, stenographer, b. St. Johns, NB, d/o

Joseph Hanna (St. Johns, NB, bookkeeper) and Sarah Logan (St. Johns, NB)

Irving M. of Barrington m. Linna M. **Buzzell** of Barrington 2/1/1897; H - 32, farmer, b. Barrington, s/o Elisha (Barrington, farmer) and Lucy (housewife); W - 19, teacher, b. Barrington, d/o Samuel (Barrington, farmer) and Nellie (housewife)

Samuel Seavey, Jr. of Barrington m. Lizzie S. **Hart** of Barrington 4/1/1911; H - 25, paper maker, b. Dover, s/o Samuel S. Locke (Rochester, farmer) and Elizabeth Faircloth (Lake Megantic, housewife); W - 37, housemaid, b. Van Buren, ME, d/o Frank Hart (Van Buren, ME, farmer) and Madeline Violette (housewife)

Stanley A. of Barrington m. Ida Belle **Thompson** of Lee Hill 6/1/1898 in Lee; H - 27, farmer, b. Barrington, s/o Samuel (deceased) and Sophronia (Barrington, housewife); W - 27, teacher, b. Lee, d/o Jonathan (deceased) and Lucy (Amesbury, MA, housewife)

Stanley A. of Barrington m. Isabelle B. **Chesley** of Barrington 5/18/1904; H - 33, farmer, 2d, b. Barrington, s/o Samuel A. Locke (farmer) and Sophronia Sherburne (Barrington); W - 27, at home, b. Boston, MA, d/o George H. Chesley (Barrington, engineer) and Elizabeth J. Snell (Lee)

Stephen A. of Nottingham m. Barbara A. **Allan** of Barrington 7/18/1982

LOGAN,

Robert K., Jr. of Jefferson City, MO m. Ruth Ann **Sessions** of Barrington 7/15/1983 in Portsmouth

LOISELLE,

Wilfred E., III of Barrington m. Lisa A. **Sanders** of Barrington 12/31/1982

LORANGER,
Roger R. of Barrington m. Jennifer O. **Loranger** of Barrington 5/29/1986

LORING,
Justin C. of Barrington m. Janice A. **Crossley** of Dublin 3/16/1972 in Durham; H - b. 8/11/1946 in NH, s/o Winthrop L. Loring (ME) and Alice V. Clay (IA); W - b. 12/6/1948 in MA, d/o Edmund Crossley (MA) and Nellie A. Smith (MA)

LOUDON,
Adam of Barrington m. Katrina **Holt** of Barrington 8/3/1985 in Portsmouth

LOVER,
Richard Peter of Milton m. Nancy Elizabeth **Swain** of Barrington 2/9/1974 in Portsmouth

LOVERING,
Frank H. of Durham m. Annie **Tylor** of Barrington 8/3/1890; H - 24, b. Deerfield, s/o Charles and Harriet Lovering; W - 18, b. Barrington, d/o Hiram and Eliza Tylor

Sidney H. of Barrington m. Mary E. **Lovering** of Barrington 4/9/1966; H - 56, clergyman, 2d, widower, b. Somerville, MA, s/o Everett L. Lovering (MA) and Ruby E. Hamilton (MA); W - 21, shoeworker, b. Waterville, ME, d/o Vernald L. Nickerson (ME) and Gladys E. Sanderson (ME)

LOW,
David T. of Barrington m. Carol A. **Howard** of Alton 10/11/1958 in Laconia; H - 22, Coast Guard, b. MA, s/o Frederick Low (NY) and Irene Beard (MA); W - 19, IBM, b. NH, d/o Frank W. Howard (NH) and Alice S. Sponberg (Sweden)

LOWRY,

Ellis C. of Barrington m. Beverly A. **McGregor** of Rochester 9/10/1955 in Rochester; H - 22, USAF, b. MA, s/o Leo C. Lowry (SC) and Ardella F. Montgomery (MA); W - 18, clerk, b. NH, d/o Ronald W. McGregor (MA) and Floris M. Prepper (ME)

Mark K. of Barrington m. Anita M. **Geldart** of Barrington 6/13/1981

William D. of Barrington m. Madeline S. **Richard** of Rochester 10/12/1950 in Rochester; H - 24, clerk, b. MA, s/o Leo C. Lowry (SC) and Ardella F. Montgomery (MA); W - 22, sales clerk, b. NH, d/o Henri E. Richard (NH) and Stella A. LeBrune (NH)

LUCAS,

John E. of Barrington m. Rose **Donahue** of Barrington 6/24/1922 in Rochester; H - 32, weaver, 2d, b. Woburn, MA, s/o Edward Lucas (Boston, MA, laborer) and Jennie Harris (Bristol, RI, housewife); W - 30, weaver, 2d, b. Medford, MA, d/o Joseph Goulette (Canada, laborer) and Rose Shortslers (NY, housewife)

LUKE,

Earle M. of Barrington m. Susan J. **LaCroix** of Dover 6/30/1979 in Dover

LUKEN,

Terry A. of Moultonboro m. Donna M. **Anderson** of Barrington 8/9/1980 in Dover

LYNCH,

Cornelius M. of Barrington m. Loretta F. **Gleason** of Barrington 7/14/1956 in Stratham; H - 33, sheet metal wkr., 2d, b. MA, s/o Cornelius M. Lynch (MA) and Elizabeth L. Blount (MA); W - 40, saleslady, 3rd, b. MA, d/o Francis Eldridge (MA) and Sophia T. Ahern (MA)

MACDONALD,
Eugene A., Jr. of Barrington m. Donna L. **Davis** of Barrington 6/26/1982 in Newmarket

MACDOUGALL,
Donald W. of Barrington m. Cathy A. **Poitras** of Exeter 7/24/1982 in Exeter

MACE,
William E. of York, ME m. Theresa H. **Lauze** of York, ME 9/6/1951; H - 28, laborer, 2d, b. NH; W - 23, beamer, b. MA, d/o Ralph A. Lauze (NH) and Alice B. Dion (NH)

MACEACHERN,
Donald J. of Barrington m. Elizabeth A. **Cole** of Barrington 12/19/1982
Donald L. of Barrington m. Michele J. **Lambert** of Barrington 4/1/1980

MACIVER,
Mark D. of Barrington m. Janet L. **Bristol** of Dover 9/5/1983 in Newmarket

MACNEIL,
Michael E. of Barrington m. Anne E. **Campagna** of Barrington 12/23/1981
Robert T. of Somersworth m. Carolyn L. **Allard** of Barrington 6/29/1985 in Dover

MACRAE,
Kenneth of Barrington m. Ethel **Brown** of Rochester 8/11/1918 in Rochester; H - 28, farmer, b. Barrington, s/o Thomas MacRae (NS, farmer) and Clarinda Richardson (housewife); W - 27, shop hand, b. Barrington, d/o Frank Brown (Haverhill, laborer) and Annie Arlin (Barrington, housewife)

MADDEN,
Michael A. of Barrington m. Mary **Thoms** of Barrington 1/4/1986 in New Ipswich

MAGADA,
Audrxez of Barrington m. Laura R. **Drapeau** of Barrington 5/12/1979 in Dover

MAGNUSON,
Gary W. of Barrington m. Jennifer A. **Coyne** of Barrington 10/26/1978 in Portsmouth

MAHONEY,
James Joseph, Jr. of Barrington m. Cheryl Lynn **Follansbee** of Durham 12/21/1974 in Durham

MAILHOT,
Ernest of Rochester m. Doris E. **Preston** of Barrington 7/27/1973 in Gonic; H - 3d, b. 11/3/1904 in Canada, s/o Omer Mailhot (Canada) and Virginia Falardeau (Canada); W - 2d, b. 11/3/1906 in NH, d/o Fred Thompson (ME) and Gertrude Knox (ME)

MAIO,
Richard E. of Dover m. Mary M. **McKenna** of Barrington 5/30/1969; H - b. 3/17/1946 in MA, s/o Angelo B. Maio (NY) and Lorraine Margaret (TX); W - b. 10/22/1949 in NH, d/o John J. McKenna (NH) and Blanche M. Perron (NH)

MALONZO,
Frank of Barrington m. Lilla **York** of Barrington 9/1/1897; H - 27, harness maker, b. Piere Ville, s/o Frederick (Piere Ville Mills) and Isador (domestic); W - 21, domestic, b. Dover, d/o Daniel (Dover, shoemaker) and Susan

MANGOLD,
Robert G. of Barrington m. Fauna C. **Kenison** of Barrington 10/21/1972 in Madbury; H - 2d, b. 8/8/1946 in MD, s/o John W. Mangold (MI) and Margaret A. Anderson (PA); W - b. 5/25/1949 in NH, d/o George M. Kenison (NH) and Dorothy L. Batchelder (VT)

MANNING,
Wayne William of Barrington m. Linda Lee **Hartford** of Rochester 9/7/1974 in Rochester

MANSFIELD,
Benjamin W., Jr. of Barrington m. Barbara L. **Mansfield** of Dover 1/17/1948; H - 26, truck driver, b. Gilford, s/o Benjamin Mansfield (Gilmanton) and Mildred Grant (Belmont); W - 19, clerk, 2d, b. Dover, d/o Irving Lucas (Dover) and Rachel Clark (Ireland)
Robert W. of Barrington m. Barbara L. **Lucas** of Dover 1/18/1946 in Dover; H - 20, US Army, b. Belmont, s/o Benjamin Mansfield (Gilmanton) and Mildred Grant (Belmont); W - 17, drug store, b. Dover, d/o Irving Lucas (Dover) and Rachel Clark (Ireland)

MARCOTTE,
Dennis J. of Rollinsford m. Connie S. **Bodge** of Barrington 1/22/1977 in Somersworth

MARIOTTI,
Judson E. of Barrington m. Linda A. **Brown** of Barrington 7/8/1967 in Dover; H - 23, tool & die maker, b. Exeter, s/o Darius C. Mariotti (NH) and Fern M. York (WI); W - 18, beautician, b. Rochester, d/o Robert F. Brown (NH) and Irene A. Meattey (NH)
Robert D., Jr. of Lee m. Nellie F. **Canney** of Barrington 10/16/1970 in Northwood; H - 2d, b. 4/9/1947 in NH, s/o Robert D. Mariotti (NH) and Irene Babineau (NH); W -

2d, b. 10/5/1946 in CA, d/o Charles Lloyd (ME) and Nellie Bowen (CA)

MARISON,
Bernard L. of Barrington m. Jeanette L. **Everson** of Eliot, ME 8/5/1950 in Eliot, ME; H - 30, tel. clerk, b. NH, s/o Lindley Marison (NH) and Mary C. Lewis (NH); W - 19, tel. installer, b. ME, d/o Ralph Everson (NH) and Dorothy Searles (MA)
Lindley J. of Barrington m. Mary C. **Lewis** of Northwood 12/21/1916 in Northwood; H - 29, shoemaker, b. Strafford, s/o John H. Marison (Barrington, farmer) and Nellie Leighton (Strafford, housewife); W - 29, shoemaker, b. Northwood, d/o Oliver Perry Lewis (Lynn, MA) and ----- Towle (Northwood, housekeeper)

MARKHAM,
Arthur C. of Barrington m. Sharon L. **Clark** of Newmarket 7/26/1980 in Newmarket

MARSH,
George H. of Barrington m. Sadie L. **Scruton** of Strafford 8/23/1899 in Strafford; H - 25, farmer, b. Boston, MA, s/o Robert (England) and Harriet; W - 25, teacher, b. Strafford, d/o Daniel (Strafford, farmer) and Vienna
Richard D. of Barrington m. Susan E. **Beaulier** of Barrington 9/12/1987 in Hampton

MARSHALL,
Benjamin of Dover m. Evelyn **Tibbetts** of Dover 6/5/1926 in Dover; H - 24, shoeworker, b. Barrington, s/o Henry Marshall (teamster) and Cora Willey (housewife); W - 19, at home, b. Dover, d/o Ernest Tibbetts (shoeworker) and Mary Boacher (at home)
George E. of MA m. Pamela-Jean J. **MacKay** of MA 9/2/1984

Paul D. of Barrington m. Janie A. **MacDonald** of Rumney 2/12/1983 in Plymouth

MARSTON,
John Wayne of Rochester m. Cheryl Ann **Neal** of Barrington 11/21/1975 in Dover

MARTEL,
Dana P. of Barrington m. Celeste M. **Mone** of Dover 9/10/1977 in Dover

MARTIN,
Mark White of Barrington m. Judith Bates **Hunter** of Barrington 6/28/1975 in Nottingham
Wilfred J. of Barrington m. Ann C. **Mooers** of Haverhill, MA 6/5/1978 in Salem

MASON,
Thomas E. of Barrington m. Madelyn E. **Webber** of Brentwood 11/7/1962; H - 20, factory wkr., b. NH; W - 18, elec. wkr., b. MA, d/o Charles E. Webber (NH) and Margaret A. Cahill (MA)
Thomas E., Sr. of Barrington m. Irene J. **Lincoln** of Somersworth 6/2/1981

MATTIN,
Michael A. of Barrington m. Marriott B. **Davis** of Barrington 8/31/1973 in Durham; H - b. 6/1/1950 in VA, s/o Albert P. Mattin (OH) and Elizabeth Lane (NH); W - b. 9/6/1944 in NH, d/o Bryan G. Davis (NC) and Eloise J. Furr (NC)

MATTOCKS,
Robert H. of Gonic m. Melanie J. **Hunter** of Barrington 6/18/1977
Robert H. of Rochester m. Ethel A. **Plante** of Barrington 6/18/1982 in Rochester

MATTOX,
William H. of Barrington m. Lottie F. **Hall** of Somerville, MA 3/30/1904 in Somerville, MA; H - 22, laborer, b. Brentwood, s/o William Mattox (Lynn, MA, laborer) and Sarah J. Davis (Raymond); W - 30, at home, b. Charlestown, MA, d/o James F. Hall (Charlestown, MA, salesman) and Harriett F. Kimball (Lynn, MA)

MAURAIS,
Marc-Andre G. of Barrington m. Margaret I. **Ross** of Barrington 5/1/1982

MAYER,
David L. of Barrington m. Paula J. **Lowry** of Dover 11/13/1982 in Dover

MAYO,
James J. of Rochester m. Donna J. **Hill** of Barrington 8/9/1980 in Rochester

MAZE,
Alvin L. of Barrington m. Ruth A. **Davis** of Barrington 5/15/1982 in Portsmouth

McCALLION,
Neal of Barrington m. Bertha May **Scott** of Rochester 8/3/1934 in Rochester; H - 24, mill laborer, b. Gonic, s/o Sarah McCallion (Calais, ME); W - 18, at home, b. Rochester, d/o George Scott (Sanford, ME) and Eva Scott

McCANN,
Paul Robert of Barrington m. Denise Janet **Gagne** of Rochester 3/19/1976 in Rochester

McCARTHY,

Franklin R. of Barrington m. Barbara C. **Spencer** of Berwick, ME 2/21/1949 in Berwick, ME; H - 26, US Army, b. NH, s/o William E. McCarthy (NY) and Dora M. Cheltry (VT); W - 24, at home, b. ME, d/o Charles W. Spencer (ME) and Hazel H. Hart (NH)

Gilbert L. of Barrington m. Muriel L. **Lowry** of Barrington 9/20/1942; H - 20, mill worker, b. Nottingham, s/o William E. McCarthy (Scotland) and Dora Cheltry (Brandon, VT); W - 18, b. Revere, MA, d/o Leo C. Lowry (Greenville, SC) and Ardella F. Montgomery (S. Boston, MA)

Leo E. of Barrington m. Patricia F. **Garland** of Farmington 6/5/1954 in Farmington; H - 19, US Army, b. NH, s/o William E. McCarthy (NY) and Dora Cheltry (VT); W - 19, shoe worker, b. MA, d/o Raymond I. Garland (NH) and Emily M. Allfrey (England)

McCLARY,

Curtis J. of Gilmanton m. Charlotte E. **McKay** of Barrington 4/9/1979 in Strafford

McCLUNIN,

Ona Ray of Washington, DC m. Bernice L. **Records** of Boston, MA 8/28/1938; H - 33, instru. maker, b. Monkton, VT, s/o Charles F. McClunin and Grace L. Johnson; W - 34, hair dresser, 2d, b. Denison, TX, d/o James P. Redick (Denison, TX) and Estella Ross (Tombeau, TX)

McCOSKER,

John F. of Barrington m. Noreen M. **Cosindas** of Barrington 8/19/1984 in Rye

McDANIEL,

Arthur W. of Barrington m. F. Mercy **Durgin** of Lee 6/4/1906 in Lee; H - 21, farmer, b. Nottingham, s/o Frank McDaniel (Barrington, lumberman) and Ruth A. Small (Epping); W - 24, teacher, b. Lee, d/o Gilman Y. Durgin (Lee, farmer) and Mary F. Caverly (Lee)

George True of Barrington m. Grace Elizabeth **Dodge** of Somerville, MA 11/24/1917 in Somerville, MA; H - 22, farmer, b. Nottingham, s/o Frank McDaniel (Barrington, farmer) and Ruth A. Small (Epping, housewife); W - 22, bookkeeper, b. Somerville, MA, d/o William H. Dodge and Elizabeth A. Ahern

Walter S. of Barrington m. Alice M. **Clement** of Newmarket 10/27/1912 in Lee; H - 25, farmer, b. Barrington, s/o Frank McDaniel (farmer) and Ruth Small; W - 21, housekeeper, b. Nottingham, d/o John Clement (machinist) and Eliza Finn

McDONALD,

Cornelius of Barrington m. Nellie E. **Whitehouse** of Barrington 7/29/1893; H - 38, farmer, s/o Cornelius (Cork, Ireland, farmer) and Nora; W - 21, at home, d/o Elias (Barrington)

Cornelius of Barrington m. Louisa E. **Wentworth** of Rochester 11/2/1899; H - 45, laborer, 2d, b. St. Johns, NB, s/o Cornelius (deceased) and Nora; W - 44, domestic, b. Portland, ME, d/o Ansel (deceased) and Mary

McGILVERY,

Ray E. of Dover m. Marie Louise **Myshrall** of Barrington 12/28/1974

McGLONE,

Daniel H. of Barrington m. Gail D. **Hodsdon** of Somersworth 4/18/1987 in Somersworth

David P. of Barrington m. Robin F. **Hayes** of Dover 5/17/1980 in Durham

Thomas E. of Barrington m. Darcy E. **Vigneault** of Dover 8/31/1979 in Dover

McKAY,

Donald A. of Barrington m. Mary E. D. **Walker** of Barrington 12/26/1892; H - 40, lumberman, b. Clyde River, s/o Donald and Martha; W - 39, domestic, 2d, b. Barrington, d/o John T. and Alice

W. H. of Barrington m. Martha E. **Dexter** of York, ME 4/7/1893 in Dover; H - 43, lumberman; W - 20, at home, d/o James (Shelburne, NS) and Annie

McKEAGE,

Claude A. of Rochester m. June J. **Jones** of Barrington 11/27/1953 in Rochester; H - 27, presser, b. NH, s/o Claude J. McKeage (NH) and Pearl J. Parkhurst (NH); W - 22, laundry wkr., b. NH, d/o Rupert L. Jones (VT) and Gertrude M. Wood (NH)

McKENNA,

Thomas H. of Barrington m. Helen V. **Glidden** of Dover 5/9/1970 in Dover; H - b. 7/2/1948 in NH, s/o John J. McKenna (NH) and Blanche M. Perron (NH); W - b. 3/28/1948 in ME, d/o George E. Glidden (NH) and Clara C. Bean (ME)

McLAUGHLIN,

Calvin E. of Nottingham m. Grace M. **Bodge** of Barrington 8/6/1906 in Gonic; H - 24, mill hand, b. Nottingham, s/o Patrick McLaughlin (Annapolis, NS, mason) and Nelly Leathers (Northwood); W - 21, at home, b. Barrington, d/o Charles Bodge (Barrington, farmer) and Mary Carley (Brighton, MA)

McLEAN,

Donald T. of Barrington m. Fay E. **Johnson** of Barrington 11/13/1947 in Dover; H - 22, chopper, b. Johnston, RI, s/o Edwin W. McLean (Mt. Hope, MA) and Emily Hargreaves (Providence, RI); W - 17, at home, b. Hopkinton, d/o Alexander Johnson (Melrose, MA) and Marion E. Ineson (Weare)

Shawn M. of Barrington m. Karen L. **Phillips** of Barrington 10/5/1986 in Dover

McLEOD,

Daniel L. of Barrington m. Nancy E. **Roy** of Barrington 3/4/1978

McMANUS,

Henry E. of Barrington m. Diane I. **Wiggin** of Barrington 6/25/1977 in Rochester

McMASTER,

John W. of Pembroke m. Elizabeth J. **Beal** of Barrington 11/7/1970 in Concord; H - b. 10/15/1945 in NH, s/o William R. McMaster (MA) and Ellen O. Lucas (NH); W - b. 5/18/1949 in NH, d/o Edward R. Beal (MA) and Margaret G. Thomas (MA)

McNEIL,

Paul J. of Barrington m. Suzanne **Wyer** of So. Portland, ME 9/8/1979 in Wolfeboro

MEATTEY,

Herbert E., Jr. of Barrington m. Lillian E. **Moody** of Dover 9/11/1954 in Dover; H - 20, machinist, b. NH, s/o Herbert E. Meattey (NH) and Mildred DeShan (NH); W - 19, shoe worker, b. NH, d/o Willie H. Moody (NH) and Grace Smith (NH)

Herbert E., Jr. of Barrington m. Justine E. **Brooks** of Rochester 6/14/1979 in Union

Herbert E., III of Barrington m. Kethleen A. **Howard** of Barrington 5/21/1979

Reginald A. of Barrington m. Norma J. **Knight** of Gonic 1/2/1969 in Exeter; H - b. 5/25/1951 in NH, s/o Herbert Meattey (NH) and Mildred Deshan (NH); W - b. 10/29/1951 in NH, d/o John W. Knight (NH) and Matilda M. Hoytt (NH)

Richard R. of Barrington m. Jacqueline A. **Stacy** of Barrington 6/13/1959; H - 21, truck driver, b. NH, s/o Herbert E. Meattey (NH) and Mildred A. Deshan (NH); W - 19, elec. worker, b. NH, d/o Earl C. Stacy (NH) and Ruth T. Bell (MA)

Ronald P. of Barrington m. Beverly J. **Cosgrove** of Rochester 11/4/1960; H - 18, machinist, b. ME, s/o Herbert E. Meattey (NH) and Mildred E. Deshan (NH); W - 18, dietitian, b. NH, d/o Elliott A. Cosgrove (NH) and Estella M. Woodbury (NH)

Russell L. of Barrington m. Mary A. **Morrow** of Waldwick, NJ 3/23/1968; H - b. 11/14/1945 in NH, s/o Herbert E. Meattey (NH) and Mildred A. Deshan (NH); W - b. 3/19/1947 in NJ, d/o John F. Morrow (PA) and Gwendolyn R. Daly (NJ)

Russell L. of Barrington m. Diane J. **Noble** of Barrington 6/30/1978 in Union

MEIKLEJOHN,
Daniel Robert of Somersworth m. Dawn Louise **Scheri** of Barrington 10/30/1976 in Dover

MELANSON,
Albert R., Jr. of Barrington m. Sharon L. **Barber** of Barrington 3/21/1987 in Durham

Richard P. of Barrington m. Helen M. **Henderson** of Barrington 3/14/1959; H - 22, fireman, b. NH, s/o Joseph

Melanson and Julia Rinaldi (Italy); W - 19, bookkeeper, b. NH, d/o Harold W. Henderson (NH) and Katherine Wiggin (NH)

MELLO,
Christopher J. of Barrington m. Mary S. **Ellis** of Durham 7/8/1973 in Durham; H - b. 3/10/1953 in NH, s/o John J. Mello (MA) and Dolores Jankowska (MA); W - b. 9/3/1952 in NH, d/o Richard Ellis (NH) and Elizabeth Torrey (NH)

MERICLE,
James E. of Atlanta, GA m. Elissa A. **Fickett** of Barrington 5/1/1972 in Portsmouth; H - b. 8/30/1949 in GA, s/o Harry E. Mericle (NY) and Mary L. Lawson (GA); W - 2d, b. 6/17/1946 in NH, d/o Owen W. Fickett (ME) and Florence E. Hoak (ME)

MERRILL,
Clayton B. of Barrington m. Patricia A. **Baud** of Dover 8/22/1981

MERTON,
Andrew H. of Barrington m. Gail J. **Kelley** of Barrington 7/30/1978

MICHAEL,
Robert, Sr. of Barrington m. Marrion E. **Perreault** of Barrington 1/22/1977 in Rochester
Robert W. of Rochester m. Natalie M. **Gagnon** of Barrington 12/22/1986 in Nottingham

MICHAUD,
Robert J. of Exeter m. Caroline L. **Lowry** of Barrington 10/23/1949; H - 25, brick maker, b. NH, s/o George Michaud (Canada) and Lydia LaFrance (Canada); W -

19, sales girl, b. MA, d/o Leo C. Lowry (SC) and Ardella Montgomery (MA)

Ronald P. of Barrington m. Sharon R. **Grenier** of Barrington 11/9/1985 in Dover

MICHELSON,
James P. of Barrington m. Denise H. **Kapsimalis** of Barrington 7/26/1986 in Kingston

MIELKE,
Robert of Detroit, MI m. Marjorie M. **Timm** of Barrington 7/5/1958; H - 21, air force, b. MI, s/o August Mielke (MI) and Mildred Wiseman (OH); W - 18, teletypist, b. NY, d/o Frederick N. Timm, II (NY) and Marjorie M. Boyce (NY)

MILLAR,
Gordon C. of Barrington m. Rowena M. **Anctil** of Rochester 1/1/1978 in Durham

MILLEN,
Wayne R. of Barrington m. Karen P. **Johnson** of Barrington 7/4/1978 in Lee

MILLER,
George B. of Barrington m. Edna B. **Fuller** of Barrington 3/1/1959; H - 54, mill worker, 2d, b. MA, s/o Arthur Miller (Canada) and Lillian Baker (Canada); W - 51, housewife, 2d, b. MA, d/o Arthur H. Walker (VT) and Phoebe Farrington (IL)

George D. of Barrington m. Doreen T. **Loranger** of Newmarket 5/13/1978 in Newmarket

George E. of Dover m. Leah E. **McKay** of Barrington 12/31/1935 in Dover; H - 49, purch. agent, b. Haverhill, MA, s/o John S. Miller (NS) and Addie Thompson (Haverhill, MA); W - 32, housekeeper, b. Strafford, d/o Victor E. McKay (NS) and Edith T. Bateman (Strafford)

Hugh R. of Barrington m. Elaine E. **McKenna** of Rochester 4/7/1958 in Rochester; H - 27, route man, b. NH, s/o Douglass F. Miller (NH) and Edith G. Jackson (NH); W - 18, packer, b. NH, d/o John J. McKenna (NH) and Blanche Perron (NH)

Michael J. of Rochester m. Linda M. **Miller** of Barrington 8/2/1969 in Dover; H - b. 8/12/1949 in OH, s/o William Miller (OH) and Bernice M. Rawley (ME); W - b. 1/16/1949 in NH, d/o Malcolm W. Miller (NH) and Mary Y. Labrie (NH)

Wayne C. of Barrington m. Carol J. **Veno** of Dover 6/26/1970 in Dover; H - b. 8/30/1951 in NH, s/o Edward C. Miller (NH) and Pearl Ballavance (NH); W - b. 4/25/1952 in NH, d/o Wilfred Veno (NH) and Alice Fager (ME)

MILLETTE,

Adam M. of Barrington m. Lorena M. **Lutz** of Rochester 5/6/1978

Donald F. of Barrington m. Rachel M. **Veilleux** of Dover 8/5/1967 in Dover; H - 20, elec. worker, b. Rochester, s/o Adam M. Millette (NH) and Julia B. King (NH); W - 19, optical tech., b. Augusta, ME, d/o Gerard P. Veilleux (Canada) and Marie R. Breton (ME)

Llewellyn M. of Barrington m. Shirley M. **Howard** of Rochester 12/16/1967 in Rochester; H - 23, b. NH, s/o Adam M. Millette (NH) and Julia B. King (NH); W - 23, 3rd, b. NH, d/o Philip J. Caplette (NH) and Mary A. Gagne (MA)

MILLIARD,

Paul G. of Manchester, CT m. Diane Louise **Milliard** of Barrington 6/18/1977

MILNE,

Jonathan of Barrington m. Cynthia F. **Palumbo** of Barrington 5/27/1979

MINER,
David M. of Lee m. Diane S. **Bruce** of Barrington 6/16/1973 in Northwood; H - b. 12/1/1948 in MA, s/o Raymond W. Miner (MA) and Edith Atherton (Canada); W - 2d, b. 1/30/1951 in NH, d/o Edgar Twombly (NH) and Ellen Smith (VT)

MITCHELL,
Robert J. of Newmarket m. Mary-Jane A. **Crawford** of Barrington 7/31/1971 in Durham; H - b. 4/8/1949 in VA, s/o Lawrence J. Mitchell (MA) and Laurette M. Lebrecque (NH); W - b. 8/8/1949 in PA, d/o James M. Crawford (IL) and Margaret A. Quinn (CT)

MOFFETT,
Nelson J. of Rochester m. Karen M. **Weeden** of Barrington 6/23/1956 in Rochester; H - 22, laborer, b. NH, s/o Leo J. Moffett (VT) and Marie Roy (Canada); W - 18, at home, b. NH, d/o Albert E. Weeden (NH) and Thelma M. Richards (ME)

MONAGHAN,
F. Wayne of Barrington m. Dorothy N. **McLeod** of Barrington 6/21/1980 in Newfields

MONTOUR,
James R. of Rochester m. Madlyn P. **Griswold** of Barrington 12/9/1964; H - 21, shoe worker, b. NH, s/o Roland E. Montour (Canada) and Pauline R. Kyanka (PA); W - 21, at home, 2d, b. NH, d/o Frank E. Walker (NH) and Blanche R. Brogan (NH)

MOONEY,
Philip A. of Barrington m. Barbara A. **Badger** of Barrington 6/28/1980 in Dover

MOORE,

John F., Jr. of Rye m. Donna L. **Fogg** of Barrington 1/31/1969; H - b. 6/2/1948 in NJ, s/o John F. Moore (NJ) and Clara L. Kooiman (NJ); W - b. 10/26/1951 in NH, d/o Russell L. Fogg (NH) and Rose L. Ellis (NH)

Michael C. of Vincentown, NJ m. Dianne M. **Watters** of Barrington 1/29/1983 in Somersworth

MORGANELLI,

Nicholas A. of Barrington m. Sharon A. **Proulx** of Barrington 2/28/1987 in Rochester

MORRELL,

Thomas A. of Greenwich, CT m. Susan B. **Halpern** of Marblehead, MA 11/16/1968; H - b. 2/10/1946 in CT, s/o Howard Morrell (CT) and Mary K. Magness (CT); W - b. 7/22/1946 in NY, d/o Benjamin B. Halpern (MA) and Virginia B. Burrows (NY)

MORRILL,

James I. of Barrington m. Linda **Todd** of Durham 11/1/1986 in Lee

MORRISSEY,

Timothy E. of Barrington m. Dianne M. **Zielfelder** of Barrington 7/15/1978

Timothy E. of Barrington m. Cheryl L. **Morrison** of Rochester 5/16/1987 in Rochester

MORRISON,

James H. of Rochester m. Betty A. **Tuck** of Barrington 6/4/1966; H - 22, ceramist, b. Rochester, s/o Harry F. Morrison (ME) and Melinda Picard (NH); W - 19, secretary, b. Rochester, d/o Gordon C. Tuck (MA) and Beatrice Beriault (Canada)

Ray D. of Barrington m. Susan M. **Thompson** of Barrington 8/6/1982

MOULTON,
Ronald A. of Berwick, ME m. Kathleen L. **Brown** of Berwick, ME 10/8/1983

MOUNTAIN,
Fulton T. of Barrington m. Lisa M. **Garran** of East Rochester 4/23/1983
Joseph F., Jr. of Barrington m. Janine F. **Landry** of Rochester 9/1/1979

MUDGETT,
John H. of Barrington m. Ella M. **Clough** of Dover 8/3/1897 in Dover; H - 25, physician, 3rd, b. Holderness, s/o Clarette (Ellsworth, domestic); W - 20, clerk, b. Dover, d/o Frank (Ossipee, retired mer.) and Julia

MUNDAY,
Floyd L. of Dover m. Julia E. **Boodey** of Barrington 6/17/1967 in Dover; H - 23, accountant, b. Dover, s/o Fred L. Munday (NH) and Lydia Woodward (NH); W - 18, stenographer, b. Rochester, d/o Ralph J. Boodey (NH) and Pauline Beauchain (VT)

MUNROE,
Raymond L. of Barrington m. Helen J. **Fisher** of Lee 12/22/1960; H - 62, truck driver, 2d, b. MA, s/o Henry E. Munroe (MA) and Ella M. Clarage (MA); W - 62, clerk, 3rd, b. MA, d/o William S. Jennison (MA) and Katherine M. Douglas (NH)

MUNSEY,
Richard N. of Rochester m. Muriel L. **Turner** of Barrington 11/27/1940; H - 28, service man, b. Hampton, s/o Harry

D. Munsey (Exeter) and Ethel Tucker (Stoneham, MA);
W - 22, office girl, b. Barrington, d/o Arthur W. Turner
(Staten Island, NY) and Alice V. Hopey (Canaan)

MUNSON,
Robert K. of Barrington m. Wendy J. **Phipps** of Barrington
8/10/1986

MURPHY,
Ivory W. of Barrington m. Sophia A. **Davis** of Barrington
2/11/1891; H - 26, b. Lyman, ME, s/o Enoch and Ruth;
W - 26, b. Craftsbury, VT, d/o Ira and Sarah
John D. of Baldwin, NY m. Irene C. **Goodhue** of Baldwin, NY
9/28/1942; H - 47, manager, b. Quincy, MA, s/o Patrick
Murphy (Ireland) and Catherine Donovan (Wollaston,
MA); W - 42, bookkeeper, 2d, b. Stoughton, MA, d/o
John H. Goodhue (Quincy, MA) and Catherine Connell
(Aldershot, England)
Leon E. of Barrington m. Crystal L. **Senter** of Barrington
8/20/1983

MURRAY,
Joseph W. of Barrington m. Susan M. **Donovan** of
Portsmouth 10/14/1978 in Portsmouth

MUSICK,
Robert G. of Barrington m. Patricia H. **Smith** of San Leandro,
CA 12/31/1982

MUSLER,
Gary T. of Barrington m. Cindy L. **Greenwood** of Barrington
8/8/1981

MYSHRALL,
Emery Alfred, Jr. of Barrington m. Heide Marie **Langley** of
Barrington 3/8/1975 in Rochester

NAGY,
David A. of Dover m. Denise D. **Greenwood** of Barrington 10/2/1982
George of Barrington m. Cecile M. **Rogers** of Somersworth 3/22/1986 in Somersworth
George S., Jr. of Barrington m. Deborah A. **St. Laurent** of Dover 10/16/1982 in Dover

NASON,
Ernest E. of Rochester m. Dorothy O. **Thyng** of Dover 4/4/1936 in Strafford; H - 21, farmer, b. Rochester, s/o Charles E. Nason (Barrington) and Winnie Foss (Rochester); W - 22, waitress, b. Barnstead, d/o John C. Thyng (Barnstead) and Grace Downs (Dover)

NASUTI,
Robert L. of Strafford m. Lorraine M. **Brown** of Barrington 1/8/1983 in Dover

NEAGLE,
Glenn G. of Rochester m. Beatrice L. **Lachance** of Barrington 5/26/1984 in Rochester

NEAL,
Alden A. of Barrington m. Constance A. **Holmes** of Fremont 1/29/1966 in Fremont; H - 23, woodsman, b. Franklin, s/o Arthur G. Neal (NH) and Ettie Cooper (NH); W - 20, inspection, b. Exeter, d/o Maurice L. Holmes (NH) and Alice I. Lewis (NH)
Daniel R. of Barrington m. Debra J. **Neal** of Barrington 6/23/1972; H - b. 5/10/1951 in NH, s/o Roger E. Neal (NH) and Laura C. Wheeler (NH); W - b. 6/5/1954 in CA, d/o Richard Neal (NH) and Janice V. Taylor (NH)
Edwin C. of Barrington m. Myra **Hanson** of Dover 2/17/1904 in Dover; H - 25, farmer, s/o Jacob S. Neal (Farmington, clergyman) and Ann M. Clark (Barrington); W - 17, at

home, b. Strafford, d/o Nathaniel Hanson (Strafford, farmer) and Olive A. Leighton (Strafford)

Frank L. m. Myrtle A. **Clark** 12/8/1929; H - 21, laborer, b. Strafford, s/o Edwin C. Neal (Barrington) and Myra Hanson (Strafford); W - 19, at home, b. Barrington, d/o Marshall Clark (Barrington) and Ada Freeman (Barrington)

Richard of Barrington m. Janice V. **Taylor** of Strafford 1/23/1953 in Northwood; H - 19, shoeworker, b. NH, s/o Vira Neal (NH); W - 18, at home, b. NH, d/o Thurlow Garnette (NH) and Avis J. Caswell (NH)

Richard, III of Barrington m. Gladys Ellen **Carlson** of Dover 12/14/1974

Robert F. of Barrington m. June G. **Cook** of Gonic 7/6/1963; H - 22, garage mech., b. MA, s/o Arthur G. Neal (NH) and Ettie A. Cooper (MA); W - 18, at home, b. NH, d/o Burly K. Cook (MA) and Lera M. Howard (NH)

Robert F. of Barrington m. Mabel H. **Tasker** of Barrington 8/16/1969 in Northwood; H - 2d, b. 5/28/1941 in MA, s/o Arthur G. Neal (NH) and Ettie A. Cooper (MA); W - 2d, b. 11/15/1944 in NH, d/o William R. O'Neil (NY) and Mabel E. Palmer (NH)

Roger E. of Barrington m. Laura C. **Wheeler** of Barrington 7/8/1948 in Dover; H - 22, lumber, b. Rochester, s/o Edwin C. Neal (Boston, MA) and Myra Hanson (Strafford); W - 21, at home, b. Hanover, d/o Carl R. Wheeler (Canaan) and Helen Devosa (Austria)

Thomas J. of Bloomington, IN m. Marion L. **Bryson** of Barrington 6/20/1959; H - 25, USAF, 2d, b. IN, s/o Virgil C. Neal (IN) and Goldie M. Walls (IN); W - 18, waitress, b. NH, d/o Melvin F. Bryson (NH) and Evelyn M. Green (NH)

NELSON,
Wayne Franklin of Rochester m. Fay Marie **Lowry** of Barrington 9/25/1976

NEMETH,
Gabor S. of MA m. Lee A-A. **Beats** of MA 6/2/1984

NESBITT,
James P. of Barrington m. Carol J. **Stead** of Barrington 9/29/1984

NEWELL,
Arlin M. of Barrington m. Emeroy F. **Brock** of Dunkin, PQ 12/1/1915 in Manchester; H - 24, farmer, b. West Shefford, s/o George O. Newell (Quebec, farmer) and Lucy Tabor (Quebec, housewife); W - 25, teacher, b. Dunkin, PQ, d/o Henry J. Brock (Dunkin, PQ, farmer) and Clisty Parsons (Dunkin, PQ, housewife)

Gerald X. of Barrington m. Audury **Corson** of Northwood 6/29/1941 in Northwood; H - 21, mach. oper., b. Barrington, s/o Arlin Newell (Canada) and Emeroy Blake (Canada); W - 21, clerk, b. Northwood, d/o Ernest R. Corson (Durham) and Charlotte U. Strachan (Barrington)

NEWMAN,
David A. of Barrington m. Margaret M. **MacDonald** of Barrington 7/6/1985 in Dover

Earl R., III of Barrington m. Elizabeth J. **Oliver** of Barrington 1/11/1986 in Portsmouth

NEWSKY,
Joseph T. of Barrington m. Sonya M. **Fortier** of Dover 5/2/1981

Michael of Barrington m. Susan V. **Labrie** of Barrington 11/10/1984 in Dover

Michael L. of Dover m. Barbara E. **Neal** of Barrington 6/29/1957 in Dover; H - 20, machinist, b. NH, s/o Joseph Newsky (NH) and Alice Timmins (NH); W - 24, office work, b. NH, d/o Frank Neal (NH) and Myrtie Clark (NH)

NEWTON,
Henry T., Jr. of Barrington m. Rosilda B. **St. Onge** of Gonic 11/24/1949 in Rochester; H - 22, dairyman, b. MI, s/o Henry T. Newton (MI) and Pauline D. Drew (NH); W - 18, shoe shop, b. NH, d/o Elizior J. St. Onge (Canada) and Marie A. Deschene (Canada)

Stephen R. of Tilton m. Joan **Gervasi** of Barrington 8/31/1984 in Portsmouth

NICKERSON,
William B. of Anson, ME m. Phyllis B. **Damberg** of Anson, ME 7/6/1982

NIEMI,
Arnold B. of Barrington m. Arleen **Locke** of Alton 7/2/1980 in Concord

NIENHOUSE,
Ralph, Jr. of Waldwich, NJ m. Linda M. **Baxter** of Barrington 7/17/1971; H - b. 7/15/1944 in NJ, s/o Ralph Nienhouse, Sr. (Netherlands) and Jeanette Dykstra (NJ); W - b. 12/13/1947 in NH, d/o Alden E. Baxter (NH) and Geraldine E. Swain (NH)

NORMAN,
Kevin J. of Lee m. Peggy S. **Scott** of Barrington 11/15/1983 in Rochester

NORRIS,
Michael A. of Ft. Scott, KS m. Kathleen A. **Cunningham** of Barrington 8/11/1973; H - b. 9/6/1952 in WA, s/o Claude W. Norris (MO) and Phyllis L. Austin (KS); W - b. 1/12/1949 in NH, d/o Wilfred M. Cunningham (NH) and Gladys F. Marden (NH)

NORRISH,
William S. G. of Ft. Wayne, IN m. Janna L. **Stevens** of Barrington 10/8/1983

NORTON,
Romeo A. of Huntington, VT m. Nellie M. **Buzzell** of Barrington 5/14/1902 in So. Barrington; H - 51, farmer, 2d, b. Huntington, VT, s/o Solomon R. Norton (Huntington, VT) and Columbia C. Ballon; W - 35, at home, b. Barrington, d/o John A. Buzzell (farmer) and Mary Daniels

NOVAK,
Patrick R. of Newton m. Norma Y. **Brown** of Barrington 6/14/1981 in Newton

NOVARA,
Daniel F. of Barrington m. Lori A. **Cantin** of Somersworth 7/27/1985 in Dover

NUGENT,
David L., Jr. of Barrington m. Gail A. **Dow** of Barrington 10/31/1981 in Nottingham

NUNEZ,
Fabian S. of Barrington m. Rita **Tijerina** of Barrington 11/3/1979

NYE,
Richard A., Jr. of Dover m. Lorraine V. **Binette** of Barrington 8/15/1980 in Rochester

NYLUND,
David A. of Barrington m. Linda J. **Kemp** of Rochester 7/18/1986 in Kingston

O'DONNELL,
William V. of Barrington m. Carole J. **Plenty** of Westfield, NJ 2/20/1971 in Durham; H - b. 9/6/1948 in MA, s/o William O'Donnell (MA) and Helen E. McKenzie (MA); W - b. 12/3/1948 in NJ, d/o George A. Plenty (NJ) and Jean E. Clark (NY)

O'MALLEY,
Desmond F. of Barrington m. Kathryn L. **Farrow** of Barrington 6/16/1973; H - b. 10/11/1943 in NH, s/o Andrew L. O'Malley (Ireland) and Nora A. O'Malley (Ireland); W - b. 9/22/1951 in NH, d/o George T. Farrow (NH) and Lugina C. Gutowski (MA)

O'TOOLE,
James P. of Barrington m. Laura L. **Cunningham** of Strafford 4/26/1980 in Lincoln

OBERTAUTACH,
Raymond E. of Barrington m. Audrey M. **Miles** of Rochester 9/29/1984 in Rochester

ODA,
Dale T. of HI m. Jane A. **Bulman** of HI 6/16/1984

OLSSON,
Raymond of South River, NJ m. Katherine E. **Elliott** of Barrington 6/26/1965; H - 22, member USAF, b. NY, s/o Eric H. Olsson (NY) and Gerda Meinicke (Germany); W - 17, cook, b. NH, d/o Charles H. Elliott (NH) and Ruth E. Forrest (ME)

OTT,
Alan R. of Barrington m. Roxanne M. **Poisson** of Rochester 9/21/1985 in Rochester

OTTO,
Lawrence E. of Barrington m. Janice E. **Hunter** of Barrington 4/16/1977

OUELLET,
Thomas A. of Barrington m. Elaine M. **Jaczuk** of Manchester 9/22/1984 in Manchester

OUELLETTE,
Bradley D. of Rochester m. Emma M. **Daigle** of Barrington 8/15/1987

Eugene J. of Berwick, ME m. Lena M. **Plourde** of Barrington 5/5/1945 in Gonic; H - 21, truck driver, b. Berwick, ME, s/o Alphonse Ouellette (Canada) and Emma Vaillancourt (Canada); W - 19, bobbin girl, b. Auburn, ME, d/o Alfred Plourde (Rochester) and Olivine Dalpe (Canada)

George Raymond of Dover m. Joan Phyllis **White** of Barrington 10/26/1974

OWENS,
Jeffrey L. of Barrington m. Amy E. **Kindler** of Barrington 2/20/1982 in Northwood

PAGE,
Andrew C. of Barrington m. Anna A. **Hollister** of Barrington 9/1/1917 in Rochester; H - 66, farmer, 2d, b. Gilmanton, s/o John W. Page (Sandown, carpenter) and Sarah Page (Gilmanton, housewife); W - 68, housekeeper, 2d, b. Long Island, d/o Alfred Hall (Long Island, farmer) and Mary Hall (Long Island, housewife)

John A. of Barrington m. Sarah **Hoitt** of Barrington 5/6/1890; H - 43, b. Rochester; W - 41, b. Barrington

PALACIOS,
Vincent of Las Cruces, NM m. Betty K. **MacIver** of Barrington 6/19/1971 in Dover; H - b. 6/9/1950 in NM, s/o Vincent

M. Palacios (TX) and Isidora Jimenez (NM); W - b. 6/16/1951 in NH, d/o Burton A. MacIver (NH) and Josephine D. Connell (NH)

PALMER,

Curtis G. of Barrington m. Cora E. **Huckins** of Rochester 11/23/1893; H - 21, blacksmith, s/o John R. (Milton, farmer) and Ellen (Dover); W - 22, dressmaker, d/o George (Strafford, farmer) and Abbie

G. H. of Barrington m. Cora B. **Hanscomb** of Barrington 10/14/1893; H - 22, lumberman, s/o Delia Sewall (Barrington, farmer); W - 16, at home, d/o Leander (Barrington, farmer) and Nellie (Barrington)

Harold W. of Barrington m. Emma B. **Ray** of Dover 8/30/1924; H - 31, fireman, b. Rochester, s/o Burton R. Palmer (Dover, RR man) and Bertha S. Folsom (Ossipee, housewife); W - 20, at home, b. Northwood, d/o Harvey Ray (Plaistow, shoe cutter) and Lucy M. Brown (Northwood, housewife)

PARADIS,

Lionel R., Jr. of Barrington m. Kristina L. **Landry** of Barrington 4/25/1987

Richard A. of Rochester m. Karen L. **Brooks** of Barrington 6/23/1972 in Dover; H - b. 10/10/1953 in NH, s/o Philip L. Paradis (NH) and Geraldine A. Vincent (NH); W - b. 9/10/1953 in NH, d/o Richard S. Brooks and Ann K. Johnson (VT)

PARENTEAU,

Dennis H. of Barrington m. Kathy J. **Fowler** of Barrington 11/12/1983

PARISH,

William L. of Barrington m. Rene M. **Field** of Lynn, MA 12/2/1985

PARKER,

Melvin F. of Barrington m. Bernice L. **Seavey** of Rochester 8/5/1933 in Rochester; H - 24, spinner, b. Charlestown, MA, s/o William H. Parker (Eastport, ME) and Alice J. Howard (Charlestown, MA); W - 22, stenographer, b. Rochester, d/o Fred L. Seavey (Rochester) and Flora B. Wentworth (Rochester)

Rufus W. of Barrington m. Minnie D. **Winslow** of Barrington 5/17/1902 in E. Barrington; H - 18, farmer, b. Raymond, ME, s/o William A. Parker (Topsham, ME, painter) and Anna A. Strout (Raymond, ME); W - 18, at home, b. Casco, ME, d/o Anson J. Winslow (Casco, ME) and Addie Tinnie (Casco, ME)

PARKS,

James Michael of Dover m. Donetta Jean **Haley** of Barrington 7/27/1974

PARROTT,

Harry A. of Barrington m. Carolyn D. **Creighton** of Barrington 5/11/1968 in Durham; H - b. 7/24/1945 in IA, s/o Carlyle J. Jones (IA) and Marietta A. Niner (IA); W - b. 2/18/1944 in PA, d/o Donald W. Creighton (ME) and Helen A. Yeager (PA)

PARSHLEY,

Joseph E. of Barrington m. Dora M. **Hayes** of Dover 5/13/1925 in Strafford; H - 20, box worker, b. Barrington, s/o Charles E. Parshley (Strafford, retired) and Mary E. Jewell (Strafford, housewife); W - 18, at home, b. Dover, d/o Frank P. Hayes (Boston, MA, jeweler) and Medora Marcotte (Dover, housewife)

Joseph E. of Barrington m. Evelyn V. **Gray** of Barrington 9/22/1961; H - 57, machine oper., 3rd, b. NH, s/o Charles E. Parshley (NH) and Mary E. Jewell (NH); W -

53, shoe worker, 3rd, b. NH, d/o George F. Littlefield (ME) and Susie E. Lyon (Canada)

Robert V. of Barrington m. Mary G. **Howard** of Barrington 1/12/1920 in Strafford; H - 28, farmer, b. Strafford, s/o Charles Parshley (Strafford, box maker) and Mary Jewell (Strafford, housewife); W - 19, at home, b. Barrington, d/o Levi Howard (Rochester, farmer) and Cora Foss (Barrington, housewife)

PARSONS,
Joel M. of Barrington m. Kimberly M. **Hikel** of Barrington 12/12/1985

PATTEN,
Leroy Stanley of Barrington m. Cheryl Lee **Campbell** of Barrington 9/4/1975 in Wakefield

PAUL,
Andrew Joseph of Barrington m. Doris Marie **Pelland** of Barrington 6/14/1975 in Northwood

PAYETTE,
George Emile of Dover m. Jane Karen **Witmer** of Barrington 10/19/1974 in Durham

PEABODY,
Bradley S. of Boston, MA m. Cydney E. **Faucon** of Boston, MA 12/23/1978

PEARSON,
Michael E. of Barrington m. Evelyn M. **Nolin** of Pembroke 7/9/1969 in Portsmouth; H - b. 1/9/1946 in ME, s/o Maurice Pearson (ME) and Florence Holmstrom (ME); W - b. 9/14/1948 in NH, d/o Armand Nolin (Canada) and Esther Macmichael (NH)

PELLETIER,
Dean D. of Rochester m. Cheryl A. **Ellis** of Barrington 10/8/1977
Marcel L. of Rochester m. Donna J. **Pinzari** of Barrington 9/14/1985 in Rochester

PERFITO,
Anthony J. of Barrington m. Denise M. **de St. Aubin** of Manchester 7/18/1970 in Manchester; H - b. 10/9/1946 in MA, s/o John A. Perfito (MA) and Jeannette LaFlamme (MA); W - b. 7/24/1950 in NH, d/o Edward de St. Aubin (NH) and Roberta Caron (NH)

PERKINS,
Daniel O. of Dover m. Dorothy S. **Brown** of Barrington 8/14/1954; H - 29, truck driver, b. NH, s/o Fred Perkins (NH) and Sarah I. Slater (CT); W - 20, clerk, b. NH, d/o Guy N. Brown (NH) and Kathryn E. Lenfest (MA)
Fenelon J. of Barrington m. Hazel L. **Cross** of Rochester 6/7/1952 in Rochester; H - 20, airman, b. ME, s/o Earl Perkins (ME) and Blanche Y. Croteau (ME); W - 18, clerk, b. NH, d/o Frank G. Cross (VT) and Doris H. Dennis (NH)
Gary W. of Barrington m. Donna M. **Elliott** of Barrington 11/4/1978 in Somersworth
George H., Jr. of Barrington m. Sheila D. **Blidberg** of Barrington 12/13/1985
Joseph C. of Barrington m. Elsie M. **Brown** of Strafford 4/8/1899 in Rochester; H - 37, farmer, 2d, b. Barrington, s/o John and Nancy; W - 20, domestic, b. Strafford, d/o Jared (Strafford, laborer) and Jennie (Strafford)
Joseph C. of Barrington m. Lizzie M. **Richardson** of Northwood 11/12/1906 in Epsom; H - 43, teamster, 3rd, b. Barrington, s/o John B. Perkins and Nancy Seavey; W - 28, domestic, 2d, b. Northwood, d/o Eben Richardson (Northwood, shoemaker) and Sophronia Richardson

Melvin R. of Barrington m. June I. **Cross** of Rochester
5/23/1947 in Rochester; H - 20, marker, b. Auburn, ME,
s/o Earl Perkins (Auburn, ME) and Blanche Y. Croteau
(Auburn, ME); W - 20, clerk, b. Lyme Center, d/o Frank
G. Cross (Meredith) and Doris H. Dennis (Lyme Center)

Randy Kay of Barrington m. Mary Ellen **Welch** of Center
Barnstead 10/26/1974 in Somersworth

PERRY,

Harry W. H. of West Barrington m. Ethel A. **Morrison** of
West Barrington 5/5/1912; H - 30, farmer, b. Lynn, MA,
s/o Oscar M. Hill (Farmer) and Frances Annabel; W - 19,
housemaid, b. Dover, d/o George Morrison and Viola
Willey (housewife)

PETTENGILL,

Robert F. of Barrington m. Geraldine A. **Hebert** of Athens,
NY 11/8/1966 in Rochester; H - 36, prod. control mgr.,
2d, div., b. Lewiston, ME, s/o Lee D. Pettengill (ME) and
Barbara N. French (MA); W - 23, key punch oper., b.
Columbia, d/o Jessie L. Cass (NH) and Lillian N. Coates
(VT)

PHENIX,

Alan R. of Durham m. Carol L. **Emery** of Barrington
8/27/1977

PHILLIPS,

Ronald M. of Barrington m. Sharon A. **Mason** of Rochester
9/15/1973; H - b. 12/9/1951 in NH, s/o Harry Phillips, Jr.
(NH) and Elizabeth King (MA); W - b. 7/8/1954 in NH,
d/o Maurice J. Mason (VT) and Alva C. Hall (NH)

PICARD,

Ronald E. of Barrington m. Dorothy A. **Haigh** of Dover
12/16/1967 in Dover; H - 23, member USAF, b. Dover,

s/o Raymond Picard (NH) and Madeline F. Trela (MA); W - 20, secretary, b. Dover, d/o William M. Haigh (England) and Doris I. Goodwin (ME)

PICKERING,
Jackie of Barrington m. Linda J. **Brulotte** of Portsmouth 10/16/1982 in Portsmouth

PIECUCH,
Gary A. of Barrington m. Debra L. **Sims** of Barrington 8/23/1986 in Epping

PIERCE,
Hal B. of Barrington m. Linda R. **Nettleton** of Barrington 3/21/1981
Philip Alan, Jr. of Hanover m. Marianne Gladys **McIntire** of Barrington 9/4/1976 in Durham
Wesley A. of Barrington m. Lucille M. **Thompson** of Lee 8/28/1946 in Lee; H - 22, farmer, b. Dover, s/o James D. Pierce (Barrington) and Edna F. Fernald (Nottingham); W - 29, home econ., b. Lee, d/o Arthur J. Thompson (Lee) and Ethel H. Durgin (Lee)

PIERSON,
Charles A. of Barrington m. Janice M. **Goudreau** of Barrington 3/1/1986 in Durham

PIKE,
Alvah B. of Barrington m. Jean M. **Meattey** of Barrington 9/6/1980
Arthur E. of Dover m. Barbara M. **Smith** of Barrington 11/28/1952 in Dover; H - 47, salesman, 2d, b. NY, s/o Arthur E. Pike (MA) and Gertrude Shields (NY); W - 41, housewife, 3rd, b. Washington, DC, d/o Charles Morriss (RI) and Helen Richards (NJ)

Frank N. of Salisbury m. Lilla F. **Hall** of Barrington 11/12/1894 in Hampton; H - 43, shoemaker, 2d, b. Salisbury, s/o Aaron (Salisbury, farmer) and Caroline (Barrington, at home); W - 26, at home, b. Barrington, d/o Gilman and Mary

L. Gerry of Barrington m. Carol-Anne **Randall** of Wakefield 9/12/1981 in Sanbornville

PLAISTED,

Robert J., Jr. of Dover m. Janice G. **Piller** of Barrington 10/7/1967; H - 18, factory worker, b. Dover, s/o Robert J. Plaisted (NH) and Dorothy Freeman (NH); W - 15, at home, b. Quincy, MA, d/o William L. Piller (MA) and Julia L. Frye (NH)

PLANCHE,

Leon H. of Cumberland, ME m. Joan E. **Lessard** of Barrington 9/30/1978

PLANTE,

Richard R. of Barrington m. Karen F. **Guthrie** of Barrington 1/18/1986

PLOTNER,

Walter E. of Brockton, MA m. Jewell M. **Redick** of Boston, MA 8/28/1938; H - 32, printer, b. Brockton, MA, s/o Fred C. Potner (Terre Haute, IN) and Florence E. Blanchard (Brockton, MA); W - 32, hair dresser, b. Denison, TX, d/o James P. Redick (Denison, TX) and Estella Ross (Tombean, TX)

PLOURDE,

Alfred E. of Barrington m. Louise L. **Chapdelaine** of Gonic 5/12/1951 in Gonic; H - 27, laborer, b. NH, d/o Alfred J. Plourde (NH) and Olivine Dalphe (Canada); W - 20,

shoeworker, b. NH, d/o Rene J. Chapdelaine (Canada) and Elzire Plamondon (Canada)
David E. of Barrington m. Debra A. **McKay** of Barrington 9/19/1981

PLUMER,
Daniel C. of Madbury m. Karen R. **Wormell** of Barrington 11/12/1977 in Durham

PLUMMER,
Charles L. of Waterville, ME m. Ethel M. **Bodge** of Barrington 10/15/1912 in Gonic; H - 29, brakeman, b. Manchester, s/o Charles Plummer (railroad man) and Priscilla Johnson (housekeeper); W - 22, housework, b. Barrington, d/o Charles Bodge (farmer) and Mary C. Carley (housekeeper)
Richard L. of Barrington m. Karen L. **Calef** of Barrington 4/26/1986

PLUNKET,
Robert J. of Barrington m. Annie M. **Bumford** of Barrington 10/21/1892; H - 46, farmer, 2d, b. England, s/o James and Sarah; W - 43, housemaid, b. Barrington, d/o Hateville and Elizabeth

PORTER,
Ronald A. of Lee m. Sharon A. **Baxter** of Barrington 12/19/1973; H - 2d, b. 12/24/1945 in VT, s/o Edward Porter (RI) and Eula Dean (VT); W - b. 4/13/1947 in NH, d/o Sherman L. Baxter (NH) and Luverne Swain (NH)

POST,
Richard J. of Barrington m. Constance R. **Arabia** of Rochester 8/18/1978 in Rochester
Richard J. of Barrington m. Kathy J. **Glidden** of Rochester 10/18/1985 in Rochester

Richard James, Sr. of Barrington m. Carol Anne **Skillin** of Barrington 10/1/1976 in Plaistow

POTTER,
Chauncey C. of Medford, MA m. Flora May **Boyle** of Saugus, MA 8/22/1931; H - 25, accountant, b. Roxbury, MA, s/o Chauncey Potter (E. Douglas, MA) and Ada J. Fulton (NS); W - 23, at home, b. Medford, MA, d/o John A. Boyle (IA) and Olive M. Berry (Milton, MA)

POULTON,
Jeffrey J. of Barrington m. Maribeth L. **Conklin** of Barrington 7/28/1984

PRATT,
Leonard D. of Barrington m. Jeanette L. **Hall** of Barrington 1/8/1983 in Rochester

PRESCOTT,
Joseph of Barrington m. Mary **King** of Barrington 6/30/1896; H - 55, farmer, 2d, b. Barrington, s/o Eben and Sarah; W - 55, domestic, 2d, b. So. Berwick, ME, d/o Mark (So. Berwick, ME) and Abbie (Lebanon, ME)

PRESTON,
Donald B. of Barrington m. Carol A. **Wood** of Rochester 3/24/1961; H - 18, member USAF, b. NH, s/o John D. Preston (NH) and Vida C. Lund (NH); W - 19, meat wrapper, b. NH, d/o Charles H. Wood (MA) and Doris P. Sirrell (NH)

Donald B. of Barrington m. Janet R. **Rose** of Somersworth 2/4/1967 in Somersworth; H - 24, rubber worker, 2d, div., b. Rochester, s/o John D. Preston (NH) and Vida C. Lund (NH); W - 26, inspector, 2d, div., b. Somerville, MA, d/o Earl E. Moore (MA) and Helen J. Nichols (MA)

John of Barrington m. Vida C. **Lund** of Strafford 7/23/1934 in Strafford; H - 39, farmer, b. Barrington, s/o Alberton Preston (Barrington) and Fannie Preston (Strafford); W - 24, housekeeper, b. Newport, d/o Frederick Lund and Lura B. Lund (Enfield)

Loren J. of Barrington m. Joan I. **Williams** of Dover 2/9/1963; H - 26, rubber ind., b. NH, s/o John D. Preston (NH) and Vida C. Lund (NH); W - 29, rubber ind., 2d, b. MA, d/o Armand Roy (MA) and Evelyn Mosley (MA)

PRICE,
Edmund L. of Portsmouth m. Sharon E. **Green** of Barrington 2/14/1970; H - b. 9/16/1947 in HI, s/o Troy Scott Price (NC) and Nathalie R. Hanson (NH); W - b. 9/23/1947 in NH, d/o Daniel M. Green (ME) and Elaine A. Turner (NH)

PRINCE,
Kenneth A. of Barrington m. Hazel W. **Bartlett** of Northwood 12/28/1963; H - 52, mechanic, b. NH, s/o George H. Prince (WI) and Mary E. Moore (NH); W - 65, sup. child., 2d, b. NH, d/o Harrison W. Tuttle (NH) and Stella B. Foss (NH)

PROULX,
Raymond A. of Candia m. Viola C. **Rogers** of Barrington 9/18/1982 in Manchester

PUFFER,
Bryant A. of Barrington m. Sharon R. **Berounsky** of Eliot, ME 6/24/1965; H - 21, carpenter, b. NH, s/o Stanwood A. Puffer (MA) and Carolyn S. Taylor (MA); W - 18, at home, b. NH, d/o Gerald W. Berounsky (MA) and Frances M. Varney (NH)

PULSIFER,

Roy of Campton m. Ida M. **Boodey** of Barrington 8/2/1926; H - 26, bookkeeper, b. Campton, s/o John M. Pulsifer (farmer) and Laura S. Worthen (housewife); W - 25, teacher, b. Rochester, d/o John V. Boodey (farmer) and Alice Arlin (at home)

PURINGTON,

Richard Blaisdell of Barrington m. Doris Mae **Sears** of Dover 6/9/1974 in Derry

PURVIS,

Carlyle S. of Barrington m. Dorothy A. **Littlefield** of Rochester 4/12/1947 in Rochester; H - 20, box shop, b. Rochester, s/o E. Leonard Purvis (Norwich, CT) and Catherine S. Clark (E. Rochester); W - 20, at home, b. Rochester, d/o Ralph W. Littlefield (Wells, ME) and Sarah M. Guptill (Berwick, ME)

RADWAN,

Steven of Rochester m. Christine E. **Felong** of Barrington 9/8/1984 in Dover

RAMSDELL,

Frederick of Barrington m. Annie N. **Taylor** of Barrington 9/1/1939 in Dover; H - 25, truck driver, b. Wareham, MA, s/o Chester H. Ramsdell (Wareham, MA) and Katheryn Besse (Wareham, MA); W - 22, invoicer, b. Chelsea, MA, d/o Harold F. Taylor (Newfoundland) and Emily J. Rowe (Newfoundland)

Gary E. of Barrington m. Faith J. **Tuttle** of Rochester 1/19/1973 in Rochester; H - b. 12/13/1945 in NH, s/o William Ramsdell (MA) and Muriel Buck (MA); W - 2d, b. 10/25/1952 in ME, d/o Roscoe Littlefield (ME) and Anita Hout (ME)

John B. of Barrington m. Janet M. **Rollins** of Manchester 11/5/1966 in Manchester; H - 23, draftsman, b. Dover, s/o William Ramsdell (MA) and Muriel Buck (NH); W - 18, secretary, b. Somerville, MA, d/o George Rollins (VT) and Alice O'Brien (MA)

RANDALL,
David E. of Barrington m. Edresa M. **Hamner** of Somersworth 11/21/1973 in Rochester; H - b. 2/15/1949 in ME, s/o Philip Randall (ME) and Cora Webber (ME); W - b. 4/14/1947 in ME, d/o Edward Hamner (ME) and Theresa Newman (MA)

RANSOM,
Donald R., Jr. of Barrington m. Christine **Patrick** of Portsmouth 2/14/1987 in Chichester

READY,
Joseph M., Jr. of Barrington m. Kathy M. **Clark** of Barrington 12/19/1983

REAGAN,
John L. of Barrington m. Sharon L. **DeAngelis** of Concord 2/14/1987 in Concord

REAKE,
Hans H. of Barrington m. Jerilynn A. **Hoffman** of Dover 12/24/1965; H - 22, univ. student, b. Germany, s/o Herman Reake (Germany) and Hildegarde Stein (Germany); W - 22, teacher, b. NY, d/o William G. Hoffman (NY) and Ruth Bedell (NY)

REED,
James W. of Barrington m. Sophronia E. **Reed** of Barrington 11/2/1914 in Dover; H - 43, fireman, 2d, b. Barrington, s/o Charles H. Reed (Barrington, shoemaker) and Annie

B. Seavey (Barrington, housekeeper); W - 79, housekeeper, 3rd, b. Barrington, d/o Joseph Hill (Strafford, farmer) and Betsy Hanson (Strafford, housewife)

REIMERS,
Richard R. of Somersworth m. Barbara J. **Littlefield** of Barrington 8/17/1985 in Somersworth

REJACK,
Michael D. of Barrington m. Cheryl A. **Morency** of Barrington 8/31/1981

REMILLARD,
Robert R. of Manchester m. Cheryl L. **Thurston** of Barrington 6/26/1982 in New London

RENAUD,
Dale P. of Barrington m. Holly M. **Fenn** of Barrington 7/2/1981

RHOADES,
Winthrop R. of Barrington m. Deborah L. **Alberts** of Barrington 12/21/1982

RICHARDS,
Thomas H. of Greenland m. Donna K. **Leeper** of Barrington 6/19/1966 in Kingston; H - 24, univ. student, b. Exeter, s/o Frank F. Richards (NH) and Ella O. Higgins (NH); W - 21, accountant, b. Exeter, d/o Durward D. Leeper (CT) and Mary L. Spies (CT)

RICHARDSON,
David Alan of Rochester m. Janet Lee **Schanda** of Barrington 5/17/1975

Edward O. of Barrington m. Jennie "Trask" **Buzzell** of Barrington 12/24/1913 in Dover; H - 48, teamster, 2d, b. Barrington, s/o Joseph P. Richardson (farmer) and Elizabeth Hall (housewife); W - 47, housework, b. Dover, d/o John Trask (shoemaker) and Elizabeth Moore (housewife)

Paul H. of Barrington m. Sandra J. **Capen** of Dover 3/23/1979 in Dover

RICHER,
Donat D., Jr. of Sanford, ME m. Vera H. **Clark** of Barrington 5/13/1967; H - 26, assemblyman, b. Sanford, ME, s/o Donad W. Richer (Canada) and Dorila M. Hamelin (Canada); W - 20, assembler, b. Cambridge, MA, d/o Major Clark (Canada) and Helen Crowell (MA)

RICKER,
George Gerald of Rochester m. Wanda Lorraine **Cossette** of Barrington 8/28/1976

RIDDOCK,
Charles M. of Boston, MA m. Irene W. **Hayes** of Boston, MA 12/23/1933 in Dover; H - 45, rubber chem., 2d, b. Aberdeen, Scotland, s/o John Riddock (Aberdeen, Scotland) and Helen Milton (Aberdeen, Scotland); W - 30, secretary, 2d, b. Strafford, d/o Henry W. Hayes (Strafford) and Nellie Hilton (Boston, MA)

RIDOLFI,
Dominic R. of Barrington m. Barbara A. **Lindsay** of Barrington 5/21/1983

RILEY,
Charles of Barrington m. Lottie **Holmes** of Barrington 3/27/1894; H - 23, brick maker, b. Lyman, ME, s/o

Charles and Ella; W - 16, housewife, b. Portsmouth, d/o Jennie

Fred E., IV of Dover m. Patricia J. **Rowell** of Barrington 3/7/1969; H - b. 4/26/1941 in NJ, s/o Fred E. Riley, III (NY) and Ruth K. Crietz (PA); W - b. 3/22/1950 in NH, d/o Edward R. Rowell (MA) and Ruth E. Taylor (MA)

Ronald Scott of Rochester m. Kim Kra-Veiling **Brooks** of Barrington 5/30/1976 in Rochester

RIZZO,

Mark J. of Nashua m. Vanessa J. **Haley** of Barrington 8/13/1983 in North Conway

ROBERTS,

John H. of Barrington m. Cheryl A. **McKay** of Barrington 1/7/1984

Lawrence Davis, Jr. of Barrington m. Helen Mary **O'Keefe** of Barrington 3/16/1974 in Lee

Warren C. of Williamsport, PA m. Leslie **Kalechman** of Williamsport, PA 6/14/1979

William H. of Barrington m. Evelyn G. **Dow** of Hartford, VT 10/2/1971 in Hartford, VT; H - b. 9/13/1949 in NH, s/o Randolph L. Roberts (NH) and Elizabeth M. Jones (NH); W - b. 9/29/1954 in CT, d/o Frank J. Dow (VT) and Donna M. McDonald (CT)

ROBERTSON,

Allan R. of Barrington m. Dorothy A. **Ambrose** of Strafford 8/15/1981 in Strafford

ROBIE,

Lawrence C. of Barrington m. Roberta H. **Bassett** of Dover 2/3/1962; H - 24, tannery wkr., b. NH, s/o Lloyd A. Robie (NH) and Bernice E. Clarkson (NH); W - 28, clerk, 2d, b. NH, d/o George Bassett (Canada) and Sadie Oates (NH)

Wayne A. of Barrington m. Phyllis I. **Seavey** of Barrington 7/22/1952 in Northwood; H - 19, US Navy, b. NH, s/o Lloyd A. Robie (NH) and Bernice E. Clarkson; W - 16, student, b. NJ, s/o Ralph J. Seavey (NH) and Grace M. Atkins (NH)

ROBINSON,
Allen P. of Barrington m. Heidi A. **Freeman** of Barrington 2/14/1987
Gordon E. of Durham m. Helen E. **Caldwell** of Barrington 5/20/1950 in Durham; H - 26, electrician, b. NH, s/o Arthur W. Robinson (NH) and Susanna E. Large (PEI); W - 18, typ. clerk, b. KS, d/o Dexter H. Caldwell (NH) and Ruth R. Ellison (NH)
Herbert L. of Barrington m. Audrey S. **Winlock** of Lexington, MA 9/24/1949; H - 17, student, b. MA, s/o Gerald N. Robinson (ME) and Pearl Lunt (ME); W - 23, student, b. MA, d/o Harvey F. Winlock (MA) and Mabel Grebenstein (MA)
Mark G. of Barrington m. Michelle A. **Lambert** of Barrington 8/1/1987 in Durham

ROGIER,
Julian G. of Barrington m. Sandra L. **Barr** of Lee 11/1/1966; H - 22, mechanic, b. Medford, MA, s/o Frank Rogier (MA) and Gussie L. Turner (Canada); W - 19, student, b. Cherry Point, NC, d/o William C. Barr (KA) and Helen M. Bishop (CT)

ROHRBACHER,
Robert Richard of Rochester m. Denise Marie **Dionne** of Barrington 6/28/1975 in Dover

ROLLINS,
Joseph W. of Barrington m. Ruth A. **Heath** of Northwood 5/27/1955 in Northwood; H - 26, US Army, b. NH, s/o

Willie H. Rollins (NH) and Lilla M. Merrill (NH); W - 19, at home, b. NH, d/o Robinson Heath (NH) and Elsie Mudgett (NH)

Walter of Barrington m. Marinda **Hanscom** of Barrington 2/25/1899; H - 27, fireman, b. Nottingham, s/o Rufus and Elizabeth; W - 24, domestic, b. Barrington, d/o Nathan and Eliza

Walter of Barrington m. Lucy Ann R. H. **Merrill** of Nottingham 5/6/1919; H - 46, farmer, 2d, b. Nottingham, s/o Rufus Rollins (farmer); W - 21, housework, b. Rochester, d/o George F. Merrill (Rochester)

ROSS,

Richard H. of Medford, MA m. Madlyn P. **Montour** of Barrington 4/27/1968 in Rochester; H - b. 4/1/1937 in MA, s/o James E. Ross (MA) and Anne L. Connors (MA); W - 2d, b. 1/13/1943 in NH, d/o Frank E. Walker (NH) and Blanche R. Brogan (NH)

Robert Thomas, Jr. of Barrington m. Carol Ann **Marino** of Barrington 11/29/1976 in Portsmouth

Ronnie W. of Gas City, IN m. Susan E. **Clark** of Barrington 11/11/1967; H - 24, member USAF, b. Marion, IN, s/o Willis N. Ross (KY) and Marcella B. Hamilton (KY); W - 19, food handler, b. Sanford, ME, d/o Ernest W. Clark (NH) and Viola G. Elliott (NH)

Shepley L., II of Barrington m. Karen M. **Decareau** of Amherst 7/15/1978

William E. D. of New Brunswick, Canada m. Marilyn A. **Clark** of Barrington 7/2/1960; H - 38, film agent, 2d, b. Canada, s/o William E. Ross (Canada) and Laura F. Brooks (Canada); W - 25, nurse, b. NH, d/o Melvin A. Clark (NH) and Olive M. Cleveland (NH)

William O. of Barrington m. Gwen M. **Miltner** of Rochester 7/14/1979 in Rochester

RO[W]E,
Charles C. of Barrington m. Susan **Layte** of Dorchester 4/20/1898 in Rochester; H - 48, farmer, b. Danvers, s/o William and Olive (Alfred, ME, housewife); W - 25, dressmaker, b. Lawrencetown, d/o S. Hiram (NS, cabinet maker) and Mary (NS, housewife)
Edgar T. of Barrington m. Grace **Harrington** of Rockford, ME 9/23/1901; H - 18, laborer, b. Barrington, s/o Henry Roe (Barrington, laborer) and Emma Roe; W - 19, housework, b. Rockford, ME, d/o James Harrington (Rockford, ME, carpenter) and Mary Harrington
George A. of Manchester m. Emma D. **Calwell** of Barrington 1/20/1919 in Gonic; H - 76, farmer, 2d, b. Gilford, s/o James Rowe (Gilford, farmer); W - 70, housekeeper, 2d, b. Kennebunk, ME, d/o Daniel Durrell (Kennebunk, ME, mechanic)
Henry E. of Barrington m. Emma J. **Henman** of Barrington 4/5/1890; H - 34, b. Barrington, s/o Nancy D. Rowe; W - 22, b. Barrington
John F. of Barrington m. Julia **Arlin** of Barrington 4/3/1904; H - 44, sawyer, 2d, b. Barrington, s/o John F. Rowe (Barrington) and Nancy D. Heath (Bristol); W - 29, housemaid, 2d, b. Van Buren, ME, d/o Frank Hart (Van Buren, ME, farmer) and Annie M. Vievlette
Laforest L. of Barrington m. Cora A. **Howard** of Rochester 9/6/1913; H - 30, laborer, b. Barrington, s/o William Kay (farmer) and Ella F. Rowe (housework); W - 39, housework, 2d, b. Rochester, d/o George N. Howard (deceased) and Elizabeth A. Howard (deceased)
Walter H. of Barrington m. Myrtle H. **Downes** of Barrington 11/16/1913; H - 28, farmer, 2d, b. Barrington, s/o Henry E. Rowe (farmer) and Emma J. Brown (deceased); W - 24, housework, b. So. Lebanon, ME, d/o Charles M. Downes (fireman) and Emma R. Roberts (housework)
Walter H. of Barrington m. Nellie M. **Foss** of Barrington 4/13/1922; H - 35, teamster, 2d, b. Barrington, s/o Henry

H. Rowe (Barrington, laborer) and Emma J. Lewis
(Dover, housewife); W - 34, housekeeper, 2d, b. Dover,
d/o Walter E. Rowe (Strafford, shoemaker) and Sadie J.
Perkins (Dover, housewife)

ROWELL,
Edward R. of Barrington m. Ruth E. **Taylor** of Barrington
6/24/1947; H - 22, lineman, b. Winchester, MA, s/o
Edward M. Rowell (Beverly, MA) and Hazel M. Shedd
(Brookline, MA); W - 20, stenographer, b. Everett, MA,
d/o Fielding Taylor (Newfoundland) and Agnes M.
Anderson (Sweden)
Peter E. of Barrington m. Lauren C. **Chase** of Goffstown
6/25/1977 in North Hampton
Stephen T. of Barrington m. Pamela J. **Small** of Barrington
4/2/1977
Timothy E. of Barrington m. Andrea E. **Conley** of Barrington
7/30/1986

ROY,
Thomas B. of Barrington m. Martha L. **Goode** of Greenland
11/20/1976 in Greenland

ROZWADOWSKI,
Thomas A. of Barrington m. Jean **Pearson** of Barrington
10/20/1977 in Portsmouth

RUEL,
David P. of Barrington m. Lisa A. **Addison** of Barrington
6/26/1982
Paul R. of Dover m. Ruth M. **Johnson** of Barrington
12/15/1954 in Dover; H - 19, US Navy, b. NH, s/o Paul J.
Ruel (NH) and Alice Forcier (NH); W - 18, sales clerk, b.
NH, d/o Alexander J. Johnson (MA) and Marion E.
Ineson (NH)

Robert A. of Barrington m. Lisa B. **Stimpson** of Rochester 7/25/1981

RUSH,
Robert B. of Barrington m. Teresa A. **Encarnacao** of Barrington 9/9/1981 in Portsmouth

RUSSELL,
Bruce A. of Barrington m. Cynthia L. **Kelly** of Barrington 6/16/1978 in Dover
Peter C. of Barrington m. Donna J. **Schemack** of Barrington 5/16/1987 in Dover

RUTHERFORD,
Peter J. of Barrington m. Rose M. **Levesque** of Rochester 6/14/1958 in Rochester; H - 24, student, b. MA, s/o Jerome J. Rutherford (ME) and Marie T. Keliher (MA); W - 21, nurse, b. NH, d/o Charles D. Levesque (NH) and Mary E. Collins (NH)

RYEA,
Allen M. of Barrington m. Vicky S. **Ryea** of Barrington 12/31/1981

ST. CYR,
Craig R. of Barrington m. Kathleen R. **O'Connor** of Barrington 9/29/1985 in Somersworth

ST. HILAIRE,
Peter C. of Somersworth m. Deborah L. **Hargreaves** of Barrington 11/22/1980 in Dover

ST. ONGE,
Steven W. of Barrington m. Patricia A. **Morin** of Berwick, ME 4/21/1979 in Somersworth

SANDERS,
Albert N. of Barrington m. Ellen **Beam** of Portsmouth 6/3/1979 in Portsmouth

Alfred E. of Barrington m. Karen M. **Moffett** of Barrington 7/28/1972 in Concord; H - b. 12/21/1947 in DC, s/o Roberta A. Sanders (MA); W - 2d, b. 6/9/1938 in NH, d/o Albert E. Weeden (NH) and Thelma R. Richards (ME)

David C. of Barrington m. Pamela M. **Horne** of Barrington 6/18/1983

John H., Jr. of Barrington m. Lynda L. **Gagne** of Nottingham 6/18/1960; H - 19, plumber, b. NH, s/o John H. Sanders (NH) and Mina M. Forrest (NH); W - 18, at home, b. NH, d/o David J. Gagne (NH) and Beulah G. Gray (NH)

John H., III of Barrington m. Karen L. **Sweezey** of Barrington 4/1/1983

SANFACON,
Gerald L. of Barrington m. Dianne M. **Lamoreaux** of Rochester 12/22/1979 in Rochester

SANFORD,
Eugene P. of Barrington m. Mary L. **Monroe** of Rochester 6/6/1981 in Dover

SAUCIER,
Roger J. of Barrington m. Cheryl A. **Dubois** of Barrington 3/24/1979 in Somersworth

SAUNDERS,
Laurence R. of Barrington m. Margaret H. **Massey** of New Boston 2/24/1973 in New Boston; H - b. 10/15/1945 in MA, s/o Norman B. Saunders (OH) and Jeanne Ott (OH); W - b. 11/17/1947 in NJ, d/o Joseph T. Massey (NJ) and Margaret Keller (VA)

Richard N. of Stratford m. Alice M. **Bryson** of Barrington 9/3/1950 in Rochester; H - 22, mechanic, b. MA, s/o

John H. Saunders (MA) and Irene M. Hebert (MA); W - 21, at home, b. NH, d/o Melvin F. Bryson (NH) and Evelyn M. Green (NH)

SCARLOTTO,
Anthony J. of Barrington m. Mary M. **Boyle** of Barrington 10/18/1986 in Portsmouth

SCHANDA,
John L. of Barrington m. Patricia L. **McCarthy** of Arlington, MA 1/22/1972; H - b. 2/15/1953 in NH, s/o John A. Schanda (NH) and Arline M. Lirette (NH); W - b. 1/16/1950 in MA, d/o Thomas F. McCarthy (MA) and Lena McElhiney (MA)

SCHENA,
John J. of Barrington m. Joan **Gervasi** of Barrington 4/2/1977

SCHERER,
Michael J. of Greenland m. Laura A. **Walker** of Barrington 9/12/1981

SCHNOOR,
William K. of Barrington m. Bettiejo M. **Souza** of Rochester 6/10/1984

SCHREINER,
Timothy J. of Barrington m. Karen L. **Patenaude** of Barrington 7/17/1982 in Durham

SCHULTZ,
Stephen E. of Barrington m. Deborah J. **Pilotte** of Barrington 5/12/1979

SCHWAB,
Dennis R. of Northwood m. Rosalie A. **Brooks** of Barrington 2/26/1966 in Concord; H - 19, student, b. Melrose, MA, s/o Maynard B. Schwab (MA) and Edythe F. Dooley (MA); W - 19, clerk-steno, b. Portsmouth, d/o Kenneth E. Brooks (NH) and Florence H. Boston (ME)

SEAMAN,
James J. of Barrington m. Florence B. **Berry** of Barrington 4/17/1986

SEARLES,
Harry W. of Rochester m. Mrs. F. E. **Wentworth** of Atkinson 12/30/1905; H - 45, laborer, 3rd, b. Hampstead, s/o Stephen S. Searles and Elmira Bailey; W - 40, housewife, b. Hampstead, d/o John Madison and Ann Brickett (Danville)

SEAVER,
George R. of Barrington m. Patricia C. **Hayes** of Barrington 6/4/1983 in Dover

SEAVEY,
Charles H., Jr. of Barrington m. Mattie A. **Roderick** of Northwood 9/18/1890 in Rochester; H - 21, b. Barrington, s/o Charles H. and Sarah Seavey; W - 17, b. Northwood, d/o Joseph and Lizzie Roderick
Sidney C. of Barrington m. Mignonette **Moore** of Hingham, MA 9/21/1892 in Gonic; H - 18, farmer, b. Barrington, s/o Charles H. and Sarah A.; W - 17, domestic, b. Mattapoisett, MA, d/o Hyman and Tamozin
Sidney C. of Barrington m. Mignonette **Seavey** of Waltham, MA 7/6/1896; H - 22, farmer, 2d, b. Barrington, s/o Charles (Barrington, laborer) and Sarah (Barrington); W - 21, domestic, 2d, b. Mattapoisett, MA, d/o Hayman and Famozine

SEGER,
Charles E., Jr. of Dover m. Geraldine C. **Preston** of Barrington 2/21/1964; H - 20, shoe worker, b. ME, s/o Charles E. Seger (ME) and Pauline Jordan (ME); W - 18, at home, b. ME, d/o Forest Preston (ME) and Laura Cottle (ME)

SHANNON,
Daniel C. of Lee m. Sharon L. **Millette** of Barrington 11/11/1965; H - 20, member US Navy, b. NH, s/o Daniel Shannon (NH) and Geraldine Gorton (NH); W - 19, factory worker, b. NH, d/o Adam M. Millette (NH) and Julia B. King (NH)

SHAW,
Loren T. of Dover m. Susan J. **Leffel** of Barrington 12/10/1960; H - 19, truck driver, b. NH, s/o Ford W. Shaw (ND) and Mary Babb (NH); W - 17, at home, b. NJ, d/o Albert W. Leffel (NJ) and Winifred Conrad (NJ)

SHEA,
Dana E. of Barrington m. Jean L. **Bergeron** of Barrington 10/17/1987

SHEDD,
Richard I. of Hingham, MA m. Lillian M. **Carlisle** of Brighton, MA 8/10/1947; H - 47, clerk, 2d, b. Brighton, MA, s/o Richard L. Shedd (Cambridge, MA) and Margaret O. Clark (Canada); W - 43, dental hyg., b. Pittsfield, MA, d/o William P. Carlisle (Albany, NY) and Hattie Patnode (Churubusco, NY)

SHEEHAN,
George B. of Barrington m. Ivy A. **Ballentine** of Barrington 9/26/1980

Gerald P. of Barrington m. Diane M. **Mucher** of Rollinsford 11/9/1963; H - 37, bank teller, b. NH, s/o Maurice J. Sheehan (Ireland) and Mary B. Brown (NH); W - 22, bank teller, b. NH, d/o Victor S. Mucher (NJ) and Jeannette A. Walters (NY)

James M. of Barrington m. Mary E. **Pease** of Barrington 9/18/1978

SHELTON,
Richard O., Jr. of Richmond, VA m. Marie C. **Gubellini** of Barrington 7/23/1977

SHERBURNE,
Joel Ralph of Barrington m. Flora Bell **Brown** of Barrington 11/17/1920; H - 37, blacksmith, b. Barrington, s/o Joel F. Sherburne (Barrington, farmer) and Nora C. Richardson (Winchester, MA, housewife); W - 19, at home, b. Barrington, d/o William Brown (Barrington, farmer) and Sarah Reed (Barrington, housewife)

SHEVENELL,
Brian K. of Barrington m. Kelly L. **Landry** of Barrington 6/9/1979

Guy P. of Barrington m. Deborah A. **Holland** of Rochester 3/3/1978

SILVA,
Jorge M. of Medford, MA m. Maryellen **DaCosta** of Somerville, MA 8/31/1972; H - b. 4/23/1946 in Portugal, s/o Serafim P. Silva (Azores) and Maria Mendonca (MA); W - b. 9/11/1950 in MA, d/o Augusto M. DaCosta (Azores) and Ellen F. Frazier (MA)

SIRRELL,
Curt F. of Barrington m. Goldie M. **Emmons** of Barrington 4/17/1943 in Meredith; H - 29, lumber oper., b. Salisbury,

MA, s/o Francis M. Sirrell (Wentworth) and Emily M. Bennett (Montreal, Canada); W - 17, housework, b. Tilton, d/o Ernest C. Emmons (Penacook) and Jennie M. Chase (Ashland)

SMALL,
Frank B. of Barrington m. Nellie F. **Howard** of Barrington 1/30/1904; H - 25, teamster, b. Pittsfield, s/o Warren A. Small (Strafford, farmer) and Ann Collins (Strafford); W - 15, at home, b. Dover, d/o Emery Howard (Barrington, laborer) and Emma Howard (Dover)

SMALLCON,
George P. of Barrington m. Louisa E. **Wentworth** of Rochester 10/25/1899 in Rochester; H - 27, clerk, b. Barrington, s/o George (Barrington, blacksmith) and Esmeralda; W - 21, typewriter, b. Rochester, d/o Frank (Rochester, ins. agent) and Emma
William E. of West Gonic m. Elmira **Emerson** of West Gonic 8/2/1915; H - 58, poultry rais., b. Barrington, s/o Henry Smallcon (Barrington, farmer) and Levina Howard (Barrington, domestic); W - 58, housekeeper, 2d, b. Barrington, d/o Benjamin Arlin (Barrington, soldier) and Hannah Sayer (Strafford, domestic)

SMALLEY,
Jerry L. of Barrington m. Sandra L. **Paquette** of Barrington 6/26/1986

SMITH,
Adriel C. of Milton Mills m. Mary L. **Locke** of Barrington 9/25/1960; H - 25, mechanic, b. NH, s/o Frederick W. Smith (NH) and Esther M. Remick (NH); W - 18, at home, b. NH, d/o Clarence B. Locke (NH) and Eva M. Clow (NH)

David W. of Barrington m. Susan J. **Post** of Barrington 4/22/1972 in Rochester; H - b. 12/30/1946 in MD, s/o Luther M. Smith (TN) and Fern C. Griffin (NC); W - b. 11/14/1953 in MA, d/o James E. Post and Shirley M. Burke

Dwight L. of Dover m. Leslie E. **Wilks** of Barrington 8/21/1982 in Lee

Frank P. of Barrington m. Jennie **Mattox** of Barrington 4/8/1903; H - 26, farmer, b. Barrington, s/o Albion A. Smith (Nottingham, farmer) and Sarah L. Brown (Nottingham); W - 17, at home, b. Lee, d/o William Mattox (Lynn, MA, laborer) and Sarah J. Davis (Raymond)

Fred D. of Barrington m. Jessie M. **Libbey** of Somersworth 4/29/1905; H - 21, laborer, b. Newmarket, s/o Joe Smith and Nancy Clay (Lee); W - 21, b. Somersworth, d/o William Libbey (laborer) and Sarah Burnham (Madbury)

Kenneth J. of Barrington m. Maureen S. **Dowd** of Portsmouth 6/2/1979 in Portsmouth

Leroy F. of Barrington m. Therese L. **Morrissey** of Newmarket 3/8/1952 in Stratham; H - 40, set-up man, 2d, b. NH, s/o Frank P. Smith (NH) and Jennie E. Mattox (NH); W - 23, housewife, 2d, b. NH, d/o Ernest T. Hamel (NH) and Diana Langlois (ME)

Leroy F., Jr. of Barrington m. Donna M. **Garland** of Madbury 8/26/1961; H - 21, lab. tech., b. NH, s/o Leroy F. Smith, Sr. (NH) and Mary C. Thomas (NH); W - 21, secretary, b. NH, d/o Frank E. Garland (NH) and Muriel B. Clark (NH)

Lewis L. of Barrington m. Stella B. **Drysdale** of Everett, MA 9/3/1903 in Malden, MA; H - 22, farmer, b. Barrington, s/o Lewis N. Smith (Barrington, farmer) and Elizabeth Locke (Barrington); W - 25, bookkeeper, b. So. Boston, MA, d/o James Drysdale (Scotland) and Susan Drysdale (Windsor, NS)

Lewis L. of Barrington m. Flora May **Howe** of Barrington 3/23/1906 in Rochester; H - 24, farmer, 2d, b.

Barrington, s/o Lewis N. Smith (Barrington, farmer) and Lizzie Locke (Barrington); W - 18, domestic, b. Exeter, d/o Edwin F. Howe (Barrington, mach. agt.) and Mary McInis (Barrington)

Lewis L. of Barrington m. Clara E. **Tileston** of Barrington 10/15/1922; H - 41, farmer, 4th, b. Barrington, s/o Lewis N. Smith (Barrington, farmer) and Lizzie Locke (Barrington, housekeeper); W - 31, clerk, 2d, b. Lynn, MA, d/o Robert Mee (Wakefield, farmer) and Ella Mee (Wakefield, housekeeper)

Lewis Locke of Barrington m. Hannah G. **Chapman** of Barrington 11/1/1916; H - 35, farmer, 3rd, b. Barrington, s/o Lewis N. Smith (Barrington, farmer) and Lizzie Locke (Barrington, housewife); W - 29, teacher, b. Coaticook, PQ, d/o Johnathan Chapman (Barnston, PQ) and Ella J. Snow (Compton, PQ, housewife)

Michael John of Barrington m. Nancy Marie **Hadley** of Barrington 6/28/1975

Paul W. of Barrington m. Lynn L. **Montana** of Meredith 7/26/1973 in Durham; H - 2d, b. 4/20/1943 in NH, s/o Ralph Smith (MA) and Barbara Bellatty (ME); W - b. 9/5/1951 in NH, d/o Robert W. Montana (CA) and Helen F. Wherret (NJ)

Randall C. of Barrington m. Debbie L. **Hendrickx** of Barrington 5/27/1983 in Portsmouth

Robert A. of Nottingham m. Janice L. **Johnson** of Barrington 2/15/1956 in Dover; H - 19, mason, b. NH, s/o George L. Smith (NH) and Gladys DeMeritt (NH); W - 16, at home, b. NH, d/o Alexander J. Johnson (MA) and Marion E. Ineson (NH)

Stephen W. of Barrington m. Carol L. **Ryan** of Barrington 9/21/1960; H - 19, laborer, b. NH, s/o Leroy F. Smith (NH) and Mary C. Thomas (NH); W - 15, at home, b. MA, d/o Daniel E. Ryan (MA) and Ruth L. Connors (MA)

Thomas F., Jr. of Barrington m. Linda S. **Hicks** of Milford 7/11/1981 in Wolfeboro

Thomas L. of Barrington m. Nancy T. **Aziz** of Dover 3/8/1957 in Dover; H - 19, machinist, b. NH, s/o Leroy F. Smith (NH) and Mary Thomas (NH); W - 19, tel. operator, b. NH, d/o Frederick A. Aziz (MA) and Sadie M. Simon (NH)

Thomas L. of Barrington m. Donna R. **Daigle** of Barrington 12/13/1985 in Rochester

SOUSA,

Frank of Dover m. Lora B. **Bates** of Dover 5/17/1936; H - 33, road work, b. Portugal, s/o Manuel Sousa (Portugal) and Mary Sousa (Portugal); W - 40, at home, 3rd, b. N'th'sth'm, MA, d/o Ernest R. Horton and Emma S. Wharf

SOUTHER,

Thomas C., III of Barrington m. Linda J. **Michelin** of Barrington 11/1/1986 in Lee

SPAULDING,

Richard M. of Belgrade, ME m. Doris L. **Brown** of Barrington 9/3/1950; H - 29, USAF, b. ME, s/o Dexter H. Spaulding (ME) and Annie Merrill (ME); W - 17, at home, b. NH, d/o Harold Brown (NH) and Irene Stimpson (VT)

SPEAR,

Daniell R. of Barrington m. Alice R. **Spear** of Barrington 5/25/1985

SPELLMAN,

Richard L. of Barrington m. Jean E. **Hey** of Barrington 10/21/1978

SPENCER,

Arthur H. of Barrington m. Florabelle **Pinkham** of Dover 4/14/1928 in Dover; H - 55, laborer, 3rd, b. Berwick, ME, s/o Henry C. Spencer (laborer) and Nellie A. Buzzell

(domestic); W - 42, domestic, 2d, b. Dover, d/o Albert S. Foster (shoe worker) and Jane W. Perkins (domestic)
Harry L. of Barrington m. Bessie M. **Chesley** of Barrington 11/9/1906 in Rochester; H - 28, farmer, b. Berwick, ME, s/o Henry C. Spencer (Berwick, ME, teamster) and Nellie Buzzell; W - 25, teacher, b. Barrington, d/o True W. Chesley (Barrington, farmer) and Mary L. Chesley (Barrington)

SPENDLOVE,
William H. of Barrington m. Mary A. **Ellis** of Barrington 9/16/1899; H - 70, farmer, 3rd, b. England, s/o Benjamin and Maria; W - 39, domestic, 2d, b. Barrington, d/o Timothy and Sarah

SPRAGUE,
Bernard C., Jr. of Dover m. Judith A. **Mears** of Barrington 11/22/1970; H - b. 3/15/1950 in ME, s/o Bernard Sprague (ME) and Virginia Smith (ME); W - b. 2/29/1952 in NH, d/o Arthur Mears (MA) and Dorothy Howard (NH)
Cyril A. of Barrington m. Jane A. **Godbout** of Barrington 12/29/1979

SPRINGFIELD,
George W. of Gonic m. Clara Lola **Meader** of Gonic 6/28/1937 in Gonic; H - 29, mechanic, b. Rochester, s/o Willard Springfield (Epsom) and Helen Spaulding (Epsom); W - 31, teacher, b. Gonic, d/o John Meader (Gonic) and Lila Malvin (Greely, IA)

SPROWL,
Jason S. of Barrington m. Kristine A. **Peterson** of Standish, MI 9/29/1987
Timothy A. of Barrington m. Pamela J. **Hasty** of Rochester 9/19/1980 in East Rochester

STABILE,
Pasquale Donald of Falls Church, VA m. Maureen Bell **Coughlin** of Barrington 10/12/1957 in Dover; H - 21, engineer, b. NY, s/o Dominick Stabile (NY) and Helen Puma (NY); W - 17, at home, b. MA, d/o David F. Coughlin (MA) and Florence E. Bell (MA)

STADIG,
Albert L. of Barrington m. Adeline M. **Swaine** of Barrington 6/19/1948; H - 28, farmer, b. Dover, s/o Albert N. Stadig (New Sweden, ME) and Gertrude Weik (Sweden); W - 23, hairdresser, b. Dover, d/o William E. Swaine (Barrington) and Mary E. Sanders (Madbury)

STANLEY,
Samuel B. of Epsom m. Evelyn Esther **Clark** of Barrington 6/17/1925 in Strafford; H - 20, poultryman, b. Holderness, s/o Herbert S. Stanley (Epsom, poultryman) and Margaret Connell (Ireland, housewife); W - 21, teacher, b. Barrington, d/o Arthur M. Clark (Barrington, grain dealer) and Emma Kendall (St. John, NB, housewife)

STANTON,
David of Barrington m. Emma **Smith** of Wentworth 11/26/1893; H - 22, mechanic, s/o Joshua (Wentworth, farmer) and Eliza; W - 15, housemaid, d/o Lewis (Wentworth, speculator) and Mary

STEAD,
Charles E. of Farmington m. Gerri E. **Christian** of Barrington 3/2/1985 in Windham

STEINHART,
Stephen L. of Barrington m. Rosanne L. **Todt** of Barrington 4/1/1984

STEVENS,
James L. of Barrington m. Barbara L. **Bryant** of Alton 8/21/1982 in North Barnstead

STEVENSON,
Lawrence of Barrington m. Constance B. **Taylor** of Farmington 11/21/1952 in Farmington; H - 27, forestry, b. NH, s/o Alexander Stevenson (MA) and Vera Thompson (NH); W - 19, office, b. NH, d/o Harold M. Taylor (MT) and Ethel L. Boles (NH)

Willis M. of Barrington m. Carol A. **Walker** of Newmarket 1/30/1957 in Rochester; H - 21, student, b. NY, s/o Marshall M. Stevenson (MA) and Freda E. Billeter (FL); W - 18, waitress, b. NH, d/o Lloyd E. Walker (NH) and Beatrice G. Phalen (Canada)

STEWART,
Lawrence J. of CT m. Laura H. **Unterspan** of CT 6/30/1984
Stephen T. of Portsmouth m. Tanara A. Lloyd of Barrington 6/20/1987 in Portsmouth

STICKNEY,
William Wallace of Ludlow, VT m. Sarah Effie **Moore** of Boston, MA 6/1/1905; H - 52, lawyer, 2d, b. Plymouth, VT, s/o John Winslow Stickney (Grafton, VT, farmer) and Ann Pinney (Plymouth, VT); W - 28, musician, b. Plymouth, VT, d/o Alfred Thomas Moore (Plymouth, VT, farmer) and Rhoda D. Pettigrew (Plymouth, VT)

STILES,
Walter F. of Barrington m. Flora E. **Cater** of Barrington 9/10/1910; H - 45, farmer, 2d, b. Lunenburg, MA, s/o Asa Stiles and Mary H. Stiles (Lunenburg, MA, housewife); W - 20, at home, b. Barrington, d/o David Cater (Barrington, farmer) and Flora Cater (East Rochester, housewife)

STIMPSON,

George A. of Barrington m. Sylvia M. **Constance** of Dover 4/4/1965; H - 20, hardware clerk, b. NH, s/o Albert Stimpson (NH) and Stella Kelley (NH); W - 21, secretary, b. NH, d/o William Constance (NH) and Claire Rodis (NH)

STINSON,

John Foster of West Lebanon, ME m. Charlotte Ruth **Downes** of West Lebanon, ME 10/22/1976

STONE,

Albert E. of Dover m. Elizabeth A. **Atwood** of Barrington 6/13/1971; H - b. 3/7/1945 in MA, s/o Richard S. Stone (MA) and Kathryn E. Lewis (RI); W - b. 6/23/1952 in MA, d/o Robert H. Atwood (MA) and Mary G. Pooler (MA)

Edward C. of Barrington m. Maureen **McNeil** of Barrington 6/12/1982 in Pembroke

Ernest J. of Barrington m. Elizabeth K. **Decatur** of Barrington 6/15/1914; H - 43, farmer, 2d, b. Newark, NJ, s/o Henry Stone (Devonshire, England, retired) and Sophia Clamp (Colchester, England, deceased); W - 52, housekeeper, 2d, b. Barrington, d/o James A. Foss (Barrington, farmer) and Martha J. Foss (Barrington, housewife)

STRACH[A]N,

Charles E. of Barrington m. Addie M. **Arlin** of Barrington 9/9/1890; H - 26, b. Barrington, s/o William and Sarah Strachn; W - 17, b. Barrington, d/o Charles E. and Charlotte Arlin

Charles E. of Barrington m. Anna D. C. **Davis** of Barnstead 6/27/1923 in Pittsfield; H - 59, carpenter, 2d, b. Strafford, s/o William Strachan (England, shoemaker) and Sarah Otis (Farmington, housewife); W - 52, housekeeper, 2d, b. Hooksett, d/o Isaac Cate (Hooksett, farmer) and Cynthia A. Davis (Hooksett, housewife)

Raymond of Dover m. Beatrice **St. Laurent** of Somersworth 11/3/1927 in Dover; H - 24, electrician, b. Barrington, s/o Charles C. Strachn (carpenter) and Addie M. Strachn (deceased); W - 18, waitress, b. Somersworth, d/o Alfred St. Laurent (electrician) and Adelaide Dumas (domestic)

STREETER,
James A. of Barrington m. Karen L. **Howe** of Barrington 5/16/1987 in Portsmouth
Jonathan S. of Barrington m. Betty J. **Dixon** of Barrington 4/29/1972 in S. Acworth; H - b. 12/17/1947 in NH, s/o Waldo R. Streeter (NH) and Frances Snow (NH); W - b. 4/20/1950 in NH, d/o Howard L. Dixon (VT) and Marion C. Marquis (NH)

STRONG,
Leonard, Jr. of Rochester m. Ruth A. **Erickson** of Barrington 7/2/1955 in Rochester; H - 23, florist, b. NH, s/o Leonard C. Strong (NH) and Dora M. DeWitt (NH); W - 17, b. MA, d/o Emrick E. Erickson (MA) and Ida A. Eveleth (MA)

STRYLIANDO,
Strutto G. of Portsmouth m. Laurel E. **Burley** of Barrington 1/5/1913; H - 23, barber, 2d, b. Turkey, s/o P. J. Stryliando (minister) and Elene Stryliando (housekeeper); W - 16, housework, b. Dover, d/o Charles Burley (mill boss) and Edna M. Tebbetts (musician)

STUELKE,
Stephen H. of Barrington m. Rosanna F. **Long** of Barrington 2/14/1987 in Rochester

STULTZ,
Peter E. of Portland, ME m. Cheryl L. **Wentworth** of Barrington 8/15/1964; H - 21, member US Army, b. ME,

s/o Howard F. Stultz, Jr. (ME) and Effie M. Patt (ME); W - 19, hairdresser, b. NH, d/o George H. Wentworth (NH) and Katherine C. Blais (NH)

SVENSON,

John P. of Morristown, NJ m. Linda L. **Calef** of Barrington 8/15/1970; H - b. 5/16/1949 in MO, s/o Oscar W. Svenson, Jr. (NJ) and Dorothy R. Rose (NJ); W - b. 9/7/1948 in NH, d/o Leon C. Calef (NH) and Arlene E. Rowe (NH)

SWAIN,

Ansel P. of Barrington m. Maud L. **Rand** of Rochester 6/10/1908; H - 32, farmer, b. Barrington, s/o Greenlief H. Swain and Sarah E.P. Boody; W - 24, tel. oper., b. Rochester, d/o Bickford Rand (farmer) and Mary A. Berry (Strafford, housewife)

Calvin B. of Barrington m. Katherine C. **Batchelder** of Rochester 5/28/1960; H - 32, farmer, b. NH, s/o William S. Swain (NH) and Mary E. Sanders (NH); W - 38, office worker, 3rd, b. NH, d/o Lawrence J. Blais (Canada) and Ruth Hodgdon (NH)

Roy Vance of Frederick, MD m. Mattie E. **Trickey** of Barrington 12/24/1907; H - 24, teacher, b. Barrington, s/o Greenlief H. Swain and Sarah E. Bodge; W - 22, teacher, b. Barrington, d/o John F. Trickey (Rochester) and Emma Chesley (Barrington)

W[illiam] B. of Barrington m. Effie A. **Locke** of Barrington 9/4/1894; H - 33, farmer, b. Barrington, s/o Bennett (farmer) and Martha; W - 32, dressmaker, b. Barrington, d/o L. A. and Sophronia

William S. of Barrington m. Mary Esther **Sanders** of Barrington 6/20/1917 in Dover; H - 21, farmer, b. Barrington, s/o William B. Swain (Barrington, farmer) and Effie Locke (Barrington, housekeeper); W - 24, nurse, b.

Madbury, d/o Frank Sanders (Madbury, farmer) and
Carrie A. Burke (Wolfeboro, housekeeper)

SWENSON,
Harold M. of Hartford, CT m. Madelyn M. **Hopey** of
Barrington 6/25/1942 in Dover; H - 22, mach. opr., b.
Everett, MA, s/o Chester L. Swenson (Roxbury) and
Agnes M. Anderson (Sweden); W - 19, saleswoman, b.
Madbury, d/o C. Walter Hopey (Staten Island, NY) and
Bessie Bradeen (Dover)
Harold W. of Barrington m. Dale E. **Arlin** of Barrington
6/26/1964; H - 19, electrician, b. NH, s/o Harold M.
Swenson (MA) and Madelyn M. Hopey (NH); W - 17,
clerk, b. NH, d/o Norman W. Arlin (NH) and Dorothy H.
Gibb (NH)

TALON,
Steven G. of Barrington m. Helen P. **Hills** of Dover 3/23/1979
in Dover

TAORONIS,
Jonathan of Dover m. Leona Denise **Leocha** of Barrington
12/14/1976

TARMEY,
John Almont, Jr. of Barrington m. Diane Marie **Heon** of
Somersworth 11/15/1974 in Somersworth
Patrick J. of Barrington m. Pamela M. **Bisson** of Dover
9/21/1973; H - b. 3/5/1954 in NH, s/o John Tarmey (NH)
and Carole Brassaw (NH); W - b. 3/22/1955 in NH, d/o
Leo Bisson (NH) and Ethel Bough (NH)

TASKER,
Cecil W. of Northwood m. Barbara J. **Corbett** of Barrington
6/29/1956; H - 20, truck driver, b. NH, s/o Lawrence N.
Tasker (NH) and Freda B. Freeman (NH); W - 18, at

home, b. NH, d/o Hollie B. Corbett (NH) and Doris M. Drake (NH)

TAYLOR,
Donald R. of Barrington m. Debra L. **Cole** of Barrington 5/18/1984 in Gonic

Harold R. of Barrington m. Mildred E. **McDaniel** of Barrington 9/21/1939; H - 24, poultryman, b. Chelsea, MA, s/o Harold F. Taylor (Newfoundland) and Emily J. Rowe (Newfoundland); W - 20, clerk, b. Barrington, d/o George T. McDaniel (Nottingham) and Grace E. Dodge (Somerville, MA)

Harold R. of Barrington m. Doris M. **Estey** of Rollinsford 9/29/1973 in Dover; H - 2d, b. 11/28/1914 in MA, s/o Fielding Taylor (Newfoundland) and Emily J. Rowe (Newfoundland); W - 2d, b. 11/27/1919 in ME, d/o William Stackpole (ME) and Olive Roberts (ME)

Robert F. of Barrington m. Doris S. **Henderson** of Rochester 6/21/1952 in Rochester; H - 22, salesman, b. MA, s/o Fielding Taylor (NH) and Agnes M. Anderson (Sweden); W - 21, at home, 2d, b. NH, d/o Harry R. Stone (NH) and Elsie M. Freeman (RI)

Robert T. of Barrington m. Marguerite B. **Mason** of Barrington 9/7/1919; H - 42, farmer, 2d, b. NS, s/o Robert T. Taylor (NS, farmer); W - 30, housework, 2d, b. Cambridge, MA, d/o William J. Mason (Cambridge, MA, teamster)

Terry A. of Barrington m. Christine **Vanscoder** of Barrington 1/28/1984

William Harold of Barrington m. Martha Lorraine **Durost** of Rochester 10/24/1975

TEBBETTS,
John J. of Barrington m. Fannie M. **Lane** of Lee 12/13/1890; H - 21, b. Barrington, s/o Richard and Nancy Tibbetts; W - 18, b. Lee, d/o Edward Lane

TEER,
Ernest J. of Yuma, AZ m. Mary F. **Norcross** of Barrington 4/24/1927; H - 31, rancher, b. Yuma, AZ, s/o William Teer (rancher) and Nancy J. Coubourn (domestic); W - 21, domestic, b. Westmoreland, d/o Charles Norcross (blacksmith) and Gertrude Krouse (domestic)

TEMPLER,
Fred of Barrington m. Bertha M. **Stiles** of Barrington 3/25/1901; H - 29, teamster, b. Boston, MA, s/o Henry Templer (Cleveland, OH, blacksmith) and Mary Templer; W - 19, at home, b. Lunenburg, MA, d/o Ansel Stiles (laborer) and Mary Stiles

TERWILLIGER,
Donald F. of Barrington m. Veronica M. **Fogarty** of Strafford 8/14/1982 in Strafford

TESSIER,
Albert J., Jr. of Gonic m. Cheryl L. **Stultz** of Barrington 7/13/1968 in Rochester; H - 3rd, b. 10/21/1936 in NH, s/o Albert J. Tessier, Sr. (NH) and Katherine B. Ham (NH); W - 2d, b. 5/25/1945 in NH, d/o George H. Wentworth (NH) and Katherine C. Blais (NH)
Albert J., Jr. of Barrington m. Cheryl A. **Cruz** of Berwick, ME 7/27/1971 in Dover; H - 4th, b. 10/21/1936 in NH, s/o Albert J. Tessier, Sr. (NH) and Katherine B. Ham (NH); W - 2d, b. 10/22/1947 in NH, d/o Ralph C. Joy (NH) and Thelma I. Livingston (NH)
Albert J., Jr. of Barrington m. Cheryl A. **Tessier** of Barrington 7/27/1981

TETRAULT,
Bernard R. of Newington m. Alice M. **Leocha** of Barrington 4/18/1980 in Dover

THOMAS,
Harvey L. of Hartford, CT m. Mary M. **Berry** of Barrington 11/20/1942; H - 48, supervisor, 2d, b. Cambridge, MA, s/o Frank H. Thomas (Silver Creek, NY) and Alice L. Stearns (Sherman, NY); W - 33, secretary, b. Barrington, d/o Flavius J. Berry (Barrington) and Nellie Glidden (Lee) Kaufhold, Jr. of Dover m. Mary P. **Tebo** of Barrington 12/27/1984 in Dover
Robert G. of Rochester m. Cynthia A. **Fritz** of Barrington 4/29/1978 in Dover

THOMPSON,
Dennis E. of Barrington m. Cynthia J. **Gilbert** of Dover 11/9/1974 in Dover
Roscoe P. of Barrington m. Fanny E. **Freeman** of Barrington 2/22/1905 in Dover; H - 27, fireman, b. Barrington, s/o Leroy Tompson (farmer) and Mary Robinson (Barrington); W - 23, at home, b. Barrington, d/o Stephen Freeman and Fanny Chamberlain

THORNTON,
Jon R. of Barrington m. Karen E. **Tanner** of Barrington 5/19/1984 in Hampton Falls

THYNG,
Herbert J., Jr. of Dover m. Diane E. **Townsend** of Barrington 2/13/1965; H - 19, greenhouse emp., b. NH, s/o Herbert J. Thyng (NH) and Hilda I. Barnard (NH); W - 18, greenhouse emp., b. NH, d/o Archie L. Townsend (MA) and Odell Clarton (IL)

TIBBETTS,
Gary Leon of Rochester m. Linda Doris **Woolson** of Barrington 4/27/1974

TILTON,
Lloyd C. of Northwood m. Florence M. **Strachan** of Barrington 12/3/1913 in Northwood Ridge; H - 22, shoe cutter, b. Deerfield, s/o Charles C. Tilton (farmer) and Lizzie N. Adams (deceased); W - 18, shoe operative, b. Barrington, s/o Charles E. Strachan (carpenter) and Addie M. Arlin (deceased)

TIMMONS,
Richard W. of Rochester m. Mary G. **Varney** of Barrington 10/21/1961; H - 23, store manager, b. NH, s/o Clarence Timmons (Canada) and Dorothy F. Gillis (Canada); W - 21, grad. nurse, b. NH, d/o Robert W. Varney (NH) and Janet C. McCrone (MA)

TINGLEY,
Frank J. of Dover m. Kathy M. **DiGiovanni** of Barrington 9/28/1974 in Rochester

TODD,
George E. of Deland, FL m. Anita L. **Land** of Summerfield, FL 12/27/1981

TOOCH,
David E. of Barrington m. Rochelle L. **Gagnon** of Barrington 8/16/1980 in Durham

TOWLE,
Wayne D. of Barrington m. Deborah **Hastings** of Barrington 6/5/1977 in Gilmanton Iron Works

TOWNSEND,
Scott T. of Barrington m. Celia M. **Baker** of Rochester 6/30/1980 in Rochester

TRASK,
    Daniel G. of Lebanon m. Gail L. **Waterhouse** of Barrington 7/29/1978

TREBLE,
    Kenneth B., Jr. of Barrington m. Jeanne M. **Gaulin** of Rochester 3/31/1956 in Portsmouth; H - 21, carpenter, b. ME, s/o Kenneth B. Treble (ME) and Geraldine B. Stone (NH); W - 22, tel. opr., b. NH, d/o Leon Gaulin (NH) and Florence M. Mace (ME)

TREMBLAY,
    Michael J. of Barrington m. Maureen C. **Labranche** of Newmarket 6/8/1974 in Newmarket

TRITES,
    Robert Earl of Rochester m. Bernice Elizabeth **Foster** of Barrington 5/5/1975 in Rochester

TROTT,
    Douglas A. of Barrington m. Joyce A. **Goode** of Dover 7/29/1970 in Somersworth; H - b. 2/29/1948 in NH, s/o Frank W. Trott (ME) and Esther M. Bickford (NH); W - 2d, b. 7/12/1950 in ME, d/o Robert S. Wheeler (ME) and Leona M. Mariner (ME)
    Douglas A. of Barrington m. Martha E. **Lamothe** of Raymond 1/22/1973 in Epping; H - 2d, b. 2/29/1948 in NH, s/o Frank W. Trott (ME) and Esther M. Bickford (NH); W - 4th, b. 7/30/1934 in MA, d/o Daniel A. Gray, Sr. (NH) and Carolina A. Wort (KS)
    Douglas A. of Barrington m. Margit E. **Dudas** of Barrington 5/18/1987

TRUDEAU,
    Bradford J. of Barrington m. Karen V. **Crotty** of Lee 6/14/1986

TRUE,
Robert B., II of Durham m. Donna L. **Chesley** of Barrington 3/2/1979 in Durham

TUCK,
Clayton G. of Barrington m. Alice E. **Heath** of Dover 11/9/1968 in Alton; H - b. 2/16/1942 in Canada, s/o Gordon C. Tuck (MA) and Rose Marie B. Beriault (Canada); W - b. 12/31/1943 in ME, d/o Carryl E. Heath (NH) and Nathalie E. Wilber (ME)

Percy H. of Somerville, MA m. Flossie E. **Griffin** of Barrington 8/13/1907; H - 21, fireman, b. Mapleton, ME, s/o Lewis C. Tuck and Clara Dale Tuck (Fairfield, ME); W - 19, stenographer, b. Barrington, d/o Herbert Griffin (Strafford, farmer) and Mamie E. Griffin (Strafford)

TUCKER,
George D. of Barrington m. Verna M. **Kidd** of Barrington 8/28/1965; H - 25, quality control, b. NY, s/o George E. Tucker (NY) and Rebecca M. Paterson (NY); W - 25, inspector, 2d, b. OH, d/o William M. McMillan (NY) and Hannah M. Cragle (PA)

TURCOTTE,
Wayne L. of Somersworth m. Gail F. **Moreau** of Barrington 4/28/1972 in Dover; H - b. 5/24/1952 in NH, s/o Leo Turcotte (NH) and Evelyn Christie (Canada); W - b. 11/4/1951 in NH, d/o Raymond Moreau (MA) and Gertrude Peavey (NH)

TURNER,
Bruce W. of Barrington m. Jean A. **Clement** of Lisbon 12/18/1959; H - 21, student, b. NH, s/o Arthur J. Turner (NY) and Virginia F. Ramsdell (MA); W - 20, student, b. NH, d/o Edgar T. Clement (NY) and Marjorie Deming (NH)

TUTTLE,

Alpha D. of Barrington m. Eva M. **Hall** of Barrington 6/24/1908; H - 30, carpenter, b. Strafford, s/o Jeremiah Tuttle (Strafford, farmer) and Sarah C. Smith (Barrington, housewife); W - 23, domestic, b. Strafford, d/o Charles S. Hall (Strafford, farmer) and Emma F. Caverly (Strafford, housewife)

Edson C. of Barrington m. Nellie O. **Small** of Nottingham 2/1/1922; H - 47, laborer, b. Strafford, s/o Jeremiah Tuttle (Barrington, farmer) and Sarah C. Smith (Barrington, housewife); W - 57, housekeeper, b. Epping, d/o Orrin W. Small (Northwood, blacksmith) and Sarah Thompson (Middleton, housewife)

Glen Roy of Barrington m. Dawn Zina **Pero** of Epsom 8/31/1974 in Epsom

John W. of Barrington m. Claire J. **Zampa** of Newmarket 7/26/1969 in Portsmouth; H - 2d, b. 9/6/1942 in ME, s/o John W. Tuttle (ME) and Elizabeth J. Jones (OH); W - 2d, b. 2/17/1936 in NY, d/o William L. Johnston (NY) and Mary D. Yuhas (NJ)

Russell S. of Barrington m. Beverly J. **Tuttle** of Northwood 9/23/1967 in Northwood; H - 22, maint. man, 2d, div., b. Northwood, s/o Chester R. Tuttle (NH) and Alice M. Clark (NH); W - 22, none, b. Rochester, d/o Lewis K. Tuttle (NH) and Mabel V. Linscott (NH)

TWOMBL[E]Y,

Albert of Barrington m. Ellen L. **Freeman** of Barrington 2/22/1908; H - 21, laborer, b. Fremont, s/o Albert H. Twombly (farmer) and Josephine Twombly; W - 20, at home, b. Somerville, MA, d/o George H. Freeman (Barrington, farmer) and Joanna Freeman (Charlestown, MA, housewife)

Albert W. of Rochester m. Helen A. **Demeritt** of Barrington 4/27/1935 in Rochester; H - 32, laborer, 2d, b. Short Falls, s/o David O. Twombly (Pittsfield) and Bernice M.

Brown (Northwood Narrows); W - 21, housework, b. Barrington, d/o John W. Demeritt (Barrington) and Alice Whitehouse (Barrington)

Charles E. of Barrington m. Sadie M. **Willey** of Barrington 10/22/1908 in Strafford; H - 37, farmer, b. Barrington, s/o Nathaniel Twombly and Mary Sanders (Barrington, domestic); W - 32, domestic, b. Barrington, d/o William H. Willey (Barrington, farmer) and Fannie S. Wentworth

Edgar C. m. Ida M. **Deslauriers** 5/30/1929 in Pittsfield; H - 22, teamster, b. Barrington, s/o Charles Twombly (Madbury) and Alice Caswell (Barrington); W - 26, shoe shop, b. Websterville, VT, d/o Joseph Deslauriers (St. Albans, VT) and Delia Delisle (Canada)

G. Clyde of Barrington m. Merle **Gerrish** of Nottingham 5/11/1918 in Epping; H - 21, saw mill operator, b. Barrington, s/o Charles Twombly (Madbury, teamster) and Alice Caswell (Northwood, housewife); W - 17, housekeeper, b. Nottingham, d/o Warren Gerrish (Nottingham, bee keeper) and Hattie Gerrish (Nottingham, housewife)

Muton D. of Barrington m. Villa M. **Johnson** of Northwood 4/21/1928 in Northwood; H - 19, lumber op., b. Barrington, s/o Charles E. Twombly (farmer) and Alice M. Caswell (domestic); W - 19, shoe wkr., b. Woodman, d/o Ernest Johnson (farmer) and Orvilla Johnson (domestic)

Stephen L. of Strafford m. Laurie C. **Robie** of Barrington 9/28/1985

Waldo m. Beatrice **Smith** 10/26/1929 in Northwood; H - 19, lumberman, b. Barrington, s/o Charles Twombly (Madbury) and Alice Caswell (Barrington); W - 18, at home, b. Deerfield, d/o Phineas Smith (Deerfield) and Natalie B. Adams (Deerfield)

TYLER,
John B. of Barrington m. Althea **Pratt** of Epping 3/11/1905; H - 20, laborer, b. Barrington, s/o George A. Tyler (Barrington, laborer) and Abbie Arlin (Shaftsbury, VT); W - 18, at home, b. Epping, d/o Samuel Pratt (farmer) and Althea Pratt

UDALL,
John L., Jr. of Barrington m. Marjorie L. **Cushing** of Belmont 6/9/1946 in Belmont; H - 24, clergyman, b. Cambridge, MA, s/o John Udall (Wolcott, VT) and Bertha Wardrier (Braintree, VT); W - 22, at home, b. Concord, d/o Russell H. Cushing (Belmont) and Carrie L. Wyatt (Tilton)

UPTON,
Robert N. of Lee m. Alice M. **Leocha** of Barrington 11/12/1966; H - 23, vending mach., b. Woburn, MA, s/o Nathaniel R. Upton (MA) and Eleanor H. Jahnke (MA); W - 20, univ. student, b. Rochester, d/o Mitchell J. Leocha (NH) and Muriel L. Turner (NH)
Robert N. of Barrington m. Alice M. **Leocha** of Barrington 6/12/1969 in Lee; H - 2d, b. 9/26/1943 in MA, s/o Nathaniel R. Upton (MA) and Eleanor H. Jannke (MA); W - 2d, b. 8/30/1946 in NH, d/o Mitchell J. Leocha (NH) and Muriel L. Turner (NH)

VALLIERE,
Mark L. of Barrington m. Joan S. **Inman** of Barrington 5/26/1984 in Newmarket

VAN SCOYOC,
Peter W. of Barrington m. Sandra M. **Wiggins** of Sanbornton 7/26/1980 in Durham

VANDER BUSSCHE,
Louis Joseph, III of Barrington m. Shirley Rose **Elliott** of Barrington 7/17/1976

VANCE,
William B. of Barrington m. Carol L. **Briggs** of Barrington 10/13/1984 in Northwood

VARNEY,
Vern V. of Barrington m. Natalie E. **Babb** of Somersworth 8/11/1951 in Somersworth; H - 21, truck driver, b. NH, s/o Carroll Varney (NH) and Marion E. Norman (NH); W - 18, clerk, b. NH, d/o Guy S. Babb (NH) and Helen G. Shute (MA)
Vern V. of Barrington m. Corina Y. **Ruest** of Dover 6/25/1954 in Rochester; H - 24, fireman, 2d, b. NH, s/o Carroll H. Varney (NH) and Marian E. Norman (NH); W - 18, shoe worker, b. NH, d/o Cleophas F. Ruest (NH) and Alice M. DeMers (NH)

VAUGHAN,
Harold J. of Billerica, MA m. Claire C. **Conway** of Barrington 5/10/1958 in Dover; H - 38, machinist, 2d, b. MA, s/o Harold P. Vaughan (ME) and Maude Zelles (MA); W - 27, dietitian, b. NH, d/o Frederick Conway (NY) and Grace B. Pierce (MA)
John M. of Dover m. Carol E. **Googins** of Barrington 9/5/1970 in Dover; H - b. 8/14/1951 in MA, s/o John M. Vaughan (MA) and Mary E. Jennings (ME); W - b. 5/1/1951 in ME, d/o John J. Googins (MA) and Margery F. Young (ME)

VENO,
Kim R. of Barrington m. Helen A. **Moore** of Barrington 2/14/1987 in Rochester

WAAL,
Stephen D. of Rochester m. Susan H. **Irving** of Barrington 9/18/1982

WAKEFIELD,
Edgar E. of Barrington m. Serena **Ball** of Northwood 4/18/1925; H - 21, shoemaker, b. E. Harpswell, ME, s/o Elgin T. Wakefield (Holbrook, MA, laborer) and Carrie B. White (Belchertown, MA, housewife); W - 18, shoe worker, b. Marmouth, NS, d/o Owen M. Ball (Queens Coutny, laborer) and Mary E. Hatfield (Digby, NS, housewife)

WALDRON,
Clarence E. of Barrington m. Elisabeth E. **Jennison** of Madbury 10/9/1977
Richard P. of Barrington m. Catherine M. **Guay** of Dover 7/28/1979 in Dover

WALKER,
Alan J. of Hancock, NY m. Melanie R. **Larocca** of Barrington 12/17/1977
Richard A. of Barrington m. Irene H. **Beaulieu** of Gonic 7/25/1959; H - 18, shoe worker, b. NH, s/o Frank E. Walker (NH) and Blanche R. Brogan (NH); W - 18, shoe worker, b. NH, d/o Elliott L. Beaulieu (ME) and Loretta D. Ramsey (NH)
Richard A., Jr. of Barrington m. Wanda L. **Chapin** of Rochester 8/29/1987 in Rochester

WALLACE,
William, Jr. of Barrington m. Ruth W. **Blumenschein** of Barrington 12/16/1950 in Durham; H - 56, retired, 2d, b. MA, s/o William Wallace (MA) and Mary C. Fuller (MA); W - 54, none, 2d, b. MA, d/o Richard Wood (MA) and Elizabeth Finnigan (Ireland)

WALSH,
Anthony A. of Barrington m. Doris E. **Ball** of Manchester 6/13/1970 in Durham; H - b. 11/26/1940 in MA, s/o Charles A. Walsh (MA) and Margaret M. Paulukonis (MA); W - b. 1/23/1947 in NH, d/o William B. Ball (NH) and Evelyn M. Conway (NH)

WALTERS,
Clifford R. of Barrington m. Lisa O. **Giglio** of Barrington 3/19/1983 in Portsmouth

WARD,
Daniel M. of Barrington m. MaryAnn F. **Abrams** of Portsmouth 6/21/1986 in Portsmouth
Geoffrey S. of Barrington m. Susan A. **Whitney** of Greenfield 12/31/1977 in Peterborough
Rogers A. of Barrington m. Pauline R. **Collins** of Dover 2/10/1947 in Dover; H - 20, farmer, b. Pembroke, ME, s/o John Ward (Eastbrooke, ME) and Dorothy Rogers (St. Paul, MN); W - 19, at home, b. Auburn, ME, d/o William H. Collins (Lubec, ME) and Ernestine Coanut (Mechanic Falls, ME)
Stephen L. of Barrington m. Deborah L. **Rogers** of Barrington 10/22/1977 in Madbury
Stephen R. of Barrington m. Dorothy A. **Norman** of Madbury 3/7/1951 in Madbury; H - 18, truck driver, b. NH, s/o John Ward (ME) and Dorothy Rogers (MN); W - 16, rose packer, b. NH, d/o Lewis Norman (NH) and Dorothy Dodge (NH)
William H. of Barrington m. Patsy R. **Ward** of Jacksonville, FL 5/15/1971; H - 2d, b. 1/14/1948 in NH, s/o Rogers A. Ward (ME) and Pauline R. Collins (ME); W - 2d, b. 5/29/1951 in CO, d/o Jack W. Collard (MO) and Patsy R. Grayson (MO)
William Henry of Barrington m. Vicki Joanne **Small** of Barrington 9/18/1976

William R. of Barrington m. Marjorie M. **Lirette** of Dover 1/4/1953 in Dover; H - 21, soldier, b. ME, s/o John A. Ward (ME) and Dorothy Rogers (MN); W - 16, shoeworker, b. NH, d/o Albert J. Lirette (Canada) and Lena Dupre (NH)

WARNER,
George C. of Barrington m. Lilla E. **Davis** of Barrington 10/19/1890; H - 18, b. Salisbury, MA; W - 20, b. NY

WARREN,
Bradley H. of Barrington m. Anita L. **Couture** of Dover 4/23/1966 in Dover; H - 22, student, b. Carlisle, MA, s/o Richard Warren (NY) and Dorothy Bowen (MA); W - 20, shoe shop, b. Dover, d/o Alcide Couture (NH) and Theresa Brown (ME)
Elmer L. of Barrington m. Madeline L. **Geldart** of Portsmouth 8/15/1970; H - 2d, b. 2/9/1924 in MA, s/o Francis E. Warren (NH) and Nellie M. Harris (MA); W - 2d, b. 8/14/1922 in NH, d/o Ernest L. Sullivan (NH) and Emma M. Brassa (VT)
Frank E. of Barrington m. Belle **Austin** of Barrington 3/30/1896; H - 29, laborer, b. So. Berwick, ME; W - 22, housekeeper, b. Hudson, d/o Charles (Nashua, laborer) and Amanda (Hudson)
Richard R. of Barrington m. Linda **Hoyle** of Lee 8/19/1972 in Durham; H - b. 3/5/1951 in NH, s/o Richard Warren (NY) and Dorothy Brown (MA); W - b. 12/6/1952 in RI, d/o Merrill Hoyle (MA) and Joyce Humphreys (MA)
Richard R. of Barrington m. Vicki J. **Cheney** of Alton 3/15/1980 in Wolfeboro

WASIEWSKI,
Mark D. of Barrington m. Cynthia L. **Kelly** of Barrington 7/19/1986 in Newmarket

WATERFIELD,
D. Allan of Barrington m. Jeanne M. **Beaulieu** of Barrington 7/9/1987 in Newmarket

WATERHOUSE,
Arthur C. of Barrington m. Mattie E. **Young** of Barrington 9/27/1899 in Dover; H - 26, farmer, b. Barrington, s/o Daniel (Barrington, farmer) and Fidelia (Strafford); W - 21, at home, b. Boston, MA, d/o George (deceased) and Addie

Charles F. of Barrington m. Mary E. **Leighton** of Barrington 4/12/1910 in Strafford; H - 50, farmer, 2d, b. Charlestown, MA, s/o Charles Waterhouse and Nancy I. Caverly; W - 50, domestic, 2d, d/o Charles P. Holmes (carpenter) and Arvilla Foss (housewife)

Charles W., Sr. of ME m. Alice E. **Weeks** of Barrington 7/19/1984 in Rochester

Henry of Barrington m. Maud T. **Stevens** of Barrington 5/1/1900 in Northwood; H - 22, laborer, b. Barrington, s/o Charles (Charlestown, MA, farmer) and Laura; W - 16, at home, b. Barnstead, d/o Calvin (Kennebunk, ME, farmer) and Jane

J. H. of Barrington m. Myra N. **Gage** of Arlington, MA 10/7/1896 in Arlington, MA; H - 21, farmer, b. Barrington, s/o William E. (Barrington, farmer) and Elizabeth (Barrington); W - 21, artist, b. Hopkinton, d/o Harlan (deceased) and Margaret

Lester A. of Barrington m. Barbara A. **Brown** of Barrington 9/1/1944 in Rochester; H - 18, soldier, b. Rochester, s/o Maurice E. Waterhouse (Barrington) and Iva L. Swaine (Rochester); W - 15, at home, b. Dover, d/o Harold G. Brown (Barrington) and Irene A. Stimpson (Dover)

Lester D. of Barrington m. Ethel C. **Pike** of Rochester 8/17/1936 in Northwood; H - 36, asst. dyer, 2d, b. Barrington, s/o Arthur Waterhouse (Barrington) and Martha E. Young (Boston, MA); W - 22, at home, b.

Rochester, d/o Edwin L. Pike (Rochester) and Mary Wentworth

Merton A. of Barrington m. Marie A. **Duquette** of Farmington 5/12/1934 in Rochester; H - 23, dyer, b. Barrington, s/o Arthur Waterhouse (Barrington) and Elizabeth Young (Roxbury, MA); W - 19, mill operator, b. Rochester, d/o Henry Douquette and Albertine Douquette (Sherbrooke, PQ)

WATSON,

Jeffrey A. of Pekin, IL m. Betty K. **Palacios** of Barrington 5/8/1982 in Portsmouth

John of Barrington m. Annie M. **Neal** of Barrington 12/21/1893; H - 51, farmer, 2d, s/o Matthew and Margaret; W - 56, housewife, 2d, d/o John and Polly

WATT,

Edward C. of Pocasset, MA m. Mary A. **Tuck** of Barrington 6/8/1968; H - b. 3/18/1942 in MA, s/o William A. Watt, Sr. (NY) and Helen M. Porter (MA); W - b. 1/13/1944 in Canada, d/o Gordon C. Tuck (MA) and Beatrice Beriault (Canada)

WEAVER,

Francis L. of Malden, MA m. Johanna M. **Terpetra** of Malden, MA 3/20/1937 in Portsmouth; H - 23, mgr. fill. sta., b. Portland, ME, s/o Joseph Weaver (Lowell, MA) and Mary O'Connor (Portland, ME); W - 16, hairdresser, b. Holland, d/o John Terpetra (Holland) and Johanna Rickett (Holland)

WECHSLER,

Bruce J. of Barrington m. Vicki L. **McCloskey** of Newmarket 10/20/1973 in Rye; H - b. 6/19/1950 in NH, s/o Herbert Wechsler (NJ) and Jennie Epstein (NY); W - b.

5/23/1949 in PA, s/o Donald L. McCloskey (PA) and Sara P. Berringer (PA)

WEEDEN,
Albert S. of Barrington m. Elizabeth **Leavitt** of Rochester 1/30/1960; H - 20, member USAF, b. NH, s/o Albert E. Weeden (NH) and Thelma M. Richards (ME); W - 18, at home, b. NH, d/o Maurice W. Leavitt (NH) and Dora V. Heald (ME)
Albert S., III of Strafford m. Deborah L. **Anderson** of Barrington 7/18/1981
Daniel F. of Barrington m. Sally A. **Forbes** of Dover 5/15/1964; H - 20, sheet metal worker, b. NH, s/o Albert E. Weeden (NH) and Thelma Richards (ME); W - 17, student, b. NH, d/o Robert J. Forbes (NH) and Bernice G. Quimby (NH)
Daniel F. of Barrington m. Sherry R. **St. Pierre** of Dover 5/1/1972; H - 2d, b. 9/30/1943 in NH, s/o Albert E. Weeden (NH) and Thelma R. Richards (ME); W - b. 8/28/1952 in NH, d/o Ernest N. St. Pierre (MA) and Marjorie R. Gilligan (NH)

WEEKS,
Albion G. of Barrington m. Gertrude **Locke** of Barrington 10/25/1916; H - 31, farmer, b. Barrington, s/o Charles W. Weeks (Barrington, farmer) and Anna M. Glidden (Lee, housewife); W - 23, at home, b. Barrington, d/o Alphonzo B. Locke (Barrington, farmer) and Mary A. Waterhouse (Barrington)
Brian R. of Barrington m. Elizabeth I. **McCarthy** of Barrington 2/10/1973 in Rochester; H - b. 9/26/1954 in NH, s/o Robert E. Weeks (NH) and Betty M. Scott (MA); W - b. 5/13/1953 in NH, d/o William E. McCarthy (NY) and Ruth A. Mills (ME)

Charles A. of Dover m. Aline E. **Hull** of Barrington 9/15/1890; H - 20, b. Dover; W - 21, b. Unadilla, NY, d/o Peter and Mary Hull

Richard A. of Barrington m. Jodian **Plante** of Cornish 9/3/1982 in Cornish

Robert E. of Barrington m. Betty M. **Grant** of Rochester 8/31/1956; H - 29, watchmaker, b. NH, s/o Albion G. Weeks (NH) and Gertrude Locke (NH); W - 23, riveter, 2d, b. MA, d/o Arthur D. Scott (MA) and Elizabeth M. Dries (MA)

Silas C. of Barrington m. Marie **Harris** of Barrington 11/4/1977

WELCH,

Philip A. of Portland, ME m. Dillie V. **Freeman** of Barrington 2/17/1924 in Rochester; H - 33, chef, b. S. Boston, MA, s/o Adam Welch (France, glass cutter) and Clara Alletzhauser (S. Boston, MA, housewife); W - 19, waitress, b. Barrington, d/o Arthur Freeman (Barrington, farmer) and Vina Freeman (housewife)

Robert S. of Barrington m. Mary R. **Nicolo** of Barrington 9/22/1985

WELLS,

Chester E. of Northwood m. Elizabeth E. **Brown** of Barrington 8/29/1937 in Gonic; H - 20, truckman, b. Northwood, s/o William Wells (Oxford, CT) and Nancy Wallace (Northwood); W - 19, maid, b. Barrington, d/o Edward E. Brown (Lee) and Margaret McDonald (Barrington)

Donald E. of Barrington m. Barbara M. **Bouchard** of Rochester 11/14/1959; H - 21, painter, b. NH, s/o Chester E. Wells (NH) and Elizabeth E. Brown (NH); W - 16, at home, b. NH, d/o George Bouchard (NH) and Irene Dubois (NH)

Donald E. of Barrington m. Shirley A. **Sault** of W. Swanzey 11/8/1969 in Troy; H - b. 8/3/1938 in NH, s/o Chester E. Wells (NH) and Elizabeth E. Brown (NH); W - 2d, b. 3/1/1939 in NH, d/o Lloyd J. Cutter (MA) and Olive A. Lancey

George A. of Barrington m. Lillian B. **Stiles** of Barrington 8/28/1937 in Rochester; H - 35, shoe shop, b. Concord, s/o George H. Wells (Hardwick, VT) and Maud Durgin (Northfield); W - 24, teacher, b. Barrington, d/o Walter Stiles (Lunenburg, MA) and Edla Cater (Barrington)

WEST,

Henry C., Jr. of Barrington m. Kathleen L. **Pettengill** of Barrington 4/1/1985

Richard W. of Barrington m. Joyce A. **Mailhot** of Barrington 11/7/1981 in Rochester

WEYMOUTH,

Daniel M. of Rochester m. Karen M. **Merrill** of Barrington 10/12/1984 in Rochester

David P. of Barrington m. Deborah J. **Tilton** of Barrington 7/16/1983

WHEELER,

Alan John of Barrington m. Karen Susan **Tarlton** of Rochester 9/11/1976 in Rochester

Arthur J. of Barrington m. Adeline J. **Norman** of Dover 11/29/1948 in Dover; H - 18, greenhouse, b. Barrington, s/o Minnie M. Wheeler (Carrabassett, ME); W - 16, at home, b. Dover, d/o John Norman (Madbury) and Clara Varney (Barrington)

Chester H. of Barrington m. Audrey L. **Norman** of Dover 4/5/1948 in Dover; H - 22, woolen mill, b. Dover, s/o Minnie Wheeler (Barrington); W - 18, at home, b. Dover, d/o John Norman (Dover) and Clara Varney (Barrington)

Joseph m. Ruth **Demeritt** 12/3/1929 in Gonic; H - 27, lumberman, b. Lewiston, ME, s/o Frederick Wheeler (Canada) and Mary Bishop (Canada); W - 18, housework, b. Barrington, d/o John Demeritt (Barrington) and Ida Whitehouse (Barrington)

Maurice J. of Barrington m. Barbara A. **Lavasseur** of Madbury 1/16/1954 in Madbury; H - 23, lumber cutter, b. NH, s/o Joseph Wheeler (ME) and Ruth E. DeMerritt (NH); W - 19, assembler (elec. parts), b. MA, d/o George J. Lavasseur (NH) and Irene E. Doucette (MA)

Maurice J. of Barrington m. Margaret **DeButts** of Rochester 5/28/1982

WHITE,

David William of Barrington m. Heather **Crafts** of Barrington 5/3/1975

James P. of Barrington m. Pamela J. **Jewell** of Barrington 6/13/1981 in Durham

WHITEHOUSE,

Gary C. of Barrington m. Shirley I. **Wiggin** of Rochester 3/31/1968 in Lee; H - b. 6/18/1949 in NH, s/o Merle C. Whitehouse (NH) and Mary G. Goundry (NH); W - b. 10/28/1948 in NH, d/o Russell C. Wiggin (NH) and Lucy M. Richards (NH)

Jeremiah of Barrington m. Mary Ellen **Caverly** of Barrington 6/30/1891 in Dover; H - 32, b. Barrington, s/o Leonard and Eliza; W - 35, b. Strafford

John T. of Barrington m. Natalie R. **Bean** of Dover 10/6/1962; H - 18, rubber wkr., b. MA, s/o Merle Whitehouse (NH) and Mary Goundry (MA); W - 17, at home, b. NH, d/o Everett Bean (NH) and Elizabeth Blood (NH)

Mark of Dover m. Nellie **Ruel** of Dover 8/5/1890; H - 45, b. Somersworth; W - 33, b. Providence, RI

Merle C. of Somersworth m. Mary G. **Whitehouse** of Barrington 7/16/1962; H - 61, retired, 2d, b. NH, s/o John T. Whitehouse (NH) and Ida M. Brown (MA); W - 42, at home, 2d, b. MA, d/o James Goundrey (NY) and Ethel M. Russell (MA)

Robert E. of Barrington m. Sharon L. **Vittum** of Rochester 9/25/1965; H - 17, poultry worker, b. MA, s/o Merle C. Whitehouse (NH) and Mary Goundry (NH); W - 18, shoe worker, b. NH, d/o Robert L. Vittum (NH) and Beatrice M. Harding (MA)

WHITNEY,
James V. of Barrington m. Ruth E. **Hubbard** of Barrington 7/21/1986

WHYTE,
Richard Vantine, Jr. of Barrington m. Jane Elizabeth **Gikas** of Barrington 7/28/1973 in Bedford

WICKEY,
John W. of Barrington m. Merl L. Seavey **Bartels** of Barrington 9/13/1964; H - 43, efficiency investigator, 2d, b. MA, s/o Walter Wickey (MA) and Bessie N. Ellis (MA); W - 40, housewife, 2d, b. NH, d/o Ralph C. Seavey (MA) and Grace M. Akins (NH)

WIGGIN,
Elmer E. of Barrington m. Bertha M. **Reynolds** of Milton 8/24/1891 in Milton; H - 30, b. Barrington, s/o George and Sophia; W - 20, b. Milton, d/o James O. and Myra

George of Barrington m. Marcelle V. **Vern** of Salem, MA 7/27/1894 in Gonic; H - 42, farmer, b. Barrington, s/o George (Durham, farmer) and Sophia, W - 22, milliner, b. Beverly, MA, d/o E. (Beverly, MA, sea captain) and Eleanor (Beverly, MA, at home)

Jasper R. of Barrington m. Frances M. **Fanning** of Barrington 8/17/1933 in Gonic; H - 33, mill wkr., b. Barrington, s/o George Wiggin (Barrington) and Marcilla Verne (Beverly, MA); W - 20, at home, b. Barrington, d/o Manson H. Fanning (NS) and Jennie Day (Cambridge, MA)

Otto S. of Barrington m. Idella B. **Dodge** of Barrington 6/28/1924 in Rochester; H - 25, farmer, b. Barrington, s/o George W. Wiggin (Barrington, farmer) and Marcella Verne (Beverly, MA, housewife); W - 16, at home, b. Barrington, d/o Herman Dodge (Rochester, farmer) and Louise Babb (Barrington, housewife)

WILDER,
Paul Bruce of Wakefield, MA m. Dawn Marie **Saunders** of Wakefield, MA 8/30/1975

WILDONER,
Terry L. of Barrington m. Janice L. **Hough** of Rochester 6/29/1973 in Rochester; H - b. 7/23/1951 in PA, s/o Archie Wildoner (PA) and Arlene Thomas (PA); W - b. 2/9/1950 in NH, d/o Godfrey Hough (NH) and Madeline Jordan (NH)

WILKINS,
Robert R. of Somersworth m. Patricia B. **Walker** of Barrington 6/28/1958 in Rochester; H - 20, shoe worker, b. NH, s/o Richard R. Wilkins (NH) and Irma Place (ME); W - 20, shoe worker, b. NH, d/o Frank E. Walker (NH) and Blanche Brogan (NH)

WILLEY,
George H. of Barrington m. Jennie **Ham** of Barrington 7/28/1903; H - 23, engineer, b. Biddeford, ME, s/o William F. Willey (Barrington, farmer) and Josephine Harris (Portland, ME); W - 18, at home, b. Salem, MA, d/o Henry Ham and Isabel Murdock

WILLIAMS,
Geoffrey M. of Barrington m. Susan J. **Moody** of Barrington 10/25/1980

Philip of Somerville, MA m. Laura **McCarthy** of Barrington 12/20/1931 in Dover; H - 39, express clerk, b. Charlestown, MA, s/o Thomas Williams (Somerville, MA) and Julia Reilly (Malden, MA); W - 16, at home, b. Danbury, d/o William McCarthy (Dunlyn, Scotland) and Dora Cheltry (Brandon, VT)

WILSON,
Michael J. of Nashua m. Mary L. **Young** of Barrington 6/30/1968; H - b. 3/2/1947 in OK, s/o Gordon J. Wilson (WI) and Nelda R. Quinn (OK); W - b. 4/4/1947 in NY, d/o Edward H. Young (NH) and Rita C. Stewart (NY)

WINGATE,
John of Barrington m. Laura A. **Jewell** of Barrington 12/25/1900 in Rochester; H - 65, farmer, 3rd, b. Strafford, s/o Joshua (Farmington, farmer) and Mary; W - 41, at home, b. Strafford, d/o Asa (Barrington, watchman) and Mariam

WINSLOW,
Ronald A., Jr. of Barrington m. Larkin A. **Warren** of Barrington 6/27/1981 in Madison

WINTER,
Timothy R. of Barrington m. Brenda L. **Roach** of Sunapee 11/27/1976 in Newport

WIRKKALA,
Kenneth W. of Newport m. Rosemary **Ellison** of Barrington 3/19/1966 in Dover; H - 21, farmer, b. Newport, s/o Arvo J. Wirkkala (NH) and Elizabeth M. Hunter (MA); W - 17,

student, b. Exeter, d/o Chester J. Ellison (NH) and Violet M. Smith (NH)

WITHAM,
George R. of Deerfield m. Bernice E. **Bigelow** of Barrington 8/30/1957; H - 49, butcher, 2d, b. NH, s/o Albert F. Witham (NH) and Salina Brace (VT); W - 47, nurse, 2d, b. MA, d/o Chester R. Ramsdell (MA) and Katherine P. Besse (MA)

WITHERELL,
Tom B. of Gonic m. Debra C. **Jones** of Barrington 6/17/1972 in Rochester; H - b. 3/12/1950 in NH, s/o Ralph Witherell (VT) and Mary Mitchell (NH); W - b. 8/26/1951 in RI, d/o Robert Jones (IL) and Phyllis Clapp (MA)

WOJTYSIAK,
Anthony W. of Barrington m. Lisa J. **Lesperance** of Rochester 10/7/1983
Dwayne M. of Barrington m. Michelle E. **Tompson** of Barrington 6/28/1985 in Rochester

WOOD,
George H. of Barrington m. Esme E. **Jackson** of Rochester 3/24/1945 in Dover; H - 23, laborer, b. Barrington, s/o Charles J. Wood (So. Berwick, ME) and Lucy M. Hall (Rochester); W - 23, nurse, b. W. Palm Beach, FL, d/o Leslie Jackson (Madison) and Amy E. Taylor (Stockport, England)
Kenneth A. of Barrington m. Pamela R. **Seekins** of Portsmouth 10/11/1980 in Portsmouth
Leslie E. of Barrington m. Frances M. **Knowles** of Rochester 6/12/1947; H - 52, farmer, 2d, b. Fitchburg, MA, s/o James H. Wood (Hanover) and Isabel Snow (Quechee, VT); W - 40, teacher, 2d, b. Central Falls, RI, d/o Malcolm C. McNeil and Julia Radloff

William A. of Barrington m. Alma R. **Jackson** of Rochester 11/25/1943 in Dover; H - 26, lumber marker, b. Barrington, s/o Charles J. Wood (So. Berwick, ME) and Lucy M. Hall (Rochester); W - 28, nurse, b. Dover, d/o Leslie E. Jackson (Madison) and Amy E. Taylor (Stockport, England)

WOODS,
John of Barrington m. Esther M. **Marden** of Dover 1/5/1931 in Dover; H - 31, laborer, b. Strafford, s/o Joseph Wood (Canada) and Mary Jeffries (Canada); W - 22, housework, b. Dover, d/o Harry Marden (Strafford) and Fanny Welch (Barrington)

WOOLSON,
John C. of Barrington m. Vicky A. **Caplette** of Rochester 5/7/1966 in Rochester; H - 19, mechanic, b. Littleton, s/o Raymond F. Woolson (NH) and Eleanor B. Haskins (NH); W - 18, unemployed, b. Rochester, d/o Leon C. Caplette (NH) and Arline T. Willard (NH)
John C. of Barrington m. Elaine A. **Kinville** of Rochester 5/16/1981 in Dover

WORLD,
James Ronald of Carmichael, CA m. Evelyn Louise **Smith** of Boxborough, MA 11/8/1975

WORMELL,
Stephen B. of Barrington m. Lee S. **Willits** of Barrington 10/25/1980 in Durham

WORMHOOD,
Leeman B., Jr. of Madbury m. Norah G. **Chapman** of Barrington 10/7/1944; H - 21, shipfitter's helper, b. Rochester, s/o Leeman B. Wormhood (Ossipee) and Blanche E. Tibbetts (Springvale, ME); W - 23, at home,

b. Dover, d/o Harris W. Chapman (PQ) and Dorothy M. Roberts (Bristol, England)

WRIGHT,
Darryl Price of Barrington m. Darlene Frances **Bailey** of Epsom 6/21/1975

WYMAN,
Joseph C., Jr. of Barrington m. Diane M. **Tarmey** of Barrington 5/12/1984

WYNN,
Edward A. of Barrington m. Nancy L. **Smith** of Dover 10/6/1979

YARRINGTON,
Eugene N., III of Barrington m. Donna C. **Anderson** of Barrington 1/17/1987

YORK,
George Kenneth of Dover m. Sally Lynn **Musler** of Barrington 8/17/1974

YOUNG,
Edward of Barrington m. Mary **Hall** of Northwood 5/11/1892 in Northwood; H - 44, farmer, b. Barrington, s/o Jonathan and Sophia; W - 33, teacher, b. Nottingham
Kenneth R. of Barrington m. Ellen M. **Innis** of Dover 2/11/1972 in Dover; H - 2d, b. 1/3/1941 in NH, s/o Kenneth F. Young (NH) and Elizabeth O'Neil (NH); W - 2d, b. 3/15/1941 in NH, d/o Raymond Comtois (NH) and Beatrice Gregoire (ME)
Ralph N., Jr. of Barrington m. Michele L. **Garland** of Barrington 9/8/1984
Steven R. of Rochester m. Jacqueline J. **Lavertue** of Barrington 10/11/1980 in Rochester

W. G. of Barrington m. Georgianna **Brown** of Barrington 5/21/1892; H - 21, farmer, b. Barrington, s/o George and Elizabeth; W - 19, housemaid, b. Barrington, d/o Julia Brown

ZANGARINE,
Dennis A. of Barrington m. Julie J. **Burovac** of Newington 3/2/1985 in Newington

ZIELFELDER,
Richard D., Jr. of Barrington m. Lucille E. **Twombly** of Dover 6/26/1965; H - 20, meat cutter, b. MA, s/o Richard D. Zielfelder (MA) and Eleanor M. Fuller (MA); W - 18, at home, b. NH, d/o Merton D. Twombly (NH) and Villa M. Johnson (NH)

Ronald J. of Barrington m. Suzanne M. **Comtois** of Dover 6/29/1968 in Dover; H - b. 7/26/1947 in MA, s/o Richard Zielfelder (MA) and Eleanor M. Fuller (MA); W - b. 1/27/1948 in NH, d/o Philippe M. Comtois (NH) and Emily A. Downs (NH)

Ross M. of Barrington m. Dianne M. **Fogg** of Barrington 6/23/1973; H - b. 11/15/1950 in MA, s/o Richard Zielfelder (MA) and Eleanor M. Fuller (MA); W - b. 5/31/1954 in NH, d/o Russell L. Fogg (NH) and Rose L. Ellis (NH)

Ross M. of Barrington m. Sharon L. **Evans** of Barrington 3/15/1985

ZWEIG,
Neal Todd of Barrington m. Gail Ruth **Peightell** of Barrington 3/20/1976 in Concord

UNKNOWN,
white male, d. 10/12/1909 at 40; struck by R.R. train; widower

ABBOTT,
Abbie M., d. 6/5/1925 at 69/11/1; Bright's disease; widow; b. Barrington; Jerry Hall (Barrington) and Elvine J. Hall (Barrington)
Alexander L., d. 5/21/1908 at 63/3/8; pneumonia; shoemaker; married; b. Dover

ADAMS,
Hannah S., d. 4/26/1905 at 74/4/6; cancer; housewife; married; b. Holderness; John W. Rowe (Holderness)
Richard A., d. 3/1/1971 at 57 in Dover; congestive heart fail.; salesman; married; b. NH

ALEX,
William J., d. 10/31/1976 at 0/2 in Rochester; b. NH; William J. Alex and Debra Hillsgrove

ALLAN,
Christabel H., d. 4/29/1971 at 59 in Rochester; cardiac arrest; housewife; married; b. NH; George Ham and Lillian Jukes; residence - New Durham

ALLEN,
George W., d. 7/21/1899 at 52/4/29; heart failure; farmer; married; b. Barrington; Benjamin Allen (Barrington) and Sarah Brown (Barrington)

AMBROSE,
Edna Viola, d. 7/8/1956 at 58 in Rochester; cerebravascular accident; housewife; married; b. Cambridge, MA; Thomas F. Jollymore and Anna Grono

Frank E., d. 8/15/1961 at 65 in Concord; coronary occlusion; ret. trainman; married; b. Haverhill, MA; Albion Ambrose and Susie Colbin; residence - Dover

Granville D., d. 2/8/1954 at 81; congestive heart disease; general labor; single; b. Deerfield; Byron Ambrose and Flora M. Watson

Lillian G., d. 3/8/1965 at 82 in MA; arteriosclerotic hrt. dis.

ARCHIBALD,
Dorothy F., d. 10/9/1982 at 83 in NY
Earle G., d. 2/22/1983 at 77; auto mechanic; married; b. MA
Joseph S., d. 3/1/1986 at 87 in Rochester; cartoonist; widower; b. NH

ARLIN,
child, d. 9/28/1890 at 0/3/6; b. Barrington; Eli A. Arlin (Barrington) and Ida Leighton (Strafford)

daughter, d. 6/18/1895 at 0/2; phthisis; b. Barrington; Eli Arlin (Barrington) and Ida Arlin (Barrington)

son, d. 1/21/1903 at 0/0/0; premature; b. Barrington; George Arlin (Boston, MA) and Laura Freeman (Barrington)

Alsea, d. 8/6/1897 at 0/7/6; cholera infantum; b. Barrington; George Arlin (Barrington) and Laura Freeman (Barrington)

Charles E., d. 3/2/1908 at 61/9/9; over-exertion; laborer; married; b. Barrington; Daniel Arlin (Barrington) and Abigail Brown (Barrington)

Charlotte, d. 12/1/1909 at 63/1/26; pneumonia; housekeeper; widow; b. Barrington; Richard Babb and Mary Ham

Daniel W., d. 7/20/1913 at 66/3/14; carcinoma of liver; farmer; widower; b. Barrington; William H. Arlin (Barrington) and Caroline E. Seavey (Barrington)

Edward A., d. 4/26/1912 at 59/8/10; neuritis; farmer; married; b. Barrington; John W. Arlin (Barrington) and Sarah Hoyt (Barrington)

Eli A., d. 12/13/1937 at 85/6/22; valvular heart; retired; widower; b. Barrington; Dill Arlin (Barrington) and Mary Robinson (Rochester)

Ellen, d. 4/14/1894 at 0/0/7; congestion of lungs; b. Barrington; George Arlin (Barrington) and Laura Freeman (Barrington)

Francis E., d. 11/3/1957 at 69; coronary heart disease; farmer; single; b. Strafford; Eli A. Arlin and Ida B. Leighton

Frank H., d. 12/23/1939 at 65/7/16; heart disease; laborer; married; b. Barrington; Daniel Arlin (Barrington) and Laura Caswell (Barrington)

George Albert, d. 1/28/1902 at 35/7/10; cerebral hemorrhage; teamster; married; b. Barrington; William Arlin

George H., d. 5/22/1930 at 70/4/21 in Northwood; mit. insufficiency; shoemaker; married; b. Chelsea, MA; Jeremiah Arlin (Barrington) and Margaret Walker (Barrington)

George W., d. 2/12/1923 at 84/9/16; widower; b. Barrington; Benjamin Arlin and Sarah Willie

Hannah, d. 12/30/1903 at 90; organic heart disease; housewife; widow; b. Strafford; Aaron Sawyer and Annie Sawyer

Harry L., d. 4/8/1974 at 88 in Dover; farmer; single; b. NH; Eli Arlin and Ida Leighton

Ida Belle, d. 3/25/1915 at 57/10/9; housewife; married; b. Strafford; Samuel Leighton (Strafford) and Adline Winkley (Strafford)

Ida W., d. 5/24/1958 at 82 in Rochester; arteriosclerosis; housewife, widow; b. Barrington; Leonard Whitehouse and Liza Brown; residence - Rochester

Ina, d. 7/28/1911 at 18/11/23; valvular heart disease; single; b. Barrington; Eli Arlin (Barrington) and Ida Leighton (Strafford)

John, d. 11/28/1890 at 88; widower; John Arlin

John W., d. 11/6/1936 at 82/8/6 in Dover; cerebral embolism; farmer; widower; b. Barrington; Benjamin Arlin (Barrington) and Hannah Arlin (Barrington)

Laura A., d. 8/1/1900 at 52/10/14; diabetes mellitus; housewife; married; b. Barrington; Timothy Caswell and Jane Cate (Northwood)

Laura E., d. 9/8/1930 at 65 in Dover; can. of stomach

Leslie C., d. 5/3/1963 at 65 in Rochester; carcinoma of prostrate gland; ret. city emp.; married; b. Barrington; Eli Arlin and Ida Leighton; residence - Rochester

Lewis E., d. 8/1/1897 at 0/7/4; cholera infantum; b. Marlboro; Charles H. Arlin (Boston, MA) and Addie S. Reed (Barrington)

Lizzie, d. 1/9/1910 at 72; mitral regurgitation; married

Margaret, d. 9/14/1891 at 62; widow; Benjamin Walker and Betsey Canney

Martha O., d. 2/22/1921 at 76/4; housewife; married; b. Barrington; Joseph Watson (Barrington) and Lydia Bumford (Barrington)

Priscilla A., d. 12/25/1925 at 79/10/23; b. Barrington; William Bodge

ATWOOD,
William, d. 7/6/1932 at 72/2/17; val. heart disease; farmer; married; b. Middleton, MA; Morrison Atwood (Thornton) and Mary A. Fairfield (Salem, MA)

AUSTIN,
Amy R., d. 5/30/1974 at 78 in Dover; nurse; widow; b. NH; James M. Calden and Minnie Casavant

AVERY,
Clifton A., d. 10/17/1986 at 78 in Rochester; woodsman, married; b. NH

Dorothy L., d. 1/2/1975 at 68 in Portsmouth; store prop.; widow; b. ME; William Tracy and Eleanor Bixby

Oscar, d. 11/27/1945 at 80/6/11; arteriosclerosis; farmer; widower; b. Barnstead; Stephen Avery (Rumney) and Mary Straw (Rumney)

AYERS,

Charles A., d. 2/12/1913 at 65/4/12; fractured skull; laborer; married; b. Barrington; Richard Ayers (Barrington) and Susan Leighton (Randolph)

Joseph, d. 12/20/1893 at 81/2/11; old age; housewife (sic); widower; b. Barrington; John Ayers (Barrington) and Keziah Swain (Rochester)

May A., d. 1/21/1900 at 45/11/14 in Rochester; spinal meningitis; widow

Richard, d. 11/3/1890 at 81/4/1; married; b. Barrington; John Ayers and Keziah Swain

William S., d. 1/10/1900 at 52/2/7 in Rochester; spinal meningitis; married

BABB,

John C. F., d. 5/19/1924 at 57/5/19; farmer; widower; b. Barrington; Joseph T. Babb (Barrington)

Joseph T., d. 5/4/1892 at 88/4/7; old age; farmer; widower; b. Barrington; Thomas Babb

Raymond S., d. 10/1/1985 at 88 in Rochester; maintenance man; married; b. NH

BABEL,

Brian J., d. 6/18/1974 at 0/1/7 in MA; (burial); b. NH; Donn R. Babel and Anita L. Dionne

BAILEY,

Abbie, d. 2/14/1897 at 0/2; suddenly in night; b. Barrington; John W. Bailey (Haverhill) and Dora M. Warren (Haverhill)

Cyrus M., d. 1/17/1894 at 0/6/7; chronic meningitis; b. Barrington; John W. Bailey (Haverhill) and Dora Warren (Chester)

Eliza S., d. 3/12/1892 at 65; embolism; housekeeper; married; b. Barrington; John Dorr

John W., d. 3/18/1900 at 85/6; old age; farmer; married

BALL,
Elizabeth M., d. 9/30/1953 at 74; cancer, bowel; housewife; widow; b. NS; Joseph Hatfield and Racheal Comeau

Owen M., d. 3/25/1941 at 54/11/29 in So. Berwick, ME; cardiac thrombosis; farmer; married; b. NS; Francis Ball (England) and Flidah Martin (England)

BALLOU,
Leland B., d. 9/10/1971 at 69 in Rochester; congestive heart failure; laborer; married; b. NH; George Ballou and Florence Dufer; residence - Rochester

BARKER,
Frank C., d. 9/26/1964 at 57; coronary thrombosis; air lines; married; b. Fulton, IN; Verd Barker and Eva M. Bair; residence - Reading, MA

BARNUM,
Ruth Hall, d. 8/14/1948 at 74/1/18 in Rochester; apoplexy; retired; widow; b. Rochester; Franklin Hall (Madbury) and Hennie Dame (Nottingham)

BARRETTE,
Valentina, d. 3/2/1984 at 31 in Dover; housewife; divorced; b. NH

BATEMAN,
John F., d. 1/19/1945 at 66/0/7 in Dover; coronary thrombosis; lumber; married; b. Strafford; John H. Bateman (Dover) and Sarah E. Foss (Strafford)
Sarah, d. 5/6/1935 at 90/9/21; arterio sclerosis; retired; widow; b. Strafford; Daniel Foss (Strafford) and Mary D. James (Lee)

BAXTER,
Alden E., d. 11/20/1972 at 57 in Kittery, ME; coronary occlusion; welder; married; b. NH; Nahan Baxter and Altea M. Mattox
Alfred W., d. 11/25/1956 at 46; coronary thrombosis; truck driver; married; b. Madbury; Nahum Baxter and Alta M. Mattox
Ethel L., d. 9/26/1970 at 79 in Rochester; cerebral thrombosis; housewife; married; b. NH; Frank Brown and Anna Allen; residence - Rochester
Evelyn M., d. 3/17/1960 at 51; myocardial infarction; cook; widow; b. Kennebunk, ME; Ransom Nason and Luella M. Cameron
Everett D., d. 3/30/1965 at 56 in Dover; coronary thrombosis; lead man; married; b. Madbury; Nahum Baxter and Alta Maddox; residence - Madbury
James A., d. 10/11/1971 at 75 in Concord; respiratory insufficiency
Leota L., d. 10/19/1945 at 34/11/12 in Exeter; generalized toxemia; housework; married; b. Barrington; Frank Davis (Dover) and Lizzie Chesley (Barrington)
Melvin S., d. 5/17/1949 at 37 mins. in Exeter; dystocia; b. Exeter; Sherman Baxter and Luverne Swain
Milton R., d. 9/15/1973 at 59; myocardial infarction; welder; married; b. NH; Naham Baxter and Alta Mattox
Wesley Irving, d. 7/2/1945 at 69/4/21; accidental drowning; wood ch'p; divorced; b. Farmington; Nahum Baxter and Jeanette Cochran

BEAL,
Morgan C., d. 12/5/1972 at -- in Boston, MA; prematurity; b. MA

BEARDSLEY,
son, d. 2/15/1958 at 4 hrs. in Rochester; immaturity; b. Rochester; Warren H. Beardsley and Rhea E. Smith

Carl H., d. 6/9/1960 at 1 ½ hrs. in Kittery, ME; atelectasis; b. Kittery, ME; Warren H. Beardsley and Rhea E. Smith

BEAULIEU,
Loretta R., d. 1/3/1982 at 70 in Rochester; housewife; widow; b. NH

BELL,
Mary C., d. 3/7/1953 at 71; pulm. fibrosis; housewife; widow; b. Trenton, NJ; William Colclough and Mary Foster

BENNETT,
Albert, d. 7/22/1940 at 74/4/2; coronary thrombosis; widower; William Bennett (Sanford, ME) and Lydia Ricker (Kennebunkport, ME)

Alfred W., d. 7/12/1946 at 79/7/28 in Dover; cerebral hemorrhage; retired; married; b. Parsonsfield, ME; Charles Bennett

Anna May, d. 8/12/1950 at 49/0/10 in Rochester; carcinoma of cervix; box maker; married; b. Barrington; Lorenzo Dow and Ida B. Waterhouse; residence - Rochester

Ellen C., d. 3/20/1965 at 94 in Dover; coronary thrombosis; housewife; widow; b. Boston, MA; James C. Knibbs and Mary C. Knibbs; residence - Dover

Olive Hall, d. 1/7/1980 at 90 in Rochester; at home; widow; b. NH

Philip S., d. 3/5/1965 at 78 in Rochester; myocardial failure; shoe worker; married; b. Springvale, ME; Albert Bennett and Carrie Sleeper; residence - Gonic

BERGSTROM,
Dorothea, d. 3/19/1983 at 77 in Dover; housewife; married; b. MA

Grace D., d. 9/9/1983 at 73 in Rochester; homemaker; married; b. MA

BERNIER,
Fred J., d. 3/30/1894 at 0/6/30; cardiac disease; b. Barrington; Theodore Bernier (Canada) and Mary Pomeleau (Canada)

BERRY,
Albert Ira, d. 2/28/1937 at 65/5/24 in Dresden, ME; disturbance valvular

Almira P., d. 2/12/1895 at 46/5/29; cardiac ascites; housemaid; widow; b. Barrington; Isaac Cater (Barrington) and Mariam Howe (Strafford)

Alonzo, d. 5/10/1929 at 82/5/29; farmer; widower; b. Strafford; Ezekiel Berry and Mary Hayes (Strafford)

Clarence L., d. 7/12/1957 at 52 in Berwick, ME; anemia; herdsman; married; b. Barrington; Lewis Berry and Sadie Perkins; residence - Berwick, ME

Clifton B., d. 6/18/1968 at 72 in Concord; cerebral hemorrhage; lumber mill oper.; married; b. NH; Alvin T. Berry and Mary Hughes; residence - Chichester

Daniel R., d. 9/10/1897 at 86/3/7; paralysis; farmer; married; b. Barrington; Daniel Berry (Barrington) and Nancy Berry (Barrington)

Eliza A., d. 2/18/1905 at 72/5/26; fatty heart; housework; widow; b. Barrington; David B. Smith (Barrington) and Annie M. Pearey (Barrington)

Elmer, d. 3/18/1931 at 67/7/18; heart disease; farmer; married; b. Strafford; James F. Berry (Barrington) and Louisa A. Foss (Strafford)

Eva M., d. 12/29/1957 at 69 in Rochester; arteriosclerotic heart disease; housewife; widow; b. Lee; William H. Mattox and Sarah J. Davis

Flavius J., d. 5/22/1942 at 83/10/19; chr. myocarditis; farmer; married; b. Barrington; Johnathan Berry (Barrington) and Mary S. Felker (Barrington)

Ivory F., d. 4/28/1893 at 73/4/9; emb. and thrombosis; farmer; married; b. Barrington; Elijah Berry and Rachel Foss

Jennie, d. 3/15/1928 at 79/3/15; angina pectoris; at home; widow; b. Strafford; Joseph Scruton (Strafford) and Louisa Brock (Strafford)

John F., d. 12/14/1963 at 33 in York, ME; hypertensive heart dis.

John W., d. 4/15/1894 at 49/7/17; dis. of hrt, liver, stomach; carpenter; married; b. Barrington; Ivory F. Berry and Mary Lee

Jonathan F., d. 9/19/1914 at 88/5/19; lumberman; married; b. Barrington; Jonathan Berry (Barrington) and ----- Fowler (Barrington)

Lewis C., d. 2/25/1915 at 45/6/13 in Rochester; laborer; divorced; b. Plymouth; Daniel R. Berry (Barrington) and Elizabeth Buzzell (Barrington)

Lura Dell, d. 4/23/1945 at 70/9/10 in Rochester; hydro-pneumo-thorax; widow; b. Barrington; Oscar Corson (Raymond, MA) and Annie Twombly (Newmarket)

Martin E., d. 5/11/1959 at 65 in Somersworth; acute cor. occlusion; machinist; married; b. Somersworth; Michael J. Berry and Mary Kittredge; residence - Somersworth

Mary J., d. 5/4/1903 at 80/2/24; uremic coma; housewife; widow; b. Barrington; John Lee (Barrington) and Clara DeMerritt (Barrington)

Mary S., d. 4/25/1921 at 86/9/8; housekeeper; widow; b. Barrington; John Felker (Barrington) and Mahitable Winkley (Barrington)

Michael J., d. 1/8/1970 at 12 in Boston, MA; cardiopulmonary arrest; residence - North Berwick, ME

Nellie N., d. 12/2/1958 at 87 in Norwell, MA; coronary sclerosis; housewife; married; b. Lee; James Glidden and Elizabeth J. Durgin

Norman J., d. 9/29/1985 at 82; const. contractor; married; b. NH

Rhoda, d. 1/29/1908 at 92/5/17; senility; domestic; single; b. Barrington; Jonathan Berry (Barrington) and Betsey Fowler (Strafford)

Warren W., d. 5/17/1955 at 67; Stokes-Adams syndrome; farmer; married; b. Barrington; Alonzo F. Berry and Olive Brown

BICKERS,

Luther, d. 8/8/1930 at 57/2/10; angina pectoris; W. U. lineman; single; b. Provincetown, MA; Joseph Bickers (England) and Elizabeth ----- (Wellfleet, MA)

BICKFORD,

John Hart, d. 3/31/1902 at 0/1/9; unknown; b. Barrington; Herbert Bickford (Rochester) and Lizzie Perkins (Barrington)

Martha L., d. 6/8/1972 at 84 in Madbury; myocardial infarction

Maurice R., d. 12/12/1980 at 65; laborer; divorced; b. NH

BIGELOW,

Victor L., d. 10/16/1950 at 51/9/25 in Rochester; Hodgkin's disease; carpenter; married; b. Bourne, MA; Ruben Bigelow and ----- Huntley

BISSON,

Shane P., d. 11/26/1987 at 33; decontamination clnr.; married; b. NH

BLAISDELL,
Evelyn E., d. 11/14/1984 at 60 in Rochester; vending hostess; married; b. NH
Oliver Y., d. 8/4/1893 at 24/2/21; tuberculosis; farmer; married; b. Barrington; Samuel Blaisdell and Ann Freeman

BODGE,
son, d. 5/31/1910 at 0/0/0; stillborn; b. Barrington; John Bodge (Barrington) and E. Josephine Daly (Brighton, MA)
Eliza (Mrs.), d. 1/6/1908 at 82/0/11; pneumonia, old age; housekeeper; widow; b. Strafford; Samuel Daniels
Gertrude G., d. 10/10/1957 at 62; carcinoma bowel; no occ.; single; b. Barrington; Charles F. Bodge and Mary Carley
Harry W., d. 9/9/1914 at 25/11/25; single; b. Barrington; Charles F. Bodge (Barrington) and Mary C. Carley (Brighton, MA)
James, d. 2/13/1972 at 73 in Concord; pneumonia
John W., d. 10/24/1958 at 74; arteriosclerosis; farmer; widower; b. Barrington; Charles F. Bodge and Mary Carley
Mary, d. 4/12/1892 at 82/3; old age; single; b. Barrington
Mary Margaret, d. 6/14/1948 at 86/11/19; cardiac failure; widow; b. Brighton, MA; James Carley (Ireland) and Margaret O'Brien (Ireland)
Winifred, d. 8/11/1939 at 55/0/20; carc. naso pharynx; housewife; married; b. Brighton, MA; Winifred Gaffey (England)

BONFIGLIO,
Frank, d. 6/29/1978 at 74; construction; married; b. Italy; Nicholas Bonfiglio

BOOD[E]Y,
A. Marilla, d. 11/14/1921 at 81/0/26; housewife; married; b. Durham; Joseph Ferneld (Durham) and Lydia Peary (Barrington)
Alice Ida, d. 1/29/1950 at 68; endocarditis; housewife; widow; b. Stratford; Eli A. Arlin and Ida B. Leighton
D. Webster, d. 9/6/1925 at 83/1/28; old age; farmer; widower; b. Barrington; Daniel Boody (Barrington) and Sara Wiggin (Lee)
Daniel, d. 5/10/1894 at 85/0/26; old age; farmer; widower; b. Barrington; John Boody (Barrington) and Susan Hayes (Northwood)
John U., d. 4/18/1949 at 80; aorticsclerosis; farmer; married; b. Barrington; D. Webster Boodey and Alice Arlin
Ralph J., d. 7/14/1987 at 64 in Rochester; farmer; married; b. NH

BOSTON,
Almira S., d. 5/13/1901 at 21/8/24; consumption; housewife; married; b. North Hampton; Joseph Marston (North Hampton) and Lottie Broderick (North Hampton)
Oliver, d. 12/19/1893 at 85/4/21; old age; farmer; widower; b. So. Berwick, ME; Joseph Boston (Wells, ME) and C. Davis (So. Berwick, ME)
Oliver F., d. 3/13/1916 at 78/2/4; laborer; single; b. Berwick, ME; Oliver Boston (So. Berwick, ME) and Dorcas Woodes (York, ME)

BOSTROM,
Alfhild E., d. 1/24/1981 at 78 in Rochester

BOTTOM,
Richard, d. 11/21/1986 at 58 in Rochester; Air Force officer; married; b. NY

BOUCHER,
Lester D., d. 6/8/1984 at 31 in Dover; brick mason; married; b. ME

BOUTHOT,
Leopold G., d. 1/4/1986 at 79; gas attendant; widower; b. ME

BOWEN,
Harold R., d. 8/25/1964 at 80 in Dover; uremia; RR conductor; widower; b. Kennebunk, ME; William F. Bowen and Mary A. Rice
Mae A., d. 5/6/1981 at 67 in Portsmouth; housewife; married; b. NH

BOYLE,
Timothy T., d. 12/29/1979 at 28 in Dover; carpenter; married; b. NH

BRASSOW,
Doris L., d. 4/24/1986 at 81 in Rochester; housewife; widow; b. NH

BRETON,
Herve, d. 1/18/1978 at 70 in Dover; weaver; single; b. NH; Emile Breton and Rosilda Cartier
John, d. 12/3/1975 at 75 in Sarasota, FL

BREWSTER,
David J., d. 7/21/1901 at 70/0/11; heart disease; farmer; b. Barrington; Joseph H. Brewster (Barrington) and Lydia Garland (Rochester)

BRIDE,
John W., d. 1/28/1914 at 71/7/12; stone cutter; widower; b. Stratham

BRIDGES,
Carleton R., d. 9/24/1979 at 55 in Somersworth

BRITTING,
Joshua, d. 6/29/1961 at 79; coronary thrombosis; truck driver; widower; b. New York, NY; John H. Britting and Delia Mullen

BRITTON,
Harry A., d. 1/24/1986 at 84 in Dover; power engineer; married; b. MA

BROOKS,
Boyd I., d. 9/23/1967 at 77 in Somerville, MA; malnutrition; residence - Somerville, MA
Ernest P., d. 5/3/1968 at 75 in Rochester; coronary thrombosis
George H., d. 11/14/1972 at 72 in Rochester; acute congestive hrt. flr.; shoe worker; married; b. NS; George Brooks and Clara Marshall
Harold U., d. 6/8/1956 at 21 in Madbury; fractured skull; salesman; single; b. Effingham; Harold G. Brown and Irene Stimpson
Kenneth E., d. 5/3/1978 at 67 in Rochester; farmer; married; b. NH; Irving E. Brooks and Pearl Gordon
Pearl H., d. 1/16/1965 at 89; arteriosclerotic dis.; housewife; widow; b. Lyman, ME; Dimon Gordon and Harriett Underwood
Percy J., d. 10/13/1971 at 78 in Rochester; respiratory infection; woolen worker; widower; b. Canada; George I. Brooks and Clara Marshall; residence - Rochester

BROWN,
Addie, d. 11/21/1891 at 30; single; Isaac Brown (Barrington) and Sarah Arlin

Benjamin A., d. 6/13/1978 at 82 in Manchester; chef; widower; b. NH; Frank Brown and Anne Allen

Charles A., d. 2/15/1901 at 26; pneumonia; laborer; b. Loudon

Chester G., d. 1/4/1986 at 86 in Rochester; sawyer; widower; b. NH

Clement R., d. 12/17/1906 at 0/8/4; ilio calitis; b. Barrington; William H. Brown (Barrington) and Sarah P.H. Reed (Barrington)

Dennis, d. 5/19/1905 at 80; pneumonia; farmer; widower; b. Barrington

Edgar F., d. 11/19/1929 at 44/6/6; farmer; married; b. Barrington; George T. Brown and Julia Waterhouse

Edna N., d. 4/23/1982 at 88 in Portsmouth

Edward E., d. 4/16/1976 at 81 in Rochester; lumberman; widower; b. NH; Henry M. Brown and Evilla Morrison

Eliza Ann, d. 5/12/1950 at 70/9/20 in Rochester; cerebral thrombosis; housewife; widow; b. Barrington; Bert Allen and Mirinda Hanscomb; residence - Rochester

Ellen A., d. 9/27/1981 at 69 in Madbury

Ezra B., d. 5/20/1911 at 50/5/11; cancer of stomach; grocer; married; b. Barrington; Lorenzo A. Brown (Barrington) and Mary A. Berry (Barrington)

George A., d. 6/1/1961 at 62 in Dover; carcinoma of stomach; ret. farmer; widower; b. Madbury; Frank Brown and Mary Brown; residence - Dover

George T., d. 1/13/1890 at 52/10/17; married; b. Barrington; John Brown (Barrington) and Lucy Willey (Durham)

George T., d. 3/27/1961 at 68 in Rochester; coronary thrombosis; trucking bus.; married; b. Barrington; Frank Brown and Eliza Allen; residence - Rochester

Gladys M., d. 4/9/1980 at 74 in Dover; seamstress; married; b. NH

Harry R., d. 10/30/1982 at 91 in Dover; shoe worker; married; b. NH

Henry M., d. 2/17/1920 at 71/0/10; shoemaker; divorced; b. Barrington; Dennis J. Brown (Barrington) and Mehitable Evans (Strafford)

Hezekiah H., d. 11/11/1894 at 74/7/11; cerebral embolism; farmer; widower; b. Madbury; Mark Brown and Olive Twombly

Ida, d. 10/28/1963 at 71 in Nashua; myocardial failure; housewife; widow; b. Canada; John Lavoie and Lumina Lavoie; residence - Nashua

Irene A., d. 9/9/1981 at 70 in Exeter; bus. emp. forms; married; b. VT

Isaac, d. 3/23/1919 at 82/3/22; farmer; married; b. Barrington; Joseph Brown (Barrington) and Susan Arlin (Barrington)

Iza May, d. 3/12/1922 at 43/7/29; housewife; married; Gershon Harvelle (Litchfield) and Mary E. Williams (Warren, ME)

James E., d. 3/3/1896 at 60/0/12; la grippe; shoemaker; married; b. Barrington; Joseph Brown (Concord) and Susan Arlin (Barrington)

John A., d. 12/3/1936 at 59/8/23; coronary thrombosis; lumberman; married; b. Haverhill, MA; George T. Brown and Julia Waterhouse

Joseph, d. 2/24/1924 at 58/5/20; farmer; married; b. Canada

Julia, d. 10/27/1923 at 76/3/23; widow; b. Barrington; Augustus Waterhouse and Eliza Hodgdon

Kathryn E., d. 5/4/1959 at 52 in Rochester; carcinoma of breast; bookkeeper; married; b. Wakefield, MA; Harry Lenfest and Theresa McDermott

Lillian B., d. 1/22/1901 at 34/11/28; phthisic pulmonary; housewife; married; b. Barrington; George W. Willey (Barrington) and Olive Hoyt (Barrington)

Mabel J., d. 6/22/1982 at 80 in Rochester

Margaret E., d. 12/16/1954 at 61 in Rochester; carcinoma of uterus; housewife; married; b. Barrington; C. McDonald and Nellie Whitehouse; residence - Rochester

Mark F., d. 9/3/1913 at 62/1/26 in Dover; acute Bright's disease

Mehitable, d. 4/3/1899 at 74/9/17; old age; housewife; married; b. Barrington; James Evans (Strafford) and Mehitable Hall (Strafford)

Melvin Henry, d. 3/11/1920 at --; b. Barrington; Edward E. Brown (Lee) and Margaret McDonald (Lee)

Nicholas, d. 9/26/1899 at 79/9/22; heart failure; farmer; widower; b. Strafford; Nicholas Brown (Strafford) and Mary Smith (Strafford)

Raymond H., d. 3/6/1983 at 64 in Rochester; heating engineer; married; b. NH

Robert E., d. 11/7/1966 at 49 in Rochester; cerebral thrombosis; woolen mill; widower; b. Barrington; Edward S. Brown and Margaret McDonald; residence - Rochester

Sarah P. H., d. 11/29/1961 at 76; adenocarcinoma of colon; housewife; widow; b. Barrington; Charles H. Reed and Annie B. Seavey

Thomas W., d. 3/30/1964 at 71 in Dover; pyelonephritis; farmer; divorced; b. Madbury; Thomas F. Brown and Mary Brown; residence - Madbury

Weston F., d. 1/28/1946 at 48/7/19 in Rochester; natural causes; mechanic; single; b. Barrington; Frank Brown (Haverhill, MA) and Eliza Arlin (Barrington)

William H., d. 6/30/1900 at 23/7/9; drowning; laborer; single; b. Barrington; Mark F. Brown (Barrington) and Lucy Brown (Barrington)

William H., d. 5/2/1951 at 84; apoplexy; laborer; married; b. Barrington; George T. Brown and Julia Waterhouse

BRYSON,
Melvin F., d. 7/27/1967 at 76 in Dover; metastesas; farmer; divorced; b. Dover; Frazer A. Bryson and Etta Norton

BUMFORD,
Charles W., d. 4/10/1943 at 92/0/12; arterio scl. heart; farmer; widower; b. Barrington; Hateville Bumford (Barrington) and Elizabeth Henderson (Barrington)
Elizabeth A., d. 6/13/1900 at 76/2/10; gangrene; housewife; married; b. Barrington; Paul Henderson and Annie Drew (Barrington)
Ellen M., d. 10/22/1904 at 52/3/28; pneumonia; housewife; married; b. Greenland; George Hodgdon (Barrington) and Nancy Hanson (Strafford)
Grace, d. 6/29/1941 at 66/10/17 in Concord; gen. arterio sclerosis; single; b. East Barrington; Charles W. Bumford (East Barrington) and Helen Hogdon
Grover C., d. 2/25/1979 at 86 in Dover; locksmith; married; b. NH
Hateville, d. 12/29/1903 at 83/8/17; Bright's disease; farmer; married; b. Barrington; John Bumford (Barrington) and Martha Tibbetts (Barrington)
Jasper O., d. 11/28/1956 at 68 in Augusta, ME; cerebravascular accident; b. Barrington; Charles Bumford and Ellen Hodgdon; residence - Augusta, ME
Regina M., d. 2/19/1965 at 81 in Rochester; cerebral arteriosclerosis; housewife; widow; b. Quebec; Joseph Lorange and Celina Jacques; residence - Dover
Roland W., d. 6/16/1969 at 83 in Berwick, ME; married; b. NH
Sarah J., d. 6/11/1921 at 33/11/6 in Dover; housewife; married; b. Boston, MA; James Townsend (Ireland) and Ella F. Robinson (Boston, MA)

BUNDZA,
Joseph T., d. 12/6/1984 at 57 in Rochester; foreman, printing press; married; b. MA

BURKE,
son, d. 1/11/1948 at 0/0/0; prematurity; b. Barrington; Everett Burke (Milton) and Ora B. Chase (Skowhegan, ME)

BURLEY,
John B., d. 5/25/1900 at 92/10/6; unknown; carpenter; widower; b. Newmarket; James Burley (Stratham) and Mariah Bennett (Newington)

BUTLER,
Maude D., d. 11/22/1964 at 80; coronary heart disease; housewife; married; b. Northfield; Stacy Durgin and Dinah Evans

BUTTRICK,
Marilyn, d. 3/19/1976 at 42 in Rochester; housewife; married; b. NH; Howard Lee and Alice M. Brackett

BUZZELL,
son, d. 5/25/1907 at 0/1/7; erisypelas; b. Barrington; Levi Buzzell (Strafford) and Bessie Arlin (Strafford)
Angie, d. 1/16/1917 at 33/0/24; school teacher; single; b. Barrington; Walter Buzzell (Barrington) and Ida M. Locke (Barrington)
Ann Martha, d. 11/19/1890 at 62/10/21; married; b. Barrington; John Fernald (Eliot, ME) and Sarah A. Paul (Eliot, ME)
Annie E., d. 6/8/1927 at 84/6/1; arteriosclerosis; at home; widow; b. Madbury; James Emerson (Lee) and Eliza Fine (Madison)
Charles E., d. 12/4/1946 at 81/2/1 in Derry; matastatic carcinoma; retired; married; b. Barrington; William H. Buzzell (Barrington) and Ellen Church (Amherst, MA)
Clarence T., d. 10/7/1909 at 8/9/24; acute indigestion; schoolboy; b. Barrington; Levi H. Buzzell (Barrington) and Bessie Arlin (Strafford)

Edith M., d. 4/30/1958 at 85 in Dover; cerebral hemorrhage; nurse; single; b. Barrington; John H. Buzzell and Ann E. Emerson; residence - Dover

Eleanor L., d. 2/26/1966 at 54 in Kittery, ME; acute coronary occlus.; single

John A., d. 1/2/1893 at 61/0/1; apoplexy; farmer; married; b. Barrington; John Buzzell (Madbury) and Sarah Willey (Barrington)

John H., d. 6/19/1907 at 74; pneumonia; farmer; married; b. Barrington; Jonathan Buzzell (Barrington) and Olive Hill (Barrington)

John S., d. 2/8/1898 at 75/11/19; disease of liver; farmer; widower; b. Barrington; Samuel E. Buzzell (Barrington) and Lydia Buzzell (Barrington)

Laura E., d. 8/28/1961 at 69 in Rochester; circulatory failure; housewife; widow; b. Colorado Springs, CO; James M. Edney and Clara Coin; residence - Rochester

Levi H., d. 6/13/1958 at 81 in Rochester; intestinal bleeding; blacksmith; widower; b. Barrington; John H. Buzzell and Ann Emerson

Martha, d. 5/5/1929 at 77/4/12; at home; widow; b. Barrington; Timothy Tuttle (Barrington) and Mary S. Buzzell (Barrington)

Martha E., d. 5/30/1893 at 70/0/14; val. disease of heart; housewife; married; b. Barrington; Samuel Robinson and Susan Shaw

Mary S., d. 5/24/1914 at 83/7/16; widow; b. Durham; Andrew Daniels and Susan Priest

Maurice T., d. 12/26/1960 at 81 in Rochester; malignant myeloma; houseman; married; b. Lee; James Buzzell and Martha Tuttle; residence - Rochester

Nellie, d. 5/25/1929 at 73/2/24; at home; married; b. Strafford; Orrin Hill and Mary E. Foss (Strafford)

Olive J., d. 12/4/1895 at 66/11/10; heart disease; domestic; married; b. Barrington; Eben Young (Barrington) and Prudence Cate (Northwood)

Orrin P., d. 4/10/1908 at 48/8/23; pneumonia; farmer; married; b. Barrington; John A. Buzzell (Barrington) and Mary S. Daniels (Durham)

Samuel C., d. 9/16/1935 at 88/0/28; myocarditis; retired; widower; b. Barrington; Samuel R. Buzzell (Barrington) and Martha Robinson (Barrington)

Samuel R., d. 2/25/1895 at 70/10/10; cancer; farmer; widower; b. Barrington; Levi Buzzell (Barrington) and Lydia Robinson (Barrington)

Solomon, d. 5/23/1905 at 71/11/27; loss of cardiac compen.; farmer; married; b. Barrington; David Buzzell (Barrington) and Lois Leighton (Barrington)

Susan E., d. 9/26/1925 at 94/9/8; old age; retired; b. Wakefield; Ithial Allen (Wakefield) and Hannah Watson (Wakefield)

Walter, d. 11/2/1933 at 78/5/4 in Dover; angina pectoris; retired; married; b. Barrington; John S. Buzzell (Barrington) and Olive J. Young (Barrington)

William H., d. 3/20/1896 at 66/9; chronic gastritis; carriage builder; married; b. Barrington; Jeremiah Buzzell (Barrington) and Ann Winkley (Barrington)

CAHOON,
A. Pearl, d. 1/24/1987 at 69; homemaker; widow; b. MA
Eckley H., d. 10/11/1982 at 74; RR carman; married; b. MA

CALDWELL,
Clara E., d. 9/24/1935 at 71/0/27; arterio sclerosis; housewife; married; b. Germany; August Biderman (Germany)

Daniel T., d. 3/15/1904 at 70/6/3; valvular heart disease; farmer; married; b. Lee; William Caldwell (Lee) and Abigail Tibbetts (Madbury)

Dexter H., d. 1/18/1977 at 65 in Dover; foreman; married; b. NH; Harold Caldwell and Mabel Kennison

Edwin, d. 5/19/1938 at 69/9/3; chronic myocarditis; farmer; widower; b. Barrington; Daniel Caldwell (Barrington) and Mary Swain (Barrington)

Harold D., d. 4/27/1961 at 66 in Manchester; metastatic carcinoma; woodsman; married; b. Barrington; Henry Caldwell and Clara Biederman

Isaiah P., d. 8/5/1922 at 71/11/10; farmer; single; b. Barrington; John Caldwell (Barrington) and Sally Langley (Lee)

Nathaniel, d. 11/26/1897 at 74/7/3; p. paralysis; tailor; single; b. Barrington; William Caldwell (Lee) and Abigail Tebbetts (Madbury)

Ransom, d. 1/17/1928 at 79/11; pernicious anemia; blacksmith; single; b. Barrington; John Caldwell (Barrington) and Sally Langley (Lee)

Ruth E., d. 1/11/1979 at 70 in Dover; housewife; widow; b. NH

Sally, d. 12/30/1891 at 83; widow; Ephraim Langley (Lee) and Annie Jones (Lee)

CALEF,

Albert J., d. 3/12/1960 at 82 in Quincy, MA; ruptured aortic aneurysm; vice president; married; b. Barrington; Josiah R. Calef and Mary A. Chesley; residence - Quincy, MA

Austin L. F., d. 7/29/1954 at 83; heart disease; store proprietor; married; b. Barrington; Josiah R. Calef and Mary E. Chesley

Clarence L., d. 2/15/1986 at 92; store owner; widower; b. NH

Clellie M., d. 7/11/1963 at 90; acute myocardial infarction; housewife; widow; b. Barrington; George O.A. Chesley and Sarah Hill

Dorothy, d. 6/6/1969 at 70 in Boston, MA; term. bronchopneumonia; single; Austin L. Calef and Clellie M. Chesley

Leon C., d. 3/29/1979 at 81 in Dover; dealer; married; b. NH

Mary E., d. 3/21/1907 at 62/4/17; paresis; merchant; married; b. Pittsfield; John Chesley (Barnstead) and Sally Jenkins (Barnstead)

Roger L., d. 7/7/1984 at 59; owner, country store; married; b. NH

CAMILLO,
Charles C., d. 12/2/1963 at 83 in Dover; heart disease; laborer; widower; b. Italy; residence - Rochester

CAMPBELL,
Inez R., d. 3/31/1972 at 65 in Exeter; respiratory failure; housewife; widow; b. Ireland; Joseph Rosborough and Mary A. Leslie

Lee V., d. 6/7/1980 at 56 in Dover; custodian; married; b. NH

CANNEY,
Elizabeth, d. 11/20/1923 at 20/2/7; housekeeper; married; b. Everett, MA; James A. McDonald (Cape Breton) and Mary Smith (Cape Breton)

Jerome E., d. 9/20/1987 at 76 in Dover; trucker; married; b. NH

Minnie, d. 6/29/1934 at 48/0/11 in Dover; carcinoma stomach; housewife; married; b. Barrington; Benjamin Waterhouse (Barrington) and Mary E. Storey (Concord)

Norman A., d. 2/3/1961 at 74 in Dover; bronchopneumonia; blacksmith; widower; b. Barrington; Charles E. Canney and Victoria Chesley

Victoria C., d. 1/8/1899 at 37/8/23; pneumonia; housewife; married; b. Barrington; Jonathan Chesley and Sarah Chesley

CAPEN,
Augustus, d. 4/14/1913 at 1/2/26 in Dover; pneumonia

Eben E., d. 8/26/1910 at 75/11/4; nephritis; married; b. Barrington; Timothy Capen and Sarah Leathers

Elizabeth, b. 9/1/1960 at 72 in Dover; chronic myocarditis; housewife; widow; b. Barrington; John Freeman and Prudence Freeman; residence - Dover

Everett, d. 9/21/1958 at 58 in Manchester; carcinoma right lung; buffer; married; b. Barrington; Levi Capen and Clara Freeman; residence - S. Lebanon, ME

James, d. 9/1/1942 at 66/6/27 in Dover; acute intestinal obst.; farmer; single; b. Barrington; Timothy Capen (Old Town, ME) and Elmira Hanscom (Barrington)

Mary E., d. 6/29/1916 at 21/5/2 in Dover; married

Ned, d. 1/24/1937 at 42 in Springvale, ME; coronary thrombosis; shoemaker; divorced; b. Barrington; Levi Capen (Cambridge, MA) and Clara Freeman (Barrington)

Rhoda, d. 12/9/1909 at 70/9/7; carcinoma of uterus; housewife; married; b. Barrington; Benjamin Arlin and Sarah Brown

Theodore, d. 2/2/1960 at 74 in Dover; perforation duodenal ulcer; retired (taxi); married; b. Somerville, MA; Levi Capen and Clara Freeman; residence - Dover

Timothy, d. 6/21/1892 at 62 in Boston, MA; peritonitis; widower; b. Barrington

CARLL,

Harry (Harriet) Marrison, d. 6/19/1917 at 26/2/19; housewife; married; b. Strafford; John H. Marrison (Strafford) and Nellie Leighton (Barrington)

Lawrence, d. 3/7/1918 at 0/11/18; b. Barrington; Irving M. Carll (ME) and Harriette Marison (Strafford)

CARRIER,

Audrey Clair Brooks, d. 12/4/1986 at 57 in Smithfield, NC; homemaker; married; b. MA

CARSON,

Clarence P., d. 4/12/1979 at 76 in Rochester; shipyard worker; married; b. MA

Cora E., d. 1/20/1901 at 44/4/17 in Rochester; pneumonia; housewife; married; b. Barrington; Charles H. Cater (Barrington) and Maria Babb (Barrington)

CARTER,
Ernest H., d. 4/6/1948 at 87/3/22; cerebral arterioscler.; retired; divorced; b. East Kingston; Aaron Carter (Newton) and Adelaide Sweat
Frederick E., d. 4/26/1959 at 22; fractured skull; truck loader; widower; b. Cambridge, MA; Wilfred Carter and Mary O'Connor; residence - Rochester

CASE,
Minnie J., d. 4/28/1980 at 97 in MA; at home; widow; b. ME

CASLER,
Lester A., d. 11/17/1974 at -- in RI (burial)
Nicholas A., d. 3/18/1956 at 0/2 in Warren, RI; pneumonia

CASWELL,
Earle W., d. 1/25/1975 at 79 in Dover; patrolman; married; b. ME; George Caswell and Daisy Sanborn
Effie A., d. 12/30/1979 at 82 in Portsmouth; at home; widow; b. NH
Frank A., d. 10/29/1954 at 67 in Dover; intestinal obstruction; shoe cutter; married; b. Goffstown; Alphonso Caswell and Susan Brackett; residence - Dover
Mary E., d. 10/9/1965 at 75 in Rochester; coronary thrombosis; machine oper.; widow; b. Barrington; Orrin Buzzell and Jennie Trask; residence - Dover
Samuel E., d. 12/25/1898 at 72/1/25; apoplexy; farmer; single; b. Barrington; James Caswell and Lydia Evans

CATE,
Clarence E., d. 1/28/1954 at 82 in Haverhill, MA; carcinoma of prostate; married; b. Strafford; Joseph W. Cate and Hannah J. -----

Harry J., d. 7/13/1946 at 50/3/26 in Rochester; acute leukemia; mach. op.; married; b. Lee; Clarence Cate (Strafford) and Mattie E. Wood (Barrington)

Herbert C., d. 4/8/1900 at 0/8/23; bronchial pneumonia; b. Barrington; Clarence E. Cate (Strafford) and Mattie E. Wood (Barrington)

James D., d. 10/3/1894 at 64; cardiac mitral disease; soldier; James D. Cate and Ann Cater

Joseph H., d. 12/16/1913 at 83/4/17; old age; carpenter; widower; b. Dover; Eben Cate (Alton) and Nancy Hunt (Barrington)

Mattie E., d. 12/9/1966 at 74 in Haverhill, MA; coronary thrombosis

Richard, d. 9/1/1892 at 57/9/16; gangrene; laborer; married; b. Franklin; James Cate and Ann Cate

Sarah A., d. 9/9/1909 at 72/1/23; cholera morbus; no occ.; widow; b. Barrington; John P. Twombly and Lois Clarke

CATER,
Daniel, d. 4/8/1895 at 72/7/5; congestion of lungs; farmer; married; b. Barrington; Joel Cater (Barrington) and Mariam Babb (Barrington)

David Y., d. 7/14/1919 at 82/7/25; farmer; widower; b. Barrington; Ephraim Cater (Barrington) and Charlotte Otis (Strafford)

Elizabeth L., d. 5/20/1905 at 78/10/28; valvular heart disease; housewife; widow; b. Barrington; Jacob Hayes (Barrington) and Margaret Hayes (Barrington)

Flora E., d. 6/5/1916 at 55/7/6; housewife; married; b. Rochester; George W. Huntoon (Lancaster) and Melvina Drew (Jefferson)

Harry B., d. 11/1/1909 at --; b. Barrington; Henry F. Cater (Barrington) and Augusta Rollins (Strafford)
Horace G., d. 4/13/1903 at 78/7/12; cerebral hemorrhage; farmer; married; b. Barrington; John Cater, Jr. (Barrington) and Abiah Babb (Barrington)
Mariam, d. 10/20/1901 at 77/8/27 in Dover; osteo-sarcoma
Sarah A., d. 3/27/1905 at 78/3/19; valvular heart disease; widow; b. Barrington; Eliphalet Foss (Barrington) and Abigal Foss (Barrington)

CAVERLY,
Catherine, d. 10/2/1895 at 92/5/29; shock; domestic; single; b. Barrington; Nathaniel Caverly (Barrington) and Abigail Daniels (Barrington)
Elsie E., d. 7/18/1956 at 93; cerebral arteriosclerosis; shoe worker; single; b. Barrington; Charles H. Caverly and Lavina Boodey
Joseph H., d. 5/12/1937 at 81/8/12 in Strafford; toxemia
Lydia A., d. 3/22/1904 at 90/6/23; cardiac enlargement; housewife; widow; b. Barrington; Moses Caverly (Barrington) and Tamsin Caverly
Mary J., d. 9/20/1892 at 76/10/29; paralysis; domestic; widow; b. Barrington; Richard Critchett and Susan Clark
Mildred S., d. 8/27/1980 at 69 in Dover
Murl T., d. 8/26/1973 at 75 in Manchester; carcinoma of lung; inspector; married; b. MA; Thomas I. Caverly and Edna Trask

CAVERNO,
Pike, d. 4/22/1900 at 0/0/13; inanition; b. Barrington; John L. Caverno (Barrington) and Mabel Harvey (Northwood)

CENTRELLA,
Daniel, d. 6/12/1966 at 9; asphyxiation by drowning; student; b. Medford, MA; Frank Centrella and Pauline Sterry; residence - Somerville, MA

CHADBOURN[E],
Aaron W., d. 8/29/1958 at 66 in Rochester; coronary thrombosis; lumberman; married; b. Somerville, MA; Henry Chadbourne and Cora J. Willey; residence - Strafford

Miriam L., d. 5/16/1964 at 80 in Rochester; acute uremia; housewife; widow; b. Somerville, MA; Frederick W. Libby and Rachel A. Fogg; residence - Strafford

CHAPLIN,
Claude W., d. 8/27/1952 at 0 in Rochester; stillbirth; b. Rochester; Harold N. Chaplin and Julia M. Styles

Julia M., d. 12/17/1977 at 54 in Rochester; shoe worker; married; b. NH; Walter Stiles and Edna Edla

CHAPMAN,
Charles C., d. 10/25/1972 at 56 in Dover; rheumatic heart disease; laborer; married; b. NH; Robert Chapman and Agnes Clement; residence - Madbury

Dorothy M., d. 6/17/1944 at 46/10/14; gen. metasteses; housewife; married; b. Bristol, England; Hugh Roberts (England) and Mary ----- (England)

Ella J., d. 6/24/1935 at 81/0/2; mitral insufficiency; retired; widow; b. Compton; Dennis Snow and Martha Crooks (No. Adams, MA)

CHARETTE,
David E., d. 5/5/1947 at 0/0/1 in Rochester; cardiac dilation; b. Rochester; Earle Charette (Rochester) and Ruth Lenzi (Barrington)

CHASE,
Fred E., d. 10/9/1946 at 76 in Exeter; coronary sclerosis; laborer; widower; b. Newfield, ME; James Chase (Newfield, ME) and Henrietta Sanborn

CHERETTE,
Frances, d. 11/13/1950 at 74 in Concord; arteriosclerosis; housewife; widow; b. ME; Steven Beneph

CHESLEY,
Clara I., d. 1/1/1905 at 56/11/29; valvular dis. of heart; housewife; married; b. Barrington; Tobias R. Hall (Barrington) and Hannah M. Temple (Quincy, MA)
Elizabeth, d. 8/17/1934 at 94/8/4 in Exeter; cerebral apoplexy; retired; widow
Emeline S., d. 6/24/1902 at 74/5/21; exhaustion; housework; divorced; b. Barrington; Asa Chesley (Barrington) and Betsey Manson (Barrington)
Eva, d. 4/24/1930 at 80/2/24 in Concord; intes. nephritis; housework; single; b. Concord; George Chesley and Irene Ham
George H., d. 3/26/1909 at 86/3/11; pul. tuberculosis; engineer; married; b. Barrington; Lemuel Chesley (Barnstead) and Mary Merrill (Barnstead)
George O. A., d. 6/2/1919 at 73/9/24; farmer; married; b. Barnstead; Samuel Chesley (Barnstead) and Maria Scruton (Strafford)
Joel M., d. 4/4/1910 at 78/0/21; senility; farmer; married; b. Barrington; Joseph Chesley (Durham) and Maria W. Canney (Strafford)
Jonathan, d. 1/26/1897 at 66/9/11; pneumonia; farmer; married; Joseph Chesley (Barrington) and Maria Chesley (Strafford)
Joshua R., d. 5/16/1902 at 73/7/9; cerebral hemorrhage; farmer; widower; b. Barrington; Joseph R. Chesley and Mariah Canney
Mary, d. 10/9/1949 at 65 in Cambridge, MA; metastatic cancer; widow; residence - Cambridge, MA
Mary E., d. 7/29/1898 at 66/10/18; gangrene; housewife; married; b. Barrington; Daniel Swain (Barrington) and Betsey Ayers (Barrington)

Roscoe H., d. 11/9/1946 at 72/1/22 in New York, NY; buyer; married; b. Barrington; George Chesley (Barrington)

Sarah A., d. 10/23/1912 at 76/9/27; valvular heart disease; widow; b. Barrington; Asa Chesley (Barrington) and Bessie Manson (Barrington)

Sarah H., d. 11/2/1941 at 92/11/1 in Dover; coronary thrombosis; housewife; widow; b. Barrington; Hiram Hall (Barrington) and Maria Waterhouse (Orford, ME)

CHISHOLM,

Esther B., d. 4/3/1961 at 67 in Wolfeboro; coronary thrombosis; housewife; married; b. Barrington; Frank Brown and Eliza Allen; residence - Rochester

Raymond, d. 3/2/1969 at 73 in Rochester; pneumonia; farmer; widower; b. NH; Fred Chisholm and Annie -----; residence - Rochester

CHOUINARD,

Arthur A., d. 3/2/1987 at 80 in Rochester; millwright; widower; b. NH

CHURCH,

Charles, d. 4/14/1899 at 79/0/6; pneumonia; farmer; single; b. Barrington; Jonathan Church (Barrington) and Nancy Morrill

CILLEY,

Clarence W., d. 4/2/1944 at 57/3/8 in Somersworth; cerebral hemorrhage; painter; married; b. Holyoke, MA; William P. Cilley (Gonic) and Emma L. Cilley

Edna, d. 3/6/1969 at 77 in Rochester; metastatic carcinoma; housewife; widow; b. NH; Frank Otis and Ida Garland; residence - Somersworth

Edna M., d. 10/17/1978 at 85 in Rochester; housewife; widow; b. NH; David Graham and Jennie McClelland

Emma L., d. 6/18/1914 at 65/0/9; housewife; married; b. Laconia; Alvah Harrise and ----- Patch

L. Etta, d. 7/1/1935 at 73/7/4 in Dover; cerebral hemorrhage; housewife; married

William P., d. 3/17/1937 at 88/8/16 in Rochester; labor pneumonia; retired; widower; b. Gonic; Suell G. Cilley (Enfield) and Ann Clough (Barnstead)

CLANCY,

Helen G., d. 12/5/1972 at 68; acute cardiac failure; housewife; widow; b. NH; John Hughes and Kate Cassily

CLARK,

Daniel B., d. 3/21/1929 at 68/11/22; farmer; single; b. Barrington; Dennis Clark (Strafford) and Myra Clark (Strafford)

Eliza J., d. 6/8/1922 at 85/8/1; no occ.; widow; b. Barrington; Joseph Daniels (Strafford) and Eliza Hill (Strafford)

Elizabeth A., d. 11/11/1935 at 82/7/28 in Dover; interstitial nephritis; retired; widow

Everett E., d. 9/19/1966 at 78 in Kittery, ME; medullary failure; farmer; married; b. NH; Frank H. Clark and Lizza Swain

Fred F., d. 1/29/1948 at 64/2/7 in Lee; heart disease; laborer; widower; b. Strafford; Royal K. Clark (Dover) and Etta Twombly (Barrington)

George M., d. 10/5/1964 at 63 in Rochester; coronary heart disease; truck driver; widower; b. Barrington; Marshall Clark and Ada Freeman; residence - Rochester

Johanna V., d. 8/30/1943 at 82/3/28 in Northwood; malig. lymphoma; housewife; married; b. Charlestown, MA; John Vaughn (Ireland) and Catherine Connors (Ireland)

Mary D., d. 10/4/1971 at 87 in Dover; cardiovascular accident; housewife; widow; b. NH; John Daniels and Cora Arlin

Polly, d. 1/6/1892 at 90/11/14; old age; housekeeper; widow;
b. Milton; Aaron Varney and Annie Clemons

Royal K., d. 1/10/1919 at 67/1/11; farmer; married; b. Dover;
Jonathan Clark (Strafford) and Ellen Hussey (Dover)

Sarah E., d. 9/13/1967 at 81 in Rochester; cerebro-vascular
acc.; secretary; widow; b. Barrington; Samuel Henderson
and Sarah Locke; residence - Rochester

Wayne S., d. 2/21/1972 at 27; cerebral hemorrhage;
assembler; married; b. NH; Charles A. Clark and Alice M.
Gallien; residence - Newmarket

CLARKE,

daughter, d. 7/29/1913 at 0/0/0; stillborn; b. Barrington;
Marshall Clarke (Barrington) and Ada Freeman
(Barrington)

Ada, d. 7/29/1913 at 39; placentic praeina; housewife;
married; b. Barrington; Wilbur Freeman (Barrington) and
Melissa Waterhouse (Barrington)

Dennis, d. 2/15/1896 at 79/3/20; bronchitis; farmer; married;
b. Barrington; John Caverly

Sarah A., d. 5/25/1915 at 82/5/10; housewife; widow; b.
Sandwich; Tobias Bean (Sandwich) and Elizabeth
Richardson (Sandwich)

Shirlie A., d. 10/6/1970 at 45 in Dover; hanging; housewife;
married; b. TX; John Robinson and Daisy -----; residence
- Dover

CLAY,

Hester V., d. 10/7/1979 at 87 in Rochester; housewife;
married; b. MA

Thomas L., d. 12/1/1986 at 62; security guard; married; b.
MA

CLEMENT,

Florence B., d. 7/27/1974 at 58 in Rochester; cook; married;
b. NH; Glenn Walker and Eva Willey

George E., d. 11/19/1961 at 73 in Madbury; cerebral thrombosis; farmer; married; b. Rollinsford; William H. Clement and Katherine Maloney; residence - Madbury

Kathleen L., d. 1/4/1961 at 27 in Dover; carcinomatosis; mach. oper.; married; b. Rockland, ME; ----- Ayer and Berdina Clark; residence - Madbury

Robert L., d. 11/5/1975 at 50 in Dover; mach. oper.; married; George Clement and Bertha Norman

CLERK,
Gladys M., d. 10/7/1981 at 85 in Rochester; housewife; married; b. NH

Smith E., Jr., d. 2/7/1981 at 53; machinist; married; b. PA

CLEVELAND,
George E., d. 8/9/1956 at 84 in Rochester; carcinoma of esophagus; machinist; widower; b. Morrisville, VT; Charles A. Cleveland and Louise Harris

CLITES,
Dale H., d. 3/14/1980 at 53 in Dover

CLOTHIER,
Martha M., d. 7/19/1982 at 76 in Dover

CLOW,
Arlington I., d. 6/22/1953 at 73 in Dover; chr. nephritis; ret. sup. sch.; married; b. Canada; Edwin Clough and Maria Ingalls

Myrtle F., d. 11/29/1969 at 85 in Dover; cerebro-vasc. acc.; housewife; widow; b. ME; Franklin J. Fenderson and Georgia A. Goss

COGSWELL,
Alva A., d. 7/23/1980 at 82 in Dover; farmer; married; b. ME

COLBY,
Bert E., d. 4/2/1957 at 66; coronary thrombosis; loom fixer; married; b. Grantham; Edwin Colby and Angie Dube
Marguerite A., d. 4/26/1966 at 54; myocardial infarc.; housewife; married; b. NS; Owen Ball and Elizabeth Hatfield

COLE,
Annie M., d. 5/1/1900 at 64/6/8; pneumonia; housewife; married; b. Barrington; Ichabod Seavey (Barrington) and Relief Corson (Lebanon, ME)

COLT,
Jennie, d. 2/5/1892 at 8/8/23; peritonitis; b. Barrington; Morris Colt and Zoe Bomke

CONNELL,
Florence M., d. 12/4/1975 at 66 in Dover; housework; single; William S. Connell and Vila M. Kimball

CONROY,
John P., d. 7/1/1978 at 60 in MA

CONWAY,
Frederick, d. 8/3/1978 at 94 in Dover; maintenance; married; b. NY; Michael Conway and Anastasia Cain
Grace B., d. 8/28/1979 at 82 in Dover; factory worker; widow; b. MA

COOK,
John W., Sr., d. 9/6/1968 at 61 in Gonic; pneumonia; retired; married; b. NH; Joshua M. Cook and Eva Gagnon; residence - Gonic

CORBETT,
Hollie B., d. 2/13/1946 at 48/8; pulmonary embolism; farmer; married; b. Colebrook; Robert Corbett (NS) and Dora Sweeney (Burlington, VT)

CORSON,
Aaron F., d. 7/28/1901 at 68/5/11; Bright's disease; shoemaker; married; b. Lebanon, ME; John Corson (ME) and Eliza Jones (ME)
Abbie, d. 1/25/1905 at 69/10/25; hemorrhage; widow; b. Rochester; George Howe (Rochester)
Annie M., d. 2/13/1913 at 73/10/16; mitral regurgitation; no occ.; widow; b. Barrington; Enoch Twombly (Strafford) and Lucinda Daniels (Strafford)
Grace E., d. 11/20/1962 at 87 in Dover; cerebral thrombosis; nurse; single; b. NH; Henry D. Corson and Cora Cater; residence - Dover
Oliver Palmer, d. 5/10/1916 at 60/7/5; farmer; married; b. Stratham; Dow Corson (East Wood) and Melinda Arlin (Strafford)
Oscar F., d. 3/20/1908 at 70/10/9; growth in bowels; farmer; married; b. Raynham, MA; James Corson (Lebanon, ME) and Delia Hathaway (S. Bridgewater, MA)

COTTERMAN,
Theodore S., d. 8/22/1953 at 75; coronary occlusion; machinist; widower; b. Crawford Co., PA; Eli Cotterman and Lovina Wagner; residence - Boston, MA

COUGHFER,
Belle R., d. 8/30/1916 at 67

COUGHLIN,
David F., d. 10/4/1980 at 0 in Farmington
Florence B., d. 10/27/1986 at 70; housewife; married; b. MA

COUTURE,
Armand, d. 2/13/1979 at 54 in Lynn, MA

COWELL,
Cornelius, d. 12/30/1906 at 34; tuberculosis; laborer; single; b. S. America

COWING,
John E., d. 8/13/1962 at 74 in Manchester; adenocarcinoma

COX,
Brian M., d. 8/26/1981 at 8; student; b. NY

CRANDLEMIRE,
Paul I., d. 6/24/1971 at 55 in North Conway; acute myocardial infarc.; machinist; married; b. ME; Fayette Crandlemire and Georgia Crandlemire

CRITCHETT,
Dwight, d. 2/5/1927 at 21/2/24 in Phoenix, AZ; chr. anthritis; at home; single; b. Barrington; J. S. Critchett (Barrington) and Emma F. Sewall (Barrington)
Emma F., d. 1/8/1954 at 86; apoplexy; housewife; widow; b. Barrington; Charles W. Sewall and Nellie E. Layne
Frank, d. 10/22/1969 at 76 in Rochester; cardiac arrest; bookkeeper; married; b. NH; Loring J. Critchett and Emma F. Sewell
Grace, d. 11/22/1944 at 58/7/20 in Washington, DC; acute dil'n of heart; US Gov't; single; b. NH; J. Loring Critchett (NH) and Emma F. Sewall (NH)
J. Loren, d. 10/8/1919 at 65/1/9; farmer; married; b. Barrington; John Critchett (Barrington) and Lucy M. Young (Barrington)
John, d. 12/27/1905 at 86/11/14; angina; farmer; married; b. Barrington; Richard Critchett (Strafford) and Susan Clark (Barrington)

Lucy M., d. 12/2/1912 at 89/10/26; acute indigestion; widow; b. Barrington; Eben Young (Barrington) and Prudence Cate (Northwood)

CROCKET,
Nettie, d. 8/14/1918 at 65/4/27; housewife; married; b. Rockport; Ephraim Harkness (Rockport) and Jane Upham (Rockport)

CROSBY,
Annie, d. 2/2/1955 at 91 in Newton, MA; coronary occlusion; widow; b. Barrington; residence - Newton, MA
Beatrice C., d. 9/11/1974 at 77 in Dover; housewife; widow; b. MA; James T. Costello and Lily Carter
Ethel May, d. 8/19/1897 at 0/11/18; cholera infantum; b. Medway, MA; Rev. J. F. Crosby (Neponset, MA) and Eva E. Hale (Barrington)
Robert S., d. 11/16/1972 at 77 in Portland, ME

CROSS,
William, d. 6/6/1936 at 21; accidental drowning; painter; single; William Cross (Canada) and Marie Benoit (Canada)

CROTEAU,
Mary R., d. 10/5/1978 at 23; cashier; single; b. NH; Robert E. Croteau and Rita Bolduc

CUMMINGS,
Harry H., d. 10/25/1959 at 77 in Dover; cerebral hemorrhage; mail clerk; married; b. Dover; Frank Cummings and Carrie Nourse; residence - Somersworth

CUNNINGHAM,
Clayton, d. 9/2/1938 at 69/2; carcinoma of liver; retired; married; b. Antigonish, NS; A. Cunningham

Wilfred M., d. 12/5/1964 at 41 in Nashua; myocardial infarction; sub contractor; married; b. Dover; M. Alfred Cunningham and Mary Foley

CURRIER,
Maude W., d. 2/17/1959 at 78 in Haverhill, MA; cerebral hemorrhage; shoe stitcher; b. Rockport, ME; Almon E. Gray and Amanda C. Kimball; residence - Haverhill, MA

CUSTEAU,
Arzelia, d. 8/20/1971 at 90 in Dover; pneumonia; housewife; married; b. Canada; Jerome Beauregard; residence - Madbury

DAIGNEAULT,
Alice F., d. 10/27/1961 at 65 in Lawrence, MA; cer. vascular thrombosis; housewife; widow; b. Dover; Edwin F. Locke and Mary E. Cary; residence - Lawrence, MA

DAME,
Mary, d. 4/17/1891 at 72; widow; Benjamin Hayes (Strafford) and Polly Littlefield (Barnstead)

DANFORTH,
Betsey, d. 1/13/1892 at 73/4/16; acute bronchitis; housekeeper; widow; b. Barrington; John Jones and Harmate Hill
Frank J., d. 10/14/1925 at 67 in Nottingham; cerebral apoplexy; laborer; widower; b. Barrington
Jane, d. 11/18/1910 at 62; bronchitis; housework; married; b. NY; George Chamberlin and Mary A. Lynch

DANIEL, (see McDaniels)
Frank A., d. 2/19/1937 at 60/1/19 in So. Portland, ME; coronary occlusion; RR engineer; married; b. Barrington;

John C. McDaniels (Strafford) and Cora Arlin (Barrington)

DANIELS,
Charles N., d. 11/22/1939 at 82/4/9 in Dover; lobar pneumonia; farmer; widower; b. Strafford; Peltiah Daniels (Strafford) and Comfort Chase (Lyndonville, VT)
Cora, d. 8/13/1929 at 74/10/6; at home; married; b. Barrington; Dill Arlin (Barrington) and Mary Robertson (Rochester)
Elizabeth T., d. 11/15/1904 at 82/9/13; heart disease; widow; b. Smithfield, RI; John Sherman
Ira T., d. 3/23/1897 at 77/0/5; hepatits and nephritis; merchant; single; b. Barnstead; Andrew Daniels (Barrington) and Susan Priest (Nottingham)
John C., d. 3/28/1931 at 78; cere. hemorrhage; farmer; widower; b. Strafford; Peltieth Daniels (Strafford) and Comfort Chase (Lindenb'g, VT)
Martha E., d. 11/23/1914 at 37/3/7 in Portland, ME; housewife; married; Allen S. Swasey (Ossipee) and Martha Plummer

DARLING,
Arlene C., d. 11/8/1980 at 54 in Rochester; LPN nurse; married; b. MA
Elva, d. 4/22/1963 at 68 in Concord; pneumonia; widow; b. Dorchester, MA; James A. McDowell and Anna F. Beck
Jeff, d. 6/11/1959 at 0/0/1 in Dover; immaturity; b. Dover; David A. Darling and Arlene C. Patrone
Susan, d. 6/12/1959 at 0/0/1-½ in Dover; immaturity; b. Dover; David A. Darling and Arlene C. Patrone

DARNELL,
George E., d. 11/29/1983 at 56 in Portsmouth; military ret.; married; b. OK

DASH,
Douglas D., d. 7/2/1974 at 15; student; single; b. MA; Douglas C. Dash and Patricia A. Kilderry

DAVIS,
Annie, d. 2/16/1971 at 95 in Pittsfield; congestive heart fail.; housewife; widow; b. MA; Cornelius O'Brien and Mary Mahoney

Beatrice M., d. 8/21/1961 at 43 in Nottingham; ventricular fibrillation; no occ.; single; b. Newfields; Charles Davis and Mabel Clark; residence - Nottingham

Bessie H., d. 6/7/1955 at 74 in Dover; intestinal obstruction; housework; married; b. Somerville, MA; Alvah Hanscomb and Prudence Arlin; residence - Dover

Clyde R., d. 2/8/1965 at 58 in Exeter; lobar pneumonia; lumberjack; married; b. Union, ME; William Davis and Linda Robbins; residence - Epping

Donald J., d. 11/21/1974 at 66 in Dover; foreman; married; b. NH; Charles S. Davis and Minnie G. Glover

Fred B., d. 1/14/1960 at 76 in Dover; arteriosclerotic hrt. dis.; laborer; widower; b. Newmarket; Horace Davis and Mary Currier; residence - Dover

George A., d. 12/12/1983 at 87 in Rochester; electrician; married; b. MA

Gerald B., d. 10/22/1955 at 82 in Portsmouth; coronary thrombosis; merchant; widower; b. Bethel, ME; Richmond Davis and Sarah M. True; residence - Portsmouth

Ira S., d. 9/26/1892 at 63; septicemia; blacksmith; married; b. Bolton, Canada; Joseph Davis and Maria Davis

Joseph E., d. 4/12/1969 at 72 in Nottingham; arteriosclerotic heart dis.

Joseph L., d. 7/22/1979 at 57 in Concord; maintenance man; single; b. NH

Joseph O., d. 2/16/1913 at 62/4/16; chronic int'l nephritis; laborer; married; b. Barrington

Lottie E., d. 4/21/1953 at 51 in Exeter; malig. lymphoma; housewife; married; b. Barrington; George Emerson and Bessie Hanscom; residence - Epping

Madeleine N., d. 6/23/1968 at 67 in Dover; cerebral thrombosis; housewife; widow; b. NH; Louis O. Hawkins and Donna Mills

Oscar H., d. 2/25/1971 at 80; respiratory arrest

Sarah, d. 8/9/1920 at 86/8/2; retired; widow; b. Canada; John Cooey (Canada) and Leafy Sweer (Canada)

Sarah O., d. 5/19/1969 at 66 in Nottingham; myocardial infarc.

Stella B., d. 7/20/1985 at 66 in Rochester; housewife; widow; b. NH

Vinnie May, d. 12/26/1950 at 77 in Portsmouth; coronary thrombosis; at home; married; b. Barrington; George A. Smallcon and Emeralda J. Howe; residence - Portsmouth

William S., d. 2/22/1945 at 70/10/28 in Rochester; ac. lymph. leukemia; retired; married; b. Walden, VT; Ira Davis (Walden, VT) and Sarah Coocy (Canada)

DAY,

Flora Belle, d. 4/15/1976 at 80 in Portland, ME

George L., d. 6/10/1967 at 88 in Rochester; myocardial failure; caretaker; married; b. Northwood; Clarke M. Day and Ida F. Emerson

DEARBORN,

Etta Belle, d. 4/10/1945 at 77/5/23; coronary thrombosis; librarian; widow; b. Lakeport; George Dow (Ashland) and Emma Bryant (Northfield)

Harriett, d. 3/2/1911 at 78/4/16; rheumatism and bronchitis; housewife; married; b. Strafford; John Clark and Polly Varney

Mary P., d. 1/13/1890 at 82/9/9; married; b. Woodstock; Elisha Locke (Barrington) and Sophia Pinkham (Durham)

Stanley S., d. 1/30/1986 at 73; health inspector; married; b. MA

DECATUR,
Georgie E., d. 8/4/1973 at 84 in Framingham, MA; cystadenoma of pancreas
Lillian L., d. 5/7/1959 at 75 in Barnstable, MA; cerebro-vasc. hem.; residence - Centerville, MA
Nellie S., d. 1/23/1924 at 72/4/10; housewife; married; b. Barrington; John B. Hall (Barrington) and Lydia S. Foss (Barrington)
Ralph, d. 12/--/1951 at 62 in Dedham, MA; coronary thrombosis

DEMERITT,
Ada T., d. 11/26/1927 at 20/3/20 in Strafford; acute gastritis; housewife; married; b. Dorchester, MA; Timothy Fuller (ME) and Evelyn Costigan (ME)
Alice M., d. 6/25/1981 at 91 in Wolfeboro
Anna F., d. 4/18/1967 at 81 in Haverhill, MA; cerebral hemorrhage; residence - Haverhill, MA
Earl I., d. 4/16/1974 at 64 in Concord; mechanic; divorced; b. NH; Walter C. Demeritt and Margaret Gallant
John Wesley, d. 6/27/1945 at 62/4/29 in Rochester; cerebral hemorrhage; wood ch'p; married; b. Barrington; Samuel Demeritt (Barrington) and Sarah Locke (Dover)
Lilla L., d. 6/22/1948 at 79/0/25 in Bridgewater, MA; coronary thrombosis; b. Barrington; Greenleaf Swain and Elizabeth -----
Mabel, d. 9/29/1918 at 24/2/5 in Manchester; nurse; single; b. Barrington; Samuel Demeritte and Elizabeth Demeritte
Margaret A., d. 6/25/1952 at 66 in Rochester; cerebral hemorrhage; housewife; married; b. PEI; Gilbert Gallant and Mary Peters

Philip O., d. 9/14/1946 at 36/5/15 in Rochester; mult. frac. & hemor.; laborer; divorced; b. Barrington; John Demeritt (Barrington) and Alice Whitehouse (Barrington)

Tamson H., d. 1/24/1898 at 88 in Loudon; exhaustion; at home; widow

Walter C., d. 12/23/1960 at 76 in Strafford; cerebral thrombosis; farmer; widower; b. Barrington; Samuel P. DeMeritt and Elizabeth S. Locke; residence - Strafford

DESHARNEIS,
Rosie, d. 12/18/1892 at 2/6; diphtheria; b. Barrington; Ferd. Desharneis and Zoe Beaucham

DESHON,
Nathaniel W., d. 1/20/1964 at 68 in Manchester; metastatic carcinomatosis; machinist; married; b. Lynn, MA; George E. Deshon and Ann Winters

DESMARAIS,
Emilien J., d. 6/13/1964 at 65; coronary thrombosis; shoe worker; married; b. Rochester; Hegisippe Desmarais and Octavie Desmarais; residence - Rochester

DEVER,
Lawrence, d. 8/12/1980 at 55 in Rochester; mechanic; married; b. MA

DEWITT,
daughter, d. 11/18/1972 at -- in Rochester; asphyxia in utero; b. NH; Henry Dewitt and Susan M. Laney

DEXTER,
John W., d. 12/21/1934 at 71/2/15; cerebral hemorrhage; farmer; married; b. NS; James Dexter (NS) and Sarah Davis (NS)

Sarah A., d. 7/29/1907 at 69/10/11; dropsy; housekeeper; widow; b. NS; Samuel Davis (Wales) and Margaret Harris (Wales)

DIONNE,
Henry A., d. 10/30/1984 at 73 in Manchester; machinist; married; b. NH

DIVIRGILIO,
Barbara A., d. 9/28/1986 at 55 in Dover; assembler; divorced; b. MA
Nicholas G., d. 1/3/1985 at 58 in Portsmouth; pipefitter; married; b. MA

DODGE,
daughter, d. 7/27/1972 at -- in Dover; unknown cause; b. NH; Elona Estes
Bernice, d. 10/9/1918 at 9/10/19 in Rochester; b. Barrington; Herman Dodge (Rochester) and Louise Babb (Barrington)
Elizabeth A., d. 6/8/1937 at 68/5/5 in East Barrington; coronary thrombosis; housewife; widow; Timothy Ahern and Mary Corcoras
Ernest E., d. 2/3/1957 at 63 in Manchester; carcinoma left lung; shoe worker; divorced; b. Barrington; Edward Dodge and Mary A. Lingard
Herman A., d. 4/30/1918 at 34/11/19; farmer; married; b. Rochester; Frank Dodge (New Durham) and Rosilla Pearl (Strafford)
Louise G., d. 8/2/1967 at 79 in Dover; coronary thrombosis; housewife; widow; b. Barrington; John F. Babb and Sarah G. Wood; residence - Dover
Robert A., d. 9/20/1978 at 67; laborer; married; b. NH; Herman Dodge and Louise Babb

Robert E., d. 3/9/1930 at 0/9/21; pneumonia; b. Rochester; Ernest Dodge (Barrington) and Pauline Williams (Berwick, ME)

Robert L., d. 1/1/1971 at 32 in Dover; exsanguination; watchman; married; b. NH; Robert E. Dodge and Mary E. Conway

DONADIO,
Francis M., d. 12/29/1979 at 46 in Rochester; electrician; married; b. MA

DONAHUE,
Robert C., d. 7/4/1953 at 22; accidental drown.; 1st C. Petty O.; single; b. Boston, MA; Walter F. Donahue and Mary L. Melanson; residence - Rollinsford

DOWNEY,
Malcomb Sidney, d. 1/28/1921 at 0/4/5; b. Rochester; ----- Downey

DOWNING,
son, d. 11/4/1976 at 0 in Exeter; b. NH; Vincent B. Downing and Donna L. Johnson
Sarah A., d. 12/1/1979 at 0 in Boston, MA; b. MA

DOWNS,
son, d. 11/19/1910 at 0/0/0; asphyxiation; b. Barrington; Myrtle Downs (Lebanon, ME)
Shirley W., d. 1/18/1985 at 57; copywriter; married; b. OR

DOYON,
Ernest L., d. 1/12/1978 at 78; beamer; married; b. Canada; Wilfred Doyon and Delina Paree

DRAPEAU,

Joseph W., d. 6/15/1927 at 40/2/24 in North Barrington; natural causes; farmer; married; b. Somersworth; Cleophas Drapeau (Canada) and Rose Duclow (Canada)

Robert J., d. 2/5/1974 at 58 in Dover; chipper; married; b. NH; Amos Drapeau and Margaret Glode

DREW,

Benjamin V., d. 7/31/1954 at 60 in Dover; coronary thrombosis; machinist; married; b. Barrington; Greenleaf S. Drew and Neoma Miles; residence - Dover

Clarence E., d. 9/10/1943 at 57/11/22 in Rollinsford; coronary thrombosis; loco. eng.; married; b. Cape Girardeau, MO; Greenleaf S. Drew (Barrington) and Neoma V. Miles (Perryville, MO)

Doris R., d. 2/1/1978 at 76 in Dover; housewife; married; b. NH; Albert A. Pray and Alice Colony

Frank E., d. 3/29/1926 at 72/6/25; chr. myracorditis; farmer; married; b. Barrington; Greenleaf Drew (Barrington) and Mary E. Chesley (Barrington)

Frederick E., d. 5/11/1968 at 79 in Kittery, ME; myocardial infarction; confectioner; married; b. MO; Greenleaf Drew and Neoma Miles

George A., d. 9/17/1894 at 31/5/14; phthisis pulmonalis; laborer; married; Charlotte Babb (Barrington)

George Manson, d. 4/1/1945 at 70/11/18; carcinoma rectum; retired; widower; b. Pittsfield; Albert R. Drew (Strafford) and Mary Merrifield (Pittsfield)

Gladys E., d. 8/23/1969 at 79 in Dover; arteriosclerotic hrt. dis.

J. R., d. 3/5/1893 at 71/10/21; penumonia; farmer; married; b. Barrington; J. Drew (Dover) and Elizabeth Winkley (Barrington)

John T., d. 2/19/1893 at 82/10; old age; farmer; widower; b. Barrington; Meshach Drew (Barrington) and Ann Twombly (Madbury)

Joseph, d. 9/19/1897 at 0/1/14; con. cyanosis; b. Barrington; G. S. Drew (Barrington) and Noma Miles (Perryville)

Joseph E., d. 7/4/1980 at 69 in Rochester; carpenter; single; b. NH

Lydia C., d. 7/9/1981 at 94 in Dover; housewife; widow

Mary E., d. 11/20/1903 at 68/8/6; apoplexy; housewife; b. Barrington; Richard Swain (Barrington) and Sally Sherburne (Barrington)

Mary Elizabeth, d. 6/12/1899 at 64/4/18; cerebral hemorrhage; at home; widow; b. Barrington; Samuel Chesley (Barnstead) and Maria Scruton (Strafford)

Nancy, d. 2/13/1896 at 80/7/9; old age; at home; single; b. Barrington; Meshick Drew (Barrington) and Emma Twombly (Madbury)

Sarah N., d. 4/22/1914 at 77 in Nashua; widow

Sophia, d. 1/26/1901 at -- in Portland, ME; pneumonia

DRINKWINE,
Joseph, d. 6/8/1952 at 69 in Dover; cirrhosis of liver; fireman; single; b. Marlboro, MA; Frank Boivin and Rose Bonlay

DUDLEY,
Evelyn L., d. 10/26/1972 at 51; acute cardiac failure; housewife; married; b. ME; Robert Enman and Lena Lane; residence - Northwood

H. O., d. 3/31/1906 at 72/3/18; lobic pneumonia; retired; married; b. Alton; Otis P. Dudley and Zmilia Pickering

DURGIN,
Mary J., d. 3/16/1958 at 86 in Strafford; toxemia-jaundice; nurse; single; b. Strafford; Darius C. Durgin and Elizabeth A. Hoyt

DUSTIN,
Mary B., d. 10/13/1903 at 78/7/3; mitral insufficiency; housewife; widow; b. Stoneham, MA; E. Noble (Stoneham, MA)

DUTTON,
Maurice W., d. 4/29/1973 at 60 in Rochester; carcinoma of lung; machine oper.; married; b. ME; Athorn N. Dutton and Willa E. Lunt
Willa E., d. 1/12/1957 at 78; uremia; housewife; married; b. Orrington, ME; William A. Lunt and Hattie Seavey

DZEN,
John E., d. 1/6/1945 at 54/3/11 in Dover; cerebral hemorrhage; farmer; married; b. Russia; Ernest Dzen (Russia)
Ruby M., d. 8/21/1981 at 79 in Dover

EASTMAN,
Margaret P., d. 10/11/1955 at 74 in McCall, ID; acute myocardial infarction; housewife; married; b. New Hampton; Frank Preston and Adelaide G. Hubbard; residence - Atascadero, CA

EATON,
Frederick A., d. 8/2/1942 at 71/2/26; fractured skull; machinist; married; b. Graniteville, MA; George Eaton (Coaticook, Canada) and Eliza Mayhew (London, England)

EDIN,
Martha J., d. 7/14/1965 at 60 in Dover; cerebral hemorrhage; electronics; married; b. Sweden; Carl A. Johnson and Tekla Ruff
Rubin E., d. 10/3/1972 at 72 in Dover; respiratory failure; inspector; widower; b. RI; Erik Edin and Anna N. Olsson

EDMUNDS,
Peter, d. 1/28/1925 at 75; hemmor. from stomach; laborer; widower; b. Canada

EDNEY,
Clara Coin, d. 5/7/1950 at 92/3/4 in Rochester; arteriosclerosis; housewife; widow; b. OH; Thomas P. Coin and Rebecca Johnston

EGERTON,
Albert M., d. 12/2/1972 at 65 in Rochester; acute occlusion; auto mechanic; married; b. MA; Francis Egerton and Helen E. Moore

EICKLER,
Anna Eva, d. 4/23/1915 at --; b. Barrington; Herbert W. Eickler (Plantsville) and Jenefer A. Wheeler (Orange, MA)

ELDRIDGE,
Celia, d. 3/12/1966 at 54 in Rochester; respiratory insufficiency; housewife; married; b. East Boston, MA; Albino Dionizio and Mary Viera
Francis W., d. 5/21/1976 at 87 in Greene, ME; policeman; widower; b. MA; Peter Eldridge and Elizabeth Cavill
Sophia, d. 3/19/1973 at 83; coronary thrombosis; housewife; married; b. MA; Daniel Ahearn and Mary Pitts

ELLIOTT,
Angela M., d. 11/22/1975 at 0/0/2 in Rochester; b. NH; Arthur Elliott and Lorraine Brown
Catherine, d. 12/30/1933 at 0/2/13; calillam bronchitis; b. Barrington; Kelley Elliott (Canaan) and Susan Sargent (Danville)
H. Murray, d. 1/12/1975 at 85 in Rochester; Episc. priest; married; b. Canada; Oscar Elliott and Linda Keddy

Henry E., d. 10/15/1939 at 89/5; cerebral hemorrhage; farmer; divorced; b. Canaan; Henry G. Elliott and Martha Elliott

Kelley E., d. 10/28/1956 at 75 in Exeter; generalized arteriosclerosis; lumber cutter; married; b. Orange; Henry E. Elliott and Hattie Hamlet

Kelly, d. 5/16/1965 at 2; asphyxiation; b. Rochester; Clayton Elliott and Priscilla Libby; residence - Rochester

Lora M., d. 7/23/1984 at 81 in Exeter; Navy Yard laborer; widow; b. NH

Mark A., d. 5/11/1974 at -- in Rochester; single; b. NH; Arthur Elliott and Lorraine Brown

Seymour M., d. 3/10/1948 at 94/5/21 in Haverhill, MA; myocarditis; shoe worker; widower; b. Gilford; Joseph Elliott (Barnstead) and Martha Tuttle

Susan N., d. 11/9/1986 at 85 in Dover; housewife; widow; b. NH

ELLIS,

Harold R., d. 5/21/1975 at 71 in Rochester; retired; married; b. NH; Harry Ellis and Etta Rogers

ELLISON,

daughter, d. 1/12/1904 at 0/0/0; premature birth; b. Barrington; Ernest Ellison (Barrington) and Maude Morrison (Nottingham)

son, d. 12/4/1905 at 0/0/0; premature birth; b. Barrington; Ernest Ellison (Barrington) and Maude Morrison (Nottingham)

son, d. 9/1/1909 at 0/0/1; premature birth; b. Barrington; Ernest Ellison (Barrington) and Maud Morrison (Nottingham)

son, d. 9/3/1914 at 0/0/0; b. Barrington; Walter Ellison (Nottingham) and Alta Grover (Nottingham)

Alta M., d. 2/21/1938 at 49/4/20; diabetes mellitus; housewife; married; b. Nottingham; Samuel Woodbury (Nottingham) and Ida Ella Leathers (Nottingham)

Charles A., d. 10/19/1986 at 74 in Exeter; horticulturist; single; b. NH

Charles O., d. 9/5/1901 at 15/9/22; appendicitis; farmer; single; b. Barrington; B. Frank Ellison (Barrington) and Georgia A. Emerson (Madbury)

Edgar E., d. 6/22/1971 at 56 in Dover; acute myocardial infarc.; machinist; married; b. NH; Ernest E. Ellison and Maude Marrison

Ernest E., d. 8/21/1964 at 78 in Rochester; myocardial failure; sawyer; widower; b. Barrington; William A. Ellison and Etta M. Drew

Etta M., d. 8/23/1955 at 88 in York, ME; coronary thrombosis; widow; b. Barrington; Martin Drew and Sarah Watson

Evelyn, d. 4/12/1959 at 42 in Boston, MA; mult. pulmonary emboli; shoe worker; married; Kelley Elliott and Susan Sargent

Frank B., d. 9/10/1908 at 69/10/29; consumption; farmer; married; b. Barrington; Joseph Ellison (Barrington) and Betsey Dow (Durham)

Georgianna, d. 4/13/1914 at 70/4/4; at home; widow; b. Madbury; James M. Emerson (Lee) and Eliza A. Drew (Madison)

John, d. 9/2/1905 at 0/8/12; whooping cough; b. Northwood; Ernest Ellison (Barrington) and Maud M. Morrison (Nottingham)

Maude N., d. 3/22/1942 at 57/5/4 in Dover; chr. myocarditis; housewife; married; b. Nottingham; John Morrison (Nottingham) and Sarah Ellison (Barrington)

Ruth E., d. 4/12/1934 at 0/1/8; asphyxia; b. Barrington; George W. Ellison (Barrington) and Evelyn E. Elliott (Kensington)

Thelma F., d. 11/3/1978 at 57 in Dover; shoe worker; widow; b. NH; George Austin and Amie R. Rose

Violet L., d. 10/28/1965 at 50 in Hanover; pulmonary edema; housewife; married; b. Concord; Caleb Smith and Della Ferguson

Walter S., d. 3/16/1959 at 89 in Dover; arteriosclerosis; wood chopper; widower; b. Nottingham; Benjamin F. Ellison and Georgianna Emerson

William A., d. 4/27/1952 at 86; coronary thrombosis; lumber operator; married; b. Nottingham; Frank B. Ellison and Georgianna Emerson

ELLSWORTH,
William, d. 12/21/1899 at 30/4 in Rochester; natural causes; single

ELSEMORE,
Charles A., d. 10/25/1967 at 60 in Rochester; hepatic-cardiac fail.; teacher; married; b. Island Falls, ME; Wyman Elsemore and Irma Vincent

EMERALD,
Emanuel J., d. 8/5/1909 at 80; organic heart disease; retired; divorced; b. Portugal

EMERSON,
Annie, d. 2/12/1907 at 1/10/4 in Somerville, MA

Belle S., d. 10/17/1953 at 90; frac. of femur; housewife; widow; b. Strafford; Martin Howard and Hannah Gray

Bert W., d. 12/12/1890 at 0/7; b. Barrington; John Emerson (Lee) and Elmira Arlin (Barrington)

John W., d. 7/18/1909 at 60; suicide, taking Paris Green; b. Madbury; J. M. Emerson

EMERY,
Harry E., d. 5/2/1900 at 1/2/16 in Northwood; pneumonia; b. Barrington; Fred E. Emery (Manchester) and Sadie L. Lingard (Barrington)

EMHARDT,
Mary C., d. 5/20/1981 at 62 in Rochester; historian; widow; b. MA

ERCOLINE,
Hattie C., d. 11/1/1966 at 77; myocardial infarction; housewife; married; b. Framingham, MA; Frederick B. King and Blanche L. Locke

ERICKSON,
Emrich E., d. 1/17/1980 in FL

EVANS,
Albert, d. 12/2/1905 at 81/4/5; shock; married; b. Strafford; Lemuel Evans (Strafford)
Eliza T., d. 9/30/1903 at 82/7/20; apoplexy; housewife; single; b. Barrington; William Evans (Strafford) and Hannah Twombly (Strafford)
Elizabeth A., d. 11/11/1910 at 90/9/27; old age; housewife; married; b. Barrington; Israel Swain (Barrington) and Susan Bennett (Northwood)
Hannah R., d. 8/12/1893 at 24/2/28; cardiac failure; housewife; married; b. Lowell, MA; Thomas Ramsey and Hannah Donahue
Nellie A., d. 8/25/1958 at 77 in Exeter; arteriosclerosis; housewife; married; b. Nottingham; George Morrison and Emma Twombley
Rebecca L., d. 4/4/1947 at 88/3/28 in Epping; arteriosclerosis; housewife; widow; b. Epping; Samuel P. Ladd (Epping) and Sarah J. Dodge (Exeter)
Rhoda, d. 3/12/1902 at 84/4/22; shock; housewife; widow; b. Farmington; Peter Twombly (Madbury) and Annie Evans (Strafford)

FAIST,
Walter H., d. 8/22/1987 at 72; carpenter; married; b. MA

FANNING,
David B., d. 2/18/1950 at 45; arteriosclerosis; painter; single;
    b. NS; James E. Fanning and Mary Sewinamer
John, d. 7/2/1954 at 79 in Tewksbury, MA; heart failure
Mary, d. 12/28/1946 at 68/0/7 in Lexington, MA; cerebral
    thrombosis; married; b. England
Monson H., d. 12/2/1916 at 42/10/11; farmer; married; b. NS;
    James E. Fanning (Madison) and Mary A. Swain (NS)

FARRELL,
John F., d. 1/22/1982 at 37 in Portsmouth; fisherman;
    married; b. MA

FELIX,
Bernice L., d. 12/15/1982 at -- in Manchester

FELKER,
Annie L., d. 8/28/1961 at 80; myocardial failure; housewife;
    married; b. Strafford; Levi W. Brown and Lydia Smith
Charles H., d. 5/24/1948 at 35/9/29; fracture of skull; lawyer;
    single; b. Rochester; Henry Felker (Rochester) and
    Grace Berry (Barrington)
Ida May, d. 6/3/1941 at 69/9/26 in Boston, MA; valv. heart
    disease; housewife; married; b. Boston, MA; Charles
    Varney
Lydia A., d. 7/12/1902 at 66/8/6; pernicious anemia;
    housewife; married; b. Dover; William H. Seavey
    (Barrington) and Rachel Corson (Lebanon, ME)
Mehitable, d. 1/28/1894 at 91/7/4; la grippe; housewife;
    widow; b. Barnstead; Benjamin Winkley (Barnstead) and
    Elizabeth Pitman
William H., d. 5/29/1969 at 94; myocardial infarc.; farmer;
    widower; b. NH; Andrew J. Felker and Lydia A. Seavey

FELTIS,
Martin, d. 8/2/1964 at 87; coronary thrombosis; police officer; widower; b. France; Andrew Feltis and Ann -----; residence - Dorchester, MA

FENDERSON,
Franklin J., d. 2/10/1947 at 94/9/25 in Dover; pulmonary embolism; violin maker; widower; b. Presque Isle, ME; Daniel Fenderson (ME) and Jeanette Sutter (ME)
Leigh J., d. 3/1/1963 at 76 in Rochester; carcinoma of bowel; music teacher; single; b. Auburn, ME; Frank J. Fenderson and Georgia A. Goss

FERNALD,
Mary P., d. 3/12/1903 at 89/5/2; old age; housewife; b. Barrington; Isaac Fernald and Mary Perry (Barrington)

FERRIS,
Ella, d. 8/9/1977 at 83; married; b. NS; Arthur Hund and Beatrice Smith
Ella, d. 8/9/1985 at 83 in Rochester; married; b. NS

FERRY,
Forest E., d. 9/4/1933 at 12/10/20 in Rochester; lobar pneumonia; b. Barrington; Eugene Ferry (Hillsboro) and Lona Strand (Barrington)

FISHER,
Guy S., d. 7/3/1976 at 23 in Dover; factory wkr.; single; b. MA; William R. Fisher, II and Shirley Blinn

FISK,
Michael J., d. 5/14/1981 at 17 in Rochester; student; b. NH

FLINT,
Corinne A., d. 9/15/1970 at 43 in Dover; carcinoma of breast; housewife; married; b. MA; Reuben E. Edin and Martha J. Johnson; residence - Dover

FLYNN,
Marie S., d. 1/25/1979 at 84; stitcher; widow; b. MA

FOGARTY,
Leonard, d. 9/11/1958 at 59 in Dover; broncho pneumonia; wood chopper; married; b. PEI; George Fogarty and Jessie O'Hara

FOGG,
Annie Martha, d. 8/20/1913 at 73/10/19 in Somerville, MA; chronic endocarditis
David R., d. 7/1/1965 at 14; acute nephritis; student; b. Dover; Russell L. Fogg and Rose Ellis
Edith A., d. 12/9/1966 at 61 in Dover; G.I. hemorrhage; housewife; married; b. Durham; Alfred Woodman and Nellie Gilman

FOOTE,
Raymond W., d. 4/3/1971 at 83; coronary thrombosis; crossing tender; single; b. ME; Jeremiah Foote and Anna Gifford

FORREST,
Erskine, d. 7/11/1963 at 90 in Rochester; arteriosclerotic heart dis.; proprietor; widower; b. NS; John Forrest and Eleanor Meek

FOSS,
Addie, d. 10/29/1951 at 82 in Concord; carcinoma of stomach; housewife; widow; John Bodge and Eliza Daniels; residence - Rochester

Almon F., d. 2/10/1958 at 87; angina pectoris; conductor; widower; b. Strafford; Mark F. Foss and Livina Berry

Charles A., d. 6/28/1893 at 78; congestion of lungs; farmer; widower; b. Barrington; Jacob Foss (Barrington) and Sally Garland (Northwood)

Emma F., d. 3/25/1922 at 67/4/24; housewife; married; b. Barrington; Hezekiah Brown (Barrington) and Augusta Silvester (MA)

Fannie Eaton, d. 3/22/1945 at 81/0/21 in Dover; arteriosclerosis; housework; widow; b. Barrington; John F. Haskell (Belfast, ME) and Orinda Crie (Matinicus Island, ME)

James D., d. 12/12/1895 at 40/2/14; amyloid nephritis; blind maker; single; b. Barrington; James Foss (Barrington) and Martha Foss (Barrington)

James S., d. 3/13/1900 at 73/10/2; pneumonia; farmer; married; b. Barrington; Eliphalet Foss (Barrington) and Mary Foss (Barrington)

Jane L., d. 4/9/1931 at 79/8/25; apoplexy; widow; b. Barrington; Joseph L. Gray (Barrington) and Joanna F. Berry (Strafford)

Joel N., d. 4/10/1912 at 70; hardening of arteries; carpenter; married; b. Strafford; Moses Foss (Strafford) and Bessie Foss (Strafford)

Juliette A., d. 3/21/1912 at 76/0/4 in Pittsfield; organic heart disease; widow; b. Lynn, MA; ----- Beede (Lynn, MA) and ----- Gutterson (Derry)

Leslie J., d. 7/24/1912 at 55/8/19; suicide; farmer; married; b. Barrington; James S. Foss (Barrington) and Martha ----- (Barrington)

Nathaniel, d. 4/5/1910 at 82/4/27; natural causes; farmer; b. Strafford; Elisha Foss (Strafford)

Oliver M., d. 12/25/1933 at 73/2; acute myocarditis; farmer; married; b. Strafford; Morrison Foss (Strafford) and Fannie Boston (Barrington)

Sylvia May, d. 6/7/1893 at 0/0/1; b. Barrington; Fred Foss (Strafford) and Esther Hayes (Strafford)

William S., d. 8/30/1922 at 96/4/17; farmer; widower; b. Barrington; Samuel Foss and Charlotte -----

FOSTER,

G. Frank, d. 9/10/1971 at 61 in Rochester; carcinoma of lung; mill wright; married; b. MA; G. Frank Foster and Addie Houghton

FREEMAN,

daughter, d. 5/6/1912 at 0/0/0; b. Barrington; Walter Freeman (Barrington) and Effie Tyler (Barrington)

Arthur, d. 3/8/1949 at 71/1/7; apoplexy; farmer; widower; b. Boston, MA; Wilbur Freeman and Melissa Waterhouse

Beatrice, d. 5/11/1911 at 0/9/14; tuberculosis of lungs; b. Barrington; Arthur Freeman (Boston, MA) and Eva Hanscomb (Barrington)

Charles, d. 6/20/1974 at 65 in Dover; no occ.; single; b. MA; John Freeman and ----- May

Charles D., d. 1/9/1928 at 73/7; val. heart disease; farmer; married; b. Barrington; David Freeman (Barrington) and Hannah Gray (Strafford)

Charlie, d. 9/5/1893 at 18/7/15; laborer; single; b. Barrington

Clarence, d. 7/14/1912 at 0/5/2; whooping cough; b. Barrington; Arthur Freeman (Barrington) and Eva Hanscam (Barrington)

David D., d. 11/6/1890 at 74; widower; b. Barrington; Stephen Freeman (Barrington) and Betsy Hanscom (Barrington)

Effie E., d. 12/3/1957 at 76 in Dover; coronary infarction; housewife; married; b. Barrington; George Tyler and Abbie Gray; residence - Madbury

Eva H., d. 2/21/1960 at 82; myocardial infarction; housewife; widow; b. Barrington; Samuel Hanscomb and Bridgett ---

Fannie R., d. 5/9/1914 at 57/7/9 in Madbury; housewife; married

George H., d. 5/5/1911 at 49/3/5 in Rochester; married

George S., d. 1/10/1964 at 90 in Dover; bronchial pneumonia; farmer; widower; b. Barrington; Steven Freeman and Fannie E. Chamberlain; residence - Dover

Gussie, d. 4/19/1902 at 0/1/2; unknown; b. Barrington; Arthur Freeman (Barrington) and Vina Stanley (Barrington)

Josephine, d. 4/19/1974 at 72; housewife; single; b. NH; Walter Freeman and Effie Gray

Mark, d. 2/7/1964 at 65 in Concord; terminal broncho pneumonia; widower; residence - Nottingham

Mary, d. 3/16/1930 at 69/8/11; arterio sclerosis; at home; widow; b. Lynn, MA; Timothy Capen (Barrington) and Elmira Hanscom (Providence, RI)

Mary E., d. 4/22/1914 at 35 in Chelsea, MA

Matilda, d. 5/23/1907 at 26; valvular heart disease; housewife; married; b. Boston, MA; John Freeman and Mary Freeman

Perley, d. 11/1/1942 at 52/6/27 in Dover; hem'hage, leg injury; woodchopper; married; b. Barrington; Charles Freeman and Mary Hanscom (Barrington)

Rose Anna O., d. 8/19/1981 at 60 in Rochester; shoe worker; married; b. NH

Stephen R., d. 7/5/1912 at 4/3/25 in Cambridge, MA; indigestion gastritis; b. Cambridge, MA; John Freeman (Barrington)

Val. B., d. 10/3/1928 at 75; val. heart disease; farmer; widower; b. Barrington; David Freeman (Barrington) and Hannah Gray (Strafford)

Walter, d. 4/7/1967 at 88 in Dover; broncho pneumonia; mason; widower; b. Barrington; Charles D. Freeman and Mary -----; residence - Dover

Walter V., d. 10/29/1908 at 0/9/1; cholera infantum; b. Barrington; Walter Freeman (Barrington) and Effie Tyler (Barrington)

Wilbur, d. 11/25/1912 at 72; senility; farmer; widower; b. Barrington

FRIARS,
Sarah E., d. 10/19/1970 at 70 in Dover; cerebral hemorrhage; housewife; married; b. MA; Joseph A. Morley and Mary Fanning; residence - Somersworth

FROST,
Doris C., d. 8/30/1963 at 49 in Portsmouth; asphyxiation - drowning; restaurant owner; married; b. Manchester, MA; Clarence Lovely and Ariel M. Twombly; residence - Farmington

FULLER,
Milton S., d. 5/31/1967 at 70 in Rochester; carcinoma of pancreas; ret. detective; widower; b. Cazenovia, NY; Bert Fuller
Sarah, d. 4/29/1966 at 74 in Rochester; sepsis gangrene; housewife; married; b. NS; John J. MacLean

FURBISH,
Martha L., d. 8/6/1950 at 65 in Dover; carcinoma of colon; housewife; widow; b. Dover; Eugene B. Foss and Fannie E. Haskell; residence - Dover

FURLONG,
Lucy E., d. 8/3/1956 at 79 in Rochester; coronary thrombosis; housewife; widow; b. Sherman Mills, ME; Silas Bryant and ----- Jellison; residence - Rochester

GAGNE,
Beulah G., d. 12/25/1983 at 62 in Rochester; doll maker; married; b. NH

GALE,
daughter, d. 3/12/1944 at 0/0/0 in Brentwood; prematurity; b. Brentwood; Frank Gale (Amesbury, MA) and Sarah Green (Rochester)

GARDNER,
Ruth, d. 9/22/1969 at 53 in Hanover; metastatic tumor (lungs); shoe worker; widow; b. ME; Mahlon C. Lloyd and Ida Davis

GARLAND,
Cheryl D., d. 11/1/1981 at 29; savings bank emp.; married; b. NH

Gladys L., d. 4/1/1976 at 82 in Rochester; housewife; widow; b. NH; Dixie Leavitt and Elmira -----

Herbert, d. 7/14/1897 at 0/0/0; stillborn; b. Barrington; James Garland (Farmington) and Nellie Henderson (Farmington)

Patience, d. 2/27/1890 at 84/6; single; b. Rochester; James Garland (Rochester) and Abagail Jenness (Rochester)

GARVEY,
Florence E., d. 5/3/1967 at 69; myocardial infarc.; housewife; married; b. Barrington; Samuel P. DeMeritt and Sarah E. Locke

William F., d. 6/10/1970 at 72 in Cambridge, MA; carcinoma left barotid; residence - Somerville, MA

GAUNYA,
Nancy B., d. 11/11/1936 at 0/0/4; gastro-enteritis; b. Barrington; Roswell O. Gaunya (Salisbury, VT) and Lillian A. Bonneau (Dover)

GEAR,
Daniel, d. 7/1/1893 at 70/4/19; rheumatic fever; farmer; married; b. Barrington

Samuel, d. 10/17/1896 at 80/0/2; old age; farmer; married; b. Barrington; George Gear (Barrington) and Deliverance Gear (Barrington)

GEER,
George M., d. 5/29/1899 at 48/9/17; org. dis. of heart; farmer; married; b. Barrington; Samuel Geer (Barrington) and Sarah Brown (Barrington)

GEIST,
Richard J., d. 11/11/1913 at 29/8/1; pulmonary tuberculosis; machinist; married; b. Hamburg, German; Michell Geist (Germany) and Elizabeth Roensling (Germany)

GELINAS,
Cordelia, d. 1/31/1893 at 5/8; inflammatory fever; b. Barrington; Albert Gelenas (sic) (Canada) and Etuti'e Lemerise (Canada)

GENDRON,
Thomas, d. 8/31/1974 at 85 in Rochester; molder; married; b. MA; Joseph Gendron and Delvina Devoe

GERDES,
Theodore J., d. 7/2/1960 at 79; coronary thrombosis; machinist ret.; married; b. Germany; residence - Rochester

GIBB,
Neil H., d. 12/28/1967 at 43 in Rochester; gastro-intestinal hem.; auto dealer; married; b. NH; Oscar Gibb and Nellie Jones

GIBLIN,
Thomas N., d. 1/14/1955 in New York, NY

GILMAN,
Ellen R., d. 9/21/1974 at 65 in Rochester; hospital emp.; married; b. NH; Alpha D. Tuttle and Eva M. Hall

GLEASON,
Hazel M., d. 8/14/1955 at 66 in Rochester; arteriosclerotic heart disease; widow; b. Rochester; Frank Hussey and Luella Wellman

GLIDDEN,
Chris E., d. 9/29/1968 at 30 mins. in Rochester; congenital anomalies; b. NH; Reynard F. Glidden and Sandra Pratt
Doris M., d. 8/22/1976 at 70 in Portsmouth; housewife; divorced; b. ME; Frank A. Dudley and Hannah McKenney
Ella L., d. 12/16/1898 at 27/5/7; phthisis pulmonalis; housewife; married; b. Barrington; Monroe Otis (Rochester) and Alice Pinkham (Milton)
Sadie J., d. 4/8/1915 at 41/9/8; retired; widow; b. Barrington; Joseph Perkins and Naney Arlin

GLOVER,
Alta G., d. 10/4/1969 at 80 in Dover; hypertensive hrt. dis.; pastry cook; b. NH; William Ellison and Etta Drew
Bernice E., d. 2/21/1902 at 8/8/4; diabetes; school girl; b. Nottingham; Woodbury Glover (Nottingham) and Ida E. Leathers (Nottingham)
Eileen M., d. 2/2/1961 at 45 in Kittery, ME; medullary failure; housewife; divorced; b. Nottingham; Bert Glover and Alta G. Ellison

GOLDEN,
Jerry F., d. 5/8/1960 at 24; fractured skull; mechanic; married; b. Indianapolis, IN; William A. Golden and Lula M. Bolton; residence - Dover

GOODWILL,
Edna P., d. 3/8/1952 at 71 in Dover; acute decubitis; housewife; widow; b. Bridgewater, NS; Jacob B. Wynott and Selina Boliver
Thomas, d. 3/15/1938 at 71/9/8; cong. heart failure; tel. foreman; married; b. NS; Daniel Goodwill (NS) and Mary Cameron (NS)

GOODWIN,
Edith M., d. 7/19/1977 at 84 in Salem, MA

GORDON,
Harriet J., d. 6/2/1905 at 49/8/16; pulmonary tuberculosis; housewife; married; Nathaniel Underwood (Saco, ME)
Louise M., d. 1/20/1956 at 51; coronary infarction; housewife; married; b. Canada; Joseph Michaud and Anna Bossey

GORMAN,
Arthur, Jr., d. 9/19/1961 at 28; self-inflicted gun shot; driver; single; b. Portsmouth; Arthur Gorman and Doris Walker; residence - Portsmouth

GOSSELIN,
Madeline M., d. 11/15/1899 at 0/2; general debility; single; b. Barrington; Ella Rowe (Barrington)
Marilyn, d. 9/10/1976 at 33 in Rochester; waitress; married; b. NH; Hollis B. Corbett and Doris Drake

GOUPIL,
Raymond, d. 10/7/1933 at 18/2/10; fracture of skull; shoe mkr.; single; b. Newmarket; Francis Goupil (Canada) and Eva Martin (Canada)

GRACE,
Elizabeth D., d. 11/3/1914 at 84/11/26; widow; b. Fryeburg, ME; Leighton Johnson (Fryeburg, ME) and Sarah Grey (Rochester)

GRANT,
George D., d. 10/6/1986 at 78 in Dover; garage owner; married; b. VT
Mabel Katherine, d. 5/3/1976 at 76 in Dover; housewife; married; b. NH; John Clark and Annabelle Stimpson

GRAUL,
Esther T., d. 12/11/1953 at 56 in Rochester; pulmonary thrombosis; homemaker; married

GRAVES,
Marguerite H., d. 12/11/1959 at 74 in Somersworth; hypostatic pneumonia; registered nurse; single; b. Sunderland, VT; Edmund A. Graves and Harriet S. Way; residence - Madbury

GRAY,
Annie, d. 2/6/1960 at 92 in Rochester; arteriosclerotic hrt. dis.; housewife; widow; b. Milton; Daniel Wentworth and Sarah A. Henderson
Arthur P., d. 12/29/1935 at 65/3/14 in Dover; lobar pneumonia; farmer; widower; b. Canada; William Gray (Canada) and Hattie Tower (Canada)
Asa, d. 5/17/1896 at 75/7/14; Bright's disease; farmer; married; b. Barrington; Daniel Gray (Barrington) and Abbie Young (Barrington)
Elvira, d. 9/28/1918 at 65/10/6; housekeeper; widow; b. Barrington; Daniel Boginton (Pomfret, VT) and Deborah Leonard (Pomfret, VT)
Frances, d. 2/11/1917 at 84; housekeeper; widow; b. Kennebunkport, ME

Frances, d. 9/22/1934 at 71/6/29; arterio sclerosis; housewife; married; b. Barrington; John Leathers (Barrington) and Abbie J. Wentworth (Barrington)

Ida May, d. 9/24/1890 at 25/6/4; married; b. Etna, ME; Jonathan S. Buzzell (New Durham) and Rhoda E. Emerson (ME)

J. Herman, d. 12/7/1896 at 14/7/14; accidentally drowned; b. Barrington; James H. Gray (Barrington) and Ida Jones (St. Albans)

James M., d. 10/27/1894 at 80/10; heart dis. and dropsy; farmer; married; b. Barrington; Gideon E. Gray (Barrington) and Olive B. Gray (Portsmouth)

John O., d. 8/8/1928 at 70/1/25; angina pectoris; farmer; married; b. Strafford; Walter Gray (Strafford) and Louisa Leighton (Strafford)

Joseph, d. 12/24/1908 at 91 in Concord; exhaustion, senile dementia; farmer; married; b. Barrington

Mary Elizabeth, d. 1/15/1903 at 44/5/12; cerebral hemorrhage; housewife; married; b. Barrington; Ezra Hayes (Barrington) and Mary B. Wiggin (Durham)

Sally, d. 6/8/1902 at 85/9/1; old age; widow; b. Barrington; Noah Thompson (Barrington) and Hannah Clark (Barrington)

Sarah F., d. 1/17/1898 at 78/9/2; senility; housewife; married; b. Dover; John Woodes and Margaret Young

William G., d. 9/22/1898 at 54/11/22; cirrhosis of liver; carpenter; widower; b. Barrington; Joseph Gray (Barrington) and Joanna L. Gray (Strafford)

GREEN,

daughter, d. 1/15/1916 at --; b. Barrington; George Green (Haverhill, MA) and Lilla Waterhouse (Barrington)

Charles J., d. 1/15/1940 at 31/8/4; heart disease; laborer; single; b. Barrington; George A. Green (Haverhill, MA) and Lilla Waterhouse (Barrington)

George B., d. 2/5/1982 at 76; lumberman; married; b. MA

Lilla W., d. 1/16/1959 at 78; arteriosclerosis; housewife; widow; b. Barrington; Benjamin A. Waterhouse and Mary Story

GREENIER,
Ted S., d. 12/16/1978 at 17; construction; single; b. NH; Robert W. Greenier and Donna L. Shea

GREENWOOD,
Alfred M., d. 1/19/1981 at 26; no occ.; single

GRIFFIN,
Herbert E., d. 8/20/1937 at 76/10/6; anemic myocarditis; farmer; married; b. Strafford; Thomas Griffin
Robert C., d. 11/11/1910 at 11/0/23; hemophilia; b. Barrington; Herbert E. Griffin (Strafford) and Mary Hanson (Strafford)

GROVER,
Bertha Jane, d. 10/8/1898 at 0/0/1; immature; b. Barrington; Charles A. Grover (Sandown) and Fanny A. Locke (Barrington)
Harry C., d. 1/3/1951 at 78 in Berwick, ME; cardiac failure; hotel operator; widower; b. Barrington; Walter S. Grover and Fannie Young; residence - Long Beach, ME
Sarah F., d. 8/5/1898 at 52/1/8; cancer; housewife; married; b. Barrington; Jonathan Young (Barrington) and Sophia Ricker (Madbury)
Walter S., d. 9/26/1912 at 67/1/11 in Dover; cerebral hemorrhage

GUSTIN,
Richard II., d. 1/5/1983 at 87 in Rochester; warehouseman; married; b. ME

HAINSWORTH,

Norman B., d. 6/17/1985 at 67 in Rochester; mason; married; b. MA

HALE,

Charles R., d. 7/31/1954 at 86 in Lowell, MA; myocardial infarction; residence - Lowell, MA

Janet E., d. 7/12/1937 at 66/1/23 in Dover; paralysis agites; at home; married; b. Dorchester, MA; Donald MacMeekin (PEI) and Anna Tingly (Sackville, NB)

Lucia C., d. 10/6/1973 at 83; coronary occlusion; housewife; widow; b. NH; Charles S. Cartland and Julia M. Wallingford

Matthew, d. 5/29/1897 at 18/11/21; pistol ball in brain; farmer; single; b. Barrington; Samuel Hale (Barrington) and Addie Roberts (Strafford)

Robert, d. 6/11/1944 at 62 in Concord; hydro thorax malig.; farmer; single; b. Barrington; Samuel S. Hale (Barrington) and Adeline Roberts (Strafford)

Samuel S., d. 9/25/1910 at 79/4/2; cystitis; farmer; married; b. Barrington; William Hale (Barrington) and E. A. Shackford (Strafford)

William T., d. 11/11/1908 at 38/2/29 in Dover; appendicitis; farmer; married; b. Barrington; Samuel S. Hale (Barrington) and Adeline M. Roberts (Strafford)

HALEY,

Cassie C., d. 7/16/1959 at 81 in Rochester; arteriosclerosis; housewife; widow; b. Nottingham; Franklin P. Hall and Hannah J. Dame

George B., d. 8/11/1923 at 76/7/21; grain dealer; married; b. Lee; John P. Haley (Lee) and Lydia A. Gile (Nottingham)

Gertrude B., d. 4/18/1973 at 81 in Rochester; cerebral vascular acc.; housewife; married; b. NH; Ivory Hayes and Martha Daniels

John Parkman, d. 6/10/1899 at 78/7/17; consumption; farmer; widower; b. Lee; John Haley (Epping) and Sally C. Butler (Nottingham)

Josephine O., d. 2/11/1974 at 85 in Rochester; housewife; single; b. NH; George B. Haley and Josephine Ham

Mary J., d. 5/25/1938 at 85/9/3; apoplexy; housewife; widow; b. Rochester; Joseph W. Ham (Rochester) and Sarah H. Roberts (Berwick, ME)

Mary J., d. 5/23/1943 at 93/0/9; senility; housewife; married; b. Rochester; Ira T. Howard (Rochester) and Mary Jane ---- (Barrington)

Philip, d. 11/11/1946 at 79/7/4 in Haverhill, MA; massive gas. hemor.; laborer (ret.); widower; b. Haverhill, MA; John Haley (Ireland) and Julia Conners (Ireland)

Sumner A., d. 2/18/1961 at 77 in Boston, MA; uremia; retired; married; b. Barrington; George B. Haley and Mary J. Ham; residence - Somerville, MA

Waldron, d. 10/4/1918 at 36/5/15; merchant; single; b. Barrington; George B. Haley (Lee) and Josephine Ham (Rochester)

William A., d. 5/24/1978 at 86 in Rochester; farmer; widower; b. MA

HALL,
daughter, d. 8/14/1918 at --; b. Barrington; Herbert Hall (Haverhill, MA) and Eunice Ross (Barrington)

son, d. 11/19/1931 at 10 mins.; b. Barrington; Kenneth Hall (Barrington) and Ruth Hall (Dover)

Abigail J., d. 9/9/1890 at 65/9; married; b. Barrington; Nathaniel Howe (Barrington) and Rebecca Howe (Barrington)

Almira, d. 10/5/1899 at 80; old age; housekeeper; divorced; b. Barrington; Silas Hall (Barrington) and Lydia Critchett (Strafford)

Almon C., d. 8/28/1980 at 77 in Dover; shoe layer; married; b. NH

Alva A., d. 6/15/1912 at 73/1/29 in Dover; cerebral hemorrhage

Anderson C., d. 9/24/1954 at 74 in Dover; arteriosclerosis; photographer; married; b. Strafford; George A. Hall and Elmira M. Berry; residence - Dover

Andrew, d. 9/30/1911 at 85/1/22; valvular heart disease; widower

Bessie A., d. 2/13/1892 at 4/2/9; diphtheria; b. Barrington; George Hall and Carrie Richardson

Charles D., d. 12/25/1937 at 75/8/20; cerebral apoplexy; farmer; single; b. Barrington; Warren L. Hall (Barrington) and Thankful Dyer (Durham)

Charles F., d. 7/25/1920 at 83/4/12; farmer; married; b. Barrington; John Hall

Charles S., d. 4/27/1938 at 76/8/2; bronchial pneumonia; farmer; widower; b. Strafford; Colby Hall (Strafford) and Mary Buzzell (Barrington)

Chloe M., d. 5/26/1937 at 82/3/19; chronic bronchitis; retired; widow; b. Strafford; Andrew J. Buzzell (Barrington) and Eliza Tuttle (Strafford)

Christina V., d. 3/16/1946 at 89/7/18 in Concord; arteriosclerosis; housewife; widow; b. Barrington; Asa Gray and Elvira Boynton

Clifton W., d. 10/19/1985 at 78 in Concord; farmer; single; b. NH

Emma F., d. 4/18/1936 at 76/9/10; toxemia; retired; married; b. Strafford; Charles H. Caverly (Strafford) and Pheby Durgin (Strafford)

Ezra T., d. 5/11/1901 at 82/8; pneumonia; wheelwright; widower; b. Barrington; William Hall (Barrington) and ----- Tasker (Dover)

Florence, d. 9/15/1910 at 0/6/22; cholera infantum; b. Barrington; Anderson Hall (Barrington) and Agnes Sternes

Frank J., d. 7/10/1921 at 63/8/26; farmer; single; b. Barrington; George W. Hall (Barrington) and Lucinda Hall (Barrington)

Fred, d. 2/9/1978 at 72 in Nashua; shoe worker; married; b. NH; Walter F. Hall and Mertie Young

Fred Colby, d. 10/24/1948 at 60/9/12; carcinoma of bowel; Navy Yard; married; b. Northwood; Charles S. Hall (Strafford) and Emma Caverly (Strafford)

George W., d. 10/27/1904 at 76/8/5; cancer of face; farmer; married; b. Barrington; Nathaniel Hall (Barrington) and Sarah Roberts (Barrington)

George W., d. 4/16/1927 at 83/4/29; apoplexy; farmer; married; b. Barrington; William Hall (Derry) and Lydia Hall (Strafford)

Grace M., d. 4/16/1900 at 24/3/4; pleurisy; housewife; married; b. Barrington; George W. Rowe (Holderness) and Elizabeth E. Brown (Salem)

Hannah E., d. 5/23/1903 at 81; arterial degeneration; housewife; married; b. Barrington; Nathaniel Hall and Sarah Patrick

Hubbard W., d. 6/2/1894 at --; tuberculosis; mechanic; widower; b. Strafford; Hubbard Hall (Barrington) and Maria Hall (Strafford)

Ianson, d. 6/7/1905 at 76/10/9; pulmonary emphysema; shoemaker; widower; b. Somersworth; Ezekiel Hall (Barrington) and Jane Ianson (Manchester, England)

Jenefer A., d. 12/11/1955 at 66 in Rochester; coronary insufficiency; housewife; married; b. Orange, MA; Alonzo Wheeler and Jenefer Mitchell; residence - Gonic

John C., d. 3/24/1977 at 87 in Dover; ret. boatmaker; widower; b. NH; Charles F. Hall and Christina V. Gray

John E., d. 6/7/1934 at 74/5/7; apoplexy; farmer; married; b. Barrington; John W. Hall (Barrington) and Lucinda Hall (Barrington)

John Frank, d. 10/8/1942 at 91/7/7 in Rochester; apoplexy; retired; single; b. Barrington; Hanson Hall (Barrington) and Martha Drew (Barrington)

Kenneth A., d. 12/9/1956 at 60; coronary thrombosis; mill worker; married; b. Barrington; Charles S. Hall and Emma Caverly

Linza O., d. 12/13/1941 at 48/11/12; pulmonary embolism; farmer; single; b. Barrington; Charles F. Hall (Barrington) and Christiana Gray (Barrington)

Lucinda, d. 3/8/1918 at 90/8/10; retired; widow; b. Barrington; Nathaniel Hall and Sarah Patrick

Lydia, d. 7/15/1894 at 80/3/3; old age and bilious attack; widow; b. Barrington; Elijah Hall (Barrington) and Deborah Hall (Barrington)

Mabel G., d. 6/1/1978 at 79 in Rochester

Maria, d. 1/14/1891 at 74; widow

Mary, d. 3/7/1906 at 92/2/27; senility; housewife; b. Dorchester; James Bunker (Durham) and Betsey Hawkins (Barrington)

Mary A., d. 2/1/1955 at 78; cardio-vascular disease; housework; widow; b. Barrington; Joseph F. Lingard and Sarah A. Hall

Mary Angelina, d. 4/1/1905 at 64/3/3; pneumonia; housewife; married; b. Barrington; Aaron Willey

Nathaniel, d. 9/24/1892 at 61; pyaenia; farmer; married; b. Barrington; Nathaniel Hall and Sarah Patrick

Nella B., d. 1/30/1969 at 65 in Rochester; acute pulmonary edema; housewife; married; Walter Fitch and Susan Gulliver; residence - Gonic

Richard B., d. 9/20/1915 at 82/2/6; farmer; widower; b. Barrington; Nathaniel Hall (Barrington) and Sarah Patrick (Durham)

Thankful, d. 5/9/1904 at 82; unknown; housewife; widow; b. Barrington; Asa Dyer and ----- Vining

Tobias R., d. 7/20/1907 at 89; merchant; widower; b. Barrington

Walter F., d. 8/4/1951 at 77; tuberculosis; woodsman; married; b. Barrington; Daniel Hall and Nellie Caverly

Warren C., d. 11/12/1959 at 82 in Dover; cerebral hemorrhage; farmer; divorced; b. Barrington; James C. Hall and Nancy Chesley; residence - Dover

Willey E., d. 4/23/1900 at 31/4/23; pneumonia; teamster; widower; b. Barrington; Benjamin F. Hall (Barrington) and Nellie Brown (Barrington)

William, d. 1/8/1894 at 84/9/24; pneumonia; farmer; married; b. Barrington; Abraham Hall and Mary Willey

HAM,

daughter, d. 12/30/1899 at 0/0/1; premature birth; b. Barrington; George S. Ham (Barrington) and Lillian E. Jukes (Andover, England)

Anna Cate, d. 9/6/1926 at 66/4/3; cer. hemorrhage; at home; single; b. Rochester; J. Plummer Ham (Rochester) and Mary C. Waldron (Rochester)

David F., d. 9/3/1900 at 71/0/29 in Rochester; cut his throat; farmer; married; b. Barrington; James Ham (Rochester) and Mary Foss (Barrington)

Delphine F., d. 3/9/1986 at 78 in Rochester; nurse; married; b. NH

Elizabeth A., d. 3/1/1951 at 74 in Bridgeport, CT; cardiac failure

Elizabeth B., d. 10/21/1902 at 87/1/18; acute bronchitis; housewife; widow; b. Barrington; Curtis Pierce (Barnstead) and Olive Woodhouse (Madbury)

Laurana J., d. 2/1/1903 at 68/0/1 in Dover; cancer of bowels; housewife; widow; b. Barrington; William Hale Young (Barrington) and Sarah Daniels (Barrington)

Samuel C., d. 3/12/1894 at 65/2/24; hemorrhage f'm l. artery; farmer; married; b. Barrington; Thomas Ham (Madbury) and Mary Caverno (Strafford)

William H., d. 12/23/1962 at 87 in CT; cardiac failure

HAMILTON,
James E., d. 11/4/1987 at 73 in Dover; truck driver; married; b. MA

HAMMOND,
Edward C., d. 4/14/1966 at 64 in Newfields; laceration of the brain; barber; married; b. Lynn, MA; Edward G. Hammond and Lottie C. Johnson

HANSCOM[B][E],
son, d. 2/27/1896 at 0/1/14; deficient vitality; b. Barrington; Leander Hanscomb (Barrington) and Nellie Rines (Boscawen)
son, d. 12/10/1899 at 0/0/1; b. Barrington; Eva Hanscomb
Adeline, d. 1/7/1974 at 79 in Dover; housewife; widow; b. NH; John Freeman and May -----
Alvey, d. 2/21/1913 at 66; malig't dis. esophagus; farmer; married; b. Barrington; Nathan Hanscom and Hannah Walker
Charles, d. 6/22/1913 at 35; pulmonary tuberculosis; laborer; married; b. Barrington; Alvey Hanscom (Barrington) and Prudence Allen (Barrington)
Frank, d. 10/25/1969 at 87 in Dover; coronary thrombosis
Harold H., d. 9/2/1973 at 61 in Dover; coronary occlusion; plumber; married; b. NH; Albert Hanscome and Adeline Freeman; residence - Dover
John H., d. 4/--/1948 at 75/10/21 in Duxbury, MA; coronary occlusion
Leander, d. 8/11/1912 at 60 in Manchester; cerebral hemorrhage; laborer; married
Lemont, d. 7/2/1897 at 25; tuberculosis; farmer; single; b. Barrington; Nathan Hanscomb (Barrington) and Liza Gray (Barrington)
Lucy M., d. 5/20/1954 at 82 in Duxbury, MA; coronary occlusion

Nathan, d. 4/23/1892 at 84; old age; laborer; widower; b. Barrington

HANSON,
son, d. 4/29/1916 at 0/0/0; b. Barrington; Clarence F. Hanson (Strafford) and Dora E. Philbrick (Epsom)
Eliza, d. 3/3/1896 at 73/11/6; apoplexy; domestic; widow; b. Barrington; Nathaniel Hanson (Barrington) and Betsy Hill (Barrington)
Frank, d. 10/31/1971 at 87 in Dover; ruptured abdominal aneurysm
John, d. 6/16/1892 at 64/1/16; apoplexy; farmer; married; b. Barrington; Caleb Hanson
Mary S., d. 3/30/1890 at 52/6; married; b. Barrington
Maude E., d. 10/22/1950 at 60/11/25 in Dover; cerebral hemorrhage; housewife; married; b. Madbury; Alphonse Davis and Jennie -----; residence - Dover
Plummer, d. 11/25/1896 at 68/6; insane; laborer; single; b. Barrington; Nathaniel Hanson (Strafford) and Betsy Hill (Strafford)
Sally, d. 1/6/1892 at 86/9/6; old age; housekeeper; widow; b. Barrington
Stephen W., d. 9/4/1894 at --; exhaustion from hemorrhage; farmer; married; b. Barrington; Nathaniel Hanson (Strafford)

HARDING,
Cora T., d. 6/15/1975 at 80 in Rochester; housewife; married; b. NH; Charles A. Tebbets and Etta Ham
Evelyn A., d. 4/22/1978 at 55 in Rochester; housewife; married; b. MA; Edward D. McGown and Pauline Prost
John A., d. 5/6/1970 at 0 in Rochester; asphyxia - fetal death; Arthur Harding and Eleanor Blaisdell

HARRINGTON,

Margaret, d. 4/22/1895 at 32; parenchymat'n neph.; domestic; married; b. Barrington; Cornelius Mahoney

HARRIS,

Jessie M., d. 2/10/1979 at 66 in Rochester; shoe worker; widow; b. CT

John A., d. 4/26/1954 at 70 in Dover; heart disease; laborer; widower; b. NB; John A. Harris and Mary -----; residence - Gonic

Pearl L., d. 7/3/1952 at 63 in Gonic; coronary heart disease; housewife; married; b. PEI; Joseph Enman and Jane Woods; residence - Gonic

Raymond F., d. 4/3/1969 at 54 in Rochester; coronary heart dis.; shipyard worker; widower; b. ME; John Harris and Pearl Erman

Sterling K., d. 5/26/1943 at 0/7/6 in Farmington; broncho pneumonia; b. Rochester; Rex W. Harris (Rochester) and Jennie Reed (Acton, ME)

Wayne G., d. 5/12/1984 at 35; nuclear refueling; married; b. NH

HARTFORD,

Elizabeth M., d. 1/17/1984 at 63 in Dover; short order cook; divorced; b. NH

Jennie, d. 4/13/1892 at 37/10/9; heart failure; housewife; married; b. Dover; Warren Seavey and Olive Seavey

Lyman, d. 1/22/1907 at 1/2/6; marasmus; b. Barrington; Wilbur Hartford (Barrington) and Marie Pearson (NS)

Samuel, d. 4/13/1892 at 0/0/1; inanition; b. Barrington; Samuel Hartford and Jennie Seavey

Samuel A., d. 2/23/1900 at 0/0/1; undeveloped; b. Barrington; Samuel B. Hartford (Hiram, ME) and Evelyn Pearson (NS)

HARVEY,
Ethel, d. 10/19/1941 at 65/4/0 in Natick, MA; metastarsis of spine; ret. teacher; single; b. Chelsea, MA; Charles L. Harvey and Adelaide Googins (Dedham, MA)

HARWAY,
Elene A., d. 4/21/1953 at 72; cerebral hem.; housework; married; b. Wakefield, MA; Frank H. Robinson and Mamie A. Berry
Mabel C., d. 7/9/1955 at 66; coronary thrombosis; housewife; married; b. Hollis, ME; George Johnson and Clara B. Brown

HASKELL,
Ezra, d. 6/23/1916 at 81/2/12; minister; widower; b. Dover; Ezra Haskell

HASKINS,
Madelyn L., d. 9/13/1982 at 81 in Dover; housewife; married; b. VT

HATCH,
Lemuel Ozro, d. 2/6/1912 at 60/7/14 in Amesbury, MA; suicide by shooting

HAYES,
Adeline, d. 2/10/1930 at 86/0/24 in Durery, CT; arterio sclerosis; divorced
Albert W., d. 10/24/1895 at 10/2/4; acute peritonitis; b. Barrington; Ivory Hayes (Newington) and Martha Daniels (Barrington)
Arthur D., d. 6/19/1970 at 87 in Wakefield, MA; arteriosclerotic hrt. dis.; residence - Somerville, MA
Bernice M., d. 6/7/1973 at 86 in Dover; arteriosclerotic hrt. dis.; housekeeper; single; b. NH; James C. Hayes and Emma F. Hayes; residence - Dover

Bertha G., d. 6/20/1974 at 89 in CO (burial); housewife; widow

Charles H., d. 3/13/1953 at 80 in Dover; arteriosclerosis; ret. farmer; married; b. Barrington; Eleazer Hayes and Lydia A. Cater; residence - Dover

Doris, d. 4/8/1969 at 52 in Rochester; diabetes mellitus; housewife; married; b. NH; Charles Ross and Florence Arlin; residence - Milton

Edward B., d. 9/14/1901 at 24/11/17; paralysis; farmer; single; b. Barrington; Eleaser C. Hayes (Barrington) and Lizzie A. Cater (Barrington)

Eleazer C., d. 2/11/1912 at 79/6/21; valvular heart disease; farmer; married; b. Barrington; Jacob K. Hayes (Barrington) and Margaret Hayes (Madbury)

Fred R., d. 7/7/1896 at 32/2/26; typhoid pneumonia; merchant; married; b. Barrington; Eleazer Hayes (Barrington) and Elizabeth Cater (Barrington)

Gerald G., d. 9/17/1986 at 78 in Dover; master machinist; widower; b. NH

Harold H., d. 4/17/1956 at 77 in Dover; myocardial infarction; farmer; single; b. Madbury; William S. Hayes and Mattie M. Hall; residence - Madbury

Helen, d. 10/6/1918 at 29/10/9 in Somerville, MA; housewife; married; b. Strafford; Charles Garland (Strafford) and Ida Thompson (Northwood)

Irving A., d. 7/3/1962 at 55; coronary thrombosis; bus driver; b. NH; David A. Hayes and Grace Pike; residence - Madbury

Ivory, d. 11/17/1893 at 63/6/6; pneumonia; farmer; married; b. Newington; Isaac Hayes and Nancy Palmer

Jeremiah, d. 1/17/1914 at 85/0/5 in Wakefield; farmer; widower; b. Milton; John Hayes (No. Rochester) and Elizabeth Plumer (Alton)

Judith J., d. 6/16/1969 at 97 in Dover; cerebral anoxia

Lizzie A., d. 3/21/1917 at 78/6; housewife; widow; b. Barrington; John Cater (Barrington) and Abiah Babb (Barrington)

Margaret E., d. 11/18/1979 at 53 in Rochester; housewife; married; b. NH

Marion B., d. 1/25/1892 at 1/4/22; pneumonia; b. Barrington; Ivory Hayes and Martha Daniels

Martha M., d. 3/22/1937 at 88/8/16 in Madbury; arterio sclerosis; b. Gonic

Maud E., d. 7/22/1956 at 79 in Haverhill, MA; cerebral hemorrhage; widow; b. Barrington; Hiram Wood and Lydia Ham; residence - Haverhill, MA

Rebecca, d. 3/22/1892 at 82/9/26; apoplexy; housekeeper; widow; b. Milton

Viola M., d. 1/10/1986 at 79 in Rochester; housewife; married; b. MA

HAYNES,

Carrie B., d. 9/30/1948 at 75/6/28 in Gonic; cerebral hemorrhage; housewife; married; b. Barrington; John Howard and Elmira Smallcon

Edith M., d. 8/12/1966 at 69 in Rochester; carcinoma of bowel; homemaker; widow; b. Madbury; Horace Haynes and ----- Howard; residence - Gonic

Horace F., Jr., d. 12/11/1965 at 59 in Portsmouth; bronchiectasis; salesman; married; b. Madbury; Horace Haynes and Carrie B. Howard; residence - Portsmouth

Laura B., d. 4/19/1981 at 76 in Portsmouth

HAZLETT,

Minnie L., d. 4/4/1947 at 72/10/6 in Dover; carcinoma of stomach; housewife; married; b. Barrington; George W. Hall (Barrington) and Chloe Buzzell (Strafford)

HEAD,
Martha T., d. 11/5/1914 at 81/6/17; widow; b. Nottingham; Joseph Leathers (Nottingham) and Susan Shaw

HEBERT,
Donald J., d. 11/16/1985 at 66 in Rochester; custodian; married; b. NH

HENDERSON,
Alba L., d. 1/1/1947 at 66/6/2 in CA; broncho pneumonia; single; b. Barrington; Samuel Henderson (Eaton) and Sarah E. Locke (Barrington)
Carold C., d. 9/3/1955 at 77 in Newburyport, MA; bronchopneumonia; b. Barrington; Samuel Henderson and Sarah E. Locke; residence - Salisbury, MA
Harold W., d. 9/6/1975 at 78 in Rochester; postmaster; married; b. NH: William H. Henderson and Amelia Jones
Jennie M., d. 5/11/1962 at 82 in Dover; cong. heart failure; housewife; widow; b. MA; John White and Anne Harkins; residence - Dover
Ruth S., d. 1/13/1976 at 58 in Conway; extension serv.; married; b. NH; Lloyd B. Smith and Edan Chapman
Samuel, d. 4/7/1919 at 78/7/26; farmer; widower; b. Eaton; Samuel Henderson (Waterboro, ME) and Hannah Hurn
Sarah E., d. 1/6/1916 at 71/4/6; at home; married; b. Barrington; Samson Locke (Barrington) and Sarah E. Canney (Dover)

HENRY,
Jessie L., d. 12/11/1982 at 90 in Rochester; housewife; widow; b. MA
William, d. 9/9/1952 at 80 in Epping; arteriosclerotic heart disease; woodsman; married; b. E. Arlington, VT; residence - Nottingham

HERSEY,
Israel I., d. 10/1/1955 at 64; coronary thrombosis; machinist; married; b. Beverly, MA; Oliver Hersey; residence - Beverly, MA

HEY,
Jesse W., Jr., d. 12/10/1982 at 27; disabled; divorced; b. MA

HIGGINS,
Carl D., d. 4/18/1964 at 60 in Kittery, ME; medullary paralysis; lumberman; married; b. Rochester; William O. Higgins and Alice Jenness; residence - Dover
Jesse M., d. 7/21/1960 at 82; myocardial infarction; housewife; married; b. NS; Siffrai Porter and Marie -----

HILDRETH,
Pauline M., d. 8/2/1976 at 67 in Dover; housewife; married; b. NH; John McCaffery and Edna Hall

HILL,
Archelaus A., d. 6/1/1938 at 76/8/8; cerebral hemorrhage; farmer; married; b. Georgeville, PQ; Richard R. Hill (Canada) and Sarah Welch (Malone, NY)
Betsy, d. 1/1/1897 at 67/7/17; pneumonia; housewife; widow; b. Barrington; Jonathan Buzzell (Barrington) and Polly Hill (Barrington)
Joseph W., d. 7/5/1900 at 68/0/13; consumption; carpenter; widower; b. Strafford
Martha L., d. 1/15/1974 at 95; housewife; widow; b. NH; Albin H. Smith and Sarah Brown

HOBBS,
Margaret L., d. 2/27/1974 at 55 in Dover; bookkeeper; married; b. NH; George A. LaBonte and Willian A. Morin

HODGDON,
Charles F., d. 12/22/1890 at 32; married; b. Northwood
Charles F., d. 10/28/1901 at 60/10/10; cardiac hypertrophy; shoemaker; single; b. Barrington; Darius Hodgdon (Barrington) and Mary Varney (Barrington)
Darius, d. 10/2/1907 at 68/5/20; epilepsy; farmer; widower; b. Barrington; Darius Hodgdon (Barrington) and Mary Varney (Barrington)
Mary, d. 6/6/1892 at 83/6/19; old age; widow; b. Barrington; Elias Varney

HOITT,
Charles E., d. 11/22/1910 at 44/5/8; consumption; sawyer; married; b. Barrington; Charles K. Hoitt (Barrington) and Rosetta P. Drew (Acton, ME)

HOLMES,
Mary E., d. 5/14/1908 at 51; cancer; housewife; married; b. Brit. Prov.; Cornelius McDonald (Ireland) and Nora O'Brien (Ireland)
Pearl Elwood, d. 4/1/1894 at 0/0/2; birth premature; b. Barrington; Fred Holmes (Portsmouth) and Jennie Hilton (No. Berwick, ME)
Rose C., d. 11/4/1932 at 53/6/9; cere. hemorrhage; housewife; married; b. Hudson, NY
Warren E., d. 7/17/1968 at 67 in Hanover; broncho pneumonia; chef; married; b. MA; Harry Holmes and Ella Erb

HOOD,
George, d. 7/31/1978 at 57 in Exeter; mechanic; widower; b. NH; Joseph Hood and Ethel Wicstead

HOOPER,
Donald S., d. 1/15/1984 at 66 in Dover; construction supt.; married; b. MA

HOPEY,
Margaret, d. 12/24/1933 at 75/7/14 in Bow; arterio sclerosis; married; b. NB; C. Essineau (PEI)

HORNE,
Eva H., d. 4/3/1975 at 86 in Rochester; shoeworker; widow; b. NH; Frank Brown and Eliza A. Allen

HOUSTON,
Abram, d. 10/1/1936 at 85/5/25; senility; farmer; widower; b. Sanford, ME; Moses Houston (Sanford, ME) and Mary Jacobs (Sanford, ME)
Mary, d. 5/25/1910 at 84/8/12; heart failure; b. Rochester; George Jacobs and Abigail Ellis
Samuel, d. 12/7-8/1923 at 69/3/5; farmer; married; b. Sanford, ME; Samuel Houston (Sanford, ME) and Hannah Hussey (Sanford, ME)

HOVELSON,
Martha C., d. 4/17/1966 at 59 in Rochester; acute myocardial infarc.; housewife; married; b. Staten Island, NY; John Haabestad and Susan Jensen

HOWARD,
daughter, d. 3/12/1905 at 0/0/0; stillborn; b. Barrington; John Howard (Barrington) and Annie Calen (Boston, MA)
Annie F., d. 4/10/1909 at 45/0/8; pulmonary tuberculosis; housewife; married; b. Boston, MA; Michael Callen (Ireland)
Celia, d. 9/15/1903 at 0/4/21; phthisic pulmonalis; b. Barrington; Ernest Howard and Lillian Reed (Barrington)
Cora B., d. 5/21/1943 at 68/9/20; angina; at home; widow; b. Barrington; Joel N. Foss (Strafford) and Jane L. Gray (Barrington)

Earl L., d. 12/20/1940 at 42/5/2 in Rochester; lobar pneumonia; box maker; married; Ernest Howard (Barrington) and Lillie May

Edmond C., d. 11/26/1908 at 10/5/15; mitral stenases; school boy; b. Barrington; Charles Howard and Denese Hart

Emery, d. 12/31/1893 at 73/8/15; la grippe; farmer; widower; b. Barrington; S. Howard (Rochester)

Genese, d. 6/1/1907 at --; ptomaine poisoning; housewife; married; b. Van Buren, ME

Ida E., d. 3/13/1956 at 80 in Wakefield; pneumonia; housewife; married; b. Bartlett; Jacob Hill and Mary Ordway; residence - Wakefield

Laura A., d. 5/26/1932 at 73/0/13; natural causes; housewife; married; b. Strafford; Asa W. Jewell and Marion Thompson

Lillian M. R., d. 8/21/1903 at 21/6/28; phthisic pulmonalis; housewife; married; b. Barrington; Charles Reed (Barrington) and Annie B. Seavey (Barrington)

Mabel M., d. 1/7/1897 at 0/0/0; stillborn; b. Barrington; Ernest Howard (Barrington) and Lilla M. Reed (Dover)

Nellie I., d. 1/22/1908 at 4/9/2; diabetes; b. Barrington; Levi Howard (Rochester) and Cora B. Foss (Barrington)

Perley Edward, d. 10/5/1900 at 0/7/20; mirasmus; b. Barrington; Charles Howard (Barrington) and Delia Hart (ME)

William H., d. 1/13/1898 at 57; consumption; farmer; married; b. Rochester; Joel Howard (Rochester) and Harriet Clarke (Barrington)

HOWE,

Daniel, d. 2/3/1906 at --; lobic pneumonia; farmer; b. Barrington; Thomas Howe (Rochester) and Betsey Rowe (Barrington)

Frank L., d. 3/4/1916 at 58/1/7 in Boston, MA; farmer; married; b. Barrington; Daniel Howe (Barrington) and Sarah A. Clay (Lee)

George A., d. 6/22/1901 at 48/0/8; pneumonia; farmer; married; b. Barrington; Daniel Howe (Barrington) and Sarah A. Clay

Ida, d. 9/13/1948 at 87 in Newtown, CT; arteriosclerosis; widow

Isaac L., d. 9/22/1902 at 43; crushed by heavy team; teamster; single; b. Barrington; Jonas Howe (Strafford) and Mary E. Gray (Strafford)

Lena M., d. 5/4/1943 at 49/8/25 in Concord; gen'l paresis; housewife; widow; b. PQ; Joseph Duqette (Canada) and Cora Lyon (Canada)

Mary E., d. 2/13/1890 at 59/8/6; widow; b. Strafford; William Gray and Polly Gray

HOYT,

Benjamin F., d. 1/24/1914 at 75/0/22; farmer; widower; b. Barrington; Benjamin Hoyt (Tamworth) and Mahala Jiles

Charles J., d. 11/14/1897 at 67/4/10; typhoid fever; farmer; married; b. Tamworth; Benjamin Hoyt (Tamworth) and Mahala Giles (Tamworth)

Elizabeth H., d. 2/3/1907 at 67/11/24; senility; housewife; married; b. Barrington; Edward Arlin (Barrington) and Matilda Perkins

Eunice D., d. 3/28/1912 at 60/3/4; apoplexy; housekeeper; married; b. Lebanon; Benjamin Blaisdell (Lebanon) and Ann Gordon (Rome)

George W., d. 1/30/1896 at 43/5/23; cerebral apoplexy; blacksmith; single; b. Barrington; Charles K. Hoyt (Barrington) and Rosetta Drew (Acton, ME)

Mahala, d. 10/14/1899 at 91/5/17; pneumonia; retired; widow; Jonathan Giles (Lee)

Rosetta P., d. 7/6/1898 at 65/4/10; consumption; housewife; widow; b. Acton, MA; Benjamin Drew (Acton)

HUCKINS,
Zachariah B., d. 11/3/1899 at 69 in Concord; ex. in organic brain; grocer; widower

HULL,
Peter A., d. 1/10/1892 at 45/1/12; gastric hemorrhage; married; b. New York, NY; John Hull and Jeannette Foote

HUNT,
Archie G., d. 3/26/1948 at 62/3/13; heart disease; lumber op.; married; b. Johnson, VT; Mary Yaw (Lowell, VT)
Ethel Eldora, d. 3/29/1914 at 0/10/4; b. Barrington; John Hunt (Greenville) and Blanche Mabery (Mechanic Falls, ME)
Marion E., d. 11/21/1961 at 69 in Plymouth, MA; uremia; residence - Plymouth, MA

HUNTINGTON,
Martha S., d. 11/10/1897 at 47/10/3; atrope of liver; domestic; married; b. Lee; Samuel Buzzell (Lee) and Samuel Pierce (sic) (Barrington)

HUNTOON,
George W., d. 11/17/1906 at 80/3/12; senility; widower; b. Franconia; James Huntoon and Abigail Whipple (Franconia)
Melvina R., d. 10/2/1906 at 76/7/17; bronchitis; housewife; married; b. Jefferson; Solomon Drew (Jefferson) and Cynthia Richardson (Lebanon, ME)

HUSTON,
Sarah M., d. 11/17/1948 at 77/7/21; inanition; retired; single; b. IN; David Huston (IN) and Catherine Winship (Rushville, IN)

HUTCHINGS,
Ida, d. 12/14/1978 at 67 in Dover; lacer; married; b. NH; George J. Charest and Anna LaJoie

HUTCHINS,
Charles W., d. 8/25/1954 at 63 in Rochester; carcinoma of stomach; laborer; divorced; b. ME; William Hutchins and Mary Glover

INGLIS,
Margaret, d. 4/15/1960 at 87 in Concord; terminal bronchopneumonia; widow; b. Scotland; John Adair and Agnes Wilson; residence - Rochester
William, d. 7/5/1946 at 77/11/19 in Concord; cancer of colon; carpenter; "Sp"; b. Scotland; William Inglis (Scotland) and Anne Rogers (Scotland)

JACKSON,
Andrew, d. 5/1/1915 at 75; laborer; b. Canada; William Jackson and Ellen Pierce
Frank James, d. 3/26/1900 at 46/5/26; accidental; laborer; divorced; b. Rochester; Asa Jackson (Lee) and Sarah J. Pearl (Farmington)
George W., d. 10/4/1905 at 58/5/22; cerebral hemorrhage; farmer; b. Barrington; George W. Jackson and Angeline Hall (Strafford)

JACOBS,
Mary B., d. 11/13/1908 at 80/0/23; old age; housewife; widow; b. Barrington; James Wiggin and Mehitable Langley

JENNISON,
Harold F., d. 5/8/1956 at 58; pneumonia; electrician; married; b. Winthrop, MA; William S. Jennison and Katherine M. Douglas

JEWELL,
Samuel F., d. 11/22/1911 at 60/8/19; dilation of heart; farmer; married; b. Strafford; Milton Jewel (Northfield) and Nancy Caslley

JEWETT,
William G., d. 4/2/1894 at 51/5/7; apoplexy; farmer; married

JOHNSON,
son, d. 9/17/1913 at 0/0/0; stillborn; b. Barrington; Charles E. Johnson (Greece) and Laurel Burleigh (Dover)

Alexander J., d. 2/19/1985 at 78 in Exeter; machine oper.; widower; b. MA (also listed as 2/19/1984)

Bertha R., d. 10/6/1980 at 77 in Exeter; tel. operator; married; b. ME

Bradbury M., d. 11/19/1890 at 86; widower; b. Barrington

Donald F., d. 9/8/1952 at 8 in Dover; tetanus; student; b. Dover; John J. Johnson and Lucille E. Wiggin; residence - Madbury

Elizabeth G., d. 4/6/1963 at 79; circulatory failure; housewife; widow; b. Sweden; ----- Glantz and Anna S. -----

Ernest Frost, d. 10/14/1944 at 17/1/13; accidental drowning; lum. wkr.; single; b. Melrose, MA; Alexander J. Johnson (Melrose, MA) and Marian E. Ineson (East Weare)

Evelyn M., d. 1/30/1970 at 58 in Dover; Brendle branch block; housewife; married; b. NH; George A. Green and Lilla Waterhouse

Frank V., d. 9/18/1952 at 76; carcinoma of rectosigmoid; mill worker; married; b. Sweden; Nils Johnson and Anna Johnson

Gertrude E., d. 10/29/1964 at 76 in Manchester; sarcoidosis; ret. shoeworker; widow; b. Barrington; Leander Hanscom and Nellie Story; residence - Manchester

Henry, d. 5/24/1947 at 86/7/13; arteriosclerotic heart; no occ.; single; b. Portland, ME; Charles Johnson (Portland, ME) and Margaret ----- (NS)

L. Melvin, d. 1/30/1958 at 90 in Dover; arteriosclerosis; store keeper; widower; b. Syracuse, NY; Marshall Johnson and Julia Johnson

Marion E., d. 1/19/1946 at 38/8/4 in Dover; toxemia of pregnancy; housewife; married; b. East Weare; John H. Ineson (England) and Edith Martin (Concord)

Melvin H., d. 11/27/1970 at 62 in Dover; myocardial infarction; store proprietor; married; b. MA; Letournier M. Johnson and Elizabeth Griffith

Milo G., d. 1/13/1918 at 68/3/19; farmer; married; b. Sweden; John Johnson (Sweden) and Steria Johnson (Sweden)

Raymond P., d. 5/6/1985 at 83; store owner; widower; b. MA

JONES,
Arnold M., d. 11/6/1983 at 72; shipping clerk; widower; b. MA

Earl P., d. 7/31/1979 at 68 in Hanover; engineer; married; b. NH

Elaine S., d. 9/10/1974 at 26; chef; married; b. NH; Oliver G. Koons and Dorothy Gould

Georgie, d. 12/2/1951 at 72; cerebral hemorrhage; teaching; single; b. W. Orange, NJ; ----- Jones and ----- Gardner

Gertrude, d. 2/9/1931 at 30/11/9 in Rochester; cere. embolism; married

Lena R., d. 7/2/1982 at 75 in Rochester; shoe worker; married; b. NH

Rupert L., d. 4/4/1943 at 45/1/24; apoplexy; box shop; widower; b. Warren, VT; Leland Jones (Warren, VT) and Etta Arnold (Warren, VT)

JORDAN,
Robert L., d. 10/7/1933 at --; shock; cln's'r, d'er; married; b. Ellaville, GA; Ely Jordan and Lena Massie

JOY,
Clarence L., d. 2/7/1948 at 72/5/2; toxemia; retired; married; b. Dover; Lovell Joy (Strafford) and Jennie Preston (Barrington)
Lena C., d. 10/10/1969 at 85 in Malone, NY; cardiac arrest; widow; b. NH

KASSOR,
Mary, d. 8/5/1981 at 72 in Dover; housewife; widow; b. NY

KEEFE,
Thomas P., d. 4/12/1969 at 61 in Rochester; coronary thrombosis; maintenance man; married; b. ME; Thomas Keefe and Anne Quigley

KELLEY,
Carrie H., d. 11/26/1914 at 54; housewife; married; b. Chatham; Frank Grace and Elizabeth Johnson (Stowe, ME)
John A., d. 8/13/1953 at 68 in Dover; conc. of brain; woodsman; widower; b. Auburn; John A. Kelley and Elizabeth A. Moses; residence - Strafford
Paul Joseph, d. 1/18/1923 at 54/11/21; machinist; married; b. Cambridge, MA; Patrick Kelley (Ireland) and Jeanette Hamilton (Scotland)
Vincent L., d. 6/14/1986 at 50; laborer; married; b. MA

KELLY,
Mary E., d. 1/31/1973 at 101 in Haverhill, MA

KERAVICH,
Peter, d. 9/22/1974 at 65 in Rochester; machinist; married; b. Poland; Frank Keravich and Anna -----

KESWICK,
Priscilla C., d. 9/30/1923 at 10 wks.; b. Rochester; John Carpenter and Ethel M. Keswick (Canada)

KEYES,
Edward J., d. 8/10/1961 at 13; asphyxiation by drowning; student; b. MA; Edward B. Keyes and Marie Hughes; residence - Hyde Park, MA

KLUESENER,
Joshua, d. 9/13/1977 at 0 in Hanover; b. NH; David Kluesener and Sherri Hull

KNIGHT,
Inez C., d. 3/25/1962 at 77 in Dover; myocardial infarct.; housewife; married; b. NH; Daniel C. Chesley and Clara I. Hall
Thomas A., d. 5/28/1968 at 76 in Togus, ME
Wayne F., d. 5/19/1980 at 43; shoe worker; divorced; b. ME

KOEHLER,
Alta E., d. 9/21/1960 at 70 in Portsmouth; Kimmelstiel-Wilson disease; housewife; married; b. Barrington; George A. Smallcon and Esmeralda J. Howe; residence - Portsmouth
Charles E., d. 5/7/1962 at 73 in Rutland, MA; bronchial pneumonia; residence - Portsmouth

KOST,
daughter, d. 8/21/1982 at 0/0/0 in Dover; b. NH

KUGAN,
Ethel Bell, d. 11/10/1899 at 0/10 in Cambridge, MA; b. Cambridge, MA

LABRECQUE,
Norma G., d. 5/31/1987 at 71 in Rochester; registered nurse; widow; b. NH

LAHAIT,
Ivai, d. 2/16/1903 at 73/10/27; arterial degeneration; laborer; widower; b. Canada

LAHEY,
Adele, d. 4/2/1932 at 72/6/22; cere. hemorrhage; housewife; married; b. Dermond, PQ; Louis Caron (Dermond, PQ) and Marion ----- (Dermond, PQ)

LAMONTAGNE,
Edmund J., d. 7/22/1983 at 72; painter; married; b. MA

LANDRY,
Francis A., d. 8/6/1983 at 74 in Rochester; service sta. mgr.; married; b. NH
James W., Sr., d. 3/26/1987 at 80 in Dover; owner and operator; married; b. NH
Lillian M., d. 12/13/1987 at 90 in Rochester; fancy stitcher; widow; b. NH
Maurice R., d. 8/28/1973 at 43 in Dover; rhabdomiosarcoma; supervisor; married; b. NH; Alfred Landry and Delvina Bouchard

LAROCHELLE,
Joseph E., d. 1/9/1954 at 53 in Rochester; coronary thrombosis; railroad emp.; married; b. Rochester; Adolphe Larochelle and Sarah Lessard

LARY,
Mary E., d. 3/14/1987 at 72; homemaker; divorced; b. ME

LAUDUCI,
Mary R., d. 5/27/1892 at 0/0/2; inanition; b. Barrington; Louis Lauduci and Lora Decatur

LAWRY,
John E. P., d. 6/12/1987 at 83 in Exeter; draftsman; married; b. NH

LAYN,
son, d. 10/5/1898 at 0/0/1; premature birth; b. Barrington; Edward S. Layn (Madbury) and Lilla Hill (Barrington)

LEAHY,
Grace M., d. 8/31/1976 at 43 in Dover; housewife; married; b. NH; Edward D. Stillwagon and Mildred Brennan

LEATE,
George P., d. 2/23/1970 at 88 in Haverhill, MA; coronary collapse
Joseph E., d. 2/22/1955 at 17 in Kingston; suffocation

LEATHERS,
Albert, d. 5/27/1893 at 42; brain disease; farmer; widower; b. Nottingham; Joseph Leathers and Susan Shaw

LEAVITT,
Arthur W., d. 8/4/1966 at 80 in Dover; cerebral thrombosis; electrical eng.; married; b. Waterville, ME; Dudley Leavitt and Bernice Cowan
Florence R., d. 1/25/1967 at 82 in Dover; cardiac decompensation; housewife; widow; b. Salem, MA; Edward B. Rowell and Annie F. Earle

LEE,
James E., d. 3/24/1983 at 56 in Hanover; heavy equip. oper.; married; b. MA

LEEPER,
Durwood D., Sr., d. 9/16/1978 at 78 in Exeter; supervisor; married; b. MA; Bartram G. Leeper and Kitty Pempleton

LEFFEL,
Alfred W., d. 10/19/1958 at 48; acute myocardial fail.; fire watch; married; b. Union City, NJ; Alfred C. Leffel and Caroline Britting

LEIGHTON,
Aimie S., d. 2/7/1907 at 22/3/15; plithysis; single; b. Nottingham; Herbert Leighton (Barrington) and Mary Holmes (Northwood)
Alberta J., d. 11/15/1890 at 0/5/2; b. Barrington; J. Herbert Leighton (Barrington) and Mary E. Holmes (Nottingham)
Ernest L., d. 8/12/1985 at 76; dairy equip. eng.; widower; b. ME
Evelyn M., d. 10/17/1979 at 70 in Rochester; ret. teacher; married; b. MA
J. Herbert, d. 6/14/1891 at 31; married; James Leighton (Barrington) and Betsey Buzzell

LEMAY,
George D., Sr., d. 11/2/1980 at 50 in Concord; programmer; married; b. NH

LEMIRE,
Avila A., d. 1/19/1971 at 77 in Dover; congestive heart fail.; maintenance man; widower; b. Canada; Daniel Lemire and Emma Plante

LENZI,
George F., d. 3/3/1960 at 68 in Dover; uremia; salesman ret.; married; b. Boston, MA; John F. Lenzi and Mary Sullivan; residence - Rochester

George R., d. 8/22/1970 at 55 in Bedford, MA; broncho pneumonia; gas sta. attendant; married; b. NH; George Lenzi and Ruth Bodge

Ruth M., d. 8/13/1980 at 87 in Rochester; at home; widow; b. NH

LEOCHA,
Mitchell J., d. 10/16/1977 at 58 in Hartford, VT; nuclear mech.; married; b. NH; Zenon Leocha and Saturnina Jasinska

LEONARD,
Chilton H., d. 3/9/1982 at 80 in Rochester; teacher; married; b. PA

Edith P., d. 2/1/1987 at 86 in Rochester; library aid; widow; b. NY

LEPINE,
Joseph, d. 4/20/1932 at 72/1; natural causes; laborer; married; b. Canada; Pierre Lepine (Canada) and Marguerite Vegina (Canada)

LESSARD,
Paul E., d. 9/9/1976 at 40 in Boston, MA; machinist; married; b. NH; Wilfred Lessard and Arlene Connelly

LETOURNEAU,
Arthur D., d. 4/16/1952 at 58; acute coronary occlusion; carpenter; married; b. Rochester; Joseph Letourneau and Celina Perrault; residence - Rochester

LEVENDAHL,
Jules E., d. 3/8/1984 at 74 in Portsmouth; musician US Navy; married; b. IA

LEVESQUE,
Benoit, d. 10 or 11/1949 at 32; body found in woods; laborer; single; b. Caribou, ME; William Levesque and Sophia Tardiff; residence - Dover

LIBBEY,
Ella E., d. 2/9/1915 at 64/3/9; at home; widow; b. England; James Dever (England) and M. Cunningham
Reuben, d. 3/25/1910 at 83/9/3; softening of the brain; farmer; married; b. Wolfeboro; Jeremiah Libby and Esther Smith
Sadie May, d. 4/18/1941 at 81/0/18; myocarditis; housewife; widow; b. Ipswich, MA; John Hubbard (Ipswich, MA) and Sarah Hoyt (Concord, MA)

LINCOLN,
Janet A., d. 1/23/1961 at 26 in Madbury; fractured skull; cashier; divorced; b. Dover; Harold W. Henderson and Katherine Wiggin

LINGUARD,
Sarah, d. 6/20/1937 at 79/2/9; arterio sclerosis; at home; widow; b. Barrington; Jerry Hall (Barrington) and Elvira J. Hall (Barrington)

LIRETTE,
Paul W., d. 7/20/1982 at 16; student; b. NH

LIST,
Annie F., d. 9/6/1901 at 18/5/1; pulmonary tuberculosis; housework; single; b. Chelsea, MA; Charles H. List and Lizzie Elliott

LIZOTTE,
Lucy, d. 5/25/1976 at 48 in Portsmouth; nurse's aid; married; b. NH; Jesse Flint and Emily Twitchell

LLOYD,
Bertha, d. 11/22/1965 at 80 in Dover; cardiovenal failure; domestic; widow; b. Palmer, MA; Willard Wade and Cora Robbins

LOCK[E],
daughter, d. 6/22/1914 at 0/0/0 in Dover; Stanley A. Locke (Barrington) and Isabel B. Chesley (Boston, MA)
daughter, d. 6/26/1964 at 0 in Haverhill, MA; stillborn
Abbie, d. 1/8/1892 at 35/4/12; pneumonia; housewife; married; b. Barrington; Ivory Young and Mary A. Seavey
Alphonzo, d. 3/20/1937 at 87/11/10; acute neph. uremia; widower; b. Dover; Alfred Locke (N. Woodstock) and Mary Seavey (Barnstead)
Angeline H., d. 3/18/1919 at 80/1/22; retired; widow; b. Rochester; Watson Hayes (Rochester) and Joanna Winkley (Barrington)
Bert A., d. 8/30/1951 at 82 in Acton, ME; coronary thrombosis; farmer; married; b. Acton, ME; Oliver Locke; residence - Acton, ME
Charles D., d. 11/12/1895 at 70/1/25; hypertrophied prostate; farmer; married; b. Barrington; Eben Locke (Barrington) and Susan Ham (Barrington)
Clarence B., d. 10/2/1955 at 57; massive acute coronary; sweeper; married; b. Barrington; Irving Locke and Linna Buzzell
Cordelia, d. 4/13/1905 at 64/5/17; tuberculosis; housewife; married; b. Barrington; Joseph Grey (Barrington) and Susan Foss (Barrington)
Daniel S., d. 11/26/1929 at 72/9/12 in Cn. Bluffs, IA; spinal thrombosis; retired; married; b. Barrington
Eben S., d. 4/10/1936 at 70/1 in Concord; heart disease; farmer; widower; b. Barrington; Samuel Locke (Barrington) and S. Sherburne (Barrington)

Edith L., d. 1/18/1954 at 82 in Rochester; Hodgkins disease; housewife; single; b. Barrington; Alfonzo B. Locke and Mary Waterhouse

Edna F., d. 11/8/1965 at 91 in Rochester; bronchopneumonia; teacher; single; b. Barrington; Ira W. Locke and Mary A. Babb

Edwin F., d. 6/16/1949 at 75/8/16 in Haverhill, MA; broncho pneumonia; residence - Windham

Elisha E., d. 12/29/1927 at 84/11/12; hypostatic pneu.; retired; married; b. Barrington; Alfred Locke (Barrington) and Mary A. Seavey (Barrington)

Eva M., d. 1/6/1970 at 64 in Rochester; myocardial infarction; widow; b. NH; T. Samuel Dow and Mary Dufway

Frank W., d. 1/5/1951 at 74 in Dover; coronary thrombosis; shoe worker; widower; b. Dover; Oliver Locke and Martha Fernald; residence - So. Berwick, ME

George W., d. 7/29/1944 at 69/7/3 in Rochester; cardiac failure; farmer; single; b. Barrington; Alphonso B. Locke (Dover) and Mary Waterhouse (Barrington)

Hannah, d. 2/13/1931 at 65/8/26; pneumonia; housewife; married; b. St. Johns, NB; Joseph Hanna (England) and Sara Hanna (Ireland)

Harriett B., d. 5/30/1958 at 87 in Rochester; broncho pneumonia; housewife; widow; ----- Berry and ----- Scruton; residence - Rochester

Henry W., d. 3/19/1895 at 67; pneumonia; farmer; married; b. Barrington; Elisha Locke and Sophia Pinkham

Henry W., d. 2/26/1956 at 86; cerebral thrombosis; lumberman; married; b. Barrington; James M. Locke and Cordelia Gray

Idabel, d. 11/15/1902 at 32/2/29; Bright's disease; school teacher; married; b. Lee; Jonathan Thompson (Lee) and Lucy Moore (Amesbury, MA)

Ira W., d. 9/26/1907 at 76/1/10; arterio sclerosis; farmer; widower; b. Barrington; Eben R. Locke (Barrington) and Susan Ham (Rochester)

Irving M., d. 7/29/1930 at 66/5/16 in Boston, MA; car. of rectum; lumber dealer; married; b. Barrington; Elisha E. Locke (Barrington) and Lucy M. Smallcon (Barrington)

Isabelle C., d. 2/21/1931 at 55/11/11; cere. hemorrhage; housewife; married; b. Boston, MA; Isaac Blackburn (Jamaica Plain, MA) and Caroline Fowne

Isabelle E., d. 8/29/1948 at 0/0/0 in Exeter; stillborn; b. Exeter; Stanley E. Locke (Barrington) and Flora Griffin (Ossipee)

James M., d. 3/23/1932 at 87/4/15; old age; retired; widower; b. Barrington; Lyman Locke and Susan Cater (Barrington)

Lavina F., d. 11/6/1890 at 78/8/11; widow; b. Barrington; Daniel French (Stratham) and Mary Tuck (Brentwood)

Linna M., d. 12/13/1962 at 84; arteriosclerotic heart dis.; housewife; widow; b. NH; Samuel Buzzell and Mary E. Hill

Lizzie A., d. 10/10/1966 at 85 in Berwick, ME

Lucy M., d. 11/15/1920 at 77/1/21; at home; married; b. Barrington; John Smallcorn (Barrington) and Lucy Seavey (Barrington)

Mary A., d. 5/21/1900 at 48/9/9; typhoid fever; housewife; married; b. Barrington; Alexander Waterhouse (Barrington) and Lucy Cate (Barrington)

Mattie E., d. 1/4/1956 at 79; coronary thrombosis; teacher; single; b. Barrington; Ira W. Locke and Mary A. Babb

Reginald, d. 10/8/1943 at 27/1/20 in Pembroke; chr. pulmonary T.B.; machinist; married; b. Northwood; Harley Locke (Northwood) and Elizabeth Arlin

Samuel S., d. 11/27/1913 at 78/11/2; acute bronchitis; carpenter; widower; b. Rochester; Alfred Locke (Barrington) and Mary Ann Locke (Rochester)

Stanley A., d. 7/5/1947 at 76/10/5; cerebral hemorrhage; farmer; widower; b. Barrington; Samuel Locke (Barrington) and Sophronia Sherburne (Barrington)

Susanna, d. 7/6/1901 at 80/5/24; old age; housekeeper; widow; b. Barrington; Joel Cater (Barrington) and Mariam Babb (Barrington)

LORANGE,
Joseph F., d. 8/24/1969 at 77 in Dover; cerebral art. insuff.

LORD,
Isadore, d. 4/21/1900 at 50/7/13; bronchial pneumonia; inn keeper; divorced; b. Canada; Albert Lord

LOVEJOY,
Arthur, d. 5/--/1933 at 56/6/25; uremea; farmer; widower; b. Lewiston, ME; Charles L. Lovejoy (Vassalboro, ME) and Sara L. Butler (Berwick, ME)

LOVETT,
Charles S., d. 4/22/1973 at 80 in Dover; acute myocardial infarc.; joiner; married; b. MA; George W. Lovett and Etta Leason

LOWRY,
Ardella F., d. 4/23/1983 at 88 in Exeter; homemaker; widow; b. MA
Kenneth R., d. 9/7/1947 at 0/0/2 in Rochester; congenital heart; b. Rochester; Leo K. Lowry (Revere, MA) and Marion Y. Benson (Whitman, MA)
Leo C., d. 7/17/1973 at 77 in Rochester; pulmonary emphysema; Navy Yard emp.; married; b. SC; William D. Lowry and Lula Clyde

LOWY,
Marie A., d. 7/11/1981 at 77 in Dover; bookkeeper; widow; b. NY

LUBY,
Minnie E., d. 8/19/1985 at 79 in Wolfeboro; housewife; widow; b. South Africa

LUND,
Lura B., d. 8/7/1965 at 83; arteriosclerotic hrt. dis.; housewife; widow; b. Enfield; Edward Johnson and Alma Cowen

MACEACHERN,
Amanda S., d. 2/8/1981 at 27 in Hampton; no occ.; single; b. NH
Suzanne, d. 4/8/1980 at 47 in Manchester; mill worker; married; b. Canada

MACINTIRE,
Joseph, d. 7/31/1937 at 48/7/31; heart trouble; single; b. Rochester; John McIntire (Rochester) and Ann Stewart (Ireland)

MACKENZIE,
George, d. 11/28/1927 at 18/10/2; tuberculosis; at home; single; b. Waterville, ME; George Mackenzie (PEI) and Alice A. Lund (Machias, ME)

MACLEAN,
Arthur D., d. 6/12/1974 at 80; engraver; married; b. NY; Alexander MacLean and Agnes MacLoven

MACRAE,
Alice M., d. 8/19/1953 at 67 in Rochester; coro. thrombosis; shoeworker; single; b. Barrington; Thomas E. MacRae and Claudia Richardson; residence - Rochester
Josephine E., d. 6/27/1965 at 77 in Rochester; myocardial infarction; reg. nurse; single; b. Barrington; Thomas

MacRae and Clarinda Richardson; residence - Rochester

Kenneth, d. 11/21/1956 at 66 in Rochester; cerebral hemorrhage; box maker; married; b. Barrington; Thomas E. MacRae and Clarinda Richardson; residence - So. Lebanon, ME

MAHONEY,
Daniel, d. 9/4/1942 at 60 in Dover; cerebral embolism; woodchopper; widower; b. Ireland

MAILHOT,
Ernest, d. 2/19/1978 at 73 in Rochester; spinner; married; b. Canada; Omer Mailhot and Virginia Farlendeau

MALONE,
Robert S., d. 11/2/1964 at 45 in Lebanon, ME

MANSFIELD,
B. W., d. 12/13/1955 at 33 in Dover; coronary thrombosis; printer; married; b. Gilford; B. W. Mansfield and Mildred Grant

Benjamin W., d. 12/24/1966 at 65 in Dover; carcinoma of lung; machinist; married; b. Gilmanton; William I. Mansfield and Cora M. Tilton

Mildred H., d. 11/27/1970 at 75 in Dover; cerebral hemorrhage; librarian; widow; b. NH; Haven M. Grant and Etta B. Dow

MANSON,
Timothy D., d. 12/7/1891 at 50; single

MARCHAND,
Alfred R., d. 6/14/1974 at 68 in Rochester; machinist; married; b. NH; Albert Marchand and Mathilda Fugere

MARDEN,
Raymond F., d. 8/24/1966 at 58 in Rochester; coronary thrombosis; maintenance; divorced; b. Dover; Harold Marden and Fannie Welsh

MARIOTTI,
Darius C., d. 2/20/1983 at 73 in Rochester; farmer; married; b. NH
Edward C., d. 2/24/1942 at 2/1/29; acute lymp. leuke.; b. Exeter; Darius C. Mariotti (Newmarket) and Fern York (Elmwood, WI)
Fern Y., d. 6/24/1984 at 76 in Rochester; practical nurse; widow; b. WI

MAR[R]ISON,
Bernard, d. 9/10/1975 at 55 in Worcester, MA
Flora L., d. 1/21/1937 at 76/0/14 in Haverhill, MA; broncho pneumonia
Joel, d. 8/31/1902 at 69/9/26; Bright's disease; postmaster; married; b. Barrington; Joel Marrison (Barrington) and Emily Underwood
John H., d. 4/30/1932 at 71/4/19; aortic insufficiency; farmer; widower; b. Barrington; Joel H. Marrison (Barrington) and Mary S. Hanson (Barrington)
Lin'y J., d. 4/23/1923 at 35/6/3; shoemaker; married; b. Strafford; John Marison (Barrington) and Nellie Leighton (Strafford)
Mary A., d. 10/19/1914 at 85/3/7; at home; widow; b. Barrington; Jonas Hanson and Sally Geer (Barrington)
Mary L., d. 4/1/1964 at 76 in Farmington; coronary occlusion; housekeeper; widow; b. Northwood Narrows; Oliver Lewis and Julia Towle; residence - Farmington
Nellie, d. 9/5/1930 at 65/0/21; aortic insufficiency; housewife; married; b. Strafford; Samuel Leighton and Adeline Winkley
Ralph, d. 11/6/1930 at -- in Bradford, MA; duodenal ulcer

MARSAN,
Maurice E., d. 5/17/1968 at 50 in Bay City, MI; basilar art.-thrombosis

MARSHALL,
Philip S., d. 8/11/1981 at 80; architect; married; b. NH
Robert, d. 11/9/1957 at 61 in Boston, MA; massive hemorrhage; residence - Dover
Sophia I., d. 9/26/1978 at 89 in Dover; housewife; widow; b. NH; Josiah I. Smith and Annie M. Hunt

MARSON,
Linda, d. 4/4/1981 at 30 in Richmond, VA

MARSTON,
Michael C., d. 6/22/1979 at 0 in Portsmouth; b. NH

MARTIN,
Benjamin H., d. 4/26/1931 at 0/0/7; heart failure; b. Barrington; Harry B. Martin (Hudson, ME) and Loretta Sardiff (Burlington, VT)

MATTOX,
Alfred Atwood, d. 9/20/1899 at 0/0/7; urenic convulsions; b. Barrington; William Mattox (Lynn, MA) and Sarah J. Davis (Raymond)
Helen A., d. 12/31/1896 at 0/3/23; pneumonia; b. Barrington; William Mattox (Lynn, MA) and Sarah J. Davis (Raymond) (see next entry)
Helen A., d. 1/1/1897 at 0/3/23; pneumonia; b. Barrington; William Mattox (W. Lynn, MA) and Sarah J. Davis (Raymond) (see preceding entry)
Leroy, d. 6/26/1905 at 0/0/6; cardiac insufficiency; b. Barrington; William Mattox (Brentwood) and Lottie Hall (Charlestown, MA)
Mertie E., d. 7/23/1980 at 96 in Dover

William, d. 12/23/1907 at 50/9/25; tuberculosis; B&M sec. hand; married; b. Lynn, MA; Henry Mattox and Catherine Mattox

William H., d. 8/9/1951 at 70 in Rollsinford; coronary thrombosis; belt maker; married; b. Brentwood; William Mattox and Sarah J. Dacis; residence - Rollinsford

MAY,

Sylvester L., d. 7/31/1922 at 54/4/4; sawyer; married; b. Burlington, VT; Lemuel May and Lucy -----

MAYNARD,

Agnes B., d. 7/10/1959 at 67 in Concord; coronary occlusion; housewife; married; b. Nashua; Joseph Brown and Rose Rouleau; residence - Nashua

Carrie M., d. 7/13/1944 at 86/4/23 in Vernon, VT; failure of cardiac; retired; married; b. Somerville, MA; Alfred M. Sibley (Holden, MA) and Caroline Newell (Royalston, MA)

Lambert S., d. 1/27/1950 at 58 in Northfield, MA; coronary thrombosis; shipping clerk; widower; b. FL; Edward K. Maynard and Carrie Sibley

MAYO,

Arthur, d. 3/17/1980 at 75 in Dover

MAZUR,

Adam, d. 9/28/1980 at 64 in Rochester; farmer; married; b. NY

McALLISTER,

Ronald, d. 10/18/1944 at 0/1/2; enteritis from birth; b. Rochester; R. J. McAllister (Eden, VT) and Addie B. Kenney (Dover)

McALPINE,
Andrew, d. 3/16/1973 at 58 in Dover; acute myocardial infarc.; buffer; married; b. NH; George McAlpine and Evlynne Wormel; residence - Somersworth
Mary M., d. 2/23/1964 at 45 in Kittery, ME

McCARTHY,
Dora, d. 1/29/1939 at 39/9/28 in Rochester; chronic nephritis; housewife; married; b. Brandon, VT
John H., d. 1/12/1949 at 12/5/14 in Boston, MA; pelvic abscess; b. Barrington; William McCarthy and Dora Cheltry
William E., d. 2/24/1958 at 72 in Concord; coronary thrombosis; laborer; widower; b. Syracuse, NY; Gilbert McCarthy and Olive Boyce; residence - Gonic

McCONNELL,
Arthur F., d. 10/22/1979 at 88 in Manchester; ret. foreman; married; b. MA

McCORMICK,
Alyce D., d. 7/9/1987 at 62 in Portsmouth; billing clerk; widow; b. MA

McDANIEL[S],
George T., d. 2/14/1984 at 88 in Rochester; widower
Grace E., d. 8/30/1968 at 73; coronary thrombosis; housewife; married; b. MA; William Dodge and Elizabeth Ahearn
Ruth A., d. 4/28/1917 at 56/0/9; housewife; married; b. Epping; Orrin W. Small (Northwood) and Sarah Thompson (Lee)
True W., d. 5/25/1892 at 79/11/5; heart failure; farmer; married; b. Barrington; John McDaniels and Sally Chapman

McDONALD,
Cornelius, d. 3/12/1895 at 87/10/12; bronchitis and old age; farmer; married; b. Ireland; Cornelius McDonald (Ireland) and Kate Hartigan (Ireland)
Cornelius, d. 1/18/1930 at 78/2; farmer; married; b. Broth't'n, NB; Cornelius McDonald (Ireland) and Nora O'Brien (Ireland)
Jessamine A., d. 8/19/1964 at 49 in Rochester; acute vaginal hemorrhage; housewife; widow; b. Wareham, MA; Chester Ramsdell and Kate Perry; residence - Rochester
Nora, d. 2/28/1905 at 87/6; pneumonia; housework; widow; b. Ireland; James O'Brien (Ireland) and Ellen Barry (Ireland)

McDUFFEE,
Frank V., d. 4/12/1983 at 67; accountant; single; b. MA

McGLONE,
Phyllis, d. 9/19/1926 at 0/0/14; fernon oval not clos.; b. Barrington; Arthur G. McGlone (Dover) and Doris Ellison (Barrington)

McGUNNIGLE,
George J., d. 4/27/1949 at 82 in Newmarket; arteriosclerosis; teamster; married; b. Manchester; John McGunnigle and Ann Ritchie; residence - Newmarket
Millie A., d. 5/28/1959 at 94 in Newmarket; arteriosclerosis; housewife; married; b. NB; Simon Belliveau and Nancy Dugay; residence - Newmarket

McISAAC,
John H., d. 9/11/1961 at 63; myocardial infarction; mechanic; single; b. Halifax, NS; Daniel McIsaac and Annie Reddy

McKAY,
Douglass E., d. 8/11/1898 at 0/1/14; deficient vitality; b. Barrington; William McKay (NS) and Martha Dexter (NS)
Martha E., d. 5/20/1963 at 88 in Dover; pneumonia; housewife; widow; b. NS; James Dexter and Sarah Davis
W. Henry, d. 7/21/1932 at 83/2/19; senility; lumber man; married; b. NS; Donald McKay (NS) and Martha Jenkins (NS)
William H., d. 2/2/1972 at 76 in Rochester; carcinoma of lung; mechanic; married; b. NH; William H. McKay and Martha E. Dexter

McKENNEY,
Corinne, d. 9/1/1943 at 5 hrs., 25 mins. in Rochester; sub. hemorrhage; b. Rochester; Thayne Champeon (Dexter, ME) and Dorothy McKenney (Lawrence, MA)

McLAUGHLIN,
Cornelius, d. 8/11/1940 at 46/4/5; pulmonary hemorrhage; barber; single; Cornelius McLaughlin (Ireland) and Catherine Hughes (Ireland)

McMAHON,
John, d. 3/13/1911 at --; natural causes; laborer

McMULLIN,
Harriet T., d. 8/24/1981 at 83; school teacher; married; b. ME

McRAE,
Clarinda, d. 7/27/1930 at 78/0/12 in Rochester; apoplexy; retired; widow; b. Woburn, MA; Joseph Richardson (Rochester) and Elizabeth Hall (Barrington)
Thomas E., d. 12/11/1903 at 70; heart failure; mason; married; b. Cape Breton; T. McRae

MEATTEY,
Herbert E., d. 3/23/1959 at 51 in Rochester; status asthmaticus; hospital worker; married; b. Fitzwilliam; Edward Meattey and Mary Plante
Mathew J., d. 6/30/1969 at 0; smoke inhalation; b. NH; Richard R. Meattey and Jacqueline Stacy

MENTEN,
Anna G., d. 12/25/1959 at 93 in Melrose, MA; arteriosclerotic hrt. dis.; housewife; widow; b. Ft. Laramie, OH; Thomas Nieberg
Gladys E., d. 6/18/1974 at 78; housewife; married; b. IL; Edward Keller and Julia Twomey

MERRILL,
Harrison, d. 5/18/1960 at 75 in Concord; terminal bronchopneumonia; laborer; single; b. Rochester; George Merrill and Nettie Howard
Raymond L., d. 8/21/1971 at 63 in Rochester; acute myocardial infarc.; truck driver; married; b. NH; Herbert Merrill and Della Wilcox; residence - Rochester

MESERVE,
Eugene S., d. 9/3/1976 at 67 in Dover; bridge super.; married; b. NH; Samuel Meserve and Grace Dixon

MILLER,
Alice C., d. 8/13/1954 at 59; myocardial infarction; housewife; married; b. Scotland; Arthur Wesley
Douglas F., Sr., d. 1/31/1969 at 68 in Rochester; carcinoma of stomach; parts manager; widower; b. NH; John Miller and Mary McArtney
Edith G., d. 6/29/1968 at 74; myocardial infarction; housewife; married; b. NH; Leslie Jackson and Laura Howard

Emily, d. 10/24/1959 at 62; gastric hemorrhage; widow; b.
    Dorchester, MA; William H. Doherty and Carrie M. Killen
Leroy C., d. 2/11/1979 at 53 in Manchester; plumber; single;
    b. NH

MILLS,
Winnifred W., d. 9/20/1982 at 90 in Dover; housewife;
    widow; b. MA

MONROE,
Robert L., Jr., d. 4/19/1947 at 22/8/12; accidental drowning;
    student; single; b. Jersey City, NJ; Robert L. Monroe
    (New York, NY) and Claire Groh (Utica, NY)

MOORE,
Florence M., d. 8/9/1974 at 88 in Dover; machine operator;
    single; b. NY; Lester W. Moore and Emily Whitto

MORAND,
Michael H., d. 8/26/1984 at 54 in Newington; electrical tester;
    married; b. MA

MOREAU,
Yvonne M., d. 12/30/1972 at 61 in Rochester; carcinoma of
    lungs; pharmacist; divorced; b. MA; Pierre E. Lacroix and
    Leone DeBellesville

MOREL,
John D., d. 6/21/1986 at 0/3/7 in Rochester; b. NH

MORENCY,
Gary P., d. 8/5/1972 at 23; accidental drowning; shoe
    worker; single; b. NH; Pearl Morency

MORI,
Paul S., d. 6/13/1982 at 23 in Dover; electrician; single; b. NH

MORLEY,
Joseph A., d. 7/27/1924 at 77/8/27; retired; married; b. NS; Thomas Morley and Ann Quinn

MORRILL,
David F., d. 6/30/1916 at 76/5/8; married; b. Chesterfield; ---- Morrill and ----- French

MORRISON,
Sarah, d. 3/31/1935 at 69/9/15; acute gastritis; retired; single; b. PEI; Kenneth Morrison (PEI) and Hannah J. Horne (PEI)
Sarah A., d. 10/5/1913 at 73/4; apoplexy; housewife; widow; b. Barrington; Joseph Ellison (Barrington) and Betsey Doe (Barrington)
Sean P., d. 5/28/1970 at 0 in Dover; prematurity; Gayle M. Morrison
Susan, d. 8/2/1979 at 86 in Boston, MA

MOSES,
Sarah, d. 9/23/1893 at 82; old age; housewife; widow; b. Barrington; S. Freeman (Barrington) and Fanny Chamberlain (Barrington)

MUDGETT,
Lilla, d. 5/2/1896 at 28/1/26; typhoid fever; housewife; married; b. Warren; Isah F. Ford (Benton) and Harriet N. Ford (Montpelier, VT)

MUNROE,
Ruth H., d. 6/21/1960 at 60 in Dover; gangrene of bowel; housewife; married; b. Northwood; Charles H. Kelley and Mary Lang

MURPHY,
Henry J., d. 1/16/1978 at 55 in Rochester; fire fighter; married; Henry Murphy and Florence Rochileau

NAGY,
Lillian, d. 5/1/1976 at 54 in Dover; packer; married; b. NY; William Michael and Florence Harrison
Tony E., d. 12/8/1978 at 35; factory worker; married; b. NH; George Nagy and Lillian Michael

NASON,
James W., d. 6/21/1900 at 0/1/8; who. cough, bron.; b. Barrington; W. H. S. Nason (Rochester) and Ellen F. Gray (Barrington)
Kenneth E., d. 8/10/1962 at 0/0/0 in Rochester; stillbirth; b. Rochester; Raymond C. Nason and Lillian A. Wilds
Laura E., d. 4/29/1907 at 44/1; obstruction of bowels; housewife; married; b. Lee; John Simpson
Maria, d. 9/29/1898 at 0/0/17; cholera infantum; b. Barrington; W. H. S. Nason (Rochester) and Ellen F. Gray (Barrington)
Mary E., d. 3/16/1909 at 21/4/16; cerebral meningitis; student; single; b. Barrington; William H.S. Nason (Rochester) and Ellen F. Gray (Farmington)
W. H. L., d. 1/21/1894 at 3/6/6; capillary bronchitis; b. Barrington; W. H. S. Nason (Barrington) and Ellen Gray

NEAL,
Carl A., d. 10/2/1952 at 0/0/1 in Dover; congenital heart disease; b. Dover; Roger Neal and Laura Wheeler

Edwin C., d. 4/10/1969 at 89 in Dover; arteriosclerotic heart
dis.; farmer; married; b. CT; Jacob Neal and Ann Clark
Elizabeth F., d. 7/14/1905 at 71/2; valvular heart disease;
housewife; married; b. Newton, MA; James Taylor
(England) and Martha Cheney (MA)
Jacob S., d. 4/19/1890 at 49/2/21; married; b. Barrington
Janice V., d. 3/20/1971 at 36 in Marlborough, MA; crush of
chest; housewife; married; b. NH; John Taylor and Avis
Caswell
Michael, d. 2/6/1954 at 29 hrs. in Rochester; atelectasis,
bilateral; b. Rochester; Roger E. Neal and Laura
Wheeler
Myra H., d. 5/25/1976 at 89 in Rochester; housewife; widow;
b. NH; Nathan J. Hanson and Olive A. Leighton
Roger, d. 6/5/1971 at 45 in Rochester; carbon monoxide
poisoning; asst. shipper; married; b. NH; Edwin C. Neal
and Myra -----
Thomas J., d. 5/17/1962 at -- in Ngong, Africa; injuries mult.
extreme; member USAF; married; b. IN

NEWCOMB,
Charles D., d. 8/4/1962 at 74 in Hanover;
bronchopneumonia; railroad man; married; b. ME; David
Newcomb and Eveline Nichols; residence - Dover

NEWELL,
Arlin M., d. 10/16/1965 at 74 in Dover; arteriosclerotic hrt.
dis.; farmer; married; b. Canada; George Newell and
Lucy Tabor; residence - Dover
Emeroy F., d. 7/27/1968 at 77 in Dover; cerebral vascular
acc.; housewife; widow; b. Canada; Harvey Brock and
Clista Parsons; residence - Dover
Robert W., d. 4/19/1947 at 23/1/2; accidental drowning;
student; single; b. Quincy, MA; Harold P. Newell
(Newton, MA) and Marie G. Wright (Boston, MA)

NEWHALL,
Joshua L., d. 4/29/1962 at 44; asphyxiation by drowning; carpenter; married; b. MA; John A. Newhall and Marguerite Hunter; residence - Newburyport, MA
Lois E., d. 7/6/1987 at 61; secretary; married; b. MA

NEWMAN,
Edwin F., d. 12/2/1955 at 61; coronary occlusion; mechanic; married; b. Henderson, LA; Walter Newman and Florence Beard; residence - Stoughton, MA

NEWSKY,
Alice V., d. 10/12/1976 at 67 in Dover; housewife; widow; b. NH; Michael Timmions and Rose A. Donnahie

NICKERSON,
Anna I., d. 2/1/1971 at 56 in Rochester; congestive heart fail.; housewife; married; b. Canada; William Keefer
Florence, d. 5/31/1958 at 69 in Rochester; coronary heart; housewife; widow; b. Barrington; Herbert Griffin and Mary Hanson

NIEMI,
Elsie H., d. 1/27/1978 at 59 in Dover; manager; married; b. MA; Gabriel Kelimola and Selma Kailemzi

NOBLE,
Zita L., d. 2/26/1961 at 62; coronary infarction; housewife; widow; b. Malden, MA; Patrick O'Laughlin and ----- O'Hara

NOE,
child, d. 12/2/1910 at 0/2; asphyxiation; b. Canterbury; Fred G. Noe

NOFTALL,
Frederick J., d. 12/30/1962 at 73 in Dover; coronary thrombosis; gov't worker; married; b. Newfoundland; Michael Noftal and Mary Gushue
Jessie, d. 2/12/1937 at 60/9/9; arterio sclerosis; at home; married; b. Newfoundland; Henry Hoffman (Newfoundland) and Sarah Duffill (Newfoundland)
Lena D., d. 12/13/1978 at 93 in Dover; housewife; widow; b. NY; Edward Allen and Elizabeth David

NORMAN,
Dorothy D., d. 12/29/1975 at 65 in Dover; assembler; married; b. NH; Herman Dodge and Louise Babb
Harvey, d. 5/5/1935 at 0/5/27; fracture of skull; b. Barrington; John Norman (Madbury) and Clara A. Varney (Barrington)
John, d. 11/13/1952 at 47 in Dover; coronary thrombosis; carpenter; married; b. Madbury; Charles Norman and Mary Nichols; residence - Dover
Lewis, d. 1/30/1980 at 72 in Dover

NORMANDY,
Emily F., d. 8/23/1956 at 88 in Dover; thrombosis; housewife; widow; b. England; David Witto and Phillipa Bennett; residence - Dover
Joseph H., d. 11/17/1953 at 71; coro. thrombosis; camp mgr.; married; b. Providence, RI; Joseph H. Normandy and Mary Eldredge

NORRIS,
Francis F., d. 11/19/1914 at 64 in Nashua; conductor; married

NORTON,
Leslie E., Jr., d. 7/15/1983 at 57 in Rochester; motor sales mgr.; married; b. NH

NUTE,
Horace I., d. 8/14/1895 at 55/8; Bright's disease; farmer; single; b. Barrington; Cyrus Nute (Barrington) and Susan Seavey (Barrington)

NYE,
Robert E., d. 12/28/1960 at 46; fract. jaw and skull; chauffeur; married; b. Manchester; George Nye and Flora Carson; residence - Manchester

O'BRIEN,
Katherine, d. 7/6/1901 at 52; valvular disease of heart; housekeeper; widow; b. Ireland
Mary, d. 12/26/1900 at 0/3/15; spinal meningitis; b. Tewksbury, MA; Mary O'Brien (Ireland)

O'DONNELL,
John P., d. 11/18/1977 at 62

O'MALLEY,
Jennifer M., d. 9/9/1979 at 0 in Hanover; b. NH

OBERLANDER,
Lester C., d. 8/6/1985 at 77 in Exeter; printer; married; b. MA

ODIORNE,
Mary W., d. 8/23/1909 at 81 in Boston, MA; cancer; Benjamin Odiorne

ORDWAY,
Leslie G., d. 9/13/1970 at 48; fracture of skull, etc.; machine crater; married; b. NH; Harry G. Ordway and Florence L. Goodwin; residence - Pittsfield

OSBORNE,
Nellie F., d. 10/1/1973 at 85 in Rochester; carcinoma of stomach; restaurant wk.; widow; b. NH; James F. Abbott and Emma Jordan; residence - Rochester

OUELLETTE,
Marie, d. 2/15/1959 at 61; fractured skull; weaver; married; b. Canada; Theophile Perron and Marie Rouleau; residence - Pawtucket, RI

PAGE,
Grace E., d. 6/5/1891 at 7; John A. Page (Rochester)
Mabel, d. 1/1/1891 at 11; John A. Page (Rochester)

PALMER,
son, d. 6/23/1957 at 0/0/2 in Rochester; prematurity; b. Rochester; Raynor W. Palmer, Jr. and Gloria LeDuc; residence - Dover
Alta R., d. 12/29/1909 at 23/1/25; acute bronchitis; at home; single; b. Barrington; John R. Palmer (Portsmouth) and Ellen A. Gray (Dover)
Barry A., d. 6/27/1956 at 6 hrs. in Rochester; premature birth; b. Rochester; Raynor W. Palmer, Jr. and Gloria F. LeDuc; residence - Dover
Burton R., d. 12/7/1954 at 84 in Hampden, ME; cerebral accident; widower; b. Dover; John W. Palmer and Ellen Gray; residence - Hampden, ME
Ellen A., d. 9/17/1930 at 83/9/12 in Dover; frac. of shoulder
Frank J., d. 11/3/1905 at 32/5; acute cong. both lungs; shipping clerk; single; b. Edg'h. MA; Henry Palmer (England) and Mary Flinn (Ireland)
Fred E., d. 5/3/1974 at 79 in Dover; laborer; single; b. MA; Eugene Palmer and Nellie Hayes
John R., d. 8/1/1900 at 63/8/6; pneumonia; farmer; married; b. Portsmouth; William Palmer (Milton) and Mary Plummer (Milton)

Katherine D., d. 12/28/1978 at 83

Lester R., d. 5/23/1982 at 81 in Dover

Nellie F., d. 10/17/1908 at 49/4/27; phthesis; housewife; married; b. Barrington; Eleazer C. Hayes (Barrington) and Lizzie A. Cater (Barrington)

Vicki Ann, d. 8/29/1955 at 0/0/8 in Rochester; immaturity; b. Rochester; R. W. Palmer, Jr. and Gloria F. LeDuc; residence - Dover

William, d. 7/19/1964 at 87 in Dover; chronic heart failure; blacksmith ret.; widower; b. Dover; John R. Palmer and Ellen Gary; residence - Dover

PAQUIN,

Miriam B., d. 7/13/1969 at 62 in Dover; arteriosclerotic hrt. dis.; registered nurse; married; b. NS; Charles Phillips and Emeline Harris

PARADISE,

Alberta M., d. 1/14/1978 at 72 in Dover; housewife; widow; b. NH; John F. Kelley and Grace M. Perkins

Charles A., d. 4/23/1960 at 74 in Dover; carcinoma; machinist ret.; married; b. Boxford, MA; Joseph Paradise and Jeannette King

PARKER,

Albert E., d. 8/3/1981 at 83 in Rochester; farmer; married; b. Canada

Melvin F., d. 8/13/1942 at 1/5/24 in Rochester; mitral insufficiency; b. Hudson, MA; Stanley Parker (Charlestown, MA) and Rose E. St. John (Suncook)

Thelma D., d. 8/3/1984 at 80 in Rochester; antique dealer; widow; b. NH

PARSHLEY,
Alice F., d. 5/16/1959 at 54 in Rochester; cerebral hemorrhage; bookkeeper; married; b. Lynn, MA; John W. French and Dellie E. Lilly
Asa L., d. 12/24/1949 at 67/9/27 in Rochester; arteriosclerotic heart disease; chef; divorced; b. Stratford; Charles E. Parshley and Nan E. Jewel; residence - No. Barrington
Greenleaf, d. 4/18/1900 at 52/7/10; pneumonia; farmer; married; b. Strafford; Stephen G. Parshley (Strafford) and Mary J. Fogg (Nottingham)
Joseph E., d. 8/16/1981 at 77 in Dover; fibre co. emp.; married; b. NH
Mary, d. 7/22/1927 at 63/11/20; cancer of stomach; housewife; married; b. Strafford; Asa Jewell (Strafford) and Marion Thompson (Barrington)
Robert V., d. 6/3/1963 at 72 in Manchester; carcinomatosis abdominal; ret. farmer; married; b. Strafford; Charles E. Parshley and Mary E. Jewell

PATRICK,
Mary E., d. 10/24/1933 at 64/3/3; cerebral apoplexy; at home; married; b. Philadelphia, PA; Gilbert H. Prindle (NY) and Elizabeth Collins (Dover, DE)

PATRONE,
May E., d. 12/3/1982 at 90 in Dover; clerk; widow; b. MA

PATTEN,
Edwin W., d. 12/10/1982 at 81 in Dover; contractor; married; b. ME

PEABODY,
Myron F., d. 8/18/1977 at 73; contractor; married; b. MA; Frederick M. Peabody and Mabel R. Towne

PELADEAU,
Lillian, d. 10/20/1977 at 81 in Rochester; widow; b. ME; Augustus Cooper and Lettie McLaughlin

PERAULT,
Julia, d. 6/7/1929 at 45; at home; married; b. America; Leon Capen (Barrington) and Clara Freeman (Barrington)

PERKINS,
Daniel G., d. 8/20/1960 at 0 in Dover; cerebral anoxia; b. Dover; residence - Dover
Daniel O., d. 8/30/1981 at 56 in Dover
Hiram, d. 12/6/1891 at 76; widower
Jessie M., d. 3/11/1896 at 36/4/25; p'r'nch nephritis an'mia; housewife; married; b. Barrington; George Willey (Barrington) and Mary Berry (Barrington)
Ursula, d. 12/24/1912 at 62; pulmonary tuberculosis

PERRON,
John, d. 7/20/1935 at 74; heart disease; laborer; widower; Ignace Perron (Canada) and Adelie Ligotte (Canada)

PERROW,
Samuel R., d. 9/11/1979 at 59 in Boston, MA

PERRY,
Abiah W., d. 2/20/1911 at 89/8/27; valvular heart disease; widow; b. Barrington; John Brown (Barrington) and Sarah Hanson (Strafford)
Charles M., d. 5/27/1913 at 77/5/29; cancer of stomach; blacksmith; widower; b. Barrington; Smith Perry (Barrington) and Betsey Canney (Strafford)
Etta C., d. 3/3/1910 at 71/10/18; hypostatic pneumonia; housewife; married; b. Northwood; John C. Hill (Northwood) and Rebecca Bartlett (Northwood)

Ocie M., d. 12/29/1895 at 11/8/17; double abscess; domestic; single; b. Lynn, MA

Pomphrette, d. 2/28/1896 at 80/9/10; cancer; farmer; widower; b. Barrington; Pomphrette Peary (sic) (Barrington) and ----- Smith (Barrington)

Ralph E., d. 5/1/1894 at 22/9/12; phthisis pulmonalis; clerk; single; b. Northwood

Sarah C., d. 12/19/1891 at 69; married; John Smith (Barrington) and Lucy Brown (Strafford)

Timothy R., d. 7/3/1966 at 3; asphyxiation by drowning; b. Quincy, MA; Frank Perry and Barbara Robinson; residence - Wollaston, MA

William, d. 7/30/1900 at 90/1; old age; farmer; married; b. Barrington; Pomfret Perry (Barrington) and ----- Smith (Barrington)

PETERS,
Raymond V., d. 6/5/1985 at 72 in York, ME; married

PETERSON,
Dorothy M., d. 7/10/1967 at 60 in Dover; bacteremic shock; housewife; married; b. Farmington; Frank Howe and Lena Duquette; residence - Madbury

Harold L., d. 8/2/1979 at 56 in Dover

John M., d. 1/15/1973 at 79 in Concord; bronchial pneumonia; widower; b. Sweden

PHILLIPS,
Charles D., Sr., d. 3/18/1979 at 86 in Rochester; switchman; widower; b. RI

Esther A., d. 6/10/1946 at 76/619 in Rochester; circulatory failure; housewife; married; b. England; John Taylor (England) and Emma Clark (England)

Wendell E., d. 4/29/1951 at 70 in Boston, MA; pulmonary embolism; retired; married; b. East Burke, VT; Edward Phillips and Etta -----

PIERCE,

Almira, d. 1/20/1899 at 75/9/18; disease of heart; single; b. Barrington; Curtis Pierce (Barnstead) and Olive Woodhouse (Madbury)

Comfort, d. 10/1/1946 at 79/1/27 in Dover; cancer of esophagus; retired; widow; b. England; James Blount (England) and Jane Marsh (England)

Edna, d. 3/8/1981 at 91 in Rochester; housewife; married; b. NH

Israel E., d. 6/18/1897 at 54/10/10; car. hypertrophy; farmer; single; b. Barrington; Hall Pierce (Barrington) and Sally Hall (Strafford)

James B., d. 1/14/1890 at 82/7/23; widower; b. Barrington; Curtis Pierce (Berwick, ME) and Olive Woodhouse (Barrington)

James D., d. 11/23/1985 at 91 in Rochester; farmer; widower; b. NH

John I., d. 12/27/1898 at 80/2/25; acute bronchitis; farmer; widower; b. Barrington; Curtis Pierce (Barnstead) and Olive Woodhouse (Barrington)

Lewis M., d. 5/22/1939 at 66/8/19; sopsis; farmer; married; b. Barrington; Moses Pierce (Barrington) and Susan E. Dunton (Whitefield, ME)

Martha M., d. 7/20/1898 at 50/2/21; conontsibus; housewife; married; b. Rochester; James S. Foss (Rye) and Sally Hodgdon (Stratham)

Moses, d. 1/12/1899 at 79/3/4; acute bronchitis; farmer; married; b. Barrington; Israel Pierce (Barrington) and Abigail Hall (Barrington)

Muriel L., d. 4/22/1969 at 39 in Brunswick, ME

Susan E., d. 5/17/1921 at 88/5/3; widow; b. Whitefield, ME; Ephraim Dunton (ME) and Abigail Williams (ME)

PIGEON,
Lloyd C., d. 9/13/1959 at 22 in Sanford, ME; shock; welder; single; b. Cornish, ME; Moses B. Pigeon and Fannie E. Wiley; residence - Madbury
Moses B., d. 11/13/1960 at 72 in Dover; myocardial infarction; lumberjack ret.; married; b. Canada; Thomas Pigeon and Mary -----; residence - Madbury

PIKE,
Alvah B., d. 11/13/1934 at 69; heart disease; laborer; b. Middleton; James Pike and Susan Cloutman

PILLER,
William L., d. 2/24/1965 at 44 in Exeter; coronary thrombosis; salesman; married; b. Quincy, MA; Aaron Piller and Esther Richmond

PINKHAM,
Annie E., d. 10/14/1962 at 81 in Newburyport, MA; cerebral thrombosis; residence - MA
Ansel E., d. 4/6/1959 at 64 in Dover; uremia, bladder obstr.; laborer, highway; married; b. Lee; George Pinkham and Belle Stimpson; residence - Dover
Frank J., d. 9/8/1967 at 88 in Salisbury, MA; coronary thrombosis; residence - Salisbury, MA
Rose M., d. 1/7/1969 at 68 in Dover; chronic pyelonephritis

PITTSLEY,
Edna, d. 3/10/1954 at 63; heart disease; housewife; married; b. Fairhaven, MA; Walter Pierce and Mary Brightman

PLONDE,
Anna, d. 2/26/1928 at 63/2/5; diabetes; at home; widow; b. Canada; Antoine Chategay (Canada) and P. Tussotte (Canada)

PLOURDE,
Desange M., d. 5/5/1949 at 79; coronary thrombosis; housewife; widow; b. Canada; Frederick Rioux and Marguerite Rousseau
Joseph F., d. 5/2/1982 at 56 in Somersworth
Olivine M., d. 10/22/1948 at 48/7/6 in Dover; thrombacy topenia; housewife; married; b. Canada; Joseph Dalpie (Canada) and Parmelle Lucies (Canada)

PLUMMER,
Charles L., d. 11/13/1948 at 65/3/3; coronary thrombosis; retired; married; b. Nashua; Charles Plummer and Priscilla Johnson (Portland, ME)

PLUNKETT,
Annie M., d. 12/7/1924 at 77/10/23; married; b. Barrington; Hateville Bumford (Barrington) and Elizabeth Henderson (Barrington)
Robert, d. 10/11/1938 at 91/11/26 in Dover; diabetes mellitus; farmer; married; b. England; John Plunkett (England)

POIRIER,
Rene, d. 7/2/1986 at 69 in Rochester; carpenter; married; b. RI

POLLETTA,
Lena E., d. 7/29/1987 at 75; house wife; married; b. MA

POORE,
Donald L., d. 11/23/1985 at 65 in Portsmouth; florist; married; b. NH

POPE,
Edmund L., d. 1/23/1935 at 65/2/2; suicide by shooting; rd. super.; single; b. Northfield, VT; Edmund T. Pope (Northfield, VT) and Harriet E. Farnham (Brookfield, VT)

PORTER,
Daisy M., d. 6/19/1984 at 75 in Dover; homemaker; widow; b. Canada
Vivian A., d. 6/2/1982 at 67 in Portsmouth; housewife; married; b. NS

PORTRIE,
Doris M., d. 7/28/1971 at 56 in Rochester; acute myocardial infarc.; cementer; married; b. NH; Cyril Mennon and Josephine Dumas

POST,
Harrison M., d. 5/2/1976 at 87 in Rochester; shoe worker; married; b. NY; James Post and Cornelia Palmer
Lillian B., d. 6/13/1981 at 91; housewife; widow; b. NS

POTTER,
Ernest R., d. 7/31/1959 at 73 in Saugus, MA; ant. myocardial infarct.; printer; widower; b. Pawtucket, RI; Charles Potter and Ann L. Childs

POWERS,
Charles, d. 7/9/1920 at 40/11

PRAY,
Albert O., d. 11/20/1961 at 82 in Dover; pneumonia; leather wkr.; widower; b. Dover; George E. Pray and Carrie M. Evans

PRESCOTT,
Jane, d. 2/25/1896 at 77/10/5; interstitial nephritis; housewife; married; b. Barrington; John Arlin and Abbie Leathers

Mary, d. 10/17/1896 at 55/0/25; general debility; housewife; married; b. So. Berwick, ME; Mark Grant (So. Berwick, ME) and Mary Grant (Lebanon, ME)

Mary Jane, d. 12/24/1893 at 68/5/14; pneumonia; housewife; widow; b. Barrington; N. Hall (Barrington) and Sarah Gilpatrick (Lee)

PRESTON,
A. B., d. 4/12/1929 at 67/2/19; married; b. Strafford; Wingate Preston (Barrington) and Mary J. Jewell (Strafford)

Addie G., d. 1/31/1931 at 76/0/7; arterio sclerosis; widow; b. No. Berwick, ME; Samuel Hubbard (No. Berwick, ME) and Lucinda Bragdon (Kennebunk, ME)

Fannie, d. 6/15/1936 at 73/7/14; chronic nephritis; retired; widow; b. Strafford; Hiram Perkins and Mary S. Young

Frank P., d. 11/9/1964 at 71; coronary thrombosis; highway worker; b. New Hampton; Frank W. Preston and Addie G. Hubbard; residence - Manchester

John D., d. 4/24/1976 at 81 in Rochester; farmer; married; b. NH; Alberton Preston and Fannie Perkins

Margaret J., d. 11/2/1899 at 72; heart failure; housewife; married; b. Barrington; James Ham and Mary Foss

Mary Jane, d. 1/30/1905 at 69/9/7; organic heart disease; housekeeper; married; b. Strafford; Milton Jewell and Nancy Colley

Nathaniel, d. 10/1/1903 at --; gangrene of feet; farmer; married; b. Barrington; Samuel Critchett and Lydia Clark

Walter J., d. 4/9/1910 at 4/3; mitral regurgitation; b. Barrington; Alburton Preston (Strafford) and Fannie Perkins (Strafford)

Wingate T., d. 3/31/1913 at 82/2/28; arterio sclerosis; farmer; widower; b. Barrington; Samuel Critchett (Barrington) and Lydia Clarke (Barrington)

PRIESTLEY,
Ralph L., d. 1/8/1972 at 88 in Dover; cardiac arrest; salesman; widower; b. NH; James H. Priestley and Agnes Wood

PRINCE,
Grace, d. 2/2/1964 at 99 in Concord; terminal broncho pneumonia; housewife; widow; b. Barrington; Joel Chesley and Elva Richardson; residence - Derry
Hazel W., d. 11/28/1987 at 89; housemother; married; b. NH

PUGNI,
Louis F., d. 8/3/1966 at 82; coronary thrombosis; maitre d'hotel; single; b. Garlasco, Italy; Peter Pugni and Angela -----; residence - Boston, MA

PURDY,
Louise G., d. 1/14/1961 at 82 in Somersworth; cardiac decompensation; housekeeper; single; b. Lowell, MA; Michael Corr and Naomi Ramsey; residence - Somersworth
Robert P., d. 5/31/1977 at 77 in Rochester; chef; married; b. MA; John B. Purdy and Louise G. Corr

PURINGTON,
Ernest T., d. 2/1/1976 at 67 in Dover; painter; married; b. NH; Walter Moody and Sadie J. Bailey
Jennie M., d. 6/19/1977 at 63 in Strafford; assembler; widow; b. MA; Clarence F. Bell and Mary Colclough

PURVIS,
Catherine S., d. 2/15/1967 at 71 in Rochester; cerebral thrombosis; housewife; married; b. East Rochester; Charles F. Clark and Jennie N. Sinclair
E. Leonard, d. 10/17/1970 at 74; carcinoma of lung; woolen worker; widower; b. CT; David H. Purvis and Grace Young

QUIMBY,
Harry, d. 10/4/1941 at 59/4/6; retired; widower; b. Troy

QUINN,
Lydia S., d. 3/2/1902 at 59/11/4; rheumatism; housewife; married; b. Strafford; Silas Drew (VT) and Eliza J. Caverly (Barrington)

RADLOFF,
John R., d. 3/5/1983 at 23 in San Juan, PR; single; b. NH

RAMSDELL,
Chester H., d. 11/16/1965 at 82 in Rochester; uremia; boat builder; widower; b. Wareham, MA; William Ramsdell and Abbie Gregory
Dana W., d. 7/24/1985 at 34 in Rochester; never worked; single; b. NH
James B., d. 6/3/1986 at 18 in Dover; proof operator; single; b. NH
Kate P., d. 7/2/1960 at 72; malignant melanoma; housewife; married; b. Wareham, MA; Franklin F. Besse and Sophia Bryant

RAND,
Mary A., d. 3/21/1928 at 75/6/7; ateres sclerosis; at home; widow; b. Strafford; Benjamin Berry (Strafford) and Nancy Hanscomb (Lebanon, ME)

RANSOM,
Reuben, d. 4/--/1921 at 82/2; moulder, ret'd; married; b. Durham; George W. Ransom (Concord) and Sophia Bunker (Durham)

RAYWORTH,
Horace B., d. 9/27/1984 at 79 in Rochester; chauffeur; married; b. Canada

READ,
Alice M., d. 5/12/1947 at 61/11/24; angina pectoris; housewife; married; b. Charlestown, MA; Joseph Morley (at sea) and Mary Swinemer (NS)
Anson D. C., d. 11/2/1962 at 86 in Dover; coronary thrombosis; mill worker; widower; b. MA; William H. Reed; residence - Somersworth
William H., d. 7/6/1937 at 91/4/6; hypostalic pneumonia; widower; b. Boston, MA; Joseph Read (Boston, MA) and Margaret Henry (Boston, MA)

REED,
son, d. 5/16/1914 at 0/0/0; b. Barrington; Dexter K. Reed and Alice Morley
Charles H., d. 7/27/1917 at 64/3/19 in Rochester; laborer; married; b. Barrington; Holmes Reed (Rochester) and Sarah A. Hall (Barrington)
James E., d. 11/18/1978 at 30 in Danvers, MA
Sophronia E., d. 3/21/1916 at 80/2/21; housewife; married; b. Strafford; Joseph Hill
William J., d. 4/4/1899 at 87/1/10; old age; farmer; widower; b. Barrington; Robert Reed and Abiah Foss

RENAUD,
Rita G., d. 5/30/1981 at 61 in Dover; housewife; married; b. ME

REYNOLDS,
Della M., d. 10/13/1917 at 55/4/6; school teacher; single; b. Dover; James O. Reynolds (Tuftonboro) and Myra J. Hill (Strafford)
John W., d. 4/1/1896 at 61/6; stricture of urethra; laborer; married; b. Barrington; Ephraim Reynolds (Barrington) and Mary P. Locke (Barrington)
Mira J., d. 5/11/1920 at 85/6/18; widow; b. Strafford; Nicholas D. Hill and Eliza Johnson

RICHARDS,
Bridget M., d. 12/27/1910 at 33; probably ac. alcoholism; housewife; married; b. Ireland

RICHARDSON,
Annie M., d. 5/5/1972 at 83 in Dover; acute heart failure; housewife; widow; b. MA; Charles Norman and Mary L. Nichols; residence - Dover
Charles F., d. 6/26/1949 at 80 in Dover; coronary occlusion
Edwin, d. 3/25/1940 at 75/6/3; cere. hemorrhage; farmer; married; Joseph Richardson (Rochester) and Elizabeth Hall (Barrington)
Elizabeth H., d. 4/30/1899 at 81/11/21; old age; at home; married; b. Barrington; David Hall (Barrington) and Alice Allen (Barrington)
Elizabeth H., d. 12/2/1912 at 55/0/17; valvular heart disease; housewife; married; b. Barrington; John A. Buzzell (Barrington) and Mary S. Daniels (Nottingham)
Jennie E., d. 2/8/1941 at 73/7/22 in Dover; chronic myocarditis; housewife; widow; b. Durham; John B. Trask (ME) and Elizabeth Moore (Ireland)
John F., d. 6/1/1946 at 90/2/7 in Dover; arterioscl. heart dis.; carpenter; married; b. Barrington; Joseph Richardson (Gonic) and Elizabeth Hall (Barrington)
Joseph P., d. 1/30/1905 at 89/0/26; senile dementia; farmer; widower

Maud C., d. 12/29/1947 at 76/3/11 in Dover; arteriosclerotic heart; retired; widow; b. Boston, MA; Oscar Phushee (Lebanon) and Sophronia Chase (Lebanon)

Olga F., d. 3/4/1972 at 80 in Rochester; arteriosclerotic hrt. dis.; housewife; widow; b. ME; John T. Peterson and Matilda Olson; residence - East Rochester

RICKER,
Willie, d. 12/26/1892 at 33/4/15; acute meningitis; laborer; married; b. Lebanon, ME; Willis Ricker and Sarah A. Hersom

RICKETSON,
Florence, d. 7/22/1943 at 93/11/2; arterio sclerosis; no occ.; widow; b. Taunton, MA; Berry W. Williams (Taunton, MA) and ----- Reed (Taunton, MA)

RILEY,
George W., d. 8/5/1921 at 17/9/9; laborer; single; b. Barrington; Charles Riley (Barrington)

RIVERS,
William, d. 5/27/1911 at 59/1/22 in Hooksett; diabetes mellitus; landlord; married; b. ME; John Rivers (Canada) and Mary Gelina (Canada)

ROBERTS,
Edward E., d. 1/18/1911 at 69/6/6; pneumonia; farmer; b. Middleton; Ira Roberts (Middleton) and Malinda Merritt (MA)

George E., d. 4/3/1929 at 78/7; farmer; single; b. Barrington; Nathaniel Roberts (Barrington) and Nancy Arnold (Barrington)

Gladys, d. 11/19/1919 at 19/2/26; mill operator; single

Meddie, d. 9/22/1944 at 65/7/29; angina; laborer; single; b. Wayland, MA; Anthony Roberts and Adelaide -----

Sherman F., d. 8/8/1946 at 70/2/10; coronary thrombosis; carpenter; married; b. Strafford; Freeman Roberts (Strafford) and Clara Brown (Northwood)

ROBINSON,
Clark, d. 5/21/1890 at 65; b. Barrington
Frederick J., d. 4/29/1985 at 66; math professor; married; b. NH
Mary S., d. 10/10/1890 at 45/10/21; married; b. Barrington; Richard Ayers (Randolph) and Susan C. Leighton (Barrington)
William F., d. 1/31/1914 at 78/6/13; laborer; widower; b. Barrington; Aaron Robinson and Rebecca Swain (Strafford)

ROLLINS,
Clifford, d. 7/9/1981 at 22; military police; married; b. IL
George A., d. 8/14/1981 at 62 in Manchester
Hannah B., d. 8/13/1951 at 90; inanition; housework; single; b. Dover; John F. Rollins and Mary Bartlett
Peter, d. 3/13/1916 at 64; single; black; b. NC
William E., d. 11/26/1979 at 72 in Dover; real estate broker; married; b. MA

ROOT,
Waldon, d. 1/26/1985 at 58 in Rochester; driver; divorced; b. VT

ROPER,
George O., d. 8/27/1961 at 59 in Rochester; coronary thrombosis; civil eng.; married; b. Sylvester, GA; Amos A. Roper and Margaret Dewey

ROSS,
Abbie M., d. 8/4/1927 at 73/2 in Rochester; Bright's disease; housewife; widow; b. Barrington; Dennis Brown (Barrington)
Albert M., d. 8/30/1964 at 79 in Dover; cerebral vascular accident; electrician; widower; b. Charlestown, MA; James J. Ross and Margaret McDonald
Bertha J., d. 12/22/1961 at 73 in Dover; cerebral thrombosis; housewife; married; b. Lynn, MA; Charles O. Lovering and Marcellas Arnold
Charles E., d. 3/30/1953 at 60 in Rochester; acute cor. occlusion; mill wkr.; married; b. Barrington; Amaca L. Ross and Abbie Brown; residence - Rochester
Fred W., d. 6/12/1958 at 68 in Madbury; heart block; stock farmer; widower; b. Barrington; Amasa L. Ross and Abbie Brown; residence - Madbury
George E., d. 1/13/1960 at 41 in Somersworth; exsanguination; laborer; single; b. Barrington; Charles Ross and Florence Arlin; residence - Rochester
Pearl P., d. 1/22/1951 at 66 in Exeter; hypertensive heart disease; housewife; married; b. Boston, MA; James Drysdale and Susan Baker; residence - Madbury
Raymond C., d. 10/7/1976 at 45 in Portland, ME
Russell L., d. 7/5/1977 at 53 in Madbury; truck driver; married; b. NH; Fred W. Ross and Pearl Drysdale

ROWE,
Charles C., d. 3/24/1923 at 79/0/11; farmer; married; b. Danvers, MA; William Rowe (Strafford) and Olive Lowe (ME)
Elizabeth E., d. 1/8/1914 at 78/3/8; housewife; widow; b. Salem, MA; John Brown (England) and Anna Stickney (England)
Ellsworth C., d. 9/4/1902 at 2/6/3; meningitis; b. Barrington; Charles C. Rowe (Danvers, MA) and Susan Layte (Lawrence, NS)

Emma J., d. 3/16/1903 at 32/10/14 in Rochester; pulmonary consumption; housewife; married; b. Barrington; George E. Hingham and Malinda Arlin (Barrington)

Iva M., d. 11/1/1895 at 29/5; epilepsy; domestic; single; b. Barrington; Charles C. Berry (Danvers, MA) and Lizzie Rowe (Barrington)

John F., d. 4/4/1908 at 49/10/9; natural causes; sawyer; married; b. Barrington; John F. Rowe and Nancy D. Heath (Bristol)

Lizzie M., d. 7/12/1894 at 48/6; cancer; housewife; married; b. Barrington; Ivory M. Berry (Barrington) and Mary J. Demeritt (Barrington)

Nancy D., d. 5/16/1916 at 84/10/5; housekeeper; widow; b. Bristol; Nathaniel Heath and Esther Thomas

Susan, d. 10/9/1950 at 78; arteriosclerosis; housewife; widow; b. NS; Hiram Layte and Mary Braselton

Wesley A., d. 4/25/1897 at 15/4/16; typ. pneumonia; school boy; b. Barrington; Alvah J. Rowe (Barrington) and May M. Perkins (Barrington)

ROWELL,
Edward M., d. 11/9/1975 at 79 in Rochester; state emp.; married; b. MA; Edward B. Rowell and Annie Earle

ROY,
Elva, d. 4/9/1925 at 30/2/24; cancer kidneys; married; b. Cambridge, MA; Louis Chamberlain (Canada) and Adeline Bolluc (Canada)

Jean L., d. 12/17/1979 at 53 in Dover

Sandra J., d. 3/28/1947 at 0/0/0 in Dover; stillbirth; b. Dover; Jean L. Roy (Dover) and Leah Richardson (Dover)

ROYA,
Evelyn, d. 9/25/1984 at 60 in Dover; housewife; married; b. PA

RUEL,
Deborah J., d. 1/29/1977 at 19 in Portland, ME; single
Delina, d. 10/29/1942 at 92/2/13; cerebral thrombosis; at home; widow; b. Canada; John Sylvain (Canada) and Caroline Simoneau (Canada)

RUSSELL,
Fred Arthur, d. 3/31/1944 at 83/6/25; apoplexy; carpenter; widower; b. Danvers, MA; Enoch Russell (Lynnfield, MA) and Mary Russell (Lynnfield, MA)

RUTHERFORD,
Jerome J., d. 8/16/1951 at 57; acute coronary occlusion; salesman; married; b. Eastport, ME; John Rutherford and Ellen Cassidy

SABOL,
Ruth G., d. 11/26/1968 at 22 in Dover; gun shot wound; married; b. NH; Ralph W. Paige and Emma Osborne; residence - Dover

SAMPSON,
Avilda, d. 7/15/1951 at 91; apoplexy; housewife; widow; b. E. Brownfield, ME; Gardner Tibbetts and Mary J. Meader
Samuel M., d. 3/18/1946 at 76/5/10; chronic nephritis; farmer; married; b. Canada

SANBORN,
Benjamin F., d. 12/30/1897 at 70; apoplexy; laborer; widower; Benjamin Sanborn and Hannah Gray (Barrington)
Troy M., d. 5/8/1983 at 15; student; b. NH

SANDERS,
Alta M., d. 3/8/1954 at 72 in Madbury; coronary thrombosis; own home; married; b. Lee; William H. Mattox and Sarah J. Davis; residence - Madbury
Charles G., d. 1/10/1951 at 81 in Madbury; arteriosclerosis; farmer; married; b. Madbury; William J. Sanders and Harriet Huckins; residence - Madbury
Frank W., d. 1/4/1951 at 87; carcinoma of stomach; farmer; widower; b. Madbury; William J. Sanders and Harriet Huckins; residence - Madbury
Gary A., d. 3/18/1967 at -- in Rochester; anencephaly; b. Rochester; John H. Sanders, Jr. and Lynda L. Gagne
John H., d. 12/27/1973 at 67 in Rochester; construction wkr.; married; b. NH; Charles G. Sanders and Emma E. Hayes
Michael J., d. 10/24/1983 at 0/0/1 in Hanover; b. NH
Mina, d. 11/17/1959 at 56 in Dover; macroglobulinemia; teacher; married; b. Dover; J. Erskine Forest and Ruth Ackerman
William B., d. 3/3/1974 at 83 in Dover; farmer; widower; b. NH; Frank W. Sanders and Carrie Burke

SANIAL,
Rene W., d. 3/17/1967 at 86 in Rochester; pneumonitis; telephone emp.; widower; b. New York, NY; Lucien Sanial and Caroline McClenahan

SAULNIER,
Thomas, d. 7/17/1983 at 68 in Portland, ME; realtor; married

SAUNDERS,
Rufford T., d. 6/17/1984 at 64 in Dover; police officer; married; b. Canada

SAWTELLE,
Grace M., d. 10/29/1964 at 93; arteriosclerotic disease; housewife; widow; b. Belfast, ME; Frank Stevens

SAWYER,
Annie, d. 11/26/1892 at 103; old age; widow; b. Barrington
Betsey, d. 10/25/1908 at --; shock; housewife; married

SCHEU,
Arnold L., d. 6/27/1982 at 73 in Rochester; lineman; married; b. MA

SCHUMAN,
Alvin R., d. 9/11/1981 at 46 in Dover; fork lift oper.; married; b. PA

SCHWARTZ,
Charles J., d. 7/21/1909 at 55/2/17; phthisis; motorman; married; b. Westbrook, ME; John C. Schwartz (Europe) and Caroline Lennan (Europe)

SCOTT,
Evelyn, d. 9/2/1962 at 48 in OH; deferred

SEAMAN,
Ernest R., d. 7/9/1965 at 68; congestive failure; molder; widower; b. Nashua; William R. Seaman and Eleanor O'Keane; residence - Rochester

SEAVEY,
daughter, d. 10/11/1917 at -- in Laconia; b. Lakeport; Charles L. Seavey (Northwood) and Bessie M. Cook (Yarmouth, ME)
Daniel A., d. 10/15/1897 at 69/4/18; consumption; farmer; married; b. Barrington; Ichabod Seavey (Barrington) and Relief Corson (Lebanon, ME)

Ralph, d. 5/14/1982 at 87 in Tilton

Sarah A., d. 10/30/1918 at 81/9/30; retired; widow; b. Barrington; Rufus Varney (Barrington) and Sally Foss (Barrington)

SECKENDORF,
Paul A., d. 5/10/1978 at 68 in MA; painter; married; b. MA; Paul A. Seckendorf and Mary Nickerson

SEELEY,
Alphenia E., d. 7/18/1966 at 78 in Kittery, ME; coronary occlusion; housewife; widow; b. NB; Peter Waltman and Nancy Antoine

SELINERR,
daughter, d. 9/28/1915 at --; b. Barrington; Joseph J. Selinerr (Shrewsbury) and Louisa Hutchinson (Bethel, ME)

SEWARD,
Ella L., d. 12/24/1943 at 89/10/12; bronchial pneumonia; housewife; single; b. Saugus, MA; Garland S. Seward and Mary Mansfield (Saugus, MA)

Ida F., d. 12/24/1943 at 92/4/17; bronchial pneumonia; housewife; single; b. Saugus, MA; Garland S. Seward and Mary Mansfield (Saugus, MA)

SHANNON,
David W., d. 10/28/1978 at 78 in Dover; shipping clerk; divorced; b. PA; David Shannon and Estella -----

SHARE,
Sarah E., d. 10/21/1954 at 67 in Dover; acute heart failure; widow; b. Barrington; Elmer A. Hall and Lucy M. Drew; residence - Rochester

SHAW,
Fred W., d. 3/10/1955 at 20; fractured skull; bulldozer operator; single; b. Dover; Ford W. Shaw and Mary E. Babb; residence - Dover
Frederick A., d. 6/4/1965 at -- in MA; Downs syndrome; residence - Dover
Mary S., d. 5/23/1918 at 77/6/18; retired; widow; b. Northwood; Sylvester Day (Northwood) and Deborah Evans (Northwood)

SHEA,
Arnold F., d. 7/23/1976 at 62; chemist; divorced; b. NH; John Shea and Maude Hall
Margaret, d. 2/26/1985 at 86 in Dover; housewife; widow; b. MA

SHEEHAN,
Joseph T., d. 1/11/1981 at 62 in Rochester; fire fighter; married; b. MA

SHENAN [or Sherar],
Alice A., d. 9/26/1969 at 81 in Kittery, ME; anoxia; housekeeper; widow; b. Sweden; Olaf Anderson

SHEPHERD,
Margaret L., d. 5/13/1977 at 55; housewife; married; b. NJ; James Trewhella and F. Blanche Clarke

SHERBURN[E],
Joel F., d. 6/26/1907 at 72/10/2; Bright's disease, dropsy; farmer; married; b. Barrington; Jacob Sherburne (Barrington) and Marinda Meserve (Barrington)
Joel R., d. 7/6/1960 at 76; cardiovascular accident; carpenter ret.; married; b. Barrington; Loel Sherburne and Stella Richardson

John T., d. 8/7/1914 at 68/11/27; laborer; single; b. So. Boston, MA; John Sherburn (Barrington) and Sarah J. Hall (Barrington)

Marilla, d. 4/9/1896 at 87; old age; housewife; widow; b. Barrington; Andrew Meserve (Barrington) and Patience Hall (Barrington)

Sarah J., d. 12/28/1892 at 77/8/28; peritonitis; domestic; single; b. Barrington; Jacob Hall and Betsey Meserve

Stella, d. 4/6/1924 at 69/9/5; housewife; widow; b. Winchester, MA; Joseph R. Richardson and Elizabeth Hall

SHERMAN,

Milton M., d. 9/15/1973 at 63 in Dover; cardiac arrest; salesman; married; b. MA; Lawrence Sherman and Elizabeth Mamley

Rowena, d. 1/18/1976 at 58; reg. nurse; widow; b. MA; Albert K. Scrivan and Sarah F. Hartshorn

SHIERE,

Lester, d. 10/2/1982 at 60 in Dover; teacher; married; b. MA

SILMAN,

John L., d. 10/27/1975 at 62; ret. farmer; married; b. PA; Grover Silman

SILVER,

Leonard A., Sr., d. 7/16/1977 at 71; engineman; married; b. ME; Leonard A. Silver and Esther Kimball

SIRRELL,

Curt F., d. 11/18/1943 at 5 hrs., 5 mins. in Rochester; premature; b. Rochester; Curt F. Sirrell (Southbridge, MA) and Goldie M. Emmons (Tilton)

Francis C., d. 11/18/1943 at 2 hrs., 12 mins. in Rochester; premature; b. Rochester; Curt F. Sirrell (Southbridge, MA) and Goldie M. Emmons (Tilton)

SKINNER,
Nora B., d. 10/22/1982 at 87 in Rochester

SLACK,
Marion R., d. 3/24/1927 at 31/3/10; mitral insufficiency; accountant; married; b. Wilton; Edmund L. Poper (Northfield, VT) and Anna E. Ballard (Brandon, VT)

SLEEPER,
Helen S., d. 12/5/1956 at 47 in Wolfeboro; accidental drowning; reg. nurse; married; b. Barrington; Frank Caswell and Mary Buzzell; residence - Wolfeboro

SLOPER,
Ada S., d. 1/12/1935 at 60/7/10; lateral sclerosis; housewife; married; b. Barrington; Benjamin Willey (Barrington) and Augusta Cater (Barrington)
Myron J., d. 4/17/1933 at 33/11/2; ulcer of stomach; farmer; single; b. Barrington; Joshua A. Sloper (Strafford) and Ada S. Willey (Barrington)

SMALL,
Frank B., d. 11/7/1916 at 45; teamster; Alden Small

SMALLCON,
George A., d. 5/26/1912 at 60/3/25; cancer of prostate gland; blacksmith; married; b. Barrington; John L. Smallcon (Dover) and Lucy Seavey (Barrington)
George P., d. 7/30/1948 at 76/5/9 in Portsmouth; myocardial failure; retired; widower; b. Barrington; George Smallcon (Barrington) and Esmerald Howe (Barrington)

Lucy, d. 9/15/1894 at 83/6/25; heart failure; housewife; widow; b. Barrington

SMART,
Laura, d. 5/10/1967 at 106 in Haverhill, MA; cerebral thrombosis; residence - Haverhill, MA

SMITH,
Adelia, d. 7/25/1937 at 59; chronic myocarditis; housewife; married; b. Keene; James Shanley (Burlington, VT) and Harriet Robson (M'nstock, NJ)
Agnes, d. 3/12/1969 at 86 in Norwood, MA; residence - Dedham, MA
Carleton O., d. 9/19/1973 at 63 in Rochester; coronary occlusion; carpenter; divorced; b. NH; Osborne Smith and Gladys Plummer; residence - Dover
Charles E., d. 5/23/1891 at 47; married; Winthrop Smith (Barrington) and Nancy Hall
Dana G., d. 8/22/1891 at --; James F. Smith (Lee) and Florence A. Clay
Donald H., d. 4/7/1982 at 70 in Rochester; inspector; married; b. NH
Dorothy A., d. 1/26/1969 at 59 in Dover; hemorrh. subarachnoid; secretary; married; b. MA; Arbra Freeman and Lillian B. Thurston
Edna B., d. 3/21/1968 at 82 in Conway; pulmonary edema; housewife; widow; b. Canada; Jonathan E. Chapman and Ella J. Snow
Elizabeth, d. 8/11/1939 at 60/0/4; coronary thrombosis; housewife; widow; b. Brentwood; Joshua Fieldsend (England) and Lydia Fuller (Brentwood)
Elizabeth S., d. 9/15/1947 at 93/6/21 in Rochester; arteriosclerosis; housework; widow; b. Barrington; Samuel Locke (Barrington) and Sophronia Sherburne (Barrington)

Frank D., d. 4/8/1919 at 67/8/10; farmer; married; b. No. Hampton; John H. Smith (Boston, MA) and Joanna Alden

H. Grace, d. 12/1/1918 at 31/7/4; housewife; married; b. Coaticook, PQ; Jonathan Chapman (Hatly, PQ) and Ellen I. Snow (Compton, PQ)

Hannah, d. 2/5/1898 at 76/7/29; interstital nephritis; at home; widow; b. Old Town, ME; Joseph Jacobs (Sanford, ME) and Kazah Thompson

Hannah F., d. 4/17/1960 at 84; arteriosclerotic hrt. dis.; housewife; widow; b. Strafford; Martin V. Howard and Hannah A. Gray

Harold M., d. 9/25/1949 at 62 in Rye; coronary occlusion; attorney; married; b. Barrington; Walter K. Smith and Flora E. Hoyt; residence - Portsmouth

James F., d. 7/21/1943 at 33/1/29 in East Derry; frac. of skull; laborer; single; b. Barrington; John D. Smith (Haverhill, MA) and Bessie Hanscom (Somerville, MA)

James W., d. 3/3/1922 at 82/10/3; farmer; widower; b. NH

John D., d. 5/15/1915 at 68; teamster; b. Barrington; Daniel H. Smith (Barrington) and Hannah Jacobs (Augusta, ME)

John G., d. 7/18/1914 at 83/11/28 in Marlboro; farmer; David B. Smith (Barrington) and Isabel B. Chesley

LaForrest P., d. 7/23/1944 at 60/10/10; lung metastosis; farmer; divorced; b. Barrington; Lewis N. Smith (Barrington) and Elizabeth Locke (Barrington)

Lewis, d. 5/18/1951 at 69 in Rochester; coronary thrombosis; farmer; divorced; b. Barrington; Lewis N. Smith and Elizabeth S. Locke

Lewis N., d. 12/27/1938 at 84/11/5; heart disease; farmer; married; b. Barrington; Winthrop Smith (Barrington) and Nancy Hall (Barrington)

Lloyd B., d. 11/12/1953 at 68 in Dover; Hodgkins disease; ret. mail c.; married; b. Barrington; Lewis N. Smith and Elizabeth S. Locke

Lyle C., d. 6/9/1966 at 75 in Dover; cerebral thrombosis; mail carrier; widower; b. Barrington; Lewis N. Smith and Elizabeth Locke; residence - Dover

Sarah Irene, d. 4/4/1945 at 48/1/1; metastatic car. of lungs; housework; married; b. Dover; James H. Smith (Dover) and Mary Merrifield (No. Berwick, ME)

Stella B., d. 7/21/1904 at 26/9/25; eclampsia; housewife; married; b. E. Boston, MA; James Drysdale (English Channel) and Susan Baker (NY)

Walter H., d. 7/4/1926 at 68/10/3; chr. bronchitis; lumberman; married; b. Barrington; Winthrop Smith (Barrington) and Nancy Hall (Barrington)

William Hall, d. 12/26/1931 at 80/6/14; arterio sclerosis; farmer; single; b. Barrington; Winthrop Smith (Barrington) and Nancy Hall (Barrington)

Wilson W., d. 9/6/1912 at 63/3/19; valvular heart; laborer; single; b. Barrington; Winthrop Smith (Barrington) and Nancy Hall (Barrington)

Winthrop, d. 5/23/1904 at 84/1/3; heart disease; widower; b. Barrington; Winthrop Smith (Durham) and Betsey Hall (Barrington)

SNELL,
Eliza C., d. 5/26/1927 at 68/11/28; chr. myocarditis; at home; widow; b. Strafford; Plummer Hill (Strafford) and Lucy Hayes (Northwood)

SNOW,
Philip, d. 3/24/1892 at 27; consumption; laborer; single; b. Barrington

SOMERVILLE,
Harold F., d. 11/10/1978 at 72 in Rochester; polaroid worker; married; b. MA

SOULE,
Emily E., d. 2/18/1895 at 0/9; croup; b. Barrington; Elmer Soule (Auburn, ME) and Genise Hart (Auburn, ME)

SPENDLOVE,
Hannah, d. 8/22/1899 at 71/6/8; blood poisoning; housewife; married; b. Barnstead; Joshua Parshley
Mary, d. 4/26/1906 at 51; chr. diffuse nephritis; housewife; married

SPROWL,
Raymond E., d. 1/16/1986 at 73 in Rochester; marine machinist; married; b. ME

SPURRELL,
Joel D., d. 5/7/1971 at -- in Bridgton, ME; fetal death

STABILE,
Denise M., d. 9/24/1977 at 16 in Rochester; student; single; b. VA; Pasquale D. Stabile and Maureen B. Coughlin

STABLER,
Edward R., d. 9/26/1971 at 65 in Dover; bronchopneumonia; professor; married; b. CT; Edward R. Stabler and Elizabeth Tubby

STACY,
Kathrina B., d. 5/22/1948 at 68/3/7 in Winthrop, MA; carcinoma of cervix; housewife; married; b. Hebron, NY; Joshia Shaw and Emiline Stark

STADIG,
Albert L., d. 4/9/1972 at 52 in Dover; hepatic failure; carpenter; married; b. NH; Albert N. Stadig and Gertrude W. Wick

STANLEY,
Charles A., d. 3/27/1950 at 3/2/9 in York, ME; brain abscess; b. Lynn, MA; Herbert Stanley and Anna Drysdale

STEPHEN,
Mary, d. 7/10/1965 at 102; uremia; housewife; widow; b. Scotland; David Anderson and Jane Keir

STEPHENS,
Annie L., d. 4/23/1901 at 0/1/27; marasmus; b. Shelburne; John W. Stevens (sic) (Franklin) and Daisy V. Sturtevant (Haverhill, MA)

STEVENS,
Lloyd E., d. 6/29/1970 at 76; cerebral contusions; barber; married; b. NH; Everett W. Stevens and Lizzie Glidden; residence - Sanbornville

Meta B., d. 4/20/1965 at 91 in Rochester; arteriosclerotic hrt. dis.; housewife; widow; b. Barrington; Jonathan Berry and Mary S. Felker

Rudd O., d. 3/15/1961 at 66; arteriosclerotic hrt. dis.; meat cutter; married; b. Durham; Frank Stevens and Caroline Smart

STEVENSON,
Douglas M., d. 7/25/1987 at 83 in Rochester; instructor; widower; b. NH

Eva L., d. 5/13/1982 at 80 in Rochester; teacher; married; b. NH

STILES,
Ella, d. 2/4/1936 at 45/4/12 in Rochester; uraemia; housewife; married; b. Barrington

Ida E., d. 5/10/1955 at 85 in Dover; arteriosclerotic heart disease; housework; single; b. Lunenburg, MA; Asa Stiles and Mary Litchfield

Walter, d. 5/27/1951 at 86; gangrene; farmer; widower; b. Lunenburg, MA; Asa Stiles and Mary Litchfield

STIMPSON,
Albert A., d. 6/14/1964 at 69; coronary thrombosis; grocer; married; b. Portsmouth; George D. Stimpson and Florence H. Langmaid

STONE,
son, d. 3/2/1928 at 0/0/0 in Rochester; stillborn; b. Rochester; Harry Stone (Barrington) and Elsie Freeman (Providence, RI)
Elsie M., d. 12/14/1979 at 78 in Rochester; housewife; married; b. RI
Frank, d. 6/6/1932 at 78; suicide by shooting; farmer; widower; b. Canada; Xavier Stone (Canada) and Margaret Fowmied (Canada)
Helen Clara, d. 5/7/1913 at 40/6/22; carcinoma; housewife; married; b. Rochester; James F. Riley (Wellington) and Margaret Seeleye (London, England)
Isabell, d. 11/17/1951 at 82 in Concord; cardiac decompensation; retired; single; b. MA
Marguerite E., d. 3/4/1972 at 73 in Lansdowne, DE; acute myocardial infarction
Oralie L., d. 8/28/1931 at 77/9/27; cere. thrombosis; housewife; married; b. Canada; Isaac Lahais (Canada) and Mari Prue (Canada)
Robert L., d. 3/26/1969 at 68 in Delaware City, PA; widower
Willie, d. 4/14/1979 at 74 in Rochester; truck driver; widower; b. NH

STRACHAN,
Addic M., d. 2/5/1912 at 37/11/22; bronchial pneumonia; housewife; married; b. Barrington; Charles E. Arlin (Barrington) and Charlotte Babb (Barrington)

Charles E., d. 3/13/1946 at 81/6/4 in Concord; hyperten. cardio. dis.; carpenter; married; b. Strafford; William Strachan

George C., d. 2/8/1964 at 59 in Rochester; rheumatic heart disease; auto mechanic; married; b. Barrington; Charles ----- and ----- Arlin; residence - Rochester

Raymond, d. 3/22/1930 at 27/3/28 in Northwood; lobar pneumonia; widower

STRATTON,

Elizabeth, d. 9/6/1909 at 85/3/14; bloody dysentery; housekeeper; widow; b. Barrington; William Seavey (Barrington) and Hannah Foss (Barrington)

Ephraim M., d. 7/28/1899 at 82/1/17; chronic cystitis; farmer; married; b. Conway; Samuel Stratton

STRONG,

Alberta R., d. 11/10/1959 at 9 hrs. in Rochester; immaturity; b. Rochester; Leonard Strong and Ruth A. Erickson

Marlene A., d. 4/11/1963 at 0 in Dover; hyaline membrane dis.; b. Dover; Leonard Strong and Ruth Erickson

SULLIVAN,

Mary A., d. 1/11/1980 at 89 in Rochester; housewife; divorced; b. VT

SWAIN,

child, d. 7/31/1934 at 3 hrs.; prematurity (7 mos.); b. Barrington; William S. Swain (Barrington) and Mary Sanders (Madbury)

daughter, d. 5/20/1936 at 0/0/1; premature birth; b. Barrington; William S. Swain (Barrington) and Mary E. Sanders (Madbury)

son, d. 3/20/1939 at --; hemorrhage; b. Barrington; Dorothy E. Swain (Barrington)

Ansel P., d. 3/5/1926 at 50/5/15; car. of s. intestine; farmer; married; b. Barrington; Greenleaf Swain (Barrington)

Bennett E., d. 2/11/1895 at 70/10/20; subacute pylonephritis; farmer; widower; b. Barrington; Israel Swain (Barrington) and Susan Bennett (Northwood)

Clara Augusta, d. 11/8/1911 at 67/9/26 in Boston, MA; chronic valvular heart dis.

Clarence, d. 8/6/1957 at 69 in Revere, MA; uremia

Effie A., d. 3/18/1949 at 87/3/29; cerebral hemorrhage; housework; widow; b. Barrington; Samuel A. Locke and Sophronia Sherburne

Elizabeth, d. 6/30/1895 at 86/5/11; cerebral apoplexy; domestic; widow; b. Barrington; Jacob Hall (Barrington) and Betsey Meserve (Barrington)

Harry E., d. 11/29/1899 at 21/2/20; typhoid fever; farmer; single; b. Barrington; Greenleaf Swain (Barrington) and Sarah Bodge (Barrington)

John Q. A., d. 3/12/1912 at 85; apoplexy; farmer; widower; b. Barrington; Mark Swain (Barrington) and Eliza Clough (Pittsfield)

Mary Esther, d. 1/25/1965 at 73; circulatory failure; housewife; married; b. Madbury; Frank W. Sanders and Caroline Burke

Maude L., d. 12/14/1951 at 67 in Dover; acute peritonitis; seamstress; widow; b. Rochester; Bickford Rand and Mary A. Berry; residence - Dover

Roy V., d. 9/15/1964 at 81 in Rochester; carcinoma of liver; ret. educator; married; b. Barrington; Greenleaf H. Swain and Sarah E.P. Bodge

Sally, d. 1/6/1898 at 83/6/3; old age; housewife; widow; b. Barrington; Gideon Sherburne (Barrington) and Betsey Chesley (Barrington)

Sarah F. P., d. 10/15/1900 at 56/7/18; consumption; housekeeper; widow; b. Barrington; Isaac Bodge (Barrington) and Hannah Pearl (Barrington)

William B., d. 9/28/1941 at 80/1/5 in Rockingham; hypostatic pneumonia; farmer; widower; b. Barrington; Bennett Swain (Barrington) and Martha J. Swain (Barrington)

William S., d. 11/27/1974 at 78; self employed; widower; b. NH; William A. Swain and Effie A. Locke

SWANSON,
George A., d. 9/1/1974 at 51; supervisor; single; b. RI; William B. Swanson and Mary Fortin

SWENSON,
Joseph C., d. 1/27/1969 at 73 in Exeter; vent. tachycardia fib.; janitor; married; b. NY; John Swenson and Gustava Kristiansen

TANNER,
Celia, d. 3/24/1974 at 97 in RI (burial)
John, d. 9/21/1891 at 80; married
Olive F., d. 7/31/1892 at 81; found dead; housekeeper; widow; b. Newmarket

TAPLIN,
Alvin E., d. 5/8/1955 at 74 in Rochester; cerebral vascular accident; painter; married; b. Utica, NY; Andrew E. Taplin and Martha Thompson; residence - Rochester
Olive B., d. 6/11/1963 at 74 in Gonic; acute myocardial infarction; housewife; widow; b. West Boxford, MA; Minander Rokes and Maria Whittier; residence - Gonic

TARBELL,
Fannie B., d. 10/1/1968 at 86; arteriosclerotic hrt. dis.; shoe worker; widow; b. NH; Daniel B. Clough and Lydia F. -----

TARBOX,
Nettie, d. 9/22/1890 at 32/11/20; married; b. Haverhill, MA; Charles H. Savage (Ashburnham, MA) and Hannah J. West (Haverhill, MA)

TARDIFF,
Louis T., d. 7/3/1975 at 72; cook-owner; married; Joseph Tardiff and Emma Trenblay

TASKER,
Elizabeth, d. 5/8/1929 at 86/0/9 in Strafford; housekeeper; widow; b. Barrington; Ezra Caverly (Strafford) and Eliza Caverly (Strafford)

TAYLOR,
Agnes M., d. 3/24/1964 at 75 in Rochester; cerebral hemorrhage; housewife; married; b. Sweden; Carl A. Anderson
Avis J., d. 3/22/1987 at 74 in Dover; accounting supervisor; widow; b. NH
Blanche, d. 11/2/1980 at 80 in Rochester
Donald G., d. 1/20/1963 at 2 in Dover; meningitis; b. Dover; Harold R. Taylor and Mildred McDaniel
Fielding, d. 11/14/1968 at 79; arteriosclerotic hrt. dis.; carpenter; widower; b. Newfoundland; Noah H. Taylor and Ann Pilgrim
Glenn R., d. 12/4/1975 at 25 in Rochester; store clerk; single; Robert F. Taylor and Doris L. Stone
Herman H., d. 6/26/1971 at 73 in Rochester; congestive heart failure; shoeworker; married; b. ME; Byron Taylor and Jennie Stoddard
John V., d. 10/5/1964 at 63; coronary thrombosis; shipfitter; married; b. Dover; John J. Taylor and Elizabeth Hagan
Judith Ann, d. 12/13/1947 at 0/1/12; whooping cough; b. Dover; Harold R. Taylor (Chelsea, MA) and Mildred McDaniel (Barrington)

Mildred E., d. 6/29/1972 at 53 in Hanover; hepatic failure; housewife; married; b. NH; George McDaniel and Grace Dodge

TEAGUE,
Harlan L., d. 5/10/1977 at 73; elec. engineer; divorced; b. ME; Charles M. Teague and Clara Beckett

TEBBETS,
Charles A., d. 5/5/1935 at 73/7/11; broncho pneumonia; farmer; widower; b. Barrington; Amos B. Tebbets (Barrington) and Catherine Wadleigh (Meredith)

TEBBETTS,
C. Belle, d. 2/9/1905 at 45/6/9; valvular dis. of heart; single; b. Barrington; Amos B. Tebbetts (Rochester) and Catherine M. Wadleigh (Meredith)
Etta J., d. 4/26/1934 at 71/7/23; coronary thrombosis; housewife; married; b. Rochester; Plummer Ham (Rochester) and Mary Waldron (Dover)
Leila K., d. 1/1/1905 at 11/9/30; Landry's paralysis; student; b. Barrington; Charles A. Tebbetts (Barrington) and Etta J. Ham (Rochester)

TEMPLE,
Bertha, d. 3/5/1904 at 21/4; pernicious anemia; housekeeper; married; b. Lunenburg, MA; Asil Stiles (Charlestown, MA) and ----- Litchfield (Lunenburg, MA)

TESSIER,
Katherine B., d. 11/23/1981 at 70 in Rochester; woolen winder; married; b. NH

THOMAS,
Eleanor B., d. 8/23/1972 at 63 in Rochester; coronary disease; housewife; married; b. NH; Oscar Terrill and Katherine E. Preston; residence - Gonic
Lawrence, Sr., d. 2/21/1974 at 76 in Rochester; truck driver; widower; b. MA

THOMPSON,
Ann, d. 8/20/1922 at 74; housekeeper; widow; b. Barrington; Lyman Locke (Barrington) and Susan Cater (Barrington)
Clarence E., d. 1/17/1905 at 16; par. after dipth., pneu.; student; b. Barrington; Hezekiah T. Thompson (Barrington) and Lanzarah Raynes (Bangor, ME)
Edith, d. 7/6/1945 at 81/8/26 in Epping; myocardial failure; domestic; single; b. Nottingham; Samuel Thompson
Eliza P., d. 5/22/1897 at 71/7/19; heart disease; domestic; widow; b. Meredith; Nathan Wadleigh and Polly Ray
Florence J., d. 7/16/1979 at 56 in Manchester; housewife; married; b. Canada
H. Tilghman, d. 3/29/1951 at 85; arteriosclerotic heart disease; farmer; widower; b. Barrington; William Thompson and Eliza Philgate
Hattie L., d. 10/14/1897 at 43/1/15; pul. tuberculosis; housekeeper; single; b. Nottingham; S. R. Thompson (Lee) and Louise Cilley (Nottingham)
Herschel C., d. 1/10/1986 at 92 in Rochester; VP engraving; widower; b. IN
Hezekiah, d. 6/13/1902 at 88/11/15; apoplexy; farmer; married; b. Barrington; Noah Thompson (Barrington) and Hannah Clark (Barrington)
Ida F., d. 1/25/1935 at 73/11; lobar pneumonia; housewife; married; b. Bangor, ME; Calvin Raynes (Bangor, ME) and Ann R. Gardner (Bangor, ME)
Isaac, d. 1/1/1893 at 59/6/1; fracture of skull; farmer; married; b. Barrington; Isaac Thompson (Barrington) and Lucy A. Brock (Madbury)

James E., d. 4/16/1922 at 77/7/3; farmer; married; b. Tamworth; Issac Thompson (Barrington) and Lucy Brock (Barrington)

Jay C., d. 1/24/1908 at 49/6/1; malignant dis. of liver; farmer; single; b. Nottingham; Samuel Thompson (Lee) and Louise M. Cilley (Nottingham)

Lanzara, d. 12/15/1940 at 81/6/3; cerebral thrombosis; housewife; married; Calvin Raynes (Bangor, ME) and Ann Gardner (Bangor, ME) (see Ida F.)

Leon, d. 8/26/1968 at 79 in Dover; broncho pneumonia; wood chopper; married; b. NH; Roy E. Thompson and Mary E. -----

Leroy S., d. 11/9/1913 at -- in Dover; heart disease

Lester, d. 1/19/1892 at 1/4/15; peritonitis; b. Barrington; H. F. Thompson and L. V. Rayner

Louisa M., d. 7/13/1900 at 77/9/1; old age; housewife; widow; b. Nottingham; Joseph Cilley (Northwood) and Nancy Malone

M. E., d. 7/22/1932 at 68/10/16; carcinoma of liver; housekeeper; single; b. Barrington; William Thompson (Barrington) and Eliza Wardley (Meredith)

Roscoe P., d. 1/29/1965 at 85 in Deerfield; myocardial infarction; b. Nottingham; residence - Nottingham

Samuel, d. 12/27/1892 at 78/6/26; old age; laborer; single; b. Barrington

William, d. 11/14/1892 at 74/2/12; cancer; farmer; married; b. Barrington; Noah Thompson and Mary Clark

Willie I., d. 8/25/1946 at 85/0/27 in Rochester; post-op. shock; farmer; widower; b. Barrington; William Thompson (Barrington) and Eliza Wadleigh (Ludlow, VT)

THOREN,

Arvid T., d. 10/20/1967 at 64 in Rochester; myocardial infarc.; teacher; married; b. New York, NY; Carl O. Thoren and Sophia Johnson

Marie W., d. 9/11/1979 at 78 in Rochester; housewife; widow; b. PA

TIBBETTS,
Catherine M., d. 2/23/1898 at 66/0/24; tuberculosis; housewife; widow; b. Meredith; Nathaniel Wadleigh (Meredith) and Polly Ray (Meredith)
Eri L., d. 8/22/1930 at 66/11/27 in Dover; carcinoma of -----
Richard B., d. 12/15/1905 at 76/10/24; senile dementia; farmer; married; b. Barrington; John Tibbetts and Anna Buzzell

TILTON,
William, d. 11/6/1957 at 79 in Concord; pneumonia; laborer; widower; b. NH; William Tilton and Ella Hilliard

TOAS,
Lucinda H., d. 6/27/1946 at 71/10/14; coronary thrombosis; housework; divorced; b. Dover; Leander Huntress (Dover) and Hannah Damm (Dover)

TOUSSAINT,
George E., d. 1/11/1980 at 68 in Rochester; contractor; married; b. NH

TRAHAN,
Ethel A. M., d. 7/4/1982 at 68 in Rochester

TRASK,
John B., d. 11/14/1902 at 65/11/21; cerebral hemorrhage; farmer; widower; b. Bangor, ME; James Trask (ME) and Martha Brown (ME)

TRELA,
John M., d. 4/3/1971 at 58 in Dover; hypoglycemia; projectionist; married; b. NH; Thomas Trela and Nellie Lichwalla

TRICKEY,
Emma, d. 8/27/1929 at 73/8/12; at home; widow; b. Barrington; Samuel Chesley (Barnstead) and Maria Scruton (Strafford)
Fred M., d. 2/15/1901 at 17/7/25; consumption; farmer; married; b. Barrington; John F. Trickey (Rochester) and Emma M. Chesley (Barrington)

TRUBENBACH,
Alfred C., d. 3/11/1976 at 88 in Dover; hotel mgr.; widower; b. Germany; Carl L. Trubenbach and Marie Myer

TUCK,
son, d. 5/3/1908 at 0/0/0; stillborn; b. Barrington; Percy H. Tuck (Mapleton, ME) and Florence E. Griffin (Barrington)

TUCKER,
Paul, d. 8/29/1898 at 0/3/29; cholera infantum; b. Barrington; Charles H. Tucker (Thornton) and Angie E. Clay (Concord, VT)

TURCOTTE,
Frederick P., d. 7/29/1975 at 52 in Dover; mach. oper.; married; b. NH; Homer Turcotte and Leonia Marceau

TURNER,
Alice V., d. 12/2/1974 at 82 in Rochester; housewife; widow; b. NH; Austin Hopey and Margaret Arsenault
Arthur J., d. 9/13/1984 at 70 in Portland, ME; retired electrician; married; b. NY

Arthur W., d. 11/13/1962 at 73 in VA; artteriosclerotic heart dis.; ldgm. machinist; married; b. NY; James Turner and Sophronia Kipling

TUTTLE,
Abby L., d. 6/1/1912 at 64/0/3; apoplexy; housekeeper; widow; b. Rochester; George W. Johnson (Strafford) and Lydia A. ----- (No. Berwick, ME)
Annie S., d. 2/1/1913 at 52/11/17; pulmonary tuberculosis; teacher; single; b. Barrington; Timothy W. Tuttle (Barrington) and Mary S. Buzzell (Barrington)
Carrie E., d. 10/24/1945 at 72/6/14 in Dover; diabetes mellitus; at home; married; b. Barrington; Daniel Arlin (Barrington) and Laura Caswell (Barrington)
Chester R., d. 7/13/1984 at 72 in Concord; UNH custodian; married; b. NH
Daniel H., d. 11/25/1910 at 17/2/15 (sic); diabetes; laborer; widower; b. Northwood; Joseph H. Tuttle (Dover) and Carrie E. Arlin (Barrington)
Ella G., d. 8/10/1960 at 77 in Biddeford, ME; hepato-renal infarction; single; b. Nottingham; Mayo G. Tuttle and Nettie Caverly
Eva M., d. 11/18/1912 at 38/0/3 in Portland, ME; uremia; widow; b. Barrington; Joel M. Chesley (Barrington)
George S., d. 12/1/1899 at 44/1; paralysis; farmer; single; b. Barrington; Timothy Tuttle (Barrington) and Mary S. Buzzell (Barrington)
John H., d. 6/13/1949 at 79 in Dover; cerebral hemorrhage; shoe cutter; widower; b. Dover; Joseph Tuttle and Nellie Hodgdon; residence - Dover
Mary S., d. 12/29/1898 at 73/2; bronchial pneumonia; housewife; widow; b. Barrington; Samuel E. Buzzell (Barrington) and Lydia Buzzell (Barrington)
Timothy F., d. 9/30/1907 at 44/8/23 in Boston, MA; intestinal obstruction; silversmith; single; b. Barrington; Timothy Tuttle (Barrington) and Mary S. Buzzell (Barrington)

Wendell T., d. 11/5/1956 at 50 in Boston, MA; multiple mycloma; b. Barrington; Joseph H. Tuttle and Carrie E. Arlin; residence - Dover

TWOMBL[E]Y,
Abiah, d. 1/18/1892 at 83/0/26; capillary bronchitis; housekeeper; single; b. Strafford; Moses Twombly and Abra Hanson

Caleb, d. 12/6/1891 at 80; married; Moses Twombly (Strafford) and Abra Hanson

Charles, d. 4/20/1929 at 63/2/18; farmer; married; b. Madbury; Daniel Twombly (Madbury) and Hannah Jackson (Madbury)

Charles, d. 1/5/1931 at 61/0/1; bronchial pneumonia; farmer; widower; b. Barrington; Nathaniel Twombly (Barrington) and Mary Sanders (Barrington)

Charles Irving, d. 9/23/1905 at 0/6/16; convulsions; b. Barrington; Charles E. Twombly (Madbury) and Alice M. Caswell (Northwood)

Clarence E., d. 3/9/1914 at 0/8/29; b. Barrington; Charles E. Twombly (Madbury) and Mary A. Caswell (Northwood)

George H., d. 5/27/1961 at 64; coronary thrombosis; mechanic; married; b. Barrington; Albert Twombly and Elizabeth Caswell

Harold G., d. 7/9/1908 at --; asphyxia; b. Barrington; Albert H. Twombly (Madbury) and Lizzie O. Caswell (Barrington)

Ida A., d. 3/13/1919 at 0/6/16; b. Barrington; Charles E. Twombly (Madbury) and Mary A. Caswell (Northwood)

Joel, d. 12/16/1903 at 0/0/10; imperfect development; b. Barrington; Charles E. Twombly

Mary A., d. 4/25/1932 at 53/7/15; cere. hemorrhage; at home; widow; b. Northwood; Irving L. Caswell and Delilah A. Foss

Mary E., d. 3/14/1909 at 76/4/8; pneumonia; housewife; widow; b. Barrington; George Twombly (Stratham) and Polly Twombly (Strafford)

Mary L., d. 10/30/1890 at 33/2/17; single; b. Barrington; Nathaniel Twombly and Mary Sanders

Nathaniel, d. 11/3/1893 at 66/10; inflammation of bowels; farmer; married; b. Barrington; N. Twombly and Mary Tanner

Ruth E., d. 4/22/1962 at 58 in Concord; subarachnoid hemorrhage; janitor; widow; b. NH; H. Weston Tuttle and Stella Foss; residence - Nottingham

Sadie, d. 2/1/1922 at 43/11/29; housewife; married; b. Barrington; William H. Willey (Barrington) and Fannie Wentworth (Strafford)

Sarah J., d. 1/2/1912 at 87/2/20; uremia; housewife; widow; b. Hartford, CT; Thomas Larrabee (Charlestown) and Phoebe Chesley (Durham)

Stephen, d. 3/7/1986 at 0/0/1 in Hanover; b. NH

Synie, d. 3/8/1900 at 0/6/3; dysentery; b. Barrington; Charles Twombly (Madbury) and Alice Caswell (Northwood)

TYLER,

Abbie, d. 1/3/1913 at 59 in Dover; chronic int'l nephritis; widow; b. Barrington

George A., d. 10/13/1909 at 51; appendicitis; laborer; married; b. Barrington; Hiram Tyler (Barrington)

Leslie, d. 12/5/1896 at 2; meningitis; Horace Tyler (NH) and Annie Hanscomb (NH)

Samuel, d. 10/30/1893 at 66; c. emb. and thrombosis; farmer; married; b. Barrington; S. Tyler and Annie Willey

VALLEE,

Edmond J., d. 4/13/1973 at 65 in Rochester; cerebral vascular acc.; bartender; divorced; b. NH; Godefroi Vallee and Josephine Britton

VAN VALKENBURG,
Richard, d. 7/9/1959 at 27; asphyxiation, drowned; shoe designer; single; b. Holyoke, MA; Wallace Van Valkenburg and Rose Giroux; residence - Andover, MA

VARNEY,
baby, d. 5/29/1937 at -- in Madbury; material jamalic
Kathleen T., d. 11/22/1985 at 72; shoe stitcher; divorced; b. NH
Marcia O., d. 11/30/1900 at 63/7/17; cerebral hemorrhage; housewife; married; b. Barrington; Nathaniel Brock and Mary Drew
Mary H., d. 3/11/1900 at 63/9/4; pneumonia; housewife; married; b. Barrington; Paul H. Hayes (Strafford) and Mary Berry (Strafford)
Rachel, d. 6/10/1897 at 84/4/11; injury to hip; domestic; widow; b. Barrington; William Felker (Barrington) and Hannah Gray (Rochester)
Rufus C., d. 6/14/1900 at 86/10/25; apoplexy; farmer; widower; b. Barrington; Elias Varney and Hannah Locke (Barrington)

WADE,
Elizabeth M., d. 11/2/1964 at 70 in Rochester; cerebral thrombosis; housewife; married; b. Winchester; Eugene Burpee and Ellen L. Russell
Elmer M., d. 3/29/1966 at 74 in Rochester; lymphalic leukemia; farmer; widower; b. NS; John H. Wade and Harriet Hall

WAKEFIELD,
Irene D., d. 4/24/1967 at 65 in Cambridge, MA; housekeeper; married; b. Saugus, MA; John Campbell and Charlotte Loyte

WALDRON,
Hariette B., d. 9/14/1894 at 58/2/10; intestinal carcinoma; housewife; widow; b. Barrington; Samuel Chesley (Barnstead) and Maria Scruton (Strafford)
John H., d. 1/5/1893 at 84/11/11; peritonitis; farmer; widower; b. Barrington; John Waldron and Comfort Haines

WALKER,
Frank, d. 4/26/1976 at 58 in Rochester; shoe worker; married; b. NH; Arthur F. Walker and Lillian Heath
Mabel T., d. 9/24/1964 at 76 in Dover; arteriosclerotic heart dis.; reg. nurse; divorced; b. NS; Nathan Trefrey and Elizabeth Scott
Robert C., d. 5/3/1970 at 18; drowning; Univ. student; single; b. NJ; Henry J. Walker and Blanche Killen; residence - Jersey City, NJ
William, d. 12/20/1954 at 49; skull fracture (accidt.); lumber operator; married; b. MA; William H. Walker and Effie McCutcheon; residence - Durham

WALLACE,
Margaret L., d. 9/28/1957 at 82; metastatic carcinoma; ed. and proof reader; single; b. Nyack, NY; William Wallace and Mary L. Wyman

WALLINGFORD,
daughter, d. 6/30/1955 at 9 hrs. in Exeter; prematurity; b. Exeter; R. E. Wallingford and Helen Elliott
Richard E., d. 12/4/1985 at 51 in Dover; silicone dryer; married; b. ME

WALSH,
James P., d. 2/26/1975 at 76 in Manchester; shoeworker; married; b. NH; Patrick Walsh and Mary Fadden

WALTERS,
Richard N., d. 3/12/1974 at 19 in Dover; shipper; single; b. PA; Richard N. Walters and Elizabeth Hollen

WARD,
Dorothy A., d. 10/17/1961 at 0 in Rochester; stillbirth; b. Rochester; Stephen R. Ward and Dorothy A. Norman; residence - Dover

Ellen I., d. 9/8/1906 at 32/5/25; tuberculosis; trained nurse; married; b. Barrington; Thomas McRae (NS) and Clara Richardson (Woburn, MA)

John, d. 6/4/1949 at 45/0/12; coronary thrombosis; woodsman; married; b. Eastport, ME; John T. Ward and Mary E. Clark

WARREN,
George, d. 3/16/1897 at 0/4; con. of lungs; b. Barrington; Frank Warren (S. Berwick, ME) and Belle Austin (Hudson)

WATERHOUSE,
A. C., d. 11/15/1948 at 75/6/5; arteriosclerosis; retired; married; b. Barrington; Daniel Waterhouse (Barrington) and Fidela Berry (Barrington)

Benjamin, d. 10/30/1928 at 70/11/18; chron. ilocolitis; farmer; widower; b. Barrington; Benjamin Waterhouse and Eliza Walker

C. F., d. 5/10/1933 at 73/10/2; apoplexy; farmer; married; b. Barrington; Charles H. Waterhouse (Barrington) and Nancy I. Caverly (Barrington)

Daniel, d. 4/24/1927 at 76/2/1; apoplexy; farmer; married; b. Barrington; Daniel Waterhouse and Delia Hathaway (Bridgewater, MA)

Delia, d. 12/4/1894 at 76/4/9; old age; housewife; widow; b. S. Bridgewater, MA; George Hathaway and Mary Knapp

Delphine, d. 8/11/1923 at 72; single; b. Barrington; Benjamin Waterhouse and Eliza Walker

Elizabeth, d. 4/2/1914 at 75/3/10; at home; widow; b. Dover; William Hale (Barrington) and Eliza Shackford (Strafford)

Fidella, d. 5/12/1929 at 80/6/16; at home; widow; b. Barrington; James Berry (Strafford) and Louise Foss (Strafford)

Laura J., d. 3/4/1909 at 57/3/25; general debility & apoplexy; housewife; married; b. Manchester; Azariale B. Hill (Strafford) and Hannah Hall (Strafford)

Martha A., d. 1/18/1894 at 74/2/9; general debility; post mistress; widow; b. Barrington; William Winkley (Barrington) and Sarah Hussey (Barrington)

Martha W., d. 11/29/1909 at 86/8/2 in Salem; cerebral softening; at home; widow; b. Barrington; Jeremiah Buzzell (Barrington) and Ann Winkley (Barrington)

Mary, d. 3/18/1935 at 76/6/10; endocarditis; housewife; married; b. Northwood; Charles P. Holmes and Anelia Foss

Mattie E., d. 5/13/1957 at 79; myocarditis; housewife; widow; b. Roxbury, MA; George Young and Adeline Lambert

William, d. 9/9/1907 at 91/0/16; senility; physician; married; b. Barrington; Jeremiah Waterhouse (Barrington) and Susan Twombly (Dover)

William E., d. 11/29/1902 at 57/9/29; chronic nephritis; farmer; married; b. Barrington; Jeremiah Waterhouse (Barrington) and Martha A. Winkley (Barrington)

WATSON,

Lydia, d. 1/25/1892 at 83/1/11; peritonitis; housekeeper; single; b. Barrington; John Bumford and Martha Tebbetts

Sarah A., d. 11/20/1892 at 58/7/20; apoplexy; housewife; married; b. Barrington; John Buzzell and Miss Willey

Sylvester, d. 1/24/1910 at 69/6/24; valvular heart disease; farmer; single; b. Barrington; Joseph Watson and Lydia Bumford (Barrington)

WEBSTER,
George K., d. 10/27/1914 at 56/7/15; farmer; divorced; b. Dover; Daniel K. Webster (Londonderry) and Elizabeth P. Downs (Dover)

WEEDEN,
Ellen F., d. 1/26/1896 at 44/5/27; tumor and dropsy; housewife; married; b. Strafford; James Currier (Sutton) and Thankful Tibbetts (Somersworth)
Peter T., d. 9/9/1975 at 11 in Portland, ME; student; Albert S. Weeden and Elizabeth Leavitt

WEEKS,
Albion G., d. 3/25/1965 at 79 in Rochester; CVA with hemiplegia; farmer; widower; b. Barrington; Charles W. Weeks and Anna Glidden
Charles W., d. 3/22/1937 at 87/14/2 (sic); labor pneumonia; farmer; widower; b. Strafford; William Weeks (Strafford) and Mariah Clark (Barrington)
Dorothy, d. 1/28/1979 at 60
Gertrude L., d. 1/6/1964 at 70; circulatory failure; housewife; married; b. Barrington; Alfonso B. Locke and Mary Waterhouse
Maria, d. 11/24/1891 at 75; married; Hezekiah Clark (Rochester) and Hannah Ham
William, d. 5/4/1892 at 79/11/23; old age; farmer; widower; b. Barrington; Elisha Weeks and Mary Potter

WELLS,
George H., d. 9/4/1932 at 70/0/18; acute uremia; b. Hardwick, VT; Henry G. Wells and Laura Strong

WELSH,
Norman W., d. 3/9/1980 at 78 in Manchester; machinist; widower; b. PA

WENTWORTH,
Abbie, d. 3/5/1896 at 67/3; pneumonia; housewife; married; b. Rochester; James Ham (Rochester) and Olive Waldron (Rochester)

Daniel, d. 2/1/1916 at 88/11/20; farmer; widower; b. Lebanon, ME; Samuel Wentworth (Lebanon, ME) and Rachel Furber (Lebanon, ME)

Lowell E., d. 6/23/1965 at 68; coronary thrombosis; electrician; married; b. Newton; Bertrand Wentworth and Alice Wormwood

Natalie M., d. 2/10/1973 at 78 in Dover; bronchopneumonia; housewife; widow; b. NH; Fred Hayes and Bessie Parshley

WESCOTT,
Harold W., d. 7/12/1954 at 56 in Rochester; chronic nephritis; spinner; married; b. Porter, ME; William H. Wescott and Joanna Swasey; residence - Rochester

WEST,
Mary Ella, d. 9/2/1930 at 64/3/27; angina pectoris; seamstress; widow; b. Somerville, MA; Roswell Brooks and Sarah F. Ordway

WHEELER,
daughter, d. 9/27/1979 at 0 in Rochester

Arthur J., Sr., d. 11/3/1976 at 46 in Wolfeboro; contractor; married; b. NH; ----- and Minnie Wheeler

Daniel J., d. 4/12/1981 at 0 in Boston, MA

Elmer F., d. 8/4/1965 at 65; multiple fracture; swine herdsman; married; b. Manchester; John Wheeler and Etta M. Swinnington; residence - Dunbarton

James, d. 6/24/1935 at 41/10/12; asphyxia; laborer; single; b. Kingfield, ME; Fred Wheeler (Canada) and Mary Bishop (Canada)

Joseph, d. 7/23/1959 at 57 in Dover; coronary thrombosis; maintenance man; married; b. Lewiston, ME; Frederick R. Wheeler and Mary Bishop

WHIDDEN,
George A., d. 9/29/1924 at 83/8/15; retired; widower; b. Melrose, MA; John Whidden (Denmark, ME) and Sally Houston (Sanford, ME)

WHITCAMB,
Don S., d. 12/27/1944 at 61/5/26; "carmocraf stomach"; farmer; married; b. Long Island, NY; Jane Solomon

WHITCHER,
Raymond C., d. 5/17/1969 at 72 in Portsmouth; myocardial infarc.; joiner; married; b. NH; William Whitcher and Fannie Strong
Sylvia E., d. 4/24/1971 at 69 in Portsmouth; acute myocardial infarc.; seamstress; widow; b. VT; Leo D. Fox and Estella Clough; residence - Portsmouth

WHITCOMB,
Delphine, d. 2/7/1948 at 67/3/5; arteriosclerosis; housewife; widow; b. Meriden, CT; Morris Bermas and Moley Bermas

WHITE,
Edith B., d. 1/27/1982 at 71 in Dover
Sadie A., d. 5/17/1950 at 76/1/28 in Dover; coronary thrombosis; ironer; widow; b. Barrington; Mark Brown and Lucy Brown; residence - Dover

WHITEHOUSE,
Andrew J., d. 1/10/1956 at 64 in Manchester; cor. pulmonalis; laborer; single; b. Barrington; John T. Whitehouse and Ida M. Brown; residence - Rochester

Charles, d. 4/3/1931 at 78; heart disease; single; b. Barrington; Leonard Whitehouse (Barrington) and Eliza J. Brown (Strafford)

Edna, d. 2/14/1897 at 0/2; cro. laryngitis; b. Barrington; John Whitehouse (Barrington) and Ida Brown (Barrington)

Eliza J., d. 1/22/1912 at 75/6/18; bronchial pneumonia; housewife; widow; b. Barrington; Joseph Brown and Eliza J. Robertson (Strafford)

James L., d. 2/28/1946 at 80/9/10 in Rochester; cancer of rectum; single; b. Barrington; Leonard Whitehouse (Barrington) and Eliza Brown (Manchester)

Jeremiah, d. 4/11/1943 at 83/5/29; arterio scl. heart; retired; widower; b. Barrington; Leonard Whitehouse (Barrington) and Eliza J. Brown (Barrington)

Mary, d. 12/6/1912 at 89/11/6; fractured hip; widow; b. Barrington; John Bumford (Barrington) and Martha Tibbetts (Barrington)

Mary, d. 4/2/1936 at 81/9/28; arterio sclerosis; retired; married; b. Barrington; Cyrus Caverly (Strafford) and Sarah Twombly (Barrington)

Merle C., d. 12/25/1963 at 63; acute coronary insufficiency; retired; married; b. Barrington; John T. Whitehouse and Ida M. Brown

Turner, d. 11/20/1896 at 85/1/20; cerebral hemorrhage; farmer; married; b. Barrington; Jeremiah Whitehouse (Rochester) and Mary Coffin (Dover)

WHITMORE,
Ada B., d. 7/4/1963 at 67 in Hanover; infarction large intestine; retired; widow; b. Boston, MA; Frederick W. Barr and Mary Ann Kennedy

WHITNEY,
Christine M., d. 7/25/1952 at 21 hrs. in Laconia; prematurity; b. Laconia; Howard A. Whitney and Irene Beard

WHITTEMORE,
Ann P., d. 5/2/1943 at 73/3/1 in Exeter; capillary bronchitis; housewife; widow; b. Barre, VT

WICKEY,
John W., d. 12/21/1976 at 55; metalsmith; divorced; b. MA; Walter Wickey and Bessie Ellis

WIECHERT,
Anna, d. 9/25/1939 at 51/8/24; phlebitis; housewife; married; b. Philadelphia, PA; Charles Kuenzel (Germany)
James E., d. 12/23/1971 at 50 in Rochester; hepatitic insufficiency; dental mechanic; married; b. NH; George Wiechert and Anna Keunzel; residence - Rochester

WIGGIN,
B. Marcille, d. 8/20/1964 at 92 in Dover; arteriosclerotic heart dis.; housewife; widow; b. Beverly Farms, MA; Reuben E. Grush and Emma Stillman; residence - Rochester
Bertha M., d. 12/26/1955 at 84; cerebral arterial occlusion; housewife; married; b. Milton; James O. Reynolds and Myra J. Hill
Elmer E., d. 3/11/1956 at 94; mesenteric thrombosis; agent; widower; b. Barrington; George Wiggin and Sophia Hayes
Etheline B., d. 4/26/1911 at 0/1/26 in Lee; pneumonia
Frank I., d. 3/4/1956 at 74 in Dover; myocardial infarction; laborer; widower; b. Lee; James M. Wiggin and Matilda Bennett; residence - Madbury
Herbert H., d. 1/21/1908 at 0/4/23; pertussis; b. Barrington; George W. Wiggin (Barrington) and Marcella V. Vern (Beverly, MA)
Kenneth A., d. 4/15/1970 at 58 in Boston, MA; fracture of skull

Marguerite, d. 1/29/1908 at 13/6/25; pneumonia; student; b.
  Barrington; George W. Wiggin (Barrington) and Marcella
  V. Vern (Beverly, MA)
Marguerite V., d. 11/23/1980 at 86 in Dover
Morton H., d. 10/31/1965 at 70 in Rochester; carcinomatosis;
  teacher; married; b. Barrington; Elmer E. Wiggin and
  Bertha Reynolds
Otto S., d. 2/17/1982 at 82 in Rochester
Sophia, d. 12/8/1893 at 70/8/16; bronchitis; housewife;
  married; b. Barrington; Jacob Hayes (Barrington) and
  Margaret Hayes (Madbury)

WILFRET,
George W., d. 3/13/1948 at 81/4/14 in Easton, MA; chr.
  myocarditis; retired; widower; b. Boston, MA; John C.
  Wilfret (Germany) and Henrietta Tanck (Boston, MA)

WILKINSON,
George M., d. 9/5/1974 at 57 in Dover; inspector; married; b.
  MA; Thomas Wilkinson and Agnes Swenson

WILLEY,
Annie A., d. 12/26/1919 at 77/0/8; housewife; married; b.
  Barrington; George Cater (Lee) and Milanda Arlin (Lee)
Benjamin F., d. 10/9/1922 at 84/3/17; farmer; widower; b.
  Barrington; Benjamin Willey (Barrington) and Sophia -----
Charles H., d. 3/18/1907 at 22; tuberculosis; farmer; single;
  b. Barrington; William H. Willey (Strafford) and Fannie
  Wentworth (Strafford)
David F., d. 8/7/1894 at 53/1/11; septicemia
Evie W., d. 6/14/1955 at 92 in Dover; chronic myocardial
  insufficiency; housework; widow; b. Vienna, ME;
  Elbridge Watson and Mary Ladd; residence - Dover
Fannie S., d. 4/7/1906 at 57/8; tuberculosis; housewife; b.
  Strafford; Israel Wentworth (Barrington) and Mary Clark
  (Canada)

Frank L., d. 2/19/1955 at 67 in Dover; coronary disease; mach. operator; married; b. Boston, MA; George W. Willey and Olive Hoytt; residence - Dover

George W., d. 6/20/1911 at 86/6/19 in Dover; senility

Ida, d. 6/9/1904 at 16; pulmonary tuberculosis; single; b. Barrington; William H. Willey (Barrington) and Fannie Wentworth (Barrington)

Norris E., d. 3/9/1958 at 71 in Dover; pneumonia; baggage master; widower; b. Barrington; Frank L. Willey and Eve Watson; residence - Dover

Olive, d. 3/14/1905 at 79/11/16; pneumonia; housewife; married; b. Barrington; Benjamin Hoyt (Tamworth) and Mahala Giles (Barrington)

Susan F., d. 8/21/1907 at 60/4/27; senile dementia; housekeeper; widow; b. Quincy, MA; William Hammond (No. Berwick, ME) and Hannah Reed (Quincy, MA)

William H., d. 4/8/1920 at 78/8/8; farmer; widower; b. Barrington; Benjamin F. Willey (Barrington) and Sophia McCoy (Nottingham)

William W., d. 4/15/1913 at 67 in Concord; diffuse nephritis; carpenter; single; b. Barrington; Hiram Willey (Barrington) and Susan Mills (Barrington)

WILLIAMS,

Oscar, d. 5/15/1897 at 15 in Boston, MA; accident; school boy; Oscar Williams

Richard L., d. 8/17/1966 at 78 in Dover; arteriosclerotic hrt. dis.; farmer; married; b. Long Branch, NJ; Richard L. Williams and Rachel B. Smith; residence - Dover

Ruth W., d. 1/8/1967 at 78 in Boston, MA; Hodgkins disease

WILSON,

Chester W., d. 11/23/1980 at 93 in Exeter; salesman; married; b. MA

Kenneth R., d. 3/4/1972 at 49; coronary thrombosis; hosp. orderly; single; b. NH; Harold Wilson and Marion Hunt

WINGATE,
John, d. 7/30/1903 at 68/5/21; cancer of stomach, bowels; farmer; married; b. Strafford; Joshua Wingate (Farmington) and Mary McNeil (Strafford)

WINKLEY,
Elizabeth, d. 1/20/1970 at 81 in Framingham, MA
Laura L., d. 5/2/1926 at 69/8/28; heart failure; housekeeper; widow; b. Barrington; Hattiville Bumford (Barrington) and Elizabeth Ham (Barrington)

WITHERELL,
Ethel, d. 4/18/1969 at 73 in Rochester; myocardial infarct.; housewife; widow; b. VT; Henry Belden and Agnes Buckell; residence - Rochester
Harry W., d. 8/26/1968 at 74 in Rochester; cerebral thrombosis; farmer; married; b. VT; Charles R. Witherell and Elizabeth Stowell; residence - Rochester
Jay K., d. 8/16/1975 at 16; student; single; b. NH; Ralph W. Witherell and Mary Mitchell

WITHERSPOON,
Anna J., d. 9/4/1957 at 85; nephritis; housewife; married; b. NS; John Grono and Elizabeth Fralick
Benjamin, d. 10/16/1972 at 89 in Rochester; myocardial infarction; farmer; widower; b. NS; residence - Rochester

WITMER,
Carl T., d. 8/15/1966 at 54 in Hanover; infarction of cerebrum; pipe fitter; married; b. Huntington, IN; Elliott Witmer and Mollie Euyert

WOLF,
son, d. 10/19/1979 at 0 in Dover; b. NH

WOOD,
Albert I., d. 9/8/1966 at 77 in Concord; myocardial infacrtion; store clerk; widower; b. Hanover; Charles H. Wood and Sarah Clifford

Arthur, d. 10/1/1918 at 20/10/28; laborer; single; b. Barrington; Joe Wood (Canada) and Mary Wood (Canada)

Celia F., d. 10/14/1965 at 73; cerebral accident; housewife; married; b. Walpole; William Gunnison and Truth E. Fisher

Charles H., d. 5/7/1975 at 64 in Rochester; cert. appraiser; married; b. MA; Henry Wood and Jennie Lavalle

Emily P., d. 7/21/1895 at 60/3/16; pneumonia; nurse; single; b. Boston, MA; Hiram Wood (Marblehead, MA) and Sarah Silver (Atkinson)

George, d. 9/26/1918 at 24 at Camp Devens, MA; soldier; single; b. Barrington; Joe Wood (Canada) and Mary Wood (Canada)

Hiram H., d. 6/13/1905 at 71/9/25; chronic bronchitis; farmer; married; b. Boston, MA; Hiram Wood (Marblehead, MA) and Sarah Silver (Londonderry)

James Henry, d. 11/21/1949 at 79 in Dover; coronary thrombosis; electrical engr.; married; b. Hanover; Charles H. Wood and Sarah J. Clifford; residence - Dover

Joseph, d. 11/29/1920 at 64/8/9; laborer; married; b. Canada; Moses Wood (Canada) and Mary Greenwood (Canada)

Julia Etta, d. 10/18/1946 at 59/7/24 in Dover; cerebral hemorrhage; housework; married; b. Clayto'n, AL; James Hicks (GA) and Sarah Conant (G'dwater, AL)

Leslie E., Sr., d. 9/20/1968 at 73 in Lakeland, FL

Lucy M., d. 2/24/1965 at 74; myocardial failure; housewife; married; b. Rochester; Charles F. Hall and Christani Gray

Margaret I., d. 5/28/1974 at 54 in Rochester; shoe worker; single; b. NH; Charles I. Wood and Lucy M. Hall

Marie J., d. 6/10/1922 at 66/3/23; housekeeper; widow; b. NS

Wilfred, d. 11/2/1918 at 27/19/29; laborer; married; b. Barrington; Joe Wood (Canada) and Mary Wood (Canada)

WOODS,

son, d. 10/13/1937 at -- in Rochester; prem. sep. placenta; b. Rochester; William J. Wood (Scotland) and Edith M. Adair

Jacob, d. 12/18/1936 at 67/7/15; heart disease; married; b. Canada; David Woods (Canada) and Delma Woods (Canada)

John, d. 2/27/1977 at 0 in Dover; b. NH; William J. Woods and Dale K. Clement

John D., Sr., d. 7/31/1957 at 57 in Dover; cardio vascular disease; truck driver; married; b. Strafford; Joseph Woods and Mary Jeffries; residence - Dover

Mary, d. 2/23/1952 at 69; arteriosclerotic heart disease; housewife; widow; b. Canada; Basil Levesque and Rose Pelletier

Mildred E., d. 9/21/1982 at 71 in Dover

William J., d. 1/26/1962 at 65 in Rochester; myocardial infarct.; ticket agent; married; b. Scotland; William Woods and Margaret Adair; residence - Rochester

WORMWELL,

Andrew K., d. 2/16/1917 at 75/8/6; retired farmer; married; b. Farmington; Amos Wormwell (Phillips, ME)

WORRALL,

Arthur E., d. 8/19/1953 at 24; imp. punc. larynx; oiler; married; b. New London, CT; John E. Worrall and Helen R. Clark; residence - Groton, CT

WRIGHT,
Robert, d. 3/25/1918 at 68; farmer; widower; b. Ireland; James Wright (Ireland) and Eliza Williamson (Ireland)

YORK,
Willie, d. 10/11/1891 at 4; Willie York (Barrington) and Jennie Brown

YOUNG,
Ada R., d. 1/19/1913 at 66/9/5; diabetes; housewife; married; b. Marshfield, MA; Jacob Ewell (Marshfield, MA) and Sarah Carnes (Hingham, MA)
Charles S., d. 11/26/1958 at 77 in Rollinsford; carcinoma of stomach; heeler; married; b. Barrington; Jeremiah K. Young and Fannie A. Locke
Dora, d. 5/14/1898 at 0/7; bronchial pneumonia; b. Nashua; Phillip Young (Somersworth) and Ida Ronlean
Dora, d. 10/6/1977 at 88 in Manchester; housewife; widow; b. NH; George Flanders and Lucy Felch
Ella A., d. 12/20/1972 at 84 in Norway, ME
Ellen M., d. 3/20/1937 at 42/4/10 in Rochester; labor pneumonia; housewife; married; b. Pittsfield; George Brock (Pittsfield) and Edith Twombly (Barnstead)
Frank C., d. 11/25/1955 at 97 in Dover; broncho-pneumonia; farmer; widower; b. Barrington; John L. Young and Mary Buzzell; residence - Dover
Frank H., d. 2/12/1914 at 64/5/22 in Madbury
Fred L., d. 3/1/1965 at 72 in Manchester; heart failure; salesman; married; b. Barrington; Kingman Young; residence - Manchester
George, d. 1/7/1935 at 54 in Concord; cerebral neoplasm; farmer; single; b. Barrington; John Young
Herman E., d. 11/16/1964 at 77 in Haverhill, MA; metastatic carcinoma; residence - Plaistow

Isaac H., d. 1/23/1934 at 87/6/15; mitral insufficiency; farmer; widower; b. Barrington; Isaac H. Young (Barrington) and Mary Seavey (Barrington)

Ivory, d. 12/15/1891 at 89; married; Isaac Young (Barrington) and Susan Kelly (Dover)

Ivory L., d. 7/10/1964 at 61 in Rochester; rheumatic heart disease; sawyer; married; b. Barrington; Nat. L. Young and Ella Thayer; residence - East Rochester

J. Kingman, d. 3/5/1895 at 40/3/16; nervous exhaustion; farmer; married; b. Barrington; Jonathan Young (Barrington) and Sophia Ricker (Madbury)

James A., d. 8/12/1981 at 66 in Rochester

John W., d. 1/21/1901 at 51 in Brookline, MA; mitral obstruction

Lendel A., d. 12/21/1966 at 86 in Rochester; myocardial infarct.; divorced; b. Salem, MA

Lewis E., d. 7/29/1900 at 21/8/22; tuberculosis; mechanic; single; b. Barrington; J. Kingman Young (Barrington) and Fannie A. Locke (Barrington)

Lewis H., d. 2/28/1949 at 85/2/13 in Dover; arteriosclerosis; widower; residence - Madbury

Mary A., d. 4/24/1893 at 76/4/19; carcinoma; domestic; widow; b. Barrington; Elijah Seavey (Barrington) and Polly Parshley

Mary S. H., d. 6/16/1947 at 75/2/15 in Concord; cerebral hemorrhage; housewife; married; b. Barrington; Samuel Hale (Barrington) and Adeline Roberts

Sophia Locke, d. 10/21/1898 at 70/0/19; chorea; housewife; widow; b. Barrington; Jacob Hall (Barrington) and Abigail Foss (Barrington)

Stella I., d. 12/8/1961 at 81 in Plaistow; myocarditis; housewife; married; b. Haverhill, MA; Frank E. Stevens and Emma E. Runnells; residence - Plaistow

W. H., d. 5/5/1891 at 82; married; William Young

William J., d. 10/6/1981 at 33 in Texas

ZIELFELDER,
Eleanor M., d. 4/17/1987 at 68 in Rochester; homemaker; married; b. MA

Other Heritage Books by Richard P. Roberts:

Alton, New Hampshire Vital Records, 1890-1997

Barnstead, New Hampshire Vital Records, 1887-2000

Barrington, New Hampshire Vital Records

Dover, New Hampshire Death Records, 1887-1937

Gilmanton, New Hampshire Vital Records, 1887-2001

Marriage Records of Dover, New Hampshire, 1835-1909

Marriage Records of Dover, New Hampshire, 1910-1937

Milton, New Hampshire Vital Records, 1888-1999

Moultonborough, New Hampshire Vital Records

New Castle, New Hampshire Vital Records, 1891-1997

New Hampshire Name Changes, 1768-1923

New Hampshire Name Changes, 1923-1947

Ossipee, New Hampshire Vital Records, 1887-2001

Rochester, New Hampshire Death Records, 1887-1951

Vital Records of Durham, New Hampshire, 1887-2002

Vital Records of Effingham and Freedom, New Hampshire, 1888-2001

Vital Records of Farmington, New Hampshire, 1887-1938

Vital Records of Lyme and Dorchester, New Hampshire, 1887-2004

Vital Records of New Durham and Middleton, New Hampshire, 1887-1998

Vital Records of North Berwick, Maine, 1892-2002

Vital Records of Orford and Piermont, New Hampshire, 1887-2004

Vital Records of Tamworth and Albany, New Hampshire, 1887-2003

Vital Records of Tuftonboro and Brookfield, New Hampshire, 1888-2005

Vital Records of Wakefield, New Hampshire, 1887-1998

Vital Records of Warren, New Hampshire, 1887-2005

Wolfeboro, New Hampshire Vital Records, 1887-1999

www.ingramcontent.com/pod-product-compliance
Lightning Source LLC
Chambersburg PA
CBHW071133300426
44113CB00009B/955